Map Use
and Analysis

Second Edition

John Campbell
University of Wisconsin–Parkside

WCB **Wm. C. Brown Publishers**
Dubuque, Iowa•Melbourne, Australia•Oxford, England

For Hazel

Book Team

Editor *Lynne M. Meyers*
Production Editor *Diane E. Beausoleil*

Wm. C. Brown Publishers
A Division of Wm. C. Brown Communications, Inc.

Vice President and General Manager *Beverly Kolz*
Director of Sales and Marketing *John W. Calhoun*
Advertising Manager/Associate Marketing Manager *Amy Schmitz*
Director of Production *Colleen A. Yonda*
Manager of Visuals and Design *Faye M. Schilling*
Design Manager *Jac Tilton*
Art Manager *Janice Roerig*
Publishing Services Manager *Karen J. Slaght*
Permissions/Records Manager *Connie Allendorf*

Wm. C. Brown Communications, Inc.

President and Chief Executive Officer *G. Franklin Lewis*
Corporate Vice President, President of WCB Manufacturing *Roger Meyer*
Vice President and Chief Financial Officer *Robert Chesterman*

Copyright © 1991, 1993 by Wm. C. Brown Communications, Inc.
All rights reserved

A Times Mirror Company

Library of Congress Catalog Card Number: 92–75544

ISBN 0–697–13579–9

Printed in the United States of America by Wm. C. Brown Communications, Inc.,
2460 Kerper Boulevard, Dubuque, IA 52001

10   9   8   7   6   5   4

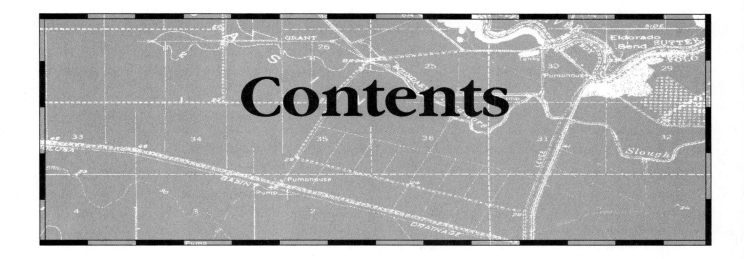

Contents

Preface xi

1   Introduction 1
Why Use a Map? 1
What Is a Map? 2
Virtual Maps 3
  Mental Maps 3
  Digital Data 7
Real Maps 7
  Planimetric Maps 7
  Topographic Maps 10
  Thematic Maps 11
  Cartograms 15
  Remotely Sensed Images 17
Summary 19
Suggested Readings 20

2   Basic Mapping Processes 21
Shape and Size of the Earth 21
  Basic Spherical Shape 21
  Locational System 21
    Meridians 22
    Parallels 23
    Graticule 23
  Refinements in Shape 23
    Ellipsoid 24
    Geoid 25
  Size 25
Mapping Process 26
  Geodetic Control Surveys 26
    Latitude determination 27
    Longitude determination 27

☐ **The Analemma 29**
☐ **Dates and Times 31**
International Date Line 31
Time Zones 33

    Deflection of the vertical 35
    Control network 35
    Horizontal datum 35
  Plane Surveys 35
    Horizontal locations 36
    Elevation determination 36
    Vertical datum 36
Topographic Mapping 38
  Aerial Photography 38
  Stereoscopic Images 38
  Ground Control 39
  Plotting 40
Summary 41
Suggested Readings 41

3   Map Projections 42
Map-Projection Concepts 42
  Projection Surfaces 42
    Plane 42
    Developable surfaces 42
  Light-Source Location 43
  Orientation and Tangency 43
Globe Characteristics 45
  Conformality 45
  Equivalence 46
  Distance 47
  Direction 48

Compromise Projections 49
  Miller cylindrical 49
  Robinson projection 49
Projection Selection 49
Summary 51
Suggested Readings 52

4 Scale and Generalization Concepts 53

Scale 53

☐ **Units of Measurement and Map Scales 53**
Linear Measurements 54
U.S. Customary Units 54
Metric Units 54
Areal Measurements 55
Nautical Measurements 56

Methods of Stating Scale 58
  Word statement 58
  Representative fraction 58
  Graphic scale 58
Large and Small Scale 59
Scale Determination 60
  Use of known features 60
  Use of lines of latitude and
    longitude 61
  Use of map comparison 61
Scale Conversion 61
  Representative-fraction (RF) and word-
    statement conversions 62
  Representative-fraction (RF) and graphic
    conversions 62
  Word-statement and graphic
    conversions 63
Generalization 63
  Selection 63
  Simplification 63
  Combination 63
  Locational Shift and Size Exaggeration 63
Summary 64
Suggested Readings 65

5 Measurements from Maps 66

Map Accuracy 66

☐ **National Map Accuracy Standards 66**
Horizontal Accuracy 66
Vertical Accuracy 66

Distance Measurement 67
  Direct Methods of Measurement 67
    Scaling 67
    Map measurer 68

Computer-assisted methods 68
Indirect Methods of Measurement 69
  Short distances 69
  Long distances 69
  Computer-assisted methods 69
Error Sources 70
  Measurement error 70
  Smoothing 70
  Slope 70
Area Determination 71
  Areal Scale 71
  Direct Methods of Measurement 72
    Scaling and computation 72
    Polar planimeter 72
  Indirect Methods of Measurement 73
    Grid squares 73
    Dot planimeter 73
    Strip method 74
    Polygon method 74
  Computer-Assisted Methods 74
    Small areas 74
    Large areas 75
Summary 76
Suggested Readings 76

6 Route Selection and Navigation 77

Basic Considerations 77
  Direction Determination 77
    True north 77
    Magnetic north 77
    Grid north 79
    Declination diagram 79
  Direction Designation 79
    Azimuth 80
    Back-azimuth 81
    Bearing 81
    Back-bearing 81
Land Operations 82
  Map Orientation 82
  Position Determination 83
  Route Selection 84
Water Operations 84
  Nautical Charts 84
    Publication date 85
    Projections 85
    Units of measurement 86
    Depth indications 86
    Special symbols 86
  Position Determination 87
    Astronomical observations 88
    Lines of position 88

Radar 88
Satellite observation 89
Radio direction finding 90
Loran 90
Dead Reckoning 92
Aviation Operations 92
Aeronautical Charts 93
World Aeronautical Charts 93
Sectional charts 95
Flight Planning 96
Summary 98
Suggested Readings 99

7 Terrain Representation 100
Symbols 100
Spot Heights 100
Land surfaces 100
Water surfaces 100
Contours 101
Contour interval 101
Contour types 102
Layer Tints 103
Illuminated Contours 104
Hill Shading 104
Physical Models 106
Physiographic Diagrams 108
Block Diagrams 109
Summary 110
Suggested Readings 111

8 Contour Interpretation 112
Contours 112
Characteristics 112
Applications 116
Elevation estimation 116
Reservoir capacity estimation 116
Flood-zone maps 117
Profiling 117
Methodology 117
Cut-line 117
Vertical scale 117
Drawing the Profile 120
Applications 120
Cut and fill 120
Intervisibility 121
Slopes 121
Slope Measurement 121
Gradient 121
Percent 121
Degree 122

Applications 123
Slope-zone maps 123
Maximum slope limitations 123
Trafficability 125
Summary 125
Suggested Readings 126

9 Topographic Features 127
Drainage Patterns 127
Type of Dissection 128
Dendritic 128
Rectangular 128
Trellis 128
Radial 129
Annular 129
Miscellaneous 130
Texture of Dissection 130
Selected Examples of Landforms 130
Coastal Features and Shorelines 134
Escarpments 135
Glaciation 135
Alpine 135
Continental 138
Mountains 141
Plains 141
Plateaus 141
Solution Features 143
Valleys 143
Volcanic Features 146
Water Features 146
Wind Features 148
Miscellaneous 148
Summary 150
Suggested Readings 150

10 Locational and Land-Partitioning Systems 151
Locational Systems 151
Latitude and Longitude Positions 151
Interpolation 152
Subdivisions of degrees 156
World Geographic Reference System 156
Grid Systems 158
Reference Grids 158
Plane Rectangular Grids 158
Universal Transverse Mercator System 159
Civilian system 159
U.S. Military Grid Reference System 163
State Plane Coordinate System 166
Land-Partitioning Systems 168

Unsystematic Subdivision 169
  Metes and bounds 169
  Bearings 170
Systematic Subdivision (U.S. Public Land
  Survey) 171
  U.S. Public lands 171
  Township, range, and section 171
  Plats 171
  Property descriptions 174
  Irregularities 174
Land Survey in Canada 175
  Patterns in areas of French
    settlement 175
  Patterns in areas of English
    settlement 176
  Westward expansion 176
  Cultural influences 178
Summary 180
Suggested Readings 181

11 Characteristics of Map Features: Shape
    and Point Patterns 182

Shape 182
  Subjective Description 182
  Numerical Indices 182
  Desired Characteristics of a Shape
    Index 182
  Specific Measures 183
    Miller's measure 183
    Bunge's measure 183
    Boyce-Clark radial shape index 185
    Advanced techniques 187
  Comment on Shape Indices 187
Point Patterns 187
  Types of Distributions 188
  Quadrat Analysis 188
    Quadrat size and orientation 189
    Weaknesses of quadrat analysis 190
  Nearest-Neighbor Analysis 190
  Spatial Correspondence of Areal
    Distributions 193
  Coefficient of Areal Correspondence 193
  Chi-Square Statistic 194
  Other Methods 197
Summary 197
Suggested Readings 198

12 Characteristics of Map Features:
    Networks and Trees 200

Networks 200
  Terminology 200
  Accessibility 201
  Connectivity 201
  Network Types 201
  Measurement 202
  Applications 202
Trees 203
  Hierarchic Order 203
  Bifurcation Ratio 203
Summary 204
Suggested Readings 204

13 Qualitative and Quantitative
    Information 205

Point Symbols 205
  Dot-Distribution Maps 205
  Nonproportional Point Symbols 205

☐ Levels of Measurement 207
Nominal 207
Ordinal 208
Interval and Ratio 208

  Graduated Point Symbols 209
Linear Symbols 209
  Nominal Information 209
  Quantitative Information 209
    Ordinal representation 210
  Flow Maps 210
Areal Symbols 211
  Nominal Distributions 212
  Quantitative Distributions 212
    Choropleth maps 212
    Classification 214
    Evaluation 215
    Unclassed choropleth maps 217
    Bivariate and multivariate maps 217
    Dasymetric maps 218
    Prism maps 218
Surfaces 220
  Isolines 220
  Types of Isolines 220
    Isometric lines 220
    Isopleths 220
Summary 222
Suggested Readings 222

14   Cartograms and Map Misuse 224

Cartograms 224
   Linear Cartograms 224
      Routed linear cartograms 224
      Central-point linear cartograms 225
   Area Cartograms 226
      Noncontiguous cartograms 226
      Contiguous cartograms 227
      Interpreting area cartograms 227
Map Misuse 228
   Map Inaccuracy 228
   Propaganda 229
      General characteristics 229
      Symbol distortion 230
      Use of imaginary events 232
      Distortion of concepts 232
      The Peters projection 233
Summary 234
Suggested Readings 235

15   Special-Purpose Maps 236

Transportation Maps 236
   Highway and Street Maps 236
      Highway maps 238
      Street maps 240
   Automated Navigation 240
   Route Maps 240
Weather and Climate Maps 241
   Weather Maps 241
   Climate Maps 243
Geologic Maps 243
Maps of the Past 246
   Historical Maps 246
   History Maps 247
Maps of the Moon and Planets 248
Journalistic Cartography 248
Television Maps 251
Summary 252
Suggested Readings 253

16   Maps and Graphs 254

Line Graphs 254
   Types of Variables 254
   Maps as Graphs 254
   Types of Scales 255
      Arithmetic line graphs 256
      Logarithmic line graphs 261

Surface Graphs 264
Bar Charts 265
   Types of Scales 265
   Use of Symbols 266
   Other Types of Bar Charts 267
      Loss-and-gain bar charts 267
      High-low bar charts 267
   Interpretation Problems 267
Pie Charts 267
Area and Solid Diagrams 270
   Proportional Symbols 270
      Graduated circles 270
      Other geometric symbols 272
      Realistic figures 272
   Volumetric Diagrams 273
Special Diagrams 273
   Scatter Diagrams 273
   Population Profiles 274
   Circular Graphs 276
      Climatograph 276
      Wind-rose 277
   Triangular Graphs 278
Summary 278
Suggested Readings 279

17   Remote Sensing from Airborne Platforms 280

Methods and Images 280
   Electromagnetic Spectrum 280
   Types of Remote-Sensing Devices 280
      Spectral range 281
      Signal source 281
      Detector location 281
Aerial Photography 281
   Types of Aerial Photographs 281
      Vertical photographs 281
      Oblique photographs 281
   Photographic Materials 283
      Negatives and positives 283
      Emulsion types 284
   Photo Characteristics 286
      Scale 287
      Planimetric shift 288
   Aerial Photo Products 289
      Single prints 289
      Photomosaics 290
      Orthophoto products 292

Photo Interpretation 292
    Visual clues 292
    Interpretive keys 294
Stereoscopic Pairs 294
    Stereoscopic viewing 294
    Interpretation 295
Other Airborne Imagery 296
    Radar 296
    Scanners 296
Summary 297
Suggested Readings 297

18   Remote Sensing from Space 299
Spectral Characteristics 299
Collection Systems 299
Ground Resolution 300
Image Creation 300
Examples of Remote-Sensing Systems 300
    Landsat 300
    SPOT 303
Image Processing 303
    Linear Contrast Stretching 304
    Edge Enhancement 304
Thematic Information Extraction 304
    Classification 304
    Change Detection 306
Interface with Geographic Information
    Systems 306
Summary 306
Suggested Readings 307

19   Computer-Assisted Cartography 308
Overview 308
    Advantages of Computer-Assisted
        Techniques to the Map Producer 308
    Implementation Problems of Computer-
        Assisted Techniques 309
    Effects of Computer-Assisted Techniques
        on the Map User 309
Format and Data Capture 309
    Digitizing 309
        Labeling 310
        Vector and raster digitizing 310
    Other Considerations 310
        Machine coordinates 310
        Geocoding 311
        Format and the user 311
Output 311
Applications 312

Microcomputer Programs 312
Larger-Scale Applications 314
    Irrigation potential 314
    Terrain analysis 314
    Other applications 314
Database Availability 314
    U.S. Geological Survey Products 315
        Digital line graphs 315
        Digital elevation models 317
        Digital land-use and land-cover data 318
        Geographic Names Information
            System 318
    Census Bureau Products 318
        TIGER 318
    World Data Banks 320
    Other Databases 320
Summary 321
Suggested Readings 322

20   Digital Geographic Information
Systems 323
Overview 323
    Definition 323
    Antecedents of GISs 323
    Formal GISs 325
GIS Components 325
    Data Input and Storage Structure 325
    Data Adequacy 326
    Data Forms 327
        Points 327
        Lines 327
        Areas 327
        Surfaces 327
    Rectification 327
    Labeling 327
    Format Considerations 327
    Manipulation and Analysis Techniques 328
        System capabilities 328
        Basic operations 328
        Reclassification 328
        Overlaying 329
        Distance functions 330
        Modeling 331
    Output Capabilities 334
        Statistical reports 334
        Maps and graphs 334
GIS Applications 334

Industrial site selection 334
Military examples 334
Other examples 335
Summary 335
Suggested Readings 336

21 U.S. and Canadian Map Producers and Information Sources 337

U.S. Federal Map Producers 337
Major Agencies 337
U.S. Geological Survey 337
Bureau of Land Management 338
National Ocean Service 338
Defense Mapping Agency 339
Other Agencies 339
Army Corps of Engineers 339
Bureau of Indian Affairs 339
Bureau of the Census 341
Central Intelligence Agency 341
Department of Agriculture 342
Department of Transportation 344
National Aeronautics and Space
Administration 345
National Park Service 345
National Weather Service 345
Tennessee Valley Authority 345
Major Map Series 345
U.S. Geological Survey Topographic
Maps 345
National Ocean Service Nautical
Charts 348
Nonfederal Map Producers 349
State Agencies 349
Major Private Firms 350
AAA Cartographic Services 350
Donnelley Cartographic Services 350
General Drafting Company, Inc. 350
Gousha/Simon and Schuster, Inc. 351
Hammond Incorporated 351
National Geographic Society 352
Nystrom 352
Rand McNally and Company 352
Information Sources for Maps and Related
Materials 353
Federal Sources of Information 353
Earth Science Information Center
Network 353

National Geodetic Information
Center 353
EROS Data Center 354
National Environmental Satellite, Data,
and Information Service 354
Nonfederal Sources of Information 355
Publications 355
Earth Observation Satellite
Company 355
SPOT Image Corporation 355
Map Collections 355
Library of Congress 355
National Archives 356
The American Geographical Society
Collection 356
Defense Mapping Agency 356
Specialized examples 356
Canadian Government Maps 357
Topographic Mapping 357
Aeronautical Charts 357
Defense Mapping 357
Other Maps and Related Publications 357
National Geographical Mapping
Program 358
Map Information and Ordering 358
Maps from Statistics Canada 358
Toponyms 358

☐ **Names on Maps 359**

Northern Land Use Information Series 360
Aerial Photography 360
Hydrographic Charts 360
Summary 360
Suggested Readings and Reference
Materials 360

22 Foreign Maps 363

Language 363
Signs and Symbols 364
Locational Systems 364
Graticule 365
Centesimal system 365
Prime meridian 365
Plane Rectangular Grids 365
Units of Measurement 366
Foreign Map Products 366
Summary 367
Suggested Readings 367

Appendixes

A Copyright 368

B Magnetic Compass Use 369

C Sources of Mapping Programs and
    Databases for Microcomputers 373

D International Map of the World 378

E Earth Science Information Center (ESIC)
    Network 380

F Map Storage and Cataloging Systems 387

G British National Grid 395

Glossary of Selected Terms 397

Index 419

Preface

This book is designed to serve as an introduction to the fascinating world of maps. It explains how to use maps to obtain information about a wide variety of topics. Throughout the book, maps are viewed in a broad framework. Thus, the discussion includes mental maps, aerial photographs, remotely sensed images, computer-assisted cartography, and geographical information systems, in addition to traditional printed maps. The writing style is neither formalistic nor casual, with an emphasis on clarity of explanation. The discussions assume that the reader has no specific prior knowledge of the topic, so that even novice map users can understand and use the information and techniques presented.

Chapter 1 explains why maps are useful and lists the many types of maps available. Then, mapping processes are discussed in Chapter 2 because an understanding of how maps are produced provides a necessary basis for their proper use. For similar reasons, important aspects of the size and shape of the earth are reviewed. Chapter 3 surveys the characteristics of map projections, especially from the standpoint of the appropriateness of certain projections for specific purposes. The link between scale and generalization is discussed in Chapter 4, as are methods of scale determination. Because maps are used for measuring distances and areas, Chapter 5 discusses techniques for carrying out these measurements.

Techniques used in route selection and navigation on land and water and in the air are examined in Chapter 6. Chapter 7 examines how the surface of the terrain is represented on maps. Contour interpretation techniques and techniques for producing profiles and determining slopes are provided in Chapter 8. Chapter 9 follows with extensive illustrations of a variety of landform types. The examples shown are, in large part, selected from the definitive U.S. Geological Survey collection *A Set of 100 Topographic Maps Illustrating Specified Physiographic Features.*

A variety of locational and land ownership systems, which are essential for specifying location and for describing land ownerships, are explained in Chapter 10. These include latitude and longitude, the Universal Transverse Mercator and State Plane Coordinate systems, metes-and-bounds surveys, the U.S. Public Land Survey System, and the similar Canada Land Survey System.

More abstract topics are introduced in the following two chapters. First, Chapter 11 surveys the characteristics of mapped distributions, such as the shape and pattern of point distributions. Second, Chapter 12 analyzes stream patterns and transportation systems through the abstract concepts of networks and trees.

Chapter 13 discusses methods by which thematic maps are used to convey a variety of qualitative and quantitative information. Cartograms, map misuse, and the use of maps as powerful propaganda tools are examined in Chapter 14. Chapter 15 surveys a variety of special-purpose maps, including highway and street maps, weather and climate maps, geologic maps, maps of the past, maps of the moon and the planets, and maps in journalism and on television. Chapter 16 is devoted to the interpretation of graphs. Graphs are important in their own right, but they are also extensively used as map symbols and as map supplements.

Remote-sensing techniques are becoming increasingly important and accessible to map users. Therefore, aerial photography, as well as remote sensing from space, are explained in Chapters 17 and 18. Chapter 19 describes modern techniques of computer-assisted cartography, and Chapter 20 examines geographic information systems. Both of these approaches are increasingly used to produce unique products and analyses of interest to map users.

A survey of U.S. and Canadian map producers and map sources is provided in Chapter 21. This chapter also includes comments on major map collections that map users will want to visit when their travels permit. The final chapter, Chapter 22, briefly discusses the special problems often encountered when dealing with foreign maps.

At appropriate points in the text, supplementary treatments of a variety of topics are provided, including discussions of the analemma, dates and time zones, units of measurement and map scales, the National Map Accuracy Standards, and levels of measurement. Finally, appendixes discuss a variety of background topics, including copyright protection, the use of the magnetic compass in the field, sources of mapping programs and databases for microcomputers, the International Map of the World, the locations of Earth Science Information Network Offices, map storage and cataloging systems, and the British National Grid.

While working on this second edition, I have been conscious of my continuing indebtedness to the many people who assisted in the production of the first. I have also appreciated and benefitted from the comments in published reviews, as well as from those submitted during the revision process. Particularly appreciated have been the less formal comments offered at meetings, and in letters and telephone calls. The following reviewers provided numerous useful suggestions: Daniel E. Turbeville, Eastern Washington University; Linda M. Marston, University of Wyoming; Kenneth W. Engelbrecht, Central Missouri State University; and Joseph W. Weidel, University of Maryland. All comments have been considered carefully and many have been incorporated into the text. However, not every suggestion has been heeded. This is not because of stubbornness but because (as always) it is impossible to please everyone. A plea for more detail on a particular topic from one reviewer, for example, has frequently been directly countered by a suggestion from another that the topic be eliminated altogether. Thus, in the end, I have had to follow my own view of what is needed. I hope that many of these decisions will prove correct.

I remain indebted to my colleagues in the Geography Department at the University of Wisconsin–Parkside for their active support and encouragement. It is hard to visualize a more congenial group of long-term colleagues. Finally, as always, I thank my wife, Hazel, for her continued loyalty and her companionship on the hiking and kayaking expeditions that have put our map use skills to the test.

John Campbell
Racine, Wisconsin

1
Introduction

WHY USE A MAP?

Maps are an ancient invention, probably having existed for over four thousand years. Remnants of clay-tablet maps dating to about 2500 B.C. have been found (figure 1.1). In addition, primitive, maplike scratchings in the sand, as well as maps in other forms, likely existed for many millennia before that.

These early maps performed useful functions for their creators, functions that maps still perform for us today. For example, maps are especially effective devices for recording and communicating information about the environment. Most importantly, they clearly preserve the locational attributes of that information; that is, they show the relationships between one feature and another. Not only do they show that there is a forest outside of town, but they also indicate the extent and limits of both forest and town. This is something that other forms of recording and communicating information, such as written descriptions, tables, and graphs, generally do not do as effectively or efficiently. Furthermore, maps can also indicate distances and directions between locations, or the areas occupied by different types of land uses or features.

In more recent times, maps have acquired additional applications. For example, they are useful for determining the patterns formed by many types of distributions on the earth's surface. The arrangements of cultural features, such as the spacing between towns or the patterns of roads and other transportation facilities, can be analyzed using maps.

FIGURE 1.1 Clay-tablet map, circa 2500 B.C. Oldest known map, discovered in the ruins of Nuzi in northern Mesopotamia by the American School in Baghdad and Harvard University. Mountain ranges are shown on the left and right. Two rivers join near the bottom of the map and flow toward the upper-left corner. Localities of special interest are designated by circles, within which the names are written. (Size of the original: 7.6 by 6.5 centimeters.) SMN 4172. Photograph courtesy of the Harvard Semitic Museum.

Similarly, the alignments of physical features, such as streams and lakes, and the crests of hills and the floors of valleys, can be determined. The arrangements of such features can be explored, organized, and analyzed by visual and statistical methods, using maps as the database. These techniques have aided investigators in the generation of hypotheses about why the patterns are as they are. These investigations have suggested, for example, that certain economic relationships underlie the locational pattern of settlement and that the pattern of some physical features affects the location of specific human activities. Similarly, regular physical relationships underlie the patterns of stream erosion, the arrangement of drumlins in glaciated regions, and the alignment of river tributaries, to name just a few of the vast multitude of possible examples.

Maps are not limited only to showing information about physical and cultural features found on the earth's surface. They are also used to show distributions of more abstract features, such as the flow of trade, the use of communications, the extent of political influence, or the areas occupied by peoples of various races, languages, or religions. They provide a major source of historical documentation and are used for regional planning and property-assessment purposes. In addition, features found on the surface of extraterrestrial bodies, such as the moon and the planets, have been mapped, as have imaginary environments used as the settings for works of fiction.

Regardless of the topic or the locale maps frequently play a role in providing information and explanations regarding topics of interest. The rest of this introductory chapter examines just what constitutes a map.

WHAT IS A MAP?

The answer to the question, What is a map? may seem rather obvious to someone who is interested enough in maps to read this book. Maps, after all, are neatly drawn, bird's-eye views of the earth's surface. They show where places and things are located and help us find our way from one place to another. We are all familiar with many kinds of maps—from those confusingly folded, multicolored road maps that are stuffed into the glove compartments of our automobiles; to the beautifully drawn illustrations in books and atlases that provide information about the distribution of climates, vegetation types, languages, income, political patterns, and myriad other topics; to the topographic sheets whose intricate contours and drainage patterns serve as guides for our hiking or fishing expeditions. A visit to the map collection of your community or university library will convince you that a tremendous variety of maps is available.

In recent years, new methods of gathering, analyzing, and presenting information about the earth have been introduced, including aerial photography and satellite-based remote sensing, as well as computer methods. These developments have made it necessary to recognize that the conventional maps mentioned previously are only part of the contemporary map picture and that the definition of maps must include an extremely broad range of "products." Some of these products show topics that are physical (such as road maps), some show more social or cultural topics (such as language maps), and some show even more abstract subjects (such as maps of income levels). In addition, many products, such as aerial photographs or satellite images, qualify as maps even though they do not resemble conventional maps. It also has been suggested that some "maps" are not even visible. Invisible maps may exist only as bits of electronic information stored in the memory of a computer, or, even more abstractly, only in our minds. Finally, maps are not limited to representing information about the earth. They are equally useful, for example, for showing features found on the moon or the other planets, and they can present patterns that exist on the ground (topographic maps), under the ground (geologic maps), or above the ground (weather maps).

Given the variety of possible maps, this text uses a broad, flexible definition: A map is any concrete or abstract image of the distributions and features that occur on or near the surface of the earth or other celestial bodies. The great variety of map concepts that fall within this definition can be classified as either (1) real maps or (2) virtual maps.[1]

[1]The classes used here are simplified from those proposed by Harold Moellering in "Real Maps, Virtual Maps, and Interactive Cartography," in *Spatial Statistics and Models,* ed. Gary L. Gaile and Cort J. Willmott (Dordrecht, Holland: D. Reidel Publishing, 1984), 109–32.

FIGURE 1.2   Map image on the screen of a cathode-ray tube (CRT).

Courtesy of Intergraph Corporation.

A **real map** is any tangible map product that has a permanent form and that can be directly viewed (often referred to as "hard copy"). Conventional drawn or printed products (traditionally called maps) fit into this category, as do maplike aerial photographic products or the end product of some other type of remote sensing, maps produced using devices controlled by computers, block diagrams and similar drawings, and relief models and globes constructed to represent some part or all of the earth's surface.

Virtual maps are related to real maps in one way or another and have qualities that allow them to be converted into real maps. They are divided into three types.

One type of virtual map consists of images that can be directly viewed but are not permanent. A map image projected onto the screen of a **cathode-ray tube (CRT)** is an example (figure 1.2). Such an image is real while the device is turned on, and the information that it presents is similar or identical to that of a real map of the same topic. The difference is that as soon as the CRT is turned off, the image vanishes.

A second type of virtual map consists simply of mental images that are in many ways the conceptual equivalent of a conventional printed map.

The third type of virtual map consists of information gathered by researchers in the field or obtained by remote-sensing methods about such topics as surface elevations, rock types, soils, ethnic types, income levels of inhabitants, types of crops, and names and locations of geographic features. Such geographic data are traditionally stored in written notes, books, or computer printouts, all of which can be directly viewed. Increasingly, however, they are stored in digital form in a computer memory or storage device, such as a magnetic disk. This form of map is common for remotely sensed information, which is often gathered and stored directly in digital form, but also frequently includes information converted from printed or written sources. Computer software and hardware systems permit this type of information to be seen in tabular form, or in the form of a visual image.

All three types of virtual maps can be converted into visible, "real" map products.

While there is not complete agreement on the use of the term *virtual map,* the label does convey the idea that a map is simply a special format for the storage of geographic data. Whether the information is called "map data" or "virtual maps," there is no doubt that it is an integral element of the mapping process. Virtual maps are discussed frequently in this book, beginning with the next section.

VIRTUAL MAPS

Mental Maps

As already noted, the current concept of maps must encompass much more than the artifacts traditionally called maps. Indeed, the most familiar but, at the same time, most unusual forms of maps are the virtual maps called cognitive maps, or mental maps.

Mental maps are images we have in our minds. These images provide us with an awareness of the location of places in the world, the relationships between places in terms of direction and distance, the size and characteristics of regions, and so on. Mental maps have been called "the environmental image, the generalized mental picture of the exterior physical world that is held by an individual."[2] Some mental

---

[2]Kevin Lynch, *The Image of the City* (Cambridge, Mass.: M.I.T. Press, 1960), 4. Much of the discussion that follows is based on this book.

FIGURE 1.3   Mental map images of the same
neighborhood, drawn by three different boys: Dave,
Ernest, and Ralph.

From Peter Gould and Rodney White, *Mental Maps* (Pelican Books, 1974).
Reprinted by permission.

maps are a kind of miniature map in the mind, sometimes rather vague and ill-formed, but sometimes
complete with accurate details. Other mental maps are
more subtle and difficult to define because they are
somewhat more abstract and are tailored to one's individual conceptions, experiences, and needs, even
to the point of distortion. Indeed, it has been suggested that mental maps "are quite unlike [real] maps
. . . because they are personal, fragmentary, incom-
plete, and presumably, frequently erroneous."[3]

One aspect of the mental map concept is easily illustrated. Simply visualize the route that you usually
follow from your home to the shopping center, or
recall the general outline of the United States and the

locations of its cities and states. Consider how easily
you move about in different environments with the
help of your mental images. The framework that
mental maps provide allows you to tell others about
the route that you follow, and they may be able to visualize it as well. Furthermore, such a mental image
provides a frame of reference to which you can add
information on the basis of your new experiences. A
mental map can be converted into a more conventional real map by sketching its image on a piece of
paper (figure 1.3). We all do this when we want to
guide our friends to our new house or to indicate to
a stranger the best route to follow to see the local
tourist attractions.

Another aspect of mental maps is illustrated by
considering where in the country you would prefer
to live if you were given a choice. You are almost sure

[3]John S. Keates, *Understanding Maps* (New York: John Wiley and Sons, A
Halsted Press Book, 1982), 53.

to have a ready answer to the question. Certain regions, states, or cities undoubtedly appeal to you, whereas others have absolutely no allure, and still others fall somewhere in between. Almost everyone, it seems, has somehow endowed different locations with images of relative attractiveness or repulsiveness. Such images are often shared with other individuals who have been exposed to the same physical and cultural environments.

A number of considerations undoubtedly affect your feelings about where you would like to live. For example, what is the climate like? Is there a year-round monotony about it, or is there a variation between summer and winter weather, with the spring and fall transitions that many people find attractive and invigorating? If you are a sports buff, you may prefer a location that promises a long snow season to facilitate skiing, or a year-round warm climate suited to swimming and other water sports.

Other factors that you may consider include scenery: Is the view that meets the eye an unvarying, flat plain, or are there mountains or seashores to bring variety? Or, how about pollution: Are the air and water clear, or is there likely to be contamination of either or both? Even the reputation of a state for having a good or bad government can enter into your mental rating.

Social contacts and preferences may also affect your mental image of the place you would like to live. Regional reputations differ with regard to the sociability and openness of the residents toward newcomers, and one may appeal to you more than another, depending upon your own social style. Economic conditions are also important. If an area has a reputation for economic growth and activity, it may appeal to you because it provides the potential for prosperity.

In the end, your mental image of a region is a composite of a whole range of considerations. Certainly, not all considerations are equally important. If one element has greater importance you will give it greater weight than another less important element. Such weighting is not necessarily systematic, but the relative importance of the factors is taken into account in forming your mental map. Obviously, not everyone's mental map will be the same. All of the preferences are subjective, but they are nevertheless real.

How are these subjective images of desirability or repulsiveness formed? Partly by direct experience. You may have traveled in certain areas, for example, and formed impressions based on your experiences and observations. Even such direct experience must be recognized as subject to error. This is especially true if the period of observation is too short, or if it occurs under conditions that are different from those of your ordinary, day-to-day existence.

Other, less direct, factors may also enter into the formation of opinions about the relative desirability of different locales. You may be influenced by geography courses, news broadcasts, maps, television programs or movies, or conversations. If the information you obtain is inadequate, inaccurate, or otherwise misleading, your conclusions will be faulty. Although opinions based on indirect sources may not be as solid as those drawn from direct experience, they are no less influential.

Experimentation has shown that there are certain similarities between people's mental maps of where they would like to live, even though they find themselves at different locations. In figure 1.4, some mental map concepts have been converted to more familiar map form. These examples summarize the spatial preferences of groups of students enrolled in universities located in different regions of the United States. The students were asked to rank the forty-eight contiguous states in terms of desirability (the higher the score, the greater the desirability).

The rating maps have general tendencies in common. For example, some parts of the country are consistently viewed as more attractive. Western California, central Colorado, and, to a lesser extent, northern New England fall into this category. Other areas, such as the South (especially Alabama and Mississippi) and the Dakotas, are generally seen as less attractive. On the other hand, the maps also show that people like areas with which they are familiar. In each case, the home territory of the raters tends to be viewed as relatively attractive. Alabamians, for example, have high regard for their home state and adjoining parts of Florida and Georgia. Minnesotans and Pennsylvanians have similar views of their home territories. Each of these ratings contrasts with the views of the other three groups. Californians also view western California as attractive, thus reinforcing the general trend. In addition, however, they extend their preference area farther north and south along the coast. You may find it interesting to compare these maps with your own preferences.

FIGURE 1.4 Mental maps representing students' views of the desirability of the forty-eight contiguous states. Views from: (*a*) California, (*b*) Minnesota, (*c*) Pennsylvania, and (*d*) Alabama.

Adapted from Peter Gould and Rodney White, *Mental Maps* (Pelican Books, 1974). Reprinted by permission.

Digital Data

Increasingly, computer methods are being used in mapping and related fields. Computers are being applied to the processing and analysis of remote-sensing data, to the production of maps (called **computer-assisted cartography**) and to the operation of **geographic information systems**. These applications are discussed in chapters 19 and 20.

Computer techniques can introduce a number of potential advantages, including speedier, easier, and more accurate map design and production. Other manipulations, including scale and projection changes and the statistical analysis of data, can also be more easily accomplished using computer techniques. Increased timeliness is also anticipated because updated information can be made immediately available to all users from a centralized database. Overall, computer methods should provide the cartographer with the flexibility to produce more innovative and effective maps.

Although the potential advantages of computer applications in cartography are not always achieved, progress is being made, and more frequent computer applications are inevitable in the future. Some of the results produced by computer methods will be indistinguishable from conventional maps. Other results, however, may be quite different, and some knowledge of the methods by which they were produced will help you to understand and evaluate them. For all of these reasons, portions of this book are devoted to computer applications in mapping.

REAL MAPS

Virtual maps have limitations that frequently make the use of more conventional real maps a necessity. "Indeed, one of the main reasons for making maps must be that 'mental maps' are inadequate as useful stores of locational information."[4] For this reason,

much of this book deals with actual, physical map products and with concepts and measures related to them. The sections that follow briefly summarize the many types of maps and maplike products.[5] The topics introduced here are discussed in greater detail throughout the rest of the text.

Planimetric Maps

A variety of information about the many types of features found on the earth's surface is shown on maps. Maps that do not attempt to show the relief features in measurable form are perhaps the simplest type and are called **planimetric maps**.

Planimetric **base maps** are often used to provide the framework for thematic maps, which present information about some special subject (see figure 1.13). Depending on the topic being presented, base maps range from very simple to very complex. Simple base maps are often adapted from existing maps and may contain only the shorelines and boundaries that outline a country or region. Other base maps may be more complex and may include rivers, political boundaries, transportation routes, and other information. The amount of detail shown on a base map depends on the purposes of the particular project.

Outline maps are outlines that provide a framework for plotting information (figure 1.5). They facilitate the preparation of quick sketch maps for study purposes or classroom use.

The information shown on **cadastral maps** usually includes the location of property-ownership lines, with their bearings and lengths, the ownership and size of land parcels, and similar information (figure 1.6). When you visit your assessor's office, for example, or purchase a piece of real estate, you almost inevitably make use of cadastral maps. Specialized maps of this general type, called **line-route maps**, are

---

[4]Keates, *Understanding Maps*, 53.

[5]Modified from Morris M. Thompson, *Maps for America*, 3d ed. (Washington, D.C.: U.S. Department of the Interior, U.S. Geological Survey, 1987), 15–17.

FIGURE 1.5 An outline map of the United States.

Source: Produced by the Department of Geography, University of Illinois.

FIGURE 1.6 Example of a cadastral map. (Village of Sturtevant, Racine County, Wisconsin, 1 inch to 100 feet, 1 February 1978.)

Courtesy of Racine County Planning and Development.

FIGURE 1.7   Example of line-route map.
Courtesy of Wisconsin Natural Gas.

used by utility companies to show the routes and rights-of-way of their transmission lines or pipelines (figure 1.7).

Topographic Maps

Maps that show the shape and elevation of terrain are generally called **topographic maps** (figure 1.8), to distinguish them from the planimetric type. The term *topographic* is from the Greek *topos* (place) and *graphien* (to describe) and means, therefore, as complete a description of a visible landscape as scale and symbol limitations allow. Similarly, **bathymetric maps** show water depths and the configuration of underwater topography (plate 1). Topographic and bathymetric maps have many uses, ranging from helping you plan the route for a hike or sailing outing to detailing the terrain of a piece of property you wish to purchase.

Within the general categories of topographic and bathymetric maps, several types can be distinguished, each produced in a wide range of scales. **Engineering maps** are detailed maps, sometimes called **plans**, used for guiding engineering projects such as bridges or dams, and as aids to estimating the construction costs of such projects (figure 1.9). If you become involved in any significant construction project, you will find it useful to be able to interpret such maps. **Flood-control maps** (figure 1.10), which are used to provide information about areas subject to flooding, are derived from topographic maps. Detailed and accurate terrain information is critical to determining flood risk.

FIGURE 1.8   Portion of a typical topographic map.
(Hyatt Gap quadrangle, Alabama, 1:24,000, 1958.)

FIGURE 1.9   Example of engineering map for landfill.
Courtesy of Racine County Planning and Development.

It may be of vital importance for you to be able to read such maps when you are evaluating a possible property purchase or other real-estate transaction. Another general type of topographic map—a **landscape map**—provides detailed site information and planting plans for gardens and parks (figure 1.11). You may want to sketch a map of this type for your own use or you may need to interpret landscaping plans that have been prepared for you by a landscape architect.

Thematic Maps

Thematic maps show information about any one of a myriad of special topics, superimposed on a base map (figure 1.12). Types of thematic maps include geologic, forestry, soil, land-use, slope, and historical. The information on these maps can be presented using a variety of techniques. The study of a selection of thematic maps provides an appreciation for the physical, historical, or social characteristics of a country or region that would be difficult to achieve in any other way. Similarly, thematic maps provide information that allows you to compare the characteristics of two or more different regions.

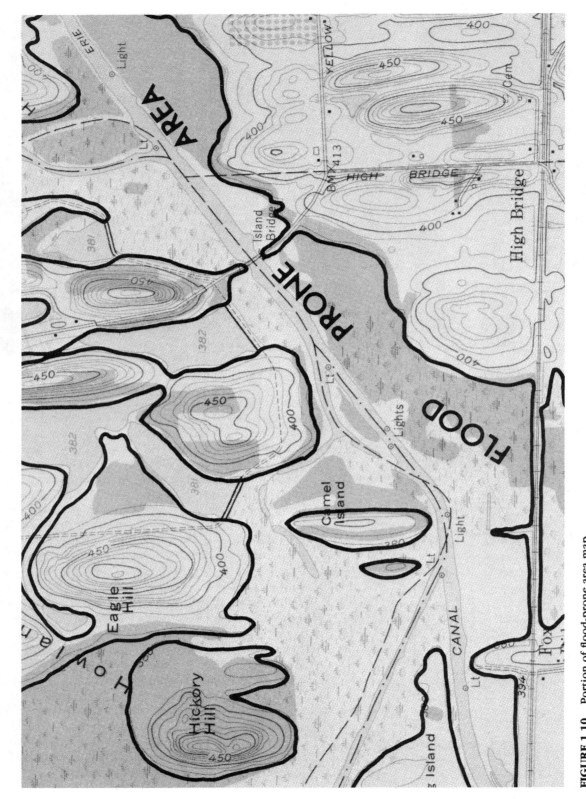

FIGURE 1.10 Portion of flood-prone area map. (Montezuma quadrangle, New York, 1:24,000.)

FIGURE 1.11   Example of a landscape map.

Courtesy of K. E. I. Kujawa Enterprises, Inc., Landscape Architecture
Division.

Thematic maps in which dots are used to represent a specific quantity of a particular variable are called **dot-distribution maps** (figure 1.13). The goal of such maps is to provide a visual image of the variation in the density of a distribution. The variables presented range from the number of cattle on farms to the distribution of human populations.

Thematic maps that show distributions summarized on the basis of areas delimited by state or county boundaries or other arbitrary boundary lines are called **choropleth maps** (figure 1.14). On a choropleth map, each area is colored, shaded, dotted, or hatched to appear as a darker or lighter tone. The darkness of the tone is designed to be proportional to the density of

FIGURE 1.12 Example of a typical thematic map.

From Ashok K. Dutt, Charles B. Monroe, and Ramesh Vakamundi, "Rural-Urban Correlates for Indian Urbanization," *The Geographical Review* 76, no. 2 (April 1986): 173–83. Reproduced by permission of The American Geographical Society.

the distribution. **Isoline maps,** on the other hand, show numerical values for continuous distributions by means of lines joining points of equal value (figure 1.15).

Variations in line width or color are used on thematic **flow maps** to show the direction and amount of movement, as well as the types of goods or services moved (figure 1.16). The placement of the flow lines sometimes indicates the actual route followed by the flow and sometimes simply shows that linkages exist between sources and destinations.

A wide variety of other types of thematic maps present quantitative information through the use of symbols such as proportional circles, pie charts, bar graphs, and other graphic methods.

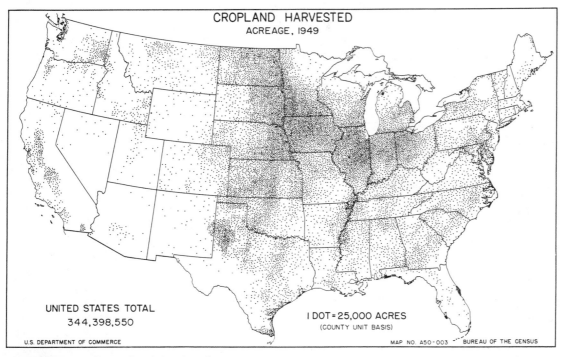

FIGURE 1.13 Example of dot-distribution map.

Source: U.S. Department of Commerce, Bureau of the Census, *Portfolio of United States Census Maps* (Washington, D.C.: U.S. Government Printing Office, 1953).

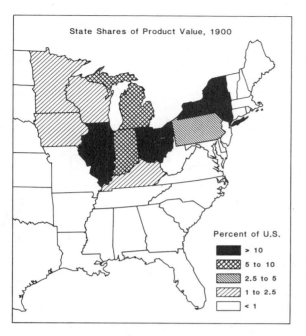

FIGURE 1.14 Example of choropleth map, showing state shares of product value, 1900.

From Mary Beth Pudup, "From Farm to Factory: Structuring and Location of the U.S. Machinery Industry," *Economic Geography* 63, no. 3 (July 1987): 203–22. Reprinted by permission.

Cartograms

Many representations of distributions are not traditional maps but are, instead, distorted representations called **cartograms**. Cartograms are created by substituting a different standard of measurement (time or cost, for example) for the distance measurement customarily used (figure 1.17). When this is done, sizes, shapes, and distances as we normally think of them are modified or distorted. Although the images thus formed show the world in a different and unfamiliar way, they often provide useful insights precisely because of their different appearance. You should know the strengths and weaknesses of cartograms.

Now that we have taken a broad overview of the many forms of maps, we can discuss in more detail how best to use them. Chapter 2 provides a basis for this discussion by reviewing some of the earth's important physical characteristics and how some of the information about those characteristics is gathered.

FIGURE 1.15 Example of isoline map. Lines join points of equal value on the Palmer Drought Severity Index (PDSI).

From Peter T. Soulé and Vernon Meentenmeyer, "The Drought of 1988: Historical Rank and Recurrence Interval," *Southeastern Geographer* 29, no. 1 (May 1989): 17–25. Reprinted by permission.

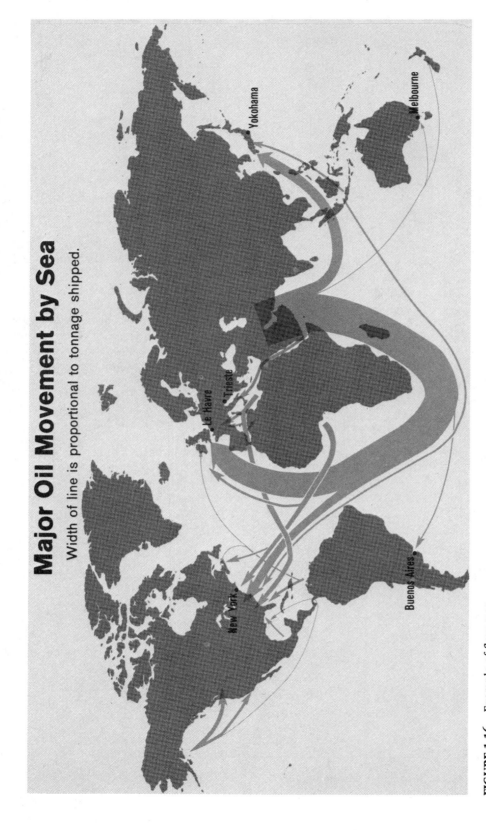

FIGURE 1.16 Example of flow map.

Source: Portion of Central Intelligence Agency map "The Persian Gulf,"
1:1,600,000, 1980.

FIGURE 1.17 **Cartogram showing countries of the Western Hemisphere drawn in proportion to their share of world total gross national product (compare with figure 14.4).**

Adapted and reprinted by permission from International Bank for Reconstruction and Development, The World Bank, *World Development Report 1984* (New York: Oxford University Press, 1984).

Remotely Sensed Images

Remote sensing consists of gathering information by means of a sensor—human vision is one example—that is not in contact with the objects in the scene being observed. The major types of remotely sensed information in the world of maps are aerial photographs, images from radar and other airborne sensors, and satellite images.

Aerial photographs are the most common remote-sensing product. They are categorized by their angle of view and by the type of photographic emulsion used.

The angle of view of aerial photographs may be either vertical or oblique. **Vertical aerial photographs** are those that are taken with the lens pointed straight down at the ground (figure 1.18a). **Oblique views** are taken with the lens pointed at an angle away from the vertical (figure 1.18b). It is important to distinguish between these two types because the uses to which they are typically put are quite different. For most mapping purposes, vertical aerial photographs are the most useful. You will find them helpful if you are evaluating real estate, for example, because they clearly show the relationships between various properties, as well as the arrangement of many of the properties' physical characteristics. For some purposes, however, oblique photographs serve equally well. If you are interested in dramatizing the location of a resort area, or showing an industrial site to advantage, an oblique aerial photograph is particularly useful. The techniques involved in the use of aerial photographs are explored in chapter 17.

In addition to angle of view, aerial photographs differ from one another in terms of the emulsion on which the image is captured. If a normal, black-and-white (panchromatic) emulsion is used, it is sensitive to a range of wavelengths within the electromagnetic spectrum that is quite similar to that seen by the human eye. The result, however, is a translation of the colors in the original scene into a range of shades of gray in the photograph. If, on the other hand, an emulsion that is sensitive to the ultraviolet wavelengths is substituted for the normal emulsion, the image obtained differs markedly in appearance and, more importantly, can be used for special applications. The use of color emulsions also permits looking at an image in special ways. Knowing the differences introduced into aerial photographs by the various emulsion types is helpful when you are using aerial photographs for a particular application.

Another type of remotely sensed product is the **radar image** (figure 1.19). To obtain a radar image, a special transmission is beamed from a power source, and the reflected energy is captured and converted into an image of the scene. The geometry and appearance of radar imagery is quite different from that

(a)

(b)

FIGURE 1.18   (*a*) Vertical and (*b*) oblique aerial
photographs of the same area in downtown Sheboygan,
Wisconsin.

Courtesy of Aero-metric Engineering, Inc.

FIGURE 1.19   Radar image of San Andreas Fault. SLAR
image (side-looking airborne radar).

Courtesy of Westinghouse Electric Corporation.

FIGURE 1.20   Satellite image of Racine, Wisconsin, and vicinity. (Landsat, color composite original, 2 April 1976.)

Source: U.S. Geological Survey EROS Data Center.

obtained by aerial photography, and there are a number of special applications for which it is particularly well suited.

Today, images can be captured by instruments taken aloft in spacecraft, with or without a human crew. Those images can be returned to earth, whether or not the spacecraft itself ever returns. The technology involved in gathering these **satellite images** from space has been improving rapidly since the early days of space flight (figure 1.20). A wide variety of images are available today, and they are used for an even wider variety of applications, some of which may be of interest to you. An appreciation for the characteristics of remotely sensed images will help you to decide if obtaining such coverage is likely to be useful to you.

Summary

Maps have been produced since ancient times because of the useful functions they perform. They record and communicate information about variations from place to place in the physical and social aspects of the environment. They record distance and direction and are useful tools for exploring, organizing, and analyzing information about the patterns formed by distributions on the earth's surface. They also provide clues for understanding the origins of those patterns. In addition, they provide historical documentation and are useful for regional planning and property-assessment purposes.

Real maps are actual images of the distributions and features that occur on or near the earth's surface. Virtual maps, on the other hand, include images that can be directly viewed but that are not permanent, mental images, and spatial information that is not in standard map form. Mental maps, for example, are images we hold of the exterior physical world. They provide a framework by which we move through and evaluate our environment.

In recent years, computers have allowed speedier, easier, more flexible, and more accurate processing and analysis of vast amounts of remotely sensed data. They have also assisted in the production of maps and in the operation of geographic information systems, and have provided the flexibility needed to produce more innovative and effective maps.

Much of this book deals with real maps and related concepts and measures. Real maps take many forms. Planimetric maps, for example, do not attempt to show relief features in measurable form. Topographic maps, on the other hand, show the shape and elevation of the terrain, and bathymetric maps show water depths and the configuration of the underwater topography. Other maps are used for guiding engineering projects, for planning flood-control measures, and for developing landscapes.

Thematic maps show information about special topics. They use a variety of symbols, including dots to represent the location and quantity of some particular variable, tones or patterns to show the arrangements of variables over areas (choropleth maps), lines to identify locations with the same data values (isoline maps), or lines to show flows and connections between locales.

Cartograms are deliberately distorted representations created by substituting a different standard of measurement (time or cost, for example) for standard distance or area measurements.

Remotely sensed images are gathered by means of a sensor that is not in contact with the objects in the scene being observed. Remotely sensed images include aerial photographs, images from radar and other airborne sensors, and satellite images. These images provide up-to-date information about features on the earth that otherwise might not be available to us.

SUGGESTED READINGS

Downs, Roger M., and David Stea. *Maps in Minds: Reflections on Cognitive Mapping.* New York: Harper and Row, 1977.

————, eds. *Image and Environment: Cognitive Mapping and Spatial Behavior.* Chicago: Aldine, 1973.

Gould, Peter, and Rodney White. *Mental Maps.* Baltimore, Md.: Penguin Books, 1974.

Harley, J. B., and D. Woodward, eds. *The History of Cartography. Volume 1: Cartography in Prehistoric, Ancient, and Medieval Europe and the Mediterranean.* Chicago: University of Chicago Press, 1987.

Lynch, Kevin. *The Image of the City.* Cambridge, Mass.: M.I.T. Press, 1960.

Moellering, Harold. "Real Maps, Virtual Maps, and Interactive Cartography." In *Spatial Statistics and Models,* edited by Gary L. Gaile and Cort J. Willmott. Dordrecht, Holland: D. Reidel Publishing, 1984, 109–32.

————. "Strategies of Real-Time Cartography." *Cartographic Journal* 17, no. 1 (1980): 12–15.

Parfit, Michael. "Putting Our Mental Demons on Maps." *Smithsonian Magazine* (May 1984): 121–31.

Robinson, Arthur H., Randall D. Sale, Joel L. Morrison, and Phillip C. Muehrcke. *Elements of Cartography.* 5th ed. New York: John Wiley and Sons, 1984, 20–36.

Thompson, Morris M. *Maps for America.* 3d ed. Washington, D.C.: U.S. Geological Survey, 1988.

Thrower, Norman J. W. *Maps and Man: An Examination of Cartography in Relation to Culture and Civilization.* Englewood Cliffs, N.J.: Prentice-Hall, 1972.

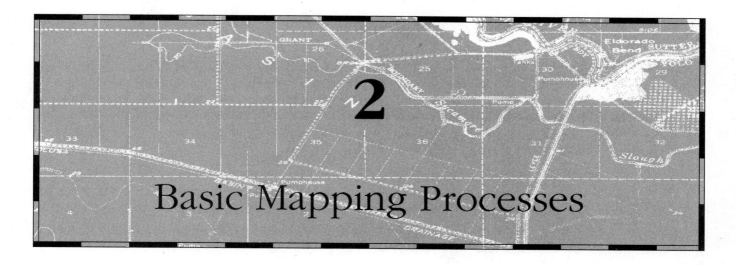

Basic Mapping Processes

This chapter examines methods for measuring the shape and size of the earth, determining locations on the earth's surface, and gathering basic information about objects located on the surface. A general background in these methods will improve your understanding of maps and the information shown on them.

SHAPE AND SIZE OF THE EARTH

Knowledge of the shape and size of the earth is crucial to understanding the relationships between maps and the world they represent. For this reason, we will discuss the basic attributes of the earth before turning specifically to the study of maps.

Basic Spherical Shape

The earth is spherical, not flat, and its spherical shape is difficult to represent on a flat map sheet. In this section, we will consider the evidence for a spherical earth. Map projections, which are used to represent the earth on maps, introduce many problems into map use. These problems, which must be understood by all map users, are discussed in chapter 3.

In recent years, astronauts observing the earth from a vantage point in space have seen convincing direct evidence that the earth is **spherical** (figure 2.1). Most of us, however, are confined to locations on or near the earth's surface. No matter where we are standing—whether on the shore of the ocean, at the base of a mountain range, on the brink of a canyon, or at the edge of a desert—there seems to be little immediate evidence of the earth's shape. But if we look methodically, we can find clues that lead to the conclusion that the earth is, indeed, spherical rather than flat.

Perhaps the simplest way to gather evidence that the earth has a spherical shape is to watch an object as its distance from us increases or decreases. Such an object, whether it is a ship that is moving out to sea, or a building that we are approaching on land, appears or disappears over the horizon in a certain manner, and that is our clue.

Consider, for example, what we see as a ship moves away from us. First, the ship appears to grow smaller as its distance from us increases. At the same time, it appears to sink over the ocean's surface, so that the bottom of its hull disappears first and the top of its mast disappears last (figure 2.2). This sequence of events occurs because the ship is moving over the curved surface of the earth. If the surface were not curved, the ship would appear to grow smaller, but its hull would always be in view. The apparent sinking movement just described is uniformly observed, regardless of one's location or the direction of one's movement. The only circumstance that would account for this universal occurrence is that the earth has a spherically-shaped surface.

Locational System

Before maps that accurately portray the locations of features on the earth's surface can be prepared, there must be a means of defining those locations. The method that has been adopted for this purpose is the

FIGURE 2.1   **Astronaut's view of earth rising over the moon's horizon (Apollo photo).**

Source: U.S. Geological Survey EROS Data Center.

FIGURE 2.2   **Successive views of a ship disappearing over the horizon.**

system of latitude and longitude. The chief characteristics of this system are briefly reviewed here because of its fundamental importance in the production and use of maps.

Because the earth is essentially a sphere, there would seem to be no unique location that would provide a natural starting point for a locational system. Fortunately, however, the earth rotates on its axis, and

the location of that axis, and of the **poles of rotation**, can be determined. The poles provide the starting point for the rest of the system.

Meridians.   Visualize a plane passing through the center of the earth. The line defined by the intersection of the plane with the earth's surface is called a **great circle** (figure 2.3a). An infinite number of great circles can be drawn, but those that pass through the poles are particularly useful. Each half of a great circle that joins the poles is defined as a line of longitude, or **meridian**. These lines are used to specify locations in the east-west direction (figure 2.3b). Because all of the meridians are identical, one must be selected as a starting point, or **prime meridian**. Most current maps use the meridian of Greenwich, England, as the prime meridian, although there are some exceptions. The

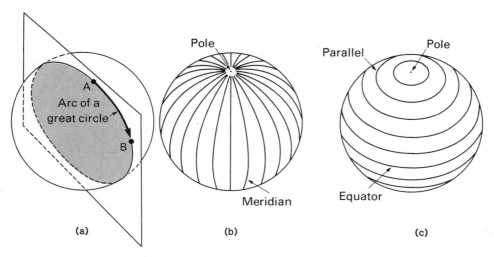

FIGURE 2.3   Characteristics of the graticule. (*a*) The arc of a great circle is the shortest distance between two points on the earth's surface. (*b*) Meridians (lines of longitude) are arcs of great circles that meet at the poles. (*c*) The equator is a great circle, located midway between the poles. Parallels (lines of latitude) are concentric small circles that are parallel to the equator.

prime meridian is given a value of 0, and the remaining meridians are numbered in degrees, east or west of the prime meridian (figure 2.4a). The highest numbered meridian is the 180th meridian, which is on the opposite side of the globe from the prime meridian.

Parallels.   A second set of locational lines is placed at right angles to the meridians. First, a great circle, called the **equator**, is located midway between the poles (figure 2.3c). Then a series of **small circles** is defined (a small circle is created when a plane passing through the earth divides the earth into two unequal portions). These small circles, which are called lines of **latitude**, or **parallels**, are placed parallel to the equator. They are numbered in degrees north and south from the equator, which is given a value of 0, with the maximum value of 90 assigned to each pole (figure 2.4b). Parallels are used to define locations in the north-south direction.

Graticule.   The pattern of meridians and parallels on the earth is referred to as the **graticule**. The following characteristics of the graticule are based on the simplifying assumption that the earth is a sphere:

1. Parallels are true east-west lines.
2. Parallels are equally spaced between the equator and the poles.
3. Parallels are always parallel to one another, so any two parallels are always the same distance apart all the way around the globe.
4. Meridians are spaced farthest apart on the equator and converge to a single point at the poles.
5. Parallels and meridians cross one another at right (90°) angles.

Refinements in Shape

A more detailed examination reveals that the earth's shape is not *exactly* spherical. (See the sources listed in the "Suggested Readings" at the end of the chapter

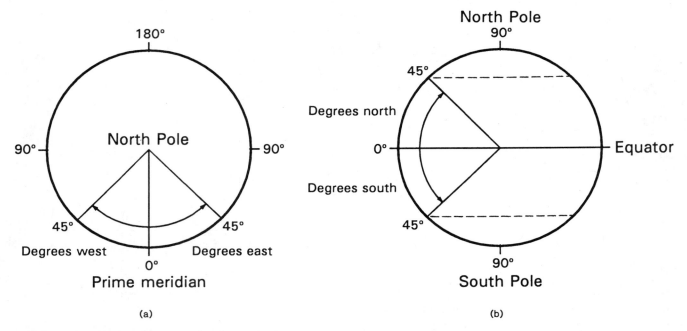

FIGURE 2.4   Numbering system for the graticule.
(*a*) Meridians. (*b*) Parallels.

for more information.) For our purposes, it is sufficient to note the general differences between the true
shape of the earth and a sphere.

Ellipsoid.   The earth revolves easterly on its axis.
This rotation generates centrifugal force, which causes
the earth to bulge slightly in the middle and to flatten
slightly at the poles, resulting in a shape called an **ellipsoid** (figure 2.5). The ellipsoid is the shape generated by an ellipse that rotates on its minor axis. It
has a slightly greater radius at right angles to the axis
of rotation and a slightly smaller radius along the axis
(figure 2.6a). This is called **polar flattening**. The difference is not great. Polar flattening amounts to about
1 part in 298, which means that the earth is very close
to the true spherical shape that results from the rotation of a circle (figure 2.6b). For this reason, many
general maps can be based on the assumption that the
earth is a sphere. Extremely accurate maps, on the
other hand, must be based on the earth's ellipsoidal
shape because of its effect on the spacing of the lines

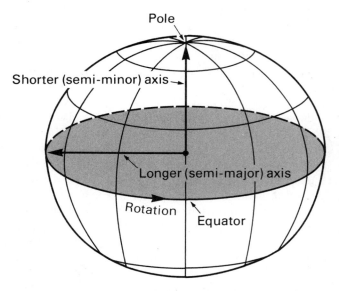

FIGURE 2.5   An ellipsoid is formed by rotating an ellipse
on its shorter axis.

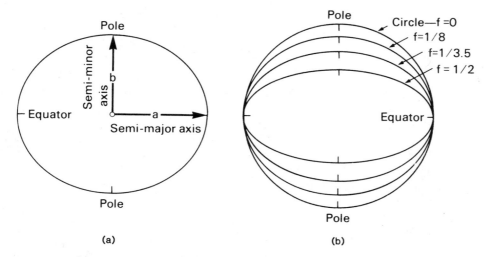

FIGURE 2.6   Characteristics of an ellipse. (*a*) The shape of an ellipse is determined by the relative lengths of its semi-minor and semi-major axes. (*b*) The flattening ratio of an ellipse representing the earth (approximately 1/298) is very close to zero, so the ellipse is almost a circle.

of latitude and longitude. The dimensions of the ellipsoid recently adopted for use in maps produced by U.S. government agencies are shown in table 2.1.

Geoid.   Accurate measurements of the earth's size and shape also reveal that it is not a "regular" ellipsoid but that it has a somewhat irregular shape, called the **geoid**. This is not a reference to the mountains and ocean bottoms that wrinkle the earth's surface. The vertical distance from the deepest part of the ocean to the highest mountain peak is about 19,880 meters (65,223 feet). The diameter of the earth is about 12,756,370 meters (41,851,481 feet), so the relief features are quite insignificant in comparison. What is more important, from the standpoint of detailed mapping and geodetic surveying, is that the earth's equigravitational surface undulates because of variations in the density of various portions of the earth's crust. These variations in mass, in turn, introduce variations in the effect of gravity and lead to the irregularities in shape. Again, for many purposes, the "lumpy" nature of the earth's surface can be ignored,

TABLE 2.1   Size of the Ellipsoid

Equatorial radius (in meters)—6,378,137	Flattening (approximate)—1/298

Source: International Union of Geodesy and Geophysics. Adopted for international use and used for North American Datum, 1983 (NAD83).

but the effects of the surface irregularities are taken into account in the detailed, geodetic surveys that provide the framework for detailed maps.

Size

How large is the earth? Obviously, knowing the earth's size is as fundamental as knowing its shape. Because maps are a representation of a portion of the earth's surface, the distances from one point to another on the earth must be determined so that they can be represented on maps or globes.

Although visualizing the earth's shape from indirect evidence is difficult, it at least seems more feasible to directly measure distances between points on the earth's surface. For relatively short spans, such as those required for local surveys, distances are measured directly, using surveying techniques. With longer distances, direct measurement is a much more difficult task. It is simply not feasible to take a measuring tape and work around the world, taking measurements along the way and totaling them at the end. The intervention of oceans, mountains, and other obstacles, coupled with a vast array of technical difficulties, make such a measurement process difficult to conceive and impossible to accomplish. Small errors that would inevitably be made along the way would accumulate and contribute to an inaccurate size determination. In addition, the earth's basic spherical shape increases the difficulty of measuring distances over its surface. How, then, can the size of the earth be measured?

The basic approach to measuring the earth is not particularly complex, nor is sophisticated modern equipment required. In fact, about 250 B.C., the Greek mathematician **Eratosthenes** measured the earth, using simple observations and applying his knowledge of basic principles of geometry. The exact methods used by Eratosthenes, as well as the accuracy of his measurements, have been debated many times, but the version presented here covers the major facts.

As a starting point for his measurement of the earth, Eratosthenes observed and measured shadows. He knew that, at the time of the **summer solstice**, the noon sun is directly overhead on the Tropic of Cancer. He then determined that the town of Syene (near present-day Aswan, Egypt) was located on the Tropic of Cancer because vertical shadows were cast there at the solstice.

He also observed that at noon on the occasion of a solstice, the sun cast an angled shadow in the city of Alexandria (which was located north of Syene on approximately the same meridian). He measured the angle of this shadow and found it to be one-fiftieth of the circumference of a circle. From geometry he knew that the angle between a pair of lines drawn vertically to the center of the earth from Syene and from Alexandria would be the same as the angle of the shadow that he had measured (figure 2.7). Because the angle between the verticals at Syene and Alexandria

amounted to one-fiftieth of a circle, it was apparent that the distance between the two towns was equal to one-fiftieth of the earth's circumference.

Eratosthenes next determined that the surface distance between Syene and Alexandria was 5,000 stadia, although accounts differ as to whether he had the distance carefully measured or whether he estimated it on the basis of travelers' reports. By multiplying 5,000 stadia by 50, he estimated the earth's circumference to be 250,000 stadia. Given modern-day estimates of the length of a stadia, the measurement appears to have been rather close to the presently accepted equatorial circumference of the earth, which is 40,075 kilometers (24,901 miles).

Details aside, what is important about the story of Eratosthenes' feat of measurement is his use of a logical, geometric method. Methods in use today employ more sophisticated equipment, but the same basic logic.

MAPPING PROCESS

Surveying involves taking measurements to determine the position of points on the earth's surface. A basic understanding of surveying helps you to see how the information used in the construction of maps is gathered. The two types of surveying are geodetic control and plane.

Geodetic Control Surveys

Detailed surveys that take into account the curvature of the earth and determine locations in terms of latitude and longitude are called **geodetic control surveys**. The principal reason for considering such surveys is that they provide the overall control, or framework, for maps. Because of the complexity of the subject, our discussion is limited to only a general consideration of geodetic control surveys.

The first step in a geodetic control survey is to establish the latitude and longitude of two starting points on the earth's surface. Such locations are determined by taking astronomic observations.

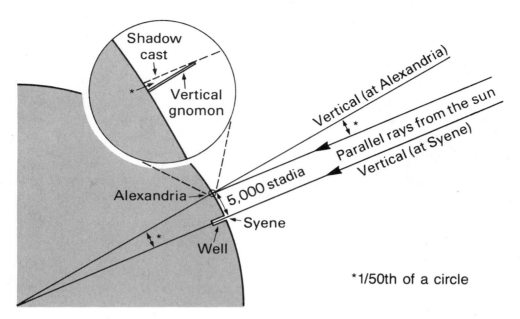

Shadow cast

Vertical gnomon

Vertical (at Alexandria)

Parallel rays from the sun

Vertical (at Syene)

Alexandria

5,000 stadia

Syene

Well

*1/50th of a circle

FIGURE 2.7 Eratosthenes' method of measuring the earth.

Latitude determination. To a present-day observer standing at the **North Pole**, the star **Polaris** is almost exactly overhead.[1] This means that Polaris is an excellent point of reference for determining latitude.

Throughout the Northern Hemisphere, measuring the angle between Polaris and the observer's horizon defines the observer's **astronomic latitude** (figure 2.8). To understand why this is so, suppose that the observer is standing at the North Pole. Polaris is, then, directly overhead. This means that the angle between the horizon and the star is 90 degrees, which is the latitude of the North Pole. In contrast, suppose that the observer is standing at the equator. At this location, Polaris falls directly on the horizon, at an angle of 0 degrees, which is the latitude of the equator. The same relationships hold, regardless of the observer's position, so that any Northern Hemisphere latitude can be determined by observing Polaris.

[1]Polaris is actually about 1½ degrees away from the extension of the earth's axis. Tables that compensate for this difference are available.

Other stars, including the sun, can be observed to determine latitude, and observations also can be made at locations in the Southern Hemisphere. The techniques involved in such observations are similar to those already mentioned, although adjustments are required to take into account differences in the location of the object observed, relative to the earth, at different times and dates.

Longitude determination. The process of determining longitude is not quite as straightforward as the method for determining latitude because, as already mentioned, longitude must be defined in relation to some arbitrary starting point on the earth's surface. The position of the sun provides the basic information for determining longitude. The moment the sun passes directly over a meridian is defined as **apparent solar noon** on that meridian. When apparent solar noon is observed at a given location, the difference between the observed time and the time of apparent solar noon at the Greenwich meridian provides a direct measure of the difference in longitude of the two locations.

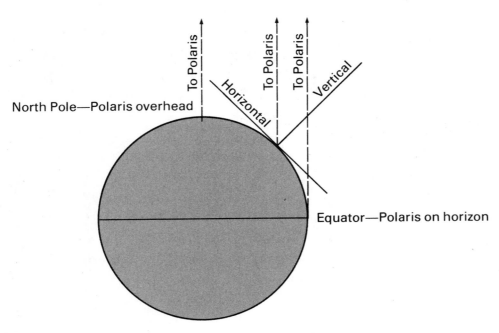

FIGURE 2.8 Measuring the angle between Polaris and the observer's horizon defines the astronomic latitude (Northern Hemisphere).

In the past, determining time and longitude was very difficult. From early maps of the world, it is apparent that the latitudes of places were fairly accurately known at quite an early stage. Longitude, however, was very inaccurately determined until the development, about 1735, of the extremely accurate clock called the **chronometer**. Indeed, the difficulty in making longitude determinations contributed to Columbus's belief that by sailing west from Europe he would, in relatively short order, reach Asia. He was overly optimistic because his estimate of the distance involved, based on longitude, fell far short of the actual distance. Fortunately, precise information regarding the time at Greenwich is now available worldwide from radio time signals. These signals provide the time information needed for determining longitude.

The relationship between time and longitude is clear. The sun appears to pass from east to west over a given meridian once every twenty-four hours. During that twenty-four hours, the sun passes over the full 360 degrees of the earth's circumference. Thus, every hour, the sun passes over 15 degrees of longitude (one twenty-fourth of 360 degrees). If, for example, it is 3:00 P.M. at the prime meridian when it is noon at the observation point, three hours have passed since the sun passed over the prime meridian. The sun has traversed 45 degrees of longitude during that time period, so the observation point is located 45° west of the prime meridian. Similarly, if it is 9:00 A.M. at the prime meridian when it is noon at the observation point, the sun will not pass over the prime meridian until three hours later. In this case, the observation point is located 45° east of the prime meridian.

THE ANALEMMA

When examining a globe, you may notice a figure-eight-shaped diagram that is usually located, simply as a matter of convenience, in the Pacific Ocean. This diagram is called an **analemma** (figure 2.9). An analemma gives information about the latitudes at which the sun is directly overhead throughout the year, as well as about the **equation of time.**

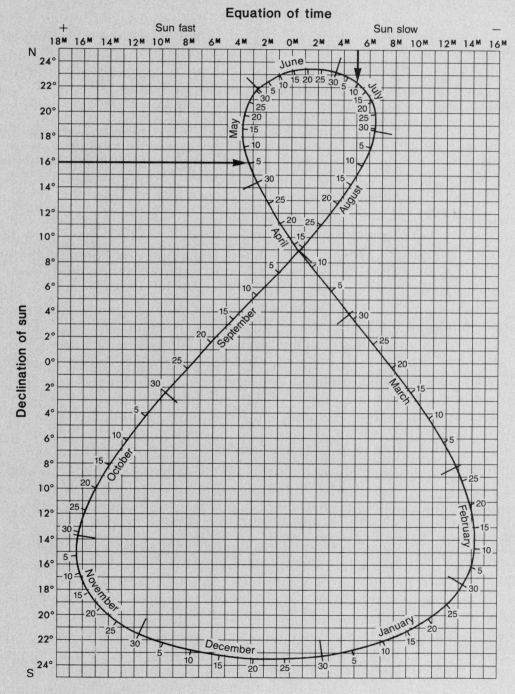

FIGURE 2.9   An analemma.

Box continued from page 29.

Although this information is provided more exactly in a set of tables, called an **ephemeris,** the analemma gives an interesting visual picture of the relationships.

The imaginary plane that passes through the sun and the earth at all positions of the earth's orbit around the sun is called the **plane of the ecliptic.** The earth's axis tilts 23½ degrees, relative to a line perpendicular to the plane of the ecliptic (figure 2.10). This tilt causes the sun to be directly over different latitudes, ranging from the Tropic of Cancer to the Tropic of Capricorn, at different times of the year. The analemma, therefore, stretches between the two tropics on the globe and indicates the parallel at which the sun is directly overhead on any given day. To use the analemma for this purpose, you must locate the date of interest on the diagram. The parallel that intersects it is the required parallel. For example, as shown in figure 2.9, the sun is almost directly over latitude 16° north on May 5th. This information, which is called the **altitude of the sun,** is used to adjust the calculation when an observation of the sun is being used to determine the latitude of a point on the earth's surface.

When the longitude of a point on the earth's surface is determined by observing the passage of the sun, the calculations must take into account the difference between apparent solar time and mean solar time. The reason for this concern is as follows. Noon—**apparent solar time**—is the precise moment at which the sun passes over the meridian

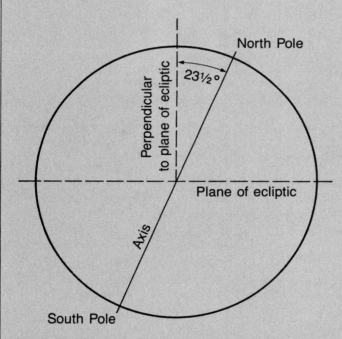

FIGURE 2.10   Earth's axis is inclined 23½ degrees from a vertical line through the plane of the ecliptic.

on which an observer is located. An **apparent solar day** is the period between one noon and the next at the same location. If the earth's orbit around the sun were perfectly circular, every day would be of the same duration. But because of the elliptical shape of the earth's orbit, the speed of the earth's movement varies. As a result, the length of an apparent solar day differs from one part of the year to another. For convenience, however, timekeeping on the earth is based on the average length of the day throughout the year. Thus, every day is taken to be twenty-four hours long. This is the concept of **mean solar time.** There is usually a difference between the time of passage of the sun over an observer's meridian (apparent solar noon) and the moment of noon on the observer's watch (mean solar time). The difference, which is obtained by subtracting mean solar time from apparent solar time, is called the **equation of time.**

The analemma is used to determine the equation of time on any given date. This is done by locating the desired date on the diagram and extending a vertical line from that date to the horizontal time scale. The intersection of the vertical line with the time scale indicates the number of minutes by which mean solar time is ahead of or behind apparent solar time. On July 10, for example, the line in figure 2.9 indicates that the sun is *slow* by 5 minutes, which means that apparent solar noon occurs 5 minutes after mean solar noon.

The equation of time is used to refine the time difference between an observation location and the prime meridian. This time difference can be important. An 8-minute time differential, for example, makes a difference of 2 degrees in longitude. Time differentials range from zero, on four occasions throughout the year, to as much as minus 14 minutes in February and more than plus 16 minutes in November.

DATES AND TIMES

It is noon (solar time) where you are when the sun passes over your meridian. At the same moment, half a world (180 degrees) away from your meridian, it is midnight. At the midnight meridian, one day ends and the next begins— it is no longer Monday, for example, but Tuesday, instead. These facts sound straightforward enough and would probably provide a sufficient set of timekeeping rules if, as in earlier periods of history, transportation and communication between different spots on the earth's surface were slow or nonexistent. The simple rules, however, lead to complications when we can travel or communicate quickly over long distances.

For example, according to the basic rules, if it is midnight, Monday at your location, it is 12:15 A.M., Tuesday a short distance to the east and 11:45 P.M., Monday the same distance to the west. The coordination of travel schedules for railroads or airlines, or broadcast schedules for radio or television stations would be hopelessly complex if we strictly followed the basic rules. The simple rules are even more confusing over long distances. If it is noon in Chicago, what time and what day is it in London? In Tokyo? In Rio de Janeiro? In the interests of simplifying this potential confusion, two special concepts—the International Date Line and the time zone—were introduced into timekeeping.

INTERNATIONAL DATE LINE

The meridian of Greenwich is generally accepted as the prime meridian (0° longitude). The 180th meridian is halfway around the world from Greenwich. Because the earth turns through 180 degrees in twelve hours, the 180th meridian is also half a day away from Greenwich. Thus, when it is noon at the Greenwich meridian, it is midnight at the 180th meridian.

Box continued on page 32.

Continued from page 31.

Wherever on earth the sun is at the meridian, morning ends and afternoon begins. Similarly, wherever on earth midnight comes, the old day ends and a new day begins. The 180th meridian has been given a special significance in relation to this event. Because it is half a day away from the prime meridian, it has been designated the **International Date Line.** What this means is illustrated by a complete, twenty-four-hour passage of times and dates (figure 2.11).

FIGURE 2.11   The progression of days around the world.
See text for details of (*a*) through (*e*).

Assume that it is precisely noon at Greenwich (0° longitude) and midnight at the International Date Line (180° longitude) (figure 2.11a). At that exact moment it is the same day (Monday for example) everywhere in the world. Then, in the next moment the day at the Date Line changes from Monday to Tuesday. As time passes Tuesday comes to additional areas of the earth. After six hours have passed (figure 2.11b), Tuesday has spread a fourth of the way around the world, west from the Date Line, and Monday has become correspondingly smaller. When the midnight line arrives at Greenwich (figure 2.11c), Tuesday is twelve hours old and has spread halfway around the world. The process continues (figure 2.11d) until Monday disappears (figure 2.11e) and Wednesday begins a new cycle of the same, never-ending progression. Except at the stroke of midnight on the Date Line, there are always two days on the earth at the same time. The 180th meridian always divides the new day from the old, which is why it is called the International Date Line.

An additional refinement that should be noted is that the Date Line does not follow the 180th meridian precisely (figure 2.12). The deviations from the meridian avoid the arbitrary division of a nation into two different days of the week. Eastern Siberia has the same day as the rest of Siberia, for example, and the western Aleutian Islands have the same day as the rest of that island chain.

The Date Line introduces a bit of potential confusion into trans-Pacific travel. If you cross the Date Line, going from east to west (toward Asia from North America for example), you advance from one day to the next (from Monday into Tuesday) (figure 2.12). If you cross in the other direction, you go from Tuesday back into Monday. There is a division between one day and the next at the midnight line as well. The midnight line, however, moves around the earth, as we have seen, whereas the International Date Line stays in place.[2]

Time Zones

The day is divided into twenty-four hours, and during a twenty-four-hour period, the earth rotates 360 degrees on its axis, at a rate of 15 degrees of longitude per hour. For convenience sake, the earth is similarly divided into twenty-four **time zones,** each spanning 15 degrees of longitude (figure 2.12). The central meridian of each of these zones is designated as a time meridian. In the conterminous United States, for example, the time meridians are 75° west, 90° west, 105° west, and 120° west. Under the time-zone concept, all localities within each zone keep the same time as the zone's time meridian.

The boundaries of the standard time zones have many jogs built in. These jogs tend to follow political boundaries (national and local) or are arranged to fall in sparsely populated areas. These accommodations reduce the necessity for persons engaged in local commerce to constantly adjust their time.

[2]Treating the polar view of the earth as a clock face provides a particularly useful way of keeping track of the progression of time and days. See David Greenhood, *Mapping* (Chicago: University of Chicago Press, Phoenix Science Series, 1964), 11–12.

FIGURE 2.12 International date line and time zones of the world. The time zone numbers indicate the number of hours by which zone time must be increased or decreased to obtain Greenwich Mean Time. Zones of small extent are omitted. (Based on Defense Mapping Agency Standard Time Zone Chart of the World, 24th ed., June 2, 1986.)

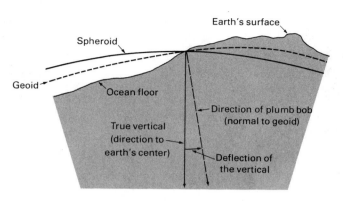

FIGURE 2.13   Deflection of the vertical.

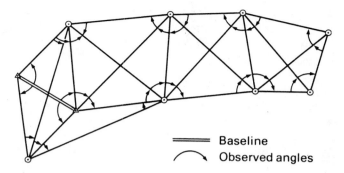

FIGURE 2.14   Typical triangulation network.

Deflection of the vertical.   The characteristics of the earth present another complication in determining location. The accuracy of the observations of the sun and stars depends in part on a precise determination of the vertical. This is because the instruments used to make the observations must be properly aligned relative to the earth. This alignment is accomplished by observing the pull of gravity using a level, a plumb bob, or a similar device. A plumb bob, for example, points toward the earth's center of gravity. Because of the variation in the earth's density, however, the direction to the center of gravity does not always coincide with the direction to the earth's geometric center. The difference at a given location between a vertical line drawn to the center of the earth and a vertical line drawn to the earth's center of gravity is called the **deflection of the vertical** (figure 2.13). During a geodetic survey, the effect of the deflection of the vertical must be taken into account.

Control network.   After the two starting locations have been determined from astronomical observations, the process of establishing a geodetic control network begins.[3] First, a baseline is carefully and accurately measured between the two known locations to serve as the basis for the remainder of the survey. A system of triangulation is then established by measuring the angles between the baseline and additional observation points (figure 2.14). From the length and direction of the baseline, and the measured angles from its precisely located endpoints, the

[3]In actual practice, the astronomic coordinates of a number of points are determined, and the relationships between them are mathematically adjusted to provide a framework that takes into account the variations from place to place of the deflection of the vertical. The methods by which this is accomplished go beyond the basic concepts presented here.

surveyor calculates the locations of the newly observed points. Additional angular measurements to new points establish a network of triangles and a series of known locations at which **monuments** are placed. Ultimately, entire countries or continents are covered with geodetic control networks.

Recent technological developments in surveying have increased the accuracy of distance measurements. Many surveys are now based on the measurement of distances instead of the measurement of angles. The **trilateration networks** established by such surveys serve the same purpose as the historically more common **triangulation networks** discussed here.

Horizontal datum.   For many years, maps of North America were based on a vast control network, called the North American Datum of 1927 (NAD27), which originated at Meade's Ranch, Kansas. Positions in the network were recalculated for use in connection with the North American Datum of 1983 (NAD83), which now serves as the standard reference for future maps of the continent. The new **horizontal datum** was necessitated by today's engineering and scientific accuracy requirements and was made possible by satellite observation methods. Datum changes resulted in the alteration of the corner points of map sheets, such as U.S. Geological Survey (USGS) quadrangles.

Plane Surveys

Even though the earth has a basically spherical shape, local limited surveys can be conducted without accounting for shape because minimal inaccuracies occur when surveying over short distances. When a city's sewer system or a county's highways are surveyed, for example, the measurements and computations are made without considering the earth's spherical shape. The term **plane surveying** is used to identify such surveys.

Horizontal locations.   Plane surveying uses a combination of distance and angular measurements to determine the relationships between feature locations. Plane surveys of local areas are tied into the geodetic network by using the geodetic monuments as precisely defined starting and ending points. Given a known, identifiable ground point, such as a geodetic monument, the distances and directions to other points can be measured and recorded (figure 2.15). From the information collected by the survey, maps are constructed to accurately show the location of selected features, which can range from the property lines of real-estate subdivisions to the alignments of highways or power lines.

Elevation determination.   Because the surface of the earth is not flat, maps must also incorporate information about the variations in its elevation. Measuring the difference in elevation between two points is not difficult, especially if the points are relatively close to one another. Using a level and a measuring rod, surveyors start at a point whose elevation is known and compare the elevations of other points to it. A level is basically a telescope that can be aimed in a perfectly horizontal direction to take readings on a measuring rod scaled in the desired units.[4]

One way in which the **leveling technique** is used is as follows: First, the level is set up halfway between the starting and ending points. The starting point is preferably a previously surveyed monument of known elevation. (More will be said shortly about the methods used to establish this starting level.) The ending point is the point whose elevation relative to the starting point is to be determined. The measuring rod is placed vertically on top of the starting monument, and the surveyor sights on the rod through the level. The cross hairs in the level intersect the measurements on the rod. The measurement at the intersection of the cross hairs indicates the elevation of

the instrument above the starting monument (figure 2.16). The rod is then moved into position at the ending point. The level is turned, and a sighting is again taken on the vertical rod. This measurement is the elevation of the instrument above the ending point. The difference between the two readings represents the elevation difference between the starting point and the ending point.

Vertical datum.   If the survey is purely local the elevations of any number of points may be determined, all relative to the elevation of the starting point. If it becomes necessary to relate these points to the points determined in other similar surveys the elevations in one survey will not necessarily have any relationship to the elevations in the other surveys. This problem can be overcome only if a common elevation, known as a **datum**, is used as the starting point for all of the surveys.

The most commonly used datums are related in a systematic way to the level of the ocean because, in general, sea level meets the requirements for a universal starting level. The determination of sea level requires a considerable amount of effort because the oceans do not maintain a constant elevation relative to the land masses that surround them. This is due to tidal movement caused by variations in the gravitational attraction of the sun and the moon as their positions change relative to the earth. This is not an easily understood set of relationships because the influence of each of these bodies varies over time in its own pattern. The distance of the sun and the moon from the earth changes, and the attitude of the earth in relation to the direction of their gravitational pull also differs. The combination of these two separate patterns of change results in an extremely complex pattern of variation.

Because of the variation in tidal levels, an averaging concept, called the **mean datum**, is used to establish the desired common starting level. The averaging is done by taking tidal observations at hourly intervals. When a sufficient number of observations has been taken to account for all of the tidal variations and fluctuations, the average is calculated. The total time period involved in this process, if maximum accuracy is required, is 18.6 years! The complete cycle of relationships between the sun, moon, and earth, called the **metonic cycle**, evolves over that period of time.

---

[4]A horizontal sighting is perpendicular to the direction of gravity at the observation point.

FIGURE 2.15 Plane survey, subdivision plat. (Town of Mount Pleasant, Racine County, Wisconsin, 28 July 1976, reduced from original.)

Courtesy of Racine County Planning and Development.

FIGURE 2.16 Determining elevation difference by differential leveling.

Other problems must be overcome in the process of determining mean sea level. For example, winds disturb the surface of the water, resulting in waves that can reach major proportions. Obviously, a "surface" existing in a body of water churned by waves is difficult to measure. These difficulties are overcome by creating a **stilling basin**, cut off from the direct influence of wind and waves. A tunnel below the depth of direct wave influence allows water pressure to establish a more easily measured level within the basin.

When a datum is established for large areas, variations *between* stations due to differences in gravity from place to place must also be taken into account. An averaging process based on a leveling survey between tidal measuring stations accomplishes this. The result of this averaging is used to establish the final mean datum. The standard North American Datum, which is used in the United States and the rest of North America, was adjusted in 1929 and again in 1988 (NAD88). Other levels, such as mean low tide or mean high tide, may be calculated for special purposes such as navigational charts or boundary surveys.

TOPOGRAPHIC MAPPING

When the required control-survey work has been done, topographic mapping is built upon the framework that the survey provides. The topographic mapping is usually accomplished by combining surveying with techniques based on aerial photography. Topographic maps are discussed here because they are important in two major ways. First, the maps themselves have many practical uses. Second, they provide information that is the basis of the other types of maps that we will be considering.

Aerial photography allows the rapid acquisition of accurate, up-to-date information about the size, location, and character of objects on the earth's surface. It also reveals the configuration of the surface itself. For these reasons, aerial photography is essential to modern topographic mapping. Since World War II, it has been used extensively in the gathering of information needed to produce new maps and to update existing maps. Also, in many instances aerial photographs substitute for maps. In the remainder of this chapter, we will discuss how aerial photographs are used in the process of creating maps. In chapter 17, we will consider the use of aerial photographs as map products.

Aerial Photography

Vertical aerial photographs for mapping purposes are taken with an **aerial survey camera**, which typically takes photographs that are 23 centimeters (9 inches) square. This large format permits the capture of a considerable amount of detail over a large image area. As the name suggests, vertical photographs are taken with the camera in as perfectly vertical a position as possible, so that the geometry of the resulting photo can be easily handled. If a photo is not perfectly vertical, corrections must be introduced to make it usable, which adds to the complexity of the process.

Stereoscopic Images

When we look at the world in the course of our normal activities, we see it in three dimensions. The major reason we have this ability is that our eyes are slightly separated from one another. Thus, one eye

FIGURE 2.17 Successive, overlapping aerial photographs used for stereoscopy. (Reduced from 9½-by 9½-inch originals.)

Source: U.S. Geological Survey photos.

sees a scene from a somewhat different angle than the other. This situation is called **parallax**. When parallax is present, the brain is able to interpret the slightly differing views so that we "see" a three-dimensional image.

Unfortunately, individual aerial photographs do not have a three-dimensional quality but simply show a flat image of features on the earth's surface. For this reason, aerial photographs used for topographic mapping applications are taken in a series, with each photo overlapping the preceding photo (figure 2.17). Overlapping photos provide two slightly differing views of each portion of the earth's surface. Photos taken in this manner are called **stereo pairs**. In use, stereo pairs are placed in a simple instrument called a **stereoscope** that allows one eye to see one view and the other eye to see the other (figure 2.18). Parallax is thus obtained, and the result is an apparent three-dimensional view of the earth's surface—a **stereoscopic image**.

When stereo pairs are used for mapping purposes, they are typically viewed in a more complex instrument, called a **stereoplotter**. Many types of stereoplotters are available. Some of them are simple, and

some are highly automated, so that operator intervention is minimal. Whatever type is used, their common characteristic is that they allow the operator to see one of the stereo-pair images with one eye and the other image with the other eye. This creates an apparent three-dimensional view of the terrain, called a **stereomodel** (figure 2.19). The discussion that follows is designed to describe the general process involved and not the details related to any particular machine.

Ground Control

In conjunction with aerial photography, **ground control points** are established at locations that are easily identifiable, both on the ground and in the aerial photos. A survey establishes the precise locations of the control points, and a map, called a **control diagram**, is prepared on the basis of the survey. The operator of the stereoplotter places the control diagram on the base of the instrument. The relationship between the stereomodel and the control diagram is then established by matching the control points on the model to the corresponding points on the diagram.

(a)

(b)

FIGURE 2.18   Two types of stereoscopes. (*a*) Pocket type. (*b*) Folding-mirror type with photos and parallax bar in place.

Courtesy of the Lietz Company.

BALPLEX PROJECTORS

TRACING TABLE

MODEL

MANUSCRIPT MAP

FIGURE 2.19   Relationship between projectors, stereomodel, tracing table, and control diagram (manuscript map) in a multiplex-type plotter.

Courtesy RFM Associates Inc.

Plotting

The stereoplotter uses a point of light, called a **floating mark**, that appears to be suspended over the stereomodel. Vertical data, such as the location of a contour line (a line joining points of the same elevation), are obtained from the stereomodel by locking the floating mark at the desired elevation. It is then moved so that it remains in contact with the apparent surface of the stereomodel and, therefore, follows a contour line. As the mark is moved, a planimetric line-image of the contour is traced on a manuscript map. Additional contours are established by raising or lowering the floating mark to the desired elevations and tracing the line of contact at each elevation.

Planimetric data, such as the alignment of a road, are obtained by moving the floating mark until it is just touching the apparent surface of one end of the feature in the stereomodel. The mark is then moved so that it follows the center line of the feature. Because the surface of the feature varies in elevation, the mark is moved up and down to keep it in contact with the surface. The planimetric location of the horizontal path followed by the floating mark is recorded on the manuscript map.

This process is repeated, as necessary, until all of the features to be mapped are recorded. Then the manuscript map is checked for accuracy and the necessary drafting, photography, and printing is done to produce a completed map. A digital file of *x-y* coordinate values is often recorded when a map is drawn. This type of file may be used later in conjunction with a plotter to create a hard-copy map (see chapter 19).

Summary

Knowing the shape and size of the earth is crucial to understanding the relationships between maps and the earth. The earth's basically spherical shape is particularly important because it is difficult to represent on a flat map sheet.

Locations on the earth are specified on the basis of the latitude and longitude graticule. Great circles that pass through the poles are the lines of longitude (meridians) used to designate east-west locations. Other graticule lines are placed at right angles to the meridians. One of these is the equator, a great circle located midway between the poles. The others are the lines of latitude (parallels), which are small circles parallel to the equator.

Because the earth rotates on its axis, it bulges at the equator and is flattened at the poles, resulting in a shape called an ellipsoid. The earth is not a regular ellipsoid but is a somewhat irregular shape called a geoid.

Surveying determines the position of points on the earth's surface. Geodetic control surveys take into account the curvature and irregular shape of the earth and are used to ascertain latitude and longitude locations. Latitude is determined by measuring the angle between Polaris, for example, and the observer's horizon. Longitude determination, on the other hand, requires knowledge of the difference in the time of occurrence of apparent solar noon at the location to be determined and at the Greenwich meridian.

The establishment of accurate locations is complicated by variations in the earth's density. The difference at a given location between a vertical line to the center of the earth and a vertical line to the earth's center of gravity is called the deflection of the vertical. This variation affects the readings of surveying instruments because they respond to the pull of gravity.

A geodetic control survey starts with an accurately measured baseline. A system of triangles is established by measuring the angles between the baseline and additional observation points, at which monuments are established. Plane surveys of local areas are tied into the geodetic network by using the monuments as starting and ending points. Information about variations in elevation is added by leveling techniques, relative to a vertical datum.

Aerial photography provides accurate, up-to-date information about the size, location, and character of objects on the earth's surface, as well as about the configuration of the surface itself. Particularly useful are three-dimensional images obtained by using stereoscopic pairs of vertical photos, which are tied to the surveyed control points.

SUGGESTED READINGS

Campbell, John. *Introductory Cartography.* 2d ed. Dubuque, Iowa: Wm. C. Brown Publishers, 1991, 61–106.

Dickinson, G. C. *Maps and Air Photographs.* 2d ed. New York: John Wiley and Sons, A Halsted Press Book, 1979, chapter 4.

Robinson, Arthur H., Randall D. Sale, Joel L. Morrison, and Phillip C. Muehrcke. *Elements of Cartography.* 5th ed. New York: John Wiley and Sons, 1984, 55–75.

Smith, J. R. *Basic Geodesy.* Rancho Cordova, Calif.: Landmark Enterprises, 1988.

3

Map Projections

As discussed in chapter 2, the earth's shape is basically spherical. Attempts to represent this spherical earth on a flat piece of paper result in distortions, although the resulting map may have useful characteristics. Knowledge of the effects of the map-projection process is therefore an important aspect of understanding maps. This chapter first discusses the general principles that lie behind the various types of map projections. Commonly encountered map projections and their characteristics are then examined. The chapter concludes with a discussion of the importance of map-projection characteristics from the perspective of the map user.

MAP-PROJECTION CONCEPTS

A **map projection** is simply a systematic rendering of a **graticule** on a flat sheet of paper, consisting of the lines of latitude and longitude. The skeleton provided by the graticule is converted into a map by adding a representation of the geographic features found on the earth.

To understand the geometric basis of map projections, visualize a transparent globe with the graticule and the coastlines and other features drawn on it. When a light source is placed inside this globe, the various lines drawn on it cast shadows on any surface placed nearby. The outline of these shadows forms the map projection.

Many so-called map projections are actually systematically arranged graticules designed to have particular characteristics. They could not be obtained with the transparent globe-and-shadow approach. The globe-and-shadow idea is useful, nevertheless, as a means of understanding the basic concepts involved in map projections.

Projection Surfaces

Three physical surfaces are commonly used for the construction of map projections. These are the plane and two developable surfaces—the cylinder and the cone.

Plane. The simplest projection surface is a **plane** (flat) surface. Projections onto such a surface are referred to as **azimuthal projections**. The most significant aspect of a plane surface is that an outline projected onto it does not have to undergo further distortion or manipulation because it is already a flat map.

Developable surfaces. Some projection surfaces are not flat at the time the projection is created, but can be flattened later by making an appropriate cut in the surface and unrolling (developing) it. When this unrolling is accomplished without stretching or tearing and, therefore, without distortion of the surface or of the patterns drawn on it, the surface is called a **developable surface**.

The **cone** and the **cylinder** are developable surfaces commonly used for mapping purposes (figure 3.1). A cylinder is developed by cutting along its length and unrolling it. A cone is developed by making a cut from its base to its apex before unrolling it.

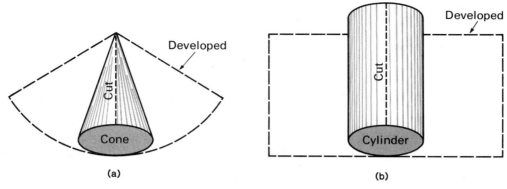

FIGURE 3.1 Developable surfaces. (*a*) Cone.
(*b*) Cylinder.

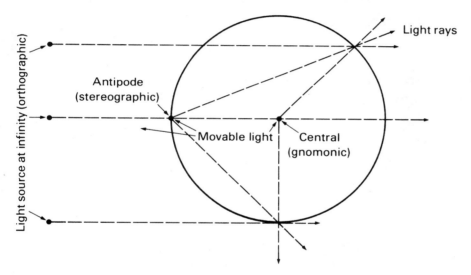

FIGURE 3.2 Three common locations for the projection
light source.

Light-Source Location

Thus far this discussion has implicitly assumed that the map-projection light source is located at the center of the globe. The light source, however, can be located at any desired point. Three common locations for the projection light source are: (1) the **gnomonic position**, at the center of the globe; (2) the **stereographic position**, at the antipode (the point exactly opposite the point of tangency of the projection surface); and (3) the **orthographic position**, at infinity (figure 3.2). Changing the location of the light source, even when the position and type of projection surface are held constant, alters the characteristics of the resulting projection. The specific effects of these changes are discussed as the appropriate projections are described.

Orientation and Tangency

The **orientation of a projection surface** may be changed as desired, although certain orientations are defined as **normal**, or regular (figure 3.3). A cylinder, for example, is normally oriented so that it is tangent along the equator. A cone is normally oriented so that it is tangent along a parallel, with its apex over the pole, in alignment with the axis of rotation. The normal orientation for a plane is tangent at the pole (polar azimuthal).

If the orientation of the projection surface is changed, the location of the point or line of **tangency** between that surface and the globe also changes. When the projection surface is turned 90 degrees from normal, the result is called a **transverse projection**. In a transverse cylindrical, for example, the cylinder is

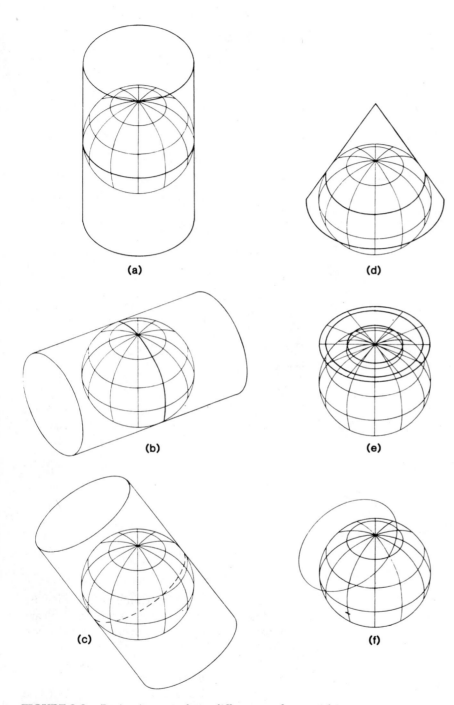

(a)

(b)

(c)

(d)

(e)

(f)

FIGURE 3.3   Projections on three different surfaces with differing orientations. (*a*) Regular cylindrical. (*b*) Transverse cylindrical. (*c*) Oblique cylindrical. (*d*) Regular conic. (*e*) Polar azimuthal (plane). (*f*) Oblique azimuthal (plane).

Source: John P. Snyder, *Map Projections Used by the U.S. Geological Survey,* 2d ed., Geological Survey Bulletin 1532 (Washington, D.C.: U.S. Government Printing Office, 1982).

tangent along a meridian. In the case of a transverse projection on a plane, the plane is tangent at the equator. A transverse conic, which is not frequently seen, has the apex of the cone on the plane of the equator. An **oblique projection** results if the projection surface lies at an angle somewhere between the normal and transverse positions.

The different orientations of the projection surface each produce a distinctive graticule and pattern of distortion. Although each graticule has a different appearance, those that are produced with the projection light source at the same location and with the same projection surface often retain the same general characteristics. The normal (polar), transverse (equatorial), and oblique cases of the stereographic projection, for example, all maintain correct shapes in small areas. A straight line drawn from the center of any of them represents a great circle. On the other hand, a transverse Mercator maintains correct shapes, as does a normal Mercator. But straight lines drawn on a transverse Mercator do not represent great-circle routes as do straight lines on a normal Mercator. (The Mercator projection is discussed later in the chapter.)

GLOBE CHARACTERISTICS

Because of its similarities to the earth, a globe is a useful reference tool. On a globe, features from the earth's surface—their shape, the area they occupy, and the distances and directions between them—are correctly shown. An "ideal" map projection would retain all of these characteristics and translate them to the map. The basic problem of making the transition from a three-dimensional globe to a flat map is that the process inevitably involves the loss of some globe characteristics, so the "ideal" projection can never be achieved. We will now review some specific qualities of the globe that "ideal" maps should have.

Conformality

The retention of correct shapes on a map is called **conformality**. The importance of conformality is that map features can be recognized by their distinctive shapes. Conformality also allows the accurate recording of direction. The requirements for a conformal map are that the lines of latitude and longitude must cross one another at right angles and that the

scale must be the same in all directions at any given point. Both of these conditions exist on a globe.

The term *conformality* is somewhat misleading because the condition can only be achieved for small areas on a map. The shapes of large mapped areas, such as continents, are always different from the shapes of those areas as shown on the globe, even on a map defined as conformal. That the shapes of small areas are retained is what leads to the classification of a map as conformal.

One example of the principle of conformality is the **Mercator projection**. Others include the **Lambert conformal conic** (which is often used for maps of the United States) and the stereographic and **transverse Mercator**. The Mercator is not obtained by geometrical construction. Instead, it is mathematically designed so that the north-south scale changes at the same rate as the east-west scale. This means that the scale on the Mercator is the same in all directions at any given point on the map. This is not the same as saying that the scale is the same everywhere, however, because the scale of a map drawn on a Mercator projection is the same as that of an equivalent globe only at the equator. At 60° north or south, the east-west distance between two meridians on the earth is half the distance between the same two meridians at the equator. On the Mercator projection, however, the spacing between the meridians is the same at 60° as it is at the equator. This means that the east-west scale along the sixtieth parallel of a Mercator map is twice as great as the east-west scale at the equator. These scale differences become increasingly exaggerated away from the equator and toward the poles.

In addition to the equality of the scale at each point on the Mercator, the meridians and parallels of the projection all cross one another at right angles. This characteristic is also true on the globe, which means that shapes on the Mercator are correct, and it is classified as a conformal projection. It must be reemphasized, however, that conformality does not mean that shapes are correct over large areas, such as continents. What it does mean is that the shapes of individual features are correct, or nearly so. This is the most that can be expected of a conformal projection because only on the globe can the scale be the same everywhere.

Other qualities of the Mercator projection, which make it particularly useful for navigational purposes, are discussed in chapter 6.

Equivalence

When a map is produced on an **equal-area (equivalent) projection**, a unit area drawn on it always represents the same number of square kilometers on the earth's surface, regardless of where it is drawn. The retention of such areal relationships is especially important on maps used to represent the areal extent of various phenomena on the earth's surface. Assume, for example, you are interested in the amount of arable land in various countries. It would be very misleading to visually compare the area of arable land in one country with the area in another country if the map showed different-sized areas for the same actual amount of land.

To retain equivalence, any scale changes that occur in one direction must be offset by suitable changes of scale in the opposite direction. For example, the three rectangles shown in figure 3.4 are equal in area even though their dimensions differ. Similarly, variations in the angles at which parallels and meridians cross one another on map projections affect the shapes of the land areas on the maps, but need not affect their areas.

FIGURE 3.4   Three rectangles that are equal in area, even though their dimensions differ.

One example of an equivalent projection is the sinusoidal (figure 3.5). Other commonly encountered equivalent projections include the Albers equal-area (which is often used for maps of the United States), the homolographic, Goode's interrupted homolosine, and the Bonne. On the sinusoidal, the scale is true along the central meridian and each parallel, which gives the projection its equal-area characteristic.

The right-angle crossing of parallels and meridians is lost in many projections, including the sinusoidal.

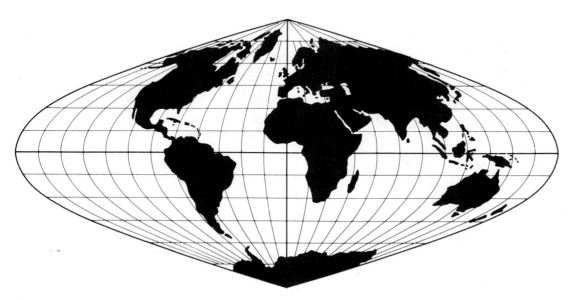

FIGURE 3.5   Sinusoidal projection.

Courtesy of Cartographic Laboratory, University of Wisconsin-Madison.

FIGURE 3.6   Goode's interrupted homolosine projection.

Courtesy of Cartographic Laboratory, University of Wisconsin-Madison.

The meridians of the sinusoidal projection have the shape of a sine curve (hence the name sinusoidal). The angles at which the meridians cross the parallels become increasingly acute toward the periphery of the projection. The result is an increasing distortion of shapes in those areas. These shape changes do not affect the ability to retain equivalence, and, in fact, retaining equivalence inevitably distorts shapes.

Because of their shape distortions, interrupted versions of equal-area projections are often encountered. **Interruption** involves separating the projection along several dividing lines. This allows the continents (or the oceans, if they are of more interest for a particular application) to be shown with correct areas, but with less distorted shapes. The Goode's interrupted homolosine is an example of this approach (figure 3.6). This projection is also unique in that it joins the sinusoidal and the homolosine projections at about 40° north and south to further improve the shapes. These examples emphasize that a projection can be either conformal or equivalent, but *not* both.

Distance

Correct distance relationships require that the length of a straight line between two points on a map represents the correct **great-circle distance** between the same points on the earth. (The path of a great circle is the shortest distance between two points on the earth's surface.) Maps that have this characteristic can be designed but, even on such **equidistant maps**, correct distances can only be measured from one or, at most, two points.

The **azimuthal equidistant projection** is an example. All points on azimuthal equidistant projections are plotted at their true distance from the center of the projection and are in their true global direction, or azimuth, from the center (hence the name azimuthal). In the polar case, which is the easiest to visualize, the parallels are concentric circles spaced the correct scale distance apart and centered on the pole (figure 3.7). Area and shape relationships are not retained anywhere on the projection and are increasingly distorted away from the center.

On the azimuthal equidistant projection, the antipodal point to the center of the projection (the point exactly opposite, on a line drawn through the center of the earth) becomes a circle with a diameter equal to the earth's circumference. This illustrates very forcefully that distance relationships, other than those measured from the center of the projection, are increasingly distorted away from the center point. Measurements between any and all points, even on an equidistant map, do *not* yield correct distances.

FIGURE 3.7   Portion of azimuthal equidistant projection, polar case.

FIGURE 3.8   Portion of gnomonic projection, polar case.

Direction

When a projection retains correct direction, a straight line drawn between two points on the map shows the correct azimuth of the line. An **azimuth** is defined by the angle formed at the starting point of a straight line in relation to a meridian. The angle is usually, but not always, measured in a clockwise direction, starting from north.

In the **gnomonic projection**, the light source is at the center of the globe. Thus, the spacing of the graticule increases rapidly away from the center of the projection, resulting in an increasingly exaggerated scale (figure 3.8). Using the gnomonic projection to cover more than a portion of a hemisphere on a single map is not practical.

The most important characteristic of the gnomonic projection is that all straight lines drawn on it represent portions of great circles. The reason for this can be visualized by remembering that a great circle is created by the intersection with the surface of a plane that passes through the center of the earth. If such a plane is continued outward, it intersects with the plane on which the projection is being made. Because the intersection of two planes always occurs

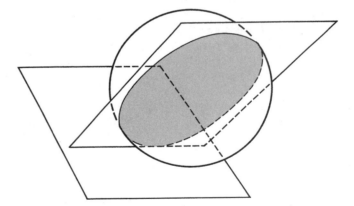

FIGURE 3.9   The intersection of two planes always occurs along a straight line. In the gnomonic projection, all projection planes pass through the center of the earth. The resulting great-circle plots are therefore straight lines on the map.

along a straight line, the result is that all great-circle routes appear as straight lines on the map (figure 3.9). Applications of this characteristic of the gnomonic are discussed in the section of chapter 6 that deals with navigation.

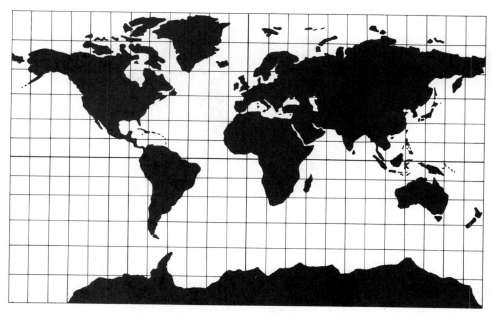

FIGURE 3.10   Miller cylindrical projection.
Courtesy of Cartographic Laboratory, University of Wisconsin-Madison.

Compromise Projections

Many map projections do not preserve any of the specific globe characteristics. They often have some useful characteristic, however, that makes them attractive for certain applications. The examples that follow illustrate these types of projections.

Miller cylindrical.   The **Miller cylindrical projection** shows the world in a rectangular format (figure 3.10). It is modified from the Mercator, so that it distorts the size of areas less, especially in the higher latitudes. It is not conformal, nor does it have the navigational usefulness of the Mercator.

Robinson projection.   The **Robinson projection** is a compromise projection (figure 3.11). It has the virtue of minimizing visually disturbing distortions that make many world projections unattractive for general uses.

PROJECTION SELECTION

As discussed earlier in the chapter, the characteristics of a particular map are determined by the projection on which it is plotted. The retention of shape,

equivalence, direction, or distance—or some compromise in relation to these characteristics—may be the most important consideration relative to the planned purpose of the map. The projection on which the map is drawn is selected accordingly. Retaining a particular characteristic inevitably results in the distortion of other, potentially important characteristics, so the choice inevitably involves some give-and-take. When selecting a map for a particular purpose, therefore, the map user must keep the characteristics of the various types of projections in mind.

The projection choices for large-scale maps, such as topographic sheets and navigation charts, have been made by the producing agencies, usually major government agencies, and the map user can be assured that the choices are rational. The Mercator and gnomonic projections are used for navigation charts, for example. The gnomonic charts are used for selecting great-circle routes and the Mercator charts for determining compass headings. Measuring distances on either the gnomonic or the Mercator is difficult because of the constant change in scale. Therefore, an azimuthal equidistant projection is usually better for distance-measurement purposes. Unfortunately, finding azimuthal equidistant projections centered on specific locations is often difficult, so the map user may have to contend with the variable scales of the gnomonic or Mercator.

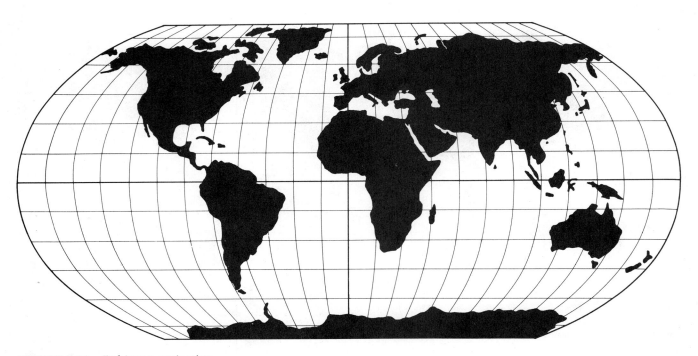

FIGURE 3.11   Robinson projection.

Courtesy of Arthur H. Robinson and Cartographic Laboratory, University of Wisconsin-Madison.

The Lambert conformal conic projection is frequently used for midlatitude air charts because straight lines drawn on it very closely approximate great-circle routes. Such charts can be used for route selection and distance determination. Similarly, in recent years, conformal projections such as the transverse Mercator have been increasingly used for topographical maps. With the methods described in chapter 5, the map user can measure short distances, determine directions between nearby points, and calculate areas on such topographic sheets.

In the case of medium- to small-scale maps (in contrast to the situation with large-scale maps), a wide range of producing agencies, companies, and individuals are involved. In these cases, projection selection may possibly be less rational. Thus, the effect of the projection on any such map should be considered before use.

The considerations involved in the selection of map projections include, for example, the size of the area of interest. If a relatively small area is involved, such as one of the counties in the United States, there is no real difficulty. The amount of distortion on virtually any projection would be difficult to detect on

map sheets even 2 or 3 feet in size, especially if the projection is centered on the area to be mapped. When an area the size of a country or a continent is involved, however, the amount of distortion can become extreme, so the selection is much more important.

The latitude of the area of interest is another important consideration in projection selection. In areas near the equator, for example, cylindrical projections tend to be favored because the cylinder, in the normal orientation, is tangent at the equator, and there is minimal distortion. The lines of tangency of conic projections, on the other hand, are along the parallels, usually in the middle latitudes. This makes conic projections a likely choice for maps of that part of the globe. Pole-centered azimuthal projections are suitable for areas near the poles because the amount of distortion at the poles is minimized and increases toward the lower latitudes. Different versions of this class of projection have special characteristics that may also be selected, including correct distances from the center or equivalence.

The shape of the area of interest also influences the choice of projections because of the different areas of minimal distortion of each particular projection. When the area is wide in one direction and narrow in the other, a map that has its area of least distortion aligned with the long axis of the area of interest should be selected. For example, the Bonne, sinusoidal, or transverse Mercator projections are usually preferred when the area that is mapped is long in the north-south direction but has little east-west extent, such as Chile. This is because the areas of least distortion of these projections lie along their central meridians. Conic projections, on the other hand, are particularly useful for maps of areas with considerable east-west extent and relatively less north-south extent because their area of minimum distortion is along their standard parallels. The Lambert conformal and Albers equal-area projections, for example, are very suitable for mapping the United States.

Maps of areal distributions are best done on equal-area projections. This is because the area occupied by a particular phenomenon in one part of the world may need to be compared with the areas it occupies in other parts of the world. Or the areal extent of one phenomenon may need to be compared with that of another phenomenon, no matter where in the world it occurs. The equal-area projections, by definition, allow such comparisons, but the map user must be careful to select maps of the same scale.

Conformal projections, on the other hand, are best when compass directions between locations are important. The Mercator, for example, is useful when it is necessary to record direction accurately, as in plotting winds and ocean currents.

Four azimuthal projections have particular applications. The azimuthal equidistant, for example, is useful when it is centered on a point from which the airline distance and direction to any other place in the world is to be determined. The oblique aspects of the orthographic projection, on the other hand, are used to represent views of the earth from space. The difference between the projection and the actual perspective of an observer in space is so slight that it is virtually unnoticeable. The stereographic projection is often used for plotting purposes when radiating patterns are involved. Any circle plotted from the globe appears as a circle on a stereographic projection. Finally, the gnomonic projection is useful for radio or seismic work because the waves involved in such studies travel in approximately great-circle directions. They are, therefore, plotted as straight lines on the gnomonic projection.

Summary

Representing the spherical earth on a flat piece of paper requires a systematic rendering of the latitude and longitude graticule, called a map projection. Although some projections are obtained by the use of the transparent globe-and-shadow approach, most are systematically arranged graticules designed to have particular characteristics. An ideal map projection would retain the characteristics of the globe and translate them to the map. But the transition from a three-dimensional globe to a flat map inevitably involves the loss of some globe characteristics.

Three physical surfaces are commonly used for the construction of projections. These are the plane and two developable surfaces—the cylinder and the cone. Three common locations for the projection light source are: (1) the gnomonic position, at the center of the globe; (2) the stereographic position, at the antipode (the point exactly opposite the point of tangency of the projection surface); and (3) the orthographic position, at infinity. The orientation of a projection surface may be changed as desired, although certain orientations are defined as normal. A cylinder is normally oriented when it is tangent along the equator, a cone when it is tangent along a parallel (with its apex over the pole), and a plane when it is tangent at the pole. When the projection surface is turned 90 degrees from normal, the result is a transverse projection. An oblique projection results if the projection surface lies at an angle somewhere between the normal and the transverse positions. The importance of the different aspects of the projection surface is that each one produces a distinctive graticule and a different pattern of distortion.

The retention of globe characteristics has different aspects. Retaining correct shapes is called conformality, whereas retaining equal-area characteristics is called equivalence. Correct distance is obtained when the length of a straight line between two points on a map represents the correct great-circle distance between the same points on the earth. Direction is retained when a straight line drawn between two points on the map shows the correct azimuth of the line.

Projections are selected on the basis of the retention of globe characteristics, or of some compromise in relation to the globe characteristics. Retaining a particular characteristic inevitably results in the distortion of other, potentially important, characteristics, so the choice involves some give-and-take.

SUGGESTED READINGS

Campbell, John. *Introductory Cartography.* 2d ed. Dubuque, Iowa: Wm. C. Brown Publishers, 1991, chapter 2.

Committee on Map Projections of the American Cartographic Association. *Choosing a World Map: Attributes, Distortions, Classes, Aspects.* Special Publication No. 2 of the American Cartographic Association. Falls Church, Va.: American Congress on Surveying and Mapping, 1988.

————. *Matching the Map Projection to the Need.* Special Publication No. 3 of the American Cartographic Association. Falls Church, Va.: American Congress on Surveying and Mapping, 1991.

————. *Which Map Is Best?: Projections for World Maps.* Special Publication No. 1 of the American Cartographic Association. Falls Church, Va.: American Congress on Surveying and Mapping, 1986.

Fisher, Irving, and O. M. Miller. *World Maps and Globes.* New York: Essential Books, 1944.

Kellaway, George P. *Map Projections.* London: Methuen, 1949 (reprinted 1970).

McDonnell, Porter W., Jr. *Introduction to Map Projections.* New York: Marcel Dekker, 1979.

Robinson, Arthur H., Randall D. Sale, Joel L. Morrison, and Phillip C. Muehrcke. *Elements of Cartography.* 5th ed. New York: John Wiley and Sons, 1984, chapter 5.

Snyder, John P. *Map Projections Used by the U.S. Geological Survey.* 2d ed. Geological Survey Bulletin 1532. Washington, D.C.: U.S. Government Printing Office, 1983.

Steers, J. A. *An Introduction to the Study of Map Projections.* 14th ed. London: University of London Press, 1965.

4

Scale and Generalization Concepts

After information has been gathered about the earth and its surface features, the cartographer must decide how the information is to be presented on a map. Two particularly important decisions are: (1) the selection of the appropriate map scale and (2) the amount of detail or generalization suitable. As a map user, you need to be aware of the effects that these decisions have on the final map.

SCALE

Physical distances on the earth's surface are relatively easy to visualize because of our experience with them. We may have to commute 7 miles (11.3 kilometers) to work, the nearest major-league baseball park may be 200 miles (321.9 kilometers) away, and we are used to watching (American) football teams play on a field that is 100 yards (91.44 meters) long. Recognizing that a half-inch (1.27 centimeter) measurement on a map may, depending upon the particular map scale, represent any one of those ground distances or, indeed, any other distance is not as easy. This variable relationship between the size of actual features on the earth and the size of the map symbols that represent those features is discussed in this section.

UNITS OF MEASUREMENT AND MAP SCALES

Units of measurement must be defined before features on the earth's surface can be mapped. In the United States, we are used to working with units of the U.S. Customary System, such as inches, feet, yards, miles, and acres. These units are familiar, but they are extremely awkward for calculation purposes. Most of the rest of the world, on the other hand, works with metric units such as centimeters, meters, kilometers, and hectares. Although the metric system is unfamiliar to many of us, it has great advantages in ease of computation.

The metric system has been approved for use in the United States since 1866. Despite this long period of approval, the process of converting to metric units continues to move slowly in this country. Nevertheless, many maps are now produced using metric units, and this trend is expected to continue. From a practical point of view, therefore, you should be familiar with metric units so that you will be able to use both foreign and domestic metric maps properly. As a learning aid, most of the measurements in this book are given in both metric units and their U.S. Customary equivalents.

Continued on page 54.

Continued from page 53.

LINEAR MEASUREMENTS

U.S. Customary Units

   U.S. Customary Units of measurement are based on the units of the older English system (see table 4.1). This system developed over a long period of history. Most of the units were established arbitrarily and have been subject to change over the centuries. The **foot,** for example, is a measure descended from numerous ancient measurements. Those measurements, which were based on different ideas about the length of a human foot, varied from about 25 to 34 centimeters (approximately 9.8 to 13.4 inches). The division of each foot into twelve equal inches was begun by the Romans.

TABLE 4.1   U.S. Customary Units—Linear Measure

LAND UNITS

---

12 inches = 1 foot
3 feet = 1 yard
16½ feet* = 1 rod
40 rods = 1 furlong = 660 feet*
8 furlongs = 1 mile* = 5,280 feet*

NAUTICAL UNITS
1,852 meters = 6,076.11549 feet (approx.) = 1 international nautical mile

---

*Survey units, not international units.

   In the United States today, there are two different definitions of a foot. From 1893 until 1959, the foot was defined as 1,200/3,937 meter (1:0.30480061). In 1959, the **international foot** was defined as 1:0.3048 meter. At the same time, it was decided that within the United States any data expressed in feet and derived from geodetic surveys would continue to use the foot as it was defined in 1893. This foot is called the **U.S. survey foot.** In day-to-day usage, the difference between the two measures is not very important, but in accurate measurements of long distances, the difference between them can be significant. For example, a measurement of 800,000 meters is 2,624,666.67 U.S. Survey Feet, but 2,624,671.92 International Feet. Given such potential confusion, it is little wonder that surveyors are encouraged to use meters instead of feet.[1]

   The concept of a **mile** is descended from a Roman measurement called, in Latin, *mille passus* (1,000 paces). A Roman pace, as it was originally defined in England, was approximately 5 feet long, so a 1,000-pace mile covered 5,000 feet. In 1593, however, a law was passed in England that brought a shorter statute foot into use. Because the physical length of a mile remained unchanged, the number of feet in the newly defined **statute mile** was increased to the familiar but awkward 5,280 feet (1,609.3 meters).

Metric Units

   The **metric system** has the major advantage of being a decimal system. This is a great convenience when conversions between units are required because they are related to one another by simple multiples of ten (see table 4.2).

---

[1]James Stern, "Do You Know Which Foot to Use?," *ACSM Bulletin,* August 1987, 36.

TABLE 4.2 Metric Units—Linear Measure

1 millimeter = 1/1,000 meter
1 centimeter = 1/100 meter
1 decimeter = 1/10 meter
1 meter
1 decameter = 10 meters
1 hectometer = 100 meters
1 kilometer = 1,000 meters

Note: This table reflects part of the International System of Units (SI), a modernized metric system established by international agreement in 1960.

In addition to their computational convenience, metric measurements are, theoretically, particularly well suited to mapping applications. This is because the **meter** was originally defined by the French Academy of Sciences in 1791 as one ten-millionth of the great-circle distance from the earth's equator to its pole. A major problem with using the earth as the standard for determining the length of a meter, however, is that determining the precise measurement of the earth is extremely difficult. The length of the original meter, which was finalized by an international conference in Paris in 1875, for example, was established on the basis of a detailed survey that was as accurate as the instruments of the period allowed. As newer, more accurate methods of measurement were introduced, however, the presumed size of the earth had to be adjusted, so that the precise relationship of the meter to that size was altered.

For this reason, the modern definition of the meter is based on a specific physical measurement that does not change over time. Since 1983, the meter has been defined as the distance that light travels in 1/299,792,458 of a second. This measurement, although it is undoubtedly impossible to visualize, can be precisely determined whenever necessary, anywhere in the world, provided that the necessary equipment is available.

The modern definition of the meter, then, is no longer based on an exact relationship between the length of the unit and the size of the earth. But the initial earth-referenced length is still influential because the standard for the modern meter was based on that earlier measurement. In practice, however, a measure established on the basis of a particular relationship to the size of the earth is really no more satisfactory than any other arbitrary measure. What is most important is the measure's practicality in use.

Areal Measurements

The areal units of the U.S. Customary System are a mixture (table 4.3). A basic unit of areal measurement, for example, is an **acre.** An acre is defined as 160 square rods, with each rod 16.5 feet long. As a result, an acre contains 43,560 square feet [160 (16.5 × 16.5) = 160 × 272.25 = 43,560].

TABLE 4.3 U.S. Customary Units—Areal Measure

144 sq. inches = 1 sq. foot
9 sq. feet = 1 sq. yard = 1,296 sq. inches
1 rod = 16.5 feet; therefore, 1 sq. rod = 272¼ sq. feet*
160 sq. rods = 1 acre = 43,560 sq. feet*
640 acres = 1 sq. mile*
1 mile by 1 mile* = 1 section of land
6 miles by 6 miles* = 1 township = 36 sections = 36 sq. miles*

*Survey foot or mile, not international foot or mile.

Continued on page 56.

Continued from page 55.

TABLE 4.4   Metric Units—Areal Measure

1 are = 100 sq. meters (10 meters on a side)
1 decare = 10 ares = 1,000 sq. meters
1 hectare = 100 ares = 10,000 sq. meters

Note: This table reflects part of the International System of Units (SI), a modernized metric system established by international agreement in 1960.

Another commonly encountered sequence of units is used in the United States Public Land Survey (USPLS) (see chapter 6). This system is based on townships that encompass thirty-six sections, with each section consisting of 1 square mile. Each square-mile section contains 640 acres and is conveniently subdivided into smaller units such as quarter sections (160 acres), quarter-quarter sections (40 acres), and quarter-quarter-quarter sections (10 acres). With the complex set of relationships among these and other areal measurements of the U.S. Customary System, it is easy to see why metric units of areal measure are an attractive alternative (table 4.4).

NAUTICAL MEASUREMENTS

Another element of complexity in linear measurements is that the **nautical mile** used for measuring distances at sea is different from the statute mile used on land. The original reason for this was navigational convenience. Navigators determine the position of their vessels in terms of latitude and longitude. It therefore made sense to measure distances between locations in units that are related to the graticule.

The concept of an earth-related, nautical measurement has been accepted for a long time. For example, the former **U.S. nautical mile,** sometimes called the **geographical mile,** measured 6,080.2 feet (1,853.24 meters). This definition was based on the length of an arc of 1 minute, measured along the equatorial great circle of the earth. Confusingly, the British used a unit called the **admiralty nautical mile,** which was equal to 6,080 feet (1,853.18 meters). The two nautical miles differed in size by this small amount because they were based on slightly different measurements of the earth.

The **international nautical mile** was established in 1959 to eliminate the confusion caused by different nations using different units of measurement. This unit, which is 1,852 meters (6,076.12 feet), is based on an idealized concept. First, a perfect sphere with a surface area equal to the surface area of the earth was defined. The international nautical mile was then determined by calculating the length of an arc of 1 minute along a great circle of this perfect sphere. Thus, the relationship between a nautical mile and a degree of latitude is, for practical purposes, 1 nautical mile per minute, or 60 per degree. Some error is involved in this relationship, however, because the earth is not a perfect sphere, and the lengths of actual degrees of latitude vary slightly, depending upon where they are located between the equator and the pole. Also, of course, degrees of longitude vary in length, from a maximum at the equator to zero at the pole, so the desired relationship between nautical miles and degrees of longitude only exists at the equator.

The nautical term *knot* is often misused. A knot is defined as 1 nautical mile per hour, so it is a measure of speed, not of distance. That is why it makes no sense to say that a ship is traveling at 15 knots per hour; the correct statement is that it is traveling at 15 knots.

Nautical depth measurements have also had, traditionally, their own unique measure—the fathom. A **fathom,** which equals 6 feet (approximately 1.83 meters), was defined by the amount of sounding line that could be encompassed between the outstretched hands of an average seafarer. Many nautical charts record depths in fathoms, but recently there has been a transition to using feet or meters. When using a nautical chart, you must be certain which of the various units is in use or grievous errors could result.

As you work with maps, you are likely to encounter many situations that require you to convert from metric units to U.S. Customary Units, or the reverse. The conversion factors in table 4.5 will assist in this task.

TABLE 4.5   Conversion Factors (U.S. Customary Units to Metric Units and Metric Units to U.S. Customary Units)

LINEAR MEASURE		
Given	Multiply by	To Yield
Nautical miles	1,852.0	Meters
Statute miles	1,609.3	Meters
Yards	0.9144	Meters
Feet	0.3048	Meters
Inches	0.0254	Meters
Meters	0.00054	Nautical miles
Meters	0.00062	Statute miles
Meters	1.094	Yards
Meters	3.281	Feet
Meters	39.37	Inches

AREAL MEASURE		
Given	Multiply by	To Yield
Sq. miles	2.59	Sq. kilometers
Acres	0.405	Hectares
Sq. yards	0.836	Sq. meters
Sq. feet	0.0929	Sq. meters
Sq. inches	6.452	Sq. centimeters
Sq. kilometers	0.386	Sq. miles
Hectares	2.471	Acres
Sq. meters	1.196	Sq. yards
Sq. meters	10.764	Sq. feet
Sq. centimeters	0.155	Sq. inches

Note: For conversions to and from other linear metric units, simply shift the decimal in the multiplication factor the appropriate distance and direction. For example, given centimeters, multiply by 0.3937 to derive inches, or, given inches, multiply by 2.54 to derive centimeters.

Units of measurement have a strong influence on the scales at which maps are drawn. A very common scale for topographic maps, especially in Great Britain and in other parts of the world that have come under British influence, is 1:63,360 (or a multiple or fraction thereof). These scales were adopted because there are 63,360 inches in a mile. At the scale of 1:63,360, then, 1 inch represents 1 mile, ¼ inch represents ¼ mile, ¹⁄₁₀ inch represents ¹⁄₁₀ mile, and so on, so it is easy to measure distances with a regular ruler that is subdivided into conventional fractions of an inch.

In the United States, on the other hand, the base scale for topographic mapping was for a long time 1:62,500. This base provided a convenient progression of scales, each of which was an equal multiple of the others (1:62,500, 1:125,000, 1:250,000, 1:500,000, and 1:1,000,000). On maps drawn at these scales, however, inches do not exactly match multiples or fractions of a mile on the scale, so a ruler cannot be easily used for direct scaling.

In recent years, the scale 1:24,000 has become dominant for topographic maps in the United States. This scale is convenient because it is equivalent to 1 inch to 2,000 feet, so a ruler is easily used for direct scaling.

In parts of the world that use the metric system, common map scales are 1:25,000, 1:50,000, 1:100,000, and 1:1,000,000. Direct scaling, using a metric ruler, is convenient at these scales. At a scale of 1:100,000, for example, 1 centimeter on the scale represents 1 kilometer on the earth's surface.

Methods of Stating Scale

The **scale** of a map is the ratio between map distances and earth distances. This scale relationship is expressed in one of three different, but equivalent, ways: (1) as a word statement, (2) as an arithmetic ratio, or (3) as a graphic symbol.

Word statement.   A **word statement** of map scale gives a quick idea of size relationships, but it is in a form that is awkward to use in many applications. Typical word statements might say, for example, that a given map is at a scale of "1 inch to 1 mile," whereas another is at a scale of "1 inch to 2 miles." The second map, then, will show considerably less detail than the first because two miles instead of one are represented by every inch.

Representative fraction.   A representative-fraction (RF) scale is the ratio between the map distance and the ground distance between equivalent points. It is expressed either as a true ratio, such as 1:100,000, or as a fraction, such as 1/100,000. Both means of notation have the same meaning; in this example, one unit of distance on the map represents 100,000 of the same units on the earth's surface.

A representative-fraction scale is "unit free." That is, the ratio between the map-distance values and the earth-distance values remains the same, regardless of whether the measurements are expressed in feet, miles, meters, kilometers, or any other unit of distance. Another way of saying this is that both portions of the ratio (or the numerator and denominator of the fraction) are always expressed in the same units of measurement.

A distance of 1 centimeter on a map with a scale of 1:100,000 represents 100,000 centimeters on the surface of the earth; or 1 inch on the same map represents 100,000 inches on the ground. To say that a scale of 1:100,000 means that 1 inch on the map represents 100,000 feet on the earth, or some other mixed measurement, is obviously incorrect. However, a word statement of the scale of a map with an RF of 1:100,000 could correctly be "1 centimeter represents 100,000 centimeters," or "1 centimeter represents 1,000 meters," or "1 centimeter represents 1 kilometer." These are all equivalent statements.

Some types of maps, including land-ownership plats, sometimes use a "mixed" scale statement, such as 1 inch to 2,400 feet. This method need not cause confusion, however, because the distance units are clearly identified.

Graphic scale.   A line drawn on a map and subdivided into units appropriate to the scale of the map is called a **graphic scale**. A graphic scale allows a distance measured on the map to be translated directly into the correct earth distance by comparing it to the scale (depending, as already discussed, on the map projection). Alternatively, the graphic scale allows the transfer of a desired earth distance directly onto the map.

Graphic scales on a single map often include a variety of scale units (such as kilometers, miles, feet, yards, meters, and so on). This arrangement allows measurements to be taken directly in the desired units without the necessity of converting from one unit of measure to another.

Graphic scales are particularly useful because they change size in proportion to changes in map size. If a map is photographically enlarged to twice its original size, for example, its scale has been altered proportionately. For this reason, neither the original word statement nor the RF scale relationship is valid for the enlargement. If a graphic scale is included with the rescaled map, on the other hand, its length is changed in the same proportion as the map, and it continues to be correct. This characteristic is beneficial if a photostatic or photographic reduction or enlargement of a map needs to be made, assuming that the map is not copyrighted or that proper permission has been obtained (copyright guidelines are presented in appendix A). If the original graphic scale is included within the image area to be copied, the reproduced graphic scale will be correct.

There are two basic styles of graphic scales. The first style consists simply of a series of major units. In addition, the first major unit of such a scale is sometimes subdivided to allow greater accuracy in measuring relatively short increments of distance (figure 4.1a). Because this arrangement is rather awkward when measuring fractional distances, a second type of scale, which has a subdivided extension added in front of the first major unit, is more easily used for that purpose (see figure 4.1b).

For the sake of accuracy and ease of use, specially drawn scales (instead of simple rulers) are almost always used for map measurements. One exception is

(a)

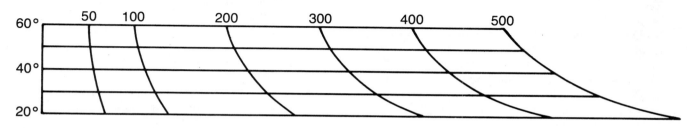

(b)

FIGURE 4.1   Types of graphic scales. (*a*) First major unit subdivided. (*b*) Subdivided extension added in front of first major unit.

Scale of nautical miles at various latitudes

FIGURE 4.2   Variable graphic scale, designed for use with polar stereographic projection.

Source: Redrawn from U.S. Weather Service, Surface Weather Map.

a map drawn at a scale of 1:63,360, on which 1 inch is equivalent to 1 mile. Another exception is a map drawn at a scale of 1:100,000, on which 1 centimeter represents 1 kilometer. In these cases, an inch or centimeter ruler can be used to measure distances directly on the respective maps. (Multiples or fractions of these scales are also conveniently measured with the appropriate ruler.)

Variable graphic scales are sometimes drawn on maps on which the scale ratio varies considerably. Variable graphic scales are simply a collection of individual scales with a separate, subdivided scale line for each specified portion of the map, and with some method of designating where each scale line should be used (figure 4.2). For example, in a typical situation, each scale line is associated with a specific parallel. In addition, it is normal to use the specified scale line in a zone on either side of the appropriate parallel (usually halfway to the next parallel). Because scale changes on maps are continuous and do not occur in steps or increments, some error is introduced by not having continuously changing graphic

scales. This error, however, is likely to be within a reasonable range for most purposes.

Large and Small Scale

It is not unusual to hear in a discussion of maps that one map is **large scale** and another is **small scale**. Unfortunately, the use of these terms is often a source of confusion, in part because there is no universally accepted definition of what constitutes a large-scale map or a small-scale map. The following definitions are generally acceptable, although many lists with different divisions may be found.[2] Large scale is 1:50,000 or larger (such as 1:10,000); Intermediate scale is 1:50,000 to 1:250,000, and Small scale is 1:250,000 to 1:7,500,000.

[2]Some U.S. Geological Survey publications use the following subdivisions: large scale, 1:25,000 or larger; intermediate scale, 1:50,000 to 1:100,000; and small scale, 1:250,000 to 1:7,500,000. This list's usefulness is limited because the list leaves gaps between categories and also does not define very small or very large scales.

In addition, city plans may be at very-large scales, such as 1:2,500, and maps in some atlases, books, and reports may be at scales in the range of 1:100,000,000 or smaller and be classified as very-small-scale maps.

Another frequent source of confusion regarding large and small scales involves a misunderstanding of what is implied by the terms. Would a large-scale map be useful for a given purpose, for example, or would a small-scale map be better? This type of concern can be dealt with by memorizing the following rule: "The smaller the number in the denominator, the larger the scale." This means that a map with a representative-fraction scale of 1/1,000, for example, is a large-scale map, as compared with a smaller-scale 1/1,000,000 map. A small-scale map of a given size, then, shows a relatively large portion of the earth's surface, with relatively little detail. It is useful for general orientation purposes. A large-scale map of the same size, on the other hand, shows a relatively small portion of the earth's surface in relatively greater detail. It is useful for determining more specific information, such as street widths or exact distances between map features.

These large- and small-scale definitions are only suggestions. Actual scales, rather than these categories, should be used to establish the scale in a particular case. The terms are useful, however, for comparing two or more maps ("This map is at a larger scale than that map") or for deciding the relative scale appropriate for a given task ("We need a very-large-scale map for this job").

In special applications, the concepts of vertical and areal scale are often encountered. For purposes of greater clarity, these concepts are discussed elsewhere—areal scale in conjunction with areal measurement (chapter 5) and vertical scale in conjunction with profiling (chapter 8).

Scale Determination

Occasionally, a map will not include a scale. This problem may appear on individual aerial photographs or with maps that have been copied on an office copy machine. The absence of a scale greatly limits a map's usefulness because you usually want to know the size of features shown, or the distances between them. When faced with such a situation, you can often create a reasonably accurate scale of your own, using whatever clues the map provides. The specific clues that you can use vary, depending on the type of map and the amount of detail it shows. The basic technique used involves proportionality.

Use of known features.   The use of proportionality involves the comparison of the size of a reference feature on the map to the size of the same feature on the earth (or on a map of known scale). For example, this type of comparison is easily visualized in the case of an aerial photograph that shows a familiar object with a well-known standard size, such as a baseball diamond, tennis court, or football field. Objects of this type can be used for scaling purposes if you are confident from other clues, such as their relationship to parking, the type of stadium, and so forth, that they are likely to conform to standard dimensions. A sandlot baseball diamond would obviously not provide dimensions as reliable as those taken from a major-league ballpark.

Assume, then, that a standard baseball diamond appears on a particular photograph. The first step in determining the scale of the photograph is to measure the distance between bases on the photograph using a convenient scale. You would then determine the standard distance between bases (90 feet) and establish the ratio between the distance on the photograph and this standard distance. If, in this case, the distance between bases on the photograph is 0.3 inch, the computation would be as follows:

$$\frac{0.3''}{90'} = \frac{0.3''}{90 \times 12''} = \frac{0.3}{1,080} = \frac{0.3/0.3}{1,080/0.3}$$
$$= \text{RF } 1/3,600$$

Notice that the photo (or map) distance is reduced to a value of one.

Unfortunately, there is seldom anything as convenient as a baseball diamond or football field on the segment of photograph or map that you are trying to scale. You must usually be prepared to be ingenious, or to work a little harder, to determine scale. The map or photo may, for example, contain section lines (see chapter 10). The standard distance between section lines is 1 mile, so if such lines are on average spaced 2.65 inches apart on a map, the scale of the map is:

$$\frac{2.65''}{1 \text{ mile}} = \frac{2.65''}{1 \times 63,360''} = \frac{2.65/2.65}{63,360/2.65}$$
$$= \text{RF } 1/23,909$$

This is, of course, very close to the standard 1/24,000 U.S. Geological Survey quadrangle scale. Indeed, it is likely in this example that the map is actually at the standard scale. The slight difference may arise because the spacing between section lines is frequently not exactly the prescribed 1-mile distance. Because of such considerations, it is good practice to take several measurements of similar map features and to use the average measurement for scale-calculation purposes. In addition, in this particular case care must be taken to be certain that quarter-section lines, or other regularly spaced divisions, are not mistaken for section lines.

Use of lines of latitude and longitude. Another useful scaling reference frequently shown on maps is the latitude and longitude graticule. The map distance between a pair of latitude or longitude lines that are spaced a known number of degrees apart can be compared to the earth distance between the same lines to determine the map's scale ratio. On an atlas map, for example, if the map distance between the lines of latitude for 40° and 41° north is 24.5 millimeters, the map scale is:

$$\frac{24.5 \text{ mm}}{111.133 \text{ km}} = \frac{24.5 \text{ mm}}{111.133 \times 1,000,000 \text{ mm}}$$

$$= \frac{24.5/24.5}{111,133,000/24.5}$$

$$= \text{RF } 1/4,536,040$$

(or for practical purposes 1/4,500,000)

You must be careful to use the correct figures for the spacing between graticule lines. In this case, 111.133 kilometers is the average length of a degree of latitude. If the lengths of degrees of longitude are used, however, the convergence of the meridians toward the poles must be taken into account. This is done by multiplying 111.133 kilometers by the cosine of the latitude (the cosines of angles are listed in standard mathematical tables). For example, at 30° north the result would be:

$$\cos(30°) \times 111.133 \text{ km} = 0.8660 \times 111.133 \text{ km}$$
$$= 96.24 \text{ km (at 30°)}$$

If greater accuracy is required, the exact lengths of degrees of latitude and longitude should be used (see tables 10.1 and 10.2).

Use of map comparison. Maps can also be compared to calculate an unknown scale. A map of known scale that covers at least a portion of the area covered on the map of unknown scale is required. In this case, select a pair of features that are likely to be accurately located on both maps, such as railroad crossings, city symbols, drainage features, section lines, lines of latitude or longitude, and so on. The choice depends partly on the scale of the maps and partly on the types of features common to both maps.

To use the map-comparison method, measure the distance between the same pair of features on each of the maps, using any convenient units. The unknown map scale is then obtained by multiplying the known RF scale by the ratio of a measurement on the map of unknown scale to the equivalent measurement on the map of known scale. For example, assume that two features are 50 millimeters apart on a map of scale 1:125,000, and the same features are 100 millimeters apart on a map of unknown scale:

$$\frac{100}{50} \times \frac{1}{125,000} = \frac{2}{1} \times \frac{1}{125,000} = \frac{2}{125,000}$$

$$= \frac{2/2}{125,000/2}$$

$$= \text{RF } 1/62,500$$

Scale Conversion

It is often helpful to convert a map scale from one form to another. You may wish to make measurements from a map that lacks a graphic scale but whose representative-fraction (RF) scale you know. Or the map may have a graphic scale that you wish to express as a word statement for ease in conversation. Other **scale conversions** may also be helpful for a variety of reasons. The procedures for making such changes are quite straightforward because each form is simply an alternative way of expressing the same relationships.

Scale conversions are facilitated if you keep certain standard units in mind. For example, if you are dealing in metric units it is helpful to remember that there are 1,000 meters in 1 kilometer, 100 centimeters in 1 meter, 10 millimeters in 1 centimeter, and so on. If you are dealing in English units, on the other hand, you should remember that there are 5,280 feet (and 63,360 inches) in 1 mile. (Maps are often produced at a scale of 1:62,500 because the multiples of 62,500, such as 125,000, 250,000, and so on, are mathematically convenient.)

Representative-fraction (RF) and word-statement conversions. If the map scale is expressed as a representative fraction, it may be more meaningful to you, or to someone with whom you are conversing, to put the scale into words. A map with an RF of 1:100,000, for example, has a word-statement scale of "1 centimeter per kilometer" (because there are 100,000 centimeters [1,000 meters] in 1 kilometer). Similarly, if a map has an RF of 1:63,360, its scale in words is: "1 inch to 1 mile."

The conversion of a word-statement scale to an RF is the mirror image of the conversion from an RF to a word statement. Thus, the RF equivalent of "2 inches per mile" is 1:31,680 (2/63,360 = 1/31,680). Several common RF/word-statement relationships are shown in table 4.6. Note that maps at the scale of 1:62,500, or its multiples, are identified as "1 inch to approximately 1 mile," and so on. Note also that alternative expressions are in common use, such as the equivalent statements: "¼ mile to an inch" and "4 inches per mile." Determining which style of expression to use is simply a matter of personal choice.

Equivalencies for values not included in table 4.6 can be easily determined. To determine how many inches to the mile, for example, divide the denominator of the RF of the map into 63,360. Thus, on a map with an RF of 1:40,000, there are approximately 1.58 inches per mile (63,360/40,000). Conversely, to determine how many miles to the inch, divide 63,360 into the denominator of the RF. Thus, on a map with an RF of 1:400,000 there are approximately 6.3 miles to the inch (400,000/63,360). If you are working in metric units, substituting 100,000 for 63,360 in the previous formulas yields centimeters per kilometer, and kilometers per centimeter, respectively. You may wish to check these relationships by recalculating some of the entries in table 4.6.

Representative-fraction (RF) and graphic conversions. If a map includes an RF scale statement, you can create a graphic scale by deciding the number of map units you wish to represent, drawing a line of the proper length, and applying the appropriate label. Assume, for example, that the RF scale of a map is 1:100,000, and you wish to draw a 10-kilometer scale. Because there are 100,000 centimeters in 1 kilometer (1,000 meters, each containing 100 centimeters), a 10-centimeter line would represent 1,000,000 centimeters, or 10 kilometers. Similarly, if the RF is 1:63,360, a 1-inch line would represent 1 mile.

TABLE 4.6 Scale Relationships

REPRESENTATIVE FRACTION (RF)	WORD STATEMENT
1:1,200	100 feet to an inch
1:4,800	400 feet to an inch
1:7,920	⅛ mile to an inch (or 8 inches per mile)
1:9,600	800 feet to an inch
1:15,840	¼ mile to an inch (or 4 inches per mile)
1:24,000	2,000 feet to an inch
1:25,000	¼ kilometer per centimeter (or 4 centimeters per kilometer)
1:31,680	½ mile to an inch (or 2 inches per mile)
1:50,000	½ kilometer per centimeter
1:62,500	1 mile to an inch (approx.)
1:63,360	1 mile to an inch
1:100,000	1 kilometer per centimeter
1:125,000	2 miles to an inch (approx.)
1:126,720	2 miles to an inch
1:250,000	4 miles to an inch (approx.)
1:253,440	4 miles to an inch
1:500,000	5 kilometers per centimeter 8 miles to an inch (approx.)
1:506,880	8 miles to an inch
1:1,000,000	10 kilometers per centimeter 16 miles to an inch (approx.)
1:1,013,760	16 miles to an inch

To convert a graphic scale to the RF form, select a convenient scale distance, such as 1 mile or 1 kilometer, and measure its length as precisely as possible. The measurement should be done in appropriate units, such as inches for miles and centimeters for kilometers. Then divide the measured distance into the distance indicated on the graphic scale, both in the same units, to obtain the denominator of the RF. If 1 mile (63,360 inches) on the graphic scale measures 2.64 inches, for example, the RF is 1:24,000 (63,360/2.64). Similarly, if 1 kilometer (100,000 centimeters) on the scale is 2.0 centimeters long, the RF is 1:50,000 (100,000/2.0).

One of the most convenient aspects of maps drawn to metric scales becomes apparent when you are making scale-conversion measurements such as those just described. On a map with a scale of 1:100,000, each centimeter represents 1 kilometer; at a scale of 1:1,000,000, each centimeter represents 10 kilometers, and so on. This means that a standard centimeter scale is easily used for scaling distances on metric-scale maps.

Word-statement and graphic conversions.
Conversions between word-statement scales and graphic scales are accomplished by combining the procedures just described. To go from a word statement to a graphic scale, for example, simply convert the word statement to an RF and then convert the RF to graphic form. Converting from a graphic scale to a word statement is easily done by first determining the equivalent RF and then converting the RF to a word statement.

GENERALIZATION

Every map has, to some extent, been simplified or **generalized**. Even large-scale topographic maps cannot possibly show every detail of the real world they represent. Because of this, cartographers adjust the content of each map to make the map as useful and recognizable a representation of the real world as they can within the limits of the space available and the scale of the map. The smaller the scale of the map, the greater the amount of generalization required because the amount of space available to show any given feature decreases as scale decreases. If the generalization is properly done, the distinguishing characteristics of the mapped features will still be effectively represented.

An awareness of the techniques that cartographers use to accomplish generalization will assist you in interpreting and understanding the level of detail presented on any given map.

Selection

One means of generalization that cartographers use is the **selection** and retention of the more important features in an area and the elimination of the less important ones. If a series of lakes is shown, for example, some of the smaller lakes in the group are eliminated as scale is reduced, so that the larger ones can be retained (figure 4.3a). Simply put, this means that you must be aware of the possibility that some of the smaller features in a given area may simply not be shown on the map.

Simplification

A second technique of generalization is the **simplification** of the shapes of the features retained on the map. To continue the previous example, this approach would mean that the shorelines of the lakes are made less complex at smaller scales. Ideally, enough detail is retained so that the major characteristics of the features are identifiable. A coastline with many bays and headlands, for example, should not be reduced to a smooth curve. Instead, sufficient complexity should be retained so that the nature of the actual coastline can be realized, even though the individual features are not all retained (figure 4.3b).

Combination

Another step that cartographers take in the generalization process is the **combination** of two or more similar features into a single symbol. If there are many small wooded areas in a region, for example, two or more of them may be combined to show as one. If the combination of features is carried too far, however, there is a danger that the map user will not be aware that the region is characterized by scattered areas of woodland, separated by unwooded areas (figure 4.3c).

Locational Shift and Size Exaggeration

The generalization of a particular map may also have required the cartographer to **shift** the location of some features. For example, a road, a railroad, and a river may all be crowded into a narrow valley, but the purpose of the map has made it necessary to show all of them. Because of the need for legibility, however, the weight of the linework on the map must be sufficient to be distinguishable, and there must be sufficient space between the lines to keep them from running together. Faced with the incompatible requirements of retaining features as well as legibility, the cartographer may **exaggerate** the size of the features to improve visibility and shift their location slightly to gain the necessary space. This combination of techniques retains legibility, even though the features lie in slightly shifted positions and occupy

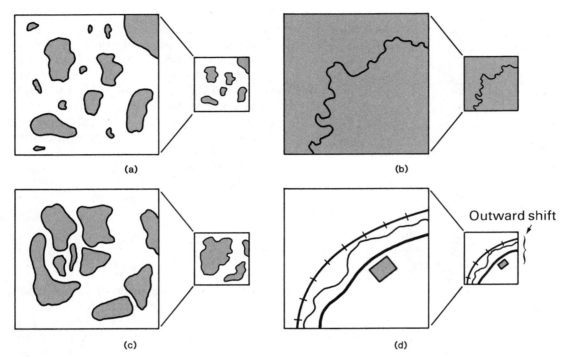

FIGURE 4.3 *Generalization techniques. (a)* Selection.
(b) Simplification. *(c)* Combination. *(d)* Locational shift
and size exaggeration.

more space than they would if they were represented
to precise scale (figure 4.3d). Keep in mind the possibility—indeed the likelihood—that the size of some
of the features on a map may be exaggerated and that
not every feature is likely to be shown at its precise
location.

In most instances, the cartographer uses one or
more methods of generalization on a given map. If
sound judgment has been exercised, the result is a
level of generalization that allows appropriate detail
for the particular map scale to be shown. You must be
aware of the existence of generalization and try to
select the most appropriate map for the purpose at
hand. Because judging the validity of a particular
map's level of simplification is difficult, the best safe-
guard is to consult a variety of maps. Maps drawn at
larger scales than the map you are currently using are
likely to be the most useful. A comparison between

the details shown on several maps, even maps of the
same scale, will improve your knowledge of the
mapped area and allow you to better judge the accuracy of any given map.

Summary

The representation of the earth's features on a map
is affected by scale and generalization.

The scale of a map is the ratio between map distances and earth distances. It is expressed in one of
three equivalent ways: as a word statement, representative fraction, or graphic symbol. Although maps are
sometimes referred to as large or small scale, the terms
are generally more useful for comparative purposes.

Because scale involves proportionality, an unknown scale may be determined by comparisons. For

example, the size of a reference feature on the map can be compared to the size of the same feature on the earth. Comparisons between maps also can be used to calculate an unknown scale. All that is required is a map of known scale that shows at least some of the same features as the map of unknown scale.

Because the three methods of stating scale are equivalent to one another, conversions from one method of expression to another are feasible. For example, if the scale is expressed as a representative fraction, it may be more suitable, in a given situation, to put the scale into words.

Every map is, to some extent, simplified or generalized because it is impossible to show every detail of the real world it represents. The content of each map must be adjusted to make it a useful and recognizable representation of the real world, within the limits of the space available and the scale of the map. The smaller the scale of the map, the greater the amount of generalization required. One method of accomplishing generalization is to retain the more important features in an area and eliminate the less important ones. A second technique is the simplification of the shapes of the features retained on the map. Another method of generalization is the combination of two or more similar features into a single symbol. Finally, the size of some features may be exaggerated, and some may be shifted in location.

SUGGESTED READINGS

Cuff, David J., and Mark T. Mattson. *Thematic Maps: Their Design and Production.* New York: Methuen, University Paperbacks, 1982, 91–94.

Dickinson, G. C. *Maps and Air Photographs.* 2d ed. New York: John Wiley and Sons, A Halsted Press Book, 1969, 143–49.

Greenhood, David. *Mapping.* Chicago: University of Chicago Press, Phoenix Science Series, 1964, 42–50.

Hodgkiss, A. G. *Maps for Books and Theses.* New York: Pica Press, 1970, 37–43.

Muehrcke, Phillip C. *Map Use: Reading, Analysis, and Interpretation.* 2d ed. Madison, Wis.: JP Publications, 1986, 408–17.

Robinson, Arthur H., Randall D. Sale, Joel L. Morrison, and Phillip C. Muehrcke. *Elements of Cartography.* 5th ed. New York: John Wiley and Sons, 1984, 60–63, 79–83.

5

Measurement from Maps

A variety of information about the earth and about the features distributed on its surface is obtained by direct measurement from maps. Two measurements of primary importance are: (1) the distances between locations and (2) the areas of regions. This chapter presents some of the techniques by which map measurements of these values are made. The determination of other factors, such as direction, shape, and slope is discussed in later chapters. This chapter also examines the importance of map accuracy in relation to measurements taken from maps.

MAP ACCURACY

The accuracy with which a map is constructed is critical when measurements are taken from it. The difference in elevation between two points on a topographic map, for example, cannot be precisely determined by merely noting the locations of the points relative to the contour lines. Instead, the level of accuracy with which the contours are drawn limits the accuracy that can legitimately be expected. (This is explained in more detail in the section "National Map Accuracy Standards.")

NATIONAL MAP ACCURACY STANDARDS

The accuracy of topographic maps has two components: horizontal and vertical. The **U.S. National Map Accuracy Standards**[1] provide the framework by which maps produced by federal government mapping agencies are judged. These standards, which were revised on 17 June 1974 and are still in use, are a good example of the type of approach often taken in the determination of topographic map accuracy.

Maps tested for accuracy are selected by the producing agency. Those that meet or exceed the established standards are published with the statement, "This map complies with National Map Accuracy Standards," included in the legend.

[1] Morris M. Thompson, *Maps for America*, 3d ed. (Washington, D.C.: U.S. Department of the Interior, U.S. Geological Survey, 1987), 104.

HORIZONTAL ACCURACY

The **horizontal accuracy** of a map produced by a U.S. government mapping agency is measured by testing the placement of "well-defined points" on the map. This involves first the selection of a number of points on the map for testing. The points selected for this purpose are limited to those that are "visible or recoverable on the ground." Examples of such points include bench marks and property boundary monuments, road and railroad intersections, the corners of large buildings or structures, the center points of small buildings, and so on.

The correct location of each of the selected points is then determined, using a survey of greater accuracy than that of the map being checked. These "correct" locations are then checked against the actually plotted location of the same points on the map being tested, and the amount of error at each location is measured. Assuming that the map being tested is at a scale larger than 1:20,000, no more than 10 percent of the points tested can be in error by more than 1/30 inch. At a scale of 1:24,000, for example, an error of 1/30 inch would be equal to 66.7 feet (20.3 meters) on the ground. In the case of maps at scales of 1:20,000 or smaller, the error allowance is 1/50 inch.

VERTICAL ACCURACY

The standards for **vertical accuracy** apply to contour maps at all scales. In this case, the points to be tested are selected and their actual elevations are de-

termined, again from more accurate surveys. The elevations of the same points are then determined on the map being tested, and the differences between the two elevations are calculated. The rule applied is "Not more than 10 percent of the elevations tested shall be in error more than one-half the contour interval."

An additional complication involved in the testing of vertical accuracy is that the tester may, in effect, shift the map location of the point being tested by as much as the permissible horizontal error for a map of that scale. Such a shift may serve to offset some or all of the vertical error that would otherwise occur.

DISTANCE MEASUREMENT

Direct Methods of Measurement

This discussion of direct methods of map distance measurement assumes that one of two conditions is met so that the measurements taken are valid. One condition is that the distances are short, so that the earth's curvature is not an important factor in the measurement. The second is that the map is on an equidistant projection and the measurements are taken along appropriate alignments (see chapter 3). To take an extreme example, it would not be valid to directly measure the distance between New York and London on a Mercator projection using the methods discussed here. A large-scale Mercator projection

might be used, however, to measure the distance between the downtown and the suburbs of a city, a matter of only a few miles.

Scaling. The simplest method of determining the straight-line distance between two points on a map is to measure the map distance directly with an engineer's scale, a pair of dividers, or marks on the edge of a strip of paper. The earth distance is then determined by checking the measurement against the appropriate map bar scale (figure 5.1). If the measured distance exceeds the length of the bar scale, several partial measurements are combined.

The paper-strip method has an advantage in that distances other than straight-line distances are easily accommodated. The distance along an irregular route

FIGURE 5.1   Measurement of straight-line distance using bar scale.

Source: Department of the Army, *Map Reading,* FM 21–26 (Washington, D.C.: Department of the Army, January 1969).

FIGURE 5.2   Measuring length of irregular route.

Source: Department of the Army, *Map Reading,* FM 21–26 (Washington, D.C.: Department of the Army, January 1969).

is measured by individually marking sections of the route, end to end, on the paper strip (figure 5.2). These sections are kept as short as is necessary to ensure that the length of each one closely approximates the curved-line distance between the marked points. Once the total length of the route is marked on the strip, the distance is scaled by the same technique as is used for straight-line distances.

Map measurer.   Another convenient method of measuring distances on a map is to use a special device called a **map measurer** (figure 5.3). The scale on the dial of the map measurer is set to zero, and the tracing wheel is placed at the desired starting point on the map. The wheel is then guided along the route to be measured, and the pointer on the dial indicates the number of centimeters or inches the wheel travels. The swivel handle of the device makes it possible to trace an undulating route, although it is a tricky maneuver to measure a path that contains numerous curves, especially if they are tightly spaced.

The map distance is converted to earth distance by multiplying the map scale denominator by the distance shown on the wheel and converting to the desired units. If the map distance is 3 centimeters (approximately 1.18 inches), for example, and the map scale is 1:100,000, the earth distance is:

3 cm × 100,000 = 300,000 cm = 3,000 m = 3 km
(or 1.18 in. × 100,000 = 118,000 in. = approx. 1.86 mi.)

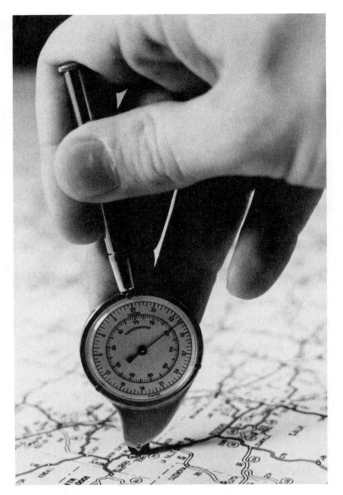

FIGURE 5.3   Map measurer.

Source: John Kehoe photo, by permission of Keuffel and Esser Company.

Alternatively, the wheel of the map measurer is placed at the zero point on the map's graphic scale and is rolled along that scale (in the direction opposite to the direction it was moved on the map), until the pointer once again rests on zero. The graphic scale reading at the stopping point gives the ground distance represented by the length of the path on the map. If the distance measured is longer than the scale, the process must be repeated as often as necessary to return the scale on the map measurer to zero, and the accumulated values indicate the total distance.

Computer-assisted methods.   Computer-assisted methods for direct distance measurement typically involve the use of a digitizing table and appropriate software. In the simplest mode, the map is fastened to the digitizing table, and the map scale is entered. The starting and ending points are then selected, and the software computes the direct, straight-line distance between them. In a more complex mode, significant points are selected along the desired route, and the distance between the endpoints is calculated, taking the twists and turns of the route into account.

Distances can be directly determined in any required units by any of the previously discussed methods if suitable scales are provided or constructed.

Indirect Methods of Measurement

When it is inconvenient or impractical to measure distances directly from a map, indirect methods of measurement are useful.

Short distances.   When two points are located within a relatively short distance of one another, within the confines of a medium-sized state, for example, the distance between them may be indirectly measured without correcting for the curvature of the earth's surface. If the UTM or state plane coordinate locations of the points are known, or can be determined, the distance between them can be easily calculated, provided both points lie within a single grid zone. The technique used in these circumstances is an application of the Pythagorean theorem. The east-west distance between the points is obtained by finding the difference between the east-west coordinates (figure 5.4). The same process is carried out for the two north-south coordinates. The required distance is then calculated by taking the square root of the sum of the squares of the east-west and north-south distances.

Distances that span two or more grid zones can be calculated by taking advantage of the overlap provided between adjoining zones. A "linking point" along the alignment of the path between the two points of interest and within the area of overlap needs to be established. The distance from each point to the linking point is then determined, using the appropriate grid values for each. The two partial distances are then added to obtain the total distance.

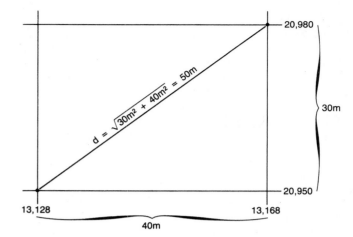

FIGURE 5.4   **Measuring distance using the Pythagorean theorem.**

Long distances.   Distances of several hundred miles or more are measured in generally the same way as shorter distances. With these longer distances, however, spherical coordinates are used instead of plane coordinates because the shape of the earth must be taken into account.

Spherical triangles have different characteristics than do the more familiar plane triangles, so the straightforward Pythagorean method cannot be used to determine distances on a sphere. Also, the spherical coordinate system involves degrees, minutes, and seconds of latitude and longitude, or decimal degrees, rather than familiar distance units. Both of these factors complicate the computations. The scope of this book does not include computations involving spherical coordinates, so they are not discussed further here.

Computer-assisted methods.   A computer may be used for indirect distance calculations if suitable software is available. A minimal system of this type simply allows the entry of the desired beginning and ending coordinates. The necessary calculations to determine the direct-route distance between the coordinates are then performed, under program control. The program can be designed to take into account as much detail about the spherical geometry of the earth as is desired. This aspect is most important when long

FIGURE 5.5   Simplification of a line results in shortening its length.

distances are calculated. In a more advanced system, a data file of available routes is required. In this case, a specification of the particular route to be followed is included, along with the starting and ending coordinates. This type of calculation is often a feature within a geographic information system.

Error Sources

Three factors influence the accuracy of horizontal distance measurements: (1) measurement error, (2) the level of generalization of the line being measured, and (3) the vertical displacements along the route.

Measurement error.   Following curved lines accurately when using a map measurer or a paper strip is difficult, but these difficulties are minimized by careful measurement. Error is also reduced when each measurement is repeated at least three times and the average of the three readings is used as the most likely distance value.

Smoothing.   Because of map generalization, routes (other than straight lines) inevitably are represented in somewhat simplified form on maps. The smaller the map scale, the greater the amount of simplification **(smoothing)** that occurs. In addition, simplification of a line results in shortening the distance between its starting and ending points (figure 5.5).

TABLE 5.1   Effects of Scale on Measured Distances (Distances in Kilometers)

	MAP SCALE		
	1:250,000	1:63,360	1:25,000
Smooth Coast	12.5	13.2	13.375
Crenulated Coast	15.0	16.2	21.75

Source: Adapted from J. P. Cole and C. A. M. King, *Quantitative Geography* (London: Wiley, 1968), 60.

For these reasons, route distance measurements taken from maps tend to underestimate the true distances between features on the earth's surface.

In the case of linear features, the more complex the shape, the greater the effect of map generalization. A straight-line feature, for example, is accurately represented by a simple straight line on a map. A linear feature made up of intricate, closely spaced curves, on the other hand, is not accurately represented by the inevitably smoothed form shown on the map.

In one experiment, the influence of generalization differences was illustrated by measuring two stretches of coastline, one smooth and the other irregular, on maps of three different scales. As shown in table 5.1, the measured length varied considerably for both stretches of coastline, but the more irregular coastline showed the greatest variation. Also, in general, the measured lengths increased as scale increased, reflecting decreased generalization. This experiment suggests that the only feasible way to avoid serious underestimation of the length of irregular features is to use a source map that is at the largest scale appropriate for the task at hand.

Slope.   When distance measurements are taken from a map, **slope errors** may occur because features are shown orthographically on the map. This means that their distances apart are not affected by elevation differences and are the same as they would be if the earth were flat. In the real world, the routes between locations almost always involve ups and downs. The actual surface distance between two objects, there-

FIGURE 5.6   When slopes exist, the surface distance is longer than the map distance between two points.

fore, is longer than the map distance, except in the exceptional case where the ground surface is perfectly flat (figure 5.6).

In many circumstances, the difference in distance traveled due to elevation differences is trivial. In traveling from Chicago to Denver, for example, there is an elevation difference of approximately 1,432 meters (4,698.4 feet). Taking this difference into account increases the 1,686 kilometers (1045 miles) travel distance by only 0.6 meter (1.97 feet) (less than 0.1 percent). In this example, the difference obviously can be ignored.

If you are planning a hike in mountainous territory, on the other hand, your origin and destination may be only a few kilometers apart in horizontal distance. The vertical distance that you have to traverse, however, may increase the total hiking distance significantly. In the Grand Canyon, for example, the horizontal distance from Yavapai Point, on the south rim, to Phantom Ranch, at the floor of the canyon, is approximately 4,660 meters (15,289.5 feet). The vertical elevation difference between these two points is 1,391 meters (4,563.9 feet), and the "actual" distance between them is 4,863 meters (15,955.5 feet), assuming that you could travel in a straight line from one point to the other. (In actuality, of course, the trail travels a very tortuous path, so that the actual total travel distance is much greater.) The elevation difference, then, adds 4.3 percent (203 meters or 666 feet) to the horizontal distance. This difference is for many purposes not of major importance, although your feet may tell you otherwise after you hike the trail.

Assuming that there is a relatively uniform slope between two points, the calculation of the distance correction for elevation involves a simple application of the Pythagorean theorem. If, for example, there is

a horizontal distance of 1,000 meters (3,281 feet) between two points, and a vertical difference of 100 meters (328.1 feet), the total surface distance between the two points is:

$$\sqrt{(1{,}000 \text{ m}^2 + 100 \text{ m}^2)}$$
$$= \sqrt{(1{,}000{,}000 \text{ m}^2 + 10{,}000 \text{ m}^2)}$$
$$= \sqrt{1{,}010{,}000 \text{ m}^2} = 1004.98 \text{ m} \ (3{,}297.3 \text{ ft})$$

Another factor to be considered in distance measurement is that undulations in the earth's surface add additional errors. These differences might be significant in very rough terrain. If great accuracy is required for the measurement of distance over such terrain, the route must be broken into a number of sections, each with a relatively uniform up- or downslope. The surface distance for each section is then calculated, and the total distance is obtained by totaling the figures for the individual sections.

AREA DETERMINATION

Areal Scale

The **areal scale** of a map is sometimes used to describe the relationship between the *area* of a feature plotted on a map and the area of the same feature on the earth's surface. The ratio between the area of a region on the map and the area of the same region on the earth is the square of the map's linear scale. On a map with a linear scale of 1:24,000, for example, each *linear* unit on the map represents 24,000 *linear* units on the earth. At the same time, however, each *square* unit on the map represents 576,000,000 (24,000²) *square* units on the earth. This areal scale is best expressed as 1:24,000².

A number of other methods are available for the measurement of map areas. These range from quick, relatively inaccurate, estimation techniques to more accurate methods that utilize special instruments and often require a longer period of time or special data to accomplish.

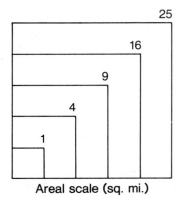

Areal scale (sq. mi.)

FIGURE 5.7   Graphic areal scale.

Direct Methods of Measurement

Scaling and computation.   The area occupied by some relatively small features can be determined with a linear graphic scale. The length and width of rectilinear features, such as a building or a city block, are easily measured. Determining the area that the feature occupies is then a matter of simple arithmetic. This method is reasonably accurate for small areas if the feature has a relatively regular geometric shape. It is not satisfactory, however, if the feature has a very irregular outline.

The size of features can be estimated directly with a graphic areal scale (figure 5.7). Ideally, such scales are provided on transparent material so that they can be laid directly over the map. This form is particularly easy to use; it is simply a matter of totaling the unit areas occupied by the feature of interest. The area of a county in square miles, the area of wheat land in hectares, or the size of a lake in square kilometers, for example, can be determined by this method, if a scale with the desired units is available. This method is inaccurate if the feature has an irregular shape.

Polar planimeter.   A polar planimeter is an instrument that measures areas on a map in terms of square inches or square centimeters (figure 5.8). These measurements are then arithmetically converted to earth measurements.

FIGURE 5.8   Polar planimeter.
Source: John Kehoe photo, by permission of Keuffel and Esser Company.

The pivot point of the planimeter is set up so that the area to be measured can be traced. (The pivot point may be either inside or outside the area to be measured, although the location affects the conversion factor that must be used.) The planimeter dial is set to zero, and the tracing point is placed at a predetermined starting point. The tracing point is then carefully guided around the perimeter of the area, returning to the starting point. When the tracing is completed, the reading on the dial is recorded. At least three readings should be taken because of the difficulty of tracing the boundary exactly. The average

Area = [(full cells) + 1/2 (partial cells)] × cell value
    = [71 + 1/2(26)] × 1 km² = 84 km²

FIGURE 5.9   Grid-square method of areal measurement.

Area = [dots within + 1/2 (dots on boundary)] × dot value
    = [75 + 1/2 (18)] × 1 km² = 84 km²

FIGURE 5.10   Dot-planimeter method of areal measurement.

value of the three map area readings is then converted into the area on the ground in the desired units. This is done by using either of the following formulas:

1.   To determine ground area in square kilometers:

$$\text{ground area (km}^2) = \frac{\text{map area (cm}^2) \times RF^2}{100,000^2}$$

2.   To determine ground area in square miles:

$$\text{ground area (mi}^2) = \frac{\text{map area (inches}^2) \times RF^2}{63,360^2}$$

where the RF value, in each case, is the denominator of the map scale.

Some planimeters are available with an adjustable tracer arm that allows direct scaling in ground units. Also, some elaborate instruments such as digitizing boards may be connected to a computer that is programmed to automatically convert instrument readings directly into the desired areal units.

Indirect Methods of Measurement

Grid squares.   The **grid-squares method** of measurement involves overlaying the area of interest with a right-angled grid of lines, spaced an appropriate distance apart (figure 5.9). It is convenient if the spacing between the lines is scaled so that the desired areal units are obtained without further calculation. If the lines are spaced 1 scale kilometer apart, for example, each grid square represents 1 scale square kilometer.

The cells that fall within the area to be measured are then counted. If a full cell falls within the area, it is counted as one. If only a portion of a cell falls within the area, one of two methods of counting is adopted. In the first approach, the total number of partial cells is divided by two and added to the total number of full cells to obtain the total area. The assumption that lies behind this approach is that, by chance, some cells fall in such a way that a large portion is within the area and others fall so that only a small portion is within the area. The expectation is that the two categories will balance one another, so that the average value of one-half cell will be relatively accurate. If the grid of lines is fine enough, this method is likely to be satisfactory. In any case, the grid-square method should not be used when extreme accuracy is required.

If the grid pattern is somewhat coarse (or if you do not "trust" random processes), a second approach is taken. In this method, an estimate is made of the fraction of each partial cell that falls within the area being measured. The total of these fractional values is added to the number of full cells to determine the total area.

Dot planimeter.   With the **dot-planimeter method** of areal measurement, which is a variant of the grid-square method, a regularly spaced pattern of dots is placed over the map, and each dot represents the center of an imaginary grid square. A total dot count is obtained by adding the number of dots that fall fully within the area to be measured and one-half of the number of dots that fall on the boundary of the area to be measured (figure 5.10).

Next, a dot unit value is determined, based on the spacing between the dots and the scale of the map. Assume, for example, that the dots are spaced 1 centimeter (0.394 inches) apart and the map scale is

Area = total length of strips × width
    = 84.2 km × 1 km = 84.2 km²

FIGURE 5.11   Strip method of areal measurement.

Total area = Areas (A + B + C + D + E + F)
    = 81.8 km²

FIGURE 5.12   Polygon method of areal measurement.

1:10,000. The imaginary square that surrounds each dot is 1 centimeter (0.394 inches) long on each side, which, at the scale of 1:10,000, represents 10,000 centimeters or 100 meters (3,940 inches or 109.4 yards). The area of each square, therefore, represents 10,000 square meters (11,968 square yards). The total dot count is then multiplied by the dot unit value, and the result is the desired areal measurement. In contrast to the grid-square and strip methods, which are exhaustive counting methods, the dot-planimeter method is a sampling procedure.

Strip method.   In the **strip method**, a series of parallel lines is drawn over the area to be measured. As with the grid-square method, it is helpful if the spacing between the lines is scaled so that the results of the measurement are obtained directly in the desired units.

The ends of each of the strips are established by drawing vertical lines at the edge of the area being measured. Because the edge of the area is uneven and not likely to cross the strip at right angles, this line is located so that it balances the portion of the area that is outside the line with the portion that is inside (figure 5.11).

The length of each strip is then measured using the same units that were used to establish the strip's width. Adding the individual lengths and multiplying the total length by the width of a single strip yields the total area.

Polygon method.   The **polygon method** of areal measurement is based on direct measurements. It is most suitable for use when the boundary of the area to be measured is made up of a series of relatively straight lines (or can be approximated by a series of

such lines). The method involves subdividing the study area into a number of regular geometric figures (rectangles, triangles, and trapezoids) (figure 5.12). The dimensions of these figures are determined, using the desired map units, and their areas are obtained by standard procedures (height × width for rectangles, ½ height × base for triangles, and height × ½ (side₁ + side₂) for trapezoids). The total of the individual areas gives the overall measurement.

Computer-Assisted Methods

A computer can be used to calculate areal measurements if suitable software is available. This greatly reduces the tedious calculations necessary using regular computational methods and usually speeds up the operation as well. As is the case with many computer operations, the preparation of a suitable data file is the major task required for the calculation of areas.

Small areas.   For relatively small areas, the curvature of the earth can be ignored. The data file in this case consists of a list of x,y coordinates (UTM or state plane coordinates, for example) and is done with a standard digitizing tablet (see chapter 19). Usually, critical points on the outline of the area to be measured are selected, and a digital file of their coordinates is created.

The physical process of digitizing is very similar to tracing the outline of an area with a standard planimeter. The advantage over using a planimeter is that a file of coordinates is created, and this is potentially useful for other operations such as creating a map of the area. Indeed, if a computer mapping coordinate file already exists, it can be used directly, and the creation of a new file is unnecessary.

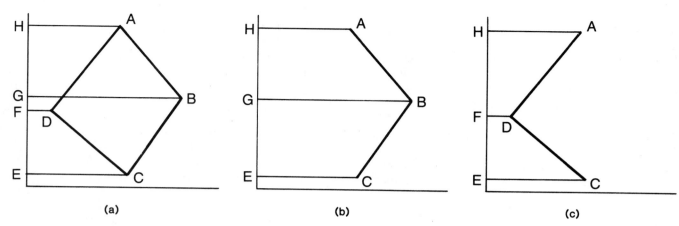

FIGURE 5.13   Computer-assisted method of areal measurement. (*a*) Area of interest (*ABCDA*) and reference framework. (*b*) Trapezoids encompassing area of interest (*HABGH* and *GBCEG*), but including excess area. (*c*) Trapezoids excluding area of interest (HADFH and *FDCEF*).

The coordinate file, whether it is newly created or already exists, is simply read into the appropriate software package, which computes the area and reports the result. The task is accomplished in somewhat different ways by different software packages, but the general approach is as follows.

Assume that we wish to compute the area of the region defined by the vertices *A, B, C,* and *D* in figure 5.13. This region can be related to the vertical axis in the figure to form four trapezoids (*HABGH, GBCEG, HADFH,* and *FDCEF*). The data file for this region would contain *x* and *y* coordinates for each of the vertices in these trapezoids.

In general, the area of a trapezoid is determined by multiplying its height by the average length of its two parallel sides, or height × ½ (side$_1$ + side$_2$). The coordinates in the data file are used in the following manner to compute the area of each trapezoid: Take trapezoid *HABGH* as an example. In this case, its height is found by subtracting the *y* coordinate of vertex *B* from the *y* coordinate of vertex *A*. The average length of its parallel sides is found by adding the *x* coordinate of vertex *A* (which is the length of side *HA*) to the *x* coordinate of vertex *B* (the length of side *BG*), and dividing the result by 2.

After the areas of the four trapezoids have been determined, they are used to calculate the area of the region of interest on the basis of the relationship of each trapezoid to that region. Some of the trapezoids encompass the region (and more), whereas others fall entirely outside it. The procedure, therefore, is to add the areas of the trapezoids that encompass the desired region and to subtract from that total the areas of the trapezoids that fall outside it. This process is shown in figure 5.13. Here, the region of interest (*ABCDA*) is shown, as is the reference framework (figure 5.13a). The region *ABCDA* is included in two trapezoids (*HABGH* and *GBCEG*) (figure 5.13b), but excess areas are also enclosed. This is resolved by excluding the area encompassed by the two outside trapezoids (*HADFH* and *FDCEF*) (figure 5.13c), which leaves the area of interest.

This may seem to be a rather roundabout method of calculation, especially when dozens, or perhaps hundreds, of trapezoids are involved. With computer calculations, however, the results are obtained very speedily.

Large areas.   A different procedure is needed for relatively large areas because the curvature of the earth cannot be ignored. In such cases, a computer-assisted method that uses a data file consisting of geodetic coordinates is available. The article "Area Computation from Geodetic Coordinates on the Spheroid," by A. J. Kimerling, which is listed in the "Suggested Readings" at the end of this chapter, gives the details of this method.

Summary

Distances and areas are often directly measured from maps, although the accuracy with which the map is constructed must be kept in mind when this is done.

Ideally, distance measurements are taken over short distances so that the earth's curvature is not an important factor in the measurement. Otherwise, they should be taken along appropriate alignments, on a map drawn on an equidistant projection. If these requirements are met, direct scaling using the map's graphic scale and dividers, scales, paper strips, or a map measurer is feasible, as are computer-assisted methods.

Indirect distance measurement methods are sometimes preferable. These include the application of the Pythagorean theorem to the grid coordinates of the endpoints of the distance to be measured. Over longer distances, computations using spherical coordinates are used.

Three factors influence the accuracy of distance measurements: measurement error, map generalization, and vertical displacements along the route. Measurement error stems from simple difficulties encountered when using the measuring devices and is minimized when measuring is done with care. Map generalization inevitably simplifies linear features, which normally results in shortening the distance between their starting and ending points. Slope errors occur whenever a route involves ups and downs, and the actual surface distance between two locations is longer than the map distance, except where the ground surface is perfectly flat. The underestimation of distances that results from generalization and slope can be corrected if it is judged to be important enough in a particular case.

Area determination can involve quick-estimation techniques or more time-consuming, but often more accurate, methods. Direct methods include simply scaling the dimensions of features and computing their area accordingly. Alternatively, the sizes of features can be estimated directly by using a graphic areal scale. Also, a polar planimeter can be used to measure areas on a map in terms of square inches or square centimeters and the measurements converted to earth measurements. Indirect methods of measurement include the use of grid squares, dot planimeters, and the strip method, all of which are relatively inaccurate. The polygon method can be more accurate, especially if the outline of the study area is relatively regular in shape. Computer-assisted methods can also be used to calculate areal measurements. These reduce the calculations and usually speed up the operation.

SUGGESTED READINGS

Herring, Bruce E., and Marguerite L. Freeman. "Areal Calculations Using an Acoustical Digitizer-Minicomputer System." *Surveying and Mapping* 45, no. 4 (1985): 319–30.

Kimerling, A. J. "Area Computation from Geodetic Coordinates on the Spheroid." *Surveying and Mapping* 44, no. 4 (1984): 343–51.

Lopshits, A. M. *Computation of Areas of Oriented Figures.* Boston: D.C. Heath, 1963.

Thompson, Morris M. *Maps for America.* 3d ed. Washington, D.C.: U.S. Geological Survey, 1987, 104.

6

Route Selection and Navigation

A primary use of maps is as an aid to route selection and navigation; maps provide indispensable information about locations, obstacles, directions, and distances. We may need to decide which roads to travel to reach an adjoining town, to lay out a compass path for an orienteering outing, to plot the course for a ship to follow to reach harbor, to pick the radio beacon that will guide an airplane to the next airport, or to perform any one of a multitude of similar tasks. Regardless of the simplicity or complexity of our route-selection problem, a map of some sort is likely to be an important part of the solution.

Although this chapter treats land, water, and air applications separately, they overlap a great deal. The basic considerations involved in planning a course by dead reckoning, for example, apply equally to all three, even though the discussion of dead reckoning has been placed in the nautical section. Therefore, keep an open mind when considering which techniques may be applicable in a particular situation.

BASIC CONSIDERATIONS

Direction Determination

The determination of direction requires a frame of reference. A baseline must be established first, then direction is expressed in terms of angular measurements in relation to the baseline. The baseline usually used for direction finding is a north-south line that passes through the viewer's position and establishes "north." Because more than one north reference can be established, however, the viewer must decide which one to use.

True north. The most commonly used north for direction-finding purposes is **true north** (sometimes called **geographical north**). True north is the northerly direction along a line of longitude.

True north is easily determined, on a clear night in the northern hemisphere, by sighting on Polaris. Polaris is a star located almost directly over the geographical north pole.[1] With a little more difficulty, observations of other stars, including the sun, may be used for this purpose.

A **gyrocompass** provides another means for determining true north. It has an advantage in that it can be used at any time of the day or night, at any point on the earth's surface, or above or below the earth's surface. Also, because a gyrocompass aligns itself with the spin of the earth's axis, its north arrow points steadily true north and is not affected by the vagaries of the earth's magnetic field, as is the more common magnetic compass.

Magnetic north. The north arrow of a magnetic compass points toward the north magnetic pole, a direction called **magnetic north**. The north magnetic pole currently is located in northern Canada, approximately 1,440 kilometers (895 miles) from the geographic pole (the pole of rotation). The two poles are

---

[1] Because Polaris is not directly on a line extended from the earth's axis of rotation, a discrepancy of approximately 1½ degrees must be taken into account when true north is determined very accurately. The required correction is obtained from the appropriate tables in a reference publication for the current year. Standard references, for this and other astronomical observations, include: *The Astronomical Almanac* (Washington, D.C.: U.S. Naval Observatory); the *Solar Ephemeris* (Morristown, N.J.: Keuffel and Esser); *The Nautical Almanac* (joint publication of the U.S. Naval Observatory and H.M. Nautical Almanac Office, Royal Greenwich Observatory); and the *Air Almanac* (by the publishers of *The Nautical Almanac*) for the current year.

not in direct alignment with one another in relation to most locations on the earth's surface. As a result, the magnetic compass does not usually point directly toward the geographic north pole and, therefore, does not indicate true north. The difference between true north and magnetic north at any given location is called **magnetic declination.**[2]

A special map, called an **isogonic chart**, shows magnetic declination (figure 6.1). The lines drawn on this chart to show locations with equal declination are called **isogonic lines**. In the western United States, as the chart shows, declination is generally eastward,

which means that the compass points east of true north. The reverse is true in the eastern United States. The isogonic line that joins points of zero declination is called the **agonic line**.

The location of the magnetic pole changes with time. The changes are somewhat predictable over a period of several years. As a result, the change in declination expected in the near future can be predicted. An isogonic chart, therefore, is drawn to show the situation at a particular time. It also usually includes an indication of the expected direction and amount of

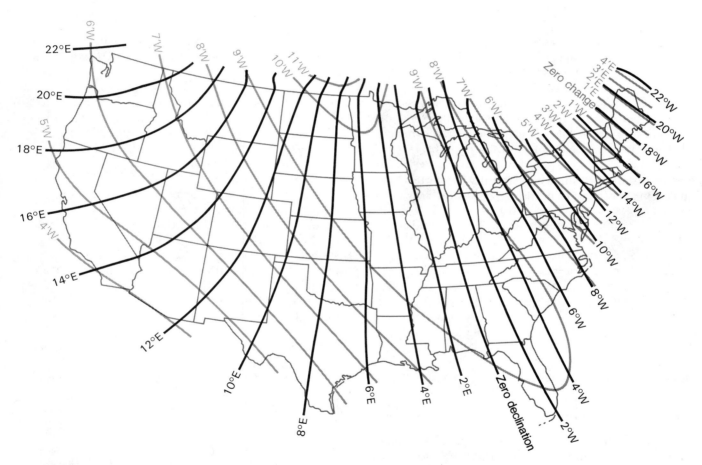

FIGURE 6.1   Isogonic chart. Black lines are isogonic lines, which join points of equal compass declination. Gray lines join points of equal annual change in declination.

Source: "Magnetic Declination in the United States—Epoch 1980," U.S. Geological Survey map I-1283, 1980.

[2]Navigators often use the term *variation* for the same concept.

annual change. This information allows the adjustment of the declination values on the chart for current use, even though the chart may be several years old.

Deviations are another complication involved in the determination of compass direction. **Compass deviation** is the difference between the direction to the north magnetic pole and the direction that the compass needle actually points. One source of deviation is the presence of ore bodies that distort the earth's magnetic field. Some such deviations are relatively well known and predictable and affect areas of considerable extent. These deviations are often included in the information from which isogonic charts are drawn. Other deviations, such as those due to power lines, are not so predictable and their effects not so widespread. This idiosyncratic type of deviation is not shown on an isogonic chart, and the user of a magnetic compass must be on the alert for the deviation's effects when operating in the field. Compass readings taken near metallic objects such as automobiles or fence lines, or near power lines are particularly likely to be inaccurate. Indeed, even keys in your pocket can lead to significant compass deviation. Magnetic compasses installed in ships are carefully located and adjusted in an attempt to minimize deviation problems, although these efforts are never entirely successful.

Grid north. Any map may have one or more specialized grids, such as the Universal Transverse Mercator (UTM) or State Plane Coordinate (SPC) grids, superimposed on it (see chapter 10). The direction of the north-trending grid lines of any such grid is referred to as **grid north.**

Meridians, which are aligned with true north, converge as one moves away from the equator and toward either pole, whereas the lines of a rectangular grid do not. Therefore, although the north-south lines of rectangular grids may coincide with true north at the grid origin (or at some other special point), they usually do not align at other locations. Thus, there is almost always a difference between the direction of the nominally north-south lines of a particular grid and *either* true or magnetic north. In addition, the grid north of two or more grids seldom matches, so there may be more than one grid north on a given map.

Declination diagram. A declination diagram is placed on a map to show the relationships between the three "norths" that have been described (figure

UTM GRID AND 1973 MAGNETIC NORTH
DECLINATION AT CENTER OF SHEET

FIGURE 6.2 Declination diagram. The star indicates true north, *GN* stands for grid north, and *MN* and the arrow designate magnetic north. Angles on the diagram show only relative directions; actual angles are plotted when making adjustments. (Randeen Ridge quadrangle, Minnesota, 1:24,000, 1973.)

6.2). True north is usually marked by a line with a star at the end, suggesting Polaris; magnetic north is often shown by a line with a partial arrowhead, representing a compass needle, or with the letters *MN;* and the grid-north line is typically indicated by the abbreviation *GN.* The angular difference between the three north directions is indicated on the face of the diagram. The date of the diagram is also usually indicated, sometimes with the expected annual amount and direction of change in declination.

Declination diagrams on maps are sometimes drawn diagrammatically, rather than exactly. This is especially true in the case of small angles of declination, which are difficult to reproduce accurately. For this reason, exact conversions from one reference direction to another are often done mathematically, rather than graphically. Nevertheless, a declination diagram is useful for keeping track of the calculations involved in converting a directional reference from true to magnetic, from grid to true, and so on. If an accurate graphical conversion is needed for direct-measurement purposes, a larger version of a declination diagram can be drawn using exact measurements. Such a diagram is often drawn directly on the face of the map so that angular measurements can be made more easily in relation to the desired base direction.

Direction Designation

Directions are usually designated as either azimuths or bearings.

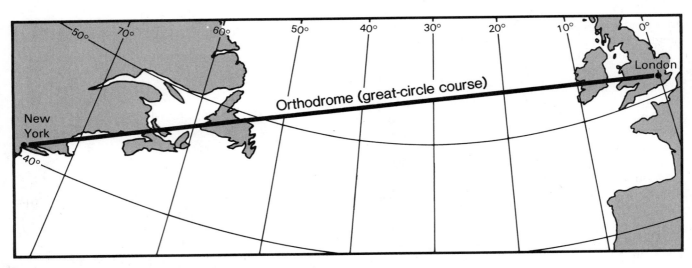

FIGURE 6.3   The orthodrome (true azimuth or great-circle route) crosses successive meridians at constantly changing angles.

Azimuth.   An azimuth is a directional designation that is usually measured in a clockwise direction from north (although south is the reference direction in some cases). Depending upon the reference direction, azimuths are stated as orthodromes (based on true north), magnetic (based on magnetic north), or grid (based on grid north). Azimuth measurements are usually stated in degrees, minutes, and seconds, and range from 000° (north), through 090° (east), 180° (south), 270° (west), to 359° (approximately north, again).[3]

Over a short distance, an azimuth is simply the angle between two sightings, one taken on the reference direction and the other on the target, or destination. It can be directly plotted, with relative impunity, when the distance between the origin and destination is relatively short. When directions over long distances are involved, however, the curvature of the earth must be taken into account because, depending upon how one defines direction, an azimuth from a starting point may or may not remain constant. The concepts *orthodrome* and *constant azimuth* are involved here and require some clarification.

[3]Occasionally, angular measurements are expressed in *grades* (see chapter 22). Also, in military applications such as aiming of artillery weapons, *mils* are used to measure angles. In this system, a circle is divided into 6,400 mils, so that each mil represents approximately one-eighteenth of a degree.

The term *orthodrome* (sometimes called the **true azimuth**) refers to the direction of a great circle (see chapter 2). This is because, when one starts out in a given direction and follows a great circle, one eventually returns to the point of beginning. In most cases, the angle at which an orthodrome crosses successive meridians constantly changes (figure 6.3). One exception to this rule occurs when the orthodrome is along the equator. In this case, it crosses all of the meridians at a right angle. Another exception occurs when the orthodrome is along a meridian. In this case, of course, no other meridians are crossed.

In contrast to an orthodrome, a **constant azimuth**, or **rhumb line**, is defined as a directional line that crosses each succeeding meridian at a constant angle.

A simple **conversion diagram** may be used to assist in the change of azimuths from one reference direction to another. A conversion diagram is a sketch that shows two reference lines (figure 6.4a). One reference line represents the original base direction (true north, for example), and the other represents the new base direction (magnetic north, for example). The diagram also shows the azimuth being converted to the new base in its correct relationship to the reference directions. The angles between each of the lines are indicated, but they need not be drawn to the exact measurements because the sketch is used simply as an organization aid, not for actual plotting.

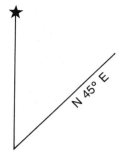

Note: In these sketches, angles are drawn in correct relative location, but are not necessarily plotted accurately.

FIGURE 6.4 (*a*) Conversion diagram. (*b*) Conversion of magnetic azimuth to orthodrome (true azimuth). (*c*) Adjustment for west declination.

FIGURE 6.5 Bearing, north 45° east.

The examples that follow illustrate some possible conversion combinations. Assume, for example, that a magnetic azimuth of 045° is to be converted to an orthodrome and that the declination is 004° east (figure 6.4b). The relationships between magnetic azimuths and orthodromes in this situation, as figure 6.4b indicates, require *adding* the declination to the magnetic azimuth to obtain the orthodrome of 049°. Obviously, the reverse would be true when converting from orthodrome to magnetic. Figure 6.4c, on the other hand, shows that a west declination requires that the amount of the declination angle be *subtracted* from the magnetic azimuth to obtain the orthodrome.

Conversions from grid to orthodrome or from grid to magnetic (or the reverse of either) require the use of the angle between grid north and true north or between grid north and magnetic north, as appropriate. In the example in figure 6.4a, the angle between grid north and magnetic north is the *sum* of the declination and the angle between grid north and true north. In other cases, the angle is the *difference* between these two angles. Once again, the conversion diagram readily indicates which situation applies.

Back-Azimuth. A **back-azimuth** is the exact reverse of an azimuth. (The regular azimuths just described are sometimes called forward azimuths for the sake of clarity.) The value of a back-azimuth is ob-

tained by adding 180 degrees to an azimuth that has a value of less than 180 degrees, or subtracting 180 degrees from an azimuth that has a value of 180 degrees or more.

Bearing. A **bearing** is a type of direction designation often utilized in metes-and-bounds surveys. Bearings are measured from either a north or south baseline, whichever is nearer to the direction being designated. Bearings may be relative to either magnetic, true, or grid north, so the baseline should be designated on the map.

Because of the manner in which they are measured, bearings have a maximum value of 90 degrees. A bearing is designated with the following form: north 45° east, for example (figure 6.5). The base direction is stated first (in this case, north). The numerical designation indicates the number of degrees that the bearing differs from the reference direction (here, 45°). If the accuracy of the measurement is sufficient, the bearing direction includes minutes, seconds, and fractions of seconds. The last portion of the designation indicates whether the bearing is to the east or west of the reference direction (east, in this case).

Back-Bearing. Just as a back-azimuth is the opposite of an azimuth, a **back-bearing** is the exact reverse of a bearing. The value of a back-bearing is obtained by changing both of the directional references of the bearing. For example, assume that the bearing to a position from an observation point is north 45° east. The back-bearing from the position to the observation point, then, is south 45° west.

LAND OPERATIONS

Movement over land is generally the simplest form of navigation. Features that can be used for orientation are usually relatively abundant, and the ground provides a stable platform for observations. These circumstances are in marked contrast to conditions frequently encountered at sea or in the air. Heavy tree cover or adverse weather conditions, on the other hand, can hide reference points and make the land navigator's task considerably more difficult.

Map Orientation

An important aspect of organizing route-finding activities on land is to orient the map being used. A simple method of **map orientation** is the process of inspection. Inspection involves selecting easily recognizable features on the landscape and locating the same features on the map. The map is then turned so that the landscape features are in the proper relationship to the mapped features (figure 6.6).

A more exact method of map orientation involves the use of a compass. In this approach, a compass is placed on the map near the declination diagram. Because the compass arrow points to magnetic north, the map and compass are rotated as a unit until the direction of the north arrow on the declination diagram matches the direction of the compass needle (see appendix B). If the rate and direction of change in declination are known, any necessary correction of the north arrow on the declination diagram is made prior to starting the orientation process.

FIGURE 6.6   Map orientation by inspection.

Source: Department of the Army, *Map Reading,* FM 21–26 (Washington, D.C.: Department of the Army, January 1969).

Position Determination

If you do not know your exact location, a properly oriented map provides the means for determining it, using a method called **resection**. Resection can be done either with or without a compass. In the compass method of resection, two or three known positions on the ground are located and marked on the map. The magnetic azimuth to one of the known positions is determined by taking a compass sighting.

The back-azimuth of this sighting is then drawn on the map from the known position toward your unknown position, using the compass to establish the direction (see appendix B). Preferably, this process is repeated for two other known locations. The crossing of the back-azimuths marks your ground position (figure 6.7).

The use of three known references for resection is preferred because, ideally, the lines from all three will

FIGURE 6.7   Resection.

Source: Department of the Army, *Map Reading*, FM 21–26 (Washington, D.C.: Department of the Army, January 1969).

intersect at the same location. If they do not, a triangle, called the **triangle of error**, is formed. A large triangle of error indicates that the measurements need to be rechecked. A small triangle of error, however, indicates that the center of the triangle is the best estimate of the correct location.

If a compass is not available, resection can be accomplished using the straightedge method. In this approach, the map is oriented by inspection. Two or three known positions are then located and marked on the map. Next, a straightedge is laid on the map, with its center at the map location of one of the known positions. With this map location as a pivot point, the straightedge is turned until its edge is aligned with the same known position on the ground. (This alignment is determined by sighting along the edge of the straightedge.) A line is then drawn along the straightedge through the map location of the known position and toward your position. This operation is repeated with one or two additional points, and the intersection of the lines is your position. Again, the accuracy of the method is indicated by the size of the triangle of error.

Route Selection

Once the map is oriented and your location determined, you can plan the route to your desired destination. Plotting your proposed path on the map allows you to select a travel route that avoids steep gradients, hazardous areas, and other difficulties, while steering you to as many points of interest as possible. You can also make note, in advance, of reference points for monitoring your progress. Your selected route may be followed by using clues provided by reference to the map, by use of a compass, or by a combination of both methods.

When no compass is available, you must use landscape features, such as hilltops or water towers that also appear on the map, as reference points. When such a reference point lies in line with your desired route, for example, you can simply keep it dead ahead and be certain that you are on the proper path. You can check your progress by periodically reorienting your map. This will verify that other visible reference points lie in the correct relationship to your estimated position. When you have reached the end of a

particular line of travel, you simply select a new target that will guide you in the appropriate direction for the next portion of your journey.

When you are using a compass, the magnetic azimuth of each portion of the route is obtained by measuring its angle from magnetic north. Aligning the compass with the desired route on a properly oriented map allows a direct reading of compass direction.[4] The compass is then sighted in the desired direction, and a target that lies on that azimuth is selected. In this case, the target can be much less prominent and need not be shown on the map. A distinctively shaped tree or a large rock, for example, often makes an excellent target. You then move in the desired direction by keeping the selected target directly ahead. When you reach one target, you select another that is on a heading appropriate to the next portion of your route and continue as before.

WATER OPERATIONS

The special maps used for navigational purposes are usually called **charts**. The two principal types of charts are nautical charts for navigation at sea and aeronautical charts for navigation in the air. Each type incorporates special characteristics suited to its particular applications.

Nautical Charts

Many different types of **nautical charts** are published to serve the varying needs of chart users (figure 6.8). The National Ocean Service (NOS), for example, publishes four major types of conventional nautical charts of U.S. waters: (1) harbor charts, (2) coast charts, (3) general charts, and (4) sailing charts.[5] These vary in scale from harbor charts at scales of 1:50,000 and larger to sailing charts at 1:600,000 and smaller. The larger scales show the detail necessary

---

[4]Compass use is discussed in appendix B.

[5]Small-craft and intracoastal waterway charts and a variety of other charts and materials are also published by the NOS. In addition, nautical charts and related products for inland waterways are published by the U.S. Army Corps of Engineers, and charts are published on a worldwide basis by the Defense Mapping Agency (DMA).

FIGURE 6.8   Portion of typical nautical chart. (Not for navigational purposes.)

Source: "Example of a National Ocean Service Nautical Chart: Potomac River," NOS Educational Publication no. 14.

for operation in relatively confined harbor and coastal situations, whereas the smaller scales are suitable for operations in less confined, offshore areas. Some of the more important general characteristics of nautical charts are described here.

Publication date.   A chart's publication date is vitally important because both navigational hazards and aids change over time. Using a chart on which such changes have not been recorded is extremely dangerous. For this reason, charts are revised at regular intervals. To ensure that the chart you intend to use is the most recent version, you should check the pamphlet *Dates of Latest Editions,* which is issued quarterly by NOS.

As an aid to chart users, a **Notice to Mariners** is published weekly by the Defense Mapping Agency Hydrographic/Topographic Center (DMAHTC).[6]

[6]Notices for the Great Lakes are published weekly by the U.S. Coast Guard.

Local notices are also published, as required, by U.S. Coast Guard District Offices. These notices specify changes to aids to navigation and other information of importance to vessel operators. The information from any notices that have been published since the effective date of the chart must be recorded on the face of the chart before it is used. Recently, the *Notice to Mariners* has been made available by means of a radio/computer interface so that ships at sea have immediate access to the most up-to-date navigational information.

Projections.   A useful characteristic of the Mercator projection is that a straight line drawn between any two points represents a line of constant heading (known as a loxodrome or rhumb line). Because of this characteristic, many nautical charts are drawn on the Mercator projection. Great-circle planning charts, however, are drawn on the gnomonic projection, and other projections are used for particular purposes.

Units of measurement. Navigators must frequently measure distances on nautical charts. For this reason, some charts contain graphic scales. Because of strong historical precedent, these scales are frequently in nautical miles. Other scales are sometimes used, however, including statute miles, meters, or feet. These scales are used in the same manner as any other graphic scale (see chapter 5).

When no graphic scale is provided, a question naturally arises as to how distance measurements are made. The answer to this question is provided by the information in the box entitled "Units of Measurement and Map Scales" (see chapter 4). As stated there, the international nautical mile is based on the measurement of an imaginary perfect sphere with a surface area equal to the surface of the earth. Specifically, it is the length of 1-minute of arc along a great circle of the sphere.

When you examine a chart, you will find that its neatline is subdivided into minutes, and fractions of minutes. This subdivision provides a built-in scale on which each minute of latitude represents one nautical mile and fractions of minutes represent equivalent fractions of a nautical mile. To measure a distance on this scale, the chart distance between two points is recorded, usually by spreading a pair of dividers between them. The dividers are then carried to the neatline and the nautical mile distance is read from the marks representing the lines of latitude. If distances are needed in units other than nautical miles, conversions are easy to carry out (see chapter 4). For example, one nautical mile = 1,852 meters, 6,076.12 feet, or approximately 1.151 statute miles.

Most nautical charts are drawn on the Mercator projection. This is convenient for navigational purposes, because a straight line on the Mercator represents a constant compass heading. However, it also means that the scale of the chart constantly changes as the latitude changes. Because of this change in scale, two limitations must be observed when taking and scaling measurements. First, both operations must be done at the same latitude. Second, degrees of latitude must be used, and not degrees of longitude.

Depth indications. Possibly the most vital safety information for anyone operating a vessel is the depth of the water under the vessel's keel. The depth of water bodies such as lakes and oceans varies as remarkably as the elevations on the earth's surface, but the undulations are hidden from view by the water.

For this reason, the depth information on navigational charts provides vital information about the conformation of the bottom.

On most charts, depth information is indicated in two ways. First, individual depths, or **soundings**, are specified by printing a number that is the equivalent of a spot height. There is usually no dot or other symbol to indicate the location of the sounding. The number that specifies the depth is simply centered at the correct location. Second, points of equal depth are indicated by lines called depth curves. Sometimes, hypsometric coloring between the contours indicates areas that fall within a particular range of depths.

Depths on charts are traditionally shown in **fathoms** (6 feet), although feet and meters are also used. The units used on a particular chart are clearly indicated on the face of the chart. One must be cautious, nevertheless, because of the potential danger of confusing depth values. If a ship draws 2 fathoms, areas that have a depth of less than 2 fathoms (12 feet), plus a margin for error, must be avoided. If the depths are marked in meters, however, the critical depth value is 4 meters (4 meters is slightly more than 2 fathoms). Heights of objects or natural features are usually recorded in feet. Both ocean and Great Lakes charts, however, are gradually being changed to a metric standard, so that depths and heights will both be recorded in meters.

The datum used for recording depths is an important variable that must also be taken into consideration when using depth indications on navigational charts. Information regarding the datum used on a particular chart is printed with the chart title. In general, depths are measured from the level of some form of average low water, in tidal waters. This means that the depths shown provide safe operating margins under most conditions. At extreme low tide, however, depths are less than those indicated on the chart. The wise mariner, therefore, takes tidal conditions into account when determining safe operating conditions.

Special symbols. The symbols used on nautical charts are selected to meet the special needs of chart users. These symbols deal in particular with such matters as water depth, the characteristics of the ocean floor or lake bottom, and the location and types of navigational aids such as channel markers. For obvious reasons, such important navigational information is presented in exhaustive detail on nautical charts. Information about land features is quite limited and is usually confined to the immediate coastal

FIGURE 6.9   Selected examples of symbols used on nautical charts.

Source: Chart No. 1, United States of America, Nautical Chart Symbols and Abbreviations, 8th ed. (Washington, D.C.: Department of Commerce, November 1984).

areas and to those features such as radio towers, bridges, railroad tracks, and cities and towns, that provide locational clues to the navigator. *Chart No. 1* is a reference booklet showing the symbols used on the nautical charts of the National Ocean Service.[7] Se-

lected examples of these symbols are shown in figure 6.9. One important additional method of symbolization on charts is the use of vertical lettering for features that are dry at high water and italics for submerged or floating features.

Position Determination

The determination of your vessel's position is a critical part of navigation because knowing where you are is fundamental to selecting the route you must

---

[7]*Chart No. 1, United States of America, Nautical Chart Symbols and Abbreviations* (Washington, D.C.: Department of Commerce, National Oceanic and Atmospheric Administration). The booklet also contains a glossary of principal foreign charting terms and information regarding aids to navigation in U.S. waters.

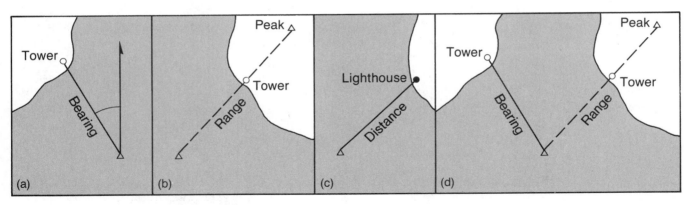

FIGURE 6.10   Lines of position. (*a*) Bearing. (*b*) Range. (*c*) Distance. (*d*) Fix.

follow to reach a new destination. Also, once your position has been accurately determined, you can check for any potentially hazardous conditions in the vicinity.

Early methods of position determination depended on visual observations assisted by various types of relatively simple instruments. Modern methods, on the other hand, often depend on sophisticated radio and electronic gear. This section describes some of the more fundamental approaches to locational determination and provides a basic understanding of how they relate to navigation.

Astronomical observations.   The traditional method by which navigators determine their position is by observing the sun and stars. This method, although relatively time consuming, is accurate and is particularly useful for navigation out of sight of land, provided atmospheric conditions allow taking the necessary observations. Depending on circumstances, a variety of other methods can supplement or take the place of direct observations.

Lines of position.   Navigators operating within sight of land maintain close watch on the location of their vessel by using **lines of position**. The use of lines of position is simply an application of the method of resection described earlier in the chapter. Lines of position may be **bearings** on known objects, such as church spires or water towers (figure 6.10). In nautical terms, a bearing is the angle, in degrees, between a reference direction and the direction to an observed feature. Nautical bearings, therefore, range from 000° to 360°, in contrast to surveyor's bearings, which were described earlier in the chapter.

Lines of position may also be **ranges**, which are alignments of two known objects (figure 6.10b), or they may be *distances* from such objects (figure 6.10c). When lines of position are plotted on a navigation chart, their point of crossing establishes the vessel's location, which is called a **fix** (figure 6.10d). Obtaining a fix is the most accurate and trustworthy method of determining a vessel's location.

Radar.   **Radar** is an active remote-sensing technique involving the transmission, reflection, and detection of radio waves that are only a few centimeters in length. It can be used regardless of weather and lighting conditions. The same general principles apply whether the transmitter is located on a ship, an airplane, or at a land base, but this section is written from the perspective of a ship-based installation.

A radar transmitter sends out pulsed signals, which are focused into a narrow beam by a special antenna. The antenna rotates as the signal is transmitted, so that a complete circle is swept every few seconds. When a pulse strikes the land surface, a tree, a building, another ship, a navigational aid, or any other object, it is reflected back to the radar antenna and is detected by a receiving unit. The returned signals are then used to create a display on a television-like cathode-ray tube. Objects that reflect signals show up on the screen as points of light, with the transmitter located at the center of the screen (figure 6.11). Each point

FIGURE 6.11 **Photograph of image on radar screen.**
(Inset shows radar unit.)
Courtesy of Raytheon Marine Company.

of light is located in the correct direction and at the correct scale distance from the ship. The appropriate location is determined by the direction from which the radar beam was reflected and by the length of time it took for it to reach the target and return.

The radar image is used to provide navigational information. Bearings are taken on identifiable objects that appear on the radar screen, for example. These bearings are plotted on the navigator's chart, in the same manner as other lines of position, to establish the vessel's location. In addition, the location, speed, and direction of movement of other ships and the location of navigational hazards can be determined by careful observation, so that collisions and groundings can be avoided.

A radar observer must have a considerable amount of training, experience, and skill. The image on the radar screen consists simply of points of light, whose meaning must be interpreted. Different objects, at different orientations, for example, reflect signals with varying strength. As a result, their images on the screen vary in brightness. In addition, because the resolution of the radar image is dependent upon the width of the radar beam, an object may sometimes look larger than it actually is. Also, the length of the pulse transmitted affects the ability to differentiate objects. Features located close to shore, for example, may merge with the shoreline. Signals may also be reflected from the surface of the water, under certain wave conditions, producing a confusing "clutter." In addition, atmospheric conditions may adversely affect the reception of the radar signals. All of these factors make the interpretation of a radar image as much an art as a science, and although radar provides a vital navigational aid, other navigational methods must be used in conjunction with it.

Satellite observation. Various types of navigational satellites have been placed in use in recent years and have made virtually automatic position determination possible. Potentially, they make accurate, worldwide position determination available on a twenty-four-hour basis, in all types of weather. Although details vary, the systems generally involve the reception and interpretation of signals transmitted by one or more orbiting satellites by a receiver located on board the vessel. (Again, land-based observations utilize the same principles.)

There are two general types of satellite navigation systems. One of these, characterized by the **Transit system**, depends on the Doppler effect. The Doppler effect is commonly illustrated by the example of a whistle of a constant pitch, sounded from a moving train and heard by a stationary observer. If the train is moving toward the observer, the pitch of the sound is increased; the greater the speed of movement, the greater the change in pitch. Then, as the train passes, the pitch of the sound that the observer hears drops, even though the whistle continues to emit a constant pitch.

In a Doppler-based navigational system, the satellite transmits a continuous radio signal with a fixed frequency. The apparent frequency of the signal received by a monitoring station varies, depending on whether the satellite is approaching the station or moving away from it. Combining the frequency information with timing and orbital data also transmitted by the satellite allows the calculation of the position of the receiving station in relation to the satellite. Simultaneous observations at two points, one of which is at a known location, increases the accuracy of the method.

The other general type of satellite navigational system is exemplified by the partly operational **NAV-STAR Global Positioning System (GPS)**. GPS depends on the reception of signals transmitted from several satellites (eighteen are scheduled for the complete system). The time difference between the transmission of each signal by a satellite and its arrival at the receiver in relation to the speed of light provides distance information. When four or more such distances are combined, the receiver's position is accurately fixed. The specific capabilities of GPS for the civilian user, including the availability of speed and time information, depend upon whether certain codes are made public or are retained as classified military information.

Satellite systems integrate information obtained from the satellite and provide a direct digital readout of the latitude, longitude, and, in some cases, elevation, of the receiver. This reading is then plotted onto the appropriate chart. The accuracy of the systems varies, but a commonly used one gives quick and reliable readings to within 200–300 meters. This accuracy is increased to within 10–25 meters when observation periods are longer so that a series of signals can be received and interpreted. Land-based stations that remain at a fixed location during several satellite passes provide even more accurate readings, with latitude, longitude, and elevation determinations accurate to less than 1 meter.

Radio direction finding. Radio direction finding (RDF) is a method of position determination that involves the use of directional information obtained from radio signals. It is used in place of visual observation of lighthouses, points of land, or other landmarks.

RDF requires a series of separately identifiable radio transmitters placed at specified locations. These transmitters operate continuously, and their signals radiate in all directions from their transmission towers. A radio receiver with a rotating-loop antenna is needed aboard the ship whose location is to be determined. The strength of the signal picked up by the receiver varies as the antenna is rotated. By relating the orientation of the antenna to the strength of the signal, the operator determines the directions to at least two

transmitting stations. The back-bearings from the known locations of those stations are then plotted to determine the position of the ship, in the same manner as was shown in figure 6.7.

An alternative method of RDF is for the ship to transmit a signal. When this signal is picked up by two or more receiving stations, the directions from those stations to the ship are determined by the use of rotating-loop antennas. When the bearings are plotted, the ship is located at the crossing points of those lines. Some receiving stations are also equipped to measure distances. One disadvantage of this system is that the locational information obtained must be relayed to the ship, which introduces a time delay, as well as a potential for miscommunication.

RDF can be utilized in weather, lighting, and distance conditions that prevent visual sightings. Unfortunately, various types of radio-wave interference sometimes make it difficult to obtain accurate readings, so the method is not totally dependable.

Loran. Another method used to determine the location of a ship or an airplane is the radio navigation system called **loran** (an acronym for *long-ra*nge *n*avigation). The loran system is based on radio-transmission travel times.

Loran employs pairs of radio-transmitting stations, called master *(M)* and slave *(S)* stations, located some distance apart. Each pair of stations transmits readily identifiable, synchronized radio pulses. These pulses are received by a special radio receiver on the ship or airplane whose location is to be determined. This receiver measures the time interval between the two pulses, which is used to determine the location of the receiver.

When the *M* and *S* stations simultaneously transmit signals, a radio located at a point equidistant from them receives both transmissions simultaneously (line *A* in figure 6.12). On the other hand, a receiver at point *B* is closer to *M* and, therefore, receives the signal from *M* earlier than it receives the signal from *S*. The same timing difference occurs at many other points which, when plotted, fall on the hyperbolic curve *C-D*. Sets of these curves, based on expected time differences between the reception of *M* and *S* signals, are preplotted on specially constructed loran charts (figure 6.13). Each individual curve on the chart represents locations at which the signals from the designated pair of stations are received at a specified time interval.

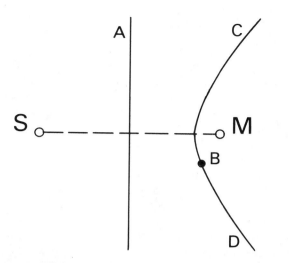

FIGURE 6.12   Relationship between loran slave (*S*) and master (*M*) stations and lines of position.

To use the loran chart, the operator first tunes to a given pair of stations. The time reading thus obtained indicates that the receiver is located somewhere along the curve that represents that interval. The measurement and plotting process is then repeated with a second pair of stations and the locational curve that corresponds to the observed time interval from those stations is identified. The intersection of the two curves indicates the location of the receiver.

The accuracy of the loran technique partly depends on the atmospheric conditions that exist at any particular time and the manner in which they affect radio transmissions. Generally, for example, transmission conditions are better at night than in the daytime. Also, the location of the transmitter pairs relative to the observer affects the angle at which the location curves intersect one another. If the angle is rather flat,

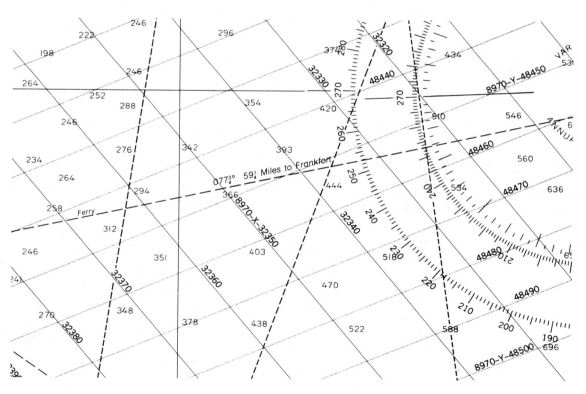

FIGURE 6.13   Portion of loran chart. Numbers printed beside loran curves are time delays from designated stations. (Not for navigational purposes.)

Source: National Ocean Service Chart 14903, 1984.

FIGURE 6.14 Angle differences affect the accuracy of the loran plot.

the amount of inaccuracy due to an error in measuring the time interval between signals is greater than if the curves intersect at an angle that is closer to a right angle (figure 6.14). Finally, the effective range and level of accuracy of the system depends on the particular frequency used and the vintage of the equipment. In general, loran accuracies are sufficient for navigational purposes on the high seas but not for determining locations within confined waterways.

Loran stations provide coverage for much of the north Pacific Ocean, the north Atlantic Ocean, and the Mediterranean Sea. The Decca and Omega systems are worldwide locational systems. The transmission frequencies and some other details of these systems are different, but they are based on the same basic principles as loran.

Dead Reckoning

Once position has been determined, the navigator's task is to plan and track the vessel's movements. The most straightforward approach to these tasks is to use a process known as **dead reckoning**.[8] This technique is used either for advance route planning or for keeping track of progress toward a destination. Dead reckoning depends on knowing the starting point and the direction, speed, and time of travel away from that point. Although the same general technique is applicable to travel by ship, airplane, land vehicle, or on foot, the description here is based on travel by ship.

To estimate current position with the dead-reckoning method, the route that has been traveled from a known starting point is divided into separate

components, called **legs**. Information about the direction of travel, as well as the length of time and the speed for each leg of the journey, is recorded. Speed of travel divided by elapsed time equals distance traveled. Thus, one simply locates the starting point and plots, in sequence, the direction and distance of each leg of the journey away from that point. The theoretical location of the ship at each stage of the voyage is shown by the resulting plot (figure 6.15).

Many inaccuracies can creep into the dead-reckoning process. For example, directions may be inaccurately recorded because of compass deviations. In addition, speeds and directions may not be accurate because of the effect of winds, currents, and tides on the motion of the vessel. If either wind or water movement works opposite to the direction of travel, for example, progress is slowed, and the distance traveled per unit of time decreases. On the other hand, influences in the direction of travel increase speed and, therefore, the distance traveled per unit of time. Similarly, a crosswind or movement of water causes a drift away from the planned course, as well as a change in speed. The exact influence of these factors on the motion of the vessel is difficult to determine.

For these and other reasons, positions obtained by dead reckoning are ordinarily used only if other sources of position information are not available. When more accurate information is obtained, such as an astronomical fix or a fix based on observed lines of position, a correction is made, and a new series of dead-reckoning position estimates is started, based on the updated location. If an accurate locational fix cannot be obtained, the navigator may estimate the effects of winds and tides and use them to adjust the vessel's dead-reckoning location. A location based on this type of adjustment is called an **estimated location**.

Dead reckoning is also useful as a method of advance route planning. In this case, the desired route of travel is laid out on the chart. Headings for each leg are then determined, and this data, combined with expected speeds, allows the calculation of estimated elapsed time en route, arrival times, and similar information.

AVIATION OPERATIONS

Earlier sections of this chapter that deal with land and water navigation are equally relevant to aerial navigation because the principles and techniques in-

[8]The derivation of the term *dead reckoning* is uncertain and has resulted in some confusion between estimated location, which takes current and wind into account, and dead reckoning, which does not. See *American Practical Navigator: An Epitome of Navigation* (Washington, D.C.: Defense Mapping Agency Hydrographic/Topographic Center, Pub. no. 9, 1984), 59. [Originally by Nathaniel Bowditch, LL.D., vol. 1.]

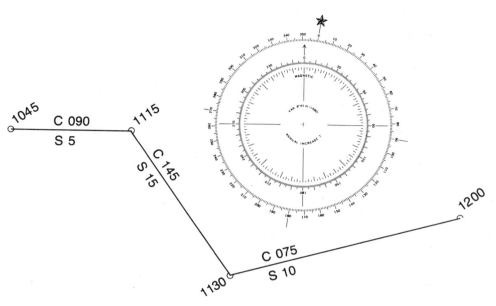

FIGURE 6.15   Example of dead-reckoning plot. Angled notations are times of observations; *S* indicates speed; *C* indicates course heading (magnetic).

volved are virtually identical. The chief difference between aerial navigation and the other types is that locations must often be determined and courses selected, very rapidly. Also, specialized charts and navigational aids have been developed for the use of aerial navigators.

Aeronautical Charts

Aeronautical charts are special maps designed to meet the needs of aviators. They are published at a variety of scales to suit different users. Charts published in the United States range from planning charts at scales of 1:2,000,000 or smaller, to airport obstruction charts at scales as large as 1:12,000.

Aids to aeronautical navigation are subject to frequent change. For this reason, aeronautical charts, like nautical charts, must be as current as possible to avoid confusion or disaster and are frequently revised. In addition, notices called *Notice to Airmen (NOTAMs)* are regularly published by the Federal Aviation Administration (FAA) and distributed by the U.S. Government Printing Office. Between chart revisions, NOTAMs provide up-to-date information about changed navigational aids.

Because of the variety of specialized charts available, the descriptions given here are limited to two commonly encountered series: the World Aeronautical Charts and the visual flight rule version of the sectional charts. These series provide good examples of the general characteristics of aeronautical charts.

World Aeronautical Charts.   The **World Aeronautical Chart (WAC)** series is based on the Lambert conformal conic projection. WAC charts are published at a scale of 1:1,000,000, which is convenient for navigation by moderate-speed aircraft. Coverage is limited to land areas. Sheet edges conform to lines of latitude and longitude, but the number of degrees covered by each sheet varies somewhat, as the index map shows (figure 6.16).

WAC charts show cities and towns as well as principal roads, railroads, and distinctive landmarks (figure 6.17). The terrain representation includes spot elevations, contours, and elevation tints, as well as the stream-drainage pattern. Information regarding aeronautical features is overprinted on the base map in dark blue or magenta ink. This includes the location of radio navigation information, airports, runways, restricted areas, obstructions, and so on. The symbols used on WAC charts are virtually identical to those described in the section that follows on sectional charts.

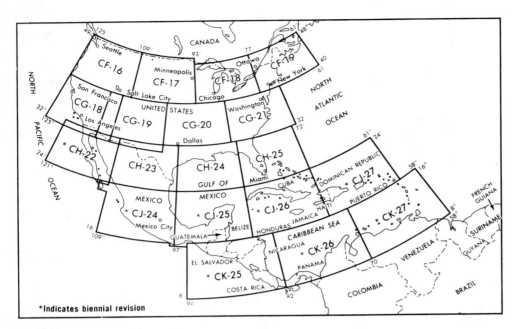

FIGURE 6.16   World Aeronautical Chart (WAC) series index for the conterminous United States, Mexico, and the Caribbean.

Source: National Ocean Service, *Aeronautical Charts and Related Publications.*

FIGURE 6.17   Portion of WAC chart. (CF-18, 1:1,000,000.) (Not for navigational purposes.)

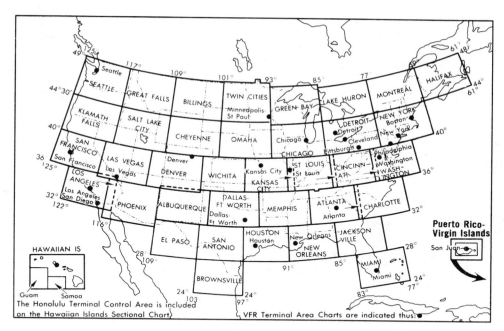

FIGURE 6.18   Sectional chart series index for conterminous United States, Hawaiian Islands, Puerto Rico, and the Virgin Islands.

Source: National Ocean Service, *Aeronautical Charts and Related Publications.*

Sectional charts.   Sectional charts are based on the Lambert conformal conic projection and are published at a scale of 1:500,000. Each chart covers an area that averages 4 degrees of latitude and 6 to 8 degrees of longitude (figure 6.18). These charts are designed for the visual navigation of slower- to medium-speed aircraft (figure 6.19).

The major classes of data shown on sectional charts include topographic data, radio aids to navigation and communication, airport traffic and airspace information, and airport information. Topographic information includes features that are useful checkpoints for visual navigation, such as cities and towns, roads and railroads, power transmission lines, as well as coastlines and drainage patterns (figure 6.20a). This type of information is printed in black or dark blue. Built-up city areas are shown in bright yellow, and elevation zones are printed in relatively subdued hypsometric tints. A detailed latitude and longitude graticule is also included.

Just as marine navigators must pay particular attention to the depth of the water under the keel of their ship, aerial navigators must be aware of the altitude of their aircraft above the earth. The elevation of the terrain must be considered before safe operating altitudes can be determined. Flying 10,000 feet above sea level, for example, is not recommended when terrain features reach the vicinity of 10,000 feet or above. For this reason, the elevation of the highest terrain elevation within each latitude and longitude quadrangle on a sectional chart is printed in boldface type (figure 6.20b). The large numbers indicate elevation above sea level in thousands of feet, and the small numbers represent hundreds of feet. Additional elevation information is provided in the form of contour lines and hypsometric tints.

Aircraft typically use **aneroid altimeters.** As altitude increases, barometric pressure decreases, and these altimeters convert the current pressure into a direct altitude reading. The altimeter must be **calibrated** so that it reflects current barometric conditions. This means that, before departure, for example, it is set so that it shows the elevation of the airport *above sea level.* Adjustments are made during a flight if conditions warrant.

FIGURE 6.19   Portion of typical sectional chart. (Green Bay, 1:500,000.) (Not for navigational purposes.)

The remaining symbols on sectional charts are printed in dark blue or magenta. This color scheme assures maximum visibility, even under the subdued red lighting used in aircraft at night.

A variety of different types of radio aids to navigation and communication are provided on sectional charts (figure 6.20c). Among these are various types of radio beacons that are of direct use in navigation. By homing in on such beacons, it is possible to follow designated routes between locations. Other radio transmissions provide traffic-control information and weather broadcasts.

Airport traffic service and airspace information includes designated airways with directional indications. Also shown are operational floors, which are designated minimum elevations above the surface, and a variety of control areas and restricted areas (figure 6.20d).

In addition, sectional charts indicate the elevations of major obstructions such as tall buildings, smokestacks, or radio towers (figure 6.20e). The elevations of such features are shown relative to sea level, and their height above the ground is also indicated. The latter information is particularly useful

when a **radio-type altimeter** is available. This type of altimeter provides direct information regarding the **absolute altitude** of the aircraft—that is, its altitude above the earth's surface, instead of simply above sea level.

Finally, sectional charts provide information about airports. This includes runway surfaces and lengths, services available, elevation, military or civilian status, hours of operation, lighting facilities, and other vital details (figure 6.20f).

Flight Planning

Two distinct types of rules govern aircraft flights. The simplest type governs flights under favorable weather conditions, in which visual references to landmarks can be used to reliably control the operation of the plane. Such flights operate under **visual flight rules**. When some or all of the flight occurs under conditions that prevent reliable visual contact, instruments must be used to determine location, direction, and altitude. Under such conditions, **instrument flight rules** are observed. If you are interested in actual aircraft navigation, you must be thoroughly

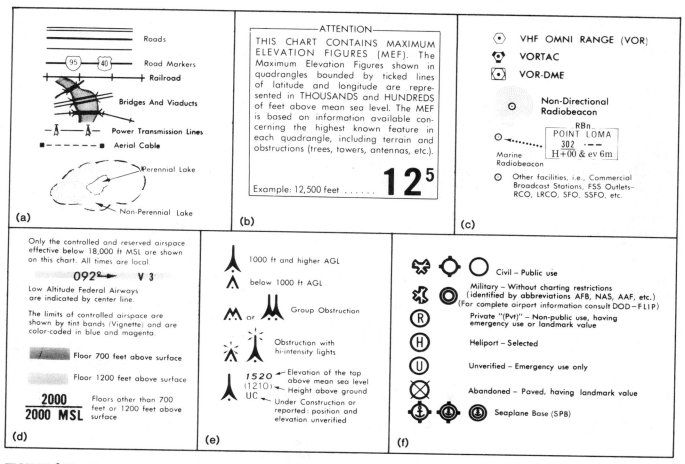

FIGURE 6.20 Examples of the symbols used on WAC and sectional charts. (*a*) Topography. (*b*) Elevation markings. (*c*) Radio aids to navigation and communication. (*d*) Airport traffic service and airspace information. (*e*) Major obstructions. (*f*) Information about airports.

trained in the use of navigational aids and equipment, have a detailed knowledge of flight rules, and learn a great deal of technical information. The discussion here is designed simply to indicate the importance of map-use skills for aerial navigation purposes.

Because there is often very little time to work out navigational matters while airborne, and because of the need for control of the use of limited airspace, air navigators usually work out a **flight plan** prior to departure. In addition, in many cases, the flight plan must be filed with the appropriate authorities.

Flight planning is based on dead-reckoning procedures. It includes determining the courses that will be flown, usually using both true and compass directions. It also notes landmarks that will be important checks on the correct route, as well as distance, estimated flying time, and altitude for each leg.

When a visual flight is under way, roads, railroads, power lines, shorelines, and other easily distinguished features are used to determine the course to be followed. In particular, the visual alignment of two objects, called a **range**, is often used to provide route alignment.

Different types of charts are used at various stages of flight planning and during the flight itself. In the planning phase, small-scale charts are used because the major concern is the selection of the best general route to follow. In the absence of other factors, this is usually the great-circle route, especially for long-distance flights. When in flight, larger-scale charts are needed so that detailed information about landmarks, hazards, and aids to navigation can be easily seen. These charts should not be at too large a scale, however, as the speed of the plane carries it across the mapped area rapidly. On an approach to a terminal, a larger-scale chart may be needed so that sufficient detail is provided. Indeed, under some conditions, a large-scale, detailed, landing chart may be used during the final stages of the landing procedure.

In addition to the World Aeronautical Chart series, other aeronautical chart series include the Jet Navigation (JN) (1:2,000,000 scale) and the Global Navigation (GN) (1:5,000,000 scale), which are designed to provide similar functions to those served by WAC. All of these are readily available, either for sale or in map libraries, provide virtually worldwide coverage, are carefully compiled, and are frequently updated and revised. Because of these characteristics, this set of map resources is also valuable to the general map user who is not involved directly with air navigation.

Summary

Maps are used extensively for route selection and navigation. The basic considerations involved apply equally to land, water, and aerial navigation, although there are special aspects to each.

Direction is expressed in terms of angular measurements from a north-south baseline. The most common reference is to true (geographical) north, the direction to the geographical north pole. In contrast, magnetic north is the direction to the north magnetic pole. Geographical and magnetic north differ at most locations by the amount of magnetic declination. Isogonic charts show declination and, usually, the expected direction and amount of annual change in declination. Points of equal magnetic declination are shown by isogonic lines, and the line of zero declination is the agonic line.

Compass deviation is the difference between magnetic north and the direction that the compass needle actually points. If this is well known and predictable, it is included on isogonic charts. However, compass readings taken near metallic objects are likely to suffer from unpredictable deviation.

The direction of the north-trending lines of a grid, such as Universal Transverse Mercator (UTM) or State Plane Coordinate (SPC) grids, is grid north. Grid north almost always differs from true or magnetic north. In addition, the grid north of two or more grids is seldom the same.

A declination diagram shows the relationships between the three "norths." A form of declination diagram, called a conversion diagram, is used to assist in the change of direction from one reference to another.

Directions are designated by either azimuths or bearings based on true, magnetic, or grid north. An azimuth is usually measured clockwise in degrees, minutes, and seconds from north. An orthodrome (true azimuth) is the direction of a great circle and, in most cases, crosses successive meridians at a constantly changing angle. A constant azimuth (rhumb line), in contrast, crosses each succeeding meridian at the same angle. A back-azimuth is the exact reverse, by 180 degrees, of an azimuth. A bearing is measured from either a north or a south baseline, whichever is nearer to the direction being designated. Bearings have a maximum value of 90 degrees.

Orientation involves aligning a map with the terrain by inspection or by compass. Position determination begins with a properly oriented map. Resection is then used to locate an unknown position by marking three known ground positions on the map. The magnetic azimuths to these positions are determined, and back-azimuths are drawn from the known positions toward the unknown position. Alternatively, visual sightings to the known positions are drawn on the map. The crossing of the back-azimuths, or sightings, marks the unknown position. If back-azimuths do not meet exactly, a triangle of error is formed. The center of this triangle is an estimate of the correct location.

Route selection involves the identification of reference points that can be used to monitor location. The route is followed by using clues provided by the map, by using a compass, or by a combination of both.

Nautical charts are designed to serve the needs of waterborne navigators. Because hazards and aids to navigation change over time, the latest edition of a chart, posted with changes listed in the *Notice to Mariners,* should always be used.

Water depths are traditionally shown in fathoms, although feet and meters are also used. The units used on a particular chart, as well as the chart's datum, must be determined to prevent confusion.

The determination of a vessel's position is critical to navigation. Navigators determine position by observation of the sun or stars or, if they are operating within sight of land, may obtain a fix by resection, using lines of position. Radar, satellite observation, radio direction finding, and loran are also used to determine location.

Dead reckoning is used to plan and track the movements of a vessel. The method depends on knowing the starting point and the direction, speed, and time of travel along the various legs of the voyage. The effect of winds, currents, and tides on the motion of the vessel may be used to adjust a dead-reckoning position to obtain an estimated location.

Aeronautical charts are specially designed to meet the needs of aviators. Because aids to aeronautical navigation are subject to frequent change, the most recent chart and information from the latest *Notice to Airmen* must be used.

Generally, aeronautical charts show cities and other distinctive landmarks and terrain features. Aeronautical information, including the location of radio navigation aids, airports, runways, restricted areas, obstructions, and so on, is overprinted in dark blue or magenta. Elevation information is emphasized, and the highest elevation within each latitude and longitude quadrangle is printed in boldface type.

Two distinct sets of rules govern aircraft flights. Visual flight rules govern flights under favorable weather conditions. When some or all of the flight occurs under conditions that prevent reliable visual contact, instruments are used to determine location, direction, and altitude, and instrument flight rules are observed.

SUGGESTED READINGS

American Practical Navigator: An Epitome of Navigation. Washington, D.C.: Defense Mapping Agency Hydrographic/Topographic Center, Pub. No. 9, 1984. [Originally by Nathaniel Bowditch, LL.D., vol. 1.]

Department of the Army. *Map Reading.* Department of the Army Field Manual FM 21–26. Washington, D.C.: Department of the Army, Headquarters (current edition).

Gardner, A. C. *A Short Course in Navigation.* New York: Funk and Wagnalls, 1968.

Haug, Moir D., Francis H. Moffitt, and James M. Anderson. "A Simplified Explanation of Doppler Positioning." *Surveying and Mapping* 40, no. 1 (March 1980): 29–45.

Maloney, Elbert S. *Dutton's Navigation and Piloting.* 14th ed. Annapolis, Md.: Naval Institute Press, 1985.

Monmonier, Mark S. *Technological Transition in Cartography.* Madison, Wis.: University of Wisconsin Press, 1985, 15–45.

Muehrcke, Phillip C. *Map Use: Reading, Analysis, and Interpretation.* 2d ed. Madison, Wis.: JP Publications, 1986, 203–16, 476–88.

Points and Positions. Torrance, Calif.: Marine and Survey Systems Division of Magnavox Advanced Products and Systems Company.

Snufeldt, H. H., and G. D. Dunlap. *Navigation and Piloting.* Annapolis, Md.: Naval Institute Press, 1970.

Stewart, John Q., and Newton L. Pierce. *Marine and Air Navigation.* Boston: Ginn and Company, 1944.

Terrain Representation

Because the earth's surface is seldom absolutely flat, mapmakers have always been challenged to convey information about its undulations to map users. And because maps are drawn or printed on flat sheets of paper, they are not particularly well suited to representing a three-dimensional surface. Three-dimensional physical models and a number of other techniques provide partial answers to the problem. Each technique has difficulties of its own, however, and does not provide the total answer. The purpose of this chapter is to describe the advantages and disadvantages of some of the terrain-representation techniques that have been used with varying success over the years.

SYMBOLS

Spot Heights

The simplest way to represent relief is to use numbers called **spot heights**. A spot height on a map indicates the elevation of the earth's surface at that point relative to some datum (see chapter 2). Sometimes, the number appears without a symbol, but often, a point symbol of some type indicates the location to which the elevation value refers (figure 7.1a).

Spot heights are typically located at the crest of a hill, a road intersection, a railroad grade crossing, or some similar, easily identifiable point. A **bench mark**, placed by geodetic surveyors, is an ideal location for a spot height because it can be precisely located in the field and then used as a reference point for additional survey work (figure 7.1b). On a map, a special symbol is usually used to distinguish a bench mark from other types of spot heights.

Land surfaces. The advantage of spot heights as a means of representing land surfaces is that they provide an exact value at an identifiable location. Their main disadvantage is that they do not provide useful information about the shape of the terrain or about the elevations *between* the spot heights. Nor do they provide any visual three-dimensional effect. Also, the same set of spot heights could conceivably represent a number of different surface configurations. For these reasons, spot heights are often combined with one or more other methods of terrain representation.

Water surfaces. Water surfaces provide readily identifiable reference levels. The elevation of the water surface above a datum is, therefore, often indicated on maps. Usually, the elevation value is simply printed on the water surface, without any additional symbols. On USGS quadrangle maps, for example, blue italic numerals indicate water-surface elevations. Different symbols may be encountered on maps produced by other agencies.

Horizontal control:

Third order or better, permanent mark ....   Neace
                                                    △

With third order or better elevation ....   BM △
                                                      148

Checked spot elevation ....   △ 64

Coincident with section corner ....   △
                                                  Cactus

Unmonumented ....   Not Shown

Vertical control:

Third order or better, with tablet ....   BM ×
                                                      53

Third order or better, recoverable mark ....   × 394

Bench mark at found section corner ....   BM +
                                                      61

Spot elevation ....   × 17

(a)

(b)

FIGURE 7.1 (*a*) Examples of spot height symbols used on U.S. Geological Survey topographic maps. (*b*) Bench mark monument.

Source for (*b*): Morris M. Thompson, *Maps for America,* 3d ed. (Washington, D.C.: U.S. Department of the Interior, Geological Survey, 1987).

Contours

A **contour** is an imaginary line that joins points of equal elevation above or below some datum (figure 7.2). The contours drawn on topographic maps are extremely important because they provide the basis for the development of a great deal of helpful information about the terrain.[1]

Contour interval. An infinite number of contours could theoretically be drawn on any given map. For example, contours could be drawn at sea level, at 1 meter above sea level, at 2 meters above sea level, and so on, for every meter of difference in elevation. Indeed, in the extreme, a contour could conceivably be drawn to represent every centimeter of elevation, or a similar, very fine interval. Closely spaced intervals are often used for detailed engineering or landscape maps. On the other hand, contours may be drawn at only 10 meters, 50 meters, or even more widely spaced intervals on smaller-scale maps.

[1]The contour definitions used here are based on Morris M. Thompson, *Maps for America,* 3d ed. (Washington, D.C.: U.S. Department of the Interior, U.S. Geological Survey, 1987), 26–28.

FIGURE 7.2 Relationship between surface and contours.

Source: U.S. Geological Survey.

(a)   (b)

FIGURE 7.3   Contour intervals vary, depending on the
characteristics of the terrain. (*a*) If the terrain is relatively
flat, a close interval is used so that the small vertical
differences can be seen. (Ten-foot contour interval,
Emerado quadrangle, North Dakota, 1:62,500, 1936
[reprinted 1943].) (*b*) If the terrain is steep, a wider
interval is used so that map details are not overwhelmed
by the contours. (Fifty-foot contour interval, Mount
Bonneville quadrangle, Wyoming, 1:62,500, 1938.)

The basic **contour interval** is the vertical distance
between contours. It is selected by the mapmaker to
clearly display for the user the predominant terrain
features in the mapped area. If the terrain is relatively
flat, a close interval is used so that the small vertical
differences can be seen (figure 7.3a). If the terrain is
more mountainous, on the other hand, a wider interval is used so that map details are not overwhelmed by detailed contour information (figure
7.3b).

The selection of the basic contour interval also
takes into account the scale of the particular map.
A closer contour interval is generally selected for
large-scale, detailed maps so that the density of contour lines is sufficient to provide a good representa-

tion of the shape of the terrain. A wider interval is
used for small-scale, generalized maps, to avoid
overcrowding.

Two basic contour intervals can be used on one
map. This is usually avoided, but it may be necessary
when an area contains abrupt contrasts in relief (see
figure 8.2). In such a case, a closer interval is used in
the areas that have relatively flat terrain and a wider
interval is used in the steep areas.

Contour types.   In an area of relatively complex
terrain, mapmakers commonly accentuate every fourth
or fifth contour by drawing it in a wider line weight.
The paths of these **index contours** are then easier to
identify and follow. Index contours usually have

FIGURE 7.4 Types of contours. (*a*) Index. (*b*) Intermediate. (*c*) Supplementary. (*d*) Depression. (*e*) Carrying.

numbers inserted at intervals along their length to indicate the elevation that they represent (figure 7.4a). Index contours are usually selected so that convenient numbering sequences result, such as 5, 10, 15, or 50, 100, 150, and so on.

Regular contours, spaced at the normal interval and drawn with a finer line weight, lie between the index contours. These **intermediate contours** may or may not be numbered, depending in part on the space available (figure 7.4b).

Supplementary contours are additional contours usually drawn at intervals that are some regular fraction of the basic contour interval (often half) (figure 7.4c). Supplementary contours are appropriate in areas of flat terrain, where contours drawn at the basic interval would be spaced relatively far apart. They are usually drawn as dashed or dotted lines to distinguish them from contours drawn at the basic interval.

When using a contour map, examine the map legend for information regarding the contour interval. At the same time, check for the possibility of two intervals or of supplementary contours. This precaution reduces the possibility of misinterpreting the contours.

When an area lies at a lower elevation than all of the surrounding terrain, it forms a depression. A depression that fills with water forms a lake. The land surface of a depression not normally filled with water, however, is mapped with contours on its surface. These **depression contours** are distinguished from regular contours by short ticks, at right angles to the contour line (figure 7.4d). The ticks point downslope, toward the bottom of the depression.

It is not always possible to draw accurate contour lines because of the inaccessibility of an area, the presence of a particularly heavy forest cover that obscures the view of the terrain in aerial photographs, or some similar problem. In these situations, contour lines may be drawn to represent the likely surface of the terrain. Such **approximate contours** are usually dashed or dotted to indicate their uncertain nature.

If a series of contours falls extremely close together, as may happen in a particularly steep area, they may not all be shown as individual lines. A single contour, drawn to represent the several contours that would be drawn if space allowed, is called a **carrying contour** (figure 7.4e). This type of representation does not occur frequently because, if the basic contour interval causes extensive crowding on a given map, a wider interval is substituted.

When a dam is constructed, a portion of the land surface behind it becomes inundated. The contours that represent the land surface that was exposed before the flooding may be retained, however. Such contours are called **underwater contours**. Underwater contours are *not* the same as depth curves, which show the depth of the water (and are discussed in the next paragraph). Instead, underwater contours indicate elevations above the same datum as the land-surface contours on the map.

When contours are drawn to represent the bottom configuration of a water body, they are called **depth curves**, or **isobaths**. Depth curves are measured *down* from the specific water surface and, therefore, are not directly related to the overall map datum. Depth curves in ocean areas are frequently the exception because they are normally related to the mean low-tide level.

LAYER TINTS

Layer tints, sometimes called hypsometric tints, are often used to fill in between contour lines or isobaths to give a stronger visual indication of general elevation or water depth zones. Suppose, for example, that there are three contour lines on a particular map at 100, 200, and 300 meters, in addition to the coastline.

Layer tints added to this map would probably consist of four different tones or colors: one between sea level and 100 meters, another between 100 and 200 meters, a third between 200 and 300 meters, and a fourth above 300 meters.

Layer tints are also commonly used in conjunction with **form lines**. Form lines are generalized contours that are frequently used on small-scale, less detailed maps. When layer tints are added to form lines, the area of the map that lies within each general elevation level is overprinted with a specific tone or color.

Sometimes, layer tints are shades of gray or of a single color, such as brown. When tones of a single color are used, the light tones are usually assigned to the lower elevation ranges and the darker tones are used at the higher elevations. When the map is printed in multiple colors, however, a color sequence may indicate the elevation zones (plate 2). One commonly used sequence begins with green in the lower elevations and proceeds through buffs and yellows to oranges, reds, purples, and, finally, white, as higher elevations are reached. The idea behind this gradation is that the warmer colors (oranges, reds) "advance" toward the eye, while the cooler colors (greens, buffs) "retreat." Presumably, then, the color sequence tends to produce a visual three-dimensional effect. Unfortunately, little evidence supports this view, and the color-sequence effect is probably of little or no help. In fact, because the colors have different *values* (that is, some are dark and some are light), the eye may even be confused by the mixture of effects due to color differences and those due to value differences.

Another problem with layer tints is that users may fall into the trap of thinking that the colors represent vegetation or climatic types. For example, map users who are unfamiliar with the layer-tint color sequence may assume that the green colors represent well-watered, fertile areas. That the Sahara Desert is usually green on this type of map illustrates the fallacy of this view.

Despite its shortcomings, this type of color sequencing is used extensively. Some mapmakers use a very effective color sequencing that *does* represent the vegetation types of different areas, which, again, points out the importance of consulting each map's legend to know the meaning of the symbols and colors being used.

Because the information provided by layer tints is usually very generalized, the tints are often used in conjunction with other techniques. Most commonly, this means that contours, spot heights, or both, may be encountered on layer-tinted maps.

ILLUMINATED CONTOURS

A method of **illuminated contours** has been developed to bring more effective visual impression of relief to what is, otherwise, a standard contour map.[2] In this method, the overall map is covered with an intermediate value of gray or of some single color, such as blue or brown. An imaginary source of light is placed at the upper-left corner of the map, and the contours on the side of the landform facing the light source are shown as white lines. The contours on the side away from the light source, on the other hand, are shown as dark lines, as though they are in shadow. The result is a strong impression of the region's surface relief (figure 7.5).

An advantage of the illuminated contour method, in addition to the visual effect of relief, is that the contours can be read in the usual way. It is still possible to measure and estimate elevation values using conventional techniques. Unfortunately, the method gives the unrealistic impression that the terrain surface is made up of layers instead of continuous slopes.

HILL SHADING

One visually effective means of indicating the shape of the terrain is to use **hill shading**.[3] Hill shading is the application of gray values to the map so that the modeling of the surface is apparent.

The idea of hill shading can be visualized by imagining that a light has been placed so that it shines on a three-dimensional terrain model. The light is angled so that it strikes obliquely, from the upper-left corner of the model, and shadows are cast toward the lower right. If a vertical photograph is taken of this illuminated model, the result is a type of hill-shaded map.

[2]Kitirô Tanaka, "The Relief Contour Method of Representing Topography on Maps," *The Geographical Review* 40, no. 3 (July 1950): 444–56.

[3]This method is also known by other names, including plastic shading, relief shading, and terrain shading.

FIGURE 7.5   Illuminated contours.

Reprinted from Kitirô Tanaka, "The Relief Contour Method of Representing Topography on Maps," *The Geographical Review* 40, no. 3 (July 1950): 444–56. Reprinted by permission of The American Geographical Society.

In reality, construction of this type of illuminated model requires considerable time and expense, and the model is difficult to properly light. For these reasons, hill shading is usually preferred to the illuminated model. Hill shading is traditionally rendered by means of an airbrush (plate 3). More recently, computer-assisted techniques have been used (figure 7.6).

One difference between an illuminated model and a hill-shaded map is that the shadows cast on the model always fall directly in the direction of the light. This means that features that trend in the same direction as the light falls often do not cast sufficient shadow to show their actual relief. With hill shading, on the other hand, the gray values are determined on the basis of angle of illumination and the amount of light striking the surface, assuming that nothing else is shadowing it. Also, in some cases, the light cast on a model can fall across the floor of a valley and cover a portion of the slope on the opposite side. This is especially true in the case of rather steep-walled, deep valleys. This results in some visual confusion because the map user tends to lose track of the valley floor. When hill shading is used, the shadows are stopped at the bottom of the valley, thus eliminating the confusion. It may seem paradoxical, but the artificial method (hill shading) can result in a more effective map than the "natural" method (the illuminated model).

FIGURE 7.6   Computer-assisted hill shading of part of
the Black Hills, South Dakota.
Courtesy of EROS Data Center.

One shortcoming of hill shading is that the successful creation of a strong three-dimensional effect
may produce very dark tonal values in some areas.
Such dark tones reduce the visibility of other symbols
printed over them, symbols that may be equally important to the map user.

Hill shading also has the disadvantage of not providing the accurate determination of elevations. The
technique of the artist who does the shading and the
characteristics of the reproduction process used
greatly affect the map's final appearance. If the shading
is relatively dark, for example, the map user may interpret the terrain slope as being steeper than it actually is, whereas relatively light shading is likely to
have the opposite effect. The interpretation of the
shading, in other words, is largely subjective. For this
reason, hill shading is often used in combination with
spot heights, contours, or both so that accurate elevations can be determined.

PHYSICAL MODELS

A **physical model** is the most straightforward means
of showing the three-dimensional aspect of the earth's
surface (figure 7.7). In a physical model, the third dimension does not have to be simulated, as it does on
maps, because it actually exists, and the hills and valleys of the terrain are directly seen and understood.

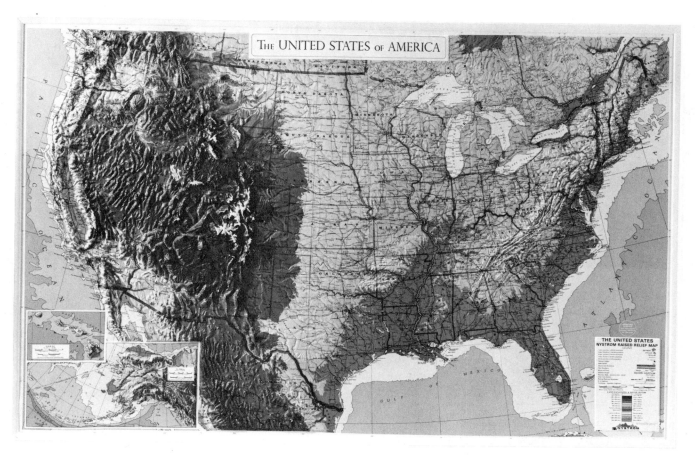

FIGURE 7.7 Terrain model in the form of a vacuum-formed relief map.

Courtesy of Nystrom, Division of Herff Jones, Inc.

Despite their visual appeal, terrain models are not used extensively. One reason is that they are expensive to build. Another reason involves handling and storage. Many models are built of layer upon layer of heavy materials, although lighter materials are often used today. Even when lighter-weight materials are used in their construction, however, the thickness and inflexibility of models make them extremely difficult to handle and store. Some models are made of vacuum-formed plastic sheets on which the appropriate map has been printed. These plastic-relief models are lighter and easier to handle but must be stored individually because stacking damages them.

Another problem with physical models is that, while they are created on the basis of quantitative measures, they are somewhat difficult to interpret. The main reason for this is that, even in areas of what would be considered severe relief, the elevations of the earth's surface are relatively slight in comparison to the immense horizontal distances usually involved. **Vertical exaggeration** is usually introduced into models to overcome this difficulty.[4] Vertical exaggeration involves using a different scale to measure vertical distances than is used, on the same model, to measure horizontal distances. The result is that the vertical relief of the area *appears* to be more realistic, even though it is not to the same scale.

Finally, the exact surface elevation at any specific point on a terrain model is difficult to determine, although the relative elevations of different areas may be quite clear. Spot heights and contours may be added to the model, but this is relatively rare.

[4]See also the section on profiles in chapter 8.

FIGURE 7.8   Physiographic diagrams. (*a*) France.
(*b*) The coastal plain of England and France.

(*a*): Reprinted from Erwin J. Raisz, "The Physiographic Method of
Representing Scenery on Maps," *The Geographical Review* 21, no. 2 (April
1931). Reprinted by courtesy of The American Geographical Society. (*b*):
From Armin K. Lobeck, *Geomorphology, An Introduction to the Study of
Landscape* (New York: McGraw-Hill, 1939).

PHYSIOGRAPHIC DIAGRAMS

Physiographic diagrams are a pictorial method of
representing the earth's surface. In general, they consist of an oblique view of a portion of the surface from
a position high above the ground (figures 7.8a and
7.8b).

There are strong elements of artistic license in the
design of physiographic diagrams. In particular, the
base map on which the diagram is drawn is a conventional, vertical view, but the symbols that represent
the terrain features are drawn from an oblique point
of view. This means that there is a problem with planimetric displacement. If the bottom of a mountain
is placed at its correct location, for example, its top is
necessarily misplaced. In addition, the oblique viewpoint may cause features that lie behind the higher
elevations to be hidden from view. Despite these
problems, the general effect of a well-drawn physiographic diagram is quite realistic.

The second element of artistic license in physiographic diagrams is that the features are drawn in a
generalized, somewhat idealized, manner. In many
cases, the landscape features are classified into groups,
and standardized symbols are used to represent
each type. Thus, each and every feature of the real-
world landscape is not realistically represented in a
physiographic diagram, although major features are
sometimes explicitly shown. In general, a physiographic diagram gives an overall idea of the extent and
types of terrain found in a region.

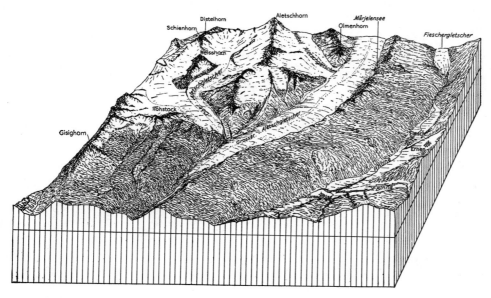

FIGURE 7.9   Block diagram of a typical portion of the Swiss Alps.

From Armin K. Lobeck, *Geomorphology, An Introduction to the Study of Landscapes* (New York: McGraw-Hill, 1939).

BLOCK DIAGRAMS

A **block diagram** is a pictorial representation of a portion of the earth's surface, drawn as though it were a picture taken at an oblique angle from the window of a high-flying aircraft (figures 7.9 and 7.10). The oblique angle of view contributes to the three-dimensional impression that is the hallmark of such diagrams. The terrain is drawn as though it were a piece of the surface, sliced from the earth in a block, and the sides of the block are usually shown in the drawing. In addition to the surface features, block diagrams often include geological profiles drawn on the sides of the block. These profiles provide information regarding the underlying geological structure of the area.

Although block diagrams are visually attractive and provide an effective three-dimensional appearance, they have similar disadvantages to those of physiographic diagrams. First, planimetric displacement occurs. The top of a hill, for example, appears to be shifted away from its map location toward the back of the diagram. Second, the oblique viewing angle causes features with high elevations to block the view of lower features located behind them.

FIGURE 7.10   Block diagram produced by computer methods.

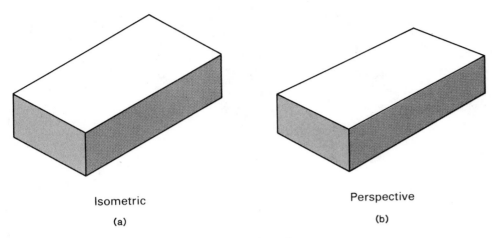

Isometric
(a)

Perspective
(b)

FIGURE 7.11   Comparison between isometric and perspective blocks. (*a*) Isometric view. (*b*) Perspective view.

In addition, block diagrams are not designed for the measurement of distances or elevations. This is because of the isometric or perspective construction methods used, as well as the vertical exaggeration usually introduced.

For ease of drawing, many block diagrams use an isometric construction method (figure 7.11a). In an isometric drawing, the corner of the drawing faces the front, and the two visible edges are aligned at 30-degree angles with the horizontal. In addition, the block appears to tilt up at the back. Because of the visual shortcomings of the isometric method, many block diagrams are drawn with a more realistic perspective view (figure 7.11b). In a perspective view, the edges taper toward the back. If one-point perspective is used, as in the example shown in figure 7.11b, one edge is parallel to the viewer, and the other tapers toward the vanishing point. If two-point perspective is used, both sides taper, each toward its own vanishing point. The use of perspective removes the appearance of tilt that occurs in an isometric view, but more distant points are relatively smaller than those closer to the viewer.

To effectively portray terrain, virtually every block diagram incorporates vertical exaggeration. The amount of vertical exaggeration introduced depends on the local relief and the scale of the diagram.

The primary purpose of block diagrams, then, is to illustrate the relationships between features and *not* to provide measurements, which are better obtained from a traditional map.

Summary

Representing the earth's three-dimensional surface on flat sheets of paper is a challenge to mapmakers. Various techniques are used in an attempt to solve this problem.

The simplest method of relief representation is the use of spot heights that indicate the elevation of points on the earth's surface. This has the advantage that exact values are provided at identifiable locations. It does not, however, provide useful information about the shape of the terrain between the spot heights, nor does it provide any visual, three-dimensional effect.

Another method of relief representation is to use contours, which are imaginary lines that join points of equal elevation. The paths of the contours provide elevation information and also a limited visual effect of relief. To improve the visual effect, contours are sometimes enhanced. One way of doing this is to add layer tints over zones of the same general elevation. Another method is to use illuminated contours. This involves making the contours on the northwest side of the landform white, as though they are directly illuminated. The contours on the side away from the light source, on the other hand, are shown as dark lines, as though they are in shadow.

The most visually effective method of relief representation is hill shading. Hill shading is simply the application of gray values to the map to simulate shadows that make the modeling of the surface apparent. This method is often combined with contours and spot heights so that measurements are available, in addition to the visual effect.

Physical models are the most straightforward means of showing the earth's surface. In a model, the third dimension does not have to be simulated, as it does on maps, because it actually exists. Models are expensive and awkward to handle and store, however. Also, even in areas of severe relief, the elevations of the earth's surface are relatively slight in comparison to the horizontal distances. This means that vertical exaggeration is usually required to obtain a visually satisfactory result.

Two pictorial methods of representing the earth's surface are also used. Both methods present an oblique view of the terrain from a position high above the ground. Physiographic diagrams involve drawing stylized representations of the terrain features on a conventional map base. Block diagrams, on the other hand, present a realistic picture of a portion of the

earth's surface. Both methods involve planimetric displacement, which means that a feature is not always located in its correct position. Also, their oblique viewpoint causes features that lie behind the higher elevations to be hidden from view.

SUGGESTED READINGS

Keates, J. S. "Techniques of Relief and Representation." *Surveying and Mapping* 21, no. 4 (December 1961): 459–63.

Lobeck, Armin Kohl. *Block Diagrams.* 2d ed. Amherst, Mass.: Emerson-Trussell, 1958.

Raisz, Erwin J. "The Physiographic Method of Representing Scenery on Maps." *Geographical Review* 21 (1931): 297–304.

Thompson, M. M. *Maps for America.* Washington, D.C.: U.S. Department of the Interior, Geological Survey, 1979.

Yoeli, Pinhas. "Relief Shading." *Surveying and Mapping* 19, no. 2 (June 1959): 229–32.

8

Contour Interpretation

In many situations, knowing the terrain characteristics of a particular area in advance is valuable. Engineering projects and military operations benefit from such prior knowledge, as do such day-to-day activities as hiking and camping. A number of map-analysis techniques are used to determine terrain characteristics. Although maps are seldom the only source of information for a terrain-analysis project, much can be learned from their systematic examination.

Topographic maps are particularly useful for terrain-analysis projects. Contour lines are the fundamental source of terrain information on such maps, and contour analysis and interpretation are discussed in this chapter. The application of contour interpretation to the classification of terrain types is covered in chapter 9.

The general approaches discussed in this chapter lend themselves to many practical applications. Computer calculations often are more rapid, flexible, and accurate than many of the more traditional approaches described here. Nevertheless, an understanding of the general characteristics of the applications is useful, whether or not computers are used, because the computer approaches are typically based on, or are the equivalent of, the more traditional ones.

CONTOURS

Characteristics

One characteristic of contours is that they all close by returning to the point from which they started. This is always the case, although the closure does not necessarily occur on a given map sheet. Contours that close on a given sheet represent either hills or depressions of relatively limited size. Depressions are differentiated from hills by the use of depression contours, with their distinctive tick-marks (see chapter 7).

The horizontal spacing of contour lines reveals the nature of the slope that the lines represent. The vertical interval between contour elevations is constant (except in the infrequent situation where two intervals are used on the same map). Variations in horizontal spacing, therefore, reflect variations in slope. If the contour lines are evenly spaced on the map, the slope is uniform. Widely spaced lines indicate a relatively flat slope (figure 8.1a), whereas closely spaced lines indicate a steep slope (figure 8.1b). If the contours are closely spaced at the top and widely spaced at the bottom, the slope has a concave shape (figure 8.1c). If the contours are closely spaced at the bottom and widely spaced at the top, on the other hand, the slope has a convex shape (figure 8.1d). Variations on these combinations can be similarly interpreted.

FIGURE 8.1   Characteristics of slopes are shown by
contour spacing. (*a*) Uniform, gentle slope. (*b*) Uniform,
steep slope. (*c*) Concave slope. (*d*) Convex slope.

Source: Department of the Army, *Map Reading*, FM 21–26 (Washington,
D.C.: Department of the Army, January 1969).

FIGURE 8.2　Two basic contour intervals used on the same map (interval is 5 feet up to 500 feet, 25 feet above 500 feet). The change in contour interval causes an exaggerated, apparent sharp change in slope. (Whittier quadrangle, California, 1:24,000, 1925 [reprinted 1932].)

As already mentioned, two basic contour intervals are sometimes used on the same map. The differences in horizontal spacing and, consequently, in appearance, that result from the different intervals influence the map user's interpretation of the terrain. In figure 8.2, for example, apparently steep terrain in the area with closely spaced contours appears to abruptly change to relatively flat terrain in the area with widely spaced contours. In actuality, terrain characteristics have not changed at all; only the basic contour interval has changed. In such circumstances, a map user who is not aware of the use of the two different basic contour intervals incorrectly interprets the terrain characteristics. Obviously, the marginal information or legend on any map should be checked to determine the contour interval (as well as other important information).

The shape of contours reflects other aspects of the terrain. For example, water-cut stream valleys frequently have what is characterized as a V-shaped cross section, whereas glacial valleys are rounded into a U-shaped cross section (see examples in chapter 9). The contours that cross valleys point in the upstream direction (point *b* in figure 8.3). The closed ends of contours that represent ridges or drainage divides, on the other hand, point in the downslope direction (point *c* in figure 8.3). The relative sharpness or rounded form of the contours as they cross the ridge line reflects the form of the ridge itself (point *a* in figure 8.3).

Thus, the shapes of ridges, valleys, hills, and depressions, as well as the characteristics of slopes, are indicated by the arrangement of contour lines on a map. The sections that follow illustrate some of the

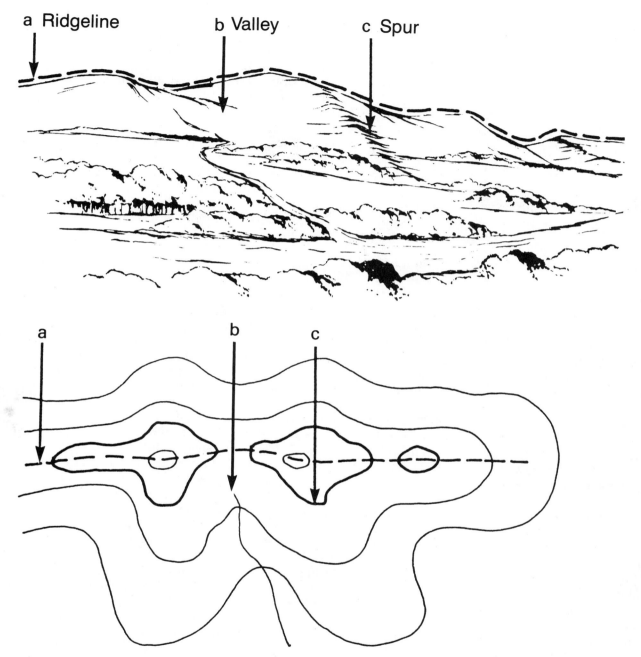

FIGURE 8.3   Contour patterns indicate locations of valleys and ridges. Contours that cross valleys point upstream, whereas those that cross ridges or spurs point downslope.

Source: Modified from Department of the Army, *Map Reading,* FM 21–26 (Washington, D.C.: Department of the Army, January 1969).

FIGURE 8.4   Linear interpolation for elevation estimation.

uses of contours. The use of contours for the identification of distinctive landforms is discussed in chapter 9.

Applications

Elevation estimation. On contour maps, the elevations of bench marks and other selected locations, such as road crossings, are often given exactly. Elevations of other locations must be estimated.

If the point whose elevation is to be estimated falls on a contour line, the elevation of that contour is the best estimate of the elevation of the point. If the point falls between contours, however, a technique called **linear interpolation** may be used to arrive at the estimated elevation.

Linear interpolation is based on the assumption that the slope between contours is constant. This assumption, which may not actually be correct, introduces potential error into the process. In the absence of additional information, however, linear interpolation is a logical procedure that involves using rules of proportionality to estimate. If, for example, a point is located halfway between two contour lines, the point's elevation is estimated as being halfway between the elevation values of those lines.

Figure 8.4 illustrates linear interpolation for estimating elevation at any location. First, draw a line through the point whose elevation is to be obtained, in the direction of maximum slope (that is, at right angles to the contour lines). Next, determine the point's distance from the lower contour as a proportion of the total distance between the two contours.

Then apply that proportion to the contour interval. Finally, add the resulting fraction of the contour interval to the lower contour elevation to obtain the point's estimated elevation.

Elevation estimates based on contour lines, whether or not the values are interpolated, usually are not completely accurate. This is because there is a certain amount of permissible error in the placement of contours, even on maps that meet national accuracy standards, and contours are often smoothed, or generalized, especially on small-scale maps. Any elevation estimate based on contours, then, usually is not completely accurate. Plus or minus one-half the contour interval is usually an accepted estimate of the possible error.

Reservoir capacity estimation. An often-encountered application of contour information is the calculation of the capacity of a proposed reservoir, the volume of a pile of stockpiled coal, or some similar problem. Such calculations can be made with the use of detailed contour maps of the features involved. Photogrammetric techniques are frequently used for these purposes and often provide more up-to-date and accurate information. In the absence of the necessary photos and equipment, however, existing maps are a useful source of information.

When estimating reservoir capacity, the area enclosed by the contour line that represents the eventual surface level of the reservoir is measured, as are the areas encompassed by each lower contour. These areas are then used to determine the approximate reservoir capacity, given the following formula:

$$V = i\,(A1/2 + A2 + A3 + \cdots + An)$$

where i is the contour interval and each A (A1, A2, etc.) is the area contained within the given contour outline.

The area of the surface contour is divided in half because the formula is based on the assumption that the contour interval is centered on the elevation of each contour line, and therefore, half of the volume is above the contour and half is below. In the case of the topmost contour, then, only half of the volume is below the water surface. Another assumption of the formula is that the effect of the sloping sides of the feature being measured will average out. This means that the greater volume above the contour, where the reservoir is usually wider, will be balanced by the smaller volume below the contour. The actual variation due to slope can be calculated if necessary but is not likely to be important if the contour interval is sufficiently close.

Flood-zone maps. Around the banks of lakes, rivers, and other water bodies, areas that lie at relatively low elevations are likely to be subject to flooding. Despite the threat of flooding, people have made, and continue to make, extensive use of the lands surrounding water bodies. Agricultural activity, settlements, industry, and transportation facilities are often situated in such areas. Information regarding flood danger, then, is extremely important.

The specific areas subject to flooding vary from time to time, depending on the water volume present and the other conditions that prevail. The factors that affect susceptibility to flooding include natural conditions, such as temperature, soil types, and vegetation, and man-made factors, such as paving and diking.

Of particular importance to flooding, of course, is the shape of the terrain surface. A topographic map, therefore, provides a starting point for the production of a **flood-zone map**. The volume of water expected to overflow the banks is calculated based on the flood level selected for planning purposes. The shape of the river valley determines the level of flooding from the predicted water volume. If the valley is broad and flat, the level of flooding from a given volume of water will be less than if the valley is narrow and steep-sided. These considerations allow the selection of the probable maximum level of the expected flood, along the length of the stream. Other factors that affect the rate of water flow out of the valley must be taken into account in refining the basic map.

The Federal Emergency Management Agency (FEMA) produces a specific type of large-scale flood-zone map in support of the national flood insurance program. These maps show, as closely as possible, the areas subject to flooding under what are called **100-year flood conditions**, as well as other, related information, such as floodways (figure 8.5).

A 100-year flood is defined as a major level of flooding that has one chance in one hundred of being equaled or exceeded in any one-year period. The term is simply a statement of probabilities and does *not* mean that such conditions occur at 100-year intervals, or, indeed, that a 100-year flood will actually occur

within a given 100-year period. Although the 100-year flood is commonly used as a standard, it is not necessarily the *maximum* flood that could occur. More serious conditions could arise, although they would be extremely rare. If greater safety is desired, the probable extent of a 500-year flood, for example, would have to be taken into consideration.

PROFILING

A **profile** is simply a cross-sectional view through a particular piece of terrain. Profiles provide a relatively quick and accurate means of determining such useful information as the relative steepness of slope of the terrain at given locations, the form of hills, the relationships of hilltops to depressions, the intervisibility of points, and the determination of hidden areas. Profiles are also used in the planning of construction projects involving earth moving, such as road, railroad, and pipeline construction, because they provide information regarding the amount of material that must be moved in grading the right-of-way.

Methodology

Cut-line. Drawing a profile begins with the selection of starting and ending points that fit the needs of the task at hand. Once these points are selected, a **cut-line** joining them is drawn on the map (or on a map overlay if the map surface must be protected) (figure 8.6).

Although the cut-line is often a simple, straight line between two points, it is perfectly feasible to draw a line that follows any desired route. It might be useful, for example, to draw a profile along a curving highway route or a twisting hiking trail. The cut-line in such a case is simply drawn on the centerline of the route. The subsequent step in the drawing process, which consists of transferring elevations to the profile drawing, is slightly more difficult. The balance of the operation is the same as for a profile drawn along a straight-line route.

Vertical scale. The next step in creating the profile involves the selection of the vertical scale. Let us assume, as an example, that the map from which the profile is being taken has a scale of 1:10,000, which

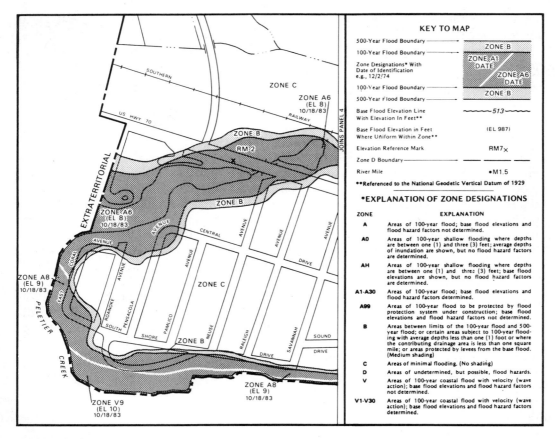

FIGURE 8.5 Portion of flood insurance rate map produced by the Federal Emergency Management Agency (FEMA) in support of the national flood insurance program. (Town of Morehead City, North Carolina, reduced scale.)

Courtesy of Federal Emergency Management Agency.

is a relatively large scale. This means that each horizontal centimeter (0.3937 inch) on the map represents 10,000 centimeters or 100 meters (approximately 328 feet) on the ground. If the same scale is used for the vertical dimensions on the profile, a rise of 100 meters (328 feet) is similarly represented by a vertical dimension of 1 centimeter (0.3937 inch). This may be satisfactory if the hills in the area rise several hundreds, or even thousands, of meters or feet above the valleys. However, if this local vertical relief is in the range of 20 meters (65.6 feet), for example, the profile's vertical dimensions will not exceed 2.0 millimeters (0.08 inch), and the surface characteristics will be very difficult to measure and interpret.

This type of problem is likely to be even more pronounced at the commonly encountered scales of 1:24,000 or 1:62,500. At 1:24,000, a rise of 1,500 meters (4,921.5 feet) is only 6 centimeters (2.36 inches) high, and at 1:62,500, the same map-profile distance represents a rise of 3,906 meters (12,816 feet).

Implicitly, the vertical scale of a map is the same as its horizontal scale because there is no *direct* representation of vertical distances on a map. Instead, some indirect method is used to indicate the elevations at various locations (as is discussed in chapter 7). With profiles, however, vertical distances are directly visible (as they are on terrain diagrams and physical models). In such cases, the vertical scale may

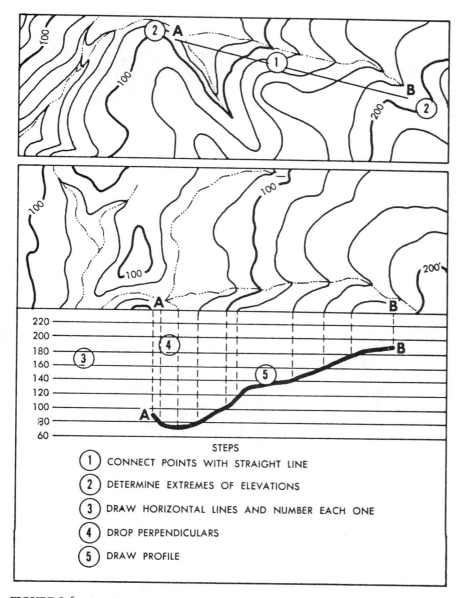

FIGURE 8.6   Drawing a profile.

Source: Department of the Army, *Map Reading*, FM 21–26 (Washington, D.C.: Department of the Army, January 1969).

not be the same as the horizontal. The cartographer may decide, instead, to exaggerate the vertical scale.

The use of a vertical scale that is greater than the horizontal scale of a cross section or model is called **vertical exaggeration**. Cartographers often use vertical exaggeration to give a visually more satisfactory appearance to the features shown or to obtain an elevation difference that can be easily measured. Gen-

erally, less exaggeration is needed in areas of greater relative relief, whereas more is needed in areas that are relatively flat.

Vertical exaggeration is both a help and a problem to map users. While it increases the visual effectiveness of the presentation, it also has the potential to give *too* strong an impression and, therefore, to be misleading. Noting the amount of relief exaggeration that has been incorporated into a presentation is helpful in interpreting the profile's appearance.

Formally, vertical exaggeration is defined by comparing the vertical earth distance represented by a unit of map distance with the horizontal distance represented by the same measurement. Assume, for example, that a profile has a horizontal scale of 1:50,000. This means that one horizontal centimeter (0.3937 inch) on the model represents 50,000 horizontal centimeters (19,685 inches) on the earth. A centimeter (0.3937 inch) measured vertically on the profile, however, may represent 10,000 centimeters (3,937 inches). In this case, the vertical exaggeration is five times (50,000/10,000 or 19,685/3,937).

Vertical exaggeration causes the slope of a hillside to look steeper than it actually is. The same thing occurs with regard to the apparent dip of a surface in the case of a geologic cross section. Slope information must be interpreted carefully when the slope is drawn with vertical exaggeration.

Drawing the Profile

When the desired vertical exaggeration has been chosen, the next step is to prepare the profile itself (figure 8.6). The profile is usually drawn on a separate piece of paper of the required length. A series of equally spaced, parallel, horizontal lines is drawn on the paper, or prepared cross-section paper may be used. The spacing between these lines is based on the contour interval and the desired vertical scale so that the correctly scaled vertical interval is represented.

The elevation lines are labeled with the appropriate elevation values so that there is one line for each contour line on the map. The bottom elevation line is usually designated at least one contour interval below the lowest point on the profile and the upper line at least one contour interval above the highest point. This procedure provides clearance for the tops of the hills and the bottoms of the valleys.

The prepared profile overlay is then taped over the map, with its upper edge aligned with the cut-line on the map. It is usually convenient at this stage to tape the map/overlay unit onto a drawing table and to align the horizontal lines using a T square.

The cut-line on the map intersects the contour lines along its path. These intersections are used in drawing the profile. The contour intersection closest to one end of the profile line is located, and its elevation is determined. A light vertical line is then drawn from

FIGURE 8.7   **Proposed gradient drawn on a profile.**

the contour intersection to the correct horizontal elevation line. The intersection of the vertical line with the elevation line is marked with a dot. This process is continued until each contour crossing on the map is transferred to the equivalent point on the profile.

The final step in creating the profile is to draw a line joining the points plotted on the profile. The path of this line represents the ground surface. The profile should not be drawn as a series of straight lines joining the designated elevation points. Instead, the ground surface is assumed to be rolling or fluctuating. The lines between the points, therefore, are drawn as relatively smooth curves that take into account the general direction of the slope on both sides of each intersection. The result is that sharp breaks in the surface are generally avoided. When hilltops or valley bottoms are encountered, the profile line should not abruptly flatten out to follow the horizontal line. Instead, the profile should be allowed to rise above or drop below the contour line, as appropriate to the terrain's general slope.

Applications

Cut and fill.   Engineers frequently need to establish road or railroad routes and gradients that minimize the movement of earth. It is generally most economical to balance the amount of material removed from the high areas (cut) with the amount of material required to fill low areas (fill).

A profile drawn along the proposed route assists in making cut-and-fill determinations. A proposed gradient is drawn on the profile (figure 8.7), and the areas above and below it are measured, using one of the methods described in chapter 5. These measurements are used as a rough estimate of the relative amounts of **cut and fill** needed along that route.[1] The

[1] Accurate determinations depend on the characteristics of the terrain for some distance on each side of the proposed route, so multiple profiles may be needed.

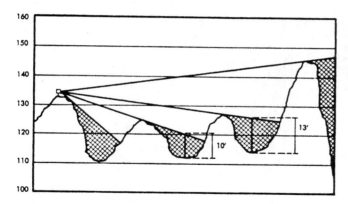

FIGURE 8.8 Intervisibility profile. Locations not visible from viewpoint are shown by cross-hatching.

Source: Department of the Army, *Map Reading,* FM 21–26 (Washington, D.C.: Department of the Army, January 1969).

gradient is then adjusted, as necessary, to come as close to balancing cut and fill as feasible. Alternative routes, with various gradient schemes along each, can be tested to determine the best choice from the standpoint of balancing cut and fill. Other factors, such as gradient limits and the directness of the route, are also considered in the final route selection.

Intervisibility. A profile is useful for determining whether or not two points are **intervisible.** The two points of interest are located, and a profile is drawn between them. A straight line is then drawn on the profile between the locations of the two points. If the line does not encounter any obstructions, the points are intervisible (figure 8.8). Points that are hidden from view (are in **defilade**) are also determined by this method.

An extension of the same technique is used to map areas hidden from the view of a given observation point. A series of profiles is drawn that radiates from the proposed viewpoint, with the accuracy of the final product governed by how close together the profiles are placed. The limits of visibility for each profile are then plotted on the map and are linked together to outline areas that are blocked from view (figure 8.9).[2]

In addition to its obvious importance in military operations, intervisibility information is useful for the evaluation of proposed sites for forest-fire lookouts, the planning of logging and other activities so that they interfere as little as possible with recreational and scenic values, and similar civilian applications.

[2]A computer-assisted method of preparing intervisibility maps is described in Pinhas Yoeli, "The Making of Intervisibility Maps with Computer and Plotter," *Cartographica* 22, no. 3 (1985): 88–103.

SLOPES

The surface slope of the terrain is an important factor in determining the feasibility of such activities as logging or installing a septic-tank sewage system. A slope map graphically depicts the steepness of the land and is useful for planning such projects.

Slope Measurement

A slope map shows, by a color or pattern, the various areas that fall within specified ranges of surface slope. The slopes are expressed in three alternative ways: (1) as a gradient, (2) as a percent, or (3) in degrees. The same slope can be expressed in any of these three forms. The particular form chosen is simply a matter of convenience in relation to the task at hand.

Gradient. The **gradient** of a slope is the fraction that represents the ratio between the vertical distance, known as the **rise,** and the horizontal distance, known as the **run** (figure 8.10). Both rise and run must be stated in the same units, whether the units used are feet, meters, inches, or yards.

To compute this ratio, a starting point and ending point are located on the map. The elevation of each point and the horizontal distance between them are determined by the measurement techniques described earlier. The slope is then written as the ratio between the (vertical) rise and the (horizontal) run, with the ratio reduced to show the horizontal distance per unit of vertical distance. If the vertical distance is 3 meters (9.843 feet), for example, and the horizontal distance is 30 meters (98.43 feet), the slope is 3/30 (9.843/98.43), which reduces to 1/10, or ten units of run per unit of rise.

Note that, when the slope is expressed as a ratio, the slope designation is unit free. Thus, a slope of 1/10 is equally valid when interpreted to mean 1 meter in 10 meters, 1 foot in 10 feet, and so on.

Percent. Slope is expressed as a **percent** by simply determining the rise per 100 units of run (divide the rise by the run and multiply the resulting decimal fraction by 100). In the previous example, the rise was 3 units, and the run was 30 units. This is equivalent to a 10 percent slope (3/30 × 100 = 0.1 × 100 = 10%).

FIGURE 8.9   Plotting masked areas for an intervisibility map.

Source: Department of the Army, *Map Reading,* FM 21–26 (Washington, D.C.: Department of the Army, January 1969).

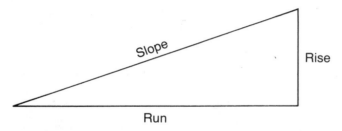

FIGURE 8.10   Relationship between rise, run, and slope.

Degree.   The third means of expressing slope is as an angle, in **degrees** from the horizontal. The angle of slope may be measured directly from a profile drawn with no vertical exaggeration. More commonly, however, the angle is calculated using the same rise and run information used to determine fractional or percentage slopes.

Dividing the rise by the run results in a decimal value defined as the tangent (tan) of the slope angle. The slope angle can be determined by locating this value in a table of trigonometric functions or by using the tan^{-1} key on a calculator. Continuing the previous example, the slope 3/30 has a tangent of 0.1, and the angle with this tangent value is approximately 6 degrees.

Applications

Slope-zone maps. The slope of the land surface is often an important factor in making decisions about land-use restrictions or the general desirability of an area for cultivation. Slope is also a major factor in the relative ease or difficulty of moving equipment or personnel over the terrain. A specialized map, called a **slope-zone map** presents slope information for such purposes.

A slope-zone map shows, by means of coloring or shading, areas of relatively homogeneous slopes (figure 8.11). The process of establishing slope zones is time consuming because it requires repeated slope determinations over the entire area of interest, and the greater the accuracy required, the more closely spaced the determinations must be. One way to create a slope-zone map is to draw a series of profiles throughout the area of interest. The profiles are then examined to determine the relative steepness of the slopes at different locations. This information is transferred back to the map, and areas with similar slopes are identified by appropriate symbols. Because of the expense of such detailed work, the U.S. Geological Survey usually prepares slope-zone maps only at the request of a government agency. In addition, some private firms produce such maps on a contract basis. Computer-assisted techniques can expedite the production of slope-zone maps.[3] As such techniques are more frequently applied, slope-zone maps may become easier to obtain.

You can prepare a slope-zone map, if only moderate reliability is required, with a simple visual method. First, you must prepare a set of templates (figure 8.12). Mark each template with a set of lines spaced to represent a specific slope at the scale and contour interval of the map to be analyzed. The number of templates required is determined by the number of zones and the fineness of classification needed and is usually limited to a few easily distinguishable categories. To produce the slope-zone map itself, visually match the templates against the contour lines on the base map, and draw an outline around areas of comparable slope. Add identifying colors or patterns to complete the project.

Maximum slope limitations. A route between two locations usually must meet certain grade restrictions. Road or railroad alignments, for example, cannot be too steep because of the limited capabilities of the vehicles that use them. Similarly, vehicles that can move directly across the terrain, such as those often used in military operations, search-and-rescue missions, logging operations, or similar activities, have maximum grade restrictions. Even hikers prefer to limit the steepness of their routes to avoid too much stress. The determination of the slopes along the path between a given starting point and destination is one method of ensuring that the capability of the particular equipment or personnel involved in a planned movement is not exceeded. If the objective is to be reached, the route must not include grades that are steeper than the operational limit.

Slopes may be determined by examining a profile taken along the planned route, as was already discussed. If no profile is available and it is not considered worthwhile to draw one, a contour map can be used to check slope limits. Both vertical distances (based on the contour interval of the map) and horizontal distances (between contours) can be determined directly from the map. These two pieces of information are sufficient for checking that the **maximum slope limit** is not exceeded.

First, the horizontal distance between contours that will satisfy the maximum slope limit is calculated. Suppose, for example, that the maximum permissible slope is 4 percent, and the contour interval of the map is 10 meters (32.81 feet). The 4 percent slope limit [4 meters (13.124 feet) of rise per 100 meters (328.1 feet) of horizontal distance] means that 25 meters (82.025 feet) of horizontal travel is required for each meter (3.281 feet) of rise. Given the contour interval of the map, a minimum horizontal distance of 250 meters (820.25 feet) must be traveled for each contour interval that is overcome.

Once the minimum horizontal distance requirement is determined, the process of checking to see that the maximum slope is not exceeded is simple and

[3]See, for example, D. A. Sharpnack and G. Akin, "An Algorithm for Computing Slope and Aspect from Elevations," *Photogrammetric Engineering* 35, no. 3 (1969): 247–48.

FIGURE 8.11   Slope-zone map. (Hershey, Pennsylvania, 1:24,000.)

Source: Melvin Y. Ellis, ed., *Coastal Mapping Handbook* (Washington, D.C.: U.S. Government Printing Office, 1978), 165.

FIGURE 8.12   Template for determining slope zones on 1:24,000-scale map with 10 ft. contour.

FIGURE 8.13 Checking maximum slope limitations on a planned route of travel by measuring minimum horizontal distance requirement.

mechanical. The example explained here assumes a continuous uphill gradient, but it is not difficult, once the basic procedure is understood, to accommodate uphill or downhill variations.

The desired route is first plotted on the map. Then a pair of dividers is set to the correct scale equivalent of the minimum horizontal distance requirement. The first leg of the route is checked by placing one divider tip at the starting point (assuming, for simplicity sake, that it is on a contour line). The dividers are then aligned so that the other tip lies on the uphill path (figure 8.13). If the dividers do not reach beyond the next contour line, the slope does not exceed the limit. The dividers are then moved to the next contour crossing, and the process is continued until the final destination is reached. If the distance between any pair of contour lines is less than the minimum horizontal distance for which the dividers are set, the maximum slope limit is exceeded. The route at that point is adjusted accordingly, and checking of the re-aligned portion is continued.

Trafficability. The ability of an area to support vehicles of a certain type is called **trafficability**. Trafficability is of particular importance in military operations because the selection of routes able to support specific types of vehicles can assist in meeting a military objective. Trafficability information is also important in peacetime engineering and forestry projects.

A trafficability map shows zones of relative ease or difficulty of travel for various modes of transportation. The determination of trafficability is based on multiple criteria. Slope is usually a major factor, but other common criteria include types of vegetation cover, surface materials, and weather conditions. Geographic information systems, which are discussed in chapter 20, are particularly useful for the analysis necessary to generate trafficability maps.

Summary

Contour lines are particularly useful for terrain analysis. The horizontal spacing of contours reveals the nature of the slope. If the contours are evenly spaced, for example, the slope is uniform. Widely spaced contours indicate a relatively flat slope, and closely spaced contours a steep one. If contours are closely spaced at the top of a slope and widely spaced at the bottom, the slope has a concave shape. If the contours are closely spaced at the bottom and widely spaced at the top, the slope is convex.

Contours reflect other aspects of the terrain. Water-cut stream valleys, for example, usually have a V-shaped cross section, whereas glacial valleys are rounded into a U-shaped cross section. Contours that cross valleys point in the upstream direction, but those that cross ridges or drainage divides point downslope. The relative sharpness or rounded form of the contours as they cross the ridge line reflects the form of the ridge itself. Thus, the shapes of ridges, valleys, hills, and depressions, as well as the characteristics of slopes, are indicated by the arrangement of contour lines.

Elevations of locations are estimated by means of linear interpolation between contours. This process is based on the assumption that the slope between contours is constant.

Practical applications of contour analysis include volume estimation and the development of flood-zone maps. In addition, profiles, which are cross-sectional views through the terrain, provide information about slope steepness, intervisibility, and so on, and are used in planning construction projects.

Slopes are expressed as gradients, percentages, or degrees. The gradient of a slope is the ratio between the rise and the run. Slope, in percentage terms, is given by the rise per 100 units of run. Slope may also be denoted as an angle, in degrees from the horizontal. Slope-zone maps show areas of relatively homogeneous slope.

A route between two locations must usually meet grade restrictions. Slopes along the proposed route may be determined by examining a profile taken along its path. Alternatively, the horizontal distance between contours that will satisfy the maximum slope limit is calculated and stepped off along the planned route. If the limit is exceeded, the minimum horizontal distance is used to discover an alternative route.

Trafficability is the ability of an area to support vehicles of a certain type. A trafficability map shows zones of relative ease or difficulty of travel for various modes of transportation, with slope a major consideration.

SUGGESTED READINGS

Department of the Army. *Map Reading*. Department of the Army Field Manual, FM 21–26. Washington, D.C.: Headquarters, Department of the Army (current edition).

Muehrcke, Phillip C. *Map Use: Reading, Analysis, and Interpretation*. 2d ed. Madison, Wisc.: JP Publications, 1986.

Speak, P., and A. H. C. Carter. *Map Reading and Interpretation*. 2d ed. London: Longman Group, 1970, 14–18.

Tyner, Judith. *The World of Maps and Mapping*. New York: McGraw-Hill, 1973, 12–21.

9

Topographic Features

Topography is the surface configuration of the earth. The **landforms** on the earth's surface are the result of the complex interactions of natural processes, working throughout the eons of geologic time. One set of processes involves movements of the earth's crust, called **tectonic activity**. These crustal movements create the basis for the landforms by causing the broad uplift or depression of the earth's crust, as well as its folding and faulting. In addition, external flows and internal intrusions of volcanic material introduce unique details into the landscape. A second set of processes sculpts the features created by the first. These involve a variety of geologic, hydrologic, atmospheric, and biotic forces, including the physical and chemical action of surface water, groundwater, ice, and wind, and even the action of plants and animals. These forces bring about weathering, mass movement, erosion, and deposition, which create the details of the landscape.

As a major environmental element, the earth's topography has many significant and diverse effects on human life and endeavors. Some of these effects are direct. Mountain ranges, for example, are barriers to transportation, but they also harbor minerals utilized by industry and provide scenic attractions and enjoyment. Valleys shelter agricultural activities. They also hold the rivers that create disastrous floods which, at the same time, bring renewal to the soils. Some effects of topography on human activity are indirect, operating through topography's interrelationship with other environmental elements. Deserts develop in the lee of mountain ranges, for example, and rain forests are created on mountains' windward flanks. Each of

these dramatically different environments has differential impacts on the activities of the human population. In addition, there are more subtle effects on plant and animal life and, therefore, on human activity. Different varieties of vegetation grow at different elevations and exposures, for example. In these and many other ways, topography influences human life and activities. An examination of landforms also helps to develop an understanding of and appreciation for the past and for the ongoing processes that have led to where we are and will continue to mold our environment.

A full understanding of how a specific topographic feature developed requires a knowledge of the nature and history of the underlying geological structures. It also requires an appreciation of a variety of physical processes, as well as the modifying effects of climate and vegetation. These matters go well beyond the scope of this book, which is limited to examining typical examples of local landforms that are recognizable on topographic maps. The book by Victor Miller and Mary Westerback listed in the "Suggested Readings" at the end of this chapter provides an excellent reference for more extensive study.

DRAINAGE PATTERNS

Drainage patterns, the arrangements of streams on the landscape, are indicators of underlying geology. Although the patterns that streams form on maps do not allow extensive analysis of underlying geology, preliminary drainage-pattern classifications can be

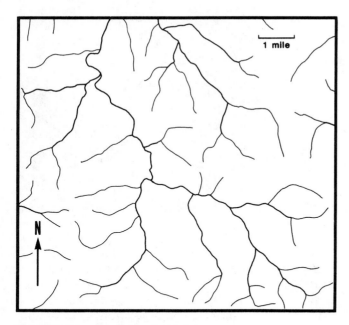

FIGURE 9.1   Dendritic drainage pattern.

Source: Traced from St. Paul quadrangle, Arkansas.

FIGURE 9.2   Rectangular drainage pattern.

Source: Traced from Hillsboro quadrangle, Kentucky.

generated in preparation for more extensive work. Drainage patterns can be classified in two ways: type of dissection and texture of dissection.[1]

Type of Dissection

The classification of drainage patterns into characteristic types is a subjective process, but several generally adopted major categories can be identified. Knowledge of these categories provides some initial clues about underlying geological structure when a map is being analyzed.

Dendritic.   The term *dendritic* means treelike, an apt analogy for this common drainage pattern that is characterized by treelike branching (figure 9.1). The tributaries (lower-order streams) of a dendritic drainage pattern join the main (higher-order) streams

[1]Douglas A. Way, *Terrain Analysis: A Guide to Site Selection Using Aerial Photographic Interpretation,* 2d ed. (Stroudsburg, Pa.: Dowden, Hutchinson and Ross; New York: McGraw-Hill, 1978), 49.

at acute angles. Dendritic patterns usually form in areas of homogeneous (uniform) soil and rock, often consisting of horizontal strata or unjointed rock masses, which exert no predominant directional control on the drainage.

Rectangular.   Rectangular drainage patterns (figure 9.2) are a variation of the dendritic type. In this case, however, the next-highest-order tributaries join highest-order streams at approximately right angles. The rectangular pattern of these major streams originates with bedrock, whose jointing or fracturing controls the pattern's development.

Trellis.   Another modification of the dendritic pattern is the **trellis drainage pattern,** which has parallel tributaries. This pattern often forms in areas of alternating parallel ridges and valleys (figure 9.3).

FIGURE 9.3 Trellis drainage pattern.

Source: Traced from Waldron quadrangle, Arkansas.

Radial. A circular pattern of channels flowing away from, or toward, a central point is called a **radial drainage pattern**. When the streams flow outward from the feature that controls the pattern, such as a volcano or structural dome, the pattern is referred to as **centrifugal** (figure 9.4). In this type, the radial streams often flow into a collector stream around the base of the feature. When the streams flow inward into a crater or similar structure, the resulting pattern is called **centripetal** (figure 9.5).

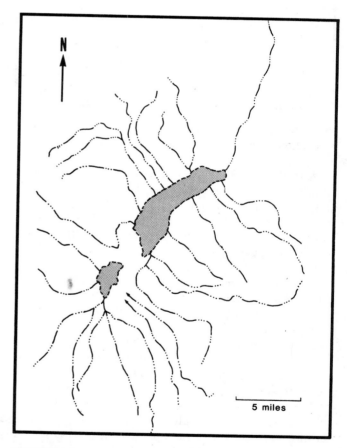

FIGURE 9.5 Radial drainage pattern (centripetal). Clayton Valley, Nevada (intermittent streams and lakes).

Source: Traced from USGS State of Nevada map.

FIGURE 9.4 Radial drainage pattern (centrifugal).

Source: Traced from Katahdin quadrangle, Maine.

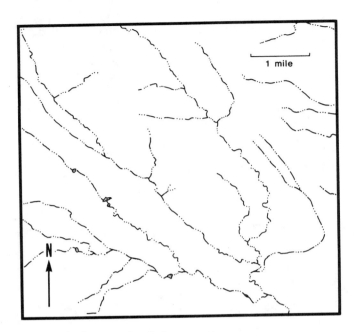

FIGURE 9.6 Annular drainage pattern.
Source: Traced from Maverick Spring quadrangle, Wyoming.

Annular. The underlying topography control that leads to a radial pattern is similar to the control that results in an **annular drainage pattern** (figure 9.6). The annular characteristic is introduced by the presence of joints or fractures that create elements of parallel drainage.

Miscellaneous. A great variety of other stream patterns form in special circumstances. For simplicity sake, these are grouped here into a *miscellaneous* category. The following examples illustrate the diversity: A disrupted pattern is characteristic of areas of poor drainage resulting from glaciation (see the discussion of glaciation later in the chapter). Disappearing streams and internal drainage occur in areas where bedrock solution results in the development of underground drainage channels (see figure 9.25). A fanlike pattern of streams often spreads out over the base of an alluvial fan (figure 9.7). A braided, meandering pattern is characteristic of a stream that is close to the level of a water body, such as a lake or the ocean (figure 9.8). The pattern evolves because the water body establishes a limit on the stream's downward cutting. As a result, the stream wanders from side to side and creates a broad, flat valley. An artificial pattern is imposed when there is human intervention in the form of channels and ditches for navigation, irrigation, or drainage (figure 9.9).

Texture of Dissection

Texture of dissection describes the relative fineness of the stream pattern.[2] The categories typically established to describe texture—fine, medium, and coarse—are indicative of its rather subjective nature. The concept, however, offers some insight into the possible nature of the underlying geology and soils.

The definition of texture is based on the spacing of first-order streams (see chapter 12). If the first-order streams are very close together, say on the order of 100 meters or less, the texture is classified as fine. If, on the other hand, the first-order streams are spaced 400 or more meters apart, the texture is classified as coarse. A pattern with medium texture would, of course, fall in the 100- to 400-meter range.

Fine texture is likely where there is relatively weak rock because in such a circumstance a small volume of water is sufficient to establish a drainage channel. An impermeable soil type, which results in a greater volume of runoff from the surface, also can be expected to contribute to a fine texture. A coarse texture, on the other hand, is more likely where there is resistant bedrock because a large volume of runoff is needed to establish stream channels. If the soil is permeable, runoff is reduced, and any tendency toward a coarse texture is reinforced. In addition, the presence of vegetation protects the surface and increases the tendency toward coarseness because runoff is decreased.

SELECTED EXAMPLES OF LANDFORMS

For descriptive purposes, landforms may be grouped into categories based on their location or origin. In this section, we discuss the following landform groupings: coastal features and shorelines, escarpments, glaciation (alpine and continental), mountains, plains, plateaus, solution features, valleys, volcanic features, water features, wind features, and the inevitable miscellaneous features.

The tremendous variety of landforms found around the world cannot be addressed in any detail here, nor can their underlying geologic origins be adequately explained. A textbook on physical geography or geomorphology should be consulted for additional examples, as well as for discussion of the influence of subsurface structure and other geologic factors on the development of landforms. In addition, the examples

[2]See, for example, Way, *Terrain Analysis,* 49, or Strahler, *Introduction to Physical Geography,* 340–41.

FIGURE 9.7 Alluvial fan. (Ennis quadrangle, Montana, 1:62,500, 1949.)

FIGURE 9.8 Braided, meandering stream. (Ennis quadrangle, Montana, 1:62,500, 1949.)

FIGURE 9.9 Human intervention: irrigation and drainage canals. (Dunnigan quadrangle, California, 1:62,500, 1953.)

133

FIGURE 9.10   Sand spit. (Provincetown quadrangle, Massachusetts, 1:62,500, 1889 [reprinted 1940].)

shown in the U.S. Geological Survey collection *A Set of 100 Topographic Maps Illustrating Specified Physiographic Features* provide an invaluable source of further information regarding typical landforms.[3] Although the examples in this collection are from the United States, similar features are found throughout the world.

[3]Extracts from the collection are presented in Richard DeBruin, *100 Topographic Maps Illustrating Physiographic Features* (Northbrook, Ill.: Hubbard Scientific, 1970).

Coastal Features and Shorelines

The features found in coastal areas and along shorelines develop in a zone where land and water meet. Sand, for example, is moved by wave and current action until it reaches a location where those actions cannot carry it any longer. Deposits of sand and other materials on the shoreline are shaped by the complex wave and current action into distinctive features, such as **sand spits** (figure 9.10).

FIGURE 9.11   Delta of the Mississippi River.

Source: Traced from Army Map Service Strategic Map (undated).

As a river enters a larger body of water, such as an ocean, a sea, or a lake, the speed of water flow decreases, and materials that had been suspended and carried by the stream are deposited. If conditions are suitable, such deposition forms a **delta** (figure 9.11).

Escarpments

Escarpments occur where erosion has worked on the underlying structures and resulted in a marked, extensive difference in elevation, often in the form of **cliffs** (figure 9.12).

Glaciation

Alpine.   Alpine areas are frequently subjected to glaciation. The actions of the ice have carved a variety of **alpine features** in the mountains (figure 9.13), including basins at the head of valleys (**cirques**) that sometimes contain lakes (**tarns**), sharp-edged ridges (**arêtes**) with passes or saddles (**cols**), and mountain peaks (**horns** or **matterhorns**). In addition, **U-shaped valleys** typically result from ice action.

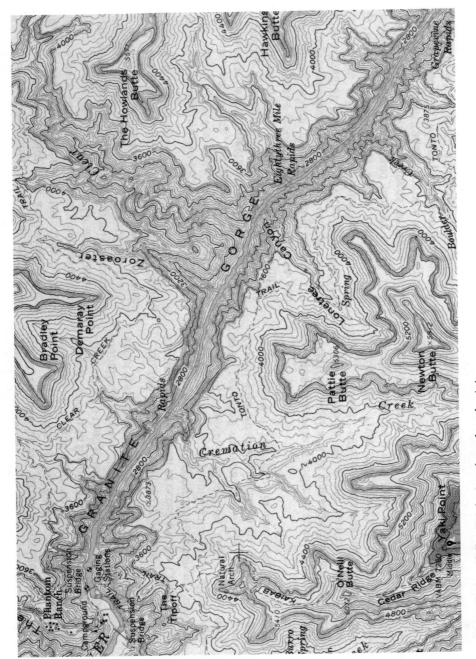

FIGURE 9.12 Cliffs. (Bright Angel quadrangle, Arizona, 1:62,500, 1962.) Cliffs abound in the Grand Canyon but are especially notable in the Granite Gorge.

FIGURE 9.13 Typical alpine glaciation features.
(*a*) Arête between Raid Peak and Mount Geikie, with col
just north of Mount Geikie. Both Raid Peak and Mount
Geikie are horns. Cirque, with tarn, southeast of Raid
Peak. (Mount Bonneville quadrangle, Wyoming, 1:62,500,
1938.) (*b*) Matterhorn (Bradley Peak). (Bradley Peak
quadrangle, Wyoming, 1:24,000, 1953.) (*c*) U-shaped
valley (Waterton Valley). (Chief Mountain quadrangle,
Montana, 1:125,000, 1938.)

FIGURE 9.14   Continental glaciation. Erosion to
bedrock, with interrupted drainage, rounded hills, and
depressions, often with lakes or marsh. (Monadnock
quadrangle, New Hampshire, 1:62,500, 1936 [reprinted
1950, with corrections].)

Continental.   Many distinctive features result
from either the removal or deposition of materials by
the action of the extensive ice sheets associated with
continental glaciation. One frequently encountered
aspect of areas subjected to glaciation is a **disrupted
drainage pattern**, in which streams run in many directions without visible pattern, often through areas
of lake and marsh. (Similar features are often found
in areas of alpine glaciation.) In areas where material
was removed, the bedrock left behind has been
formed into smoothed depressions and hills (figure
9.14). In areas where deposition was dominant, numerous depressions and small lakes called **kettles**
often formed when large fragments of ice lying within

the glacial debris **(till)** melted and left cavities behind
(figure 9.15). **Drumlins**, which often occur in groups
called **drumlin fields**, are lozenge-shaped hills with
steep slopes facing in the direction from which the
ice advanced and more gradual slopes in the opposite
direction (figure 9.16). **Terminal moraines** were left
at the margins of the furthest advance of the glaciers
(figure 9.17), and lakes frequently occupied the space
behind them. The resulting terrain features may include a line of small hills and hummocks at the location of the moraine, with a broad, flat **lacustrine
plain** in the area of the former lake bottom (figure
9.18).

FIGURE 9.15   Continental glaciation: Kames (hills) and
kettles (depressions). (Kingston quadrangle, Rhode
Island, 1:24,000, 1957.)

FIGURE 9.16   Continental glaciation: Drumlins.
(Palmyra quadrangle, New York, 1:62,500, 1902
[reprinted 1948].)

FIGURE 9.17   Continental glaciation: Terminal moraine, with interrupted drainage, kames (hills), and kettles with marshes and lakes. (Jackson quadrangle, Michigan, 1:62,500, 1935 [enlarged].)

FIGURE 9.18   Continental glaciation: Lacustrine plain, with characteristically gentle slopes and strand lines of glacial Lake Agassiz. (Emerado quadrangle, North Dakota, 1:62,500, 1936 [reprinted 1943].)

FIGURE 9.19 Hogbacks (Piney Mountain and Ross Mountain). (Waldron quadrangle, Arkansas, 1:62,500, 1939.)

Mountains

The features related to mountains include a great variety of ridges, hills, faults, and folds. Extensive concave or convex slopes may occur (see figures 8.1c and 8.1d), or a distinctive formation may result from the erosion of particular types of folded bedrock. A **hogback**, for example, is a sharp-crested ridge formed by the eroded edge of steeply inclined strata (figure 9.19). In other locations, streams may have eroded **water gaps** (figure 9.20). Where the river has not been able to keep up with the uplift of the bedrock, partial gaps, called **wind gaps**, are left (figure 9.20).

Plains

Features associated with plains may occur where lakes or streams have deposited materials to form an **alluvial plain** (figure 9.21). Features of plains also may be formed in desert conditions or as a result of glaciation.

Plateaus

Plateaus frequently result when a relatively horizontal resistant rock layer is gradually eroded away, and less resistant materials are removed more rapidly

FIGURE 9.20   Water gap (stream at Little Mountain) and wind gap (road at Little Mountain). (Harrisburg quadrangle, Pennsylvania, 1899 [reprinted 1948].)

FIGURE 9.21   Alluvial plain, with low relief, lakes, meandering streams, abandoned meanders, and swampy areas. (Philipp quadrangle, Mississippi, 1:62,500, 1957.)

FIGURE 9.22   Portion of Coconino Plateau, at the edge of the Grand Canyon. (Bright Angel quadrangle, Arizona, 1:62,500, 1962.)

from its edges (figure 9.22). A variety of related features may become apparent as the edges of the plateau recede. A **mesa** is similar to a plateau, although less extensive, whereas a **butte** is an isolated remnant with very small surface area and clifflike sides (figure 9.23). Where the resistant layer is tilted, a low ridge called a **cuesta** may form instead of a plateau. A cuesta has a steep slope on one face and a more gently sloping surface (the equivalent of the plateau surface) on the other (figure 9.24).

Solution Features

Certain types of rock, such as limestone, are susceptible to solution by water. Where such underlying bedrock is dissolved by water action, underground drainage may develop. As a result, the surface drainage pattern in such areas is irregular and disrupted, with streams sometimes sinking from view. In addition, **sinks** may appear as the roofs of the underground streams and caverns collapse, and some sinks may be deep enough to form lakes (figure 9.25). This situa-

tion emphasizes the need for more knowledge than can be gained from a topographic map alone. The kettles mentioned in the discussion of glacial features, for example, may take a form that looks very similar to solution features, even though their origins are entirely different.

Valleys

There is a tremendous variety of valley features resulting from the action of water in either removing or depositing materials. For example, a typical stream valley is **V-shaped** where downward cutting is active (figure 9.26). Where streams are near to grade and downward cutting is minimal, however, **meanders** and natural **levees** form, and **oxbow lakes** develop in remnants of the changing river channel (figure 9.27). In other areas, water action may deposit **alluvial fans** as water movement slows where it leaves steep, restricted channels, and empties into a valley bottom (see figure 9.7).

FIGURE 9.23   Butte (Promontory Butte) and mesa
(tableland north of Promontory Butte). (Promontory Butte
quadrangle, Arizona, 1:62,500, 1952.)

FIGURE 9.24   Cuesta, with gentle slope to the north and
steeper south-facing slope. (Delaware quadrangle,
Michigan, 1:24,000, 1948 [photo-revised 1975].)

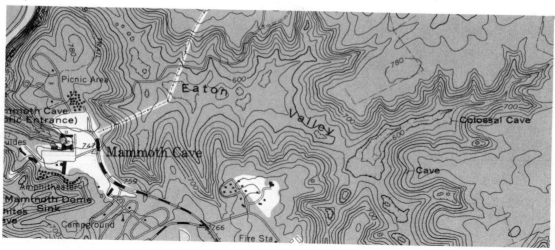

FIGURE 9.25 Solution features: Depressions (sinks) (in Eaton Valley), cave entrance (Colossal Cave), and disappearing (sinking) stream (adjacent to Colossal Cave). (Mammoth Cave quadrangle, Kentucky, 1:24,000, 1965.)

FIGURE 9.26 V-shaped valley (valley of Carbon River). (Lake Tapps quadrangle, Washington, 1:62,500, 1942.)

FIGURE 9.27 Stream features. (*a*) Meanders. (Strasburg quadrangle, Virginia, 1:62,500, 1947.) (*b*) Oxbow lakes. (Caspiana quadrangle, Louisiana, 1:62,500, 1955.) (*c*) Natural levees on the riverbanks, supplemented by man-made levees (labeled "LEVEE"). (Somerset quadrangle, Louisiana-Mississippi, 1:24,000, 1963.)

Volcanic Features

Features produced by volcanic action that are of sufficient size to be visible on a contour map include **cinder cones**, sometimes with **craters** at the top (figure 9.28). Large **volcanic cones** dominate many landscapes (figure 9.29).

Water Features

Another broad category of features comprises those distinctive forms created by the action of water. Many of the forms associated with lakes and streams are strongly interrelated with features already discussed, such as oxbow lakes, disappearing streams, and water gaps. Among the other forms are **rapids** and **springs** (figure 9.30).

FIGURE 9.28   Cinder cone, with crater. (Menan Buttes quadrangle, Idaho, 1:24,000, 1951.)

FIGURE 9.29   Volcanic peak, with radial drainage pattern. (Mount Rainier quadrangle, 1:125,000, 1924.)

FIGURE 9.30   Rapids and springs. (Thousand Springs quadrangle, Idaho, 1:24,000, 1949.)

(a)

(b)

FIGURE 9.31   Wind features. (*a*) Sand dunes. Undulating surface and stippled symbol indicate sand. (Provincetown quadrangle, Massachusetts, 1:24,000, 1958.) (*b*) Sand hills. (Ashby quadrangle, Nebraska, 1:62,500, 1948.)

Wind Features

The wind is a powerful force for the transportation and deposition of materials. Features formed by the action of wind include **dunes** (figure 9.31a) and ancient **sand hills** (figure 9.31b).

Miscellaneous

Because of the enormous variety of landforms, some types fall into a category that must be labeled *miscellaneous*. Features in this category range from **natural bridges** (figure 9.32) to **fall lines** (figure 9.33).

FIGURE 9.32   Juanita Arch natural bridge. An intermittent stream flows under the arch. (Juanita Arch quadrangle, Colorado, 1:24,000, 1960.)

FIGURE 9.33   Fall line. (Washington West quadrangle, D.C.-Maryland-Virginia, 1:24,000, 1965 [photo revised 1983].)

Summary

Landforms are the result of the complex interactions between the tectonic movement of the earth's crust and the geologic, hydrologic, atmospheric, and biotic forces that bring about weathering, mass movement, erosion, and deposition. As a major environmental element, topography has direct and indirect effects on human life.

Drainage patterns are classified in terms of the type and texture of dissection. Types of dissection include the treelike dendritic pattern and the related rectangular and trellis types. The circular patterns of channels flowing away from, or toward, a central point are called radial patterns; those that flow outward are centrifugal, and those that flow inward are centripetal. Annular patterns are circular patterns modified by the presence of joints or fractures that create elements of parallel drainage.

A great variety of stream patterns form in differing circumstances. Disrupted patterns, for example, are characteristic of areas of poor drainage resulting from glaciation. Disappearing streams and internal drainage occur in areas of bedrock solution. Fanlike patterns of streams often spread out over the bases of alluvial fans. Braided, meandering patterns are characteristic of streams that are close to the level of a water body that establishes a limit on their downward cutting. Also, human intervention is seen in the artificial patterns of irrigation and drainage ditches, or navigation canals.

Texture of dissection describes the relative fineness of the stream pattern. The concept offers some insight into the nature of the underlying geology and soils.

For descriptive purposes, landforms are grouped into categories based on their location or origin. The features described in this chapter represent only a sample of the tremendous range and variety of existing landform features. In particular, the challenging study of the influence of geologic structure and other factors on the formation of these features has been largely ignored because of lack of space; a separate book would be needed to do justice to the topic. The goal of this chapter, therefore, is simply to show that the contours on topographic maps provide useful information for the identification and initial study of distinctive landform features.

SUGGESTED READINGS

Brunsden, D., and J. Doornkamp, eds. *The Unquiet Landscape*. Bloomington, Ind.: Indiana University Press, 1974.

DeBruin, Richard. *100 Topographic Maps Illustrating Physiographic Features*. Northbrook, Ill.: Hubbard Scientific, 1970.

Garner, H. F. *The Origin of Landscape*. New York: Oxford University Press, 1974.

Miller, Victor C., and Mary E. Westerback. *Interpretation of Topographic Maps*. Columbus, Ohio: Merrill Publishing Co., 1989.

Pitty, W. F. *The Nature of Geomorphology*. London: Methuen, 1982.

Way, Douglas A. *Terrain Analysis: A Guide to Site Selection Using Aerial Photographic Interpretation*. 2d ed. Stroudsburg, Penn.: Dowden, Hutchinson and Ross; New York: McGraw-Hill, 1978.

10
Locational and Land-Partitioning Systems

Humankind has always needed to describe the locations of features on the earth's surface. In the earliest times, primitive and relatively immobile humans could use word descriptions to convey the locations of hunting or fishing sites, attractions or dangers, or other features that were of importance to them. Their descriptions could be simple word pictures of the location, such as "the hill with snow on top" or "the hole of gushing waters." As mobility and the complexity of life increased, however, it became increasingly necessary to identify more and more features and to differentiate between many features of the same type. This caused a great increase in the number of place names and feature names.

Today we must be able to describe the location of thousands of places on earth in accurate and unequivocal terms. Commonly, we must locate some object or locale of interest on a map, given its locational description. In addition, we frequently need to provide such locational information to others so that they can find their way. Regardless of which task we face, there are a number of methods of specifying locational information. The commonly used locational methods described in this chapter range from the latitude and longitude coordinate system to the State Plane Coordinate (SPC) system. They also include the World Geographic Reference System (GEOREF) and the Universal Transverse Mercator (UTM) and Universal Polar Stereographic (UPS) systems.

As land-ownership concepts evolved, land-ownership description systems were developed to accurately describe the limits of property tracts. Situations in which we need to convey land-ownership information to someone else or to plot a land-ownership description onto a map are common. Both of these abilities are vital to anyone involved in real-estate transactions, even when the transaction is as relatively simple as the purchase of a home, and are useful in many other situations as well. This chapter, therefore, also describes two major types of land-partitioning systems. The first is the unsystematic subdivision of land using metes-and-bounds descriptions. The second is the systematic subdivision system utilized by the U.S. Public Land Survey (USPLS) and the similar system used by the Canada Land Survey.

LOCATIONAL SYSTEMS

Latitude and Longitude Positions

The latitude and longitude graticule on a map is used for determining positions in two different ways. First, the latitude and longitude of a specific map location may need to be calculated so that it can be recorded and communicated to someone else. Second, the latitude and longitude of a feature may be given so that the map user can locate the feature on the map.

TABLE 10.1 Length of Degrees of Longitude

LATITUDE	KILOMETERS
0	111.319
5	110.899
10	109.639
15	107.551
20	104.647
25	100.950
30	96.486
35	91.288
40	85.394
45	78.847
50	71.696
55	63.994
60	55.800
65	47.176
70	38.187
75	28.902
80	19.393
85	9.735
90	0.000

Source: Computed from data supplied by National Geodetic Survey, based Geodetic Reference System 1980 ellipsoid.
Note: This table shows the length of a degree of arc along the latitude named.

TABLE 10.2 Length of Degrees of Latitude

LATITUDE	KILOMETERS
0	110.574
5	110.583
10	110.608
15	110.649
20	110.704
25	110.773
30	110.852
35	110.941
40	111.035
45	111.132
50	111.229
55	111.324
60	111.412
65	111.493
70	111.562
75	111.618
80	111.660
85	111.685
90	111.694

Source: Computed from data supplied by National Geodetic Survey, based Geodetic Reference System 1980 ellipsoid.
Note: The table shows the length of a degree of arc centered on the latitude named.

In this section, we discuss how to accomplish the first of these tasks. Although the second task is not specifically discussed, it is simply the reverse of the first.

If a location falls on the lines of latitude and longitude that are printed on the map, it is a simple matter to read off the coordinates. The difficulty comes in the more usual situation in which the location lies somewhere *between* the graticule lines. When this occurs, a process of **interpolation** is used to estimate the intermediate coordinate value.

Interpolation.   A simple case illustrates the interpolation process. Assume that a feature is halfway between 10° and 20° north, for example. Clearly, its latitude is 15° north. When features do not fall in such convenient locations, however, the interpolation process becomes more difficult.

Obviously, interpolation requires a graticule as a starting point. Some maps do not contain a full graticule but use short lines, called **ticks**, to indicate the intersection of the graticule with the map outline (called the **neatline**). When using such a map to determine locations, you must first establish the graticule by joining the ticks with a lightly drawn pencil line. If the graticule of the map projection that you are using is curved, joining the ticks with straight lines introduces some error into the estimation process. To partially alleviate this problem, some maps contain additional reference ticks that indicate the intersection points of the graticule within the map. USGS 1:24,000-scale quadrangle maps, for example, use this method. If the map you intend to use lacks both a graticule *and* grid ticks, you must obtain a more suitable map before proceeding.

One complicating factor in the measurement of latitude and longitude is that the graticule spacing varies from place to place. This is particularly apparent in the case of the lines of longitude, which converge toward the poles (table 10.1). It is also true, however, that the parallels are slightly farther apart toward the poles because of the slight flattening of the earth. The effect of this flattening is sufficient to be apparent at large map scales (table 10.2).

The variation in spacing between the graticule lines means that a simple scale that works accurately for subdivisions of a degree of longitude at 40° latitude, for example, will not work at 50°. Nor can it be used at other latitudes or for subdividing latitude readings.

FIGURE 10.1 Use of ruler for graphically interpolating latitude. The same approach is used for determining longitude. Any ruler with an appropriate number of subdivisions can be used, but this Geo Ruler is conveniently divided into minutes and seconds.

Courtesy of Elamco, P.O. Box 301, Lincolnton, GA 30817.

This means that different scales must be used for each latitude and longitude subdivision. Three methods flexible enough to deal with this complication are described here.

A simple ruler or engineer's scale, subdivided in either inches or metric units, can be used for interpolation. (An even more useful device for this purpose is the special ruler shown in figure 10.1.) Assume, for example, that the latitude of point *A* in figure 10.1 is to be determined. As is the case with USGS 7.5'-quadrangles, the lines of latitude are 2'30" apart (42°37'30" and 42°40' north). First, select a scale that comfortably spans the distance between the two lines of latitude. You will probably have to place the ruler

on a slant to accomplish this. Next, align the ruler so that it passes through point *A*, with the 0-mark on the lower graticule line and the 2'30"-mark on the other. Each unit on the ruler represents 1 second of latitude. In this case, point *A* is at the 1'10"-mark, which means that it is that amount north of 42°37'30" north, or 42°38'40" north.

Another method of expediting the interpolation process, in the case of USGS 7.5'- and 15'-topographic quadrangles, is to use another type of commercially available transparent template. This template allows for the subdivision of degrees of latitude or longitude, regardless of the latitude range involved. It is used as shown in figure 10.2.

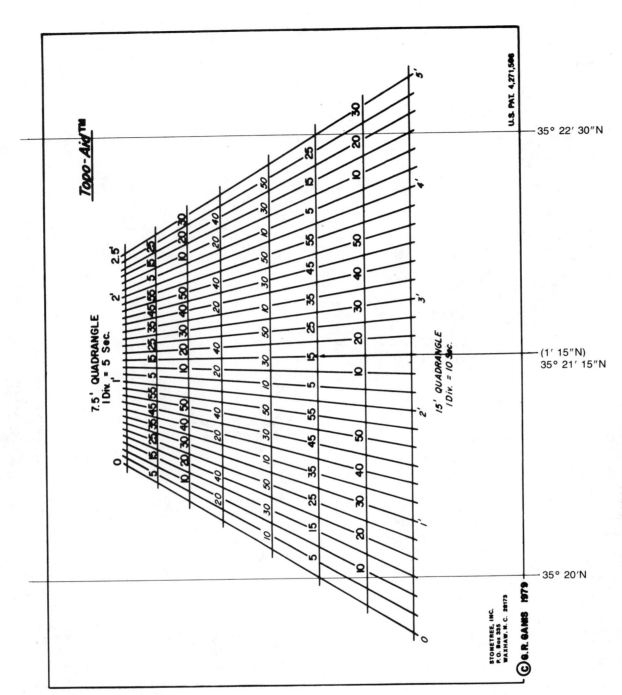

FIGURE 10.2 Use of Topo-Aid/TM/ transparent subdivision template.

Courtesy of Stonetree, Inc., P.O. Box 335, Waxhaw, NC 28173.

Other scale selections are convenient for different graticule spacings. As already mentioned, on USGS 1:24,000-scale quadrangle maps, for example, the spacing between grid ticks is 2′30″, which totals 150″ of arc. In this case, if a scale with 150 units is used, each unit on the scale is equivalent to 1 second on the map.

Another method of interpolation involves using a pair of **spacing dividers** (figure 10.3). Suppose, for example, that the latitude of the dot in figure 10.4 is to be determined and that the graticule lines for 10° north and 20° north are on the map. The spacing dividers have eleven points, so when the endpoints are placed on the two parallels, the space between them is divided into ten equal parts. In this example, then, the dot is four spaces north of 10° north, at 14° north.

Spacing dividers have the advantage that they can be adjusted to any length (up to their maximum

FIGURE 10.3   Spacing dividers.
Courtesy of Charvoz.

FIGURE 10.4   Use of spacing dividers for latitude/ longitude interpolation.

reach). In addition, division into anywhere from two to ten units is easily done by selecting a different number of points. Using five points, for example, gives a division into four units.

Subdivisions of degrees. The system of degrees, minutes, and seconds used for latitude and longitude designations is awkward because of the subdivision of each degree into 60 minutes and of each minute into 60 seconds. One way to avoid this complexity is to use decimal fractions of a degree instead. When this method is used, 10°30', for example, is converted to 10.5°.

When decimals are not used, minutes and seconds can be located by subdividing in a sequential manner. Locating 57°10', for example, would require first locating 57° and 58° and then interpolating between them to locate 10'. Since 10' is one-sixth of the 60' that make up 1 degree, it would be sufficient to divide the space into six parts. When this is done, the first space north of 57° is 57°10' north. If accuracy to the level of seconds is required, a further subdivision of the 1-minute spacing is done in a similar manner.

World Geographic Reference System

Specifying a location on the earth's surface in terms of degrees, minutes, and seconds of north and south latitude, and of east and west longitude, is somewhat cumbersome. The **World Geographic Reference System (GEOREF)** allows more convenient and rapid reporting and plotting of locations.

In the GEOREF system, which is used primarily for military air operations, latitude and longitude designations are replaced by a simple set of letters and numbers. The world is first divided into 15-degree-wide north-south and east-west bands, using the lines of longitude and latitude (figure 10.5a). The twenty-four longitudinal zones are lettered in an eastward direction, beginning at the 180th meridian. The first zone to the east of 180° is identified by the letter *A*. The identifying letters continue in alphabetical order with the letter *Z* applied to the zone immediately to the west of the 180th meridian (*I* and *O* are omitted).

The twelve latitudinal bands begin with *A*, for the first band north of the South Pole, and end with *M*, for the last band south of the North Pole (*I* is omitted).

Establishing the 15-degree zones and bands results in the formation of 288 quadrangles, each uniquely identified by a pair of letters. The first letter of the pair identifies the vertical zone and the second letter identifies the horizontal band. This follows the general rule of grid systems: "Read right and then up." The British Isles, for example, fall largely within square *MK,* using this system.

When more accurate location descriptions are required, additional subdivisions are used. The first increase in accuracy is provided by subdividing each of the 15-degree quadrangles into 225 1-degree quadrangles (figure 10.5b). Each of these quadrangles is identified by adding a third and fourth letter to the original pair of letters. The north-south zones are identified by the third letter, using *A* through *Q* (omitting *I* and *O*), beginning at the western edge of the 15-degree quadrangle. The east-west bands are identified by the fourth letter, using the same letter sequence, and beginning at the southern edge of the 15-degree quadrangle.

The use of the four identifying letters described so far allows the full identification of any 1-degree quadrangle in the world.

More accurate identification of locations within a 1-degree quadrangle is accomplished by adding a numerical component to the letter codes. In the case of a four-digit number, the first two digits specify the number of minutes the location is to the east of the indicated degree line. The last two digits specify the number of minutes the location is to the north of the indicated degree line. In effect, this divides each 1-degree quadrangle into 3,600 1-minute quadrangles. Further accuracy is provided by using decimal designations. Thus, a GEOREF coordinate with four letters and six numbers identifies any 0.1-minute quadrangle in the world. The first three digits indicate easting and the last three digits indicate northing (the decimal point is not actually written) (figure 10.5c). Similarly, any 0.01-minute location is identified by four letters and eight numbers.

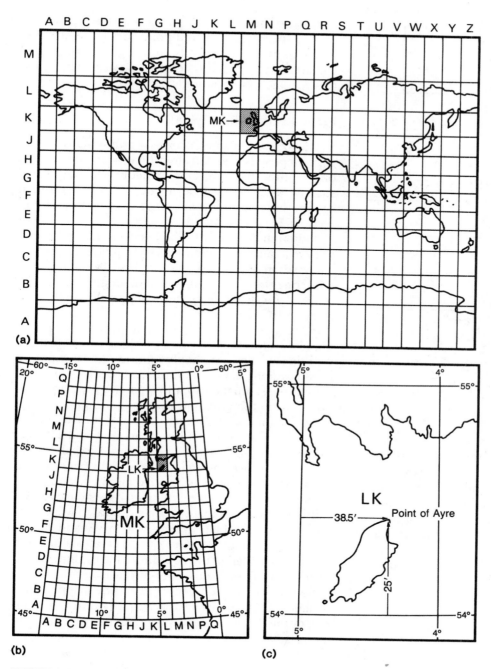

FIGURE 10.5 Determination of a reference using the GEOREF system. (*a*) Worldwide 15-degree-wide zones and bands. (*b*) Isle of Man: 1° Square MK LK. (*c*) 1 Point of Ayre: MK LK 385250.

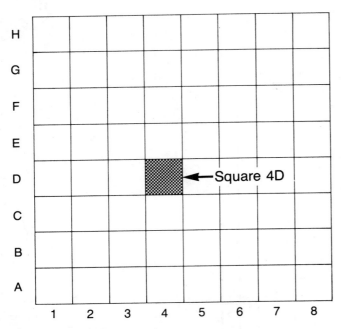

FIGURE 10.6   Simple reference grid.

GRID SYSTEMS

Reference Grids

Maps often include special reference grids. Some grid systems are very easily understood because they are designed simply as a supplement to a map index. Examples of this type are commonly encountered in atlases and on street maps. The index lists cities, towns, rivers, streets, and other features and designates the grid square in which each feature appears (in the case of an atlas, the page number is given as well). To find a feature, you first locate the designated square, using the identifying letters and numbers printed around the outside border of the map (figure 10.6). You then search within the square for the feature. Reference grids of this type often use letters to designate the horizontal bands and numbers to designate the vertical ones, with both series beginning at the lower-left corner of the map. The numbering and lettering patterns are not standardized, however, so each system must be examined individually. The major shortcoming of such grids is that they are specific to each map and, therefore, do not tie into any overall locational system.

A more important type of grid system allows the user to specify any desired point in relation to other locations within a relatively large region. The general characteristics of such systems are described next, and two specific examples are examined.

Plane Rectangular Grids

One or more **plane rectangular grid systems** may be superimposed on a map after it has been constructed on a latitude and longitude graticule. The purpose of such grids is to provide an easily used locational system that does not require the introduction of corrections for the curvature of the earth.

Although details vary, plane rectangular grids tend to have a number of elements in common. In the typical case, an origin is established first. Two sets of parallel lines are then established, beginning at the origin, with one set perpendicular to the other, thus forming the rectangular grid. The grid lines are not directly associated with the latitude and longitude graticule, although they may be aligned with it at the grid origin; they are simply arbitrary lines, superimposed over the map. In addition, a systematic labeling system is established to allow users to specify locations within the grid system.

In rectangular coordinate systems, measurements of locations are specified in terms of distances away from the origin, along the grid lines. Typically, measurements above (north) or to the right (east) of the origin are designated as positive numbers, and those below (south) or to the left (west) are negative. Because negative designations are awkward to work with, most plane coordinate grid systems are established in the equivalent of the first quadrant of a Cartesian system, so that all of the coordinate measurements are positive. In other words, the origin is usually established south and west of the area to be mapped, and distances are measured eastward and northward from that point.[1] There are exceptions to this rule, but they are relatively easy to deal with once the more usual arrangements are understood. One simply has to be careful when measuring distances to increase or decrease the numbers in the correct directions.

[1]Such an origin is often called a **false origin** because it lies outside the area being mapped.

Reference lines for plane coordinate grids are often drawn on maps. They are usually at a regular spacing, such as 1,000 yards, 1,000 meters, or 10,000 feet. The spacing is selected so that the grid does not interfere with other information on the map. If the scale is relatively large, the grid lines are spaced at a closer interval than if the scale is relatively small. Other than convenience, there is nothing to prevent the map placement of grid lines at *any* arbitrary interval.

A numbering system is needed so that the location of a grid reference can be quickly determined. A variety of systems is used involving letters, Arabic numbers, Roman numerals, or some combination of letters and numbers.

The general rule for plane coordinate grid systems is that locations are defined by giving the east-west coordinate first and the north-south coordinate second. Usually, the coordinates are simply distance values, measured from the system origin. They are frequently written as a single number block, with the division into east-west and north-south components merely implied. Suppose, for example, that a point is located 642,000 meters east and 195,000 meters north of the origin. One way to represent the coordinates for this point is by the number 642000–195000. Alternatively, the hyphen is omitted, so that the number is shown as 642000195000. In addition, trailing zeros are often omitted on a grid reference, but always as an equal number of digits from each half. When this is appropriate, the example coordinate is conveniently shortened to 642195. An abbreviated coordinate of this type indicates that the feature is located in the grid square that lies to the east and north of the point that is 642,000 meters east and 195,000 meters north of the origin.

Leading digits in coordinate strings are also sometimes omitted when work is being done in a limited region. Continuing with the previous example, a location that is 1,642,000 meters east and 2,195,000 meters north might normally be listed as 16422195. When the leading digits are omitted, the reference is shortened to 642195. However, this same set of numbers is the full reference for the point located at 642,000 meters east and 195,000 meters north. It could also be the shortened reference for other points located at 1,000,000-meter intervals. Obviously, this shorthand approach depends on an agreement by all parties involved that prevents a shortened reference from being confused with other possible locations. In

some systems, the preceding digits and trailing zeros that may be omitted are printed as smaller-sized numbers on the face of the map.

More accurate designations of points to be located are often given by using decimal places to indicate subdivisions between grid lines. Thus, a point located at 642,500 meters east and 195,300 meters north could be designated as 642.5–195.3. Other systems call for running decimal numbers together, again without specifically dividing them into east-west and north-south components. In this case, the decimals are implied rather than written (64251953). Obviously, the user of any grid system must know that system's numbering conventions to interpret a particular coordinate.

Universal Transverse Mercator System

The **Universal Transverse Mercator (UTM) grid system** is based on the **transverse Mercator projection**, with two standard lines. It covers the earth's surface between 80° south and 84° north. The UTM system is used in conjunction with the **Universal Polar Stereographic (UPS) grid system**, which covers the polar caps.

The UTM system involves establishing sixty north-south zones, each of which is 6 degrees of longitude wide. In addition, each zone overlaps ½ degree into the adjoining zones. This allows easy reference to points that are near a zone boundary, regardless of which zone is used for a particular project.

Two methods of location identification are used in the UTM and UPS systems. The first is intended for civilian use and the second for military use. The basic framework, however, is the same for both schemes. Because the civilian system is most commonly encountered, it is described first, and the military system is compared to it.

Civilian system. First, a false origin is established 500,000 meters west of the central meridian of each UTM zone (figure 10.7a). In the Northern Hemisphere, this origin is on the equator; in the Southern Hemisphere, it is 10,000,000 meters south of the equator. A square grid, with the lines extended north and east from the origin, provides a basic locational framework. With this framework any point on the earth's surface, within each zone, has a unique coordinate.

FIGURE 10.7 (*a*) Universal Transverse Mercator (UTM) zone. (*b*) Universal Polar Stereographic (UPS) zones.

A locational grid system is imposed on the two polar (UPS) projections as well (figure 10.7b). Grid north is arbitrarily established so that the prime meridian is at the top-center of the south zone, and the 180th meridian is at the top-center of the north zone. The origins of these grids are located at the lower-left corner of each grid, 2,000,000 meters to the left and 2,000,000 meters down from the pole.

The first step in locating a feature, using the UTM system, is to identify the zone and hemisphere in which it lies. Assume, for example, that the location of the Kenosha, Wisconsin, airport is to be specified. Kenosha is located in zone 16 in the Northern Hemisphere, so this is the first portion of the locational description. The specific location in relation to the origin is then determined. This location is designated in terms of eastings (distances measured from west to east) and northings (distances measured from south to north).

UTM coordinates are shown on the edges of many topographic maps. A portion of the USGS 1:24,000 Pleasant Prairie quadrangle is shown in figure 10.8. A considerable amount of extraneous marginal information is deleted from this figure so that the UTM system is clearly shown. Note that the UTM grid designations are abbreviated in most locations by omitting the last three zeroes and showing designations of 100,000 or more in smaller type. In figure 10.8, for purposes of clarity, the full identification numbers for a portion of the grid are added. The grid itself is also

FIGURE 10.8 Use of UTM coordinate grid. (Portion of U.S. Geological Survey Pleasant Prairie quadrangle, Wisconsin, 1:24,000, 1971.)

shown, although it is indicated only by short blue ticks in the margins of the original map.

The northernmost tip of the runway of the Kenosha Airport is identified in figure 10.8. It is located in the UTM grid square that lies between 423,000 meters east and 424,000 meters east, and between 4,716,000 meters north and 4,717,000 meters north, as is indicated by the grid lines. In this case, the exact location of the point of interest, within the nearest 10 meters, is 870 meters east and 510 meters north of the southwest corner of the grid square. The full UTM coordinates of the location, then, are 423,870 meters east and 4,716,510 meters north (Northern Hemisphere, zone 16).

Determination of UTM coordinates is facilitated by the use of a Metric Coordinate Reader, which is available from the U.S. Geological Survey (figure 10.9).[2] The device can be used with any map containing a UTM grid. Most USGS maps, for example, have UTM grid ticks around the map margin. A full grid is constructed by drawing lines that connect these ticks. After the full grid has been drawn, the UTM coordinates of any given point on the map are obtained by using the coordinate reader in the following manner.

[2]There are two versions of the reader. The CR-2 is designed for use on maps with scales of 1:24,000, 1:25,000, 1:62,500, 1:125,000, and 1:250,000. The CR-1 is designed for use on maps with scales of 1:2,500, 1:5,000, 1:10,000, or decimal multiples of these scales.

FIGURE 10.9 U.S. Geological Survey Metric Coordinate Reader (reduced).

In this example, the feature of interest is the building symbol shown in figure 10.10. First, note the UTM grid zone in which the feature lies, as given in a marginal note on the map. In this example, it is zone 16. Then draw in the coordinate grid in the area of interest, and locate the southwest corner of the grid square that surrounds the building symbol. The designations of the grid lines that form the southern and western edges of this grid square provide the general coordinates (429,000 meters east and 4,720,000 meters north). Next, select the appropriate scale on the co-ordinate reader and hold the reader so that the scale

designation (1:24,000, in this case) is in normal reading orientation. Place the bottom edge of the scale so that it is aligned on the southern edge of the se-lected grid square. Slide the scale right or left, until the vertical scale line passes through the center of the school symbol. Then read the fine grid designations from the scales. In this case, each small tick indicates a distance of 20 meters, so distances can be accurately estimated to the nearest 10 meters. The east-west dis-tance between the grid line and the building symbol is approximately 450 meters, and the north-south dis-tance is 150 meters. Add these values to the general

FIGURE 10.10 **Use of Metric Coordinate Reader.**
(Superimposed on portion of U.S. Geological Survey
Racine South quadrangle, Wisconsin, 1:24,000, 1958,
UTM grid lines added. Illustration reduced.)

coordinates to obtain the final UTM designation of the location of the building symbol: 429,450 meters east, 4,720,150 meters north, Northern Hemisphere, zone 16.

Because the civilian location reference uses only numbers, it is easily handled by computer systems, which is an advantage in many applications.

U.S. Military Grid Reference System. The military versions of the UTM and UPS systems are identical to the civilian systems already described, except for the method of identifying grid zones. The U.S. Military Grid Reference System is used for this purpose. Because this system avoids the long strings of numerals that occur in the civilian systems, it is believed to be preferable for military use.

In the military system, the area of the world lying between 84° north to 80° south is subdivided into grid zones that are 6 degrees east-west by 8 degrees north-south (with some exceptions north of 56° north). Each grid zone is identified by a column number and a row letter (figure 10.11). The column numbers, 1

FIGURE 10.11 **Grid-zone designations of the UTM and UPS military grid system.**

Source: Department of the Army, *Grids and References,* TM 5–241–1 (Washington, D.C.: Department of the Army, March 1983).

FIGURE 10.12   Basic plan of the 100,000-meter square identifications of the UTM military grid system zones.

Source: Department of the Army, *Grids and References*, TM 5–241–1 (Washington, D.C.: Department of the Army, March 1983).

through 60, are the UTM zone numbers. The zone letters, *C* through *X* (with *I* and *O* omitted), start at 80° south and continue to 84° north. The grid zone for a given location is identified by its column and row designation, such as 3N. In addition, grid zones *A* and *B* are assigned to the south zone of the UPS system and *Y* and *Z* to the north zone.

The grid zones are subdivided by a pattern of 100,000-meter squares, each of which has a two-letter identifier (figure 10.12). The identification pattern is set up so that repeated combinations of the identifying letters are as far apart as possible. The first identifying letter indicates the column, and the second letter designates the row. The pattern is not completely regular. Details of the variations, which are numerous, are found in the Department of the Army Training Manual TM5–241–1. (See the "Suggested Readings" at the end of the chapter.)

The column identification letters for the 100,000-meter squares apply both north and south of the equator. The first group begins with *A,* east of the 180th meridian, and continues easterly for 18 degrees (*I* and *O* are omitted), after which it is repeated every 18 degrees. As a result, in the 6-degree UTM zones 1, 2, and 3, for example, the letter *A* is located in the westernmost column of zone 1, *Z* is located in the easternmost column of zone 3, and the first column in zone 4 begins again with the letter *A.* The tapering of the UTM zones toward the poles affects the columns on the western or eastern sides of the zones. As the tapering of the zones progresses toward the poles, the outer columns gradually become narrower or are eliminated.

The pattern for the row letters is somewhat more complex, and, again, there are variations that are not described here. The twenty letters *A* through *V* (omitting *I* and *O*) are used to identify the rows, with a different pattern applied to even- and odd-numbered UTM zones. In odd-numbered zones, the first row north of the false origin (the equator, in the Northern Hemisphere, and 10,000,000 meters south of the equator in the Southern Hemisphere) is designated as *A.* In even-numbered zones, the same pattern is used, except that the sequence is advanced five letters, so that squares with the same identification are

farther apart than they would be if the offset was not introduced. Thus, the first row in an even-numbered zone is *F* instead of *A.* Thereafter, the sequence of letters is the same as that already specified. In each case, the sequence of letters progresses northward and is repeated every 2,000,000 meters.

The UPS zones also have two-letter grid-square designations. The pattern for the north zone is shown in figure 10.13; the south zone has a similar pattern with different letter designations.

Locations within each 100,000-meter square are given in meters as coordinate distances from the southwest corner. The location is defined by the easting, which is given first, and by the northing, which is given second. The digits are written in sequence without punctuation. The number of digits used in the coordinates depends on the accuracy required, or that is possible, given the scale of the map. A ten-digit number is the maximum, and it indicates a location within a 1-meter square. This level of accuracy is seldom reached. At the other extreme, if no grid coordinates are given, the location simply lies somewhere within the designated 100,000-meter square.

A full grid reference consists of the grid-zone designation, the 100,000-meter square identification, and the grid coordinates (written to the desired degree of accuracy). The reference (within 100 meters) for Kent Point, in figure 10.14, for example, is 18SUT916091. If a less accurate location is required, the coordinate portion of the reference is shortened accordingly. Within 1,000 meters, the reference is 18SUT9109, and within 10,000 meters, it is 18SUT90. If the scale of the map permits greater accuracy, coordinates are adjusted accordingly. Within 10 meters, for example, they might be 18SUT91620914, and within 1 meter, 18SUT9162309143.

If there is no danger of confusion, as would be the case if operations were being carried out within a limited area, the full grid reference is not required. If the area is restricted to one grid zone, for example, the grid square and its coordinates is sufficient (UT916091) or, if it is restricted to one 100,000-meter square, the coordinates alone can be used (916091).

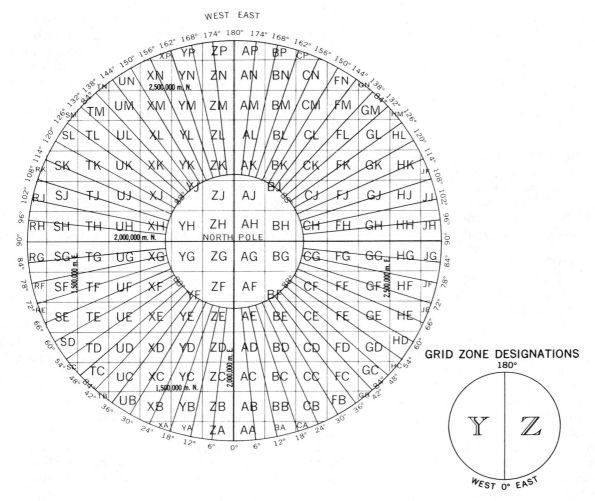

FIGURE 10.13   Two-letter identifications of the
100,000-meter squares and partial squares of the UPS
military system grid (north zone).

Source: Department of the Army, *Grids and References,* TM 5–241–1
(Washington, D.C.: Department of the Army, March 1983).

State Plane Coordinate System

The **State Plane Coordinate System (SPCS)** is a rectangular coordinate system that is individually applied
to each of the United States. The system is designed
to simplify local surveys and at the same time tie them
into the national geodetic network. As the name indicates, the system uses plane coordinates. This is
done so that the surveyor does not have to take the

curvature of the earth into account, which greatly
simplifies the survey computations. This simplification is acceptable for the small areas usually involved
in local surveys because the amount of error introduced is quite small.

A separate SPCS is established for each state. The
larger states are subdivided into zones, with the
number of zones determined by the distortion limits

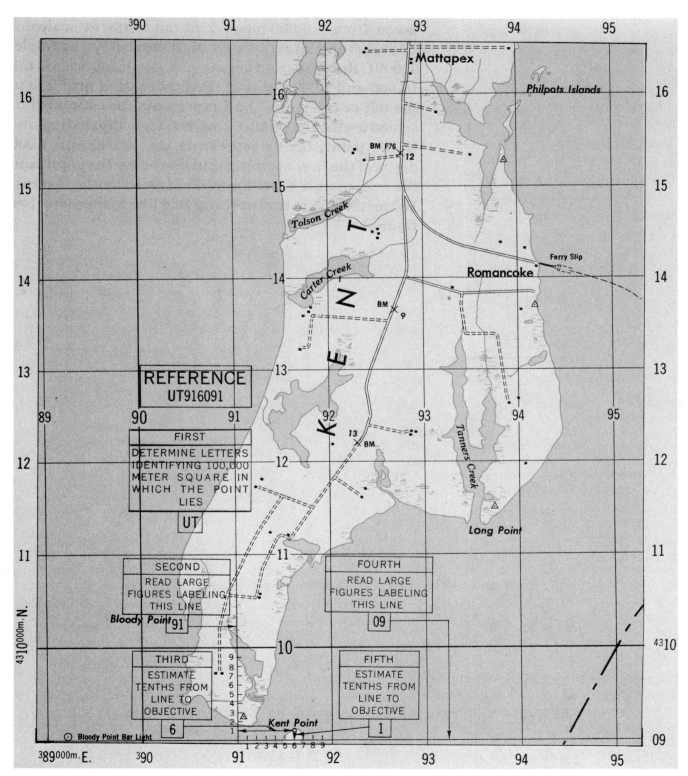

FIGURE 10.14   Method of reading a military grid
reference from a large-scale map.

Source: Department of the Army, *Grids and References,* TM 5–241–1
(Washington, D.C.: Department of the Army, March 1983).

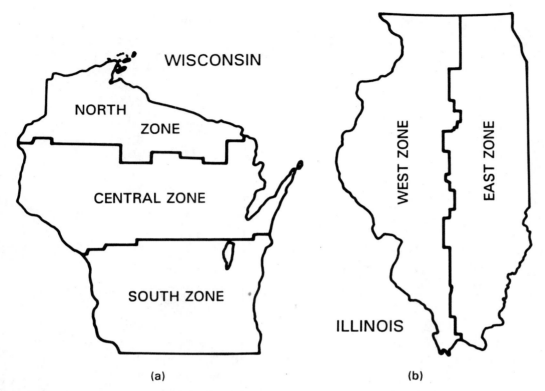

(a)

(b)

FIGURE 10.15   State Plane Coordinate System (SPCS) zones. (*a*) In a state covered by the Lambert projection. (*b*) In a state covered by the Transverse Mercator Projection. Zone boundaries fall on county boundaries.

Source: Joseph F. Dracup. *Fundamentals of State Plane Coordinate Systems.* Rockville, Maryland: U.S. Department of Commerce, National Ocean Survey, 1974 (reprinted 1977).

that have been established for the SPCS (figure 10.15). A map of each zone is then drawn on a projection selected to reduce distortion. With some exceptions, the Lambert conformal projection is used for east-west trending states and the transverse Mercator is used for north-south trending states.[3]

For purposes of designating locations, a false origin is established for each zone. This false origin is located outside the zone and is placed so that all of the measurements based on it are positive numbers. The typical false-origin location is west of the central meridian of the zone. The location is 2,000,000 feet west in the case of the Lambert projection and 500,000 feet west for the transverse Mercator projection. It is south of the southern edge of the zone in both cases. Location coordinates are measured from the false origin

in feet. They are measured to the right (called false eastings) and upward (called false northings). A full SPCS location designation consists of the easting, the northing, the name of the state, and the designation of the zone, such as north, south, east, west, or central. The designation of the identified point in figure 10.16, for example, is 2,557,910 feet east, 225,360 feet north, Wisconsin, South Zone.

LAND-PARTITIONING SYSTEMS

Two basic types of surveys used to determine land-ownership boundaries and property descriptions in the United States are described in this section.[4] Surveys that serve these purposes are generally referred

[3]A revised SPCS system is in use in some states, based on the transverse Mercator projection and with distances expressed in meters.

[4]The survey terms used here follow the glossary in *Definitions of Surveying and Associated Terms,* revised, American Congress on Surveying and Mapping and the American Society of Civil Engineers, 1978.

FIGURE 10.16 Use of state plane coordinate grid. (Portion of U.S. Geological Survey Pleasant Prairie quadrangle, Wisconsin, 1971. Original scale 1:24,000— illustration reduced.)

to as **cadastral surveys**. In the United States, however, the use of the term *cadastral survey* is preferably reserved to describe land-ownership surveys of the public lands. The term **land survey** is used to describe such surveys outside the public lands.

Unsystematic Subdivision

In most of the originally colonized portions of the eastern United States, land-ownership patterns developed in an unplanned manner called **unsystematic subdivision**. Property boundaries were established on the basis of the claims of the settlers who had occupied, cleared, and farmed specific plots of land. Typically, the boundaries of these properties were defined first, and surveys were later carried out to record the ownership claims.

Metes and bounds. The method of land survey used to describe these unplanned land ownerships is called **metes-and-bounds surveying**.[5] A metes-and-bounds survey records the direction and length of

[5]Metes-and-bounds surveys are also used in certain situations elsewhere in the United States, including areas with systematic subdivisions.

FIGURE 10.17   Metes-and-bounds survey.
On file at the Georgia Department of Archives and History.

each portion of the boundary line of the property in sequence, as though one were walking around the perimeter of the parcel. Distinctive markers, such as trees of particular species, are often used for such surveys (figure 10.17).

Bearings.   Directions in metes-and-bounds surveys are indicated by the use of bearings. A **bearing** is the angular difference between a north or south reference and the direction of the surveyed line. The ref-

erence line, and hence the bearing, may be expressed as a true, magnetic, or grid direction. The listing of a bearing consists of three parts: the designation of the reference direction (either north or south), the angle between the reference direction and the surveyed direction (not to exceed 90 degrees), and the direction of the angle (east or west). If, for example, the line being described lies at a 45-degree angle to the east of a north reference line, its bearing is north 45° east (see figure 6.5).

Systematic Subdivision
(U.S. Public Land Survey)

In New England, in contrast to other colonial areas, there were instances of organized land-ownership plans. Towns were often surveyed prior to settlement. They were usually laid out along a riverbank or some other transportation artery, were of a fairly uniform size, and were divided into lots that were mapped prior to settlement. The lots were of variable shape and size but were frequently bounded by straight lines. New England town plans were the predecessors of the public land-survey system that was later extended throughout much of the United States.

U.S. Public lands.   The Treaty of Paris in 1783, which ended the Revolutionary War, gave control of the territory east of the Mississippi River and south of the Great Lakes (except Spanish Florida) to the United States. In addition, during the period from 1780 to 1802, the original thirteen colonies ceded their western land claims to the newly formed United States. The impending sale and settlement of these public lands created a need for a systematic method of determining and recording land ownership. As a result, in 1785, Congress passed a land ordinance that established a procedure for disposing of lands in the Western Territory. This act provided the initial framework for the **rectangular survey system** that was begun when the settlement of the western portion of the nation was in its early stages. This system, which has come to be called the **United States Public Land Survey (USPLS)**, was started in Ohio and ultimately was extended throughout most of the western states and parts of the south.[6]

Many variations in the details of the USPLS were introduced as the system evolved. For this reason, different specifics may be encountered when actual surveys are examined. When variations occur, it is necessary to consult other sources, such as those listed in the "Suggested Readings" at the end of the chapter, to determine their origins. The basic outline of the system as it is described here has nevertheless remained quite constant.

[6]The rectangular survey system is not used in Connecticut, Delaware, Kentucky, Maine, Maryland, Massachusetts, New Hampshire, New Jersey, New York, North Carolina, Pennsylvania, Rhode Island, South Carolina, Tennessee, Texas, Vermont, Virginia, or West Virginia.

Township, range, and section.   In the USPLS, an initial point is first established for the particular region to be surveyed. Astronomical observations are used to determine the location of this initial point. A north-south **principal meridian** is then established, and an east-west **baseline** is set at right angles to it, with both lines passing through the initial point. The actual arrangement of the thirty-four principal meridians and primary baselines, and the territory governed by each, is shown in figure 10.18.

A grid of lines, spaced at 6-mile intervals, is established next. The east-west lines in this grid form rows, called **townships**. They are numbered in sequence, both north and south of the baseline (figure 10.19). The north-south lines in the grid form columns, called **ranges**. They are also numbered in sequence, both east and west of the principal meridian. The intersection of the township rows and the range columns creates a pattern of squares, also called **townships** (an unfortunate repetition of the word). Townships are subdivided into thirty-six **sections**, each containing approximately 1 square mile (640 acres); the exact size of actually surveyed townships often differs from this standard, however. The sections are numbered in alternating rows, beginning at the northeast corner of the township. The reasons for the variation in township size are discussed next, along with an explanation of the subdivision of sections.

Plats.   Detailed maps that show the boundaries of USPLS land ownerships within a township are called **township plats**. The subdivision of the sections, as recorded on the plats, varies considerably. The basic system, however, uses the so-called **aliquot parts**. Aliquot parts result from the division of a section into quarters (160 acres) and, subsequently, of the quarters into quarter-quarters (40 acres). In addition, half-sections are sometimes used (either northern and southern, or eastern and western, halves).

Special units, called **lots**, are used when the normal system of fractional sections cannot be applied. Lots frequently occur along the northern and western edges of townships, for example, because measurement errors are adjusted along these edges. They are also used when a navigable stream, or a lake that is

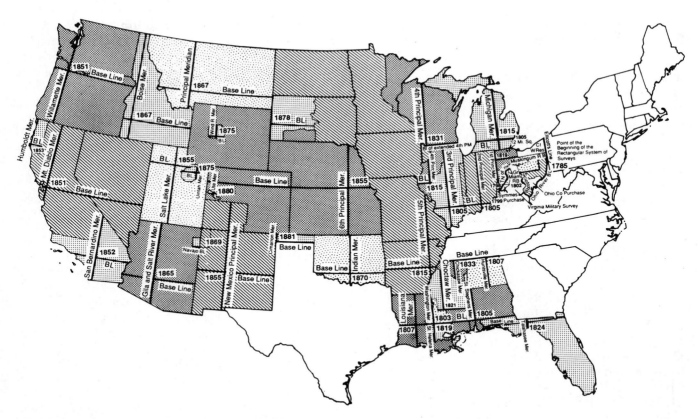

FIGURE 10.18   USPLS principal meridians and baselines, and the territory governed by each.

Source: U.S. Department of the Interior, Bureau of Land Management, *Surveying Our Public Lands* (Washington, D.C.: U.S. Government Printing Office, 1980).

25 acres or more in extent, is encountered. This is because a settler purchasing public land would generally not want to pay for a full section when a considerable area is under water and not usable for farming.

When lots are established, a line called a **meander line** is surveyed along the water body's mean high-water elevation. Then, as many standard quarter-quarter sections as possible are designated, and the remaining land is subdivided into lots. The lots are kept as close to 40 acres as possible, although subdivisions as small as 2.5 acres are sometimes encountered. The lots are identified by sequential numbers within each section. Although meander lines are used to determine acreages, high-water lines are used to establish property boundaries.

There are also instances in which preexisting claims are incorporated into the USPLS, such as in portions of California, Oregon, and Florida. Because these claims are usually irregular in shape and alignment compared to the units of the USPLS, they are incorporated into the system as lots. Other special units that were established were the so-called "French Tracts" in Orleans Territory (now Louisiana). These tracts were arranged to provide frontage on navigable waterways, an approach that was traditional with the

TOWNSHIP GRID

TOWNSHIP 2 SOUTH, RANGE 3 WEST

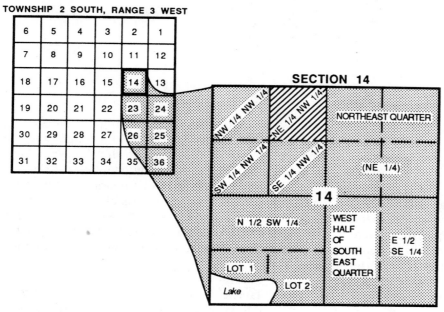

FIGURE 10.19 Townships, ranges, sections, and further divisions of the U.S. Public Land Survey.

Source: Modified from the U.S. Department of the Interior, Bureau of Land Management, *Surveying Our Public Lands* (Washington, D.C.: U.S. Government Printing Office, 1980).

FIGURE 10.20   ''French Tracts'' in Louisiana. (Portion of New Roads quadrangle, Louisiana, 1:62,500, 1939.)

French settlers in the region (figure 10.20). More information about this type of tract is provided in the discussion of Canadian land survey systems, later in this chapter.

Property descriptions.   Rectangular survey system designations are used to describe a tract of land for legal purposes. Consider, for example, the 40-acre tract marked with the diagonal line pattern in figure 10.19. This tract covers the northeast quarter of the northwest quarter of Section 14 and is located in the township that is at the intersection of Township 2 South, Range 3 West, within the area of survey that is based on a particular principal meridian. This description would normally be written in abbreviated form as: NE 1/4, NW 1/4, Sec. 14, T 2 S, R 3 W, ___P.M.

Assume, then, that you wish to locate the same tract, on the basis of its description. This task involves working from the broadest category down to the narrowest. You would first determine the area covered by surveys based on the particular principal meridian.

Then you would need a map showing the intersection of the second township south of the origin and the third range west. Within that township, you would first find section 14, then the northwest quarter of the section, and, finally, the northeast quarter of the northwest quarter. This system is valuable because such a brief description allows a specific small piece of land, within the extensive area of the United States that is covered by the USPLS, to be unambiguously defined and located.

Irregularities.   The curvature of the earth affects the size of townships in the USPLS because lines of longitude converge toward the poles. As a result, although range lines are spaced 6 miles apart along a baseline, they come closer together as they are extended north along their meridian. For this reason, corrections must be made to prevent spacing between the range lines from deviating too much from the 6-mile standard. This is accomplished by establishing correction lines, called standard parallels and guide meridians. Generally, a **standard parallel** is established every 24 miles north or south of a baseline. Along this standard parallel, north-south lines, called **guide meridians** are surveyed, at a starting spacing of 24 miles. The southern, western, and eastern boundaries of each of the blocks formed by the guide meridians and the standard parallels are nominally 24 miles long. Surveying discrepancies almost always cause the actual measurements to deviate somewhat from the desired standard. In addition, the guide meridians converge, so that the northern boundaries of the blocks are less than 24 miles long.

The imposition of a rectangular survey system onto the spherical surface of the earth, then, faces fundamental problems that result in unavoidable deviations from a strictly right-angled system of property lines. In addition, for a variety of reasons including inaccurate instruments, difficult terrain, poor work, and, unfortunately, occasional dishonesty, irregularities are often found in the pattern of USPLS survey lines. In the early years, for example, some surveyors lacked the skills or the instruments with which to measure horizontal distances between points, instead of distances over the irregular surface of the ground (see chapter 5). Such discrepancies introduced inaccuracies into the system, especially in areas with steep terrain.

Similarly, the early use of the magnetic compass, which is an unreliable tool for determining directions, often resulted in survey errors. Standard USPLS practice, therefore, excludes the use of the magnetic compass for establishing the direction of survey lines. Instead, readings from a special instrument called a solar transit, or observations of Polaris, are used to establish true north. Other directional readings are related to the reference direction thus established.

Land Survey in Canada

Different land-ownership systems have been used at various stages in Canadian history. Each system resulted in a distinctive landscape pattern in the region to which it was applied. It is not feasible to describe these systems in detail here, but some of their major characteristics can be noted.

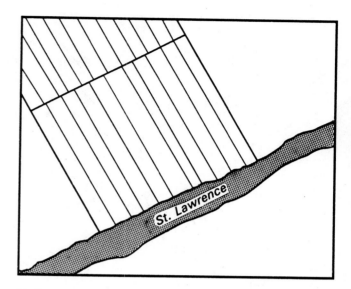

FIGURE 10.21   Example of lots (rotures) within a seigneury, in area of French settlement in Canada.

Patterns in areas of French settlement.   In the seventeenth century, the region that is now Quebec and the Maritime provinces, except Newfoundland, was under French domination. The French government granted large land holdings. called **seigneuries**, often to noblemen, but sometimes to yeomen or farmers. The **seigneurs**, as the land holders were called, had the obligation to promote settlement and development. To this end, they subdivided the seigneuries into lots, called **rotures**, that were allocated to individual farmers.

The pattern of land subdivision in the seigneuries was largely controlled by the rivers, the principal highways and communication links of the time. In the valley of the St. Lawrence River, for example, the general pattern consisted of tiers of long, narrow lots. These lots were arranged in a northwesterly, southeasterly alignment, at right angles to the trend of the river (figure 10.21). The first tier of lots fronted on the river. Although there was considerable variation, the typical river frontage of a lot was three arpents[7] (approximately 575'). They usually had a depth of

[7]One arpent equals 191.838 ft.

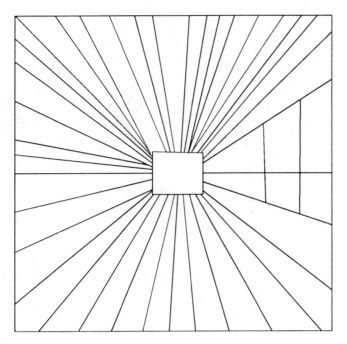

FIGURE 10.22   Example of lots within a village with a fortified central square, in area of French settlement in Canada.

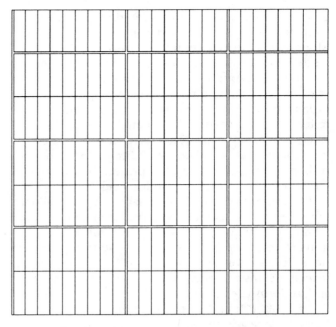

FIGURE 10.23   Example of township and lots in area of an English settlement in Canada.

thirty arpents (5,755') or more. The favorably located riverfront lots were usually settled first and the tiers of lots away from the river were settled later.

The pattern of lots differed when a village was laid out. Villages often consisted of a square, perhaps 40 arpents (approximately 1-½ miles) on a side. Forty farms, each containing 40 square arpents (34 acres), might be laid out in a radial pattern around the fortified central square (figure 10.22).

Patterns of long lots were also established by French settlers in the United States. They are found, for example, in areas around Detroit and Green Bay, and in Louisiana.

Patterns in areas of English settlement.   In later years, in areas settled by the English, lots of 100 to 300 acres were often surveyed in large, rectilinear blocks. As with the seigneuries, the patterns of these blocks frequently began with a first tier of lots approximately paralleling the irregular bank of a river. The lots in the other tiers were then arranged in rows parallel to the rear-line of the first tier. A variety of systems was used at different times, so township and

lot sizes are found in a variety of forms.[8] In one example, the township contained 36 square miles (six by six miles) (figure 10.23). It consisted of 25 lots along the river bank, each 19 chains wide (1,254'). The pattern extended inland for seven tiers, with each tier 68 chains 25 links (4,356') deep, plus a road allowance of 2 chains 25 links. The total township contained 175 lots of 120 acres each, plus provision for roads.

Westward expansion.   Still later, in the 1860s and 1870s, Canada was faced with a rapid expansion to the west. The situation was similar to that in the United States about eighty years earlier. During the early part of this period, townships were surveyed on the north shore of Lake Huron, following U.S. practices.

In 1870, to provide an orderly framework for expansion into the prairies and the mountains of the

---

[8]Don W. Thomson states that seven land surveying systems were used in present day Ontario (*Men and Meridians,* v. 1, 237).

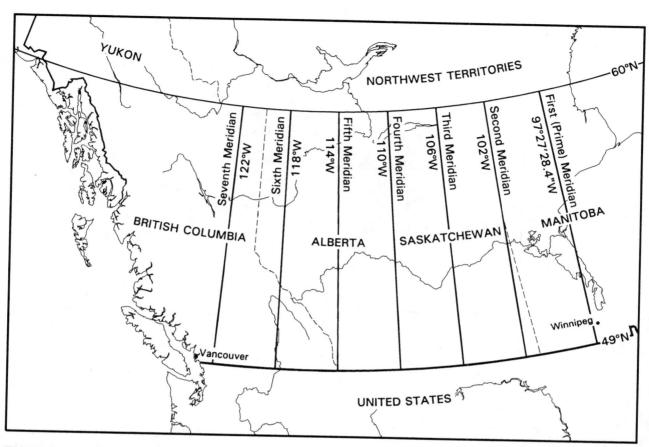

FIGURE 10.24   Principal meridians of the Canada Land Survey System.

west, the Dominion Lands Survey System was established. This system, now called the Canada Land Survey System (CLSS), uses principal meridians and base lines, townships, ranges, sections, and subdivisions of sections. It is basically the same as the USPLS pattern. The measurements of these features are the same as in the USPLS, although serious consideration was given to making the townships larger. In 1869, for example, a recommendation was made that townships contain 64 sections, each containing 800 acres, plus 40 acres for roads. The system extends from the eastern boundary of Manitoba to the Pacific Coast. Within its area of coverage, however, already occupied and surveyed lands are usually omitted from the new system.

In Canada, the survey system that was finally adopted provides a more organized, overall framework than is the case in the United States. The first

element of the CLSS is a pattern of regularly-spaced principal meridians. This contrasts with the heterogeneous scattering of principal meridians used in the USPLS. The initial principal meridian, called the First, or Prime Meridian, is located approximately 15 miles west of Winnipeg, Manitoba, along 97° 27′ 28.41″ W. A round-numbered meridian, such as 98° W, would have been simpler. However, the historical sequence of events led to the adoption of an already surveyed meridian. Other principal meridians were established with a regular, four-degree spacing (figure 10.24). In addition, there is an irregular meridian called the Coast Meridian. This meridian is located near Vancouver, British Columbia along 122° 45′ 39.6″ W.

Another departure from the USPLS style is that only one base line is used. This base line is 49° N, the parallel that defines much of the Canada-U.S. boundary.

(a)   (b)

FIGURE 10.25 (*a*) Convergence of meridians without correction. (*b*) Correction lines, as used in CLSS, to compensate for convergence.

For this reason, there are no ranges with "south" designations. Additional standard parallels are established at regular intervals to correct for the convergence of the meridians (figure 10.25). At these parallels, the north-south dividing lines jog to compensate for the convergence of the meridians.

The numbering of ranges also deviates from the USPLS pattern. Starting with the Principal Meridian, ranges are numbered in sequence to the west, until the next initial meridian is reached. This pattern is repeated over the span of each initial meridian. Therefore, to the west of the First Meridian, there are no ranges with "east" designations. The opposite

holds true to the east of the First Meridian, where ranges are numbered in sequence to the east, until the eastern boundary of Manitoba is reached.

The final differences from the USPLS involve the numbering sequence and the subdivision of the sections. In the CLSS, the numbering of the 640-acre sections zigzags from the southeast corner of each township (figure 10.26), instead of from the northeast corner as in U.S. Sections are sometimes divided into 160-acre quarter-sections, as in the USPLS, but may be divided into legal subdivisions, instead. When they are used, there are sixteen 40-acre **legal subdivisions** in a section, numbered as shown in figure 10.26. The legal subdivisions are the equivalent of quarter-quarter sections in the USPLS. Finally, legal subdivisions are infrequently subdivided into 10-acre quarters.

There are many variations on the general plan outlined above because of the special circumstances or history of particular locales. It is not possible to describe these variations here, but they are explained in the publication, *Understanding Western Canada's Dominion Land Survey System,* which is listed in the "Suggested Readings."

Cultural Influences

The existence of the rectangular survey system has had a significant influence on the cultural landscape of the western United States and Canada. Most of the world was settled without a preexisting land-ownership system. For that reason, the size and arrangement of property ownerships, the alignment of roads and railroads, the boundaries of political jurisdictions, and the alignment of similar cultural features in such areas has a relatively random appearance. The appearance of such areas is more attuned to the relatively free-form alignments of the physical landscape than to the artificial rectilinear arrangements of a man-made system. This difference in appearance is readily recognized by anyone who has traveled to different portions of the country, especially by air. The rectilinear patterns of the west and the "natural" patterns of the east are in distinct contrast with one another (figure 10.27).

FIGURE 10.26   Standard subdivision of a township in the Canada Land Survey System.

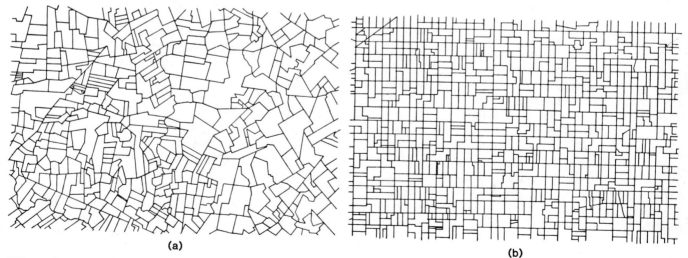

(a)

(b)

FIGURE 10.27   Contrasting land-survey patterns of physically similar areas in Ohio. The irregular boundaries of the area of unsystematic survey (*a*) contrast sharply with the rectilinear pattern that developed under the influence of the U.S. Public Land Survey (*b*).

From Norman J. W. Thrower, *Original Survey and Land Subdivision* (Chicago: Published for the Association of American Geographers by Rand McNally and Company, 1966). Reprinted by permission of the Association of American Geographers.

The effects of land subdivision on the landscape are long lasting and pervasive. We can, for example, see traces of the Roman method of land division, called "centuriation," in the landscape of rural central Italy. There is, even today, a "persistent orthogonal layout of roads, fences, and irrigation canals and even in the orientation of houses and barns" that has persisted for some two thousand years.[9]

Although not easily documented, direct influences on human activities of these differences in cultural landscapes certainly exist. The influences are as subtle as in the use of a phrase such as "plowing the south forty," which indicates the pervasiveness of the system. Such a phrase would have no meaning in much of the world, but it is easily understood by farm dwellers in areas settled under the influence of the USPLS or CLSS.[10]

Summary

The locational systems commonly used to describe locations on the earth's surface include latitude and longitude, the World Geographic Reference System (GEOREF), the Universal Transverse Mercator (UTM) and Universal Polar Stereographic (UPS) systems, and State Plane Coordinates (SPC). Other systems, including metes-and-bounds surveys and the U.S. Public Land Survey (USPLS), are used to record land-ownership information.

Positions on the latitude and longitude graticule are relatively easily determined by interpolation. The main requirement is to keep in mind the division of the circle into 360 degrees, each containing 60 minutes that are further divided into 60 seconds.

The World Geographic Reference System (GEOREF) uses 15-degree-wide north-south and east-west bands. Each quadrangle formed by the intersection of these bands is uniquely identified by a pair of letters. The quadrangles are each subdivided into 1-degree quadrangles, identified by a second pair of letters. Thus, four letters allow the full identification of any 1-degree quadrangle in the world. Closer identification of locations is provided by subdividing each 1-degree quadrangle into 1-minute quadrangles. These are identified by a four-digit number and can be further subdivided into decimal parts, if necessary.

Simple reference grids that do not tie into any overall locational system are commonly encountered in atlases and on street maps. More important grid systems, such as the UTM system and its companion UPS system, or the SPC system, designate locations within a large region.

The UTM system extends between 80° south and 84° north, and the UPS system covers the polar caps. The UTM system involves sixty north-south zones, each 6 degrees wide. Two false origins are established in each zone: one for the Northern Hemisphere and the other for the Southern Hemisphere. A square locational grid, measured in meters, is extended north and east from each origin, so that any point within each zone has a unique coordinate. A similar grid is used in the UPS system. The full UTM or UPS coordinates of a location contain its easting and northing, the hemisphere, and the zone number.

The U.S. Military Grid Reference System is a modification of the civilian UTM and UPS systems. The area covered by the UTM system is subdivided into grid zones that are generally 6 degrees east-west by 8 degrees north-south. Each grid zone is identified by a column number and a row letter and is subdivided into 100,000-meter squares, each of which has a two-letter identifier. Locations within each 100,000-meter square are given as coordinate distances, in meters, from the square's southwest corner. A full grid reference consists of the grid zone designation, the 100,000-meter-square identification, and the grid coordinates, written to the desired level of accuracy.

The SPCS system is a rectangular coordinate system that is individually applied to each state in the United States, with the larger states divided into zones. It is designed so that it is unnecessary to take the earth's curvature into account. The amount of error thus introduced is usually acceptable for the small areas involved in local surveys. In this system, a false origin is established for each zone, and location coordinates are measured east and north from it, in feet. A full SPC location designation consists of the easting, northing, name of the state, and designation of the zone (such as north, south, east, west, or central).

[9]Samuel Y. Edgerton, Jr., "From Mental Matrix to *Mappamundi* to Christian Empire," in *Art and Cartography: Six Historical Essays*, ed. David Woodward (Chicago and London: University of Chicago Press, 1987), 21.

[10]For more extensive examples of cultural influences, see the books by Norman J. W. Thrower and John F. Rooney, Jr., Wilbur Zelinsky, and Dean R. Louder, listed in the "Suggested Readings" at the end of the chapter.

Land partitions are based on either unsystematic or systematic subdivision. The method used to describe unplanned land ownerships is metes-and-bounds surveying. In this system, the direction (bearing) and length of each portion of the boundary line of the property is recorded in sequence, as though one were walking around its perimeter.

The predominant type of systematic subdivision in the United States is the USPLS system. In this system, an initial point is established, by astronomical observations, for each of thirty-four regions. A north-south principal meridian is then established, and an east-west baseline is set at right angles to it, both passing through the initial point. Six-mile-wide east-west rows (townships) are established next, as are similar north-south columns (ranges). The intersection of the townships and ranges creates a pattern of squares, also called townships. Townships are subdivided into thirty-six 1-square-mile (640 acre) sections. The sections are numbered in alternating rows, beginning at the northeast corner of the township, and may be subdivided into halves, quarters, quarter-quarters, and lots. Detailed maps of these USPLS land ownerships are called township plats.

SUGGESTED READINGS

Department of the Army. *Grids and Grid References*. TM5–241–1. Washington, D.C.: Headquarters, Department of the Army.

———. *Universal Transverse Mercator Grid*. TM5–241–8. Washington, D.C.: Headquarters, Department of the Army, April 1973.

Department of Energy, Mines and Resources. *The Universal Transverse Mercator Grid: As Applied to National Topographic System Maps of Canada*. Ottawa, Ont.: Department of Energy, Mines and Resources, 1969.

McKercher, Robert B., and Bertram Wolfe. *Understanding Western Canada's Dominion Land Survey System*. Saskatoon, Saskatchewan: University of Saskatchewan, Division of Extension and Community Relations, 1986.

Rooney, John F., Jr., Wilbur Zelinsky, and Dean R. Louder, eds. *This Remarkable Continent: An Atlas of the United States and Canadian Society and Cultures*. College Station, Tex.: Texas A & M University Press, for the Society for the North American Cultural Survey, 1982.

Sebert, L. M. "The Land Surveys of Ontario, 1750–1980." *Cartographica:* 17, 3 (1980), 65–106.

Stewart, Lowell O. *Public Land Surveys*. New York: Arno Press, 1979.

Thomson, Don W. *Men and Meridians: The History of Surveying and Mapping in Canada:* Vol. I, Prior to 1867. Ottawa: Queen's Printer and Controller of Stationery, 1966; Vol. II, 1867 to 1917. Ottawa: Information Canada, 1967; Vol. III, 1917–1947. Ottawa: Information Canada, 1969.

Thrower, Norman J. W. *Original Land Survey and Land Subdivision*. Chicago: Rand McNally, for The Association of American Geographers, Monograph 4, 1966. (Compares patterns of cultural features, such as land-ownership units; administrative districts, such as counties and school districts; and transportation facilities in two areas of Ohio: one settled under the influence of the USPLS and the other not.)

White, C. Albert. *A History of the Rectangular Survey System*. Washington, D.C.: U.S. Department of the Interior, Bureau of Land Management, 1983.

11

Characteristics of Map Features: Shape and Point Patterns

The features shown on maps often have distinctive characteristics, particularly of shape, pattern, and arrangement. Indeed, maps are frequently used as a tool for the discovery of such characteristics. Once the characteristics are identified, various methods can be applied to measure the spatial patterns, to generate hypotheses about their origins, and, ultimately, to test the hypotheses and draw conclusions regarding their validity. This chapter presents some common methods by which shape and pattern are measured.

SHAPE

A feature displayed on a map, whether it is a physical object, a political unit, or the market area of a manufacturer, is often described in terms of its *shape*.

Subjective Description

Some regions or features on maps can be described in terms of regular, geometric shapes, such as squares, circles, ovals, triangles, and octagons. The shortcomings of these descriptors quickly become apparent, however, when irregular shapes need to be described. In these cases, more exotic terminology, such as the "bootlike" shape of Italy, may be necessary. Professional map analysts often resort to similar subjective shape descriptions. They have compared various atolls, for example, to a "stretched-out diamond," a "heron," or a "headless goose without legs."[1] Shape

descriptions of this type are vaguely defined and undoubtedly mean different things to different observers. Also, this descriptive approach does not provide index numbers that an observer can consistently assign. Such index numbers would objectively distinguish one shape from another and would allow, for example, sorting into groups of similar shapes or analyzing the origins of particular shapes.

Numerical Indices

Investigators in many fields have developed numerical indices for the more scientific description of shape. Boyce and Clark reviewed examples of geographical approaches to the description of urban form, trade areas, political areas, and physical features, and of shape measures in other disciplines, dating from the 1920s.[2] They found that most of the approaches in their review were descriptive, except in physical geography, the biological sciences, and mineralogy, where they found various methods of more objective measurement. The difficulty with all of these methods was their ambiguity. Areas with different shapes could generate identical index values. In addition, these methods did not possess the other desirable characteristics described in the next section.

Desired Characteristics of a Shape Index

One requisite of a satisfactory shape index is that all investigators obtain the same value when applying the index to the same task. The methodology should

---

[1]Quoted in D R. Stoddart, "The Shape of Atolls," *Marine Geology* 3, no. 5 (1965): 370.

[2]Ronald R. Boyce and W. A. V. Clark, "The Concept of Shape in Geography," *The Geographical Review* 54 (1964): 561–72.

ensure that the outcome is not affected by scale, starting location, orientation, or translation. A second requisite is that the index provide sufficient information to permit the regeneration of the original shape. We will now consider each of these requirements in more detail.

A satisfactory shape index yields the same value for a city, for example, whether the outline is plotted on a scale of 1:100,000 or on a scale of 1:250,000. This assumes that the amount of detail in the outline remains the same at both scales so that we are truly measuring the *same* shape. Although the amount of generalization of two maps at such different scales is likely to vary considerably, this requirement refers to the result that would be obtained if the same image were simply enlarged or reduced without changing the amount of generalization. This is equivalent to saying that the same value would be obtained when comparing shapes of different sizes. A large island that has the same outline as a small island, for example, should have the same shape-index value.

When tracing the outline of a shape, you are not likely to find a preordained starting point on its perimeter. On a square, for example, the northeast corner is as logical a starting point as the southwest corner, either of the other two corners, or, for that matter, any other point, such as the middle of one of the sides. A satisfactory shape measure, then, should yield the same value, regardless of what starting point is selected.

When the shapes of two regions on a map are so similar that a tracing of one of them could be placed over the other and would match it perfectly, the shapes can be said to be identical, even if one is "upside down" on the map, as compared to the other—in other words, is in a different orientation. Similarly, if the position of the tracing is changed (translated), the shape of the outline is obviously not affected. A satisfactory shape index, then, should yield the same result for two identical, but differently oriented or translated, shapes.

A shape index should also contain enough information so a person familiar with its characteristics could *regenerate* the original shape using only the index as a basis. One of the requirements for regeneration is that there be a one-to-one correspondence between shapes and indices. This means that each shape is represented by a unique index value, and each index value describes only one shape.

Specific Measures

Unfortunately, it is not an easy task (in fact, as we shall see, it may very well be impossible) to devise a measure that provides clear and unambiguous definitions of shapes. This section describes some of the existing measures used to define shapes and considers their strengths and weaknesses.

Miller's measure. One common approach to the measurement of shape is to establish a specific reference figure and to determine how much the figure being measured differs from it. A frequently used reference figure is the circle, because the circle is the most *compact* two-dimensional shape. That is, any other figure of equal area to the circle has a greater perimeter than the circle. A measure of this type is **Miller's measure**, which was developed for the study of the shape of drainage basins.

In Miller's measure, the shape of the drainage basin (C) is the ratio between the area of basin (A_b) and the area of a circle with the same perimeter (A_c)—that is, $C = A_b/A_c$. With this approach, the basin shape indices range from almost 0, in the case of a very elongated basin, to 1, in the case of a perfectly circular basin (figure 11.1a). While this range in values provides a very convenient index, Miller's measure (and similar methods based on the same general idea) has a major problem. The problem is that the values used in the calculation of the index are based on the areas and perimeters of the two different figures and *not* their shape. The result is that many *different* shapes can yield the same index value (figure 11.1b).

Bunge's measure. William Bunge suggested a measure of shape that does not depend upon area. **Bunge's measure** is based on a set of distance measurements taken between systematically placed vertices on the perimeters of the shapes to be studied. In Bunge's example application, the outlines of ninety-seven Mexican communities were measured.

The same number of vertices must be used for all of the shapes involved in a particular study. If the shapes are generally very irregular, a closer spacing is required than if the shapes are uncomplicated. The shapes being measured may be of different sizes, and the influence of size (or scale) is excluded from the measure by giving a value of 1 to the standard distance established between the vertices for each shape. This same distance is then used for all of the measurements of that particular shape.

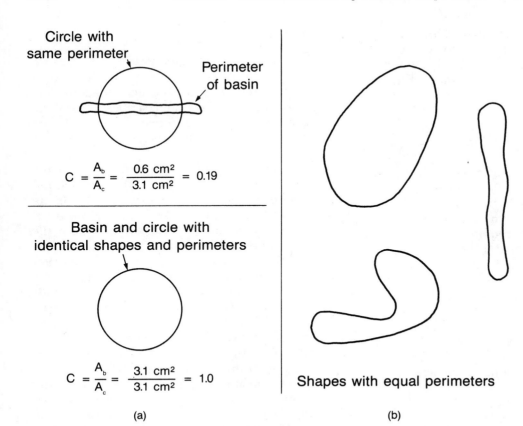

Circle with same perimeter

Perimeter of basin

$$C = \frac{A_b}{A_c} = \frac{0.6\ cm^2}{3.1\ cm^2} = 0.19$$

Basin and circle with identical shapes and perimeters

$$C = \frac{A_b}{A_c} = \frac{3.1\ cm^2}{3.1\ cm^2} = 1.0$$

(a)

Shapes with equal perimeters

(b)

FIGURE 11.1   Characteristics of shape—Miller's measure. (*a*) Index values range from almost 0, in the case of a very elongated shape, to 1, in the case of a perfectly circular shape. (*b*) Various shapes can have equal perimeters and, therefore, equal index values.

After the vertices and the standard distances are established (figure 11.2a), the shortest straight-line distances between different pairs of vertices are measured for each shape. A "lagging," or skipping, technique is used for this purpose. A starting vertex is selected (any vertex may be used), and measurements are taken in one direction (either clockwise or counterclockwise) around the outline. The first distance measured is between the starting vertex and its "lag-1" neighbor, which means that the starting vertex's immediate neighbor is skipped (figure 11.2b). The distance is recorded in the standard units previously established. Similar lag-1 measurements are then taken from the vertex next to the original starting vertex. This process is repeated until all of the vertices have served as starting points. The values thus obtained are added to obtain the lag-1 measure.

The distances between each vertex and its lag-2 neighbor are taken next (figure 11.2c) and added, and the process is continued until all of the unique lagged values (lag-2, lag-3, and so on) have been obtained.[3] Finally, each of the lag measures is squared, and these values are summed, to create lag-1², lag-2², lag-3² measures, and so on.

[3]The total number of "laggings" required depends on the number of vertices used because only unique results are desired. In the case of eight vertices, for example, the maximum number of lags required is three, whereas sixteen vertices require seven lags, and so on.

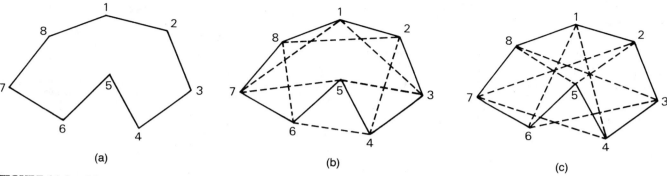

FIGURE 11.2   Distance measurements for Bunge's measure. (*a*) Numbered vertices of eight-sided polygon. (*b*) Distance between starting vertex and "lag-1" neighbors. (*c*) Distance between vertex and "lag-2" neighbors.

The value of Bunge's measure is that the set of all of the values derived for each shape is unique for that shape. This means that the shapes can be grouped on the basis of similar sets of values, as Bunge did with the Mexican communities. There are, however, a number of problems with the technique. The results obtained, for example, depend on the number of vertices chosen. This is an arbitrary number, governed by the investigator's judgment regarding how many line segments are needed to adequately describe a given group of shapes. Similarly, the locations of the vertices are arbitrary. They depend on the starting location selected by the investigator, as well as the standard distance between vertices. Finally, significant changes of direction in the outline may or may not be identified as the location of vertices. Again, this depends on the selected location of the starting vertex and the chosen standard distance between vertices. The existence of all these variables means that there is likely to be a lack of consistency from study to study in some of the choices made. As a result, different values may be obtained for the same shape. Also, there is no way that the values obtained can be used to regenerate the original shape.

Boyce-Clark radial shape index.   The Boyce-Clark radial shape index is based on the lengths of radials extending outward from a node at the center of the shape.[4] The center node is located first, usually

[4]Boyce and Clark, "The Concept of Shape in Geography," 561–72.

at the shape's center of gravity. A set of equally spaced radials is then drawn outward from the center node to the perimeter of the shape (figure 11.3). The length of each of these radials is measured in any convenient units. Then, these lengths are added to obtain the total length of all of the radials. The percentage of the total that each radial represents is then computed, and the absolute value of the difference between that value and the percentage that each radial would represent if the shape were a circle is obtained. If there are eight radials, for example, each radial in the circle represents 12.5 percent of the total length. The index value for the shape is obtained by totaling the absolute differences between the actual and the expected percentage values. This procedure is summarized by the following formula:

Boyce-Clark radial shape index = sum of the following values, where i ranges from 1 to n
$$|[(r_i / \text{sum of } r_i, i = 1 \text{ to } n) \times 100] - (100/n)|$$

The index values that result from using this method range from 0 to 175, with 0 representing a perfect circle and 175 the value that would presumably be associated with a straight line (figure 11.4). Other shapes have values that lie somewhere between. A square has an index of 12, a star 25, a specific rectangle 28, and so on.

The Boyce-Clark radial shape index suffers from several shortcomings. It does not, for example, have a one-to-one correspondence between its value and

Radial Shape Index

$$\sum_i^n \left| \left(\frac{r_i}{\sum_1^n} \times 100 - \frac{100}{n} \right) \right|$$

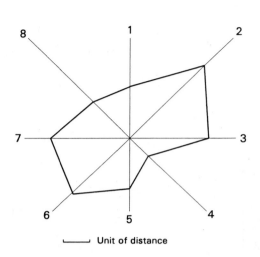

Radial No. (r)	Length (r_i)	Actual % of Total $\left(\frac{r_i}{\sum_i^n} \times 100 \right)$	Theoretical % of Total $\left(\frac{100}{n} \right)$	Absolute Difference in % $\left(\left| \left(\frac{r_i}{\sum_i^n} \times 100 - \frac{100}{n} \right) \right| \right)$
1	2.0	10.0	12.5	2.5
2	4.0	20.0	12.5	7.5
3	3.0	15.0	12.5	2.5
4	1.0	5.0	12.5	7.5
5	2.0	10.0	12.5	2.5
6	3.0	15.0	12.5	2.5
7	3.0	15.0	12.5	2.5
n = 8	2.0	10.0	12.5	2.5
$\sum_i^n = 20$				Radial Shape Index = 30.0

FIGURE 11.3   Setup for determining Boyce-Clark radial shape index.

FIGURE 11.4   Index values for Boyce-Clark radial shape index range from 0 to 175.

Modified from Ronald R. Boyce and W. A. V. Clark, "The Concept of Shape in Geography," *The Geographical Review* 54 (1964): 561–72. Reprinted by permission of The American Geographical Society.

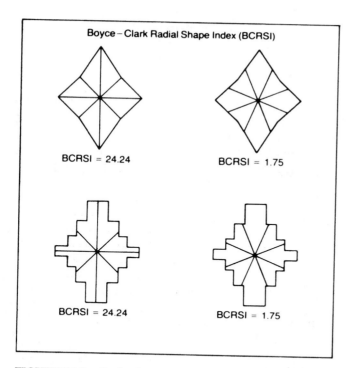

FIGURE 11.5 Lack of one-to-one correspondence between value of Boyce-Clark radial shape index and the shape of the figure. Different shapes can have the same index value, and the same shape can have different index values, depending on the method of measurement.

From Daniel A. Griffith, Michael P. O'Neill, Wende A. O'Neill, Lloyd A. Leifer, and Rodric B. Mooney, "Shape Indices: Useful Measures or Red Herrings?" *The Professional Geographer* 38, no. 3 (August 1986): 263–70. Reprinted by permission.

the shape of the figure (figure 11.5). This means that different shapes can have the same index value. Also, changes in the orientation of the radii in relation to the orientation of the figure result in different index values for the same shape. Changes in the number of radii used also result in different index values for the same figure, as do changes in the location of the center node. Finally, the index value does not permit regeneration of the original shape.

Advanced techniques. Other approaches to the measurement of shape have been developed, including a technique called Fourier analysis. The mathematics involved in the use of such methods goes considerably beyond the scope of this book. The complex measure resulting from Fourier analysis permits regeneration of the original shape, but even it does not have a one-to-one correspondence between the shape and the index values.

Comment on Shape Indices

It has been suggested that "the growing number of shape indices reflects the inability of any one measure to capture all elements of a given characteristic surface configuration. If one accepts this assessment, shape indices may represent a 'red herring' in geographic research."[5] If after reading the preceding discussion, you have the feeling that the shape measures described are not particularly satisfactory, you can at least be assured that your feeling is shared by others.

POINT PATTERNS

Point symbols may be thought of as individual indications of the locations at which a particular type of feature is found. The features represented range from man-made phenomena, such as cities, towns, manufacturing plants, stores, or shopping centers, to natural phenomena such as specific plant or animal species. At times, however, it is useful to consider a set of point symbols as a group, rather than as individual points, to see whether or not their distribution exhibits a regularity, or pattern. Although the eye provides a visual suggestion about whether or not a pattern seems to exist, analyzing the distribution of the symbols using a less subjective approach determines whether or not the apparent pattern is real.

A demonstrated order to the arrangement of points may signal that some process is at work to produce the arrangement. Further study may lead to an understanding of what this process is and how it operates. You may notice, for example, that the cities in a region seem to be rather uniformly distributed. Application of an analytic test may show that there is, indeed, a measurable order to their distribution, which may help in the development of a theory about

[5]Daniel A. Griffith, Michael P. O'Neill, Wende A. O'Neill, Lloyd A. Leifer, and Rodric G. Mooney, "Shape Indices: Useful Measures or Red Herrings?" *The Professional Geographer* 38, no. 3 (August 1986): 263–70.

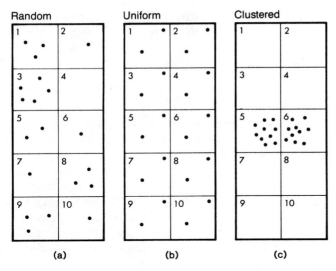

FIGURE 11.6   Standard types of point distributions.
(*a*) Random (*b*) Uniform (*c*) Clustered

why the pattern exists. One such theory, called central place theory, attempts to describe and explain just such an ordering process and is discussed in almost any economic geography textbook.

Types of Distributions

Theoretically, point distributions can assume three general types of patterns: random, uniform, and clustered. Many of the measures used to describe distributions are based on a comparison of the actual pattern of points to a pattern that would be developed randomly. A **random pattern** on a plane (such as a map surface) satisfies two conditions (figure 11.6a). First, any point is equally likely to occur at any location, and, second, the position of any point is not affected by the position of any other point. In such a pattern, then, there is no apparent ordering of the distribution. Instead, some points are clustered close to their neighbors, some are more remote from other points, and some are spaced at intermediate distances from one another. Completely **uniform patterns**, on the other hand, are distinguished by every point being as far from all of its neighbors as possible (figure 11.6b). Finally, in a **clustered pattern**, many points are concentrated close together, and there are large areas that contain very few, if any, points (figure 11.6c).

Point-distribution patterns are classified by comparing the specific pattern being tested to the basic patterns just discussed. Two techniques that take this approach are introduced here—quadrat analysis and nearest-neighbor analysis. Both of these approaches have shortcomings, especially in the simple form presented here, but they provide useful examples of analysis techniques. More advanced methods, or refinement of the methods discussed here, may be pursued through the study of some of the "Suggested Readings" at the end of the chapter.

Quadrat Analysis

Quadrat analysis is based on a measure derived from data obtained after a uniform grid network is drawn over a map of the distribution of interest. The openings in this grid, which are usually, but not necessarily, square, are called quadrats. The frequency count, which is the number of points occurring within each quadrat, is recorded first. These data are then used to compute a measure called the **variance**. The variance compares the number of points in *each* grid cell with the average number of points over *all* of the cells. The greater the difference between the value for a given cell and the average, the greater its effect on the variance.[6] Finally, the variance of the distribution being tested is compared to the characteristics of a distribution that consists of a random scatter of the same number of points over the same area. This comparison is done by using the variance-mean ratio because research has demonstrated that the mean and variance of a random distribution are equal.

The simple example that follows shows the basic application of quadrat analysis, based on a test of the "random" map in figure 11.6a.[7] To begin the process of computing the variance-mean ratio, an arbitrary 2-by-5-square grid is superimposed on the map (the importance of deciding on the appropriate number and size of quadrats is discussed later). The number of points contained in each of the resulting ten quadrats is determined and the values entered in column

[6]Additional information about the variance may be found in any introductory statistics textbook, but, for our purposes, we will simply accept it as an appropriate measure.

[7]A random process was actually used to generate this map, but because of the small number of points involved, the results must be considered to only approximate a random distribution.

TABLE 11.1 Calculation of Variance-Mean Ratio for "Random" Distribution

(1) QUADRAT NUMBER	(2) x (NUMBER OF POINTS PER QUADRAT)	(3) x^2
1	3	9
2	1	1
3	5	25
4	0	0
5	2	4
6	1	1
7	1	1
8	3	9
9	3	9
10	1	1
	$\Sigma x = 20$	$\Sigma x^2 = 60$
	$(\Sigma x)^2 = 400$	

N = number of quadrats = 10

$$\text{Variance} = \frac{\Sigma x^2 - [(\Sigma x)^2/N]}{N-1}$$

$$= \frac{60 - (400/10)}{10-1} = \frac{20}{9} = 2.22$$

$$\text{Mean} = \frac{\Sigma x}{N} = \frac{20}{10} = 2$$

$$\text{Variance-mean ratio} = \frac{\text{variance}}{\text{mean}} = \frac{2.22}{2} = 1.11$$

TABLE 11.2 Calculation of Variance-Mean Ratio for "Uniform" Distribution

(1) QUADRAT NUMBER	(2) x (NUMBER OF POINTS PER QUADRAT)	(3) x^2
1	2	4
2	2	4
3	2	4
4	2	4
5	2	4
6	2	4
7	2	4
8	2	4
9	2	4
10	2	4
	$\Sigma x = 20$	$\Sigma x^2 = 40$
	$(\Sigma x)^2 = 400$	

N = number of quadrats = 10

$$\text{Variance} = \frac{\Sigma x^2 - [(\Sigma x)^2/N]}{N-1}$$

$$= \frac{40 - (400/10)}{10-1} = \frac{0}{9} = 0.0$$

$$\text{Mean} = \frac{\Sigma x}{N} = \frac{20}{10} = 2$$

$$\text{Variance-mean ratio} = \frac{\text{variance}}{\text{mean}} = \frac{0.0}{2} = 0.0$$

2 of table 11.1. The individual values in column 2 are totaled to give the sum of x, and this value is squared (sum of x)^2. Each of the x values is then squared, and the results are entered in column 3; the total of column 3 provides the (sum of x^2) value.

The formula shown in table 11.1 allows the computation of the variance—in this case, 2.22. The next step is to interpret the meaning of this value. As mentioned previously, in a random distribution the variance and mean number of points per quadrat are the same, which means, of course, that the ratio between them is 1. In the example shown in table 11.1, the variance-mean ratio is 1.11, which is very close to 1.0, so the distribution is, indeed, likely a random one. (If required, the statistical significance of the ratio may be determined with appropriate tests.)

Because the variance-mean ratio for a random distribution is 1, any other ratio indicates that the distribution being tested is *not* random. The calculation of the variance-mean ratio for two additional distributions—one uniform (figure 11.6b and table 11.2) and the other clustered (figure 11.6c and table 11.3)—shows that this is a correct assumption. Furthermore, the nature of the results obtained when the patterns exhibit uniformity or clustering assists in explaining the manner in which different values are interpreted.

Quadrat size and orientation. The size of the quadrats, as well as their orientation, affects the outcome of the quadrat method. If the quadrats are too small, for example, they may each contain only one or two points. This means that any clusters that exist

TABLE 11.3 Calculation of Variance-Mean Ratio for "Clustered" Distribution

(1) QUADRAT NUMBER	(2) x (NUMBER OF POINTS PER QUADRAT)	(3) x^2
1	0	0
2	0	0
3	0	0
4	0	0
5	10	100
6	10	100
7	0	0
8	0	0
9	0	0
10	0	0
	$\Sigma x = 20$	$\Sigma x^2 = 200$
	$(\Sigma x)^2 = 400$	

N = number of quadrats = 10

$$\text{Variance} = \frac{\Sigma x^2 - [(\Sigma x)^2/N]}{N - 1}$$

$$= \frac{200 - (400/10)}{10 - 1} = \frac{160}{9} = 17.78$$

$$\text{Mean} = \frac{\Sigma x}{N} = \frac{20}{10} = 2$$

$$\text{Variance-mean ratio} = \frac{\text{variance}}{\text{mean}} = \frac{17.78}{2} = 8.89$$

will escape detection because no quadrats will have large numbers of points. On the other hand, if the quadrats are too large, a single quadrat may contain all, or almost all, of the points, thus giving the appearance that a cluster exists even if it does not. One recommendation for deciding on an appropriate quadrat size—one that will not be likely to veer toward one or another of these extremes—is to make each quadrat approximately twice the size of the mean area per point.[8] An alternative is to test several quadrat

[8]Based on P. Greig-Smith, *Quantitative Plant Ecology*, 2d ed. (London: Butterworths, 1964).

sizes, observing the effect of each test on the results obtained. Similar tests using different quadrat orientations may also be useful because shifting the grid, or placing it at different angles to the distribution, introduces some variation into the results.[9]

Weaknesses of quadrat analysis. In addition to the quadrat-size and orientation problems just discussed, quadrat analysis has some other weaknesses. One weakness is actually a matter of terminology. Although the technique is considered a method for measuring pattern, it is actually more appropriately described as a method for measuring dispersion. This is because it is based on considerations of the density of points and not of their arrangement in relation to one another. Another problem is that it has been shown that different probability models can yield the same values, casting some doubt on the interpretation of the results. Finally, quadrat analysis results in a single measure for the entire distribution, so any variations *within* the region are not recognized. This problem can only be dealt with by subdividing the region, which would probably be done on the basis of a visual inspection indicating that variation in pattern seems to exist.

Nearest-Neighbor Analysis

A second method of analyzing distributions of point symbols is the **nearest-neighbor technique**. This method, unlike quadrat analysis, uses distances between points as its basis. Specifically, the mean of the distance observed between each point and its nearest neighbor is compared with the expected mean distance that would occur if the distribution were random. The underlying theme of testing against a random distribution occurs here, just as in quadrat analysis, because a random pattern is the outcome that would normally be expected if no ordering process was at work. In other words, something has likely caused the distribution pattern to deviate from a

[9]See Arthur Getis and Barry N. Boots, *Models of Spatial Processes: An Approach to the Study of Point, Line, and Area Patterns* (New York: Cambridge University Press, 1978), 24–25, for more discussion of these concerns.

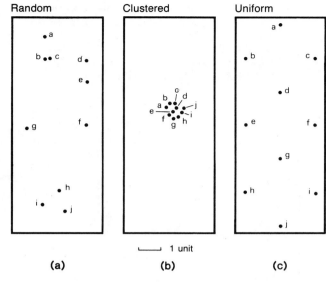

FIGURE 11.7   Source maps for calculation of nearest-neighbor statistic. (*a*) Random (*b*) Clustered (*c*) Uniform

TABLE 11.4   Calculation of Nearest-Neighbor Statistic for "Random" Distribution

(1) POINT	(2) NEAREST NEIGHBOR	(3) DISTANCE TO NEAREST NEIGHBOR (r)
a	b	1
b	c	0.1
c	b	0.1
d	e	1
e	d	1
f	e	2
g	f	2.7
h	j	1
i	j	1
j	i	1
		$\Sigma r = 10.9$

Number of points = n = 10

$$\bar{r} = \frac{\Sigma r}{n} = \frac{10.9}{10} = 1.09$$

Area of region = 5 × 10 = 50 sq. units

$$\text{Density} = d = \frac{n}{\text{area}} = \frac{10}{50} = 0.2$$

$$\text{Expected mean spacing} = \bar{r}(e) = \frac{0.5}{\sqrt{d}}$$

$$= \frac{0.5}{\sqrt{0.2}} = \frac{0.5}{0.447} = 1.12$$

$$\text{Nearest-neighbor statistic} = R = \frac{\bar{r}}{\bar{r}(e)} = \frac{1.09}{1.12} = 0.97$$

random arrangement if either a clustered or a uniform arrangement is found, and further investigation may reveal the cause.

Once again, three distinctly different distribution patterns are analyzed here to demonstrate how the nearest-neighbor statistic is calculated and to show the interpretation of the range of values that can result (figure 11.7). In the case of the random pattern, which is analyzed first, the nearest neighbor of each point in the distribution is determined, as shown in column 2 of table 11.4. The distance (r) from each point to its nearest neighbor is then recorded in column 3. Distances may be measured in any convenient units, although kilometers, meters, or similar units are usually selected, and the graphic scale of the map is used. In any case, the same units must be used throughout the process, including the calculation of density described in table 11.4. The average spacing ($\bar{r}$) between the nearest neighbors is obtained by adding all of the individual spacing values (sum of r) and dividing the total by the number of points (n) in the distribution.

The *expected average spacing* [$\bar{r}(e)$] is then calculated. This calculation is based on the spacing of points that would occur in a random distribution containing the same number of points scattered over the

same area. In general, the value of $\bar{r}(e)$ is $0.5/\sqrt{d}$, where d is the density of points over the study area (in other words, the number of points per unit area). In this case, there are 10 points in an area of 50 square units, so $\bar{r}(e)$ is 1.12.

Finally, the nearest-neighbor statistic (R) is calculated by dividing the actual by the expected average distances [$\bar{r}/\bar{r}(e)$]. If the two values are identical, as they obviously are if the distribution being tested is also random, R has a value of 1. In this case, the value of R is 0.97, which is very near to 1, so the distribution very closely approximates a random arrangement.

TABLE 11.5   Calculation of Nearest-Neighbor Statistic for "Clustered" Distribution

(1) POINT	(2) NEAREST NEIGHBOR	(3) DISTANCE TO NEAREST NEIGHBOR (r)
a	b	0.1
b	c	0.1
c	d	0.1
d	e	0.1
e	f	0.1
f	g	0.1
g	h	0.1
h	i	0.1
i	j	0.1
j	i	0.1
		$\Sigma r = 1.0$

Number of points $= n = 10$

$$\bar{r} = \frac{\Sigma r}{n} = \frac{1.0}{10} = 0.1$$

Area of region $= 5 \times 10 = 50$ sq. units

$$\text{Density} = d = \frac{n}{\text{area}} = \frac{10}{50} = 0.2$$

$$\text{Expected mean spacing} = \bar{r}(e) = \frac{0.5}{\sqrt{d}}$$

$$= \frac{0.5}{\sqrt{0.2}} = \frac{0.5}{0.447} = 1.12$$

$$\text{Nearest-neighbor statistic} = R = \frac{\bar{r}}{\bar{r}(e)} = \frac{0.1}{1.12} = 0.09$$

TABLE 11.6   Calculation of Nearest-Neighbor Statistic for "Uniform" Distribution

(1) POINT	(2) NEAREST NEIGHBOR	(3) DISTANCE TO NEAREST NEIGHBOR (r)
a	c	2.2
b	d	2.2
c	d	2.2
d	e	2.2
e	g	2.2
f	g	2.2
g	h	2.2
h	j	2.2
i	j	2.2
j	i	2.2
		$\Sigma r = 22.0$

Number of points $= n = 10$

$$\Sigma r = \frac{\Sigma r}{n} = \frac{22}{10} = 2.2$$

Area of region $= 5 \times 10 = 50$ sq. units

$$\text{Density} = d = \frac{n}{\text{area}} = \frac{10}{50} = 0.2$$

$$\text{Expected mean spacing} = \bar{r}(e) = \frac{0.5}{\sqrt{d}}$$

$$= \frac{0.5}{\sqrt{0.2}} = \frac{0.5}{0.447} = 1.12$$

$$\text{Nearest-neighbor statistic} = R = \frac{\bar{r}}{\bar{r}(e)} = \frac{2.2}{1.12} = 1.96$$

Let us now consider what the R values are for distributions that are not random. If all of the points in the distribution are clustered close together, their $\bar{r}$-value approaches 0, and R also approaches 0, as is shown in table 11.5.

In contrast, if all of the points are dispersed so that they are as far from one another as possible, $\bar{r}$ approaches its maximum value. This tendency is illustrated in table 11.6, which shows the calculation of R for the uniform distribution. R, in this case, is 1.96. It has been shown that the theoretical maximum value of R, which would occur in a completely uniform distribution, approaches 2.1491. In table 11.6, then, the distribution shows a strong tendency toward a uniform pattern. That it is not completely uniform is related to the boundary problems discussed later in this section.

The nearest-neighbor method has some advantages over the quadrat method for analyzing point distributions. First, there is no quadrat-size problem to be concerned with in the nearest-neighbor method, and, second, it takes distances into account.

The principal difficulties with the nearest-neighbor method, on the other hand, are related to determining the limits of the area to be analyzed. If the area in which the points are distributed has a logical or absolute boundary, such as the shoreline of an island, that boundary can be used. If no such logical boundary exists, the boundary must be defined in other ways. The reason for this concern with establishing boundaries is that the value of the measure varies, depending on the density of the distribution, and the density, itself, obviously varies with differences in the size of the study area.

The importance of boundaries is illustrated by two of the previous examples of uniform and clustered distributions. The distances between nearest neighbors in the clustered distribution (table 11.5) are all equal to one another, just as in the uniform pattern (table 11.6). The only difference between the two sets of data is in the absolute values of the distances.[10] This means that if you placed the clustered distribution from table 11.5 inside a smaller region, the nearest-neighbor statistic would indicate a more uniform distribution. (You may wish to try doing this, if it is not obvious to you.) The values obtained from a nearest-neighbor analysis, then, are dependent on the specific area analyzed.

The necessity for setting appropriate study-area boundaries is also apparent in the case where more than one distribution occurs within the analysis area. When this occurs, a nearest-neighbor statistic can be developed for each distribution, and, in addition, one distribution can be said to be more or less uniform, for example, than the other.

If the appropriate boundaries for the study area are not clear from the context of the study, some method is needed to determine them. One method for doing this is to select the extreme points in each direction of the distribution, and to draw the limiting lines through them. In this approach, all of the points are contained within the limits.

Another boundary problem is that the measure may be biased if the nearest-neighbor distance for a point is greater than the distance from that point to the study-area boundary. The reason for this is that there may be a *nearer* neighbor on just the other side of the boundary. This is not encountered if it has been possible to establish a boundary that encloses all the points, as already suggested. In other cases, this may not be possible because the limits of the particular phenomenon being studied extend far beyond the area to be analyzed. Consider, for example, the study of the distribution of grass clumps in a specific field that lies in the middle of a grassland hundreds of hectares in extent. In cases of this type, measurements can be taken to nearest neighbors *whether or not* they are in the study area. When this is done, measurements *from* points outside the study area are not taken.

[10]Such uniformity would seldom be encountered in a clustered distribution. The example was purposely designed to illustrate this problem.

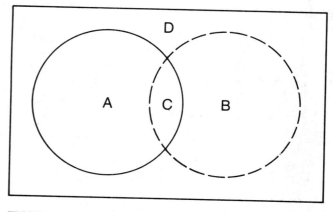

FIGURE 11.8 Composite map of two overlapping distributions.

Other methods of dealing with boundary problems have been developed, but this example at least points out the nature of the problem.

Finally, an *R* value of 1 does not necessarily indicate that the distribution is purely the result of chance because other factors may result in a distribution that has such a characteristic. It is usually safer to say that values toward the extremes (0 and 2.1491) indicate tendencies toward, respectively, uniformity and clustering and, therefore, require some explanation.

Spatial Correspondence of Areal Distributions

Quadrat and nearest-neighbor analysis deal with the analysis of a single distribution. On occasion, however, two (or more) distributions must be compared. Various techniques are designed for that purpose. The coefficient of areal correspondence and the chi-square statistic are discussed here.

Coefficient of areal correspondence. The **coefficient of areal correspondence** is a simple measure of the extent to which two distributions correspond to one another. It might be used, for example, to compare the extent of wheat farming in a region with the area that receives some minimum level of rainfall. The approach is based on a technique called **overlay analysis**. In overlay analysis, the two distributions of interest are mapped at the same scale, and the outline of one is overlaid (superimposed) on the outline of the other (figure 11.8). The regions formed

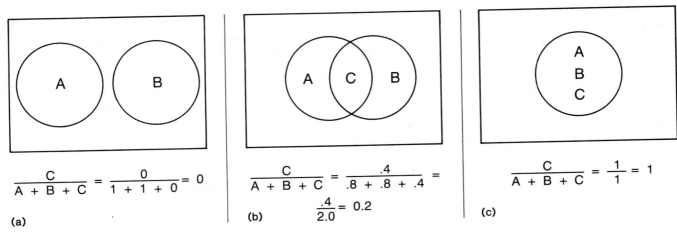

$$\frac{C}{A + B + C} = \frac{0}{1 + 1 + 0} = 0$$

(a)

$$\frac{C}{A + B + C} = \frac{.4}{.8 + .8 + .4} =$$

$$\frac{.4}{2.0} = 0.2$$

(b)

$$\frac{C}{A + B + C} = \frac{1}{1} = 1$$

(c)

FIGURE 11.9   Range of values of coefficient of areal correspondence. (*a*) With no overlap. (*b*) With partial overlap. (*c*) With complete overlap.

on the resulting composite map fall into three different categories: (1) those that fall into only one category (*A* and *B* in figure 11.8); (2) those, if any, where the two categories overlap (*C*); and (3) those that fall outside either category (*D*). The area of each of these regions is measured and the coefficient is computed on the basis of the measurements.

Specifically, the coefficient of areal correspondence is the ratio between the area of the region where the two distributions overlap (*C*) and the total area of the regions covered by the individual distributions and the region of overlap (*A* + *B* + *C*). Region *D*, which falls outside either category, is ignored. The computation takes the following form:

$$\frac{\text{Area of } C}{\text{Area of } A + B + C}$$

The three examples in figure 11.9 show the range of values of this coefficient. Where there is no overlap, the value is 0. At the other extreme, where the two categories completely overlap, the value is 1. In situations where the amount of overlap lies somewhere between the two extremes, the value of the coefficient lies between 0 and 1. Where the three regions are of equal size, for example, the value is 0.33. The value of the coefficient of areal correspondence, then, provides a simple measure of the extent of spatial asso-

ciation between two distributions, but it cannot provide any information about the statistical significance of the relationship.

Chi-square statistic.   If additional data are available, it may be possible to use other measures to indicate the strength of the association between two distributions. For example, to examine further the relationship between wheat yield and precipitation in a region, assume that data are available in the form of two simple maps (both drawn to the same scale). One map shows regions of high and low precipitation, and the other shows regions of high and low wheat yield (figures 11.10a and 11.10b). On visual inspection, it seems that there is some level of correspondence between the two maps, with wheat yield generally higher where there is more precipitation. We can, therefore, reasonably compute a **chi-square statistic** to tell us more about the relationships between the two distributions, which is made clearer by plotting the two distributions on a combined map (figure 11.10c). For simplicity sake, this example is limited to two characteristics of two distributions, but the same technique can be applied to more complex situations.

The analysis process begins with the drawing of a square grid over the map of the combined distributions. The finer the grid, the more precise the measurements (and the greater the amount of work

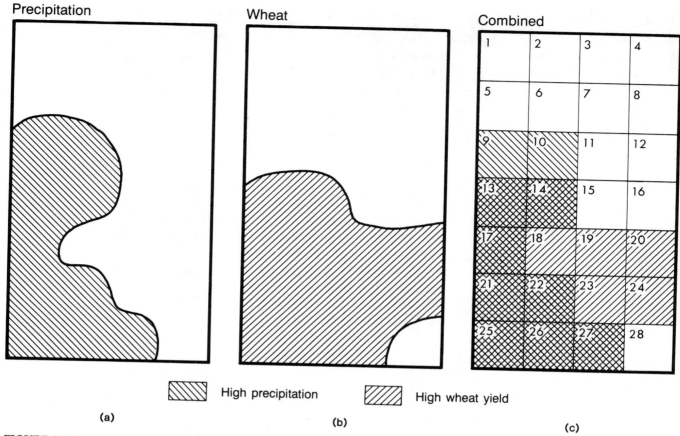

FIGURE 11.10 Relationships between precipitation and wheat yield. (*a*) Regions of high and low precipitation. (*b*) Regions of high and low wheat yield. (*c*) Combined map of the two distributions.

required for the analysis). Two values are then recorded for each quadrat of the grid: one for the precipitation class and one for the wheat production class (table 11.7). One problem with this counting process is that some cells fall on the dividing line between the categories. The usual way of dealing with this is to count the entire cell in the category that covers 50 percent or more of the cell area. The inaccuracy introduced by this procedure is reduced by using a finer-grid mesh.

In this case, four data combinations are possible: low rainfall, low yield; low rainfall, high yield; high

rainfall, low yield; and high rainfall, high yield. The total number of occurrences of each of these combinations is recorded in a **table of observed frequencies** (table 11.8). In this example, we have a simple 2-by-2 table. Its four cells represent the four possible data combinations just mentioned. The column and row totals in the table are obtained by summing across each row and down each column, after the cells have been filled in. The value in the lower-right corner is the sum of either the rows or the columns and equals the total number of cells in the study area.

TABLE 11.7 Tabulation of Quadrat Characteristics

(1) QUADRAT	(2) RAINFALL CATEGORY	(3) WHEAT YIELD CATEGORY
1	L	L
2	L	L
3	L	L
4	L	L
5	L	L
6	L	L
7	L	L
8	L	L
9	H	L
10	H	L
11	L	L
12	L	L
13	H	H
14	H	H
15	L	L
16	L	L
17	H	H
18	L	H
19	L	H
20	L	H
21	H	H
22	H	H
23	L	H
24	L	H
25	H	H
26	H	H
27	H	H
28	L	L

TABLE 11.8 Observed Frequencies

WHEAT YIELD

RAINFALL	High	Low	Total
High	8	2	10
Low	5	13	18
Total	13	15	28

TABLE 11.9 Expected Frequencies

WHEAT YIELD

RAINFALL	High	Low	Total
High	5	5	10 (35.7%)
Low	8	10	18 (64.3%)
Total	13	15	28

Comparison of the observed frequencies with a similar **table of expected frequencies** (table 11.9) provides the basis for computing a **chi-square statistic**, which gives a measure of the relationship between the two distributions. Determining these expected frequencies involves a **null hypothesis**, which states that there is *no* relationship between the two variables. This means that if the null hypothesis is correct, wheat yield will not vary in relation to rainfall. Of course, the null hypothesis can be rejected by demonstrating that rainfall (which is the **independent variable** in this example) has a strong effect on wheat yield (the **dependent variable**).

Each of the four entries in the interior of the table of expected frequencies (table 11.9) is calculated on the basis of the null hypothesis. The same row and column totals that occurred in the table of observed

frequencies (table 11.8) are used as the starting point (the calculation of the table may be based on either the column or the row totals). In this case, for example, the "high rainfall" category represents 35.7 percent of the total number of cells (10/28 = 35.7%). This percentage is applied to the thirteen cells that have "high yield" to determine that five cells would be expected to fall in the "high rainfall, high yield" category (13 × 35.7% = 5).

The remaining entries in the expected-frequencies table could be calculated in the same way, using either column or row data. In the case of table 11.9, however, the table has limited degrees of freedom, which means that once the value of a single cell in the 2-by-2 matrix has been calculated, the values of the other three cells are determined. The entry for "high rainfall, low yield" (5) is determined by subtracting the "high rainfall, high yield" value (5) already calculated from the total number of high-rainfall cells (10), and so on for the remaining entries. With larger matrices, of course, many more entries must be calculated before the degrees of freedom are exhausted.

Next, the observed-frequency table (table 11.8) is compared with the expected-frequency table (table 11.9). The measure used for this purpose is called the **chi-square statistic**, which is given by:

χ^2 (chi-square) $= \Sigma[(O - E)^2/E]$ where O = observed number of occurrences and E = expected number of occurrences.

In our example, the statistic is calculated as follows:

$$\frac{(8 - 5)^2}{5} + \frac{(2 - 5)^2}{5} + \frac{(5 - 8)^2}{8} + \frac{(13 - 10)^2}{10}$$
$$= 5.625$$

The interpretation of the chi-square statistic is based on its value. Zero indicates no relationship between the variables, whereas a larger number indicates a stronger relationship. A table of significance can be consulted to determine whether or not the specific value is statistically significant—that is, is not likely to occur by chance.[11] Unfortunately, the significance of the chi-square value varies with the size of the table itself, as well as with the actual number of cases involved. For this reason, a correction factor that eliminates the influence of those two variables is calculated. Of the several correction procedures available, one known as **Kendall's Q** can only be used on 2-by-2 tables.[12]

Kendall's Q is given by:

$$\frac{ad - bc}{ad + bc}$$

where $a, b, c,$ and d are the cell values in the table of observed frequencies (the order of the cells is shown in table 11.8). In this case, the value would be:

$$\frac{(8 \times 13) - (2 \times 5)}{(8 \times 13) + (2 \times 5)} = \frac{104 - 10}{104 + 10} = \frac{94}{114} = 0.82$$

[11]See any introductory statistics textbook.

[12]See Hubert M. Blalock, *Social Statistics* (New York: McGraw-Hill, 1960), 228–34, for a discussion of the available correction procedures, including those for larger tables.

The value of Kendall's Q always lies between $+1$ and -1, which makes its interpretation much more straightforward than that of the chi-square statistic. A Q value of 0, for example, indicates that there is no relationship between the two variables. Such a value would uphold the null hypothesis stated, and we would have to look elsewhere for explanations of the variations in wheat yields. A value of $+1$, on the other hand, would indicate a perfect positive relationship between the two variables. Because the rainfall is the independent variable and the wheat yield is the dependent variable, a perfect positive relationship would mean that a high level of rainfall is associated with a high yield. In this case, 0.82 is quite close to 1.0, and rejection of the null hypothesis is justified.

If the value of Q was negative, it would mean, in this case, that higher rainfall values are associated with lower wheat yields. In that case, we would want to rethink the problem and consider whether, for example, high rainfall is causing conditions that are too wet for the wheat to grow. For our purposes, it is sufficient to assume that, if the value of Q lies closer to 1 (either positive or negative), the relationship between the two variables is relatively strong, whereas if it lies closer to 0, the relationship is relatively weak. More specific interpretations lie beyond what can be explained here and could be pursued further in a standard statistics textbook.

Other methods. The comparison of distribution patterns can be carried much further than discussed here. The correspondence between isoline maps (see chapter 13) of two distributions can be measured, for example. This is shown in a study by Arthur H. Robinson, in which the relationship between farm population density and average annual precipitation is examined.[13] Studying this paper and other examples listed in the "Suggested Readings" at the end of the chapter will provide the basis for expanding your concepts with regard to pattern comparisons on maps.

Summary

The description of shape is often subjective, and there has been a search for numerical indices that express shape objectively. Ideally, such an index always

[13]Arthur H. Robinson, "Mapping the Correspondence of Isarithmic Maps," *Annals of the Association of American Geographers* 52 (1962): 414–25.

uses the same value to describe a given shape. Further, it provides sufficient information to permit the regeneration of the original shape. Unfortunately, the shape measures available are not totally satisfactory.

In Miller's measure, the shape index is the ratio between the area of a region and the area of a circle with the same perimeter. It ranges from almost 0, in the case of a very elongated shape, to 1, in the case of a perfectly circular shape. Unfortunately, different shapes can yield the same index value, and the original shape cannot be regenerated from the index value.

Bunge's measure is based on distances between vertices on the perimeter of the region. The same number of vertices must be used for all the shapes in a particular study, but the shapes may be of different sizes. Shapes can be grouped on the basis of similar index values. Among other problems, the results depend on the number and location of the vertices chosen, and, therefore, different values may be obtained for the same shape. Also, the index value cannot be used to regenerate the original shape.

The Boyce-Clark radial shape index is based on the lengths of equally spaced radials extended from a node at the center of the shape. The characteristics of these radials are compared with those of a similar set of radials superimposed on a circular region with the same area. The index values range from 0 for a perfect circle to 175 for a straight line. Unfortunately, changes in the orientation or number of radii or in the location of the center node result in different index values for the same shape. Also, the index value does not permit the regeneration of the original shape.

The three general types of point patterns are random, uniform, and clustered. Many of the measures for analyzing the distribution of point symbols are based on a comparison of the actual pattern with a random pattern to determine if there is an order to the arrangement of points. If the arrangement is other than random, investigation may lead to an understanding of the underlying processes leading to the establishment of uniformity or clustering.

One measure of point-distribution patterns is based on quadrat analysis. In this approach, a count is made of the number of points within each cell (quadrat) of a uniform grid drawn over a dot-distribution map. The variance is computed by comparing the number of points in each quadrat with the average number of points over all of the quadrats. This value is then compared to the variance of a random distribution of the same number of points over the same area to produce the variance-mean ratio. Because the variance-mean ratio for a random distribution is 1, any other ratio indicates that the distribution being tested is not random. In this measure, the size and orientation of the quadrats influence the outcome. Although used as a method for measuring pattern, the quadrat method is more appropriately described as measuring dispersion.

A second method of analyzing distributions of point symbols is the nearest-neighbor technique. In this method, the mean of the distances observed between each point and its nearest neighbor is compared with the mean distance that would occur if the distribution were random. If the tested pattern is also random, the resulting value is 1. If the pattern is dispersed, the value approaches its maximum (2.1491), and if the pattern is clustered, the value approaches 0. This method has the advantage that there is no quadrat-size problem, and it takes distances into account. On the other hand, the value of the measure varies with differences in the limits of the study area.

Measures of the spatial correspondence of areal distributions are used to compare two (or more) distributions. The coefficient of areal correspondence, a simple measure of this type, is the ratio between the area of overlap and the total area of the regions covered by the distributions, including the overlap. When there is no overlap, the value of the coefficient is 0. When the two regions completely overlap, the coefficient's value is 1. When the amount of overlap lies between these two extremes, the coefficient's value lies between 0 and 1. A chi-square statistic is sometimes used to tell more about the relationships between the two distributions. Because the significance of the chi-square value varies with the size of the table itself, as well as with the actual number of cases involved, a correction factor (such as Kendall's Q) is needed.

SUGGESTED READINGS

Austin, R. F. "Measuring and Comparing Two-Dimensional Shapes." In *Spatial Statistics and Models,* edited by G. L. Gaile and C. J. Willmott. Boston: D. Reidel, 1984, 293–312.

Boyce, Ronald R., and W. A. V. Clark. "The Concept of Shape in Geography." *The Geographical Review* 54 (1964): 561–72.

Bunge, William. "Theoretical Geography." *Lund Studies in Geography,* Series C, General and Mathematical Geography, No. 1. Lund, Sweden: The Royal University of Lund, Department of Geography, C. W. K. Gleerup, 1962, 72–88.

Getis, Arthur. "Temporal Land-Use Pattern Analysis with the Use of Nearest-Neighbor and Quadrat Methods." *The Annals of the Association of American Geographers* 54 (September 1964): 391–99.

Griffith, Daniel A., Michael P. O'Neill, Wende A. O'Neill, Lloyd A. Leifer, and Rodric G. Mooney. "Shape Indices: Useful Measures or Red Herrings?" *The Professional Geographer* 38, no. 3 (August 1986): 263–70.

Lee, David R., and G. Thomas Sallee. "A Method of Measuring Shape." *The Geographical Review* 60, no. 4 (1970): 555–63.

McConnell, H. "Quadrat Methods in Map Analysis." Discussion Paper No. 3. Iowa City, Iowa: Department of Geography, University of Iowa, 1966.

Miller, Victor C. "A Quantitative Geomorphic Study of Drainage Basin Characteristics in the Clinch Mountain Area, Virginia, and Tennessee." *Department of Geology, Technical Report No. 3.* New York: Columbia University, Department of Geology, 1953.

Moellering, H., and J. N. Rayner. "The Dual Axis Fourier Shape Analysis of Closed Cartographic Forms." *The Cartographic Journal* 19 (1982): 53–59.

———. "The Harmonic Analysis of Spatial Shapes Using Dual Axis Fourier Shape Analysis (DAFSA)." *Geographical Analysis* 13 (1981): 64–77.

Rogers, A. *Statistical Analysis of Spatial Dispersion: The Quadrat Method.* London: Pion, 1974.

12

Characteristics of Map Features: Networks and Trees

This chapter continues the discussion begun in chapter 10 of the measurement of map features. Many types of linear features are found on maps, including roads, railroads, rivers, and boundaries. Analysis of such features requires additional techniques.

NETWORKS

In the field of geography, a **network** is generally defined as "a set of geographic locations interconnected in a system by a number of routes."[1] Many phenomena shown on maps, such as roads, railroads, airlines, pipelines, and river systems, fit this general definition. Describing and understanding the characteristics of these networks, then, is a legitimate part of map analysis. The field of mathematics known as graph theory provides a number of concepts useful for the analysis of networks that appear on maps. This type of analysis can serve a variety of purposes, some examples of which are presented in this section.

Graph theory introduces an element of abstraction into the world of reality shown on the map. The points and lines of the graph show **topological positions**, not real-world, geographical locations. This abstraction is often beneficial, however, because it focuses on the

structure of relationships between locations, rather than on the more usual concerns of distance and direction. Another advantage of graph theory is that the structure is analyzed in an objective manner. Also, values are placed on the specific elements of the relationships of interest, and the meanings of the values can be methodically interpreted.

Terminology

The terms used in network analysis show considerable diversity because workers from a variety of disciplines have contributed their unique terminology. The terms used most in geographic applications are defined here.

A **graph**, or **network**, is simply a figure composed of points and lines (figure 12.1). The points are usually referred to as **places** because that is what they most

[1]K. J. Kansky, "Structure of Transport Networks: Relationships between Network Geometry and Regional Characteristics," University of Chicago, Department of Geography, *Research Papers* 84 (1963): 1.

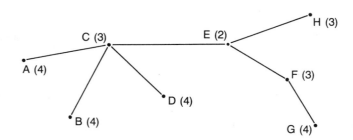

FIGURE 12.1 A graph, or network, with associated numbers.

frequently represent on maps. On occasion, the more general term *node* is substituted. The connecting line between two places is called a **route**, and a series of routes linking a series of places is called a **path**.[2] Again, the general term *link* may be substituted for route. The **length of a path** is given by the number of routes it contains. Also, the **topological distance** between two points is the length of the shortest path between them in terms of the number of routes.

Accessibility

Measures based on paths and routes are used to determine how well places are connected to other places. In other words, they show relative **accessibility**.[3] The **associated number** of a place, for example, is the topological distance from that place to the most remote place in the network. Associated numbers are indicated for each place in figure 12.1. Notice that places *A, B, D,* and *G,* which are on the fringes of the network, have the greatest topological distances. The most central place in the network, then, is the one with the lowest associated number. In figure 12.1, this is place *E.*

The highest associated number is called the network's **diameter**. The centrality or remoteness of any place in the network is evaluated in terms of its associated number relative to the associated numbers of other places and to the diameter of the network. Again, in figure 12.1, places *C, F,* and *H* fall between the distant and central places already mentioned.

A frequently encountered real-world problem is the evaluation of possible locations for a warehouse or similar facility that will serve a distribution network. Preliminary ideas about the suitability of various potential locations can be obtained by as simple a process as comparing the associated numbers of the possible sites with one another. Locations with lower numbers usually merit more consideration than those with high numbers.

[2]Points are also called junctions, intersections, terminals, or vertices, and routes are called links, arcs, sides, segments, branches, or edges.

[3]Although it is not discussed here, for the sake of simplicity, matrix algebra is frequently used in the analysis of graphs. See, for example, Ronald Abler, John S. Adams, and Peter Gould, *Spatial Organization: The Geographer's View of the World* (Englewood Cliffs, N.J.: Prentice-Hall, 1971), 258–72.

Connectivity

A different type of network analysis is the comparison of the level of development of the transportation or communication systems in two regions. A study of this type might proceed by comparing the level of completeness, or **connectivity**, of the systems.[4] In this context, a highly connected network is presumably a sign of a greater level of development than is a poorly connected one. An industrialized, economically developed country, for example, is likely to have much more fully developed road, railroad, and power networks than is an economically underdeveloped nation. Instead of being content with a subjective statement about the completeness of such networks, one can derive a numerical value that defines the level of development in the two situations, in network terms, and allows for a meaningful comparison.

The completeness of a network is measured by the **connectivity index**. The connectivity index provides a comparison between the actual connections, or routes, that exist in a given network, as compared to the total number of routes possible. A simple connectivity index is given by the formula $100(A/P)$, which converts the ratio between the actual number of routes (A) and the possible number of routes (P) to a figure that represents the percentage of completeness. To calculate this index, you must, of course, first determine the values of A and P. A is obtained by simply counting the number of connections that actually exist. P, however, must be computed. This is somewhat more complex than it might seem at first glance, because different types of graphs have different maximum numbers of possible routes.

Network Types

Assume, for the moment, that we are dealing with highway patterns. Considering the different highway configurations that we might encounter illustrates the types of networks that can be defined. First, a normal, two-way street pattern is called a **symmetric, planar network**. Such networks have two distinguishing

[4]See, for example, E. J. Taaffe, R. L. Morrill, and P. R. Gould, "Transport Expansion in Underdeveloped Countries," *Geographical Review* 53 (1963): 503–29.

characteristics: First, you can, for example, travel from point A to point B on a two-way street, and you can also travel the reverse, from point B to point A, which is the symmetry characteristic. Second, every place where two or more roads meet is a node, and you can enter or leave that intersection along any of the roads, which is the planar characteristic. The maximum number of possible links in a symmetric, planar network is $3(n-2)$, where n equals the number of nodes.

If the highway network is modified by the installation of overpasses and underpasses, the planar portion of the definition in the previous paragraph no longer holds because not every crossing point is necessarily a connecting point. You can drive across an overpass over another road and not be able to get from one road to the other. A network with this limitation is called a **symmetric, nonplanar network**. An airline system is another example of a symmetric, nonplanar network. You cannot branch off to another destination every time the airplane you are on crosses another air route! The number of possible connections in a symmetric, nonplanar network is given by $[n(n-1)]/2$.

If the highway system not only includes overpasses and underpasses but has a one-way-travel restriction on it, it becomes a **nonsymmetric, nonplanar network**. That is, you can travel from A to B, but not from B to A, over any given route. The number of possible connections in a nonsymmetric, nonplanar network is given by $n(n-1)$. In contrast, a **nonsymmetric, planar network** has one-way connections, but the paths are not allowed to cross without joining at a node. This is the equivalent of a one-way street system without overpasses or underpasses. The number of routes in such a network is given by $6(n-2)$.

Measurement

Returning to the measurement of connectivity, let us assume that the map in figure 12.2a represents a symmetric, planar highway network. On this map, there are fifteen actual connections between cities. Because there are twelve cities in the network, the total possible number of connections is $3(12 - 2) = 30$, and the connectivity index is $100(15/30) = 50$. This indicates that only 50 percent of the potential direct, city-to-city linkages are in place. The interpre-

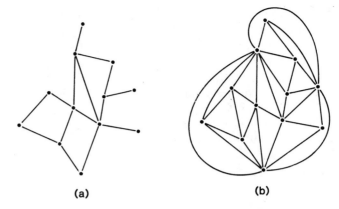

FIGURE 12.2   (a) **Symmetric, planar highway network.** (b) **Example of fully connected, symmetric, planar network—nonoptimum.**

tation of the connectivity index is somewhat ambiguous, however, because a fully connected symmetric, planar network would not be particularly desirable. Figure 12.2b shows, for example, one way in which the thirty possible connections could be achieved. Clearly, this arrangement is not an optimum one for a highway network because of the circuitous nature of some routes. In addition, not every pair of places is directly connected—such complete connections would require a nonplanar network. Also, other considerations, such as cost, relative accessibility, importance of the various places involved, and so on, need to be taken into account. The connectivity index is useful, nevertheless, as a measure of network completeness.

Applications

Many other measures are used for the analysis of networks, but space does not permit discussing more than the few preliminary ideas presented here. Such studies can be applied to such concerns as the analysis of the hierarchy of cities, the location of a railroad route to maximize net revenues, the characteristics of the interstate highway system, the shortest route for a traveling salesperson to follow to serve a series of customers, and so on. References in the "Suggested Readings" at the end of the chapter provide a variety of examples.

TREES

Up to now, we have implicitly assumed that networks include loops, so that there is more than one possible path between some pairs of places. Networks that permit such loops are called **circuit networks**. In contrast to circuit networks are **branching networks**, or **trees**, that do not contain circuits. In geographic terms, a river system is a particularly apt analogy for a graph-theoretic tree. Some transportation and distribution systems, including electrical transmission networks, are other examples of trees likely to be found on maps.

A tree with a given number of vertices always has a predetermined number of links. Specifically, because it consists simply of lines successively added to existing lines, a tree with n vertices has $n - 1$ edges, or links. For this reason, the concept of completeness, or connectivity, does not apply to branching networks as it does to circuit networks. The analysis of trees does, however, introduce additional graph-theoretic concepts.

Hierarchic Order

When a stream network, for example, is treated as an abstract tree, each stream segment assumes a specific level of importance or **hierarchic order**. Such order numbers assist in the description and analysis of the characteristics of different types of stream-development patterns. The approach applies equally well to other treelike networks.

Different schemes are used to assign order numbers to trees, each with a somewhat different outcome. The **Strahler method** of stream ordering is a suitable example of such schemes. In this method, each headwater link in the network (in other words, the smallest tributary streams) is identified as being of order 1 (figure 12.3). When two headwater (order-1) links join, the downstream link formed is classified as order 2. This process continues, and whenever two links of the same order join, the order assigned to the downstream link is that of the tributaries, *plus one*. When two links of different order join, however, the downstream link is assigned an order number the *same* as that of its higher-order tributary. Counting and recording the number of links of each order provide information useful for analyzing the characteristics of the stream network.

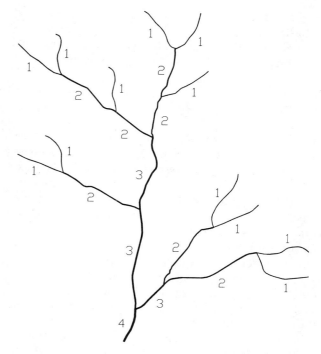

FIGURE 12.3 Strahler method of stream ordering.

Bifurcation Ratio

One use of the stream-order data obtained by the Strahler method is the calculation of **bifurcation ratios**. A bifurcation ratio is the ratio between the number of links of one order and the number of links of the next higher order:

$$\text{Bifurcation ratio} = R_b = \frac{N_{s1}}{N_{s2}}$$

where N_{s1} is the number of links of a given order, and N_{s2} is the number of links of the next higher order.

A single bifurcation ratio taken by itself has little meaning. Computing the mean bifurcation ratio for an entire drainage basin and matching the result with the same figure for other drainage basins, however, provides a method of comparing the characteristics of the various basins.[5] Differences in the patterns found from one basin to another, when compared with

[5]The mean bifurcation ratio for basin 1, for example, equals $R_{bs1} = [(N_{s1}/N_{s2}) + (N_{s2}/N_{s3}) + \cdots + (N_{sn-1}/N_{sn})]/K$, where K is the number of such ratios for the whole basin.

the geological and climatological characteristics of the basins, provide initial insights into differences in stream-development patterns under different conditions.

Summary

Graph theory provides methods for the objective analysis of networks on maps. Map networks consist of places (nodes), joined by routes (links), and paths, which are a series of routes linking a series of places.

Accessibility measures based on paths and routes are used to determine how well places are connected to other places. The associated number of a place, for example, is the topological distance (number of links) from that place to the most remote place in the network. This provides a measure of the centrality or remoteness of any place in the network. The highest associated number, which is the maximum topological distance in the network, is called the diameter.

Connectivity is a measure of the level of completeness of a network. The connectivity index provides a comparison between the actual connections, or routes, that exist in a given network, as compared to the total number of routes possible.

Networks are described in terms of their symmetric and planar characteristics. A pattern of two-way connections is symmetric, whereas a one-way pattern is nonsymmetric. If every place where two or more routes cross is a node, the network is planar, whereas if every crossing point is not a connecting point, the network is nonplanar.

Networks that include loops, so that there is more than one possible path between some pairs of places, are called circuit networks. In contrast, branching networks (trees), such as river systems, do not contain circuits. A tree always has a predetermined number of links, and each link has a specific hierarchic order.

The Strahler method is an example of hierarchic ordering of trees, applied to streams. In this approach, each headwater link is of order 1. When two order-1 links join, the downstream link formed is classified as order 2, and so on. A bifurcation ratio may be computed using the Strahler order. This is the ratio between the number of links of one order and the number of the next higher order. The mean bifurcation ratio for a drainage basin may be compared with the same measure for other basins. Differences in the ratios from one basin to another may be compared with the geological and climatological characteristics of the basins to provide initial insights into differences in stream-development patterns under different conditions.

SUGGESTED READINGS

Abler, Ronald, John S. Adams, and Peter Gould. *Spatial Organization: The Geographer's View of the World.* Englewood Cliffs, N.J.: Prentice-Hall, 1971, 255–78.

Garrison, W. L. "Connectivity of the Interstate Highway System." *Papers and Proceedings of the Regional Science Association* VI (1960): 121–37.

Haggett, Peter. "Network Models in Geography." In *Models in Geography,* edited by R. J. Chorley and Peter Haggett. London: Methuen, 1967, 609–68.

Haggett, Peter, and Richard J. Chorley. *Network Analysis in Geography.* London: Edward Arnold; New York: St. Martin's Press, 1969, chapter 15.

Kansky, K. J. "Structure of Transport Networks: Relationships between Network Geometry and Regional Characteristics." University of Chicago, Department of Geography, *Research Papers* 84, 1963.

Nysteun, J. D., and M. Dacey. "A Graph Theory Interpretation of Nodal Regions." *Papers and Proceedings of the Regional Science Association* VII (1961): 29–42.

Ore, Oystein. *Graphs and Their Uses.* New York: Random House, New Mathematical Library, 1963.

13

Qualitative and Quantitative Information

The modern postindustrial world thrives on the collection and dissemination of statistical information. Indeed, so much information of this type is gathered that finding the time to interpret and understand much of it is difficult. Graphics help to organize and interpret statistical information. Maps are a form of graphics, not totally dissimilar from graphs and statistical charts. The main feature that distinguishes maps from other graphics is that maps automatically incorporate locational information.

Various symbolization schemes are used to present quantitative information on maps. This chapter deals with the characteristics of some of the more common approaches. Other aspects of the presentation of statistical information are included in the discussions of cartograms (chapter 14) and graphs (chapter 16).

POINT SYMBOLS

Many variables that appear on maps occur at single locations (points) on the earth's surface. The symbols used to represent such data are referred to as **point symbols**.

Dot-Distribution Maps

The most straightforward type of point symbolization is used on **dot-distribution maps**. Placing a dot on a map at the location of each person's home in a city, for example, would result in a dot-distribution map.

Most dot-distribution maps do not use a simple, one-dot-for-one-occurrence approach. Instead, a single dot may represent twenty people, factories, cows, or whatever (figure 13.1). Or, one dot may represent a thousand items, or even a million or more. The number of items represented by each dot depends both on the scale of the map and on the size of the population represented. Maps drawn at small scales necessarily provide less room for symbol placement than maps drawn at large scales. Space limitations alone, then, may result in a need for *grouping* the data. In addition, large numbers, such as those encountered on population maps, often make generalization a necessity. Assume, for example, that a population map of the United States is being drawn. If one dot is used to represent each person, over 300 million dots are needed, which is obviously impractical. Any fairly complex set of data is inevitably condensed, or grouped, in some way before it is mapped. When such grouped data are used, a single symbol stands for a predetermined number of items.

The use of the term *point symbol* must be interpreted rather broadly because most objects that are mapped as points obviously do not actually occur as dimensionless points. A city, for example, is often represented on a map as a single dot. This does not imply that the city occupies no space. It simply means that, at the scale of the map, the amount of space the city takes up is very small, relative to the area of the state or nation within which the city is located.

Nonproportional Point Symbols

When a phenomenon occurs at an identifiable point, its location can be indicated by the placement of a **nonproportional point symbol**. Point symbols are

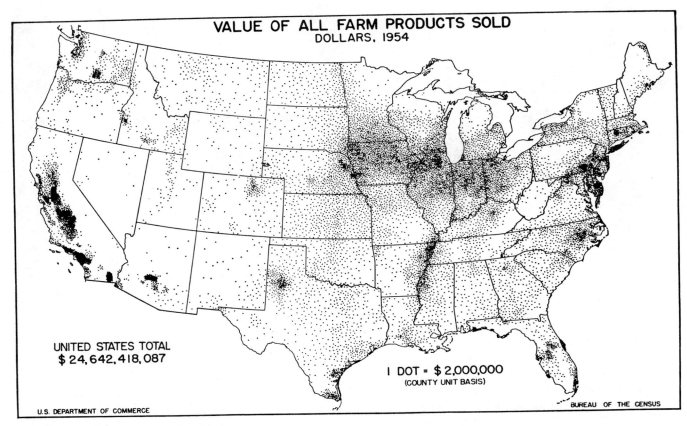

VALUE OF ALL FARM PRODUCTS SOLD
DOLLARS, 1954

UNITED STATES TOTAL
$ 24,642,418,087

I DOT = $ 2,000,000
(COUNTY UNIT BASIS)

U.S. DEPARTMENT OF COMMERCE

BUREAU OF THE CENSUS

FIGURE 13.1   Dot-distribution map.

Source: Bureau of the Census.

used to show two different characteristics of points: (1) the type or category of the phenomenon that occurs there and (2) the value (population, amount produced, and so on) connected with it. The first type of information is nominal, whereas the latter is quantitative (see the section "Levels of Measurement" in this chapter).

Suppose, for example, that the locations of alcoholism treatment programs are plotted on a map of Oklahoma, with the location of each program indicated by a point symbol. The different types of programs are nominally differentiated by using different types of point symbols (figure 13.2).

In addition to shape variations, variations in color are also often used to distinguish between nominal categories. On an agricultural map, for example, blue dots may indicate milk cows, and red dots may indicate beef cattle.

Nominal symbols do *not* indicate any quantitative differences between the various categories. The in-

troduction of size differentiation requires at least an ordinal level of information and the use of some type of proportional symbol.

Map scale is an important consideration with regard to point symbols. On a large-scale city map, for example, the city itself may cover an area of several square feet and obviously cannot be represented by a dot. Indeed, the purpose of such a map is to provide information about the internal arrangement of city streets, buildings, and other features. On a small-scale map, however, the city may occupy only a minuscule amount of map space, and any internal information about the city is not likely to be shown. Thus, a single dot can be used to indicate the city's location within the state on the small-scale map. In addition, the size, shape, or color of the dot can be varied so that statistical information, such as population, is also represented.

FIGURE 13.2   Nominal point symbols used to show types of programs providing alcoholism treatment centers in Oklahoma, 1980.

From Christopher J. Smith, "Locating Alcoholism Treatment Facilities," *Economic Geography* 59, no. 4 (October 1983): 368–85. Reprinted by permission.

LEVELS OF MEASUREMENT

The measurements used to present statistical information on maps provide different levels of information. The possible types of interpretation differ, depending on the information level of a particular set of measurements. The four levels of measurement discussed here are nominal, ordinal, interval, and ratio.[1]

NOMINAL

Sometimes the information available simply divides a group into subgroups. This type of **qualitative information** carries no implication that one subgroup is more or less important than another. The level of measurement involved in qualitative information is called **nominal measurement.**

A simple example of nominal measurement is the separation of thirty people in a room into groups on the basis of eye color. If there are twelve people with blue eyes, fourteen with brown eyes, three with black eyes, and one with green eyes, there are, then, four eye-color groups in the room. There is no logical basis, however, for saying that the green-eyed people should be ranked ahead of the brown-eyed and behind the blue-eyed. Any ordering in such a case is purely arbitrary. What you *can* do with the groups with different eye colorings is to count the members of each group

[1]Adapted from S. S. Stevens, "On the Theory of Scales of Measurement," *Science* 103 (1946): 677–80, and Jacques Bertin, *Semiology of Graphics* (Madison: University of Wisconsin Press, 1983), 34–39.

Box continued on page 208.

Box continued from page 207.

so that you know the number of people with eyes of each particular color. From these simple counts, you can also calculate the proportion or percentage of the total group that falls into each category. Nominal information of this type is used to create maps showing, for example, city classifications, types of pipelines, crop types, or soil categories.

ORDINAL

Assume that you line up the people in a room so that the tallest person is at one end of the line and the shortest is at the other. In addition, you make certain that each person is standing between someone who is taller and someone who is shorter. When you do this, you have classified the members of the group on an **ordinal basis,** using relative height as a logical ordering criterion. Notice, however, that you are only comparing one person with another to see who is taller and who is shorter. You are not obtaining measurements, in centimeters, for example, so that you know each person's exact height.

Many types of ordinal information are used on maps. Boundaries, for example, are usually classified according to the level of the political entity that they define. County boundaries are less important than state boundaries, and national boundaries are more important than either state or county boundaries. Similarly, roads are classified according to their level of jurisdiction: county road, state highway, or federal interstate highway. Any such arrangement is organized around the concept of more or less important, but does not include a quantitative measurement.

INTERVAL AND RATIO

The data levels beyond ordinal measurement are interval and ratio. These levels provide the exact dimensions, on some standard scale, of the particular phenomenon of interest. Interval and ratio levels of measurement are very similar, but the difference that exists between them affects the way in which each type of information can be used. We will discuss the ratio type first and then compare the interval type to it.

Taking a **ratio measurement** requires the use of a regularly spaced scale that begins at zero and extends out without any specific limit. For example, distance is measured using a scale such as millimeters, centimeters, or meters (or inches, feet, or yards). A meter stick, with a zero point at one end and with millimeter subdivisions marked, is a kind of scale typically used for such measurements. The zero mark on its scale indicates the total absence of length. If the scale is appropriately subdivided, an object of very small dimension can be measured and its size recorded. Such a scale can also be extended to measure objects of greater and greater size. Theoretically at least, the scale can be extended to any length necessary, conceivably to include interplanetary distances.

A metric distance scale allows you to say that B is, for example, 10 meters east of A, or that C is 20 meters south of A. In this case, you can also say that A is twice as far from C as it is from B. This latter capability gives the measure its name because it allows the ratio between two measurements to be determined.

The characteristic that distinguishes an interval scale from a ratio scale, then, is that an **interval scale** allows you to determine values according to a particular measure but does not allow you to determine the ratio between two values. Such scales are relatively rare, but one type that commonly occurs on maps is temperature information on either the Celsius or Fahrenheit scales. If two temperature readings are taken using the Celsius scale, such as 20° and 40°, we can say that 40° is warmer than 20° (an ordinal statement). We can also say that there is a 20-degree difference between the two readings, which is the same as can be done using a ratio scale. What we *cannot* say is that 40° is *twice* as warm as 20°. The reason that the latter statement makes no sense is that the starting point of the Celsius scale is an arbitrary zero point. That is, 0° Celsius represents the freezing point of water but *does not* represent an absolute zero, which would occur in the complete *absence* of heat.[2]

[2]The Kelvin scale, on the other hand, starts at absolute zero, which *does* represent the absence of heat. It is, therefore, a ratio scale.

Graduated Point Symbols

Graduated point symbols are often used to indicate the values associated with various locations. The population range of each city within a region, for instance, can be shown by appropriately varying the size of the dot that represents each city.

When dot-size variations are used, the cartographer must provide a key that indicates their meaning. Usually, a large dot indicates a city with a relatively large population, whereas a small dot indicates one with a smaller population (figure 13.3). However, whether the symbol simply reflects the *extent* of the geographical area encompassed by the city or whether it reflects the city's population may be unclear. The specific populations involved, and whether one city's population is only slightly larger than the others' or, perhaps, much larger, may also be uncertain. For these reasons, the map legend must be read carefully to determine the specific population, or population range, indicated by each size symbol.

LINEAR SYMBOLS

Because of their nature, many features such as railroads, roads, telephone or power lines, political boundaries, and rivers, are best represented on maps by **linear symbols**. Two general types of linear symbols are used. One type differentiates between nominal categories of features, and the other presents quantitative information.

Nominal Information

Nominal linear symbols simply allow the map user to recognize that one line represents a river and another a railroad. Differences in line color (or gray value), shape, or pattern are the most common nominal linear symbols. When color is used, the line representing a river may be printed in blue; whereas a black line of similar width may represent a highway. When shape is used, two lines may be the same color, but a dashed black line may indicate a trail and a solid black line a road. Combining colors and shapes produces a great variety of symbols, so that a variety of features can be uniquely identified.

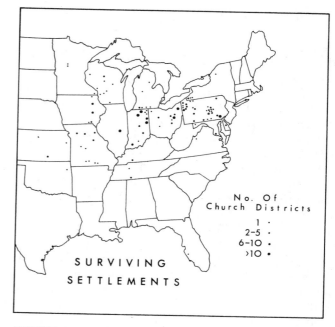

FIGURE 13.3   **Map using graduated point symbols to show sizes of known Old Order Amish settlements in the United States, 1976.**

From William K. Crowley, "Old Order Amish Settlement: Diffusion and Growth," *Annals of the Association of American Geographers* 68, no. 2 (June 1978): 249–64. Reprinted by permission.

The map legend specifies what the nominal linear symbol—for example, the solid red line, the dashed green line, or the dotted black line—represents on that particular map. Consulting the legend is necessary because the same symbol may stand for entirely different things on different maps; secondary highways are not always the *Blue Highways* implied by the book title.[3]

Quantitative Information

In addition to indicating what is being represented, linear symbols often represent quantitative information.

[3]William Least Heat Moon, *Blue Highways: A Journey into America* (Boston: Little, Brown, 1983).

Ordinal representation. Linear ordinal symbols are often used to differentiate the relative importance of what they represent. For example, different line symbols may represent the various levels of importance of political boundaries. There is obviously a range of importance from less important county boundaries to increasingly important state and national boundaries. A similar hierarchy often applies to road designations, from local through county and state to national levels. When hierarchies such as these are mapped, the style and weight of the lines used to represent each level is typically altered to represent the appropriate level of prominence. Flow maps also often use ordinal symbolization, but they frequently are extended to show ratio levels of information.

Flow maps. **Quantitative linear symbols** are found on **flow maps**, which show connections of various types that exist between locations on the earth's surface. A trade exchange between two cities, for example, may involve the movement of a certain quantity of products worth a given amount of money. Either of these pieces of quantitative information—volume or value—can be the basis of a flow map.

The usual convention regarding the use of flow lines to convey ordinal or quantitative information is to vary the width of the line in relation to the amount or value of the flow, with a wider line indicating a greater quantity. Flow-line symbols may also indicate nominal information such as the types of goods or services involved in the exchange, in combination with an indication of the value.

Line widths on flow maps are often drawn in direct proportion to the value represented. The scale in such a case might show, for example, that a line 1 millimeter wide represents 10,000 tons of product and a line 10 millimeters wide represents 100,000 tons of product (figure 13.4). This approach is feasible when the range of values is not too great.

When the flows range from very small to very large values, the data are often divided into several categories. These categories may simply be small, medium, and large when ordinal information is being presented. The various line widths represent specific data ranges such as 1–10, 11–100, and over 100, when ratio information is involved. In either case, a particular line width is used to represent each range of values, so the symbols are referred to as **range-graded**[4] (figure 13.5). When symbols are range-graded, the line that represents ten times the value may only be five times as wide (or some other multiple). When range-graded symbols are used, therefore, it is particularly important to check the legend to determine the values represented by each width.

[4]This is the same approach used for classed choropleth maps and range-graded circle symbols.

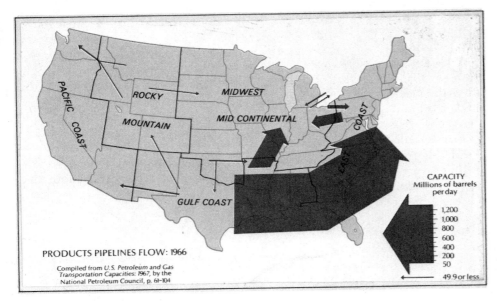

FIGURE 13.4   Flow map with proportional line widths.

Source: The National Atlas, 235.

Symbols are sometimes used instead of width variations, to represent different quantities in flow lines. For example, a dotted line may indicate a minimal-value flow, a dashed line a greater flow, and a solid line the maximum flow.

One additional style variation in flow maps has to do with the placement or routing of the flow lines themselves. In some cases, the placement of the lines indicates the actual routes followed. The lines may follow the alignments of the highway or the railroad along which the goods are moved, for example. In many instances, however, the scale of the map relative to the widths of the lines involved does not allow this type of exact alignment. When this occurs, the flow lines may simply indicate the general route followed. The annual monetary value of ocean trade between countries, for example, can be shown with flow lines. Because of the variety of routes used, though, using a line that indicates the existence and value of the connection but not the actual route may be the best way to represent the flow.

In cases of more abstract connections such as monetary exchanges, no actual route of exchange such as a road or a railroad, may be involved. In such cases, the lines drawn on the map simply indicate an interchange of some sort between place *A* and place *B,* and a certain value associated with that interchange. For these reasons, the meaning of the routes shown on flow maps must be interpreted with caution.

AREAL SYMBOLS

Areal symbols are used to represent phenomena that are spread out over the earth's surface. A vast array of subjects falls into this category, ranging from climatic-zone data to areas where certain crops predominate, or from regions occupied by specific ethnic groups to counties with specific income levels. The common characteristic of these subjects is that they occupy some more or less precisely defined area on the earth's surface. Similarly, the symbols used to represent them are spread out over the two-dimensional surface of the map.

FIGURE 13.5   Flow map with range-graded line widths.
Source: The National Atlas, 227.

FIGURE 13.6   Map using nominal areal symbols.

From Andrew Herod, "From Rag Trade to Real Estate in New York's Garment Center: Remaking the Labor Landscape in a Global City," *Urban Geography* 12, no. 4 (1991): 324–28. Reprinted by permission.

Nominal Distributions

As is true with other types of symbols, areal symbols can represent either nominal, ordinal, or quantitative information. With **nominal areal symbols**, the appropriate area on the map is covered with a pattern or color that differentiates it from the surrounding areas (figure 13.6). The map may indicate the different types of crops grown in a county, for example. The area in which wheat is the predominant crop may be shown as a stippled pattern, whereas the area in which corn is predominant may be striped, and the soybean area may have another pattern. The same goal may be accomplished on a color map by using three different colors, one for each of the categories. Any differences in the textures or colors used to designate

the different areas, however, do not imply any hierarchy or order of importance. A red area representing potato cropland is no more or less important, for example, than a green area representing turnip cropland.

Some level of generalization is to be expected on maps of nominal distributions. For example, an area identified as a wheat-growing region may contain subareas that support other crop types. Depending upon the scale of the map, however, these subareas may be omitted so that only the predominant crop type is indicated. If the number of subareas of different types is significant, the classification scheme should include suitable mixed categories.

Quantitative Distributions

The presentation and understanding of ordinal, interval, or ratio areal data is more complex. The symbolization for this purpose must indicate either the relative importance of one area compared to another or the actual values involved. Also, the symbols must often simultaneously present nominal information regarding the various types of variables being shown.

When **quantitative areal symbols** are used, subareas on the map are distinguished from one another by different color shades or different gray values that indicate the rank or numerical value of the phenomenon in each subarea.[5] Commonly, darker shades indicate greater values, and lighter shades indicate lesser values. In the case of rank information (ordinal data), the symbols indicate the relative importance of some phenomenon in each area on the map. The information is limited to an indication of a range from low to high, without any precise values attached (figure 13.7). When specific numerical values (interval or ratio data) are associated with the areas, the information is presented on a choropleth map.

Choropleth maps.   A common type of areal quantitative map is the **choropleth map**. On a choropleth map, the subdivisions are preexisting units; census tracts and county, state, or national boundaries are frequently used. If the map shows textile and apparel workers by county, for example, each county is

---

[5]Different hues (colors) usually indicate differences in kind, not differences in value.

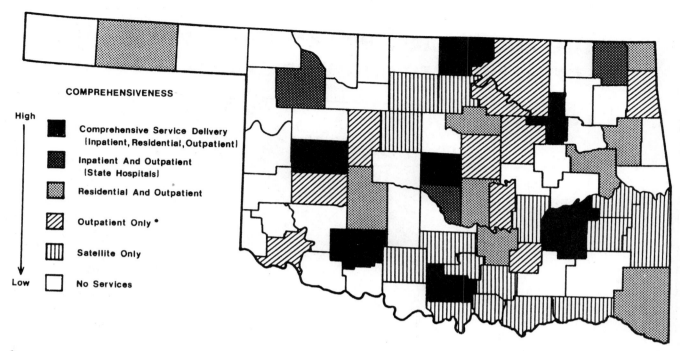

*Delaware And Washita Counties Have One Residential Facility (Halfway House) Each, But No Outpatient Facility

FIGURE 13.7   Ordinal areal symbols used to show alcoholism treatment comprehensiveness in Oklahoma, 1980.

From Christopher J. Smith, "Locating Alcoholism Treatment Facilities," *Economic Geography* 59, no. 4 (October 1983): 368–85. Reprinted by permission.

printed in a pattern that indicates the particular level of employment associated with it (figure 13.8).

The numerical values used on choropleth maps must be properly based on **areal averaging**. Areal averaging means that the information presented is *not* a simple total value. Instead, the average value for each areal unit is calculated and symbolized. In general, ratio values, such as population density, yield per acre, or average income, are used for choropleth maps, instead of absolute values like total population, total volume of agricultural production, or total income. An example will clarify the reasons for this practice.

Figure 13.9 is an example of the improper use of a choropleth map. In this case, the symbol applied to each state is based on the state's *absolute number* of hazardous waste sites. Montana, for example, appears to be at much greater risk from hazardous waste than does Connecticut, even though both states have ap-

proximately the same number of hazardous waste sites. The reason for this is that Montana's much greater physical area overwhelms Connecticut's small size and influences the apparent importance of the values being mapped. Choropleth maps that use absolute values, then, should be interpreted with caution; in most cases they convey a false impression.

One method of portraying data regarding states, counties, and other divisions involves combining the values into only a few groups so that a range of values is included in each group. The desired goal of such a classification system is to produce groupings that minimize the differences within each established category and maximize the differences between the categories. When grouped data are used, the result is a conventional choropleth map that makes it easier for the map user to understand the nature of the distribution pattern because fewer symbols are needed.

FIGURE 13.8   Example of a choropleth map.

From Merrill L. Johnson, "Postwar Industrial Development in the Southeast and the Pioneer Role of Labor-Intensive Industry," *Economic Geography* 61, no. 1 (January 1985): 46–65. Reprinted by permission.

Classification.   When classification is done, the cartographer must first decide how many groups to use. This is a necessary decision, but frequently an arbitrary one, that greatly affects the resulting map. Map users must be sensitive to the choices made by the cartographer to effectively evaluate the resulting map.

The cartographer's dilemma in trying to decide how to group the data on a map can be illustrated by considering two extreme possibilities. One extreme would be to use a separate symbol for *every* individual value. This approach would result in a large number of symbols on the map.[6] In fact, so many symbols would be needed that some cartographers feel that map users might be unable to tell the symbols apart, no matter how conscientiously they try. The

other extreme would be to show only one group; that is, the data could be completely aggregated and would show, for example, *all* of the counties with the same symbol. The resulting map would be useless, of course, because map users would be unable to distinguish between the counties at all.

Rather than take either extreme, cartographers frequently try to find some satisfactory middle ground. This involves establishing enough categories to provide meaningful distinctions between groups, but not so many that the amount of information provided is overwhelming and confusing. A typical solution is to settle on some *manageable* number of groups or divisions, frequently somewhere between five and eleven, which allow the various gray values, or colors, used as symbols to be distinguished.

[6]This type of unclassed choropleth map is discussed later in the chapter.

Hazardous waste sites
Number of Sites on National Priorities List: August 1983

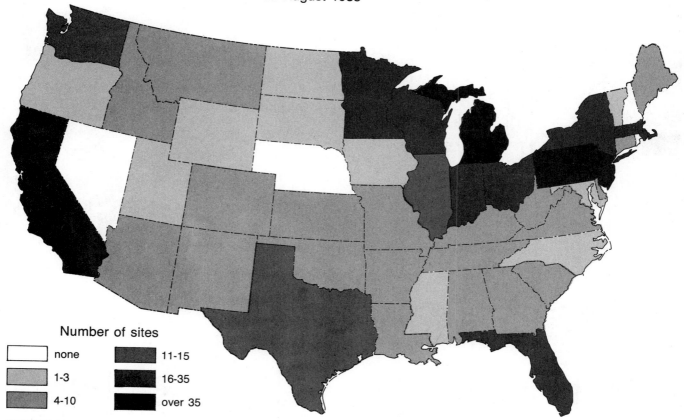

Number of sites

none	11-15
1-3	16-35
4-10	over 35

FIGURE 13.9   Choropleth map improperly based on absolute values.

Source: Redrawn from *Statistical Abstract of the United States, 1984* (Washington, D.C.: U.S. Department of Commerce, Bureau of the Census, December 1983), 212.

Classification is important because the class intervals selected determine the appearance and meaning of the final map, and a poor selection results in a misleading product. Figure 13.10 shows four maps that look very different from one another. What is not apparent is that all of these maps are based on exactly the same set of data. The differences in appearance are the result of the variations in data classes that resulted from using different classification schemes. Map users, unfortunately, do not usually have the luxury of choosing a map from among several alternatives.

Evaluation.   With a choropleth map, you usually have no way of knowing whether or not the class divisions used represent the best choice. When examining a given map, keep in mind the potential pitfalls. You can, for example, examine the map's classification system by looking at the legend. From the legend, you may be able to visualize how the appearance of the distribution is being affected by the classes selected. To do this effectively, you must go beyond the map itself. You may be able to find other maps based on the same data, for example, so that you can compare the results. Or, you may be able to find written

INDIANA: Number of Inhabitants per km², 1980

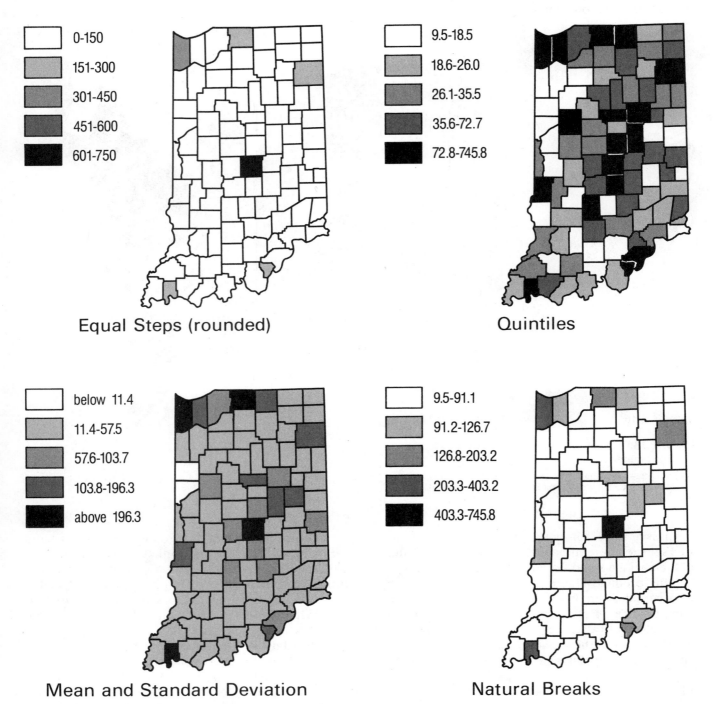

FIGURE 13.10   Different-appearing maps based on exactly the same data set.

descriptions of the distribution. You may be able to find the data that were used to construct the map in question and, in the extreme, could even experiment with your own system of classification.

You may occasionally encounter a choropleth map with overlapping categories, such as 0–10, 10–20, 20–30. The problem with this is that some values could be placed in either of two categories. In this example, 10 could be placed in either the 0–10 or the 10–20 range. This type of classification is ambiguous and does not reflect a basic understanding of appropriate procedures. The map on which it is used, therefore, is likely to have minimal value.

Unfortunately, there are no other helpful guidelines for you to follow in evaluating choropleth maps, but, as an educated map user, you can at least maintain a healthy skepticism toward what you see on them.

Classification problems are as important for other types of maps as they are for choropleth maps, although the discussion of the subject has been concentrated in this section for convenience. You should also consider the question of appropriate data subdivisions, however, when using maps that incorporate proportional circles, flow lines, or any other symbols grouped by classes.

Unclassed choropleth maps. Imagine a map depicting the average income level of persons in the United States, by county. The income-level value of each county is likely to be at least slightly different from the values associated with the other counties. If each of the counties is shaded with a symbol that indicates its average income level, a very large number of different symbols is needed. Some cartographers feel that using such an "infinitely divided" range of symbols is an effective way to present information.[7] They believe that the method has the advantage of

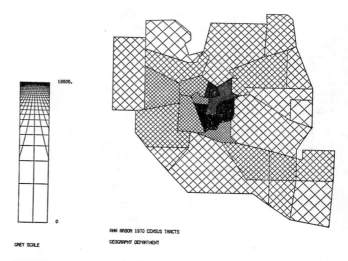

GREY SCALE

ANN ARBOR 1970 CENSUS TRACTS
GEOGRAPHY DEPARTMENT

FIGURE 13.11 Unclassed choropleth map.

giving a strong visual impression of the distribution of the variable mapped. Maps that show specific values for each area are called **unclassed choropleth maps** (figure 13.11).

Bivariate and multivariate maps. The maps discussed so far in this chapter are **univariate maps**; that is, they show variations from place to place of a single factor, such as wheat production. In many situations, however, there is a geographic relationship between two variables, such as wheat production and average rainfall. An appropriate **bivariate map** illustrates such relationships.

The discussion here focuses on a bivariate map that uses continuous shading created by crossed-line patterns (figure 13.12). The interpretation of this type of symbolization is based on the characteristics of the network created by the intersecting lines.[8] One aspect

[7]The seminal paper on this topic is W. R. Tobler, "Choropleth Maps without Class Intervals?" *Geographical Analysis* 5, no. 3 (July 1973): 262–65. A summary of arguments for and against the unclassed approach, as well as useful citations of the discussions in the literature, is contained in Michael P. Peterson, "An Evaluation of Unclassed Crossed-Line Choropleth Mapping," *The American Cartographer* 6, no. 1 (1979): 21–37.

[8]Bibliographic information, as well as research into aspects relating to the symbolization, interpretation, and measurement of such maps, is reported in a number of publications of Laurence W. Carstensen, Jr., which are listed in the "Suggested Readings" at the end of the chapter.

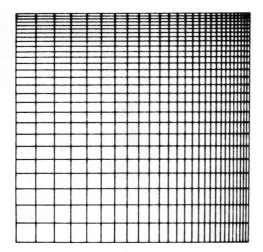

FIGURE 13.12   Key for bivariate map using continuous shading created by crossed-line patterns.

of the network is that, where the lines are closer together, a darker gray value is produced and, by implication, the density of the particular variable is greater. Another aspect of the network is that differing relationships between the two distributions result in a different pattern appearance. To illustrate, if both values are high, the lines are close together, and the openings in the network are relatively square. On the other hand, if both values are low, the lines are far apart, but the network openings are still square. These relationships are shown on the diagonal from the lower-left to the upper-right of figure 13.12. In contrast, if one value is high and the other low, the network openings take on a rectangular appearance, with the wider spacing for the low-value variable and the narrower spacing for the high-value variable. These relationships are shown in the upper-left and lower-right corners of figure 13.12.

Although only black-and-white patterns have been discussed here, the same general approach applies to color maps, on which a different color is used to represent each variable (blue for one and red for the other, for example). As usual, lighter tones represent lower data values, and darker tones represent greater data values. Printing one color over the other results in mixed colors that reflect the relationships between the variables. In the case of blue and red, for example, relatively equal values of both variables result in a purple color. Where the values of the variables are low, the purple is light; the purple is dark where the values of both variables are high. Mixtures of high values of one variable and low values of the other pro-

duce bluish-red or reddish-blue tints. The specific intensity and tint that result are dependent on the relative importance of one value or the other. **Multivariate maps**, which show the relationships between more than two variables, are sometimes produced by introducing additional colors for the additional variables. The major difficulty with color bivariate and multivariate maps is that the correct interpretation of the meanings of the color combinations is sometimes difficult.

Dasymetric maps.   A major problem with choropleth maps is that the entire area of each subdivision is symbolized the same way because any internal variations in the distribution are not recognized. In fact, as has already been indicated, internal variations are automatically eliminated by the calculation of average values for each unit. This may be satisfactory for some types of information, such as the distribution of rainfall, which may not vary in intensity to a great extent over a relatively small unit area. It may be entirely unsatisfactory, however, for showing the distribution of population or other information that can vary significantly in intensity within a similar unit area.

When they wish to show internal distributions, cartographers sometimes use a technique called **dasymetric mapping** to partially overcome the problem of areal averaging. The dasymetric technique recognizes that what is being mapped varies in intensity within the mapping units. To accommodate this, each mapping unit is divided into a number of smaller areas. Each of these subdivisions is defined so that it is relatively homogeneous in terms of the phenomenon being mapped. Although the value associated with each subdivision is still based on an areal average, the internal variation within each subdivision is much less than it would be on a choropleth map. A dasymetric map has a recognizable general appearance. The subdivisions no longer follow county boundaries or similar outlines so their shapes are likely to be much less uniform or regular than those of a choropleth map (figure 13.13).

Prism maps.   A prism map is based on a bird's-eye view, looking down at the region at an angle, from an elevated viewpoint. Each data unit on the map is raised above the base level an amount proportional to the value attached to it. The result is a series of columns, or prisms, of variable height, each with the outline of the appropriate mapping unit (figure 13.14).

FIGURE 13.13 caption and parts within figure:

CAPE COD. POPULATION MAPS
DENSITIES, 1930

(a) By townships

Scale 1 : 1,240,000

(b) By townships with "uninhabited" areas differentiated

0   5   10   15 mi
0   5 10 15km
For key to symbols see Fig. 3

(c) By subdivisions of townships

Scale 1: 945,000

0   5   10   15 mi
0   5 10 15 km

Approximate number of persons

Per mi²	Per km²
0 - 4	0 - 2
5 - 19	3 - 5
20 - 49	6 - 19
50 - 99	20 - 38
100 - 199	39 - 77
200 - 499	78 - 133
500 and over	194 and over

FIGURE 13.13 Development of dasymetric map of Cape Cod population, 1930. (*a*) Township population densities. (*b*) Township population densities after elimination of "uninhabited" areas. (*c*) Final dasymetric map after taking into account other factors affecting population distribution.

From John K. Wright, "A Method of Mapping Densities of Population with Cape Cod as an Example," *The Geographical Review* 26, no. 1 (January 1936): 105. Reprinted by permission of The American Geographical Society.

INDEPENDENTS: PERCENT OF TELEPHONES WITHIN EACH STATE

60
40
20
0

FIGURE 13.14 Prism map.

Courtesy of Laboratory for Computer Graphics, Harvard Graduate School of Design.

The heights of the prisms are difficult to judge, especially if their base is hidden. Furthermore, if the cartographer has not been careful in selecting the viewpoint, some prisms may be hidden from view entirely. Despite these possible difficulties, prism maps are often an effective means of presenting quantitative information.

SURFACES

The idea behind a map of a surface is perhaps most easily illustrated by a topographic map of the earth's surface. A topographic map shows, by contour lines or some other technique, the variations in the elevation of the earth's surface above a datum level. Maps are drawn of many other, more abstract, surfaces, however. In this section, we will discuss the use of surfaces as a means of representing statistical information.

Isolines

It does not require too great a stretch of the imagination to visualize surfaces that are more abstract than the surface of the earth. For example, during a rainstorm, different amounts of precipitation fall at different locations. If the amounts that fall at a number of points are recorded, the values obtained can be used as the basis for mapping. The amount of rain at each location is simply treated as a vertical distance above a datum, and the representation of the values of all of the points taken together, creates an abstraction of the "rainfall surface." One way that this surface can be mapped is by using each recorded value as the equivalent of an elevation control point. **Isolines** are then drawn to join points that have received equal amounts of rainfall.

The chief difference between such a rainfall map and a topographic map is that the rainfall does not create an actual *physical* surface to observe and map. It does, however, provide an abstract, conceptual surface. In a similar way, even more abstract measurements, such as population densities, crop yields, temperature statistics, and a variety of other types of information, represent **statistical surfaces**. A contour map, or a map that uses some other appropriate type of symbolization, can be created to represent these abstract concepts.

Types of Isolines

As is implicit in the preceding discussion, two types of isolines are commonly recognized. These are usually called isometric lines and isopleths, although other names for the same concepts exist.

Isometric lines. Isometric lines are isolines based on control points located on a **continuous surface**. Such control points have actually observed values associated with them. The earth's surface provides an example of this type of situation because it is higher here or lower there, but it exists everywhere. This characteristic of continuous surfaces means that every point on the surface has *some* value connected to it. Furthermore, the values that exist between two points are fairly predictable, and interpolation techniques can be used, with reasonable confidence, to determine what those values are. Contours, then, are isometric lines, as are isolines showing temperature, rainfall, barometric pressure, or other continuous variables (figure 13.15).

Isopleths. Isopleths, on the other hand, are drawn on the basis of areal averages assigned to arbitrary control points and *not* directly observable on a continuous surface. An isopleth map of population density for a given state, for example, might be based on county-level data. To construct the map, the cartographer has to obtain or compute the average population density for each county. Each of these average values is then assigned to control points, usually located at the centers of each county, and the isopleths are constructed around these control points (figure 13.16).

The values used for constructing an isopleth map do not exist on a continuous surface in the same sense as the earth's surface is continuous. There may be an area with a densely packed human population, for example, located immediately adjacent to another area completely devoid of population. For this reason, values cannot be interpolated between isopleths in the same way that they can be interpolated between isolines. Also, the shapes of the mapping units affect the locations of the control points and, consequently, the form of the isopleths themselves.

FIGURE 13.15   Isometric map showing average annual snowfall in Missouri.

Source: Walter A. Schroeder, *Missouri Water Atlas* (Jefferson City, Mo.: Missouri Department of Natural Resources, 1982).

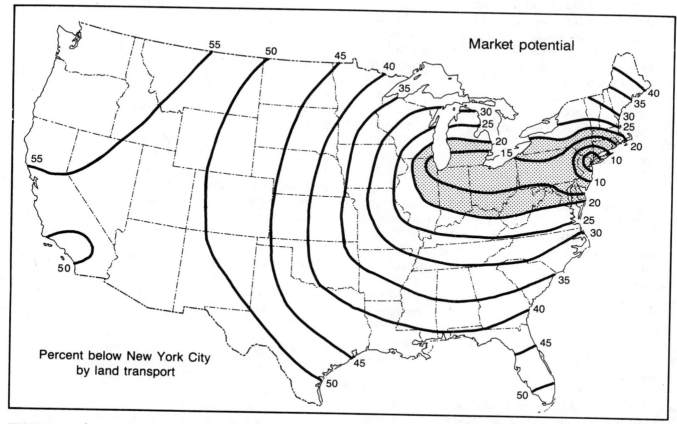

FIGURE 13.16   Isopleth map of market potential.

Redrawn from Chauncy D. Harris, "The Market As a Factor in the Localization of Industry in the United States," *Annals of the Association of American Geographers* 44, no. 4 (December 1954): 315–48. Reprinted by permission.

These characteristics of isopleths have caused some to conclude that they are not a valid means of representing areal averages.[9] The arguments against isopleths are not universally accepted, however, so you are likely to encounter many maps that fall into the isopleth category. When examining such maps, you should keep in mind the questions that have been raised and consider how they affect the usefulness of the map for your purposes.

Summary

Various symbolization schemes are used to present qualitative and quantitative information on maps.

Many variables occur at specific locations (points) on the earth's surface. The most straightforward type of point symbolization is the dot-distribution map, in which each dot indicates the location of one item or, in a form of generalization, many items.

When a phenomenon occurs at an identifiable point, its location may be indicated by a nonproportional point symbol. This shows the type of phenomenon that occurs there (qualitative information). Graduated point symbols, on the other hand, indicate the values (quantitative information) associated with various locations. This may be done by varying the size of the symbol in relation to the value it represents.

Linear symbols differentiate linear features of various types (qualitative and ordinal information) or to show flows or connections between locations (quantitative information). Flows are symbolized by varying the width of the line in relation to the amount or value of the flow.

Areal symbols represent phenomena that are spread out over the earth's surface. In the case of qualitative information, the appropriate area on the map is symbolized so that it is differentiated from the surrounding areas. When quantitative information is mapped, the symbols are designed to indicate the relative importance of the areas. This is done by using gray values or color shades that reflect a hierarchy of importance. One map category of this type is the choropleth map, in which the values presented are average values for preexisting subdivisions, such as counties.

Sometimes, the values shown on choropleth maps are grouped. When this is done, the first decision is how many groups to use in the classification system.

A typical solution is to settle on some manageable number of groups or divisions, perhaps between five and eleven. Classification is important because the chosen class intervals determine the appearance and meaning of the final map, and a poor selection results in a misleading product.

When the values on a choropleth map are not grouped, an unclassed choropleth map is produced. Such maps depict an "infinitely divided" range of symbols.

A major problem with choropleth maps is that the entire area of each subdivision is symbolized in the same way. Dasymetric mapping is used to partially overcome this often unrealistic presentation. This technique recognizes that the phenomenon being mapped varies in intensity within the mapping units. Each unit is divided into a number of smaller areas that are relatively homogeneous in terms of the phenomenon being mapped.

Both choropleth and dasymetric maps may be produced in bivariate and multivariate forms that illustrate relationships between two or more distributions at one time.

A prism map is an angled view in which each data unit is raised above the base level an amount proportional to the value attached to it.

Surfaces, both physical and statistical, are often represented by isoline maps. Two types of isolines are recognized. Isometric lines are based on control points located on a continuous surface and have actually observed values associated with them. Isopleths, on the other hand, are drawn on the basis of areal averages assigned to arbitrary control points and not directly observable on a continuous surface. There is some controversy regarding the legitimacy of isopleth maps.

SUGGESTED READINGS

Birch, T. W. *Maps: Topographical and Statistical.* 2d ed. Oxford, England: Clarendon, 1964, part II.

Carstensen, Laurence William, Jr. "A Continuous Shading Scheme for Two-Variable Mapping." *Cartographica* 19, nos. 3 and 4 (Autumn and Winter 1982): 53–70.

———. "Perceptions of Variable Similarity on Bivariate Choroplethic Maps." *The Cartographic Journal* 21, no. 1 (June 1984): 23–29.

———. "Bivariate Choropleth Mapping: The Effects of Axis Scaling. *The American Cartographer* 13, no. 1 (January 1986): 27–42.

---

[9]See, for example, David Unwin, *Introductory Spatial Analysis* (New York: Methuen, University Paperbacks, 1981), 158.

————. "Hypothesis Testing Using Univariate and Bivariate Choropleth Maps." *The American Cartographer* 13, no. 3 (July 1986): 231–51.

"Commentary." *Annals of the Association of American Geographers* 70 (1980): 106–108.

Crawford, P. V. "Perception of Grey-Tone Symbols." *Annals of the Association of American Geographers* 61 (1971): 721–35.

Dickinson, Gordon Cawood. *Statistical Mapping and the Presentation of Statistics.* London: Edward Arnold; and New York: Crane, Russak, 1973.

Dobson, Michael W. "Refining Legend Values for Proportional Circle Maps." *The Canadian Cartographer* 11, no. 1 (June 1974): 45–53.

Flannery, James J. "The Relative Effectiveness of Some Common Graduated Point Symbols in the Presentation of Quantitative Data." *The Canadian Cartographer* 8, no. 2 (December 1971): 96–109.

Jenks, George F. "Contemporary Statistical Maps— Evidence of Spatial and Graphic Ignorance." *The American Cartographer* 3, no. 1 (1976): 11–19.

————. "Optimal Data Classification for Choropleth Maps." *Occasional Paper No. 2.* Lawrence, Kans.: Department of Geography, 1977.

Jenks, George F., and F. C. Caspall. "Error on Choropleth Maps: Definition, Measurement, Reduction." *Annals of the Association of American Geographers* 61 (1971): 217–44.

Mackay, J. Ross. "Dotting the Dot Map." *Surveying and Mapping* 9, no. 1 (January-March 1949): 3–10.

————. "Some Problems and Techniques in Isopleth Mapping." *Economic Geography* 27, no. 1 (January 1951): 1–9.

McCleary, George F., Jr. "How to Design an Effective Graphics Presentation." In *How to Design an Effective Graphics Presentation,* Harvard Library of Computer Graphics, 1981 Mapping Collection, vol. 17. Cambridge, Mass.: Harvard University, Laboratory for Computer Graphics and Spatial Analysis, 1981, 34–48.

Muehrcke, Phillip C. *Thematic Cartography.* Resource Paper No. 19. Washington, D.C.: Association of American Geographers, Commission on College Geography, 1972.

Muller, Jean-Claude. "Perception of Continuously Shaded Maps." *Annals of the Association of American Geographers* 69, 2 (1979): 240–49.

Peterson, Michael P. "An Evaluation of Unclassed Crossed-Line Choropleth Mapping." *The American Cartographer* 6, no. 1 (1979): 21–37.

Sibert, John L. "Continuous-Color Choropleth Maps." *Geo-Processing* 1, no. 3 (November 1980): 207–16.

Smith, Richard M. "Comparing Traditional Methods for Selecting Class Intervals on Choropleth Maps." *Professional Geographer* 38, no. 1 (1986): 62–67.

Stevens, S. S. "On the Theory of Scales of Measurement." *Science* 103 (1946): 677–80.

Tobler, Waldo R. "Choropleth Maps without Class Intervals?" *Geographical Analysis* 5, no. 3 (July 1973): 262–65.

Williams, Robert L. *Statistical Symbols for Maps: Their Design and Relative Values.* New Haven, Conn.: Yale University Map Laboratory, 1956.

Wright, J. K. "A Method of Mapping Densities of Population with Cape Cod as an Example." *Geographical Review* 26, no. 1 (January 1936): 103–10.

14

Cartograms and Map Misuse

Maps are designed to serve a great variety of purposes. The cartograms described in the first portion of this chapter are unusual because they are modifications of the relationships that we are used to seeing on maps. Cartograms are produced by deliberately enlarging or reducing the size (area or length) of the data-collection units in proportion to the data value attached to each unit. These modifications reveal information about the data that would otherwise be difficult to observe. Unfortunately, distortions can also mislead the map user. For that reason, this chapter also examines map misuse, including the deliberate misrepresentations of propaganda.

CARTOGRAMS

A **cartogram** is a maplike diagram that is purposely modified so that locations, distances, and areas are no longer the same as they are on the globe. The nature of the differences between maps and cartograms must be kept in mind when interpreting cartograms. Two general types of cartograms are described here: linear cartograms and area cartograms.

Linear Cartograms

Linear cartograms, which are also called distance-transformation maps or distance cartograms, are designed to show relationships between locations, but not in the usual distance terms. Instead, they show *relative* distances based on various measures, such as the cost of travel between points or the time it takes to travel between points.

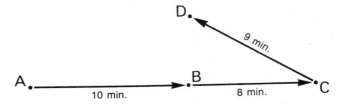

FIGURE 14.1   Routed linear cartogram.

Routed linear cartograms.   Routed linear cartograms show certain characteristics of specific paths from one point to another. A typical routed linear cartogram shows the average travel times between various points (figure 14.1). This is accomplished by drawing the length of each connecting segment so that it is proportional to the time required to negotiate it. If the scale is 1 centimeter per 10 minutes of travel, for example, a segment that takes an hour to traverse is drawn 6 centimeters long.

One complication with routed linear cartograms is that the time it takes to travel between two locations may vary, depending on the direction one is moving. For example, if there is an uphill gradient from point *A* to point *B*, it probably takes longer to negotiate the route from *A* to *B* than it does from *B* to *A*, especially if one is riding a bicycle or walking. Similarly, if the cartogram is designed to show cost of travel, the freight rates may be less in one direction than in the other because the transport company wishes to attract traffic in a particular direction (perhaps to reduce the need for shipping empty cars on that leg of the network).

Such differences in the cost or time connected with traveling in opposite directions along the same route create difficulties in cartogram construction. The problem is that the connecting line between the two

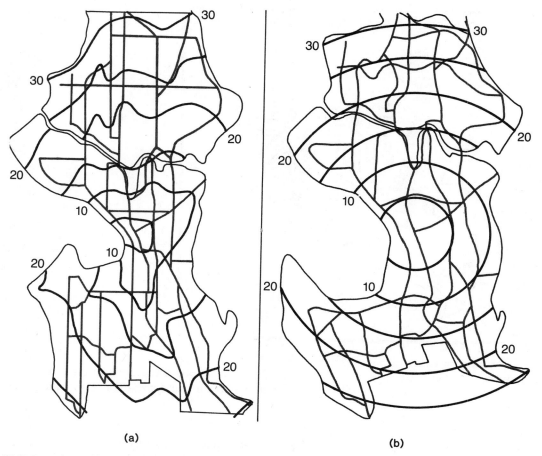

(a)   (b)

FIGURE 14.2   Conversion of conventional map to
central-point cartogram. (*a*) Conventional map of peak-
hour travel times from central Seattle, 5-minute intervals.
(*b*) Cartogram of "real" time distances from downtown
Seattle, 5-minute intervals.

Redrawn from William Bunge, *Theoretical Geography,* Lund Studies in
Geography, Series C, General and Mathematical Geography, no. 1 (Lund,
Sweden: C. W. K. Gleerup, Publishers, for The Royal University of Lund,
Sweden, Department of Geography, 1962), 55. By permission.

points *should* be drawn to two different lengths, to reflect the differing values. One solution is to use two
lines, one for each direction, each drawn to its appropriate length and with the direction of movement
specified by arrowheads. Obviously, when this is done,
the lines cannot follow the exact paths followed in
the real world, so distortions are introduced.

Even if the cost or time of travel between two points
is the same in either direction, it is likely to be different for different segments of the cartogram. The
airfare between two large cities may be less, for example, than the fare between two smaller cities located the same distance apart. If cost is being used to

scale distances, the line connecting the smaller centers will be longer than the line connecting the larger
ones. The result is that the points representing the
cities have to be shifted to accommodate the different
line lengths. As the number of connecting lines increases, accommodating their lengths through the
shifting of locations may become impossible.

Central-point linear cartograms.   A central-
point linear cartogram is based on a single starting
point and shows equal units of time or cost for
reaching other locations from that central point (figure
14.2). (Alternatively, it can show the values associ-

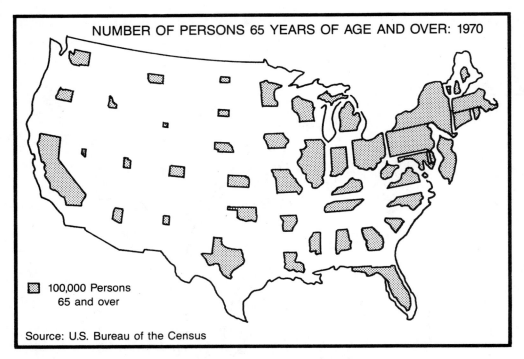

FIGURE 14.3 Noncontiguous, value-by-area cartogram. The area of each state represents the number of persons sixty-five and older in that state.

From Judy M. Olson, "Noncontiguous Area Cartograms," *The Professional Geographer* 28, no. 4 (November 1976). Reprinted by permission.

ated with reaching the central point from the other locations.) On cartograms of this type, the relative direction from the center to the other points is often retained, but directions and distances between other points on the cartogram are not correct.

Area Cartograms

Cartograms in which areas are distorted are called **area cartograms** or, sometimes, value-by-area cartograms. On such cartograms, the areas of the various regions are not constructed in proportion to their actual areas on the earth's surface, as they are on conventional equal-area maps.[1] Instead, each region is drawn to a size that is proportional to some *other*

[1]Many map projections also introduce areal distortions. These distortions are derived in a systematic way from actual earth locations and dimensions and are, therefore, quite different from the scaling variations used in cartograms. It has been suggested, however, that cartograms "can be regarded as maps based on some unknown projection," so the distinction may be moot. See Waldo R. Tobler, "Geographic Area and Map Projections," *The Geographical Review* 53 (1963): 59–78.

value associated with it, such as income, population, crop yield, or one of a myriad of other measures.

The rescaling involved in the construction of area cartograms introduces graphic difficulties. What happens is that the shapes of the regions and their locations in relation to one another cannot both be maintained when their sizes are varied in different proportions. One possible solution to this problem is to draw a noncontiguous cartogram, which retains shapes by separating the regions from one another. Another solution is to produce a contiguous cartogram, which retains the relationships between the regions but varies the regions' shapes.

Noncontiguous cartograms. In a **noncontiguous cartogram**, the regions are easy to recognize because their shapes are retained, even though they are usually shown in a simplified outline form (figure 14.3). Retaining the shapes, however, requires shifting the locations of the regions. This results in open areas of various sizes that reflect the discrepancy between the density in the most-crowded unit and the density

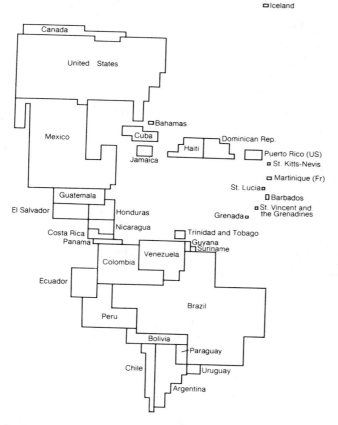

FIGURE 14.4   Contiguous cartogram showing countries of the Western Hemisphere drawn in proportion to the number of births in 1982. (Compare with figure 1.17.)

Source: Adapted and reprinted by permission from International Bank for Reconstruction and Development, The World Bank, *World Development Report 1984* (New York: Oxford University Press, 1984).

in other units.[2] What is missing, of course, is the sense of the relationships between regions—for example, where they are adjacent to one another.

Contiguous cartograms.   Some cartograms retain the desirable trait of contiguity and thus show the spatial relationships between regions. In such **contiguous cartograms**, the shapes of the regions must be changed, often drastically, to accommodate their differently proportioned areas and, at the same time, keep neighbors adjacent to one another (figure 14.4). Not only are the shapes distorted, but the details of their outlines are also usually simplified. In some extreme cases, the end result is a diagram made up of a

series of areas that look nothing like the regions represented. Such a cartogram is often somewhat confusing and difficult to read because shape is one of the major clues used to identify regions.[3] An additional difficulty with some contiguous cartograms is that, because they are rather difficult to draw, the relationships between regions are not always completely retained. Regions may touch along boundaries that differ somewhat from their real boundaries, for example.

Interpreting area cartograms.   Area cartograms are drawn as though the distribution of the phenomenon being represented is uniform within each region. They do not take into account that the density of occurrence may be very great in one area within a region and very sparse in another. Thus, on a population cartogram of the United States, the size of California is greatly affected by the major population concentration in the Los Angeles area. If the Los Angeles area were shown separately, the remainder of the state would shrink in relative importance. In the interpretation of an area cartogram, no assumptions can be made about the internal distribution of the phenomenon shown within the various regions.

The main point to keep in mind regarding either noncontiguous or contiguous area cartograms is that the *sizes* of the regions have been drawn in proportion to their relative importance in terms of whatever value is being represented. One aid to the interpretation of an area cartogram is to compare it to an equal-area map of the same area. Indeed, cartographers sometimes include such a map as an adjunct to the cartogram. The map reference assists in identifying the internal divisions of the cartogram, the geographical relationships between them, and the size distortions introduced by the cartogram. If no map is included with the cartogram, an atlas or other source can be used as a reference. Comparing the cartogram to an equal-area map is important because the cartogram's message is contained in the contrast between the true size of the geographic areas, shown on the map, and the quantity of the variable in each area, shown on the cartogram.

Cartograms usually include a small, rectangular symbol with a value attached. This key shows the specific number of units associated with a given area on

[2]Judy M. Olson, ''Noncontinuous Area Cartograms,'' *The Professional Geographer* 28, no. 4 (1976): 377.

[3]Borden D. Dent, ''Communication Aspects of Value-by-Area Cartograms,'' *The American Cartographer* 2, no. 2 (October 1975): 154–68.

FIGURE 14.5   Distribution of histosols (soils with a
surface layer of accumulated organic matter that is usually
acid and wet) in the conterminous United States.

From Philip J. Gersmehl, "Soil Taxonomy and Mapping," *Annals of the
Association of American Geographers* 67, no. 3 (September 1977):
419–28. Reprinted by permission of the Association of American
Geographers.

the cartogram and allows the determination of the approximate (but not exact) value associated with each
region. Exact information is more readily and accurately obtained from census data or other sources.
Thus, the key gives a sense of the general magnitudes
involved, and the body of the cartogram gives an
impression of the *importance* of the various regions
relative to the variable mapped.

MAP MISUSE

Because they can be complex, and because the
public generally lacks knowledge about their characteristics, maps provide seemingly endless opportunities for misuse. Some misuse is accidental and
simply stems from lack of knowledge. That it is accidental, however, does not make misuse any less unfortunate or important. On the other hand, when
the misuse is part of a systematic effort to influence
opinions or beliefs, it can be a very effective type of
propaganda.

Map Inaccuracy

Things are not always as they appear on maps. An
interesting example of the truth of this statement is a
dot map published in 1977, showing the distribution
of histosols in the United States (figure 14.5).[4] Histosols are a category of "soils with a surface layer of
accumulated organic matter that is usually acid and
wet."[5] The general category includes peat but also
encompasses many other types with characteristics
that differ significantly from those of peat. The original map of histosol distribution was copied for a series
of other maps. At the end of this process, a modified
version of the original map eventually appeared in a
1981 planning document as a shaded-area map with
the title "Principal Peatlands of the United
States"(figure 14.6). Unfortunately, many misinterpretations, distortions, and errors had been introduced into the final map. Examples of these problems

[4]Philip J. Gersmehl, "The Data, the Reader, and the Innocent Bystander—
A Parable for Map Users," *The Professional Geographer* 37, no. 3 (1985):
329–34.
[5]Gersmehl, "The Data, the Reader, and the Innocent Bystander," 331.

PLATE 1 Example of topographic-bathymetric map. Information shown in water areas includes: Universal Transverse Mercator (UTM) grid lines (see chapter 6); land-management areas (numbered red rectangles) based on Bureau of Land Management survey; and depths based on hydrographic surveys indicated by underwater contours, with depth zones shown by blue tone values.

Source: Portion of U.S. Geological Survey NI 18–4, 1:250,000, 1953 (shoreline revised and bathymetry added, 1972).

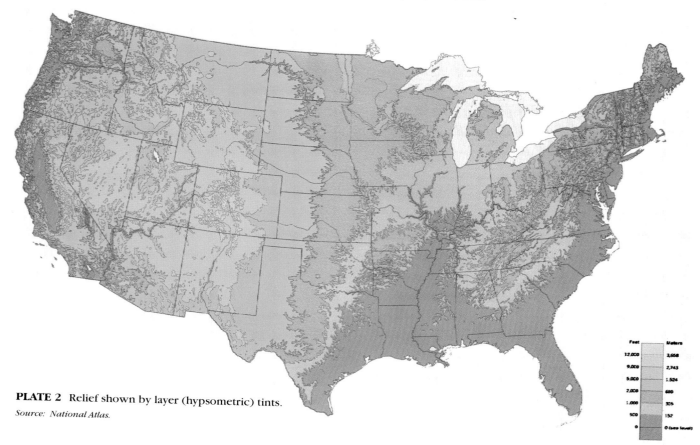

PLATE 2 Relief shown by layer (hypsometric) tints.

Source: National Atlas.

PLATE 3 Portion of hill-shaded version of a standard U.S. Geological Survey topographic map (reduced). (Fairbanks, Alaska, 1:250,000, 1956 [revised 1976].)

PLATE 4 A portion of the New York City subway map.

Source: Copyright © New York City Transit Authority. Reprinted by permission.

PLATE 5 Airline map.

Courtesy of United Air Lines, Inc.

PLATE 6 Portion of the U.S. Geological Survey geologic quadrangle map. (F. H. Olmsted, Geologic Map of the Laguna Dam 7.5-Minute Quadrangle, Arizona and California, 1:24,000, 1972.)

PLATE 7 Oblique aerial photograph.

Courtesy of Aero-metric Engineering, Inc.

PLATE 8 Portion of color-infrared aerial photograph, near Footeville, Wisconsin, 1986.

Source: USGS National High Altitude Program (NHAP).

PLATE 9 Portion of U.S. Geological Survey orthophotomap. (Randeen Ridge quadrangle, Minnesota, 1:24,000.)

PLATE 10 Portion of false-color remote-sensing image, Phoenix, Arizona. (Landsat Thematic Mapper, 30 meter ground resolution, 1:100,000-scale.)

Source: Department of the Interior, U.S. Geological Survey. "Landsat and SPOT Image Display: Phoenix, Arizona Area" Miscellaneous Investigations Series I-1941, 1987.

PLATE 11 Classified Landsat image, Lewiston, Idaho.

Source: J. W. Christenson, C. Anderson, and P. Grumbmann. *Environmental Assessment Using Remotely Sensed Data.* Intralab Project No. 75-5. Greenbelt, Maryland: National Aeronautics and Space Administration, Goddard Space Center, undated.

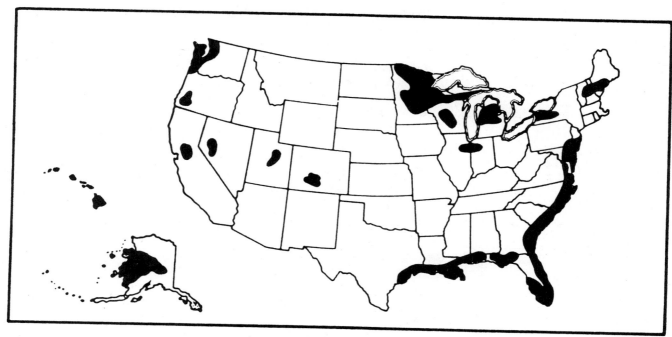

FIGURE 14.6   ''Principal Peatlands of the United States.''

Source: U.S. Department of Energy, Division of Fossil Fuels Processing,
Peat Prospectus (Washington, D.C.: U.S. Department of Energy, 1979).

included the loss of southern New England's peat resources and the creation of an important peatland in
the Nevada desert.

Cartographers can certainly learn some revealing
lessons about their responsibilities in map compilation from this "parable." For a map user, the message
is also clear, although what to do about it is less obvious. Basically, map users need to be aware that maps
are *not*, unfortunately, always as accurate as they
should be, even when produced by well-intentioned
cartographers.

Frankly, it is difficult to know what advice to give a
map user in this regard. The most useful approach may
be simply to not depend entirely on one source when
seeking information. At the very least, the map user
should consider the sources listed as the basis of each
map and, if possible, compare the copied map with
them. Any major departures of the copy from the
source should be detected by this kind of check. If
no sources are given, there is double reason to be wary
because one has no idea where the information was
obtained (even if it was accurately copied). In such
a situation, the map user should seek additional
information.

Propaganda

Maps are excellent vehicles for **propaganda** because the public puts great faith in map information.
They are, therefore, often used to convey impressions
that are helpful to a given cause, regardless of the truth
of the information shown. A number of devices are
common to propagandistic presentations.[6]

General characteristics.   The major general
characteristic of propaganda maps is the use of simple
design, with background and other detail that is extraneous, from the standpoint of the propagandist,
omitted. This often includes scale, latitude and longitude lines, roads, and other items that would provide an accurate frame of reference. Also, an
unsuitable projection is often used (and is usually un-
named). Projections that are not equal-area or conformal are particularly common. The exaggeration of
the polar areas on the Mercator projection may be employed, for example, to show the threat (or dominance, depending upon the point of view to be

[6]Louis O. Quam, "The Use of Maps in Propaganda," *Journal of Geography*
42 (January 1943): 21–32; Judith A. Tyner, "Persuasive Cartography,"
Journal of Geography 81, no. 4 (July/August 1982): 140–44.

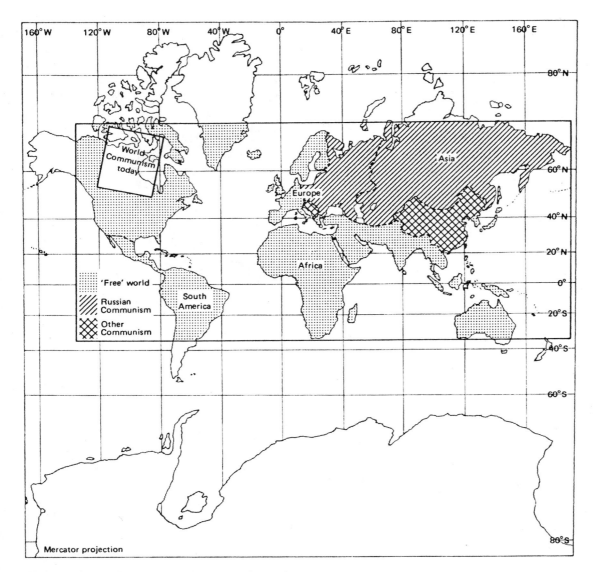

FIGURE 14.7   Mercator projection used for propaganda purposes.

From Roger Prestwich, "Maps and the Perception of Space," in *An Invitation to Geography,* eds. David A. Lanegran and Risa Palm (New York: McGraw-Hill, 1973), 35–60. Reprinted by permission.

expressed) of countries located in the higher latitudes. In figure 14.7, the projection is used to show the threat of "World Communism, as it was perceived at the time." The position of the map neatline excludes non-Communist areas, such as Antarctica, Greenland, and Alaska, and much of Canada is covered by the label. On the other hand, virtually all of the exaggerated area of the former Soviet Union is included.

Symbol distortion.   Symbol distortion is a dominant approach in propaganda maps and involves the use of strong colors and bold symbols that make the map appear to represent reality. Only those few viewers who take the time and effort to check the accuracy of the data discover whether or not the information presented is correct. In one small, recently published atlas, the maps were drawn using this approach. In this case, however, the authors include, in

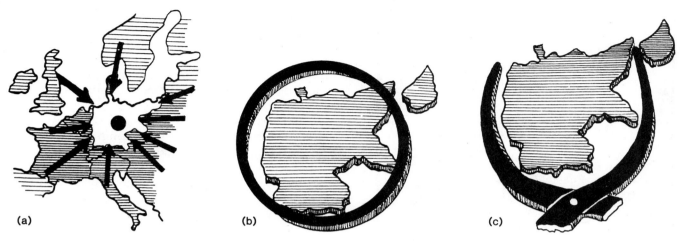

FIGURE 14.8 Typical propaganda map symbols.
(*a*) Arrows, representing pressure from all sides.
(*b*) Circle, showing the encirclement of Germany before
and after the First World War. (*c*) Pincers, signifying
pressure against Germany from France and Poland.

Source: Karl Springenschmid, *Die Staaten als Lebewesen: Geopolitisches
Skizzenbuch* (Leipzig: Verlag Ernst Wunderlich, 1934).

an explanatory section at the end of the atlas, such
statements as: "Some of the allegations recorded may
be mere figments of propaganda," or "The information falls far short of being complete."[7] The producers of propaganda maps are not likely to provide
such candid statements to explain their distorted
maps.

Action symbols are used extensively on propaganda maps (figure 14.8). Arrows, for example, exemplify speed of movement, emphasizing the rapid
movements of modern war, with its use of tanks, mo-
torized infantry, and aircraft. Pincers, concentric rings,
or pictorial symbols of chains, shown around areas
threatened by encirclement, imply the certainty of
defeat and the uselessness of resistance.

In addition, symbols are often designed to confuse
the relative importance of topics. Oversized symbols,
for example, can make it appear that an area is dominated by a certain ethnic group. In one case, thirteen
large symbols were imposed on a German map of
Latvia, giving the impression that the country was
dominated by a German population (figure 14.9). In
reality, Germans comprised only 3.7 percent of the
total population;[8] other nationalities were simply

[7]Michael Kidron and Dan Smith, *The War Atlas: Armed Conflict—Armed
Peace* (New York: Simon and Schuster, Pluto Press, 1983).

[8]John Ager, "Maps and Propaganda," *Bulletin of the Society of University
Cartographers* 11, no. 1 (1977): 1–15, quoting Hans Spier, "Magic
Geography," *Social Researcher* 8 (1941): 310–30.

FIGURE 14.9 Oversized symbols in this map make it
appear that Latvia is dominated by a German population.

Source: Facts in Review, 1 no. 16 (30 November 1939): 3.

FIGURE 14.10 "Secret map" showing purported plan for the reapportionment of South America into five republics.

Courtesy of Franklin D. Roosevelt Library.

omitted from the map. A similar approach can suggest that weapons cover every square foot of land, thus emphasizing (or, perhaps, exaggerating) the threat that the weapons represent.

When graphs are drawn, either separately or as map symbols, a common type of distortion is to use inconsistent scales to represent statistical data. The result is that one cannot obtain a correct visual impression of the relative numbers involved.

Use of imaginary events. Frequently, propaganda maps are simply the product of a creative imagination. An example of the "what might be" approach is provided by the "secret map" that showed purported plans for the reapportionment of South America into five republics (figure 14.10). The aim of this map was to elicit support for the Nazi regime from

the major South American countries that would, presumably, benefit from the addition of territory previously under other jurisdictions. There was a twist to this particular case because British intelligence apparently modified a copy of the Nazi map to show a more drastic change in national boundaries than the Nazis had actually proposed. U.S. President Franklin Delano Roosevelt then used *this* version "to generate support for the de facto war being waged in the Atlantic by the United States Navy against German submarines."[9]

Propaganda maps are also frequently used to support national territorial claims. The appearance of such claims presumably adds to their validity or, at least, reflects a certain element of national pride. Even tiny postage-stamp maps have served this purpose. Recently, for example, Argentina advanced its claim to sovereignty over the Falkland Islands (Islas Malvinas) through the publication of a postage stamp with a map showing the islands as Argentine territory.[10]

Distortion of concepts. In 1904, Professor Halford J. Mackinder published a scholarly paper, "The Geographical Pivot of History."[11] The paper included a map that showed a pivot area, or "heartland," in a protected position in north-central Asia (figure 14.11). Mackinder presented the concept that this heartland had been the source of dominant forces in world history and, furthermore, would continue its importance. For our present purposes, the most interesting aspect of this map was its manner of construction, which was designed to support Mackinder's concept.

The base of the heartland map was a Mercator projection, which exaggerated the size and importance of northern Asia. In addition, the map was enclosed within an unusual elliptical border, which bears no regular relationship to the projection itself. Because of the placement of this border, portions of North and South America appeared *twice* on the map, whereas the polar regions were not shown at all.[12] Mackinder elaborated on the relationships based on

[9]John F. Bratzel and Leslie B. Rout, Jr., "FDR and the 'Secret Map,'" *The Wilson Quarterly* 9, no. 1 (New Year's 1985): 167–73.

[10]Bruce Davis, "Maps on Postage Stamps As Propaganda," *The Cartographic Journal* 22, no. 2 (December 1985): 125–30.

[11]Halford J. Mackinder, "The Geographical Pivot of History," *Geographical Journal* 23, no. 4 (April 1904): 421–37.

[12]S. W. Boggs, "Cartohypnosis," *The Scientific Monthly* 64, no. 6 (June 1974): 471.

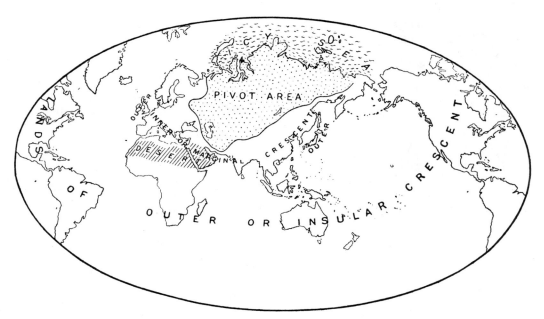

FIGURE 14.11   Mackinder's pivot area or "heartland."

From Halford J. Mackinder, "The Geographical Pivot of History,"
Geographical Journal 23, no.4 (April 1904): 435. © Royal Geographical
Society. Reprinted by permission.

this unusual map design. In addition to the heart-land, for example, he identified an "outer crescent," consisting of North and South America, Australia, and southern Africa. This crescent was illusory because, on the globe, the region is anything but crescent-shaped and, furthermore, did not seem to be related to the heartland in at all the manner of Mackinder's interpretation.

Mackinder's map, and his heartland concept, attracted considerable attention, despite what, in retrospect, seem to be rather strained interpretations. The map, in particular, "was reproduced at least four times in the Nazi literature . . . , with perversions of the author's original intent which were designed to serve malevolent purposes in propaganda."[13]

Other **distortions of concepts** are also utilized on propaganda maps, but the previous examples illustrate the major techniques. The overall result is often very similar to the style of the journalistic maps discussed in chapter 15.

Map users need to be wary of accepting every map as correct. It was recently acknowledged, for example, "that, for the last fifty years, the Soviet Union had falsified virtually all public maps of the country, misplacing rivers and streets, distorting boundaries, and omitting geographical features. . . ."[14] Map users must always be careful to evaluate the maps they use, either on the basis of information provided by the producer or, preferably, by checking independent information sources. Indeed, map users must decide whether or not a particular presentation is a valid picture of reality, or simply a propaganda trick.

The Peters projection.   It may be somewhat harsh to cite the **Peters projection** as an example of a propaganda map. The atmosphere in which the use of the projection has been advocated, however, does fit the definition rather well.

The Peters projection is promoted as a substitute for the Mercator projection, for purposes of thematic mapping. The Mercator projection has, over the years, been consistently used as a general-purpose map. This practice has continued, despite the fact that, because of its scale exaggeration, it is *not* suitable for use as a general reference map or for presentation of most thematic information (see chapter 3). With the scale

[13]Boggs, "Cartohypnosis," 471.

[14]"Which Way to Lenin's Tomb?" *Time* 132, no. 11 (12 September 1988): 49.

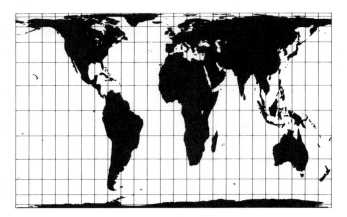

FIGURE 14.12 Peters (Gall) projection. Areas toward the poles are stretched east-west and compressed north-south, whereas equatorial areas are stretched north-south and compressed east-west.

Courtesy of Cartographic Laboratory, University of Wisconsin-Madison.

exaggeration of the Mercator in mind, German historian Arno Peters has promoted the substitution of a particular equal-area projection for the Mercator. The main advantage claimed for the Peters projection, as compared to the Mercator, is that it represents the continents and countries at their correct relative size. In addition, Peters claims that the Mercator is based on "a colonialist and racist mentality" and that its continued use fosters those abhorrent views. This statement is, at best, extremely doubtful. The popular use of the Mercator is more likely the simple result of uncritical acceptance based on familiarity and, possibly, the fact that its rectangular shape easily fits a wall-map format.

In recent years, the shortcomings of the Mercator have resulted in the increasing use of a variety of other projections for wall maps and for illustrations in textbooks and atlases. The truth of the matter is that Peters is raising a rather false argument by consistently comparing the Peters to the Mercator, and only the Mercator, as though it were the predominant (or, indeed, the only) alternative projection.

On the Peters projection, areas toward the poles are stretched east-west and compressed north-south, whereas equatorial areas are stretched north-south and compressed east-west (figure 14.12). It has been suggested that "the land masses are somewhat reminiscent of wet, ragged, long, winter underwear hung out

to dry on the Arctic Circle."[15] Only in the middle latitudes are the general shapes of the landmasses relatively undistorted. This is because the Peters projection is actually a cylindrical equal-area projection with standard parallels at 45°.[16] A large number of other equal-area projections are available, all of which provide the proper size relationships, and many of them have much less distorted shapes than those on the Peters projection.

Above all else, map users should remember that *no* single projection provides the best answer for all purposes, regardless of what boasts may be generated. This is as true of the Peters projection as of any other.

Summary

Cartograms are maplike diagrams that are purposely modified so that distances or areas are no longer the same as on the globe.

Linear cartograms show relationships between locations in terms of relative distances, based on such measures as travel cost or time. Routed linear cartograms show the characteristics of specific paths from one point to another, sometimes with separate lines to represent each direction of travel. Central-point linear cartograms show equal units of time or cost for reaching other locations from a single starting point.

In area cartograms, the areas of regions are proportional to some value associated with them, such as income or population. A noncontiguous area cartogram retains shapes by separating the regions from one another, whereas a contiguous area cartogram retains the relationships between regions but varies their shapes.

Map misuse may be accidental, or it may involve systematic propaganda. The existence of accidental inaccuracy points out that care should be taken when deciding whether or not a map presentation should be believed, even when the map is not a propagandistic product.

[15]Arthur H. Robinson, "Arno Peters and His New Cartography," *The American Cartographer* 12, no. 2 (October 1985): 104.

[16]The Peters projection is "one of a family of cylindrical equal-area projections initially developed by Johann Lambert in 1772," and is also "indistinguishable" from a cylindrical equal-area projection exhibited by Reverend James Gall in 1855. See Phil Porter and Phil Voxland, "Distortion in Maps: The Peters Projection and Other Devilments," *Focus* (Summer 1986): 27.

Propaganda maps share some general, recognizable characteristics, such as simple design and lack of a scale, graticule, or other frame-of-reference elements. They may use inappropriate projections, especially those that exaggerate size or distance. Strong colors and bold symbols are used to imply speed of movement, threat of encirclement, or dominance. Purely imaginary events or features may be mapped as well. Given all of the possible ploys, map users must be wary of propagandistic products.

SUGGESTED READINGS

Ager, John. "Maps and Propaganda." *Bulletin of the Society of University Cartographers* 11, no. 1 (1977): 1–15.

Boggs, S. W. "Cartohypnosis." *The Scientific Monthly* 64, no. 6 (June 1947): 469–76.

Cole, John P., and Cuchlaine A. M. King. *Quantitative Geography.* New York: John Wiley and Sons, 1968, 218–25.

Dent, Borden D. "Communication Aspects of Value-by-Area Cartograms." *The American Cartographer* 2, no. 2 (October 1975): 154–68.

Dougenik, James A., Nicholas R. Chrisman, and Duane R. Niemeyer. "An Algorithm to Construct Continuous Area Cartograms." *The Professional Geographer* 37, no. 1 (1985): 75.

Fleming, Douglas K. "Cartographic Strategies for Airline Advertising." *Geographical Review* 74, no. 1 (January 1984): 76–93.

Griffin, T. L. C. "Recognition of Areal Units on Topological Cartograms." *The American Cartographer* 10, no. 1 (April 1983): 17.

Haushofer, Hans. "Magic Geography." *Social Research* 8 (1941): 310–30.

Loxton, John. "The Peters Phenomenon." *The Cartographic Journal* 22, no. 2 (December 1985): 106–8.

Monmonier, Mark. *How to Lie with Maps.* Chicago: University of Chicago Press, 1991.

———. "Maps, Distortion, and Meaning." *Association of American Geographers Resource Paper 75–4.* Washington, D.C.: Association of American Geographers, 1977.

Olson, Judy M. "Noncontinuous Area Cartograms." *The Professional Geographer* 28, no. 4 (1976): 371–80.

Pickles, J. "Bibliography on Propaganda Maps." Special Libraries Association, Geography and Map Division, *Bulletin,* no. 146 (December 1986): 2–7.

Porter, Phil, and Phil Voxland. "Distortion in Maps: The Peters Projection and Other Devilments." *Focus* (Summer 1986): 22–30.

Quam, Louis O. "The Use of Maps in Propaganda." *The Journal of Geography* 42 (January 1943): 21–32.

Raisz, Erwin. "The Rectangular Statistical Cartogram." *The Geographical Review* 24 (1934): 292–96.

Robinson, Arthur H. "Arno Peters and His New Cartography." *The American Cartographer* 12, no. 2 (October 1985): 103–11.

Thomas, Louis B. "Maps As Instruments of Propaganda." *Surveying and Mapping* 9, no. 2 (April, May, June 1949): 75–81.

Tobler, Waldo R. "Geographic Area and Map Projections." *The Geographical Review* 53 (1963): 59–78.

Tufte, Edward R. *The Visual Display of Quantitative Information.* Cheshire, Conn.: Graphics Press, 1983.

Tyner, Judith A. "Persuasive Cartography." *Journal of Geography* 81, no. 4 (July/August 1982): 140–44.

15
Special-Purpose Maps

This chapter discusses the advantages and disadvantages of some of the more common types of special-purpose maps. The advantages of a special-purpose map are enhanced if the map's special properties are understood before they are used. On the other hand, a special-purpose map may possess shortcomings for other applications, so such maps must be used cautiously.

TRANSPORTATION MAPS

Maps are ideal aids for traveling, both when you are planning the trip and while you are en route. The type of map that is particularly useful for a specific journey depends, in large part, upon your mode of travel. If you are using an automobile, bicycle, or motorcycle, for example, a street or highway map is usually preferable. If you are walking along roads or highways, the same types of maps are useful. If, on the other hand, you are traveling by public transportation, a route map is indispensable. In this section, we discuss each of these types of maps. The use of nautical and aeronautical navigation charts is covered in chapter 6. Also, off-road travel on foot generally requires techniques described in sections on navigation and compass use (chapter 6 and appendix B).

Highway and Street Maps

For convenience, maps used for intercity travel are referred to here as **highway maps** (figure 15.1), while maps used to show the road layout within cities are

called **street maps** (figure 15.2). **Road atlases** are bound volumes that usually contain maps of both types, so they are not dealt with separately.

Although the details of particular highway or street maps vary widely, these two types of maps share a number of common characteristics. It is feasible, therefore, to consider some generally useful approaches to their use.

The amount of information shown on a highway or street map can be extensive. The map legend indicates the types of features shown on the map and the symbols used to represent the features. There is, of course, an emphasis on roads. On highway maps, national, state, county, and local roads are identified with distinctive route symbols. Types of road surface may be shown, and information such as whether or not the highway is divided, how many lanes it has, and whether or not it is limited access is often included. In addition, towns, cities, parks, and other points of interest are usually shown, as are the more important rivers, lakes, and other water bodies. On street maps, major arterials and one-way streets are usually distinguished from secondary arterials and residential streets. Major buildings and water bodies typically are shown.

Street and highway maps do not usually contain much information about terrain, although hill shading or spot heights of major features may be included. Topographic maps are needed for detailed terrain information.

Scale considerations enter into the use of street and highway maps, just as with other classes of maps. This means that one map cannot serve all of your needs. If

FIGURE 15.1   Portion of typical highway map.

Source: Wisconsin State Department of Transportation, Wisconsin Highway Map, 1985–1986.

FIGURE 15.2   Typical street map.

Source: Wisconsin State Department of Transportation, Wisconsin Highway Map, 1985–1986.

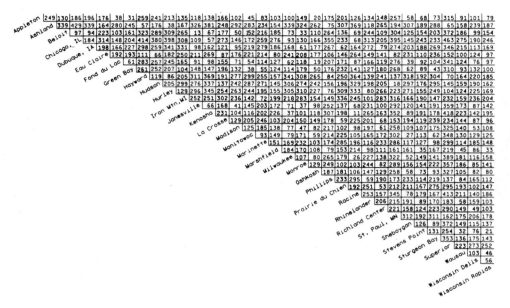

FIGURE 15.3   Typical distance matrix.

Source: Wisconsin State Department of Transportation, Wisconsin Highway Map, 1986–1987.

you are planning a trip between two major cities, for example, you may select your general route by using a map that shows the major highways of all, or a large region of, the country. Such a small-scale map does not show local roads, however, so you will need larger-scale state or regional maps to pick the best route into or out of cities, parks, and other destinations. Also, you will need street maps to find your way to specific addresses or points of interest within each city you visit.

Highway maps.   Generally speaking, the relationships between features on highway maps are reasonably accurate, but exact locations of many features cannot be maintained. Because road widths on highway maps must be exaggerated to maintain legibility, city symbols and highway alignments are often shifted and generalized.

A general strategy for trip planning using a highway map involves first finding the starting point and destination. You may have to refer to an index if you are not familiar with the specific locations. You can then select the most convenient route by scanning the available roads. At this stage, you can also include any desired intermediate destinations. Planning should

take into account the class of roads you wish to use. You may want to take a scenic route offered by secondary roads, for example, or you may prefer to use the faster, more direct route usually provided by major highways. The map key will contain a detailed indication of the various road types. These are typically symbolized by different-colored lines and line symbols. You can write down the route numbers or street names, in the order that they will be traversed, as well as other information, such as the direction of turns that you will have to make and freeway exit and entrance numbers. You may also wish to note features along the way that may be important landmarks. A written travel plan is a useful supplement to your map and will help you to keep track of your travel progress and to anticipate the necessary turns.

Highway maps often include some indication of distances and travel times between major locations. The specific form of table or diagram used varies from map to map. A **distance matrix** is one common form. A typical distance matrix requires locating the names of your origin and destination. The names may be on two outside edges, or they may be consolidated on the diagonal (figure 15.3). The box at the intersection

MILEAGE TABLE

This table shows distances between cities along state or federal routes. To find a distance, locate the two cities in the table at left. Find the smaller of the two index numbers in red in the table below. Read down the blue column to find the second index number.   Mileage between the cities is in black to the right of this number.

1. Appleton
2. Ashland
3. Beloit
4. Chicago,IL
5. Dubuque, IA
6. Eau Claire
7. Fond du Lac
8. Green Bay
9. Hayward
10. Hudson
11. Hurley
12. Iron Mountain,MI
13. Janesville
14. Kenosha
15. La Crosse
16. Madison
17. Manitowoc
18. Marinette
19. Marshfield
20. Milwaukee
21. Monroe
22. Oshkosh
23. Phillips
24. Prairie du Chien
25. Racine
26. Rhinelander
27. Richland Center
28. St. Paul,MN
29. Sheboygan
30. Stevens Point
31. Sturgeon Bay
32. Superior
33. Wausau
34. Wisconsin Dells
35. Wisconsin Rapids

FIGURE 15.4   Typical mileage table.

Source: Wisconsin State Department of Transportation, Wisconsin Highway Map, 1987–1988.

of the column and row associated with these locations contains the desired distance information in miles, kilometers, or both. Distances are usually specified from city center to city center and assume the use of the most direct major route.

A **mileage table**, or **distance log**, is another form of mileage indicator. A mileage table consists of columns of mileage figures. Each city incorporated in the table is given an identification number. You determine the numbers assigned to your origin and destination, and then follow the instructions provided to find the mileage data in the table (figure 15.4).

Another method of providing distance information is a special inset map. A map of this type is usually a simple diagram with straight lines between locations. Distances are printed next to each route segment (figure 15.5), and you simply total the distances for the appropriate segments between your origin and destination.

To determine distances between locations not shown on a distance table or diagram, you may use the map's graphic scale. This is rather awkward for any but the most direct route, so you may prefer to use the

FIGURE 15.5   Simple distance diagram.

Source: Wisconsin State Department of Transportation, Wisconsin Highway Map, 1986–1987.

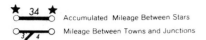

FIGURE 15.6   Distances printed next to route segments.
Source: Oregon Official Highway Map, December 1986.

distance indications often placed along highway segments. Different symbols are used to indicate mileages, but those in figure 15.6 are typical. Here, distances between intersections and towns are shown by a black number next to the highway segment. Longer distances, which may encompass several intersections, are indicated by a star at the start and end of the segment, with the distance printed in red (on the original) adjacent to the middle of the segment. Simply adding the distances corresponding to each segment of your planned route gives you the total distance.

Travel-time information is also often indicated on highway maps, usually on inset maps or in tables similar to those used for distance information. Travel times are only estimates, however, because speeds vary under different conditions.

Street maps.   On street maps, the roads within a city are usually identified by name and route number and are sometimes classified as major or minor arterials and neighborhood streets. Access roads and interchanges are usually shown, frequently with enough detail so that you can determine in advance whether or not you can transfer from one highway to another in the direction you wish to go. Address ranges may also be included so that you can determine the general location of a street address.

Street maps also include many other features, such as city and town names and boundaries, post offices, libraries, parks and zoos, cemeteries, museums, public and technical schools, colleges and universities, hospitals, major office buildings, major retail stores, shopping districts and centers, airports, bus and train stations, churches, convention centers, stadiums, golf courses and country clubs, yacht clubs and moorages, racetracks, and city, county, and other administration buildings. Suitable indexes are usually provided so that specific features can be located.

Automated Navigation

For many years, we have looked forward to having **automated navigation aids** in our cars. These aids would automatically determine and display our location. In addition, they would determine the best route to follow from that location to a selected destination and would guide us along that route by providing directional information. Systems that partially fulfill these visionary ideas now exist, but a great deal of development is necessary before all of the hoped-for capabilities are attained.

A number of systems are under development, or are available, and the details of their operation vary considerably.[1] The dominant feature of most of these systems is the capability of monitoring and displaying the vehicle's location.

Some locational systems require the user to ascertain the vehicle's initial position. Subsequent locations are determined by monitoring vehicle movement with some type of inertial navigation device. In other cases, an external location determination capability is involved. This feature may use a satellite-based global positioning system, Loran-C, or special radio-broadcast information so that the vehicle's location is available at all times, without operator input. In one such system currently available, vehicle position information is relayed to a radio receiver at a central location. The position is then displayed on the screen of a computerized mapping system that incorporates the locations of streets, addresses, and other features. Dispatch and routing orders are then radioed to the vehicle as needed.

Route Maps

Route maps designed for bus, train, subway, and, to a lesser extent, airline passengers are similar in that their content is sharply limited. Usually, they show only the locations served by a particular carrier. They are often diagrammatic, rather than realistic. The simplified routes are usually just lines joining stations, and directions and distances are often not shown accurately (plate 4). Different colors or line symbols may

[1]For summary descriptions of some of these systems and of the issues that must be faced in their development, see Matthew McGranaghan, David M. Mark, and Michael D. Gould, "Automated Provision of Navigation Assistance to Drivers," *The American Cartographer* 14, no. 2 (April 1987): 121–38.

be used to distinguish routes. Route maps are often used in conjunction with timetable information.

Airline maps may be somewhat more colorful than other types of route maps because they are often printed on a background representation of the terrain (plate 5). They usually show their routes as curved lines connecting the cities they serve.

WEATHER AND CLIMATE MAPS

Weather is the state of the atmosphere at a given moment in time, and a weather map presents a snapshot of those atmospheric conditions. Climate, on the other hand, is the average state of the weather over a long period of time. **Climate maps**, therefore, are classification maps that provide a summary of data gathered over time, rather than specific conditions at a given moment in time. If you are not familiar with the weather elements or climatic classifications, you may wish to consult a standard physical geography or weather and climate textbook for further information while reading this section.

Weather Maps

Information on a variety of elements is included on **weather maps**. Some weather maps are limited to individual topics, such as precipitation or temperature. A standard weather map, used for forecasting purposes, however, depicts a wide range of information. The information is gathered from many reporting locations and must be quickly read and understood by large numbers of people (weather forecasters, climatologists, and members of the public with an interest in the weather) located all around the world. For these reasons, weather maps use an internationally adopted set of standardized symbols designed to present information as clearly and succinctly as possible, without written language. Most weather maps are based on these symbols. Modified symbols often appear on newspaper and television weather maps, but even they usually bear a strong resemblance to the standard symbols. Familiarity with the standard symbols, then, allows understanding of the basic information shown on most weather maps.

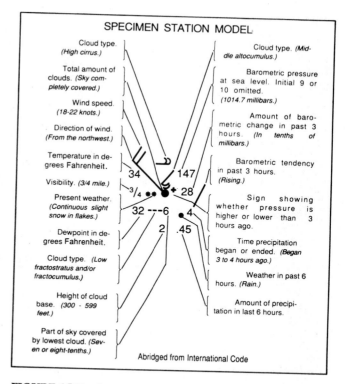

FIGURE 15.7 Specimen weather station model.

As already suggested, the gathering of weather information involves a worldwide network of reporting stations. Observations are taken at all of these reporting stations at the **synoptic hours**: 0000, 0600, 1200, and 1800 Greenwich Mean Time. The observed information includes temperature, dew point, precipitation (type and quantity during past six hours), visibility, clouds (types, and percentage of sky covered), wind (direction and speed), sea-level barometric pressure (observed barometric pressure adjusted to take into account temperature and elevation of the station), and the change in barometric pressure during the past three hours. These data are plotted to create the basis for a weather map, using a prescribed format and special symbols.

A selection of the many symbols used on standard weather maps, and a specimen plot for a single station, are shown in figure 15.7. The central point in the format is a circle that is blackened to indicate the amount of cloud coverage. Attached to this circle is a

FIGURE 15.8   Standard weather map, Tuesday,
20 September 1988.

Source: Daily Weather Maps: Weekly Series September 19–25, 1988
(Washington, D.C.: Climate Analysis Center, National Oceanic and
Atmospheric Administration).

line that indicates the direction from which the wind is blowing. Tags of different types are added to the wind line to indicate the wind speed. If conditions are calm, there is no wind line, and the cloud-coverage symbol is enclosed by a second circle. The station symbols also indicate temperature, visibility, dew point, current barometric pressure, and a variety of other information, as indicated in figure 15.7.

After the individual station observations have been plotted, two items are added to complete the map (figure 15.8). The first of these are **isobars**, which are lines of equal barometric pressure. These indicate the locations of high- and low-pressure centers and pressure gradients. The locations of warm, cold, occluded, and stationary fronts are added next. These indicate the zones of contact between air masses with different characteristics, which are often the principal areas of cloudiness, precipitation, and the more violent forms of weather activity, such as thunderstorms and tornadoes.

FIGURE 15.9   Map of individual climatic element. Mean growing season length (in days) based on the 76-year period 1911–1986.

From Philip W. Suckling, "Freeze Dates and Growing Season Length for the Southern Piedmont, 1911–1986," *Southeastern Geographer* 28, 1 (May 1988):34–45. Reprinted by permission.

Climate Maps

Climate is the summary of day-to-day weather conditions over a long time. Climatic types are based on the analysis of long-term patterns of such factors as temperature range, precipitation amounts (total and seasonal), and evapotranspiration. Locations with similar patterns of variation in the climatic factors are grouped to form climatic regions.[2] Maps of any or all of the climatic factors are produced (figure 15.9), as are maps of the climatic regions (figure 15.10).

Boundary lines on maps are usually shown as firm lines with a definite path that indicate that one region stops at the line and another begins. For example, political boundaries are definite dividing lines in that, on one side of the line, you may be in Canada and, on the other, in the United States. Boundaries between climatic regions, however, are not exact be-

cause there is almost always a transition zone between the core areas of adjoining climatic regions. This type of difficulty is associated with most maps that show boundary lines between regions with different characteristics.

GEOLOGIC MAPS

Geologic maps provide information about the structure of the earth. Many types of maps fall within this general category. Some geologic maps show the types of rocks and other materials exposed at the earth's surface. Others use cross-sectional views to show the types of bedrock that underlie the surface materials. Still others illustrate the occurrence of petroleum or other mineral deposits, the arrangement of faults, the location of earthquake epicenters, the occurrence of fossils, the availability and quality of

[2]It is not surprising, given the large number of factors to consider and the variety of conditions found worldwide, that several climatic classification systems have been developed.

CLIMATE

DESERT
☐ TROPICAL & SUBTROPICAL

▤ MIDDLE LATITUDE

STEPPE
▨ TROPICAL & SUBTROPICAL

◪ MIDDLE LATITUDE

HIGHLANDS
▨ MESOTHERMAL FOREST

◩ MICROTHERMAL SNOW
        FOREST

Source: Atmospheric Lab, Univ. of
Arizona.

FIGURE 15.10   Map of climatic zones in Arizona.

Source: Stephen Bahre, ed., *Atlas of Arizona* (Yuma, Arizona: Arizona
Information Press, 1976).

groundwater, aspects of the earth's thermal and magnetic characteristics, the location of different soil types, and many other topics.

Geologic maps are used for many purposes, including mineral exploration, searches for water sources, investigation of the suitability of different locations for dams or other structures, soil classification, and the selection of appropriate landfill garbage-disposal sites. They are also used as background for zoning studies related to groundwater percolation and to the ability of underlying structures to support major buildings.

The interpretation and use of most types of geologic maps requires training in the field of geology. For this reason, the treatment of geologic maps in this section is limited to those similar to the geologic quadrangle type produced by the U.S. Geological Survey. Such maps, which show the nature of surface deposits, are produced on a standard, topographic-quadrangle base. Cultural features are eliminated on the topographic map, leaving only locational infor-

mation and the contours. This base is overprinted, using a variety of colors, gray values, or patterns, to distinguish the various types of surface deposits (plate 6). The colors give a good visual impression of the materials' distribution pattern. Because of the difficulty of exactly identifying the often somewhat subtle color differences, however, a supplementary letter code is often used to further identify the various materials.

The classification categories used on geologic maps first distinguish materials on the basis of their geologic age, such as Cretaceous or Carboniferous. Then, subcategories describe the composition of the material, such as gravel or sandstone. The result is a detailed description of what is often a large variety of materials (figure 15.11).

Other information typically shown on geologic quadrangle maps includes the location of any fault, or fracture lines. Also, information that helps to describe the attitudes of different beds or strata of rock is shown. One aspect that is indicated is the **strike** of

FIGURE 15.11 Generalized geologic map showing various types of surface materials. (Snowbank Lake area, Minnesota.)

Source: P. K. Sims and S. Viswanathan, "Giants Range Batholith," in *Geology of Minnesota: A Centennial Volume,* eds. P. K. Sims and G. B. Morey (St. Paul, Minn.: Minnesota Geological Survey, 1972), 120–96.

the surface, which is the compass bearing of the intersection of the surface of the bed or strata with an imaginary horizontal plane (figure 15.12). The second aspect, shown in conjunction with the strike, is the **dip**, which is the downward inclination of the bed relative to the same imaginary horizontal plane (also in figure 15.12). The dip value ranges from 0° for a horizontal bed to 90° for a vertical bed.

Geologic maps sometimes indicate the surface configuration of any underlying structures. Such surfaces are shown by a separate set of contour lines, usually in a different color or with a distinctive line pattern. Finally, geologic cross sections frequently accompany the map, to reveal additional information

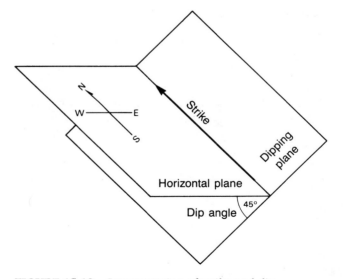

FIGURE 15.12 Interpretation of strike and dip.

FIGURE 15.13   Generalized geologic cross section. (Fillmore County District, Minnesota.)

Source: Rodney L. Bleifuss, ''The Iron Ores of Southeastern Minnesota,'' in *Geology of Minnesota: A Centennial Volume,* eds. P. K. Sims and G. B. Morey (St. Paul, Minnesota: Minnesota Geological Survey, 1972), 498–512.

about the structures found below the surface (figure 15.13). The location and direction of each cross section is marked on the map.

MAPS OF THE PAST

Maps of the past fall into two categories. In the first category are maps that were produced at some time in the past and that have been preserved for examination today. These are called historical maps. In the second category are modern maps, produced to show some aspect of past events. These are called history maps.

Historical Maps

It has been suggested that, because of progress and change in every field of knowledge, every map is out-of-date from the moment it is produced. When a map is not only out-of-date but is also ''old,'' it may fall into the historical category. **Historical maps** are useful because they show things as they existed, or at least as they were represented, in the past. They were, as are modern maps, products of the knowledge, beliefs, and biases prevalent at the time of their production. A study of historical maps, therefore, is useful for understanding past knowledge and beliefs. Through the study of historical maps, for example, we can envision the extent of the knowledge that was available to Christopher Columbus regarding the shape, size, and location of the continents. Given that knowledge, we can better understand his belief that a route to Asia could be found by sailing west from Europe.

FIGURE 15.14   T-in-O map by Isidore of Seville. Diameter of the original: 64 cm.

Source: Isidore of Seville, *Etymologiarum sive originum libri xx* (Augsburg: Günther Zainer, 1472). Courtesy of the Newberry Library.

Careful analysis of historical maps also reveals some of the beliefs that people held when those maps were made. The **T-in-O maps** of the medieval period are an example (figure 15.14). The name of these maps reflects their stylized appearance. The Mediterranean Sea formed the vertical portion of the ''T'' and the Don and Nile rivers constituted its crosspiece. The world ocean created the ''O,'' which surrounded Asia, Africa and Europe—the continents that were known at the

FIGURE 15.15   Historical map of the Washington Mall, 1792.

Source: Looking for an Old Map (U.S. Department of the Interior, Geological Survey, National Cartographic Information Center).

time. This arrangement probably did not represent the actual dominant view of the true size and shape of the earth. Instead, it supported prevalent religious views. For example, the placement of Jerusalem at the center of maps indicated its religious primacy. In addition, an imaginary Paradise was often shown at the top of the map, in the east, or *orient*. This pattern led to the use of the term **orientation** to describe the alignment of a map in its proper relationship to the earth's features. Today, north is usually at the top of the map, but the term persists.

Historical maps were subject to error and deliberate distortion, just as much as are contemporary maps. The careful interpretation of historical maps, therefore, requires equally careful investigation of other sources.

Many people enjoy collecting historical maps.[3] For some collectors, the map's information value is significant to the evolution of a branch of study in which they have an interest.[4] Frequently, however, maps are

collected simply because old objects, such as antique furniture, dolls, cars, or trivets, are interesting and, sometimes, valuable as well. As with other types of antiques, reproductions of historical maps provide colorful and interesting collectibles and have the advantage of being much more affordable than the originals (figure 15.15).

History Maps

History maps are different from antique, historical maps. They are modern products, produced to show what present-day researchers, in whatever field, believe happened in the past. Indeed, history maps are often based on antique maps produced at the time of the event. The topics included on history maps range from routes of exploration to summaries of the history of medicine, and from battle diagrams to maps of migration patterns. Whatever the topic, a history map shows, to the best of current knowledge, the status of the subject at some specific time period in the past (figure 15.16). A series of history maps on a particular topic can provide a very useful summary of the topic's historical evolution. They are a tool for the study and explanation of past events and trends.

[3]If you collect maps, you will find *The Map Collector* magazine interesting. For information, write to the publishers at Church Square, High Street, Tring, Hertfordshire HP23 5AE, England.

[4]If you are researching historical topics, the National Mapping Program brochure *"Looking for An Old Map"* provides useful source information. See also the sections on map collecting in Mark Monmonier and George A. Schnell, *Map Appreciation* (Englewood Cliffs, N.J.: Prentice-Hall, 1988), 313–19, and Joel Makower (ed.), *The Map Catalog* (New York: Vintage Books, 1986).

FIGURE 15.16   History map.

From Richard Mansfield Haywood, *The Ancient World* (New York: David McKay Company, Inc., 1971). Reprinted by permission.

MAPS OF THE MOON AND PLANETS

Simple maps of the moon have been drawn throughout history because the general arrangement of its surface features is visible from earth. Similarly, maps of Mars have been produced since the telescope brought its surface into view. Maps of the moon and Mars were sometimes as much the result of fantasy as of reality but, as science progressed, their accuracy and usefulness improved. With the dawn of the age of space exploration, interest in producing detailed maps of the surfaces of the moon, Mars, and other bodies in our solar system intensified.

The increased interest in nonterrestrial mapping stemmed, in part, from the need for detailed maps to assist in the selection of landing sites for both manned and unmanned exploration vehicles. Areas with suitable terrain for landing and with structures of interest to scientists could be more easily located with the help of accurate maps. In addition, the very technology that produced a need for better maps provided an increased ability to gather the necessary data. Early efforts at such mapping involved photogrammetric techniques and maps that were similar to topographic maps of the earth (figure 15.17). Later, orbital and fly-by probes used remote-sensing systems to send back to earth detailed, digital information regarding detected features.

Since the 1960s, the U.S. Geological Survey has produced maps showing geologic information about the moon and planets. Maps available in this series include geologic maps of Mars and the moon and shaded-relief maps of Mars, Mercury, and Venus. Overall, nineteen planets and satellites had been mapped by remote-sensing methods by 1987, and data acquisition for two more was planned for 1989.[5] Remotely sensed information is used to produce digital photomosaic images whose appearance and accuracy rival similar images of the earth's surface (figure 15.18). As space exploration continues, maps of other bodies in the solar system will be produced, and with improving accuracy.

JOURNALISTIC CARTOGRAPHY

The term *journalistic cartography* refers to maps that appear in newspapers, weekly newsmagazines, and general and popular weekly or monthly magazines.[6] These maps are similar in some ways, but the publication circumstances faced by each of the media also result in some differences in how the maps are handled.

Daily newspapers typically lack the time and resources to develop detailed, fully researched map products. Newspaper maps are frequently limited to

[5]R. M. Batson, "Digital Cartography of the Planets: New Methods, Its Status, and Its Future," *Photogrammetric Engineering and Remote Sensing* 53, no. 9 (September 1987): 1211–18.

[6]Walter W. Ristow, "Journalistic Cartography," *Surveying and Mapping* 17 (1957): 369–90.

FIGURE 15.17   Map of a portion of the surface of the moon.

Source: Macrobius Chart (LAC 43), 1:1,000,000, Aeronautical Chart and Information Center, 1965.

FIGURE 15.18   Digital mosaic image of part of the south polar region of Mars.

Courtesy of R. M. Batson, U.S. Department of the Interior, Geological Survey, Geologic Division, Branch of Astrogeology.

showing the locations of places in the news, whether proposed highway routes, accident sites, hijacking scenes, or battlefields. Maps that would effectively illustrate more complex situations are all too frequently missing. One informal study of maps that appeared in British newspapers revealed characteristics that seem to correspond to maps often encountered in their American counterparts.[7] This study pointed out the general lack of information regarding projection, scale, and orientation, in addition to frequent clutter and small size and, not infrequently, errors in boundaries and other information. These factors made it difficult to assess sizes and distances. Overall, the maps were less useful than they might have been.

Immediacy, especially when bad news is involved, is vital to the inclusion of maps in newspapers. A study of the use of newspaper maps during the Vietnam War, for example, found that the area devoted to maps, and the number of maps appearing, peaked sharply during the period that saw four coastal provinces fall under Communist control.[8] In addition, the "worse" or more dramatic the news, the larger the map's scale. On the other hand, maps are often used in newspapers to illustrate a feature article that is not faced with the same time constraints as the fast-breaking news of the day. In such cases, maps can present more complex subject matter, such as the evolution of a political campaign or the growth of world trade.

In addition to tight deadlines, newspaper maps are faced with reproduction limitations that preclude the use of fine lines and delicate tones. These restraints, coupled with the desire to sharply focus the reader's attention on the topic at hand, result in maps with recognizable characteristics (figure 15.19). They tend to be generalized and often do not have a specified scale or show the graticule. The symbolization tends to be bold and evocative, with elements such as graphic bomb bursts and tapered arrows, indicating action and movement. In addition, explanatory labels are often incorporated to convey specific details of the event. Finally, color is sometimes used to provide even greater visual impact.

[7]W. G. V. Balchin, "Media Map Watch," *The Geographical Magazine* 57 (August 1985): 408–9.

[8]Philip W. Porter, University of Minnesota, "Ten Years Ago Today— Vietnam and the Uses of Cartography" (Poster Session at Annual Meeting of Association of American Geographers, Detroit, 24 April 1985). This display presented an analysis of maps of the Vietnam War that appeared in the *Minneapolis Tribune,* January through August 1975.

FIGURE 15.19   Typical newspaper map.
Courtesy of the *Milwaukee Journal.*

Weekly newsmagazine maps share some of the characteristics of newspaper maps. They, too, are usually generalized and use bold graphic techniques. On the other hand, they tend to be more sophisticated (figure 15.20). This is partly because more time and resources are devoted to their production and partly because they can use finer linework and, frequently, can take advantage of excellent color presentations.

Maps in other types of magazines run a wide gamut in terms of subject matter and style, from simple locational diagrams to maps that present statistical information, show climatic distributions, and represent trade flows. Overall, however, journalistic cartography tends to retain the predominant characteristics of simplicity, direct presentation, and dynamic style.

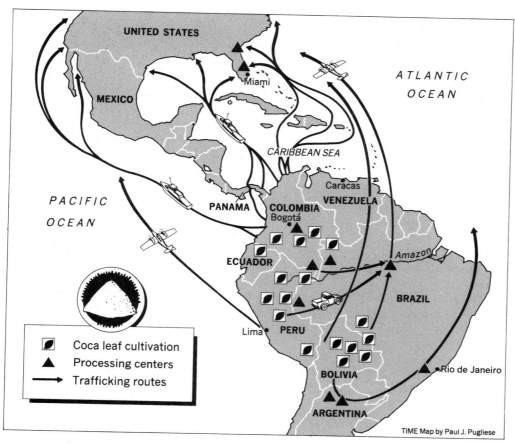

FIGURE 15.20   Black-and-white conversion of weekly
newsmagazine map for a story about cocaine.

TELEVISION MAPS

Maps are frequently used in conjunction with television broadcasts. They seem to show up most frequently on news and weather reports, although they
are also used on travelogues and other types of programs. Most **television maps** are similar to the maps
that often appear in newspapers and newsmagazines.
That is, they are usually highly generalized, with simplified (often oversimplified) coastlines, boundaries,
and other features. They usually lack scales, and even
when a latitude and longitude graticule is shown, the
viewer often has no idea what map projection is being
used.

Given the circumstances under which television
maps are produced and viewed, their style characteristics are not surprising. For one thing, the maps are
likely to be on the screen for only a very brief time,
making it difficult for a viewer to absorb a great deal
of map detail, so generalization is necessary. Similarly, because the map is on a screen and not in the
viewer's hands, it is impossible to effectively measure
distances, except by visual comparisons, so a scale is
not likely to be particularly useful.

The frequent misuse of projections is probably the
single most serious concern with television maps. The
Mercator projection is frequently used, for example,

even though its characteristics make it totally unsuitable for most circumstances. This type of misuse, however, is not surprising because the characteristics of projections are obscure to the viewing public (and, in some cases, to the person responsible for creating the map). This does not make the problem any less serious, however.

One unique aspect of television is its ability to animate images, which is often used effectively to show motion and change on maps. News maps, for example, frequently use moving arrows to show the maneuvers of military forces or trade flow over time. On weather maps, the same techniques are used to show the movement of storm systems and weather fronts. In particular, the use of sequential satellite images gives a dramatic impression of the movement of cloud patterns, even over continental-size areas.

Map viewers must be as alert to misleading maps on television as they are when using other forms of maps—perhaps even more so. On the other hand, the medium provides unique opportunities for developing distinctive map forms, and these opportunities probably will be used more extensively in the future.

Summary

Maps are designed for many special applications. The types described in this chapter are often encountered but are only a sample of the vast variety produced.

Transportation maps include highway, street, and route maps. Because highway maps are designed to assist in intercity travel, they emphasize highways and roads. They tend to be highly generalized, and the locations of other features are often not accurate. Highway maps usually include distance and travel-time information, as well as insets of special features. Street maps concentrate on roads and routes within urban areas but also include supplementary information regarding scenic attractions and urban facilities. To a limited extent, automated navigation aids are beginning to supplement traditional highway and street maps. These aids are generally capable of monitoring and displaying the location of the vehicle in

which they are mounted. Route maps focus on the routes and facilities of public transportation systems, usually to the exclusion of other information. They are often diagrammatic and may include schedule information.

Weather maps show the state of the atmosphere at a given time, using a standard format to present detailed information gathered from many reporting locations. Included on these maps are the location of various types of fronts, temperature, wind speed and direction, cloudiness, isobars showing barometric pressure, and other factors useful for weather forecasting. Climate maps, in contrast, show the average distribution of various climatic factors or the extent of climatic regions.

Geologic maps show surface materials, bedrock types, or other information, ranging from the location of earthquake epicenters to groundwater quality. U.S. Geological Survey geologic quadrangle maps show surface deposits on a standard, topographic quadrangle base. The maps record the locations of any fault lines, as well as other information, such as the strike and dip of rock strata.

Historical maps were produced in the past and reflect the state of knowledge, beliefs, and biases prevalent at the time of their production. They provide useful insights into the past. History maps, on the other hand, show what present-day researchers understand about events or conditions in the past.

Maps of the moon and planets have been produced in greater quantity, and with greater accuracy, since the advent of manned and unmanned space exploration. This partially reflects the greater need for detailed maps to assist in space flights and landings but also is a result of the great increase in the amount of information available.

Journalistic cartography refers to the maps that appear in newspapers and magazines. As a rule, these maps are highly generalized, often without a scale or graticule. They also tend to use bold and dramatic symbols and, unfortunately, often include errors. Typical television maps share the characteristic shortcomings of journalistic maps. They do, however, frequently use animation to effectively show motion and change.

SUGGESTED READINGS

Bagrow, Leo. *History of Cartography.* 2d ed. Revised and enlarged by R. A. Skelton. Chicago: Precedent Publishing, 1985.

Balchin, W. G. V. "Media Map Watch." *The Geographical Magazine* 57 (August 1985): 408–9.

———. "Media Map Watch: A Report." *Geography* 70 (October 1985): 339–43.

Batson, R. M. "Digital Cartography of the Planets: New Methods, Its Status, and Its Future." *Photogrammetric Engineering and Remote Sensing* 53, no. 9 (September 1987): 1211–18.

Brown, Lloyd A. *The Story of Maps.* Boston: Little, Brown, 1949; New York: Dover, 1979.

Claussen, Hinrich. "Vehicle Navigation Systems." In *Geographic Information Systems: The Microcomputer and Modern Geography,* edited by D. R. Fraser Taylor, vol. 1, *Modern Cartography.* Oxford: Pergamon Press Inc., 1991.

Crone, G. R. *Maps and Their Makers.* 5th ed. Folkestone, England: William Dawson and Sons; Hamden, Conn.: Archon Books, 1978.

Gauthier, Majella-J., ed. *Cartographie Dans Les Medias* (Cartography in the media). Québec: Presses de l'Universite du Québec, 1988.

Gilmartin, Patricia. "The Design of Journalistic Maps: Purposes, Parameters and Prospects." *Cartographica* 22, no. 4 (1985): 1–18.

Harley, J. B., and David Woodward. *History of Cartography.* Volume 1, *Cartography in Prehistoric, Ancient, and Medieval Europe and the Mediterranean.* Chicago: University of Chicago Press, 1987.

Hodgkiss, Alan G. *Understanding Maps: A Systematic History of Their Use and Development.* Folkestone, England: William Dawson and Sons, 1981.

Holmes, Nigel. *Pictorial Maps.* New York: Watson-Guptill Publications, 1991.

MacEachren, Alan M., and David DiBiase. "Animated Maps of Aggregate Data: Conceptual and Practical Problems." *Cartography and Geographic Information Systems* 18, no. 4 (October 1991): 221–29.

McGranaghan, Matthew, David M. Mark, and Michael D. Gould. "Automated Provision of Navigation Assistance to Drivers." *The American Cartographer* 14, no. 2 (April 1987): 121–38.

Monmonier, Mark S. *Maps With the News: The Development of American Journalistic Cartography.* Chicago: The University of Chicago Press, 1989.

———, and George A. Schnell. *Map Appreciation.* Englewood Cliffs, N.J.: Prentice-Hall, 1988, chapters 8 and 9.

Moreland, Carl, and David Bannister. *Antique Maps: A Collector's Handbook.* London and New York: Longman, 1983.

Ristow, Walter W. "Journalistic Cartography." *Surveying and Mapping* 17 (1957): 369–90.

Skelton, R. A. *Maps: A Historical Survey of Their Study and Collecting.* Chicago: University of Chicago Press, 1972.

Thrower, Norman J. W. *Maps and Man: An Examination of Cartography in Relation to Culture and Civilization.* Englewood Cliffs, N.J.: Prentice-Hall, 1972.

Tooley, R. V. *Maps and Map Makers.* 6th ed. London: Holland Press; New York: Richard B. Arkway, 1980.

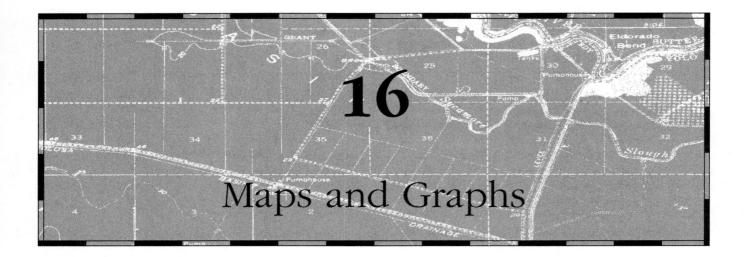

16

Maps and Graphs

Graphs are often associated with maps, either as map symbols or as supporting illustrations (figure 16.1). The ability to read graphs properly, therefore, is an important map-use skill. In this chapter, we will discuss types of graphs commonly used in conjunction with maps, interpretation of these graphs, and frequently encountered interpretation difficulties. Some of these difficulties are due to deficiencies in graph design and others to misinterpretation on the part of the user. An additional benefit of this chapter is that its information is useful whenever graphs are encountered, whether or not they are associated with maps.

LINE GRAPHS

Line graphs are one of the most straightforward and commonly encountered types of graph. Although their general appearance is likely to be familiar, a review of their characteristics will help avoid misinterpretations.

Simply stated, a line graph consists of a line joining points plotted on a grid. The path of the line shows the value of one variable relative to the value of another.

Types of Variables

Different types of variables are plotted on the axes of line graphs. For example, time periods commonly are placed on the *x*-axis, and another variable, such

as trade volume, the birthrate, automobile production, the wholesale price index, output per worker-hour, or total employment, is placed on the *y*-axis (figure 16.2a). Line graphs may also have variables other than time on both axes. Such pairs of variables can show, for example, the number of students with different intelligence quotients or the number of towns of different size classes. In such cases, the categories themselves are usually shown on the *x*-axis and the number of occurrences in each category on the *y*-axis (figure 16.2b).

Sometimes, one of the variables shown on a line graph is believed to be independent and to influence the value of the other (dependent) variable. In these situations, the independent variable is usually plotted on the *x*-axis and the dependent variable on the *y*-axis. The following list of paired variables illustrates the concept (the independent variables are listed first in each pair): temperature and disease rate; unemployment rate and frequency of strikes; alcohol consumption and accident rates; the thickness of glacial ice and its rate of flow.

Maps as Graphs

An even closer link exists between graphs and maps than has been suggested so far. For example, a line graph in which the longitude of an occurrence is plotted on the *x*-axis and the latitude on the *y*-axis could also be called a map. Another example along the same lines is the idea that a profile is also a line graph. In this case, the graph shows elevations at given distances along a line.

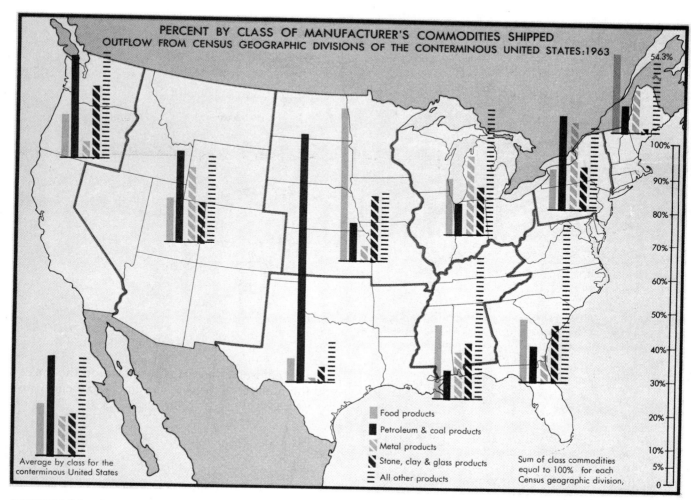

FIGURE 16.1   Graphs used as map symbols.

Source: Map sheet entitled "Shipments of Commodities by Manufacturers in the Conterminous United States, Outflow from Census Geographic

Divisions: 1963," Department of Commerce, Bureau of the Census (Washington, D.C.: U.S. Government Printing Office).

One fundamental difference between maps and graphs involves the notion of interdependence. On many graphs, one value (for example, age) may be related to another (for example, mobility). On maps, however, there is no implication that latitude is related to longitude.

We do not pursue this discussion further here because, after all, the rest of the book is about maps, but you may wish to give the matter some further thought.

Types of Scales

Line graphs may have either arithmetic or logarithmic scales, and each type has unique characteristics. The next two sections discuss the similarities and differences between the two types.

First, however, the general point needs to be made that graph scales are arbitrary. Suppose, for example, that a graph shows fluctuations in prices, ranging from one hundred to one thousand dollars, spread over a

**FERTILIZER NUTRIENTS
USED PER ACRE**

POUNDS PER CROPLAND ACRE

(a)

**DISTRIBUTION
OF FOOD STAMP PARTICIPANTS
BY HOUSEHOLD SIZE**

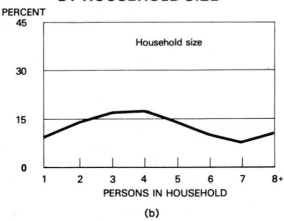

(b)

FIGURE 16.2　Typical simple line graphs. Such graphs usually show (*a*) time periods or (*b*) categories on the *x*-axis and the number or rate of occurrences on the *y*-axis.

Source: 1978 Handbook of Agricultural Charts, Agriculture Handbook No. 551 (Washington, D.C.: U.S. Department of Agriculture, November 1978).

span of ten years. There is no predetermined way to decide how far apart the years should be spaced on the graph or how much space should represent a value of one hundred dollars. Instead, the scales for these values may simply be determined by how many units must fit into the available space. In some instances, however, graph scales are deliberately selected to emphasize or de-emphasize the importance of a particular aspect of the data.

Whatever considerations determine scale selection, the results are crucial to the graph's interpretation. If one axis is long, relative to the other, for example, a specific change in value will look very different than if the same axis is made relatively short (figure 16.3). The user must determine whether the scale of the graph is reasonable in relation to the range of values in the data or if some distortion is being introduced by the graph's dimensions.

Arithmetic line graphs.　On an arithmetic line graph, the spacing between values is constant. That is, equal vertical (or horizontal) distances indicate equal changes in value, anywhere on the graph.

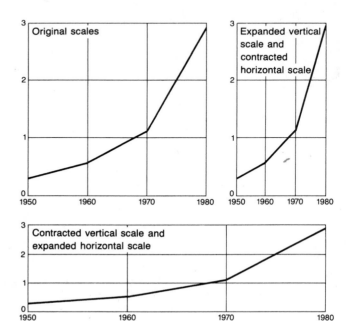

FIGURE 16.3　If one axis is long relative to the other, a specific change in value will look very different than if the same axis is made relatively short. Here, the same data are plotted using three different scale relationships.

FARM POPULATION

(a)

EMPLOYMENT OF FARM RESIDENTS

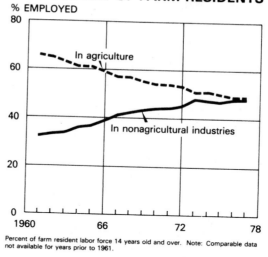

Percent of farm resident labor force 14 years old and over. Note: Comparable data not available for years prior to 1961.

(b)

FIGURE 16.4 Line graphs using (*a*) absolute and (*b*) percentage scales.

Source: 1978 Handbook of Agricultural Charts, Agriculture Handbook No. 551 (Washington, D.C.: U.S. Department of Agriculture, November 1978).

Some arithmetic line graphs are drawn using **absolute scales**, which means that each unit of distance on the graph represents the same *quantity* of a given variable. In figure 16.4a, for example, a given vertical distance indicates a change of a given quantity, regardless of where on the graph it occurs. Other arithmetic line graphs are drawn using **percentage scales**. In this type, equal spacings indicate equal percentage ranges. For example, in figure 16.4b, a given vertical distance indicates a certain percent difference, regardless of where on the graph it is measured. The comments on interpretation that follow apply equally to these two types of scales.

The spacing of the scale on either axis of an arithmetic line graph should usually be uniform. If the scale shows the passage of time, for example, a five-year period should cover five times as much distance as a one-year period. Similarly, if the scale shows values in dollars, every unit of distance should represent the same number of dollars. A nonuniform spacing on an arithmetic line graph often indicates that the graph is poorly drawn or purposely exaggerated and, therefore, is misleading. Logarithmic scales, which are discussed later, are a special exception to this.

A common fault in line-graph design that affects interpretation is the failure to start the vertical scale at zero. This often occurs when high total values are involved and the differences in those values are relatively small. In such cases, the omission of the zero baseline decreases the range of values that must be accommodated within the height of the graph. This allows variations in the values to be shown more clearly but also makes it difficult to judge the relative importance of the value changes (figure 16.5).

An alternative way to deal with the problem of small changes in large total values is to show the zero baseline but break the vertical scale to indicate missing values (figure 16.6). This is less likely to be misinterpreted because it calls attention to what has been done.

In either type of presentation, however, graph interpretation must be done cautiously because the importance of the changes in value is exaggerated. The best thing the user can do is to visualize (or measure) where the baseline *should* be or what the total length of the scale should be. This gives a perspective on the amount of exaggeration present and on the real importance of the changes. Unfortunately, there seems to be a trend away from showing the zero baseline if

WORLD PRODUCTION AND CONSUMPTION OF RAW WOOL

Clean-content weight.   Production on marketing-year basis.

FIGURE 16.5   Omission of the zero baseline allows variations in the values to be shown more clearly but makes it difficult to judge the relative importance of the value changes.

Source: 1978 Handbook of Agricultural Charts, Agriculture Handbook No. 551 (Washington, D.C.: U.S. Department of Agriculture, November 1978).

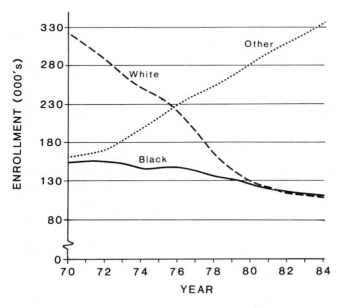

FIGURE 16.6   Zero baseline, with break in vertical scale to indicate missing values. (Total pupil enrollment in the Los Angeles school system, 1970–1984.)

From W. A. V. Clark, ''The Roepke Lecture in Economic Geography: Urban Restructuring from a Demographic Perspective,'' *Economic Geography* 63, no. 2 (April 1987): 103–25. Reprinted by permission.

the result would be ''inartistic'' and if the user can be assumed to be knowledgeable enough to realize that a zero origin does exist.[1]

Another interpretation problem is introduced when several different lines are plotted on a single graph. Normally, the main difficulty in this situation is simply keeping track of the trends of the separate lines as they intermingle with one another (figure 16.7a). The problem is more complicated when the different lines are measured in different types of quantities. Such a graph might include population, measured in numbers of people; gross national product, petroleum prices, and stock-market averages, all measured in dollars; and gasoline and crude oil production, both measured in barrels. The interpretation of such a **multiple-scale graph** requires that the user must, first, be alert enough to realize that different scales are being used and, second, be careful to use the proper scale for each variable (figure 16.7b).

With a multiple-scale line graph, the relationships between the scales are arbitrary and would apparently change if the scale values were shifted. This means that little can be inferred from a comparison of the different lines, other than whether or not a trend relationship exists between them. A trend relationship, however, does not necessarily indicate a causal relationship between any of the variables. For example, if stock market prices and gasoline production seem to follow a similar pattern of ups and downs, is it because one is affecting the other? If so, which one is the cause and which the effect? Or is it possible that some *other* variable, perhaps one not shown on the graph, is affecting *both* stock-market values and gasoline production? In other words, various explanations for the patterns seen on a graph should be carefully considered. A graph, of whatever type, may suggest a variety of relationships, but the interpretation of those relationships cannot stand on its own without adequate theory.

One special type of single-scale line graph is a **bilateral graph**. A bilateral graph uses a single arithmetic scale to portray the values of two related variables. The overlap of the lines that represent these variables is then interpreted in terms of either positive or negative values. An excess of births over deaths

[1]Cecil H. Meyers, *Handbook of Basic Graphs: A Modern Approach* (Belmont, Calif.: Dickenson, 1970), 39.

U.S. COTTON PRICES

¢ PER POUND

(a)

SHEEP NUMBERS AND LAMB AND MUTTON PRODUCTION

MIL. HEAD

(b)

FIGURE 16.7   Multiple-line graphs. (*a*) Several different lines plotted, all using the same scale. (*b*) Two lines plotted, each line showing a different type of quantity, and each with its own scale. In this case, one line shows numbers of sheep on farms and the other shows lamb and mutton production in billions of pounds.

Source: 1978 Handbook of Agricultural Charts, Agriculture Handbook No. 551 (Washington, D.C.: U.S. Department of Agriculture, November 1978).

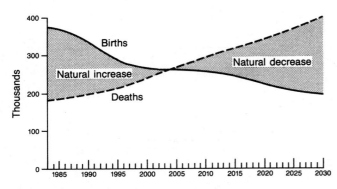

FIGURE 16.8   Bilateral graph. Population forecast for Canada.

Source: Redrawn from "Speaking Graphically," *Population Today,* 13, 12 (December 1985), 5 (Population Reference Bureau, Inc: Washington, D.C., 1985).

FIGURE 16.9   Accumulative line graph (Lorenz curve), showing families ranked by personal income, United States, 1954.

Source: Frederick V. Waugh, *Graphic Analysis in Agricultural Economics* (Washington, D.C.: U.S. Department of Agriculture, Agricultural Marketing Service, 1957), 9.

yields a natural increase in population, for example, whereas an excess of deaths over births indicates a natural decrease (figure 16.8).

Another special type of single-scale graph is a **silhouette graph.** This is simply a standard line graph in which the area below the curve is shaded or colored to give a silhouette effect. The shading highlights the trend of the line on the graph but has no other significance. Silhouette graphs should not be confused with the similar-appearing surface graphs discussed later in this chapter because the two types are interpreted quite differently.

Accumulative line graphs, often called **Lorenz curves,** are special arithmetic line graphs used to determine the degree of concentration in one variable, as compared to another. Lorenz curves are frequently used on maps in connection with interregional comparisons of a variety of population, economic, or other information.

A Lorenz curve is constructed with equal percentage units on each axis (figure 16.9). In this example, if income were equally distributed among all families, 20 percent of the families would have 20 percent of the income, 50 percent would have 50 percent of the income, and so on. The graph of these values would follow the diagonal straight line. In actuality, however, in 1954, the lower 20 percent of families received only about 6.5 percent of the income, 50 percent received about 27 percent, and 80 percent received about 57 percent. The plot of these values is

shown by the solid, curved line in figure 16.9. The greater the disparity in a distribution, the greater the departure of the Lorenz curve from the diagonal line of equality.

Some single-scale line graphs are plotted on the basis of **index values** instead of absolute numbers. Some appropriate base period is selected, and index values for each category are then computed by dividing the individual data values by the base-period value and multiplying the results by 100. An increase from a base-period quantity of gasoline production of 85 million barrels to 170 million barrels in a later period, for example, represents a doubling of production. The index values for the two periods would be 100 and 200, respectively. On the other hand, the same index values might express a doubling in average wages from a base-period value of $19,500 to $39,000 in the later period. Index values, therefore, express the ratio between base-period absolute numbers and absolute numbers for other time periods.

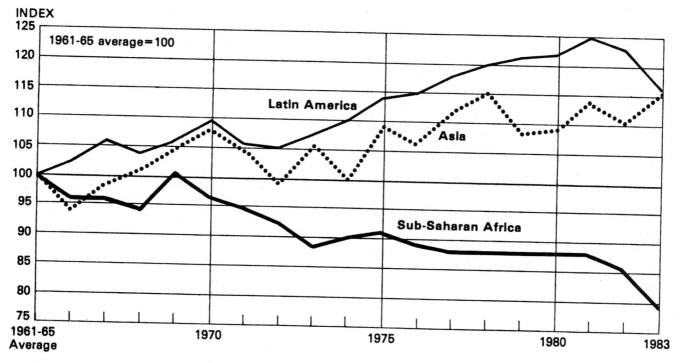

INDEX

1961-65 average = 100

Latin America

Asia

Sub-Saharan Africa

1961-65 Average   1970   1975   1980   1983

FIGURE 16.10   Line graph using index values. (Index of per capita food production, 1961–1965 to 1983: Sub-Saharan Africa, Latin America, and Asia.)

Source: Thomas J. Goliber, "Sub-Saharan Africa: Population Pressures on Development," *Population Bulletin* 40, no. 1 (1985): 16 (Washington, D.C.: Population Reference Bureau).

Index values make it possible to compare relative changes in the values of different variables by using the same base period for all of the categories, even when the units in which the variables are reported are different from one another.

When index values are plotted, the baseline of the graph is set at 100—the base-period value—not at zero. The index values of the different variables for other periods, which can be more or less than 100, are plotted above or below the baseline, as appropriate (figure 16.10).

Different types of indexes are used in line graphs. Price indexes, for example, are based on the cost of goods purchased, in dollars. Quantity indexes, on the other hand, measure the volume of variables such as coal production in tons, number of workers employed in construction, or consumption of goods in units. Finally, value indexes are based on the total dollar volume of variables such as income, payroll, or sales.

Logarithmic line graphs.   The second major type of line graph uses a logarithmic, or ratio, scale. On a **logarithmic scale**, there is no zero.[2] Instead, the value range starts at some suitable value, such as one, and increases until it reaches ten times the starting value—in this case, ten. A range of values with a multiple of ten is called a **cycle**. If the values shown on a graph cover more than a multiple of ten, additional cycles are required (such as one hundred and one thousand).

[2]See any standard mathematics textbook for a definition of logarithms.

Population (thousands)

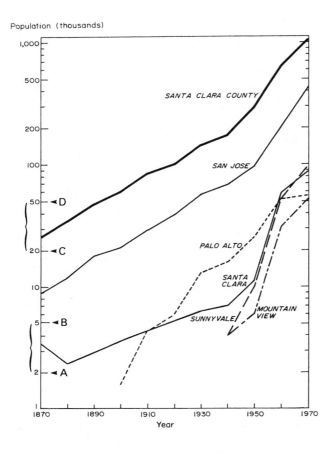

Because of their variable scale spacing, equal distances on logarithmic scales obviously do not represent equal absolute-value differences. Instead, equal distances indicate the same *percentage change* in value. In figure 16.11, for example, a given distance represents a population range of 3,000 persons between points *A* and *B,* but represents a range of 30,000 persons between points *C* and *D.* Notice, however, that *B* is two and one-half times the value of *A,* and *D* is two and one-half times the value of *C.* In other words, the ratio between the values is the same.

When a logarithmic scale is used on one axis of a graph (usually the *y*-axis), and an arithmetic scale is used on the other, the graph is called a **semilogarithmic**, or **semilog**, **graph.** The most useful characteristic of a semilog graph is that the shape and slope of the lines plotted on the graph reveal trends in the changes of the values (figure 16.12). A downward-sloping straight line on a semilog graph represents a

FIGURE 16.11   Graph using logarithmic cycles for the vertical scale, showing population growth in Santa Clara County, 1870–1970. On a logarithmic scale, equal distances represent equal percentage changes.

From Richard A. Walker and Matthew J. Williams, "Water from Power: Water Supply and Regional Growth in the Santa Clara Valley," *Economic Geography* 58, no. 2 (April 1982): 95–119. Reprinted by permission.

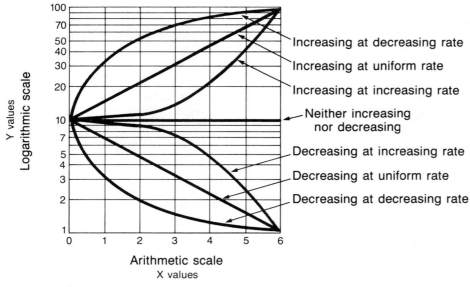

FIGURE 16.12   Slope and direction of lines on a semilogarithmic graph reveal trends in the rates of change of the values.

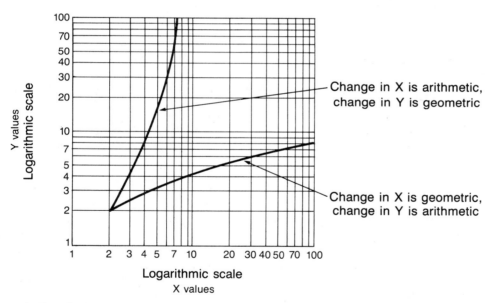

FIGURE 16.13   Shape and slope of lines on log-log graphs reflect percentage rates of change in both variables.

constant rate of decrease, for example, whereas an upward-sloping straight line represents a constant rate of increase. Also, curved lines on a semilog graph indicate increasing or decreasing rates of change.

A semilog graph shows the *relative* rate and direction of change, and parallel lines anywhere on the graph indicate equal rates of change. The absolute magnitudes of value changes are difficult to discern on a semilog graph. Arithmetic graphs, on the other hand, are appropriate for the interpretation of absolute magnitudes, but not of rates of change.

Log-log graphs use logarithmic scales on both axes and show percentage changes in both variables simultaneously (figure 16.13). A straight-line plot sloping upward at a 45° angle on a log-log graph indicates that the percentage rate of increase in both variables is the same. If the line slopes upward at greater than 45°, the percentage increase in the y-variable is greater than the percentage increase in the x-variable. If the upward slope is less than 45°, the opposite relationship is true. Downward-sloping lines indicate decreases in the value of the y-variable. Curved lines on log-log graphs indicate that one of the rates of change is geometric and the other is arithmetic.

SURFACE GRAPHS

The discussion of the types of values and scales used with arithmetic-scale line graphs applies equally to **surface graphs.** Because line graphs and surface graphs look very similar, they are sometimes confused. But how the two types are plotted and interpreted is significantly different. The values displayed on surface graphs are expressed as spaces, or bands, *between* the lines on the graph, whereas on line graphs, the values are measured from the baseline to each data line.

In contrast to line graphs, most surface graphs have a distinctive color, pattern, or shade of gray applied over each data band to call attention to the bands and emphasize the nature of the graph. If the bands are not marked in this way, the location of the graph labels should help to determine whether the graph is a line graph or a surface graph. In a line graph, the lines are labeled, as in the preceding illustrations. In contrast, on most surface graphs, the areas are labeled. (One exception is that the top line on a surface graph, which indicates the total value of the variable being graphed, is often labeled.)

Figure 16.14 shows how surface graphs are set up. The distance between the baseline and the top of the first band is based on the " 'European'/More Developed Regions" population for each year of the period.

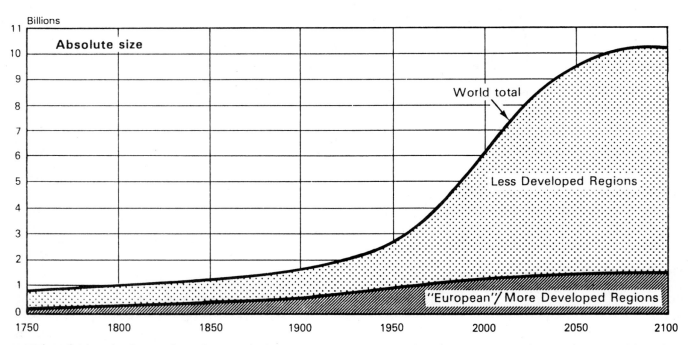

FIGURE 16.14   Absolute-scale surface graph showing world population growth (actual and projected) from 1750 to 2100. The two subcategories that are labeled (less developed and more developed regions) yield total world population (labeled line).

Source: Thomas W. Merrick, with Population Research Bureau staff, "World Population in Transition," *Population Bulletin* 41, no. 2 (1986): 4 (Washington, D.C.: Population Reference Bureau).

Similarly, the distance between the top of the first band and the top of the second band is based on the population of "Less Developed Regions." The line that defines the top of each band, then, is measured from the top of the band just below it, *not* from the baseline, as would be the case on a line graph. This method of construction results in the graphs's top line reflecting a total value that is an accumulation of all of the values below it—"World total," in figure 16.14. When interpreting a surface graph, users should be aware that sharp changes in the value of a given band make it difficult to judge the widths of the bands above it.

Surface graphs are sometimes presented in percentage form. In these situations, the total distance between the baseline and the straight line across the top of the graph represents 100 percent. Each band within the graph, then, represents a proportional share of the 100-percent total and not an absolute data value.

BAR CHARTS

A **bar chart** consists of bands or bars, each one representing a particular data range, such as an age grouping or a time period. The bars may be arranged

either horizontally or vertically, and are interpreted in the same way. Because the bars are kept a constant width, the area of each one, and hence its visual impact, is proportional to the value represented.

Types of Scales

Bar charts may show either absolute or percentage values, and either type may be subdivided. On maps, either a single bar or multiple bars may be shown for each region. A single bar represents the value of a certain category in a given time period. Multiple bars, on the other hand, show either the values of a single category for different time periods or the values of different categories during a single time period.

When an absolute-value chart is not subdivided, each bar is drawn to a length proportional to its value (figure 16.15). When such a chart is subdivided, the length of the bars, and of each segment of each bar, is proportional to the value each represents (figure 16.16).

California from 1860 to 1985

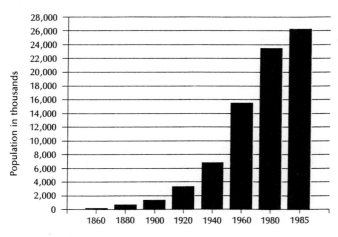

FIGURE 16.15   Bar chart with absolute-value scale (undivided). Notice that, in this example, the time intervals between observations vary, and, ideally, the spacing between bars should vary in proportion to the actual intervals.

Source: "Speaking Graphically," *Population Today* (1984): 15 (Washington, D.C.: Population Reference Bureau).

FARM DEBT

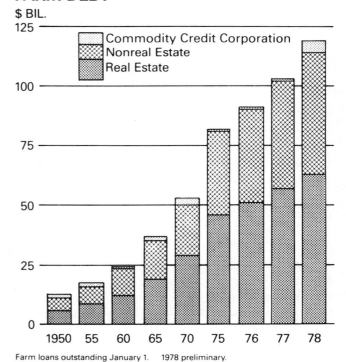

Farm loans outstanding January 1.   1978 preliminary.

FIGURE 16.16   Bar chart with absolute-value scale (subdivided).

Source: 1978 Handbook of Agricultural Charts, Agriculture Handbook No. 551 (Washington, D.C.: U.S. Department of Agriculture, November 1978).

MAJOR LAND USES BY OWNERSHIP

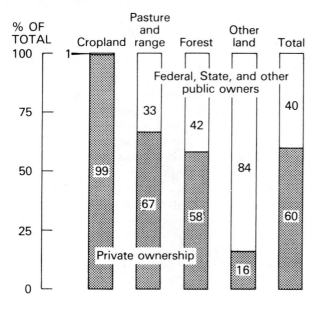

1974 data.

FIGURE 16.17   Bar chart with percentage-value scales (single variable).

Source: 1978 Handbook of Agricultural Charts, Agriculture Handbook No. 551 (Washington, D.C.: U.S. Department of Agriculture, November 1978).

Bar charts are also drawn with percentage scales. In one common type of percentage-value chart, each bar shows the subdivision of a single variable (such as a land-use type in figure 16.17). All of the bars are the same length, which represents 100 percent, and are subdivided in proportion to the percentage of the total value represented by each subcategory (such as type of ownership).

Use of Symbols

Symbols, such as oil barrels or silhouettes of people, are often used in place of simple bars to introduce an element of interest into the graph. The proper use of such symbols should not interfere with the graph's interpretation. Each symbol is assigned a value, and the number of whole or partial symbols required to equal the total is lined up in a row (figure 16.18). The result is that the row of symbols is the equivalent of a bar.

WISCONSIN

Population by Race and Residence
NUMBER IN THOUSANDS

Ŷ WHITE   ♦ NEGRO   Ŷ OTHER RACES

THE STATE

Total   4,259   128   31

FIGURE 16.18   Chart with symbols used to create the equivalent of a bar.

Source: General Population Characteristics: Wisconsin (Washington, D.C.: U.S. Department of Commerce, Bureau of the Census, 1970 U.S. Census of Population).

Other Types of Bar Charts

Loss-and-gain bar charts. Loss-and-gain bar charts differ from regular bar charts in that they have a central axis that is established as a zero line (figure 16.19). The bars on the chart are drawn above and below a horizontal axis (or to the right and left of a vertical axis). Negative values (losses) are measured below the axis or to the left. Positive values (gains) are indicated by bars that lie above the axis or to the right.

High-low bar charts. High-low bar charts usually are drawn as vertical bars representing a series of dates or times. Each bar shows the high and low values for each time period and may also include an average value.

Interpretation Problems

A zero baseline is always needed on a bar chart because if it is missing, the relative importance of the values is very difficult to interpret. Similarly, a scale break is generally unacceptable because it can be very

misleading. Such breaks are sometimes introduced, however, if some of the values represented are significantly greater than the rest (figure 16.20).

The introduction of a three-dimensional thickness to a bar chart presumably makes the bar look more interesting (figure 16.21). Unfortunately, it also makes interpretation more difficult because of the visual impression of added height that the thickness gives to the portion of the bar closest to the top.

Each bar on a chart should represent an appropriate period of time or category of data. When time is involved, each bar must represent the same length of time. If lack of data causes the last bar to represent a shorter time period than the others, distortion is introduced (see figure 16.15). In such a case, a projected figure should be used to create a comparable value for the full time period or the spacing between the bars should be adjusted.

PIE CHARTS

A **pie chart** is simply a circle that is subdivided into proportional segments. For example, each subdivision of a particular chart could indicate the percentage of land ownership represented by different

CHANGE IN PER ACRE VALUE FROM PREVIOUS YEAR

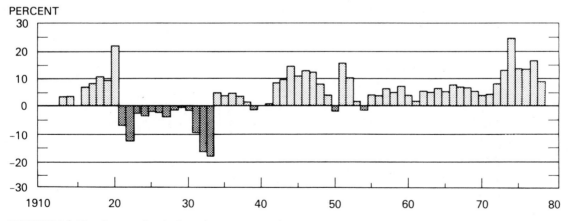

FIGURE 16.19 Loss-and-gain bar chart.

Source: 1978 Handbook of Agricultural Charts, Agriculture Handbook No. 551 (Washington, D.C.: U.S. Department of Agriculture, November 1978).

CHURCH BY CHOICE

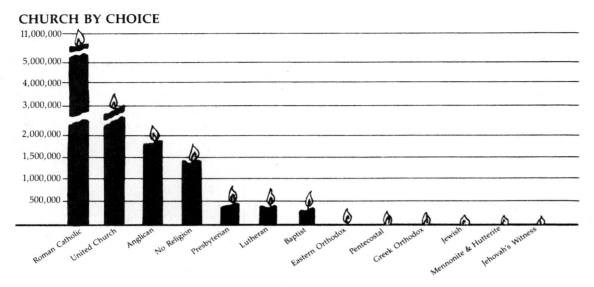

FIGURE 16.20 Scale breaks are sometimes used to make it easier to plot the differences in values. Doing so, however, de-emphasizes the amount of change taking place, so the technique is not generally acceptable.

Source: Canada Today/d' aujourd' bui 15, no. 2 (1984): 8.

U.S. Regional Populations 1987 and 2010 (Projected)

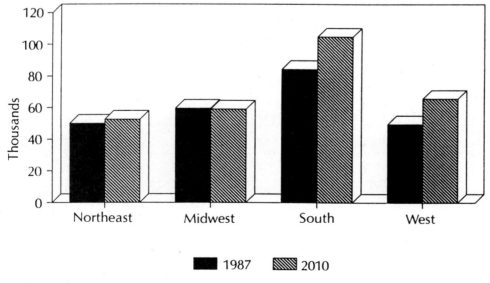

FIGURE 16.21 Bar chart with three-dimensional thickness.

Source: "Speaking Graphically," *Population Today* 16, no. 5 (May 1988): 2 (Washington, D.C.: Population Reference Bureau).

groups (figure 16.22). On maps, pie charts are often used to represent values associated with different regions.[3]

Two common pieces of window dressing introduce difficulties into the interpretation of pie charts. One of these is the use of tilt, so that the pie is drawn as an ellipse, as though it were a circle being viewed from an elevated angle. Although this may look more "interesting," it is also more difficult to interpret. In figure 16.23a, for example, each gray segment of the pie chart represents the same proportion of the total (20 percent). The use of an oblique viewpoint, however, makes it appear that the segment that lies at the top position represents a smaller value than the segment that lies at the sides.

A second common visual enhancement is the addition of thickness to the pie chart (figure 16.23b).

[3]When this is done, the circles are frequently drawn so that the area of each one is proportional to the value associated with its particular region. This use of size variation is discussed in the section "Proportional Symbols," later in the chapter.

LAND OWNERSHIP IN THE UNITED STATES

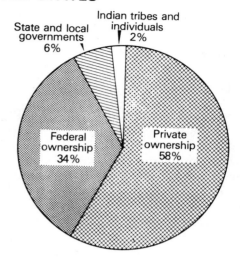

FIGURE 16.22 Pie chart.

Source: 1978 Handbook of Agricultural Charts, Agriculture Handbook No. 551 (Washington, D.C.: U.S. Department of Agriculture, November 1978).

WHAT MAKES UP THE FARM-FOOD MARKETING BILL

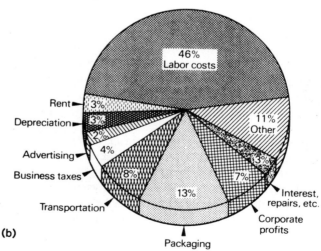

(a)

(b)

FIGURE 16.23 Enhanced pie charts. (*a*) Use of an oblique viewpoint. (*b*) Addition of thickness.

Source: 1978 Handbook of Agricultural Charts, Agriculture Handbook No. 551 (Washington, D.C.: U.S. Department of Agriculture, November 1978).

Thickness increases the visual importance of the chart's bottom segment relative to the other segments.

AREA AND SOLID DIAGRAMS

Proportional Symbols

Numerical data, such as the number of airplanes in an air force, the number of soldiers in an army, the amount of a region's agricultural output, or the quantity of energy resources available to a country, can be represented on a map in many different ways. One way is to use repeated symbols. In this approach, each symbol represents a given quantity, and the total number of symbols placed in each region represents the relevant total (see, for example, figure 14.9). This is essentially the same as the use of such symbols in a bar chart, except that the arrangement may be in a square or rectangular pattern instead of in a bar format.

Still another approach is to use proportional symbols, such as graduated circles, other geometric figures, or realistic figures.

Graduated circles.   The basic idea behind **graduated circles** is that the area of the symbol is proportional, more or less, to the value of the data that it represents. (The implication of the phrase *more or less* is discussed shortly.)

Following this rationale, a circle with one square unit of area may be used to signify one hundred tractors. Then, if another circle is to represent nine hundred tractors, it should cover nine units of area. The *area* of the circle is important, not the circle's diameter.

When proportional circles are used, the cartographer should provide a legend. This allows the map user to compare the sizes of the symbols on the map with the samples in the legend to determine the value that each symbol represents.

There are two methods of sizing proportional circles. In one method, the sizes of the circles are continuously variable, and in the other, they are arranged in a graded series. When **continuously variable symbols** are used, each circle is mathematically scaled in proportion to the value associated with the particular point it represents (figure 16.24a). This means that symbol sizes are extremely varied, with a separate size for each individual value. Because many cartographers feel that such continuously variable symbols are difficult to interpret, range-graded symbols are often used instead.

In the **range-graded approach**, a number of specific symbol sizes are established, and each size represents a particular range of values (figure 16.24b). Thus, on a given map, there may be only five circle sizes, even though a large number of different values are represented. The amount of information conveyed by such a range-graded symbol is less than that conveyed by a continuously variable symbol. This loss of information is, hopefully, offset by the greater ease of interpreting the range-graded symbol. This view is reinforced by evidence that indicates that map users do not, in any case, accurately perceive the differences in value represented by continuously variable symbols.

Map users must examine the map legend to determine what type of graduated-circle symbol is being used and what level of detail can be ascribed to it. If range-graded symbols are used on the map, the information is generalized and, as the name implies, only a range of values can be applied to any given point and *not* an exact value. If continuously variable symbols are used, on the other hand, measuring the size of the symbols to obtain an exact data value is not recommended. It is more useful to interpret the symbols visually and to observe their spatial distribution, but to refer to tabular information for exact values.

The preceding discussion implies that circle symbols are sized in direct proportion to data values. This is not always the case, however. It has been found that map users tend to underestimate the values represented by larger symbols, relative to smaller ones. If a given circle represents a value of 200, for example, a circle that occupies twice as much area is likely to be seen as representing *less than* a value of 400. In an attempt to offset this tendency toward underestimation, some maps are drawn using symbols that are not directly proportional in size to the values they represent. In this **psychological-scaling approach**, the symbols representing larger quantities are exaggerated in size, rather than being drawn in absolute pro-

(a)

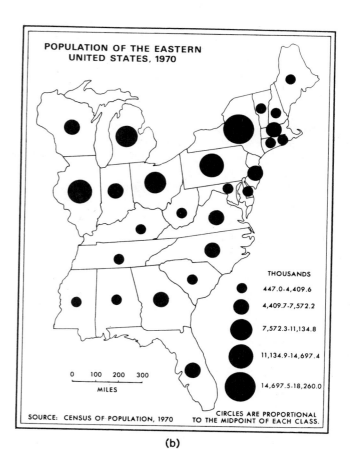

(b)

FIGURE 16.24   Proportional circle symbols.
(*a*) Continuously variable symbols used to show
Palestinian refugees registered with UNRWA (United
Nations Relief and Works Agency), late 1987. (*b*) Range-
graded symbols used to show population of the eastern
United States, 1970. Notice that each circle represents a
range of values and is scaled in proportion to the
midpoint of that class.

(*a*) From *Focus* 37, no. 4 (Winter 1987). Copyright The American
Geographical Society. Reprinted by permission. (*b*) Borden D. Dent,
"Communication Aspects of Value-by-Area Cartograms," *American
Cartographer* 2, no. 2 (October 1975): 154–68. Reprinted by permission
of the American Congress on Surveying and Mapping.

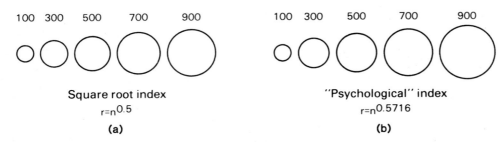

100 300   500   700   900   100 300   500   700   900

Square root index
$r=n^{0.5}$

(a)

"Psychological" index
$r=n^{0.5716}$

(b)

FIGURE 16.25   Principle of proportional circles, using two different methods of scaling. (*a*) Square root index. (*b*) "Psychological" index.

portion (see figure 16.25). The result is that, if a symbol representing 100 tractors occupies one unit of area, one representing 900 tractors occupies *more* than nine units of area.[4]

The size of pie graphs often varies in proportion to the overall data value, in exactly the same manner as simple graduated circles. On a map showing timber harvested by region, for example, the overall size of each pie graph might be proportional to the value or volume of the total harvest for a given region. The types of trees contributing to each region's harvest could then be shown by the subdivisions of the pie graphs. The same interpretation problems apply to proportionally sized pie graphs as to simple proportional circles.

Other geometric symbols.   Other proportional symbols, such as squares, rectangles, hexagons, octagons, and so on, are sometimes used on maps. The area of such geometric symbols is usually proportional to the value they represent, just as with proportional circles. The interpretation of such symbols is quite straightforward if they are properly done. If not correctly scaled, however, their appearance may be very misleading. In either case, only careful comparison of the symbols on the map with the legend will result in accurate judgment of their size and value.

Realistic figures.   Instead of geometric figures, many maps use **realistic figures** to represent data values. These two-dimensional figures are chosen on the basis of the map topic and are meant to increase the map's graphic appeal. Airplanes are used to represent air power, soldiers to stand for military forces, shocks of wheat to indicate agricultural output, and

oil tanks to illustrate energy resources, to cite a few typical examples. Unfortunately, such symbols often result in inadvertent errors in the presentation and may even introduce deliberate distortions.

The concept involved in the use of realistic figures is precisely the same as for geometric figures. That is, the size of each symbol varies in relation to the values of the data associated with it. The use of irregular figures suffers from the same problems as the use of geometric figures, but it is even more difficult for the map user to compare the areas of the irregular symbols.

A major problem with realistic figures is when their size is determined incorrectly. This happens when the heights of the symbols are changed to represent different values and, at the same time, the symbols' width is changed proportionally. Thus, for example, a figure that is made twice as tall also becomes twice as wide, and its area is four times as great (figure 16.26). The

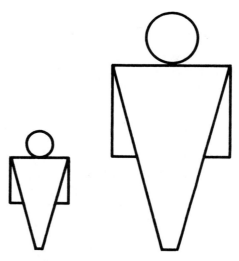

FIGURE 16.26   Interpretation problem with proportional realistic figures (see text for explanation).

[4]The exact ratio used varies. For information on this aspect, see John Campbell, *Introductory Cartography* 2d ed, (Dubuque, Iowa: Wm. C. Brown Communications, Inc., 1991).

person reading the map responds to the area of the symbol, rather than just its height. The impression is given, then, that the second figure in this example represents four times the value of the first, instead of only double.

Because this problem of misscaled symbols occurs frequently, it would be wise, for example, to measure some of the symbols on such a map and to compare the measurements with the values represented. If it is apparent that the areal scale is not consistent, the map is best disregarded.

Volumetric Diagrams

Sometimes, "solid" figures are used to represent values. These are drawings designed to look as much as possible like a sphere, a cube, or some other three-dimensional figure (figure 16.27). Such diagrams are drawn so that the volume of each figure is proportional to the value that it represents; hence, the term **volumetric diagrams**.

Map users usually find it very difficult to correctly estimate the volumes represented. In particular, larger values are likely to be seriously underestimated. At a

minimum, users should carefully compare each figure to the key provided to estimate the quantities represented. In addition, any numerical values that accompany the figures should be studied because they give exact information. Indeed, it might be better to ignore volumetric diagrams entirely because they are likely to be *less* informative than a table of data or some other form of graph, such as a bar chart.

SPECIAL DIAGRAMS

Scatter Diagrams

A special type of graph, called a **scatter diagram**, is often used to display the relationship between two variables. A scatter diagram consists of a set of points plotted on the basis of paired observations of the variables. The value of the independent variable is measured on the *x*-axis and the value of the dependent variable on the *y*-axis. For example, the use of multiple cropping techniques in agriculture might be the independent variable and grain yields the dependent

FIGURE 16.27   A portion of a classic example of the use of volumetric symbols for cities, combined with a dot map of rural population. Legend is at lower left.

From Guy-Harold Smith, "A Population Map of Ohio for 1920," *Geographical Review* 18, no. 3 (July 1928): 422–27. Reprinted by permission of The American Geographical Society.

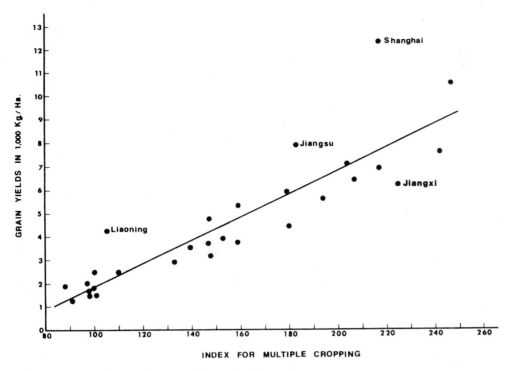

FIGURE 16.28   Scatter diagram with trend line, showing relationship between multiple cropping and grain yields in China, 1979.

From Clifton W. Pannell, "Recent Chinese Agriculture," *The Geographical Review* 75, no. 2 (April 1985): 170–85. Reprinted by permission of The American Geographical Society.

variable (figure 16.28). Other examples from a practically endless set of possibilities include labor costs and product prices; percent of the labor force employed in primary activities and per capita gross national product; ground slope and percentage of woodland; distance from the capital city and population density; and amount of fuel used and amount of power output.

A **trend line** is often superimposed over the cloud of dots on a scatter diagram, as in figure 16.28. The line represents a summary of two aspects of the relationship between the variables: its direction and its strength (figure 16.29).[5] If the trend line slopes upward, from lower left to upper right, the relationship is positive. This means that, as the value of the independent variable increases, the value of the dependent variable also increases. A trend line that

slopes downward, from upper left to lower right, indicates a negative relationship. A negative relationship is one in which the value of the dependent variable decreases as the value of the independent variable increases. If the cloud of points is closely grouped around the trend line, the relationship between the variables is strong. If the points are widely scattered, however, the relationship between the variables is weak.

Population Profiles

A **population profile** (sometimes called a population pyramid) is a graphic display of the age-sex distribution of a given region's population. Population profiles are commonly placed on maps to facilitate the comparison of the population characteristics of different countries or regions.

The basic structure of a population profile consists of a horizontal baseline divided by a vertical centerline. Horizontal bars project from either side of the

[5]This trend line should be determined by a statistical technique, such as regression. Consult any introductory statistics textbook for information about regression computations and their interpretation.

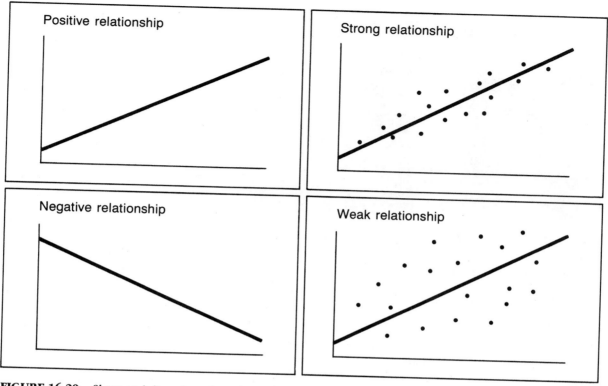

FIGURE 16.29   Slope and direction of trend line, and grouping of cloud of dots, summarize direction and strength of relationship between variables.

centerline, with the length of each bar representing the population in a specific age group. The bars on one side indicate the female segment of the population, and those on the other side represent males. The length of the bars may be based on either absolute numbers or on percentages, and the two types are interpreted differently.

When absolute numbers are used, the length of each bar is proportional to the population of that age-sex group (figure 16.30). The result is that the overall size of each profile varies in proportion to the size of the population represented. If there is a great disparity in the population of the regions involved, the resulting variation in the size of the profiles makes it difficult to compare the population structures. When percentage values are used, on the other hand, the length of each bar is proportional to the percentage of the population represented (figure 16.31). The overall size of each profile, however, is the same, regardless of the total population involved. Thus, a bar that represents 10 percent of a population of one thousand is the same length as the bar that represents

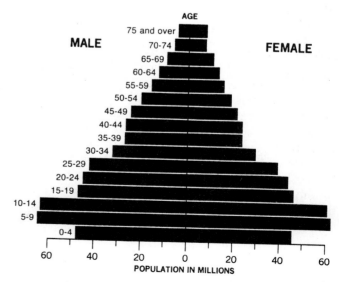

FIGURE 16.30   Population profile, using absolute scale, for China, 1978.

Source: H. Yuan Tien, "China: Demographic Billionaire," *Population Bulletin* 38, no. 2 (1983): 18 (Washington, D.C.: Population Reference Bureau).

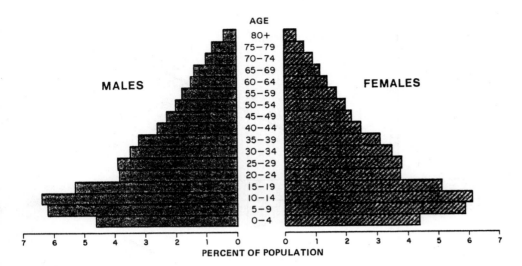

FIGURE 16.31   Population profile, using percentage scale, for Cuba, 1979.

Source: Sergio Diaz-Briquets and Lisandro Perez, "Cuba: The Demography of Revolution," *Population Bulletin* 36, no. 1 (1981): 23 (Washington, D.C.: Population Reference Bureau).

10 percent of a population of ten thousand. This means that the proportion of the population in each age-sex group is emphasized, and the population structures of regions with different population sizes are more readily compared.

A population profile is an important tool for understanding the social and economic position of a region. A profile that is broad at its base and tapers rapidly to a peak, for example, is typical of the less-developed countries and regions. The high birth rates of such regions produce the profile's broad base, and the high death rates produce its rapid taper (figure 16.32a). Regions with this type of population structure have a heavy social and economic burden because of their large, unproductive, young population. In contrast, the population profiles of economically advanced countries and regions display a relatively narrow base because of their lower birth rates. In addition, their relatively low death rates are reflected in the slower taper of the profile (figure 16.32b and 16.32c). In these regions, the economic and social problems tend to focus more on the needs of the large older population.

Marked variations in the shape of a profile at certain age levels result from population changes imposed by shifts in birth rates or death rates, reflecting changing socioeconomic conditions or war or civil disturbances (see, for example, West Germany in figure 16.32c).

Circular Graphs

Information about events that occur during a specific time period, such as the number of accidents per day, is often displayed on a **circular graph**. Averaged information about events of a recurring nature, such as weather and climate data, is also conveniently presented on circular graphs. Two examples of circular graphs used for the presentation of weather and climate information are described in this section because they are frequently plotted on maps to show the variations in conditions from place to place.[6] Other types of circular graphs have similar characteristics.

Climatograph.   A **climatograph** is a circular graph that shows climatic information such as temperature and rainfall. The data, which often consist of averages taken over a long time period, are plotted along axes radiating outward from a central origin. Mean monthly temperatures, for example, are plotted

---

[6]Regular weather and climate maps are described in chapter 15.

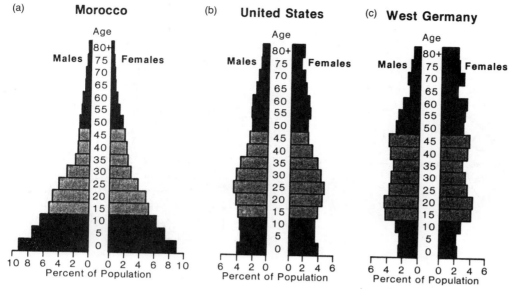

(a) Morocco **(b) United States** **(c) West Germany**

FIGURE 16.32 Comparative population profiles.
(*a*) Morocco, a lesser-developed country with high
fertility and death rates. (*b*) United States, an
economically advanced country with relatively low
fertility and death rates. (*c*) West Germany, an

economically advanced country with the world's lowest
fertility rate and a low death rate.

From Carl Haub, "Understanding Population Projections," *Population
Bulletin* 42, no. 4 (December 1987) (Washington, D.C.: Population
Reference Bureau). Reprinted by permission.

from the center of the circle, which represents the
minimum expected temperature (figure 16.33). The
outer circle then represents the maximum expected
temperature. The plotted values are joined to form
closed curves, and regions within the temperature
circle are often shaded or colored to emphasize seasonal regimes. A climatograph is particularly useful
for the depiction of seasonal changes because the
graph is continuous throughout the year.

Wind-rose. A **wind-rose** is a circular graph used
to show the average frequency and direction of wind
at one location over a given period of time. The top
of the wind-rose is oriented to the north, and bars are
extended outward from the center (figure 16.34).
Many symbol systems are used on wind-roses, but it
is typical for the length of each bar to be proportional
to the frequency of winds from the direction it is
pointing. Barbs added to the bars, or variations in the
width of the bars, are often used to indicate average
wind speed in each direction. Some indication of the
frequency of calms is also commonly incorporated.
Because of the variation in symbols and in the specific
information shown, the key that accompanies any
given wind-rose must be examined to interpret it
correctly.

FIGURE 16.33 Circular climatograph for a hypothetical
station.

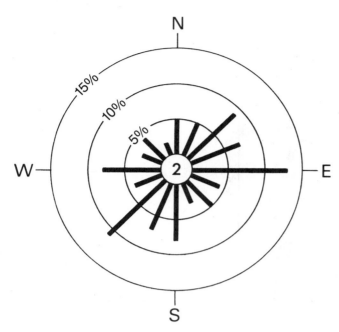

FIGURE 16.34 Wind-rose for a hypothetical station. Lengths of bars denote percentage of wind from indicated direction. Figure in center circle denotes percentage of calm periods.

Triangular Graphs

Triangular graphs, plotted on equilateral triangles, are used to show three components of some total (figure 16.35). Each location on the graph indicates a particular mixture of the three components that make up the total. Topics such as the composition of soils in different locations (silt, clay, or sand) or the composition of the work force in different countries (primary, secondary, or tertiary employment) are ideally suited for presentation on a triangular graph.

The values associated with a location on a triangular graph are read from the scales located along each side of the triangle. Point *A* in figure 16.35, for example, has a value of 50 percent on the clay scale, 20 percent on the silt scale, and 30 percent on the sand scale. It is only necessary to read two values from the graph because the third value always brings the total to 100 percent. Reading all three values and determining their sum, however, ensures that they have been read accurately.

Triangular graphs are frequently used to determine whether or not groupings of observations with similar structures exist. In figure 16.35, for example, the soil

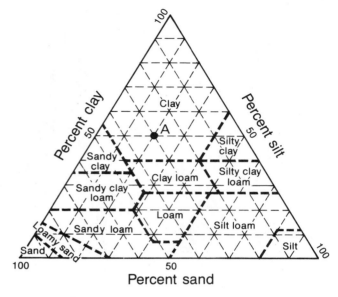

FIGURE 16.35 Triangular graph of standard soil types.

groupings within the area identified as sand are similar because they have small amounts of silt (0 to 15 percent) and clay (0 to 10 percent) and large amounts of sand (85 to 100 percent). Silt soils, on the other hand, have large amounts of silt (80 to 100 percent) and small amounts of clay (0 to 12 percent) and sand (0 to 20 percent). Groupings in other portions of the graph have similarly distinctive characteristics.

The same information shown in figure 16.35 could be displayed in other ways, such as pie charts or bar graphs. The triangular graph, however, has distinct advantages. First, the other forms require a separate graph for each observation, which is much more unwieldy. Also, groupings of similar observations are easier to see on a triangular graph than on other types of graphs.

Summary

Graphs are often associated with maps, either as map symbols or as supporting illustrations.

A line graph consists of a line, or lines, showing variations in the value of one or more variables (independent variables on the *x*-axis and dependent on the *y*-axis). Arithmetic or logarithmic scales are used. On arithmetic scales, equal distances indicate equal absolute (or percentage) changes in value. On logarithmic scales, equal distances represent equal percentage changes in values.

Semilog graphs use a logarithmic scale on one axis and an arithmetic scale on the other. On these graphs, the shape and slope of the lines reveal trends in the changes of the values. Sloping straight lines, for example, represent constant rates of change—the steeper the slope, the more rapid the rate of change. Curved lines, on the other hand, indicate increasing or decreasing rates of change.

Graphs that use logarithmic scales on both axes are called log-log graphs. The interpretation of these graphs is more complex, but a straight line sloping upward at a 45° angle, for example, indicates that the percentage rate of increase in both variables is the same, whereas a curved line indicates that one of the rates of change is geometric and the other is arithmetic.

There are several specialized types of line graphs. A bilateral graph, for example, portrays the values of two related variables. The relationship between the lines that represent these variables indicates either positive or negative net values. A silhouette graph is simply a standard line graph, with the area below the curve shaded to give a silhouette effect. Accumulative line graphs (Lorenz curves) are used to determine the degree of concentration in one variable, as compared to another. Surface graphs differ from other line graphs because the values are expressed as bands, between the lines on the graph. Measurements are taken from one edge to the other of each band, not from the baseline. Thus, the top line in the graph reflects the accumulation of all of the values below it.

Bar charts consist of bands or bars, each representing a particular data range. On an absolute-value chart, the length of each bar, and of each segment of each bar, is proportional to the value it represents. Bar charts are also drawn with percentage scales. In one common type of percentage-value chart, all of the bars are the same length, which represents 100 percent. The bars are subdivided in proportion to the percentage of the total value represented by each subcategory.

Loss-and-gain bar charts have a central zero line. The lengths of the bars, measured from the zero line, indicate negative values in one direction and positive values in the other. On high-low bar charts, in contrast, each bar shows high and low values for one time period and may include an average value.

A pie chart is a circle that is subdivided into proportional segments. The circle may or may not be proportional in size to the data value.

When proportional symbols such as graduated circles are used, the area of each symbol is proportional to the value it represents. The sizes may be continuously variable or arranged in a graded series and may be determined on the basis of true proportions or on a psychological-scaling approach.

Realistic, two-dimensional figures, such as airplanes or soldiers, may be used to represent data values. When the symbols are properly drawn, their areas are proportional to the quantities represented.

Volumetric diagrams are designed to look like three-dimensional figures. In these diagrams, the volume of each figure is proportional to the value it represents. The values represented by volumetric diagrams are difficult to estimate correctly.

A scatter diagram consists of a set of points, each of which represents a paired observation of two variables. The independent variable is measured on the x-axis and the dependent variable on the y-axis. A trend line is often superimposed on a scatter diagram, to represent the relationship between the variables.

A population profile, or pyramid, displays the age-sex distribution of the population of a given region. The length of each bar in the profile is proportional to the population of the age-sex group it represents, or to the percentage the age-sex group is of the total population.

Circular graphs can be used to present information related to time periods. A climatograph, for example, is a circular graph that shows temperature or rainfall variations. A wind-rose is a circular graph that shows the average frequency and direction of wind over a given period of time.

Finally, triangular graphs show the relationships between three components of some total value.

SUGGESTED READINGS

Holmes, Nigel. *Designer's Guide to Creating Charts and Diagrams.* New York: Watson-Guptill, 1984.

Meyers, Cecil H. *Handbook of Basic Graphs: A Modern Approach.* Belmont, Calif.: Dickenson, 1970.

Rogers, Anna C. *Graphic Charts Handbook.* Washington, D.C.: Public Affairs Press, 1961.

Schmid, Calvin F. *Statistical Graphics: Design Principles and Practices.* New York: John Wiley and Sons, 1983.

Schmid, Calvin F., and Stanton E. Schmid. *Handbook of Graphic Presentation.* 2d ed. New York: A Ronald Press Publication, 1979.

17
Remote Sensing from Airborne Platforms

The field of cartography is undergoing rapid changes due to the introduction of advanced technology. These changes involve new techniques for acquiring and analyzing data, as well as new methods of producing maps. This chapter, and the three following, describe how the use of high technology affects map users and map-related data. The emphasis in these chapters, therefore, is more on description and explanation, and less on direct, "hands-on" methods, than has been the case in other chapters. This chapter and chapter 18 discuss remote sensing, whereas chapters 19 and 20 deal with computer-assisted cartography and digital geographic information systems.

METHODS AND IMAGES

Remote sensing involves gathering information by means of a sensor that is not in contact with the object being detected. Remote sensing is not new; for millennia, humans have relied on visual images for gathering information about their environment. Remarkable as they are, however, visual images have two specific limitations in terms of mapping applications. First, they reveal only a very small portion of a wide range of potentially useful information. Second, they are not recorded in a form that is easily and accurately measured, stored, or analyzed.

Since 1850, when the first experimental aerial photographs were taken, and especially within the last fifty years, technology has greatly expanded capabilities for detecting and using remotely sensed information for mapping purposes. The discussion here focuses on the characteristics and uses of remotely sensed data about the earth, with emphasis on **remotely sensed images**.

Electromagnetic Spectrum

The **electromagnetic spectrum** consists of wavelengths of electromagnetic radiation. Everything on earth, living or inert, reflects electromagnetic radiation, and, in addition, some objects emit radiation. In either case, each source object has a characteristic radiation pattern associated with it. These patterns of energy reflection and emission are called **signatures**. Signatures are recorded by remote-sensing devices, and the information thus obtained is stored and analyzed to obtain knowledge about the properties of objects, and to distinguish between objects of different types. The information is also used to produce images.

The radiation commonly used for remote-sensing applications ranges from relatively short (ultraviolet) to relatively long (microwave) wavelengths. This includes the narrow range of wavelengths of the **visible spectrum** (figure 17.1).

Types of Remote-Sensing Devices

Remote-sensing devices are generally categorized by two sets of characteristics. The first category is based on the range of wavelengths the device detects. The second is based on the source of the signal detected.

FIGURE 17.1   The portion of the electromagnetic spectrum commonly used for remote-sensing applications.

Spectral range.   The **spectral range** of wavelengths used by remote-sensing devices may be broad, narrow, or multispectral. **Broad-band devices** use a sensor that receives energy from many wavelengths and integrates the information into a composite signal. A common broad-band sensor is the panchromatic film used in aerial photography. **Panchromatic film** forms an image through the action of a range of wavelengths that generally duplicates those involved in human vision. A **narrow-band device**, on the other hand, transmits and receives a limited range of frequencies, as is the case with radar. Finally, a **multispectral device** simultaneously records radiation in two or more separate wavelength bands, as is the case with Landsat satellite images.

Signal source.   The **signal source** of a detected signal determines whether a sensor system is classified as active or passive. An **active remote-sensing system**, such as radar, includes special equipment that transmits signals of the required wavelength. When the transmitted signal strikes the surfaces of objects, a portion of the energy is reflected back to the receiving station, where it is detected and converted into an image. **Passive remote-sensing systems**, in contrast, rely on the detection of naturally generated energy that is either reflected or emitted by an object. Aerial photography is an example of a passive system that uses reflected energy. Some sensors, on the other hand, detect the varying amount of electromagnetic energy radiated by all objects that have a temperature above absolute zero. Such systems operate without either visible light or a special source of transmitted energy.

Detector location.   Remote sensors operate in a variety of locations, on, under, or above the earth's surface. The types that are mounted in aircraft or satellite vehicles above the earth's surface are emphasized here because they are most commonly used for mapping applications.

AERIAL PHOTOGRAPHY

In chapter 2, aerial photography's prominent role in the creation of maps was discussed. Aerial photographs are equally important in their function as "real" maps. In this section, we will discuss some of the types, characteristics, and uses of aerial photographic products.

Types of Aerial Photographs

The two major types of aerial photographs are vertical and oblique.

Vertical photographs.   Vertical photographs, as the term implies, are taken with the camera pointed as nearly perpendicular to the earth's surface as possible (figure 17.2). The use of stereo pairs of vertical photos for mapping purposes was discussed in chapter 2, but they are also of major importance as maps. For this reason, most of the discussion that follows deals with vertical photos.

Oblique photographs.   Oblique photographs are taken with the camera lens deliberately pointed at a nonperpendicular angle to the earth's surface.

FIGURE 17.2   Vertical aerial photograph. (Little Gypsum
Valley, Colorado.)

Source: U.S. Geological Survey photo.

(a)

(b)

FIGURE 17.3   Oblique aerial photographs. (*a*) High oblique of downtown Chicago. (*b*) Low oblique of downtown Sheboygan.

Courtesy of Aero-metric Engineering, Inc.

High-oblique photos include the horizon, whereas **low-oblique photos** do not (figure 17.3). Both high and low obliques are used for their visual effect, in advertising or publicity photographs, for example, but they are also useful for feature-recognition purposes. We are accustomed to viewing our surroundings from near ground level and, therefore, usually see the sides, rather than the tops, of most objects. Oblique aerial photos, for this reason, provide a more familiar perspective than do vertical photos.

Photographic Materials

The relationships between the various components involved in the creation of photographic images strongly influence the final product. Photographic materials, including transparent films and opaque materials like photographic paper, are coated with light-sensitive emulsions. Various emulsions are available, each sensitive to specific electromagnetic wavelengths. The images obtained from the different types differ greatly from one another. Most of this discussion of aerial photography deals with the effects of wavelengths within the visible spectrum on panchromatic film. Some aspects of the use of film that is sensitive to shorter or longer wavelengths are also mentioned, as are color films.

Negatives and positives.   When the film in a camera is exposed to light, and later developed, the usual result is a photographic **negative**, made on a transparent medium. In the scene being photographed, objects vary in the amount and wavelength of light that they reflect. Objects that have a high level of energy reflection are recorded on the negative film as dark images, whereas those that reflect very little energy appear as transparent areas.

For most mapping purposes, a **positive print** or **transparency** is made from the photographic negative. In a positive print, the areas in the original scene that emit high levels of energy are light, whereas those that emit little energy are dark. In other words, the

(a)

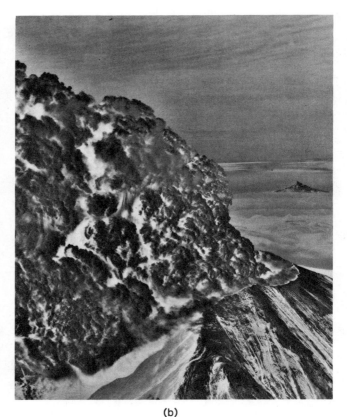

(b)

FIGURE 17.4   The tones in a positive (*a*) are the reverse of the tones in a negative (*b*). (Mount St. Helens during eruption.)

Source: U.S. Geological Survey photo.

tones in a positive are the reverse of the tones in a negative (figure 17.4). The descriptions that follow are based on the characteristics of positive prints made from photographic negatives of different types.

Emulsion types.   Many aerial photographs are made on film coated with a black-and-white, **panchromatic emulsion** that is sensitive to approximately the same range of wavelengths as the human eye. Although the images obtained with this emulsion lack color, they are useful for many purposes. In prints made from panchromatic negatives, the visual brightness of objects in the original scene is closely duplicated. The resulting image is familiar and rather easily interpreted. Black-and-white images from panchromatic film, therefore, are in common use. In fact, for

a long time, panchromatic images were the predominant type produced. Other types of emulsions are often encountered, however, because their characteristics make them useful for particular purposes.

A second type of black-and-white film emulsion is sensitive to the **infrared wavelengths**. These wavelengths, which fall outside the range of human vision, are particularly useful in the analysis of vegetation conditions and the identification of water bodies. Broadleaf vegetation is highly reflective in the infrared range, whereas coniferous vegetation is less so. On infrared print images, then, the two types of vegetation can be differentiated because broadleaves show up in light tones and evergreens in darker tones. Also, water bodies are usually very dark on infrared photos, which assists in determining the locations of

(a)

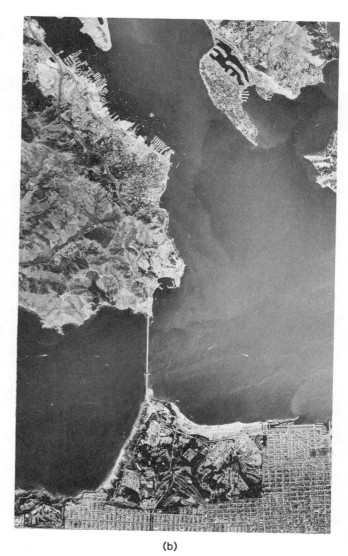

(b)

FIGURE 17.5   (*a*) Panchromatic and (*b*) black-and-white-infrared photographs of the same area.

Source: National High Altitude Program photos.

shorelines. This is especially helpful in swampy or marshy areas that have indistinct margins on panchromatic film (figure 17.5). Infrared film also has some haze-penetrating ability that is useful when conditions are not suitable for regular panchromatic film.

Features that have distinctive colors may appear in similar shades of gray on black-and-white film, which makes them difficult to identify. Because color film is

particularly helpful in identifying soil types, rock outcrops, water bodies, and other features that exhibit distinctive coloration, **color film emulsion** has supplanted panchromatic black-and-white film emulsion for many purposes (plate 7). This is feasible because, although color film is more costly to purchase and process than black-and-white film, the differences are often negligible when the total cost of an aerial photography project is considered.

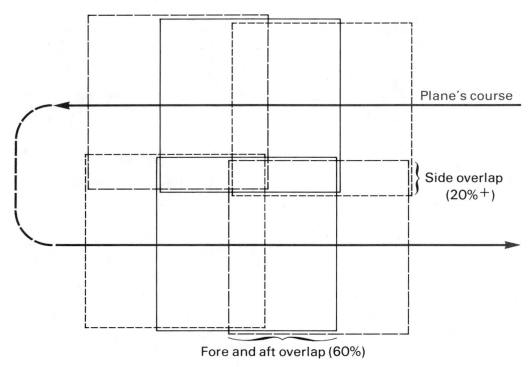

Plane's course

Side overlap
(20%+)

Fore and aft overlap (60%)

FIGURE 17.6   Flight plan provides overlap of
photographs.

Color film is also available with an infrared-sensitive emulsion (plate 8). The image obtained from **color-infrared emulsion** has colors unlike those we are used to seeing. The colors are also different from those that appear on regular color film. As with black-and-white-infrared, the sensitivity of color infrared beyond the visible spectrum makes it useful for vegetation studies. Healthy deciduous plants show up in red tones on color-infrared images, whereas evergreens range into the bluish-purple colors. The result is that different plant types can be differentiated quite easily. Also, plants that are under stress due to disease or insect infestation appear as bright green on color-infrared film. This allows detection of the stress, which may not even be visible or show up on other types of film.

Photo Characteristics

Aerial photographs to be used for mapping purposes are taken using a flight plan and equipment that provide for a high-quality product with certain desired characteristics. The **flight plan** is designed so that each photograph in a sequence overlaps the next by approximately 60 to 65 percent (figure 17.6) and, in addition, so that the photos are taken in a zigzag sequence of **legs**. The photos in one leg overlap those in the adjacent legs by approximately 20 to 35 percent. These conditions assure that the area of interest is completely covered and that the photos may be viewed stereoscopically, as is discussed later in the chapter (see also chapter 2).

Although it may not be apparent to a casual observer, aerial photographs invariably contain distortions. Some of these distortions are due to technical irregularities in the camera system, but these are likely to be very slight. Conditions encountered at the time the photos are actually taken, however, may result in photographs that are less than perfect. The aircraft may deviate from the desired course, for example, or the timing between photos may not be accurate. Either of these conditions may result in inadequate coverage between photos. Other conditions may cause variations in the elevation and altitude of the airplane at the moment the picture is taken. The aircraft may have to crab into the wind, for example, resulting in photos

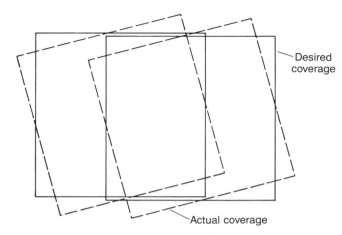

FIGURE 17.7   Effect of crab on aerial photo coverage (exaggerated).

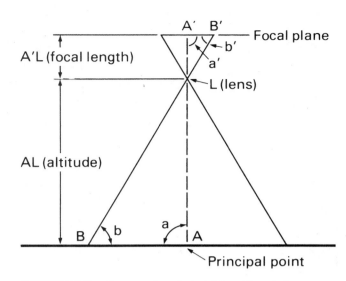

FIGURE 17.8   Geometric relationships of scale in an aerial photograph.

that do not overlap properly (figure 17.7). Similarly, the aircraft may tilt, or change altitude unexpectedly, causing scale variations.

Most aerial photographs are produced under government or commercial contracts. Because of the high standards required, such photos are not likely to suffer significantly from the distortions just described. For purposes of this discussion, aerial photographs are assumed to be free from significant technical flaws. They are also assumed to be close to absolutely vertical and to have been taken from the correct elevation (or to have been corrected to remove flaws from either of these sources). In particular, **rectified prints** have been specially processed to correct such irregularities.

Nevertheless, distortions are introduced into aerial photos through variations in topography and are particularly important when aerial photos are used as maps. An understanding of these distortions requires consideration of those aspects of the geometry of aerial photography that relate to scale determination and variation.

Scale.   The scale of an aerial photo depends on two factors: (1) the focal length of the lens used to take the photo and (2) the elevation of the camera above the surface of the earth when the photo is taken. The scale results from the following simple geometric relationships, which are shown in figure 17.8.

1.   The angles a and a' are right angles because the photograph was taken vertically.

2.   The film in the camera is parallel with the surface of the earth. The lines in figure 17.8 that represent these features are, therefore, parallel to one another.

3.   Given items 1 and 2, angles b and b' are equivalent angles.

4.   Given items 1, 2, and 3, triangles ABL and $A'B'L$ are similar triangles.

5.   Because of their location in the similar triangles, the ratio between the lengths of sides AL and $A'L$ is the same as the ratio between the lengths of sides AB and $A'B'$. This is equivalent to saying that the scale of the photo is given by the ratio between the altitude and the focal length of the lens ($AL{:}A'L$), provided that both are in the same measurement units:

$$\text{Scale} = \frac{f\,(\text{focal length of lens})}{H\,(\text{altitude above ground})}$$

Once the scale of a photo is known, the distance between two points on the photo (such as A' and B') can be measured. The scale ratio is then applied to this measurement, and the distance between the equivalent points on the ground (A and B) can be calculated. The reverse is also true. This means that the scale of an aerial photo can be determined by taking the ratio of a known distance between two objects on

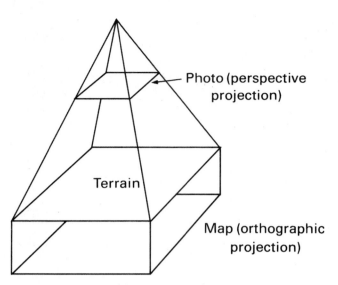

FIGURE 17.9   Relationship between the terrain, an orthographic map projection, and the perspective projection of an aerial photograph.

the ground to the distance between the same objects on the photo. The known distances for such a calculation can be determined either by direct measurement in the field or by scaling from a map. It can also be derived from other knowledge, such as knowing that the football field on a photo is 100 yards long or that the gauge of the railway tracks is 4 feet, 8½ inches.

Unfortunately, scale varies throughout an aerial photograph (the reasons for this are discussed next). Because of these scale variations, several known distance relationships are usually measured, and the resulting scales are averaged to produce the photograph's average scale. The scale obtained by use of the focal length and altitude formula is also an average scale.

Planimetric shift.   Why do variations of scale occur in aerial photographs, and what effect do these variations have on the use of the photos as maps? The answers to these questions can be obtained by looking at some simple geometric relationships. The key factor is that an aerial photograph is a **perspective view,** which is a view from a single viewpoint (figure 17.9). A map, on the other hand, is an **orthographic view,** which is a view drawn as though every point were seen from directly overhead. The perspective nature of

photographs would pose few problems if the terrain were always perfectly flat. When it is not, which is most of the time, the perspective view results in the **planimetric shift** of features that are above or below the base level of the photograph.

The amount of planimetric shift of a feature is related to its height above the datum level of the photograph and its distance from the center (called the **principal point**) of the photograph. In figure 17.10a, the top of the tower *(T)* appears, on the photograph, to be located at T′. This point is shifted away from the location of the bottom of the tower *(B).* On a map, in contrast, both the top and the bottom of the tower would be located at *B.* The farther the feature is from the principal point and the greater the height of the feature above the datum, the greater the amount of shift that occurs (figure 17.10a–c). On the other hand, the amount of shift from either source decreases as the altitude of the camera above the earth's surface increases (figure 17.10d). Planimetric shift also increases with increasing distance from the principal point and is distributed in a radial pattern around the principal point. Figure 17.11 shows the direction and amount of displacement of the images of several objects of the same height that are located at varying distances and directions from the principal point.

Planimetric shift applies not only to tall towers or buildings that appear in an aerial photograph; it also applies to the earth's surface and the location of any objects on that surface. Thus, on an aerial photograph, trees, road intersections, buildings, rock outcrops, fence lines, or any other features may be shifted some distance from their correct map location.

Planimetric shift results in scale variations within an aerial photograph because the ratio of the distance between objects on the photograph and the distance between the same objects on the ground varies from place to place. As a result, the representative fraction that expresses the scale of the photo also varies from place to place.

The errors introduced by planimetric shift cannot be corrected without specialized training and equipment. Map users, however, should at least be aware of planimetric shift and that features on an ordinary aerial photograph do not always line up properly with the same features on a map that is nominally of the same scale. For this reason, specially processed aerial

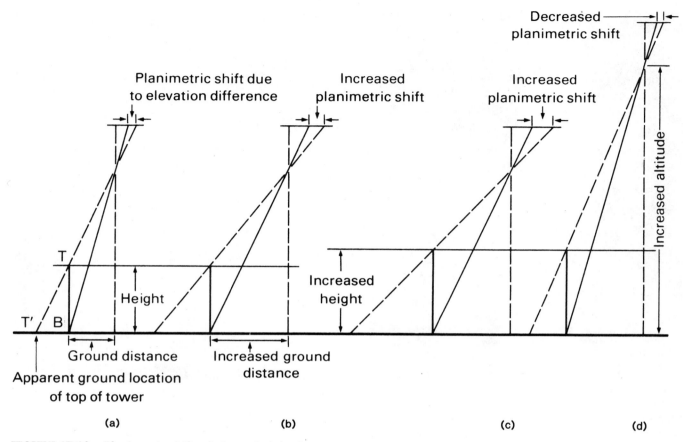

FIGURE 17.10   Planimetric shift relative to height above datum level of the photograph and distance from principal point. (*a*) Planimetric shift due to elevation difference between top and bottom of tower. (*b*) Increased planimetric shift due to increased distance of tower from principal point. (*c*) Increased planimetric shift due to increased height of tower. (*d*) Decreased planimetric shift due to increased altitude of camera.

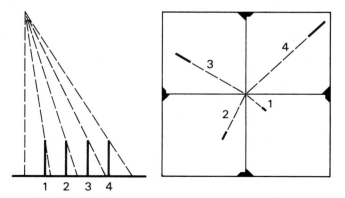

FIGURE 17.11   Planimetric shift increases with increasing distance from the principal point and is distributed in a radial pattern around the principal point.

photos, called orthophotos, are often useful. **Ortho-photos** are aerial photographs that have been processed in a special way to remove the effect of planimetric shift. Figure 17.12 shows the type of locational shift that exists in a normal aerial photograph in comparison to an orthophoto.

Aerial Photo Products

Single prints.   The basic product in any aerial photography project is a single print of the specific area photographed (or a set of single prints of a larger area). Most single prints measure 9 by 9 inches, although other sizes are sometimes encountered. As already indicated, single prints are often used as map

(a)

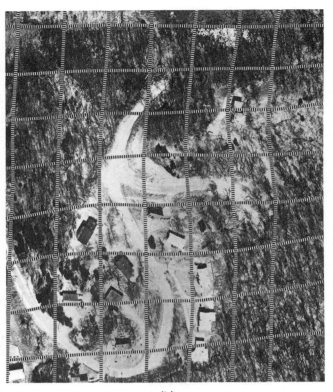

(b)

FIGURE 17.12   Locational shift in normal aerial photograph (*a*), in comparison to orthophoto (*b*).

Courtesy of Aero-metric Engineering, Inc.

substitutes, although the problems of scale variation and locational displacement must be dealt with if the photos are not orthophoto products. One thing to keep in mind when using such prints is that what appears to be the top, based on the orientation of numbering and lettering on the print, is not necessarily north.

Photomosaics.   When a single aerial photo does not cover all of the area of interest, adjoining photos can be pieced together to cover the larger area with a composite image called a **photomosaic**. The photographs used to construct a photomosaic must overlap one another. Usually, this is not a problem because standard procedures for most aerial photography flown for mapping purposes provide such overlap.

Photomosaics may be either uncontrolled or controlled. The assembly of an **uncontrolled photomosaic** is begun by fastening the print of the center of the area in the middle of a flat board. An adjoining print is then overlapped with the first one, so that features common to both are aligned with one another as closely as possible. The excess portions of the overlapping photo are trimmed away, and it is temporarily fastened in place. The same procedure is followed with additional photos, with each one matched as closely as possible with those previously put in place. Aligning the additional photos usually requires some adjustment in the locations of the photos already positioned. After the necessary adjustments are made, everything is glued in place. The result resembles a large aerial photograph of the area (figure 17.13).

FIGURE 17.13 Mosaic of aerial photographs, covering a large area in northeastern Illinois.

Courtesy of Aero-metric Engineering, Inc.

Assembling a photomosaic in the manner just described quickly results in difficulties due to the scale variations in the photos. Assume, for example, that a road intersection that shows in the first two photos is selected as one matching point. The scale variations within the two photos may make it impossible to line up the images of other features when the road intersections are aligned. An arrangement that comes as close as possible to aligning the desired points may be a necessary compromise. The alignment problems become more and more difficult to resolve as additional photos are matched to one another, progressing farther and farther from the starting point. In the end, therefore, very few points are likely to match precisely.

Using rectified photos for the mosaic results in fewer problems than using photos that are not rectified. Orthophotos, if they are available, produce an even better end product. Nonetheless, some means of structuring the mosaic's assembly is desirable, even when orthophotos are used.

Structure is provided for a **controlled photomosaic** by introducing a base map, drawn at the average scale of the aerial photos. This need only be a simple, skeletal map, either an existing one or one drawn for the purpose. The primary requirement is that it show the correct planimetric location of major features that are recognizable on the aerial photographs. These include, for example, road and railroad alignments and intersections, fence lines, property corners, and major buildings.

A controlled mosaic is assembled by securing the base map to the mounting board and fastening the individual photos over it, as with an uncontrolled mosaic. The difference is that the features on the photos are matched to their plotted map locations as closely as possible before they are fastened in place. Individual features may not line up exactly when this is done, but any errors do not accumulate, as they do in an uncontrolled mosaic. As before, overlapping areas are removed so that adjoining photos blend together as well as possible before the photos are glued down.

FIGURE 17.14   Portion of U.S. Geological Survey orthophotoquad. (Frederic SE quadrangle, Wisconsin, 1974, 1:24,000.)

Completed photomosaics are frequently photographed and reproduced and, with information such as place names and boundary lines added, make a form of photomap.

Orthophoto products. Because their locational characteristics are the equivalent of those of maps, orthophoto products have been incorporated into the map series published by the U.S. Geological Survey. One such product is an orthophotoquad, and another is an orthophotomap. These products are similar to regular quadrangle maps in that they are produced at a scale of 1:24,000 and cover 7.5 minutes of latitude and longitude. **Orthophotoquads** are orthophoto images, printed in black and white (figure 17.14). They show photographic detail, but very little cartographic treatment is added, and contours are not shown. **Orthophotomaps**, in contrast, include contour lines and feature names and are color-enhanced to improve readability (plate 9).

Photo Interpretation

The image captured in an aerial photograph can be subjected to detailed interpretation and analysis. The field of **photo interpretation** involves the recognition and identification of the great variety of natural and man-made features on the earth's surface. Feature identification is achieved by considering such attributes as the shape, size, tone, color, texture, pattern, relative locations, and shadows visible in the photo. Photo interpretation supports a great variety of applications, including archaeology, waterway charting, crop-yield predictions, fire protection, glacial studies, land-use analyses, mapping, range management, real-estate zoning, transportation studies, and wildlife management, to name only a few examples. In addition, in any field of application, photographs taken at different times can be compared to determine the nature and extent of changes in either the natural or man-made environment.

Effective photo interpretation requires a considerable amount of training and experience. The sections that follow examine some of the basic aspects of the subject to give some idea of what can be accomplished. Some of the sources in the "Suggested Readings" at the end of the chapter provide information about more advanced applications.

Visual clues. Usually, in aerial photographs, certain features can be positively identified, even if the interpreter does not have any previous experience or training. Other features, which may not have been immediately recognizable, can be identified as the interpreter gains experience. Various clues in aerial photographs assist this type of interpretation (figure 17.15). Aerial photos that are of as large a scale

FIGURE 17.15   Examples of aerial photo interpretation clues. (*a*) Major-league baseball park. (*b*) Farmstead with house, barn, silo, and outbuildings. (*c*) Agricultural land with moist and dry areas. (*d*) Different crops result in a variety of textures. (*e*) Regular pattern of orchard, contrasting with natural woodlots. (*f*) Office complex. (*g*) Distinctive shadow of the Statue of Liberty.

Photos *a, c, d, f,* and *g,* courtesy of Aero-metric Engineering, Inc. Photos *b* and *e* courtesy of Racine County Planning and Development.

as possible are preferable. Large-scale photos, supplemented by the use of a magnifying lens, allow the interpretation of many details that might otherwise be overlooked.

Even in the absence of other clues, some features are immediately recognizable because of their distinctive shape. A baseball park is an obvious example (figure 17.15a), but other, more subtle, features are also often revealed by their shape. Different features may have similar shapes, however, so that an assessment of the size of the feature may be necessary. Size can be described in two ways: relative and absolute. Relative size is the size of one object as compared with another, and it helps to distinguish between what might otherwise appear to be similar features. Two buildings, for example, may have similar rectangular outlines, but the house on a farmstead is readily distinguishable from a barn, simply on the basis of relative size (figure 17.15b). Absolute size, on the other hand, refers to the actual measurement of features, based on knowledge of the photo's scale. A railroad car, for example, may look like a simple rectangle, but measurement of its size will indicate its probable capacity and may give a clue to its use.

Other, slightly less obvious, clues assist the photo interpreter. One of these is that the features on the earth are of different colors and appear in black-and-white photographs as different tones, or values, of gray. The darker areas in figure 17.15c are areas of wet soil, for example, whereas the lighter areas are dry. When a color photo is available, of course, differences in color are more immediately obvious and are usually easier to interpret than are differences in tone (plate 8). The shade of green associated with evergreen trees is usually different from that of deciduous trees, for example. Another useful identifying characteristic is texture, which is the relative coarseness or smoothness of areas in the image. Fields planted to different crops display a variety of textures (figure 17.15d). The disparate textural characteristics help the photo interpreter to measure and tabulate the fields planted to each crop, or left fallow, throughout the area.

The arrangement of features can create patterns that are clues to their identification. The orderly pattern of the orchards in figure 17.15e distinguishes them clearly from the random-appearing pattern of a natural woodlot. Features with regular patterns and straight edges are almost certain to represent human intervention in the environment. Also, the relative location of certain features gives a clue to their identity, even though their shape or other characteristics may

not. An example of this is the large building in figure 17.15f. The extensive parking lots around this building complex mean that it is more likely to be an office structure than a school, despite the adjoining softball diamond and football field.

As was previously mentioned, vertical views may not reveal the distinctive features of some objects that would be obvious in a ground-level view. In such cases, a shadow cast on the surface provides the equivalent of a side view. The shadow of the Statue of Liberty is certainly distinctive (figure 17.15g), and the shadow of a smokestack, for example, looks distinctly different from that of a church steeple.

Interpretive keys.   Extensive **interpretive keys** have been developed that list logically organized clues that assist an interpreter in the analysis of particular environmental features. Some keys are useful for understanding agricultural environments, some are designed for use in industrial settings, and so on. The detail provided by keys often allows quite specific interpretations that would be impossible if the interpreter relied strictly on personal knowledge of particular feature types.

Stereoscopic Pairs

The use of stereoscopic pairs of aerial photographs assists in the interpretation of scenes, as well as with the measurement of elevations. A **stereoscopic pair** consists of two sequential photographs that normally overlap one another by approximately 60 percent.

Stereoscopic viewing.   We see in three dimensions. Individual aerial photographic prints, in contrast, show only two dimensions. Special techniques for viewing aerial photos, however, provide apparent three-dimensional views. Such **stereoscopic viewing** is vital to the production of topographic maps and is also a valuable adjunct to the interpretation of aerial photographs.

The three prerequisites for stereoscopic viewing of aerial photographs are: (1) a stereo pair of prints, (2) some type of stereoscope, and (3) normal vision. A **stereo pair** consists of two overlapping photographs of the same scene, usually consecutive prints from a single flight line. In the area of overlap, the features in the scene are imaged from a different viewpoint on each photograph, just as each of our eyes registers a slightly different view of the scene before us.

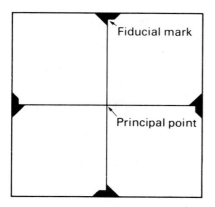

FIGURE 17.16   Relationship between fiducial marks and principal point.

A **stereoscope** is a simple instrument that permits the simultaneous viewing of a stereo pair so that the desired three-dimensional effect is achieved. Stereoscopes are arranged so that one eye focuses on objects in one photograph and the other eye focuses on the same objects as they appear in the other photograph (see figure 2.8). Individuals with normal binocular vision should experience no difficulty in viewing a stereo pair through a stereoscope.

When you wish to prepare photographs for stereoscopic viewing, first draw light lines joining the **fiducial marks**, which are located in the margins of each photo (figure 17.16). The crossing of these lines identifies the **principal point** of the photograph, which is the point on the ground that was directly below the vertical camera. Put a pinprick at the principal point, and, for clarity, draw a small, inked circle (about 5 millimeters in diameter) around the point.

After the principal point has been identified, locate and mark the equivalent point, which is called the **conjugate principal point**, on the adjoining photo.[1] Then draw a straight line between the principal point and the conjugate principal point on each photograph. This line is called the **flight line** because it joins consecutive points over which the airplane flew while taking the photographs.

Place the prepared photographs side by side on a flat surface, with the shadows falling toward you. The shadows must fall toward you to avoid a **pseudoscopic**

effect, which causes hills to look like valleys and valleys to look like hills. (You may wish to test this effect by viewing a pair of photographs with the shadows falling away from you.) Move the photographs so that the flight line is aligned horizontally. Overlap the photographs so that the principal point on one and the conjugate principal point on the other are the correct distance apart for the type of stereoscope being used. This distance varies but is usually about 6.0 centimeters (2.36 inches) for pocket stereoscopes and about 25.4 centimeters (10 inches) for the mirror type. Then place the stereoscope over the prints so that the left-hand lens is over the principal point of the left-hand photograph and the right-hand lens is over its conjugate principal point on the right-hand photograph. Looking through the lenses of the stereoscope then produces a three-dimensional view of the terrain in the area of overlapping coverage. Small adjustments of the prints usually remove any difficulty with focus.

Stereo pairs viewed through a stereoscope appear dramatically three-dimensional because the photos were taken many meters apart, as the airplane moved between exposures. Our brains, in contrast, are accustomed to interpreting scenes viewed through our eyes, which are only about 65 millimeters (2½ inches) apart. The result is a much-exaggerated three-dimensional effect in the stereoscopic view.

Interpretation.   The addition of the third dimension to aerial photographic images is an important adjunct to their interpretation. The relative elevations of points on the surface, as well as the heights of objects, become distinctive features. Also, relatively slight slopes stand out clearly. An obvious disadvantage is that the actual slope may be overestimated. Experience, however, assists in making the correct interpretation. In addition, drainage patterns, fence lines, ditches, changes in slope, types of trees, relative heights of buildings, and similar details become much more apparent.

The availability of stereoscopic images also allows the mapping of relief and the measurement of elevations. These useful techniques fall outside the scope of coverage provided here. Consult the references listed in the "Suggested Readings" at the end of the chapter for information on measurement and mapping techniques, as well as for further discussion of the interpretative uses of aerial photographs.

---

[1]This is best done using stereoscopic viewing. It can be done with reasonable accuracy, however, simply by visual inspection.

FIGURE 17.17   Portion of radar image mosaic, prepared
from synthetic-aperture side-looking radar image strips.
(Harrisburg quadrangle, Pennsylvania, 1982,
experimental edition.)

OTHER AIRBORNE IMAGERY

Radar

Radar is an active remote-sensing technique involving the transmission of microwave signals that are
reflected back to a receiver from objects in the viewing
area. Aircraft-mounted radar systems provide information that can be mapped to indicate the location of
objects, the texture of surfaces, the presence of subsurface moisture, surface temperatures, and so on.
Radar signals penetrate clouds effectively, a characteristic that allows the acquisition of images under
conditions that would prevent the use of aerial photography. Side-looking airborne radar (SLAR) is particularly useful for mapping purposes, as the image
in figure 17.17 suggests. Because of the technical

nature of radar images, we do not explore their use
further. Consult the *Manual of Remote Sensing* listed
in the "Suggested Readings" at the end of the chapter
for more information.

Scanners

Scanners are passive devices that detect and record
energy reflected or emitted from objects within their
range. They can be mounted on aircraft or space platforms, and the information they generate can be converted into an image form.

Infrared scanners depend on the detection of infrared energy emitted by any object, whether animal,
vegetable, or mineral. The amount of radiation
emitted at the longer, invisible wavelengths is related
to the temperature and surface characteristics of the

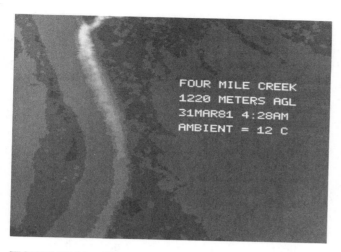

FIGURE 17.18 **Thermal infrared scanner image of a thermal plume. (Savannah River, South Carolina, 31 March 1981.)**

From John R. Jensen, *Introductory Digital Image Processing: A Remote Sensing Perspective* (Englewood Cliffs, N.J.: Prentice-Hall, 1986). Reprinted by permission.

object. Cooler surfaces within the target area appear as dark areas on the image, and warmer surfaces are lighter (figure 17.18). Infrared images, therefore, are useful for applications in which temperature differences are important, such as detecting forest fires, monitoring volcanic activity, determining the status of irrigation moisture, monitoring the decay of sea ice, counting animal populations, checking the thermal characteristics of buildings, and so on.

Summary

Remote sensing consists of gathering information by means of a sensor that is not in contact with the object being detected. The radiation commonly used for remote sensing ranges from relatively short (ultraviolet) to relatively long (microwave) wavelengths, including the visible spectrum.

Remote-sensing devices are categorized according to the range of wavelengths they detect (broad, narrow, or multispectral) and the source of the signal detected (passive or active). The devices operate in a variety of locations, but those mounted in aircraft or satellites are most important for mapping applications.

Aerial photographs, especially vertical ones, are important for mapping purposes and as map substitutes. Various film emulsions are available, each sensitive to specific electromagnetic wavelengths. The images obtained from the various types differ greatly. Black-and-white panchromatic emulsion is sensitive to approximately the same range of wavelengths as the human eye. Prints made from it closely duplicate the visual appearance of the original scene, which aids in photo interpretation. Black-and-white infrared emulsion is useful in the analysis of vegetation conditions and the identification of water bodies. Normal color film is helpful in identifying features that exhibit distinctive coloration, and color-infrared is useful for vegetation studies.

Aerial photographs for mapping are taken so that each photograph in a sequence overlaps the next by approximately 60 to 65 percent, and photos in one leg overlap those in adjacent legs by approximately 20 to 35 percent. These requirements are particularly important in relation to stereoscopic viewing.

The scale of an aerial photo depends on the focal length of the lens used to take the photo and the elevation of the camera above the surface of the earth. Distortions in scale and planimetric locations of features are introduced through variations in topography. This means that regular aerial photos are not identical with maps of the same area.

The amount of planimetric shift of a feature is related to the feature's height above the photo's datum and its distance from the photo's principal point. The amount of shift increases as the altitude of the camera above the earth's surface decreases. It also increases with increasing distance from the principal point and is distributed in a radial pattern around that point. Planimetric shift results in scale variations within an aerial photograph because the ratio of the distance between objects on the photograph and the distance between the same objects on the ground varies from place to place.

A single aerial photo may not cover all of an area of interest, so uncontrolled or controlled photomosaics may be assembled. Uncontrolled mosaics are subject to difficulties, but controlled mosaics, especially when made from orthophotos, are effective map substitutes. Orthophoto products published by the U.S. Geological Survey include orthophotoquads and orthophotomaps.

Photo interpretation involves the recognition and identification of natural and man-made features on the earth's surface. The process uses shape, size, tone, color, texture, pattern, relative location, and shadow.

Stereoscopes permit the simultaneous viewing of a stereo pair so that a three-dimensional effect is achieved. This is an important adjunct to photo interpretation. It also allows the mapping of relief and the measurement of elevations.

Radar is an active remote-sensing technique involving transmitted microwave signals that are reflected back to a receiver from objects in the viewing area. Aircraft-mounted radar systems provide a variety of information that can be mapped. Scanners, in contrast, are passive devices that detect and record energy reflected or emitted from objects within their range.

SUGGESTED READINGS

Avery, Thomas Eugene, and Graydon Lennis Berlin. *Fundamentals of Remote Sensing and Airphoto Interpretation,* 5th ed. New York: Macmillan Publishing Company, 1992.

Burnside, Clifford D. *Mapping from Aerial Photographs.* New York: John Wiley and Sons, A Halsted Press Book, 1979.

Dickinson, G. C. *Maps and Air Photographs.* 2d ed. New York: John Wiley and Sons, A Halsted Press Book, 1979.

Moffitt, Francis H., and Edward M. Mikhail. *Photogrammetry.* 3d ed. New York: Harper and Row, 1980.

Reeves, Robert G., ed. *Manual of Remote Sensing.* Washington, D.C.: American Society of Photogrammetry, 1975.

Slama, Chester C., ed. *Manual of Photogrammetry.* 4th ed. Falls Church, Va.: American Society of Photogrammetry, 1980.

Thrower, Norman J. W., and John R. Jensen. "The Orthophoto and Orthophotomap: Characteristics, Development, and Applications." *The American Cartographer* 3, no. 1 (April 1976): 39–52.

18

Remote Sensing from Space

Since the early 1970s, a number of space programs have produced imagery that has been made available to the public. Many such images are products of the U.S. **Landsat program** or, more recently, the French **SPOT program**. Some characteristics of these two programs are briefly described here because they are good examples of the methods by which space images are obtained and of the types of products available (see chapter 21 for information regarding the purchase of products).

Astronauts have brought many photographs back to earth, and some photographic film has been parachuted from satellites. Most information collected from space, however, is encoded on board the spacecraft and then transmitted by radio to earth stations for conversion into the form required for interpretation. Knowledge of the basic characteristics of the processes involved in obtaining information from instruments in space gives some idea of what can and cannot be expected from the information.

Imagery from space is usually acquired and interpreted with the help of computers. If images are created from the information (which is not necessary for many applications), they are frequently viewed on a computer screen, and hard-copy images are produced only occasionally. This text provides a broad overview of the process of obtaining and processing remotely sensed information, and the discussion concentrates on visual images. Although remotely sensed images are often spectacular in appearance, the information contained in them is often more useful in digital, rather than visual, form. The "Suggested Readings" at the end of the chapter provide some guidance for further study in this complex and important field.

SPECTRAL CHARACTERISTICS

Only a portion of the tremendously wide range of electromagnetic radiation wavelengths is used for remote-sensing purposes (see figure 17.1). The most frequently used wavelengths fall between about 0.4 micrometers and 22 centimeters because these wavelengths are more useful than others. Some objects are most easily detected by the use of radiation in certain ranges. For example, healthy vegetation is a strong reflector of energy in the infrared wavelengths, whereas vegetation under stress is not. For this reason, a project involving the detection of areas of unhealthy vegetation is likely to use imagery based on the infrared wavelengths. In addition, the atmosphere scatters and absorbs some wavelengths of energy, whereas other wavelengths pass easily through so-called atmospheric windows. Appropriate wavelengths that match these **atmospheric windows** are used to obtain as much useful information as possible.

COLLECTION SYSTEMS

Systems for collecting remotely sensed information involve the use of sensors that respond to electromagnetic radiation. The systems are arranged so that, at any given moment, each detector receives the radiation gathered from a specific area on the ground. The amount of radiation received affects detector voltage. This voltage is sampled frequently so that a series of values is obtained. Subsequently, each of these values is converted to a numerical value, which is assigned to the appropriate image area, called **a pixel**. The pixel values frequently range from 0 to 255, with 0 indicating no signal in the particular band and 255 indicating a very strong signal. Thus, each pixel value reflects the strength of the signal received for a particular ground location, within a specific band of the electromagnetic spectrum. A single value is recorded for each pixel, for each band. When the pixel values have been encoded, they are transmitted to a ground station. At the ground station, the information is stored on a computer-compatible tape, which is subsequently read into a computer for processing.

GROUND RESOLUTION

Ground resolution is the size of the area on the ground that is imaged at any one time. It determines the size of objects or areas that can be detected.

A remotely sensed image is composed of a myriad of individual pixels, which are minuscule rectangular units, each representing a specific area on the ground. Each pixel is imaged as a single shade of gray, or a single color, determined by the numerical value attached to it. The size of objects that can be detected by an examination of such an image is a function of the system's ground resolution. The rule of thumb is that the smallest dimension of an object must be at least twice as great as the system's ground resolution before there is a good likelihood of detection. One commonly used system, for example, has a ground resolution of about 30 by 30 meters. This means that a football stadium that surrounds a 50-by-100-yard (approximately 46-by-92 meter) playing field is likely to be detectable, whereas a large house that measures 10 by 15 meters is not.

The resolution capability of commercial systems is improving, however. Another, newer system has a maximum resolution of 10 by 10 meters. Military systems have greater resolutions than those available to the public, thus allowing the detection of smaller objects. The specific capabilities of military systems are subject to speculation and are undoubtedly often exaggerated. The former Soviet Union, however, marketed satellite images with a resolution of 5 by 5 meters, and such resolution probably will become common in the relatively near future.

IMAGE CREATION

One use of remotely sensed information that is particularly important in the context of this book is the creation of images for visual interpretation. This is done by using a computer-controlled exposure device. The gray tone assigned to each pixel in the image is determined by the numerical value associated with the corresponding pixel in the original scene. Pixels that have a value of 0, for example, appear white in the image, whereas those with a value of 255 appear black. Cells with values lying between 0 and 255 have intermediate gray values proportionate to their numerical value.

An image can be created for each band for which information is available. By assigning a different color to each band, a composite color image is produced on color film. The colors that result from this process are *not* necessarily the colors that would be visible to an observer of the original scene. Some portions of the image might even be made from data from the infrared, microwave, or other bands that are not visible to the human eye. Microwave detectors, for example, are useful for applications such as determining the relative roughness of the surface of the sea, monitoring the extent of sea ice, estimating the extent of snow cover, locating oil films on water surfaces, and so on (figure 18.1).

To take advantage of the information gathered from invisible wavelengths, remote-sensing images are typically reproduced in false color. In a **false-color image**, the colors assigned to each wavelength band are shifted. One typical false-color arrangement, for example, reproduces the green band as though it were blue, the red band as though it were green, and the near-infrared band as though it were red. In this type of image, healthy vegetation appears as bright red, clear water is black, sediment-laden water is powder blue, and urban centers are blue or blue-gray (see plate 10). Other color assignments are used for special purposes.

EXAMPLES OF REMOTE-SENSING SYSTEMS

Landsat

Since 1972, a series of **Landsat satellites** has been providing information regarding the earth's surface. Landsat 1, 2, and 3 were launched into orbits with an altitude of 919 kilometers (570 miles). They orbited the earth fourteen times per day, with repeated coverage of any given location once every eighteen days. Since 1982, Landsat 4 and, later, Landsat 5 have orbited at an altitude of 705 kilometers (437 miles). These systems have provided repeat coverage every

FIGURE 18.1   Microwave image, produced from Special
Sensor Microwave Imager (SSM/I) data. The purpose of
such low-resolution images (12 by 12 kilometer
resolution) is the remote sensing of atmospheric and
surface parameters, not of terrain detail.

Courtesy of Benjamin Watkins, National Environmental Satellite, Data, and
Information Service (NESDIS).

sixteen days. The major sensor systems used on
Landsat are the multispectral scanner and the thematic mapper.

The **multispectral scanner (MSS) system** has been
used on all five Landsat satellites and has collected a
vast amount of information. The MSS multidetector
array records data for four spectral bands, designated
as bands 4, 5, 6, and 7 (see table 18.1). Because the
four bands are scanned continuously and six lines of
the image are recorded at a time, a total of twenty-four
sensors is required.

TABLE 18.1   Landsat MSS Spectral Bands

BAND*	FREQUENCY
4	0.5–0.6 micrometers (green)
5	0.6–0.7 micrometers (red)
6	0.7–0.8 micrometers (reflective infrared)
7	0.8–1.1 micrometers (reflective infrared)

*Renumbered as bands 1 through 4 on Landsat 4 and 5.

The Landsat MSS scans a 185-kilometer-wide field, using a **whisk-broom scanning movement**, in which an oscillating mirror scans the ground across the satellite's direction of movement (figure 18.2a). The MSS scanner has a ground resolution of 79 by 79 meters, and sampling is conducted in such a manner that each of the final picture elements covers an area of 56 by 79 meters.

Portions of the same MSS scene, using bands 4, 5, 6, and 7, are shown in figure 18.3. Comparison of these scenes gives a sense of the variations in the images, such as the relative sharpness of the shorelines in band 6. Detailed analysis of the data that lie behind the

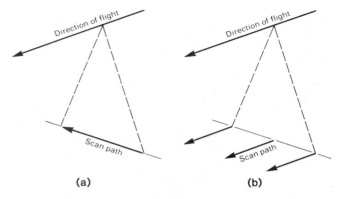

FIGURE 18.2   (*a*) Whisk-broom scanning. (*b*) Push-broom scanning.

FIGURE 18.3   Portion of Landsat MSS scene of Milwaukee, Wisconsin, and vicinity, 2 April 1976. (*a*) Band 4. (*b*) Band 5. (*c*) Band 6. (*d*) Band 7.
Source: U.S. Geological Survey EROS Data Center.

TABLE 18.2   TM Spectral Bands

BAND	FREQUENCY
1	0.45–0.52 micrometers (blue)
2	0.52–0.60 micrometers (green)
3	0.63–0.69 micrometers (red)
4	0.76–0.90 micrometers (reflective infrared)
5	1.55–1.75 micrometers (mid-infrared)
6	10.40–12.50 micrometers (thermal infrared)
7	2.08–2.35 micrometers (mid-infrared)

TABLE 18.3   SPOT Multispectral Mode Bands

FREQUENCY
0.50–0.59 micrometers
0.61–0.68 micrometers
0.79–0.89 micrometers

scenes is necessary, however, to gain more than a general impression of the possible uses of such images. Composite false-color images provide easier recognition of features such as urbanized areas, wetlands, forested areas, geologic structures, and so on.[1]

The **thematic mapper (TM) system** has been installed on Landsat 4 and 5, with images available since 1982. It has a ground resolution of 30 by 30 meters (except the thermal-infrared band, band 6, which has a resolution of 120 by 120 meters). The TM detector arrays are arranged to scan the 185-kilometer-wide ground track in whisk-broom fashion. The frequencies of the TM spectral bands are shown in table 18.2.

Landsat 6, when it is launched, is expected to carry three sensor systems. The first is an Enhanced Thematic Mapper (ETM), which has the same multispectral bands as Landsat 5, plus a 15-by-15-meter resolution panchromatic capability. In addition, this system will have a more efficient data-handling capability. The second system is a Thermal Infrared (TIR) system, which will be especially useful for such tasks as the evaluation of groundwater resources and the monitoring of global volcanic activity, snow cover, flood and erosion, and crop yield. The third system is the Sea-Viewing, Wide-Field-of-View Sensor (SeaWIFS), which will provide information on ocean chlorophyll, color, and temperature. Applications for this system include monitoring the location of warm/cool boundary areas, which are rich in marine life, as well as the study of a variety of ocean dynamics.

[1]See, for example, the many scenes included in the *Atlas of North America: Space Age Portrait of a Continent* (Washington, D.C.: National Geographic Society, 1985).

SPOT

A French, Belgian, and Swedish consortium operates a satellite observation system called *Systeme Probatoire d'Observation de la Terre* (**SPOT**). The SPOT system carries sensors that operate in either panchromatic or multispectral modes. In panchromatic mode, the spectral band is similar to that of a black-and-white photograph. In multispectral mode, three separate bands are recorded (table 18.3). The SPOT sensors are arranged in linear arrays that scan along a 60-kilometer-wide ground track of the satellite in **pushbroom fashion**, in which a complete line of the ground scene is imaged at one time (figure 18.2b). The ground resolution in panchromatic mode is 10 by 10 meters, which produces extremely detailed images. In multispectral mode, the resolution is reduced to 20 by 20 meters.

A unique feature of the SPOT system is a ground-controlled mirror system that can be pointed away from the vertical. This capability makes it possible to view selected areas across a 950-kilometer-wide path. The result is that observations can be made more frequently than the twenty-six day interval between successive passes of the satellite over a given ground location. This more frequent viewing capability is useful when cloud cover interferes with normal vertical viewing or when other circumstances make more frequent viewing desirable. Changing the angle of view also allows the production of stereo pairs for photogrammetric applications.

IMAGE PROCESSING

Simple conversion of remotely sensed pixel values into an image does not usually produce a particularly useful product. Computer-aided manipulations of the original data, however, improve the viewing quality of the final product. Some of these manipulations are typically done before the data are released to the prospective user. These **preprocessing techniques** are not discussed here because the user is not involved in them. Other manipulations are left to the user's discretion because they must be modified to suit particular applications. These processes are referred to as **image enhancements**. In the past, image enhancements required large-scale computer facilities. Recently, however, useful work has been performed on minicomputers and microcomputers.

Data adjustments often enhance the quality of the image for visual analysis purposes. Representative operations of this type include linear contrast stretching and edge enhancement. Other enhancements, such as density slicing and band ratioing, are sometimes used but are not discussed here.

Linear Contrast Stretching

Certain detector characteristics, or the presence of atmospheric haze or of certain types of materials on the surface, may result in a low-contrast image. In a **low-contrast image**, the values of the pixels in the image fall in a relatively narrow range, so that variations in the gray tones are very difficult to discern (figure 18.4a). **Linear contrast stretching** expands the range of tones so that they cover the entire available range and are much easier to differentiate (figure 18.4b).

Edge Enhancement

Edge enhancement increases the contrast between the values on either side of a dividing line, rendering shapes and details along the edges of areas more conspicuous (figure 18.4c).

THEMATIC INFORMATION EXTRACTION

The major value of remotely sensed data is that they provide information about conditions on the earth's surface. Interpretative work with the data, however, is necessary to extract this type of **thematic information**. This is often done without the aid of images, using computer-controlled statistical methods. Manipulation of the images themselves, however, is also an important aspect of analysis because the images reveal the spatial arrangement of different land-use types, surface elevation, and biophysical information, such as vegetation types and conditions, soil moisture, temperature, and texture. The extraction of thematic information is sometimes difficult. For example, different surfaces may have signatures that are similar enough that they cannot be reliably separated. Or, similar surfaces may not necessarily appear the same because of slightly varying conditions at different locations or at different times.

Classification

The data signature of a given image pixel is a composite mixture of the energy wavelengths and signal strengths of the ground surface within the area in the pixel. These data signatures range from uniform to highly mixed in any given region. In a nonurban region covered by a single crop type or by a uniform forest cover, surface signatures and image values may be quite uniform over many pixels.

Mixed uses, on the other hand, result in a greater diversity of signatures and a more complex range of values. In an urban area, for example, a great variety of cover types exist in close proximity to one another. In such areas, asphalt, concrete, and other building materials are mixed in greater or lesser proportions with vegetation of various types, as well as with areas of water. Because each surface has its own signature, the end result is a great variety of signal combinations among the various pixels. An image produced from the original, unprocessed pixel data in such an area, therefore, is also extremely variable.

The goal of **data classification** is to group pixels so that each one is associated with others that have relatively similar characteristics and is separated from those with distinctly different characteristics. This classification is done by statistically analyzing the characteristics of the radiation collected for each pixel and assigning the pixel to the appropriate category. This information can be easily mapped (plate 11). How classification is accomplished is not of direct concern to us here. Regardless of the method used, however, pixels are not always placed in the appropriate category, that is, the category they would be placed in if the classification were checked on the ground. These **classification errors** obviously reduce to some extent the usefulness of the image for particular applications.

(c)

(b)

(a)

FIGURE 18.4 Enhancements of a remote-sensing image.
(*a*) Unprocessed image. (*b*) Image after linear contrast
stretching. (*c*) Image after linear contrast stretching and
edge enhancement.

Courtesy of U.S. Geological Survey EROS Data Center.

Change Detection

The concept of **change detection** is simple. Suppose that two remotely sensed images of a specific region exist. One of these images may have been obtained prior to the current planting season and the other during the season. Change detection involves the careful alignment of the two images, followed by comparing the two on a pixel-by-pixel, or area-by-area, basis. This comparison should make it possible to determine which areas were planted (were changed) and which areas were not (were unchanged).

Many problems are encountered with real-world applications of change detection. Changes in the environment other than those that are under study may well have occurred during the time period between the two images. Weeds may have grown, brushfires may have eliminated vegetation, heavy rain may have soaked the soil or drought may have dried it, and so on. Any such changes affect the data values recorded, and their effects must be separated from changes due to the process of interest.

Other problems must also be considered, including equipment variability from one image to another, the fact that the pixels in one image are not aligned perfectly with the pixels in the other, and so on. Ideally, these factors are eliminated by appropriate processing so that *actual* changes, rather than *apparent* ones, are located. All in all, change detection is not an easy task.

INTERFACE WITH GEOGRAPHIC INFORMATION SYSTEMS

In recent years, geographic information systems (GISs) have come into use. The data used in such systems are drawn from many sources, including maps, aerial photography, field investigations, and statistical studies. Incorporation of remote-sensing data into a GIS adds an additional dimension to the system's capabilities. Remote-sensing systems collect data from the same area on multiple dates, for example. This allows the analyst to not only inventory surface characteristics on an up-to-date basis, but also to monitor changes in them. The characteristics of GISs, and the types of applications for which they are used, are discussed in chapter 20.

Summary

The electromagnetic radiation wavelengths in atmospheric windows within the range from about 0.4 micrometers to 22 centimeters are most frequently used for remote sensing from space. Detectors mounted in satellites receive signals gathered from a specific area on the ground, and the strength of radiation in specified bands is converted to digital values. Each value, which often lies between 0 and 255, is assigned to an image area, called a pixel. The encoded pixel values are transmitted to a ground station, where they are stored on tape.

Ground resolution determines the size of objects that can be detected. The smallest dimension of an object must be at least twice as great as the ground resolution of the system before it is likely to be detectable.

Images are produced by assigning a different color to each data band. In typical false-color images, the green band may be reproduced in yellow, the red band in green, and the near-infrared in red. Although images of this and other types are frequently created, the information from which they are constructed is often more useful in digital than in visual form.

Landsat satellites have been in operation since 1972. The major sensor systems used are the multispectral scanner (MSS) and, since 1982, the thematic mapper (TM). The MSS whisk-broom scanner records data for four spectral bands, from a 185-kilometer-wide field, with a ground resolution of 79 by 79 meters. Sampling is conducted in such a manner that the final picture elements cover 56 by 79 meters. TM also scans a 185-kilometer-wide ground track in whisk-broom fashion, but in seven bands. It has a ground resolution of 30 by 30 meters (except 120 by 120 meters in the thermal-infrared band).

The SPOT system, developed in France, carries sensors that operate in either panchromatic or multispectral modes. Its push-broom sensors scan a 60-kilometer-wide ground track, with ground resolution of 10 by 10 meters in panchromatic mode and 20 by 20 meters in multispectral mode.

Data manipulations, such as linear contrast stretching and edge enhancement, modify images for visual analysis purposes. Linear contrast stretching expands the range of tones so that they are easier to differentiate, whereas edge enhancement increases the contrast between the values on either side of a dividing line.

Thematic information extraction may be done without the aid of images, using computer-controlled statistical methods. Image interpretation is also important, however, because a human observer can often detect spatial arrangements that a computer routine may not. On the other hand, data differences that are meaningful to the computer are often too subtle to be seen, even on enhanced images. Data classification is used to group pixels so that each one is associated with others with similar characteristics and is separated from those with different characteristics.

Change detection involves comparisons of remotely sensed images taken at different times, to determine changes in conditions related to some factor under study. Extraneous changes, however, may mask those due to the factor of interest, and their effects must be separated if the study is to yield useful results.

SUGGESTED READINGS

Barrett, E. C., and L. F. Curtis. *Introduction to Environmental Remote Sensing.* London: Chapman and Hall; New York: John Wiley and Sons, A Halsted Press Book, 1976.

Campbell, James B., *Introduction to Remote Sensing.* New York, London: Guilford Press, 1987.

Colwell, R. N., ed. *Manual of Remote Sensing.* 2d ed. Vols. 1 and 2. Falls Church, Va.: American Society of Photogrammetry, 1983.

Curran, Paul J. *Principles of Remote Sensing.* New York: Longman, 1985.

Jensen, John R. *Introductory Digital Image Processing: A Remote-Sensing Perspective.* Englewood Cliffs, N.J.: Prentice-Hall, 1986.

19

Computer-Assisted Cartography

An important trend in the world of maps and map products is an increasing use of computers. The search for the realization of two different objectives has led to this trend. The first objective is simply to use computers directly in map production. This can involve making the same types of maps that have always been made or making new types of maps that were not possible without the computer's computational power. This approach, which is called **computer-assisted cartography**, is designed to improve the speed and accuracy of production. The second objective is the development and use of cartographic databases in geographic information systems. In this approach, computers are used to improve the analysis of geographic data. Some of the results obtained from this approach have the same appearance as traditional map products, but others can be quite different products or applications. Some of the results may never have been thought of before or, if they had been visualized, could not be produced by conventional means.

OVERVIEW

The boundary between computer-assisted cartography and digital geographic information systems is indistinct. To the extent that a separation is possible, however, the discussion in this chapter focuses on maps and map-related products produced using computer-assisted techniques. Chapter 20 deals with

the extension of those techniques into geographic information systems, so-called "smart-maps" or maps that have "come to life."[1] "Smart-maps," in this context, are systems that provide interactive capabilities.

Advantages of Computer-Assisted Techniques to the Map Producer

Computer-assisted techniques promise considerable production advantages that have attracted the attention of cartographers and have absorbed considerable research effort and financial resources. While map-production considerations are not discussed in detail here, awareness of certain aspects is helpful in understanding the impetus behind the trend toward computer assistance, as well as the nature of the map products that result.

Computer-assisted mapping methods are considered advantageous because the necessary cartographic database is in digital form. Computer techniques enable the cartographer to quickly and easily manipulate the digital data to produce the required **output**, including any necessary mathematical or statistical operations, scale or projection changes, and symbol selection. The ease of using such a system may even encourage the testing of alternative designs aimed at producing the best possible product. If a

[1]D. P. Bickmore, "Objectives in Digital Mapping," in *Proceedings, International Seminar on Computer-Assisted Cartography,* organized by the Survey of India in collaboration with the International Cartographic Association, New Delhi, India, 22–29 November 1983, 39.

permanent copy of the map is desired, a computer-driven drafting machine produces it with accuracies that far exceed the accuracy of manual drafting. Another advantage of such a system, provided the database is kept current, is that each new map produced incorporates information that is correct and up-to-date. Finally, computers allow map data to be rapidly transmitted and exchanged between users. This ease of interchange assures the production of better, more complete, and up-to-date maps. The end result of all of this should be the economic production of a greater variety of more accurate and better-quality maps.

Beyond map production, digital techniques allow textual or tabular information to be tied to cartographic features. This allows the system user to analyze selected features, recall information about them, examine the relationships between features, carry out measurements, and so on, by simply calling the appropriate functions from the computer terminal. This aspect of computer-assisted cartography blends into the digital geographic information systems discussed in chapter 20.

Implementation Problems of Computer-Assisted Techniques

Given the promises outlined in the previous section, the attractiveness of digital production techniques is easy to understand. Unfortunately, these promises have not always been met. The relative newness of the field is the primary problem. There has been little time to analyze and understand the problems involved in digital techniques or to train people in their implementation. Also, the computer technology that provides the underpinning for digital mapping has been, and still is, in a stage of rapid growth and development. As a result, many problems that have little to do with map considerations have had to be resolved. These problems include the difficulty of using many different kinds of computer systems, data formats, and computer languages. Nevertheless, as these problems are resolved, an ever-increasing volume of computer-assisted map products is likely.

Effects of Computer-Assisted Techniques on the Map User

One aspect of the application of computer techniques that may be unexpected is that many of the resulting products are simply replications of traditional map products. Such products not only look the same but are used in the same way. Frequently, however, computer-assisted methods result in nontraditional products that provide opportunities for new applications.[2]

To the extent that they are developed, new forms of map products will force some changes in the way users approach maps. For one thing, they will need to become familiar with the use of computer screens for viewing both data and maps. Also, they may have to use systems that provide databases and mapping software, rather than printed maps. In such systems, users will have access to the desired information and will be able to format it as they wish, thus producing do-it-yourself interactive maps. This possibility provides further incentive for learning about those aspects of computer-assisted mapping techniques that are important to the effective use of interactive map products.

FORMAT AND DATA CAPTURE

Data input techniques and data storage structures differ from system to system, depending on the type of data needed, the form in which the data exist, and the system's operating characteristics. Most of these matters are beyond the control of the system user, and some make little practical difference in terms of system capabilities, so they are not discussed here. An understanding of the methods used to capture the data used in computer-assisted cartography, however, will help you to gain an appreciation for the differences between two distinctly different types of systems: vector (or polygon) and raster (or gridded). These systems are discussed after the data capture methods are introduced.

Digitizing

Maps act as storehouses for spatial information about features on the earth's surface. This information consists of the locations of points, the paths of lines, the outlines of areas, and the complex interrelationships between all of the various types of features. The process of converting map data from its original, visual form to a digital format that can be handled by a computer is called **digitizing** or **conversion**.

[2]Some excellent examples of unusual computer-assisted maps are included in Mark Monmonier and Alan M. MacEachren, guest editors, "Geographic Visualization," *Cartography and Geographic Information Systems* 19, no. 4 (October 1992).

Vector image

Raster image

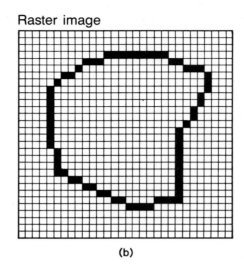

(a)   (b)

FIGURE 19.1   (*a*) Vector and (*b*) raster versions of the same image.

Labeling.   A detailed discussion of the digitizing process is not presented here because digitizing is completed before map users' use of the system. However, one aspect of digitizing that is important to map users is that, as the various map elements are recorded, they must have an identification code attached to them so that they can be selectively retrieved from the data file. This is done by **labeling** each record with a standardized set of characters, such as "050 0412" for a stream, or "170 0201" for a class-1 highway.[3] Some knowledge of these labels is helpful as you work with a geographic information system so that you understand the contents of its files.

Vector and raster digitizing.   Another aspect of digitizing that map users should understand is the difference between vector and raster methods. In **vector digitizing**, the records consist of the coordinates of specific points (or a series of points, in the case of linear features or the outlines of areas) (figure 19.1a). Traditional maps are vector products, drawn using point symbols, along with lines connecting points or outlining areas.

As an alternative to vector digitizing, maps may be digitized as **rasters**. This means that the map is divided into a myriad of tiny cells. These cells, each of which may be as small as 0.001 inch square, contain the feature records (figure 19.1b). A major difference between vector and raster digitization, then, is that a

raster image is presented as a set of individual cells, and the appearance of such an image is quite different from that of a traditional line map. The smaller the cells in a raster image, however, the more its appearance resembles that of a vector image.

Other Considerations

Maps are not the only source of data used in computer-assisted cartography. Original survey data, aerial photos, and data obtained from remote sensing are also used. Aerial photos are typically digitized in much the same manner as conventional maps. On the other hand, data obtained from original surveys and remote-sensing systems may already be in digital form. This means that they are particularly suited to incorporation into a digital-mapping process.

Machine coordinates.   The types of coordinates used in digitizing need further clarification. The coordinates obtained directly from many digitizing methods are arbitrary **machine coordinates**. This means that they are recorded in inches or centimeters, measured from a control point, such as the corner of the digitizing board. Coordinates of this type have the shortcoming that they do not have any direct relationship to locations on the earth's surface. In practice, therefore, machine coordinates are usually converted to some more general coordinate system, such as latitude/longitude or Universal Transverse Mercator (UTM) or State Plane Coordinates (SPC), in a process called geocoding.

[3]One set of codes, the standard U.S. Geological Survey attribute codes for digital line graphs, is found in appendix D of US GeoData, *Data Users Guide 1: Digital Line Graphs from 1:24,000-Scale Maps* (Reston, Va.: U.S. Geological Survey, 1986).

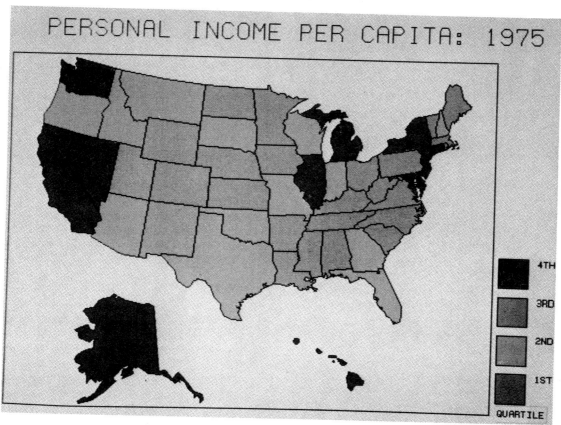

FIGURE 19.2   Map image photographed directly from computer screen.

Courtesy of Laboratory for Computer Graphics and Spatial Analysis, Harvard Graduate School of Design.

Geocoding.   Geocoding is accomplished by first determining the actual coordinates of known points on the map using the desired coordinate system. The machine coordinates of these control points are then obtained and compared to their actual coordinates. The relationship between the two sets of coordinates is subsequently used to automatically record actual coordinates as features on the map are digitized, instead of simply using machine coordinates.

A major advantage of geocoding is that data from a variety of sources are recorded in a single locational system. This allows materials mapped at different scales or on different projections to be brought to a common scale and projection so that they can be used in conjunction with one another.

Format and the user.   Whether a GIS user would prefer a raster or vector format depends on both the application at hand and the scale at which the work is being done. This is particularly true regarding output, which is discussed next. On the other hand, the selection of the system format is beyond the user's control because the system is already in existence and must be accepted as it stands, regardless of the data format. For this reason, and acknowledging the importance of differences between raster versus vector systems, we now move on to a consideration of other aspects of computer-assisted cartography.

OUTPUT

One simple and direct way of producing hard-copy maps in a computer-assisted cartography system is simply to photograph the image displayed on the computer screen. Direct photography is useful for either black-and-white or color images and has the advantage of being quick and easy. High-quality products can be produced by this method (figure 19.2).

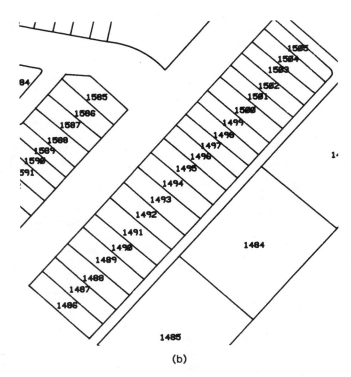

FIGURE 19.3   (*a*) Raster plotter image and (*b*) line plotter image of same area. Each address contains a node that is linked to a data base containing attributes associated with that parcel, such as acreage, ownership, and zoning.

Courtesy of City of Boston and Donohue Intelligraphics.

Probably the most common method of producing hard-copy maps, however, is to print or plot them, using a peripheral device that is part of the computer system. Depending on the characteristics of the particular system, either raster or vector devices can be used.

Raster output consists of an image produced by creating a pattern of dots on the paper (figure 19.3a). The **dot-matrix printers** that are often used with word processing and similar office systems can be used to produce graphic images, including maps. Special **raster plotters**, however, can produce larger images. **Line plotters** are vector output devices that draw an image using continuous lines, in the manner of traditional drafting (figure 19.3b). Most users seem to prefer the quality of line-plotter output, but raster devices with fine resolutions are also capable of producing high-quality images. Raster plotters have the advantage of operating much more rapidly than vector plotters. Devices of both types are capable of producing color as well as black-and-white products.

APPLICATIONS

Microcomputer Programs

A number of computer-mapping programs that run on microcomputers have been marketed recently. Many of these programs allow the user to create special-purpose maps without elaborate equipment (figure 19.4). These programs typically limit the user to thematic databases, such as population and income data, supplied by the software manufacturer. In addition, the manufacturer usually supplies base-map data for a variety of areas, ranging from the entire country, through states, counties, Standard Metropolitan Statistical Areas (SMSAs, used in U.S. census), and zip-code areas. More flexible programs provide utilities that permit the user to create and use diverse data sets and map bases and to produce a variety of map types.

Because of the lack of standardization in the computer field, programs may only operate with particular

(a)

(b)

FIGURE 19.4   Sample output from microcomputer mapping programs. (*a*) ATLAS*GRAPHICS map. Original plotted in black on an electrostatic plotter. (*b*) MAP-MASTER®. Original is a color slide.

(*a*): Courtesy of the developer, Strategic Locations Planning, Inc. ATLAS*GRAPHICS is a trademark of STSC, Inc. (*b*): Used by permission of Borland International, Inc.

computers, printers, plotters, and other hardware. This can be a severe limitation. Recently, however, the list of equipment that each program can accommodate has become quite extensive. There is, therefore, little point in going into detail on such matters here. If you are planning to implement a computer-assisted mapping project, first find the software that can produce the products you need. Then you will know what hardware to purchase to use the program effectively. Buying hardware first and then looking for software to do the job you require is likely to lead to extra expense and frustration.

Larger-Scale Applications

Numerous actual applications of digital cartographic information have been undertaken or are in the development stages. We look at a few examples of such applications here to provide some insight into the range of problems for which such techniques are helpful and to illustrate the concept of the "smart-map."

Irrigation potential.   In a study of the Umatilla River basin in Oregon, a map showing the irrigation development potential of areas within the basin was produced by computer-assisted methods.[4] First, digital elevation models (DEMs) were used to compute surface slopes in the region (DEMs are discussed later in the chapter). This information was then combined with land-cover, soils, and land-ownership data, also in digital form. The results were used to produce a map of irrigation potential in the study area. The elevation and location data in the DEMs were also used to help determine the costs of irrigation. This calculation was based on the simple fact that higher elevations and greater distances from the water source require greater amounts of energy to deliver water to a site. This factor, combined with pumping-plant data, determined the total energy requirements for bringing irrigation to the land. Then, information on the cost of energy was incorporated, and a map of the relative cost of irrigation was developed. The maps of irrigation potential and irrigation costs were used to produce the final map of irrigation development potential. This map, in turn, was used in making resource-efficient water-development decisions.

[4]"Survey of Oregon Irrigation Development Potential," in T. R. Loveland and Ben Ramey, *Applications of U.S. Geological Survey Digital Cartographic Products, 1979–1983* (Washington, D.C.: U.S. Government Printing Office, U.S. Geological Survey Bulletin 1583, 1986), 29–33.

Terrain analysis.   In military applications, digital-analysis methods produce important tactical information used in making a variety of important decisions. Such information was previously obtained by traditional map-analysis methods, but with less accuracy and with much less speed. The digital methods can provide information about sites that are screened from the enemy's electronic line of sight, that are away from enemy high-speed avenues of approach, or that have more than one access route.[5] Such information is vital to conducting an effective military operation.

Other applications.   A great variety of other applications of digital cartographic techniques has been developed. Examples that give an idea of the range of such applications include studies of intervisibility for forest-fire lookout sites; selection of the optimal areas for clear-cut logging; military observation, access, and concealment studies; selection of locations for microwave towers and of routes that would hide power lines; engineering applications, such as cut and fill, and overburden and reservoir volume calculations; forest-fire hazard evaluation; earthquake hazard prediction; rangeland management; and nuclear disaster planning.

Although these examples are classified as digital cartography applications, they cannot be clearly separated from applications of geographic information systems. The main distinction is that geographic information systems provide a higher level of data handling and analytic capabilities, as is discussed more fully in chapter 20.

DATABASE AVAILABILITY

The creation of digital databases for use in computer-assisted cartography applications is time consuming and expensive, especially because of the cost of the hardware required for some of the operations. In addition, because of the repetitive nature of many mapping projects, users may waste resources (both time and money) if they create databases that are essentially the same as those created by others. Indeed, the capability of sharing data is one of the advantages of computer-assisted cartography. For these reasons, already-prepared databases (both base-map data and thematic information) are increasingly becoming

[5]Tom Hills, "Terrain Information Used by Field Artillery," *Tech-Tran* 11, no. 2 (Spring 1986): 2.

FIGURE 19.5   Sample digital line graph.

Source: US GeoData, ***Data Users Guide 1: Digital Line Graphs from***
1:24,000-Scale Maps (Reston, Va.: U.S. Geological Survey, 1986).

available for purchase. This development, especially given the often very reasonable prices of the available databases, frequently renders the production of new individual files not cost efficient. The availability of materials of this nature is constantly changing, so only some of the more important products are described here.

U.S. Geological Survey Products

The U.S. Geological Survey sells a number of digital cartographic products.[6] The brief descriptions that follow provide a general idea of the characteristics of each.

Digital line graphs.   Digital line graphs (DLGs) contain digital map data in vector format (figure 19.5

[6]Details of these products are provided in US GeoData *Data Users Guides*, published by the U.S. Geological Survey.

TABLE 19.1   Digital Description of Topological Elements and Relationships of a Digital Line Graph (See Figure 19.5)

| | NODES | | | AREAS | |
Internal ID Number	x Coordinate	y Coordinate	Internal ID Number	x Coordinate	y Coordinate
N1	1	28	N2	13	14
N3	23	28	N4	13	1
N5	13	7	N6	22	10
N7	6	5	N8	10	4
N9	11	24	N10	23	1
N11	1	17	N12	1	1
N13	9	9			
A1	0	0	A2	6	24
A3	3	10	A4	8	7
A5	18	14			

| | | | | LINES | | |
| | Nodes | | Area | | Coordinates | |
Number	Starting	Ending	Left	Right	(First x, y)	(Last x, y)
L1	1	3	1	2	1, 28	23, 28
L2	3	10	1	5	23, 28	23, 1
L3	4	12	1	3	13, 1	1, 1
L4	11	2	2	3	1, 17	13, 14
L5	2	3	2	5	13, 14	23, 28
L6	2	5	5	3	13, 14	13, 7
L7	5	4	5	3	13, 7	13, 1
L8	13	7	4	3	9, 9	6, 5
L9	7	8	4	3	6, 5	10, 4
L10	4	10	5	1	13, 1	23, 1
L11	5	6	5	5	13, 7	22, 10
L12	9	9	2	2	11, 24	11, 24
L13	12	11	1	3	1, 1	1, 17
L14	11	1	1	2	1, 17	1, 28
L15	8	13	4	3	10, 4	9, 9

Source: U.S. GeoData, *Data Users Guide 1: Digital Line Graphs from 1:24,000-Scale Maps* (Reston, Va.: U.S. Geological Survey, 1986).

and table 19.1). They are of three types: (1) large scale, primarily digitized from 1:24,000-scale quadrangle maps; (2) medium scale, from 1:100,000-scale quadrangle maps; and (3) small scale, from the 1:2,000,000-scale *National Atlas* sectional maps.[7] The files contain point, line, and area data, with each category of information (boundaries, hydrography, Public Land Survey System, or transportation) stored as a separate file or subfile. The features are coded by size and type so that it is possible to group or select on the basis of those characteristics.

The files currently being distributed have been spatially structured to define all of the topological relationships that exist between the component elements of the file, and are designed for use in geographic information systems.

Small-scale DLGs are divided into twenty-one multistate blocks. They are available in a special graphics format designed specifically for visual products, as well as the standard format suited to carrying out digital operations on the files. The files contain boundaries, hydrography, and transportation information.

Medium-scale DLGs are provided in groups that cover 30-by-30-minute areas, corresponding to the east or west half of the 1:100,000-scale source map. Each 30-minute area group usually consists of four 15-by-15-minute files, although as many as sixteen files may

[7]See U.S. Geological Survey *Data Users Guides:* (a) *Digital Line Graphs from 1:24,000-Scale Maps,* (b) *Digital Line Graphs from 1:100,000-Scale Maps,* and (c) *Digital Line Graphs from 1:2,000,000-Scale Maps.*

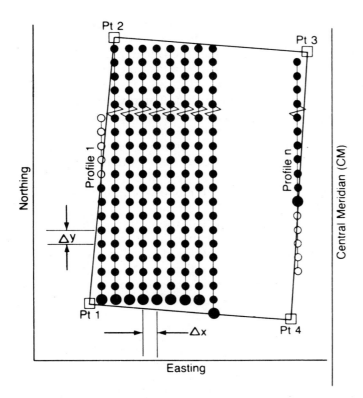

FIGURE 19.6   **Structure of a 7.5-minute digital elevation model.**

Source: US GeoData, *Data Users Guide 5: Digital Elevation Models* (Reston, Va.: U.S. Geological Survey, 1987).

be used in areas of high feature density, such as roads and trails in large cities. Current medium-scale DLGs contain hydrography and transportation files.

Each large-scale DLG file covers the same area as a U.S. Geological Survey 7.5-minute quadrangle map. The geographical extent of large-scale coverage is presently quite limited, although it will eventually include the entire country. Most current, large-scale DLGs contain boundary, hydrography, U.S. Public Land Survey (USPLS), and transportation files.

The extensive, computer-compatible data contained in DLG files are a great boon to users. The files provide the raw material on which to base the production of customized maps, without the necessity of creating new base files. Once the DLGs are read into a computer-mapping system, they can be extensively modified. Information can be added or deleted, and entirely new overlay files can be created as well. Hardcopy maps can be produced from various combinations of these files, as desired.

DLG files, in their original form, are designed for use on computer systems that include tape drives for reading the data into the system. Now, however, the DLG files are also available in a floppy-disk format that is compatible with microcomputers. Service bureaus perform the necessary transformation, for a reasonable charge, and the microcomputer user can proceed with the use of the files.

Digital elevation models. Digital elevation models (DEMs) provide elevation values in machine-readable form.[8] Computer-compatible tapes contain the data for DEMs, which are available for selected 1:24,000-scale 7.5-minute quadrangles in the United States and for 1:250,000-scale sheets, which are available for most of the country.

Each 7.5-minute DEM corresponds to the equivalent U.S. Geological Survey quadrangle. The files contain elevation values, in meters, spaced at regular, 30-meter intervals (figure 19.6). The location of each value is referenced to the Universal Transverse Mercator (UTM) coordinate system.

[8]US GeoData, *Data Users Guide 5: Digital Elevation Models* (Reston, Va.: U.S. Geological Survey, 1986).

The 1:250,000-scale DEMs are produced by the Defense Mapping Agency (DMA) and are distributed by the U.S. Geological Survey.[9] They cover 1-degree-by-1-degree blocks, which are the east or west half of the 1:250,000-scale source maps from which they are digitized. The spacing between the data values is generally 3 arc-seconds, which means that the east-west ground-distance spacing varies with latitude. At the equator, the spacing is approximately 90 meters in each direction, for example. At 50° latitude, however, the spacing is approximately 90 meters north-south by 60 meters east-west. Elevation values are recorded to the nearest meter and are referenced by latitude and longitude coordinates.

DEMs provide data that can be used for the production of contour maps and slope maps. They also provide the raw material for intervisibility maps and profiles. As with DLGs, DEMs in their original form are designed for use on large computer mapping systems. Conversions to microcomputer-compatible formats, however, are feasible.

Digital land-use and land-cover data. Digital land-use and land-cover data are produced by the U.S. Geological Survey from 1:250,000- and, occasionally, 1:100,000-scale U.S. Geological Survey land-use and land-cover maps.[10] The files contain information on up to thirty-seven categories of land-use and land-cover data. They have a minimum-size polygon of 16 hectares (40 acres) in rural areas and of 4 hectares (10 acres) in urban and built-up areas, water areas, and some other types of land use. Separate files provide the outlines of state and county boundaries and of census tracts within Standard Metropolitan Statistical Areas (SMSAs) and minor civil divisions outside SMSAs. A hydrologic file contains watershed boundaries, and a file of federal land ownership delimits areas that contain 16 hectares or more. In some cases, a file of state land ownership is also produced.

Digital land-use and land-cover data are often used in connection with land-use planning studies, such as the irrigation study mentioned earlier. They are also frequently incorporated into digital geographic information systems.

Geographic Names Information System. An additional element of the U.S. Geological Survey digital cartographic data is the **Geographic Names Information System (GNIS)**.[11] This automated system is designed to provide an index of standardized geographic names in the United States, as well as other information about the names. The system is comprised of five interrelated databases. It provides information in the form of alphabetized listings for each state or territory, either as spiral-bound books, microfiche, or magnetic tapes. Specialized searches can also be conducted to suit the needs of individual users.

GNIS now contains information about most of the named features on all of the maps in the U.S. Geological Survey topographic map series. The names were edited by comparing them with the records of the U.S. **Board on Geographic Names (BGN)**; and names from other sources, including historical data, are currently being added.

A particularly useful product from this project is the *National Gazetteer of the United States of America* (U.S. Geological Survey Professional Paper 1200). The gazetteer is produced on a state-by-state basis. Each listing contains place, feature, and area names for a given state. A condensed version of the *National Gazetteer* provides information about the geographic names contained in the U.S. Geological Survey's *National Atlas of the United States of America*. It includes the name, type of feature, location on maps in the atlas, geographic coordinates, and population statistics.

GNIS publications are an unmatched source for the verification of place names and feature names. Although the cost of the publications is relatively high for the occasional user, many libraries carry the volumes that apply to the state or region in which they are located.

Census Bureau Products

TIGER. In support of its 1990 Census of Population, the U.S. Census Bureau developed a digital cartographic database for the United States. This database is called **TIGER**, an acronym for Topologically Integrated Geographic Encoding and Referencing system. The goal of TIGER is to provide a geographical database for the entire country.

---

[9]Digital terrain tapes (DTTs) at 1:250,000-scale are also distributed by the U.S. Geological Survey. These tapes are the predecessors of the 1:250,000-scale DEMs; they are not produced in the standard DEM format, and other problems are associated with them.

[10]US GeoData, *Data Users Guide 4: Land-Use and Land-Cover Digital Data from 1:250,000- and 1:100,000-Scale Maps* (Reston, Va.: U.S. Geological Survey, 1986).

[11]US GeoData, *Data Users Guide 6: Geographic Names Information System* (Reston, Va.: U.S. Geological Survey, 1987).

FIGURE 19.7   Portion of a Census Bureau Enumerator Assignment Map generated from a TIGER file.

Source: FDC Newsletter **8** (Summer 1988).

TIGER database information was digitized from a variety of sources. The two most important of these were the Census Bureau's **geographic base file/dual independent map encoding (GBF/DIME)** files from the 1980 census and the USGS 1:100,000-scale DLGs. Other supplemental sources were used, as needed, to bring the information up-to-date. These sources included local governmental units, private mapping organizations, and census enumerators who discovered errors as they were conducting census activities.

At the Census Bureau, TIGER is used to assist in the collection, tabulation, and dissemination of census data. This includes the assignment of location codes to addresses, and the provision of a geographic structure for the tabulation and publication of census data. Also, it involves the production of cartographic products to support both collection field work and publication efforts.

For persons outside the Census Bureau, TIGER represents a valuable database for a wide range of applications. For this reason, TIGER files are being offered for sale. The first TIGER products to become available are the TIGER/Line files. These are records

of topologically consistent networks of line segments, produced on a county by county basis.

For general mapping purposes, as the name suggests, line segments are the most important part of the TIGER/Line files. Each linear feature contained in the file is represented by one or more segments, identified by a unique record number. Each of these segments has a recorded beginning and ending point. If needed, shape points are added to the record to represent the path followed by the line segment. The coordinates of each of these points is recorded in degrees of latitude and longitude, expressed to six decimal places. Additional information is recorded for each line segment to describe its attributes. This includes the source of the information; the type of feature (census feature class code-(CFCC)); topological information, including the state, county, and census divisions to the left and right of the line; and, in certain urban areas, address and ZIP code information.

In the urban areas that were covered by GBF/DIME files in 1980, each record in a TIGER/Line file describes a segment of a street (figure 19.7). The record includes the name of the street, the range of addresses on both sides of the street segment, and the node numbers that occur at each end of the segment. Also included are the numbers that identify the block, census tract, county, or other areal units that adjoin either side of the segment.

One somewhat controversial aspect of TIGER/Line files is their accuracy. When people have printed out the files and compared them with other maps or remotely-sensed images, such as SPOT, some features were not located accurately, did not have the proper shape, or were missing altogether. Often such problems occurred when information about new subdivisions or similar changes had been entered from field notes without surveyed data. The presence of apparent inaccuracies does not necessarily indicate that the census is based on faulty maps. Instead, it is more a matter of the level of accuracy that is needed for a particular purpose. For example, in the conduct of the census, the absence of a highway on ramp or the exact location of a street in a subdivision is not particularly significant. To a company using the files as the basis for delivery routing, however, the absence of the on ramp would obviously be troublesome. Similarly, exact street location would be of importance to many map users. As is the case with any database, potential users of TIGER/Line files should be certain that they meet their accuracy requirements.

One result of user dissatisfaction with TIGER accuracy has been the preparation, by private companies, of enhanced files based on TIGER. These files have been improved by additional checking and correction of locational data and updating of details on roads and highways. Often, the enhanced files are improved enough to be worth their higher cost.

TIGER/Line files may be used to produce maps of roads and other features within counties. In addition, they may be combined with statistical information, such as population, housing, and income, obtained from the census or from other sources. With proper software, various types of thematic maps may be produced for use in market research, routing problems, address matching problems, redistricting plans, and many other purposes. Application software that permits such uses is not available from the Census Bureau. There are, however, several private companies that produce software capable of using the TIGER/Line files. These same companies usually provide TIGER/Line files that have been converted to floppy disk from the original Census Bureau tapes or CD-ROMs (Compact Disk-Read Only Memory). In some cases these files have also been enhanced by additional editing as mentioned above.

To order tapes and CD-ROMS directly, contact:

Customer Services
Data User Services Division
Bureau of the Census
Washington, DC 20233
Phone: (301)763–4100

World Data Banks

Two worldwide databases are **World Data Bank** I and II. World Data Bank I contains data about coastlines, national boundaries, and place names. It was digitized from 1:12,000,000-scale source maps. World Data Bank II contains data about coastlines, major rivers, national boundaries, state or province boundaries, and place names. It was digitized from 1:3,000,000-scale source maps, supplemented by some larger-scale coverage. Both databases are available from the National Technical Information Service (NTIS):

National Technical Information Service
U.S. Department of Commerce
5285 Port Royal Road
Springfield, VA 22161
Phone: (703)487–4807

Other Databases

The field of computer-assisted cartography is changing rapidly, and a large number of government agencies, university researchers, and private companies are involved in new developments. Indeed, new products are introduced (and some old ones disappear) with great frequency. For this reason, a book of this nature cannot provide the latest information about available materials. Current information on these topics is provided more efficiently through software reviews and information about databases that appears in periodical publications. *Cartography and Geographic Information Systems, Cartographica,* and *The Professional Geographer,* for example, regularly publish information of this nature.[12] In addition, newsletters, such as those issued by the Canadian Cartographic Association, the Cartographic Specialty Group, and the Computer Specialty Group of the Association of American Geographers, are helpful sources of current information.

[12]One useful source is Dean T. Edson, "Data Bases," in Section 5, "Automation in Cartography," *U.S. National Report to ICA, 1984,* ed. Judy M. Olson (Falls Church, Va.: American Congress on Surveying and Mapping, 1984), 51–54.

Catalogs that provide references for locating computer software and digital spatial data for mapping applications are also available.[13] Although the printed versions of these catalogs are necessarily somewhat out-of-date, they do provide a good overview of the materials available from various federal, state, and local government agencies, as well as the private sector. The National Cartographic Information Center maintains a computerized version of these catalogs and is, therefore, an excellent source of information.

Summary

Computer-assisted cartography involves the direct use of computers for map production. The anticipated advantages of this approach include quick and easy map design, integrated mathematical or statistical operations (including scale or projection changes), and symbol selection. Also, the rapid exchange of data between users means that each new map can incorporate information that is correct and up-to-date. Beyond simple map production, digital techniques allow textual or tabular information to be tied to cartographic features. Most of these advantages stem from the use of digital cartographic databases. Implementation problems, however, have resulted in the advantages not always being achieved, although this situation is rapidly improving.

Digitizing is the process of converting map data from its original visual form to digital form. For maximum benefit, the various map elements must be labeled with an identification code during the digitizing process so that they can be selectively identified in the data file.

Digital records in vector form contain the coordinates of specific points. Linear features, including the outlines of regions, consist of linked coordinates of a series of points. In contrast, digital records in raster form consist of information about whether or not features fall within individual cells in a matrix. Arbitrary machine coordinates, recorded in inches or centimeters, are measured from a control point on the digitizing board. More usefully, however, machine coordinates are usually converted to latitude and longitude, or Universal Transverse Mercator or State Plane Coordinates, a process called geocoding.

Output methods include photographing the image on the computer screen; but printing or plotting, using either raster or vector devices, is more often used. Raster output devices, either printers or plotters, produce an image by creating a pattern of dots. Line plotters are vector output devices that draw an image, using continuous lines, in the manner of traditional cartography.

Computer mapping programs that run on microcomputers allow the user to create special-purpose maps without elaborate equipment. Larger-scale computer systems are usually needed for major applications, mostly because of the greater database capacity and higher operating speeds that they offer.

Because the creation of digital databases is time consuming and expensive, already-prepared databases of both base map data and thematic information are becoming increasingly available. U.S. Geological Survey products are among the more important of these digital cartographic products. Digital line graphs (DLGs) contain digital map data in vector format, and digital elevation models (DEMs) provide elevation values. Digital land-use and land-cover data are also available, as are Geographic Names Information System (GNIS) data.

The U.S. Census Bureau has developed a digital cartographic database for the United States, called TIGER (Topologically Integrated Geographic Encoding and Referencing system). This database supplants the geographic base file/dual independent map encoding (GBF/DIME) files used for the 1980 census. TIGER is used by the Census Bureau to assist in the collection, tabulation, and dissemination of census data. It also provides other users with a database for a wide range of applications. In general, TIGER/Line files include street names and address ranges, as well as block, census tract, county, and ZIP code data.

World Data Banks I and II are other examples of easily obtainable files that contain data about coastlines, national boundaries, and other features. The field of computer-assisted cartography is changing rapidly, and a large number of government agencies, university researchers, and private companies are involved in new developments. Therefore, additional map data and thematic-information files are continually becoming available.

[13]*Sources for Software for Computer Mapping and Related Disciplines* (February, 1990) and *Sources for Digital Spatial Data* (February, 1990). Available from National Cartographic Information Center, Reston, Va. (see appendix C).

SUGGESTED READINGS

Bauer, Michael. "Value-Added Data Bases Are Foundation for Diverse AM/FM/GIS Applications," *Geo Info Systems* 2, no. 5 (May 1992): 36–41.

Bickmore, D. P. "Objectives in Digital Mapping." In *Proceedings, International Seminar on Computer-Assisted Cartography.* Organized by the Survey of India in collaboration with the International Cartographic Association, New Delhi, India, November 22–29, 1983, 38–40.

Carter, James R. *Computer Mapping: Progress in the '80s.* Washington, D.C.: Association of American Geographers, Resource Publications in Geography, 1984.

Computer Mapping of Natural Resources and the Environment, Plus Satellite-Derived Data Applications. Vol. 15. Cambridge, Mass.: Harvard University, Laboratory for Computer Graphics and Spatial Analysis, 1981.

Douglas, David H., and A. Raymond Boyle, eds. *Computer-Assisted Cartography and Geographic Information Processing: Hope and Realism.* Ottawa, Canada: Canadian Cartographic Association, Department of Geography, University of Ottawa, 1982.

Groot, Richard. "Computer-Assisted Mapping and Charting: A Manager's View." In *Computer-Assisted Cartography and Geographic Information Processing: Hope and Realism,* edited by David H. Douglas and A. Raymond Boyle. Ottawa, Canada: Canadian Cartographic Association, Department of Geography, University of Ottawa, 1982, 29–32.

Guptill, Stephen C. "1:100,000-Scale Digital Cartographic Data Base for Federal Requirements." In *United States Geological Survey Yearbook,* Fiscal Year 1984. Washington, D.C.: U.S. Geological Survey, 1984.

McEwen, R. B., and H. W. Calkins. "Digital Cartography in the USGS National Mapping Division." *Cartographica* 19, no. 2 (1982): 11–26.

Monmonier, Mark S. *Computer-Assisted Cartography: Principles and Prospects.* Englewood Cliffs, N.J.: Prentice-Hall, 1982.

Olson, Judy M., ed. *U.S. National Report to ICA, 1984.* Falls Church, Va.: American Congress on Surveying and Mapping, 1984, Section 5, "Automation in Cartography."

Peucker, Thomas K. *Computer Cartography.* Washington, D.C.: Association of American Geographers, Commission on College Geography, Resource Paper No. 17, 1972.

Peuquet, Donna J., and A. Raymond Boyle. *Raster Scanning, Processing and Plotting of Cartographic Documents.* Williamsville, N.Y.: Spad Systems, 1984.

Taylor, D. R. Fraser, ed. *The Computer in Contemporary Cartography.* Vol. 1., *Progress in Contemporary Cartography.* New York: John Wiley and Sons, 1980.

20

Geographic Information Systems

OVERVIEW

Before discussing the applications of **geographic information systems (GISs)**, we need the answer to a very basic question: Just what *is* a GIS?

Definition

A GIS is an information system, which means that it provides a specific set of facts (the information), arranged in an orderly manner (the system). It also provides facilities to help the user work with the facts it contains. Many types of information systems are used today. They deal with concerns such as payroll, financial information, library holdings, and many other matters. A GIS, however, has another primary characteristic that distinguishes it from the bulk of such information systems—it deals with information that has a spatial, or geographic, component. This means that each piece of information in the system includes a reference to its location. In most GISs, the availability of this spatial component means that the system can produce maps from the data. It also means that variations from place to place in a particular variable, or geographical interrelationships between different variables, can be analyzed.

A GIS, or any other type of information system, need not be computer operated. Today, however, the use of digital data in computer-based systems is the rule, rather than the exception. In this chapter we will assume, unless otherwise indicated, that the term implies that the systems under discussion use a computer to work with **digital data**. Digital information processing is of particular importance because it provides increased speed and expanded capabilities in the analysis of spatial information.

In summary, we may accept a definition of a GIS used by the U.S. Geological Survey. "A GIS is a computer system capable of assembling, storing, manipulating, and displaying geographically referenced information."[1]

Antecedents of GISs

Relatively simple GIS procedures have been in use for a long time. Even rudimentary elements of digital techniques for the recording and analysis of geographic information were in use as early as the 1800s. Probably the most notable early example of such techniques was Hollerith's use of a punched card system for the manipulation and analysis of data during the 1890 U.S. Census of Population.

Early GIS methods are exemplified by the techniques that geographers, planners, geologists, and others have used over the years to analyze mapped information. One such method is **map-overlay analysis**. This technique involves tracing the outline of some variable of interest, such as soil types, from a

[1]Brochure, "Geographic Information Systems," U.S. Department of the Interior, U.S. Geological Survey, [1992].

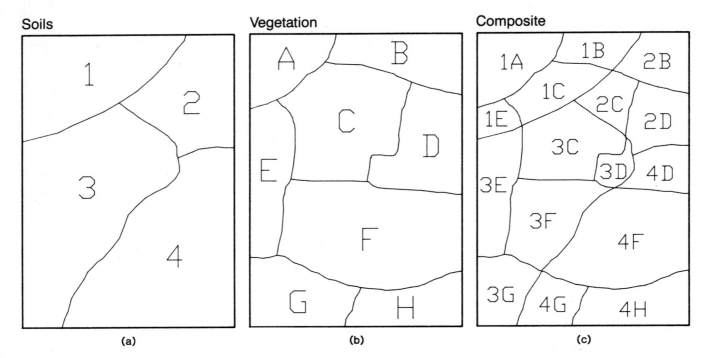

FIGURE 20.1   Relationship between sample soil and vegetation maps. (*a*) Soil map. (*b*) Vegetation map. (*c*) Overlap between maps.

source map onto a transparent overlay. The overlay is then placed over another map of the same area at the same scale, such as a vegetation map. The overlap of the soil and vegetation types shows the relationship between the two phenomena (figure 20.1). The investigator might go further and apply statistical techniques to determine the level of coincidence between the two distributions (for example, the coefficient of areal correspondence) (see chapter 11). Although such methods are useful, they are cumbersome and time consuming and provide only a limited type of analysis.

A particularly well-developed extension of map-overlay analysis techniques was the **photographic-overlay method**, used by planner Ian McHarg in the late 1960s.[2] This technique used maps as tools for analysis, taking into account the physical and social environments, and thus qualified as a GIS approach.

The photographic-overlay method was aimed at finding "the solution of maximum social utility" for the particular problem being studied. It involved

[2]See Ian L. McHarg, *Design with Nature* (Garden City, N.Y.: Doubleday/ Natural History Press, Doubleday and Company, 1969).

transparent, photographic overlays on which information was represented in shades of gray. Physiographic factors were recorded so that higher dollar costs and higher social values were both represented by darker tones. When the various overlays were placed over one another, the resulting map showed a complex pattern of gray values, ranging from light to dark. The areas that could best be used for a particular project, such as a highway, were the areas with the "least social cost." These areas, which were generally zones of lower dollar cost and of lesser social value, were shown by the lightest tone, whereas those of higher dollar cost and/or greater social value were shown by the darkest tone.

This method was used in real-world decision making, such as route selection for the Richmond Parkway in New York in the 1960s. A wide variety of factors was considered in this study, resulting in a very complex analysis. Factors considered included surface drainage, soil foundation and drainage, bedrock foundation, susceptibility to erosion, land values, tidal inundation, historic values, scenic values, recreation values, water values, forest values, wildlife values, residential values, and institutional values.[3] The Tri-State Transportation Commission ultimately accepted the least-social-cost alignment developed in McHarg's study.

Useful as the photographic-overlay approach was, there were technical problems, such as determining the appropriate weighing of factors (a problem that continues, even with computer-assisted methods). Also, the method had reached "the limits to the photographic resolution of many factors." McHarg felt that "it may be that the computer will resolve this problem, although the state of the art is not yet at this level of competence."[4] As indicated here, the "level of competence" of computer techniques has increased significantly in the two decades that have passed since these words were written, providing greatly expanded capabilities.

Formal GISs

Many early GISs were developed for land-use planning purposes. These typically involved mapping and recording various natural resources at the state, regional, or national level. The first full GIS of this nature, used on a production basis, was the Canada Geographic Information System (CGIS). The CGIS was authorized in 1964 and put into operation in 1969. The system involved a land-inventory database that was used to locate and identify marginal lands currently being used for agricultural purposes. This information was particularly useful for resource management projects, such as erosion control.

Throughout the 1960s, similar projects proliferated, including early projects in New York, Minnesota, and Kentucky. The complexity of these projects meant that large agencies were required to put them into action. A 1979 report listed eighteen state-level natural resource information systems,[5] The number of such systems continues to grow, because a broad range of functions can now be carried out on microcomputers.

[3]The maps of these factors, which cannot be reproduced here, are shown on pages 36–41 of *Design with Nature* by McHarg.

[4]McHarg, *Design with Nature*, 115.

[5]National Conference of State Legislatures, *Remote Sensing: A Review of State Landsat Applications* 2, no. 9 (February 1979).

GIS COMPONENTS

A GIS acts as a link between the real world and the user. The real world is the source of the information stored in the system. The user employs the GIS to analyze the information and applies the results to the solution of a problem. The essential considerations in any GIS, from the standpoint of such a user, are data input and storage structure, manipulation and analysis techniques, and output capabilities. We will now examine these components in somewhat more detail. Other aspects, such as input processing and data management, are extremely important but generally fall outside the focus of this discussion.

Data Input and Storage Structure

The data incorporated into GISs are obtained from sources that are either graphic and spatial in nature or that are nongraphic and nonspatial. Examples of graphic, spatial sources include existing maps, charts, graphs, and aerial photographs and other remotely sensed images. Nongraphic, nonspatial sources include tabular information, digital databases, and textual materials. Data from each type of source are converted into computer-compatible form, using techniques ranging from typing tabular data at a computer terminal to scanning source maps on a digitizer. The details of these techniques lie beyond the scope of this discussion, although the "Suggested Readings" section at the end of the chapter provides sources of information about them.

In a GIS, data are divided into separate themes, chosen from the multitude of topics possible. Typical themes include physical phenomena, such as landforms, climate, soils, or vegetation. They also include social aspects, such as income levels, racial heritage, population density, and zoning designations. Information about the characteristics of each theme throughout the region covered by the system is stored in a separate file, called a **data plane**. Data planes are the computer equivalent of map overlays. The data planes do not exist in the system as physical entities, of course; instead, they are in digital form.

The number and specific contents of the data planes in a particular GIS depend partly on the applications anticipated and partly on the resources, including computer capacity, devoted to the system. In a simple situation, for example, separate data planes could

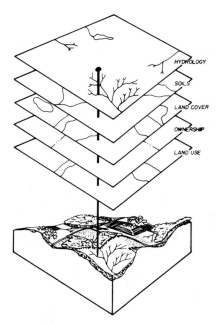

FIGURE 20.2   Example of multiple data planes in a database.

Source: Reproduced with permission of Joseph K. Berry.

record water features, vegetation, urbanized areas, roads, pipelines, railroads, and so on (figure 20.2). On the other hand, it might be desirable to include a number of data planes within each of the broad categories. For example, road classes might include separate data planes for local, county, state, federal, and interstate highways. Water features might be similarly separated into intermittent and permanent streams, lakes, marshes, and other wetlands, and vegetation categories might include deciduous trees, conifers, brush, grassland, and so on. In a real-world GIS, then, a multitude of data planes may break the information about the region into finely dissected categories.

Data Adequacy

The characteristics of the data in a GIS place the ultimate limits on what can and cannot be accomplished within the system. Even a system with excellent data storage, manipulation, and other characteristics cannot provide useful information if its data are inadequate. There are, however, practical limits to the level of detail contained in any given GIS. Greater detail means higher costs (in both time and

money) of acquiring, storing, maintaining, and using the GIS. As a potential user of a GIS, therefore, you need to know the specific topics included in a particular system to see whether or not your data needs are met. In addition, you need to evaluate the accuracy and timeliness of the data content.

Data accuracy can be generally evaluated if enough is known of the manner in which the data were collected. If remotely sensed data are used, for example, resolution (that is, how small an area on the earth's surface can be discriminated) is specifically limited. If an application demands the detection of objects that measure 10 meters on a side, and the system contains image pixels that are 79 meters on a side, the resolution is obviously inadequate for that specific application. Evaluations of accuracy are *relative,* however. That is, data may be sufficiently accurate for one use, even though inadequate for another.

If existing maps are used as a database, their scale, accuracy, and date of production are important quality-control factors. In the case of one county, for example, it is claimed that the base map currently used for recording property locations was created many years ago by gluing together the 1899 U.S. Geological Survey 1:62,500-scale topographic maps for the county. The resulting mosaic was then photographed onto a 2-by-2-inch slide, which was projected onto a sheet of paper tacked on the wall. The resulting outline was traced to create the base map! Digitizing a base map of this "quality" would not result in a very useful database, either in terms of locational accuracy or of timely information.

The information contained in a GIS must be timely, in addition to sufficiently accurate. Information on most topics is subject to more or less frequent change. The management capabilities of a GIS, therefore, must include procedures for incorporating new information, as well as for deleting obsolete information. Also, information is often published years after it is gathered. The date of publication must not be confused with the date of acquisition, which is the relevant one. Old data, however, are not necessarily bad data. If a study includes an historical dimension, the use of older material may be essential. Data showing the land-use patterns of a region at ten-year intervals, for example, would be invaluable for conducting a study of land-use evolution. For each application, it is necessary to decide which date, or dates, are relevant to the task at hand.

Data Forms

Each data plane contains information that occurs in some combination of four basic types: points, lines, polygons (areas), and surfaces. A few comments about these types are appropriate, in the context of GISs.

Points.   Features that are small in areal extent are thought of as occurring at a point in space. The classification of a feature as a point is relative and is dependent on the scale of the data plane. A city, for example, may be considered to occur at a "point" on the earth's surface if the data plane is at a small scale. On the other hand, if the data plane is at a large scale, the same city would cover a relatively large area and could no longer be considered a "point" feature.

Lines.   When features have length but lack significant width, they are treated as lines. Line features include roads, railroads, canals, pipelines, power lines, and national, state, or county boundaries.

Areas.   Features that cover a region on the earth's surface are represented as areas. Such regions are defined on the basis of distinctive characteristics, such as specific crop types, dominant religious denominations, climatic type, income per capita, population density, and so on.

Surfaces.   Finally, features that cover an area but that also have a vertical dimension are called **surfaces.** The earth's surface is probably the easiest to visualize. A surface has an outline, whether it is the shoreline of an island, or a political boundary. Within that outline, however, a surface also has a series of elevation values, one for each point defined on the surface. Other phenomena that vary in value from place to place, such as rainfall, temperature, or total income, are also represented as surfaces.

Rectification

Each data plane also includes locational information about the features recorded. Part of the input processing involves the **rectification** of the various data planes so that the features recorded are in correct alignment from one data plane to another. Locational information is specified either in terms of latitude and longitude or according to a locational grid, such as the Universal Transverse Mercator (UTM)

or State Plane Coordinate (SPC) systems. Positions also can be recorded using a special-purpose, localized reference system. Such a system is a problem, however, when the data need to be related to other sources of information that are organized around one of the standard locational systems.

Labeling

In addition to locational information, the various elements in a data plane each have an identification code so that they can be selectively retrieved from the data file. This is done, as in computer-assisted cartography, by **labeling** each record with a set of identifying characters called an **attribute code.**

Format Considerations

The discussion of vector and raster formats in chapter 19 also applies to GISs, but some additional points need to be made. Some GISs are vector-based, some are raster-based, and mixed systems are not unusual. Part of the reason that this mixture of types exists is that different sources of information are used as input into GISs. For example, many GISs are built on a base of remotely sensed information. Because such data are usually already in raster format, such systems often are built on raster methods.

On the other hand, maps are also a major source of GIS data, and they may be digitized in either mode. The influences favoring one or the other format in systems based on map inputs are less obvious. One influence is that, in the early phases of the development of computer-assisted cartography, most digitizing was done using vector-based digitizers. This influence naturally carried over to related systems in the GIS arena. As more emphasis was placed on automating and speeding up the digitizing process, however, raster-scanning devices were developed. As these devices became more important, the development of raster-based systems was emphasized.

Another important factor that influences the vector versus raster decision is that some operations are performed more efficiently in one mode than in the other. For example, a raster format is favored when overlaying operations are performed. Routing and network linkage problems, on the other hand, are handled more efficiently within a vector format. When geographic accuracy and the appearance of a traditional map are important, vector systems tend to be favored. Improvements in output devices and an increase in the accuracy levels of raster digitizing seem to be reducing the importance of this factor, however.

Finally, because many different types of operations are performed within a given GIS, it is desirable to have data in one format to facilitate some operations and in the other format for other operations. For this reason, some systems provide for raster-to-vector and vector-to-raster conversions. This flexibility allows the use of the format best suited to each particular operation.

Manipulation and Analysis Techniques

A GIS is supposed to provide a storehouse of information for use in the analysis and solution of a variety of problems. To provide the flexibility required for such applications, the system must include capabilities for manipulating, comparing, or combining the data in various ways. This section describes some techniques typically available for these purposes.

System capabilities.   GIS capabilities usually include the following:[6]

1. Comparing the distribution of two types of data within the study area
2. Searching for a selected set of characteristics that occur together, either with or without some other specific characteristic
3. Searching for the nearest neighbor of a specific feature, with added criteria regarding the presence or absence of other characteristics
4. Handling comparisons between data recorded at different scales or on different projections

The basic operations that support these capabilities include reclassification, overlaying, distance functions, and modeling.

Basic operations.   The user of a GIS calls selected data planes from the computer memory and carries out any operations desired. In the process, new data planes are created and, henceforth, are treated as separate entities. These data planes are subjected to further manipulation, discarded, or stored, as desired. However, the original data planes are almost invariably retained in the system, in unchanged form,

[6]R. F. Tomlinson, "A Geographical Information System for Regional Planning," in *Land Evaluation,* ed. G. A. Stewart (New York: St. Martin's Press; South Melbourne: Macmillan of Australia, 1968), 200–210.

so that they are available for future applications. This protection of the original data is usually assured by the use of a "read-only" arrangement, which allows the user to access and manipulate the original data, but prevents any changes to the original files by anyone but system maintenance personnel.

Reclassification.   One method of altering an existing data plane to create a new one is **reclassification**. Reclassification is the replacement of the initial category designations by new values, based on specified criteria. Assume, for example, that one data plane includes soils in several categories, with designations like *1* for gravel, *2* for clay loam, *3* for silt loam, and *4* for loam (figure 20.3a). The areas suitable for agriculture could be delineated by arbitrarily giving them a value of *1* and giving all of the other areas a value of *0*. The reclassified data would be stored as a new, separate overlay of areas of soil suitable for agriculture (figure 20.3b).

Reclassification may also be done on the basis of the relative importance of a particular type of feature for a specific purpose. For example, conifers might be considered more suitable than deciduous trees for high-quality recreational facilities, and brushland might be altogether unsuitable. To represent this situation in the GIS, the vegetation data plane could be reclassified so that areas designated as conifers are shown with a value of *2*, deciduous trees a value of *1*, and brushland a value of *0*. Although there would not necessarily be a difference in the map's general appearance, the assigned numerical values would represent an ordinal classification of the vegetation types in terms of recreation potential.

Still another type of reclassification requires simple arithmetic or statistical operations. A data plane recording average temperatures in degrees Fahrenheit could be converted to one of temperatures in degrees Celsius by applying the appropriate conversion factor to the original values. Although there would be no difference in the appearance of the two maps, the difference in values would be important in relation to any subsequent calculations.

In another situation, reclassification might be done on the basis of feature size. Woodland areas, for example, could be reclassified on the basis of the number of acres contained in a contiguous forested area. The new data plane would have entries indicating feature size, rather than simply indicating wooded sites (figure 20.4).

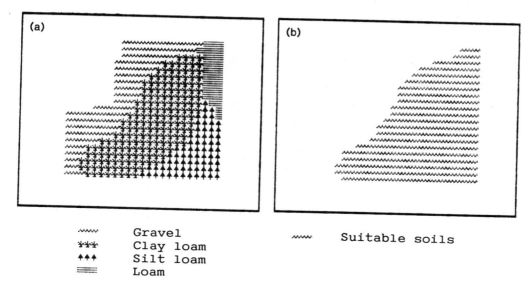

ᨃᨃᨃ	Gravel
✝✝✝	Clay loam
♦♦♦	Silt loam
▦▦▦	Loam

ᨃᨃᨃ   Suitable soils

FIGURE 20.3 Reclassification by renumbering.
(*a*) Original classification. (*b*) Reclassified data.
Source: Map by Dean Boyer.

Number of cells

ᨃᨃᨃ	31
✝✝✝	116
♦♦♦	140
▦▦▦	227
▨▨▨	438

FIGURE 20.4 Reclassification on the basis of feature size.

Overlaying. Another way of generating a new data plane is to **overlay** two or more existing data planes on one another. This is the digital equivalent of carrying out map-overlay analysis by physical methods. In a GIS, however, the task is accomplished much more quickly and easily. In addition, other considerations, such as weighing the various factors, can be accommodated.

Overlaying may be done in several ways, including establishing some minimum, maximum, or other specific value as a requirement. A certain minimum average rainfall might be required for a specific crop,

for example. For planning purposes, a map could be generated to show only those areas that meet or exceed that minimum requirement. In another situation, several complementary characteristics might be desired for development purposes, such as selected soils, certain vegetation types, and specific zoning. Overlaying the data planes for each of these categories gives those areas that contain the three required categories a value indicating that they are suitable (figure 20.5). Those areas that do not contain all three categories are given a value indicating that they are unsuitable.

Suitable soils

Suitable vegetation

Suitable zoning

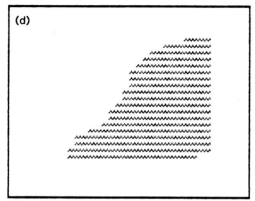

Area suitable for development

FIGURE 20.5   Overlaying to determine areas that meet or exceed a minimum requirement. (*a*) Suitable soils. (*b*) Suitable vegetation. (*c*) Suitable zoning. (*d*) Area suitable for development.

Source: Map by Dean Boyer.

Alternatively, ratings can be obtained by weighting the categories on the basis of their relative importance and adding the layers together. If slope is the most important limiting factor for a particular project, for example, slope ratings might be given a weight of *3,* whereas vegetation ratings, which are slightly less important, might have a weight of *2,* and so on with other factors. In this type of application, a range of ratings for each location would be possible. Those locations with the lowest total value would be most suitable, and those with higher values would be less suitable.

In another application, industrial development activities might need to be excluded from wildlife habitat areas. In that case, areas for potential industrial development could be evaluated on a variety of characteristics. The information on wildlife habitat areas, however, would be used to exclude development from a given area, even if the other characteristics of that area indicated suitability for industrial use.

Distance functions.   **Distance functions** are also available and are used for a variety of purposes. Assume that a particular location is being considered

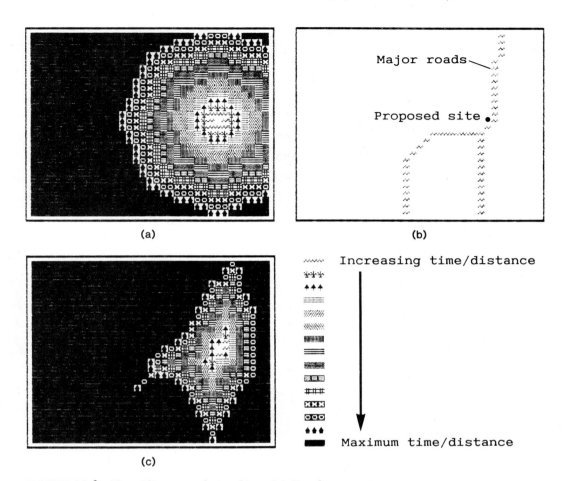

FIGURE 20.6   Time/distance relationships. (*a*) Simple distance. (*b*) Principal roads. (*c*) Weighted distance (travel time).

for a shopping center, for example. With a distance function, each point in the region can be assigned a value based on its distance from the proposed site (figure 20.6a). The resulting information can then be analyzed along with population and income information to determine the new shopping center's potential market zone. In situations where travel time is more important than simple distance, the calculation of the zone of influence can be modified. By incorporating road network information (figure 20.6b), in particular, distance can be expressed in terms of travel time, rather than in direct distance (figure 20.6c).

Other types of analysis of the effects of distance are equally possible. A cost analysis can be used, for example, to compute the minimum cost path from a factory to a number of potential warehouse locations. Or,

in another application, a distance function can determine the location and extent of desirable environmental buffer zones. Such zones are often used to protect an important aspect of the environment, such as bald-eagle nests, scenic areas, or high-quality water sources (figure 20.7). In a GIS, a buffer zone is established by appropriately renumbering locations within a specified distance of the protected feature. The designated buffer zones can then be excluded from any development or activity plan that might affect them.

Modeling.   The production of new data planes and statistics is one of the basic tools of a GIS. The utility of such a system is based on its capability for handling a logical sequence of analytical operations, called **modeling**. Models use the database, in a series

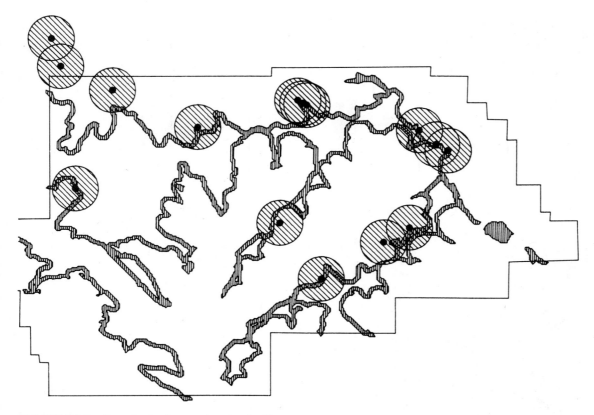

FIGURE 20.7   Sample final map showing buffers away from cliff edges (bands) and around raptor sites (circles) in the Tar Sand Lease Unit, Utah.

Source: FDC Newsletter 3 (Winter 1986): 7. Contributed by Harvey Fleet, National Park Service.

of steps, to produce information regarding the alternative outcomes that would result from different courses of action.

The sequence of operations in a model varies from case to case. The appropriate model is determined by the analyst, who takes into consideration the relationships between the variables of importance in a particular situation. A simple model for the selection of the optimal corridor for a highway is an example. In this case, it is assumed that it is preferable for the highway to avoid steep slopes and, also, to be as well hidden as possible.[7]

[7]Based on Joseph K. Berry, "Computer-Assisted Map Analysis: Fundamental Techniques" (Paper presented at National Computer Graphics Association, Computer Graphics 1985 Conference, Fairfax, Va., 1985).

In this example, the model is designed to select a minimum-cost highway alignment between two towns. To accomplish this the model uses information about topography and residential housing locations. A portion of the cost is measured in dollars, reflecting the higher construction costs encountered in areas with steeper slopes. Also involved, however, are the social costs associated with having a highway built within view of residential locations. Costs of the latter type cannot be converted directly into dollar terms. One portion of the model, therefore, uses a sequence of steps to develop an appropriate cost surface, based on exposure to view. Each location is then assigned a relative cost based on its particular combination of steepness and exposure.

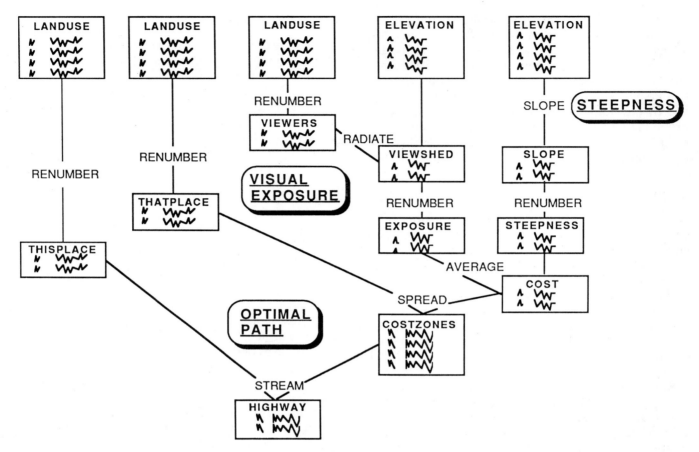

FIGURE 20.8   Example of simple modeling.

Source: Reproduced with permission of Joseph K. Berry.

The model works as follows (figure 20.8). First, it uses elevation information to develop data on steepness of slope. The same elevation information is used to produce an intervisibility map that shows areas within view from existing residential areas. Values on the cost surface are then determined. They are low in areas that are flat and not visible from houses and reach a maximum in visually exposed areas on steep slopes. Finally, the model identifies the minimum-cost route between the two towns, taking into account the values on the cost surface.

A particular advantage of computer-assisted modeling is its flexibility, which encourages the testing of a variety of possible approaches to a problem, allowing the addition of new considerations or the refinement of existing ones, as desired. The highway-siting model could be modified extensively. Several different relative weighings of the criteria could be tested, for example, including variations in the relative weighing of the terrain steepness and visual-exposure factors. In addition, new factors, such as the barrier nature of lakes, could be recognized. In each case, the effect of the changes on route selection would be determined. Thus, the response of the model to various possible factor relationships provides information useful for informed decision making. This is a more rational approach than simply providing a single "take-it-or-leave-it" outcome, with no alternative options.[8]

Determining the relative importance of the various factors involved in any problem is the most difficult aspect of modeling techniques. This problem is just

[8]Berry, "Computer-Assisted Map Analysis."

as severe as it was when McHarg used the photographic-overlay method. Although the GIS provides the capabilities of dealing with ranks and weights, the system itself cannot determine what those values should be. Decisions of that nature can only be made by persons who have the necessary technical expertise in the fields of study pertinent to a particular problem. Even then, the decisions are subjective and must be exposed to some type of societal evaluation before they are accepted.

Output Capabilities

In addition to their complex information processing and modeling capabilities, GISs incorporate large amounts of data. This fact places a premium on an adequate means for getting the information and analyses to the user. Typically, the data planes can be viewed, one at a time, directly on the computer screen (CRT). At times, however, some type of relatively permanent (**hard-copy**) output is needed for distribution purposes, and most systems provide methods for producing such copy.

Statistical reports.   A GIS database is often used for the production of **statistical reports**, as well as for the creation of maps. Depending on the data available in the system, such statistics might include calculations of average income level, average elevation, maximum elevation, and similar information. In addition, total land values within a specific distance of a given origin, total hectares of agricultural land, total area in a forest with percentages of different tree types, or any of a myriad of other possible pieces of statistical information could be generated. Such statistical information is typically printed out in the form of tables, using a typewriter-like printer attached to the computer system.

Maps and graphs.   The methods available for the production of hard-copy maps in a GIS are identical to those mentioned in chapter 19 in connection with computer-assisted cartography. These methods include photographs of the CRT image, raster prints, or vector plots (see figures 19.2 and 19.3).

In addition to statistical reports and maps, GISs commonly have the capability of converting the statistical information into various graphs, such as pie, bar, and line graphs. Hard-copy graphs are produced by the same methods as are used to produce hard-copy maps.

GIS Applications

To bring this discussion to a conclusion, some real-world examples of applications serve to illustrate the usefulness of GIS techniques.

Industrial site selection.   A multilayered database was developed for an area in north-central Connecticut.[9] An Industrial Site Selection Model was one of the applications included in the project. A number of factors of concern in the selection of sites appropriate for industrial development were available in the database and were evaluated as part of the selection process. These factors included areas of wetland, locations subject to flooding, and sensitive environmental areas. The availability and quality of the water supply and of sewers and transportation facilities were also examined for each site, as were the site's zoning classification and size. By excluding or including sites with specific characteristics, potentially useful industrial sites were selected for industrial development consideration.

Other uses of the same database included a Public Water Supply Groundwater Exploration Model. This model took a variety of relevant factors into consideration to determine whether a given location should be accepted or rejected as a potential well site. In addition, two other water resource models were developed for use in the prediction of groundwater flows and for water resources planning and management programs.

Military examples.   The physical environment is overwhelmingly important to military operations. For this reason, the armed forces are very much involved in developing applications of GIS techniques to assist in analyzing potential environmental influences. Three examples give some idea of the scope of such applications.

Mobility studies are a traditional type of military terrain analysis, in which various surface characteristics are studied to determine their effect on the ability of various types of military vehicles to negotiate the terrain. Traditional mobility mapping begins with the production of individual factor maps, often using aerial photographs as an information source. Typically, these factor maps show such information as the surface configuration (slope), surface drainage, vegetation, transportation routes, obstacles, and surface materials (soils). By combining the individual

[9]"GIS Tested in Connecticut," *FDC Newsletter,* no. 3 (Winter 1986): 5.

factor maps in different ways, mobility maps are produced. One type of mobility map is called a "go-no-go" map. Because it uses appropriate weighings of the different factors, each "go-no-go" map indicates the ability of a particular type of vehicle to negotiate the terrain. Such analysis would benefit greatly from the introduction of GIS techniques, and work is being done in this regard.[10]

In another application, a climatic database has been developed to provide information about worldwide climatic conditions. The data include temperature, wind speed and direction, precipitation, sky cover, barometric pressure, visibility, and so on that are typical at different time periods.[11] When an operation is planned for a selected area and month, this information is used for planning equipment needs and for predicting the effect of climate on equipment performance and human factors. Equipment-performance variables include parachute-drop capabilities; effects on aircraft, such as the length of runway needed and load-carrying capabilities; and maximum anticipated off-road vehicle speed. Human factors include the possibilities of frostbite, heat stress, or increased water requirements. Estimates that reflect the possible need for additional personnel due to climatic influences on the ability to perform tasks can also be generated.

The army is also using a GIS approach for the evaluation of potential well sites in advance of the occupation of an area.[12] This technique uses a water-resources database of geological factors and geophysical data. The information made available through this system aids in making complex technical judgments and increases the odds of finding water at the selected sites.

Other examples.   GIS techniques have also been applied to projects as varied as national park planning, the selection of new town sites, the analysis of deer habitat utilization, and the siting of coal-fired power plants, to name only a few.[13]

[10]See, for example, Richard L. Taylor, "Cross-Country Movement Synthesis Using a Geographic Information System" (Unpublished Master of Science thesis in Geographic and Cartographic Sciences, George Mason University, Fairfax, Va., 1983).

[11]Mark Ross, "USAETL Researches the Effect the Environment Has on the Battlefield," *Tech-Tran* 11, no. 2 (Spring 1986): 1 and 3–4.

[12]"Detection Team Supports Brightstar 85," *Tech-Tran* 10, no. 4 (Fall 1985): 5–6.

[13]See, for example, "GIS Aids National Park Planning," *FDC Newsletter* 3 (Winter 1986): 7; and E. Teicholz and B. Berry, eds., *Computer Graphics and Environmental Planning* (Englewood Cliffs, N.J.: Prentice-Hall, 1983).

Summary

Geographic information systems (GISs) are defined as computer systems capable of assembling, storing, manipulating, and displaying geographically referenced information. This implies an automated, digital system that provides an orderly set of facts, as well as facilities for file-handling and data-processing operations. Each piece of data is tied to a locational reference system so that the system can produce maps from the data.

Information in a GIS is classified according to physical or social themes and stored on separate data planes on the basis of points, lines, polygons (areas), and surfaces. Each data plane is rectified so that it is in correct alignment with the other data planes. In addition, the various elements are assigned attribute codes so that they can be identified and selectively retrieved.

GIS capabilities usually include the comparison of distributions, searching for features with selected characteristics, finding nearest neighbors, and comparing data recorded at different scales or on different projections. The methods used include reclassification, overlaying, distance functions, and modeling.

Reclassification is the replacement of the initial categories by new values, based on such criteria as relative importance, arithmetic or statistical specifications, or feature size. Overlaying is the digital equivalent of carrying out map-overlay analysis by physical methods and is based on some minimum, maximum, or other specific value requirement. Distance functions assign values based on simple distance, travel time, or minimum cost paths. Modeling pulls the capabilities of the system together by establishing a logical sequence of analytical operations, and using the database to produce information regarding the alternative outcomes that would result from different courses of action. The output from this analysis is made available by direct viewing on the CRT or in the form of hard-copy maps and statistical reports.

Geographic information systems entail, in one way or another, virtually all of the topics discussed earlier in this book. The techniques involved in the use of conventional maps, of remote-sensing products, and of computer-assisted cartographic output are all used. These range from the determination of scale and the interpretation of symbols, to the measurement of distances, areas, and other characteristics of features on the earth's surface. In addition, GISs bring greater flexibility and accuracy to the analysis of the relationships between such features. Indeed, when one considers the capabilities of geographic information systems, it is apparent that they constitute the "state of the art" in the field of map use and analysis. It is not surprising, therefore, that GISs are currently being applied to a wide variety of "real-world" projects. In addition, the hardware and software that support such systems are becoming more refined and less expensive. For these reasons, GISs are becoming more widely available. These developments virtually assure the increased use of geographic information system technology and concepts in a more varied range of applications.

SUGGESTED READINGS

Aronoff, Stan. *Geographic Information Systems: A Management Perspective.* Ottawa, Canada: WDL Publications, 1989.

Berry, J. K. "Computer-Assisted Map Analysis: Extending the Utility of the GIS Technology." *Proceedings,* Tenth Canadian Symposium on Remote Sensing, Ottawa, Ontario, 1986, sponsored by the Canada Centre for Remote Sensing.

Douglas, David H., and A. Raymond Boyle, eds. *Computer-Assisted Cartography and Geographic Information Processing: Hope and Realism.* Ottawa: Canadian Cartographic Association, Department of Geography, University of Ottawa, 1982.

Huxhold, William E. *An Introduction to Urban Geographic Information Systems.* New York: Oxford University Press, 1991.

McHarg, Ian L. *Design with Nature.* Garden City, N.Y.: Doubleday/Natural History Press, Doubleday and Company, 1969.

Parry, J. T., J. A. Heginbottom, and W. R. Cowan. "Terrain Analysis in Mobility Studies for Military Vehicles." In *Land Evaluation,* edited by G. A. Stewart. New York: St. Martin's Press; South Melbourne: Macmillan of Australia, 1968, 160–70.

Puequet, Donna J., and Duane F. Marble, eds. *Introductory Readings in Geographic Information Systems.* New York: Taylor & Francis, 1990.

Star, Jeffrey, and John Estes. *Geographic Information Systems: An Introduction.* Englewood Cliffs, N.J.: Prentice Hall, 1990.

Taylor, D. R. Fraser, ed. *Geographic Information Systems: The Microcomputer and Modern Cartography.* Vol. 1, *Modern Cartography.* Oxford: Pergamon Press, 1991.

Tomlinson, R. F. "A Geographical Information System for Regional Planning." In *Land Evaluation,* edited by G. A. Stewart. New York: St. Martin's Press; South Melbourne: Macmillan of Australia, 1968, 200–10.

21

U.S. and Canadian Map Producers and Information Sources

A tremendous variety of mapping programs, both public and private, exists in the United States and Canada. This chapter provides some basic background data about the major map producers and the types of maps they publish. In addition, some of the libraries and depositories where maps can be consulted are discussed, as are sources from which maps can be purchased. Additional information about these and other mapping programs can be obtained by consulting the sources listed in the "Suggested Readings" at the end of the chapter.

U.S. FEDERAL MAP PRODUCERS

Major Agencies

U.S. Geological Survey. The U.S. **Geological Survey (USGS)** is an agency of the Department of the Interior. Its role is to gather, analyze, and make available information about the composition and structure of rocks, data about surface water and groundwater, knowledge of earth history and natural processes, and appraisals of potential energy and mineral resources. In addition, USGS classifies federal lands for mineral and water-power purposes and supervises oil, gas, and mineral lease operations on federal and Indian lands and the outer continental shelf.

In connection with its assigned tasks, USGS publishes a wide variety of reports and maps and is probably the preeminent U.S. map producer. A listing of the types of products the agency publishes includes topographic maps; floodplain maps; geodetic control data; geologic maps (general geology, minerals, coal, oil, gas); land-use, land-cover, river basin/watershed studies; the *National Atlas of the United States;* aerial

photographs; orthophotomaps; seismicity maps; clinometric (slope) maps; gravity survey charts; isogonic charts; water-availability maps; hydrologic maps; Landsat scenes and mosaics; and digital data. Examples of these products appear frequently throughout this book, especially in chapter 9. USGS is also involved in U.S. production of the **International Map of the World (IMW)**, which is described in appendix D.

A monthly catalog of USGS publications, entitled *New Publications of the U.S. Geological Survey,* includes information about the various books, professional papers, reports, and special maps published each month, as well as about new and revised topographic maps produced by the agency. The catalog, which is free, is available from

> Department of the Interior
> U.S. Geological Survey
> 582 National Center
> Reston, VA 22092

Distribution services for all USGS maps are provided by

> U.S. Geological Survey, Map Sales
> P.O. Box 25286
> Denver, CO 80225

Distribution services for text products (books and open-file reports) are handled by

> U.S. Geological Survey, Books and Open-File Reports
> P.O. Box 25425
> Denver, CO 80225

Many USGS products, especially topographic maps, are also available from private map dealers throughout the nation.

FIGURE 21.1   Bureau of Land Management map of surface-minerals management status. Tones (colors on original) indicate public land-management status, and patterns indicate federal mineral rights. (Cass Lake quadrangle [planimetric], Minnesota, 1:100,000, 1978.)

Information regarding the maps and related products produced by USGS and other government agencies is available from the National Cartographic Information Center and the EROS Data Center. Both of these organizations are described later in the chapter.

Bureau of Land Management.   Another Department of the Interior agency with extensive mapping responsibilities is the **Bureau of Land Management (BLM)**. The BLM is the final authority on all matters pertaining to the survey of public lands. The BLM surveys and maintains the U.S. Public Land Survey monuments and publishes the township plats described in chapter 10.

Maps and related products produced by the BLM include maps of civil subdivisions, reservations, and lands administered by the BLM; wildlife and scenic-river jurisdictions; aerial photographs; and recreation

maps (figure 21.1). Information about these products is available from the National Cartographic Information Center or from the BLM.

U.S. Department of the Interior
Bureau of Land Management
Washington, D.C. 20240

National Ocean Service.   The **National Ocean Service (NOS)** is a component of the National Oceanic and Atmospheric Administration, in the U.S. Department of Commerce. The NOS produces aeronautical charts, hydrographic surveys, nautical charts, geodetic control data, aerial photographs, orthophotomaps, gravity survey charts, and storm evacuation maps. Examples of aeronautical and nautical charts are shown in chapter 6. Information can be obtained from

Distribution Division (OA/C44)
National Ocean Service
Riverdale, MD 20737

FIGURE 21.2   Portion of Defense Mapping Agency Southeast Asia Briefing Map. (Series 5213, Edition-2, original scale, 1:2,000,000—reduced.)

Defense Mapping Agency.   The **Defense Mapping Agency (DMA)** provides mapping, charting, and geodetic support to Department of Defense components. The agency produces worldwide topographic maps, aeronautical charts, nautical charts, precise positioning data, and digital data for military purposes. Some of these products are available to civilian users (figure 21.2).

Information regarding the availability of DMA products and their purchase, which varies among the various products, can be obtained from

DMA Office of Distribution Services
Attn: DOA
Washington, D.C. 20315
Phone: (202) 227–2816

Other Agencies

Army Corps of Engineers.   In connection with its mission to maintain navigable waterways, the **Army Corps of Engineers** produces Mississippi River System nautical charts and maps showing small-craft facilities. Two distinct types of maps are produced for public distribution. The first type are free and provide information about recreational areas and facilities at Army Corps of Engineers projects. The second type—navigation charts—are for sale. The navigation charts are designed to provide a measure of safety to the boating public since they depict underwater hazards and safe main channels. Samples of both types of products are shown in figure 21.3. Information regarding these maps and charts can be obtained from the appropriate district office of the Corps.[1]

Bureau of Indian Affairs.   Maps and surveys of Indian lands are produced by the **Bureau of Indian Affairs.** Information can be obtained from

Bureau of Indian Affairs
Department of the Interior
Eighteenth and C Streets NW
Washington, D.C. 20240

[1]U.S. Army Corps of Engineers district office addresses are listed in Morris M. Thompson, *Maps for America*, 3d ed. (Reston, Va.: U.S. Department of the Interior, U.S. Geological Survey, 1987), 226.

(a)

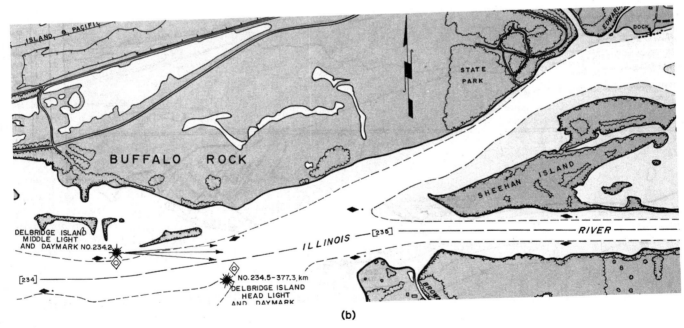

(b)

FIGURE 21.3   Sample Army Corps of Engineers products.
(*a*) Portion of guide to recreation facilities, "Lakeside
Recreation in the Midwest." (*b*) Navigation chart.
(Reduced from original scale, 1 inch to 1,000 feet.) (Not
for navigational purposes.)

Source for (*b*): Portion of Chart 52, *Charts of the Illinois Waterway*
(Chicago, Ill.: U.S. Army Engineer District, Corps of Engineers, 1974).

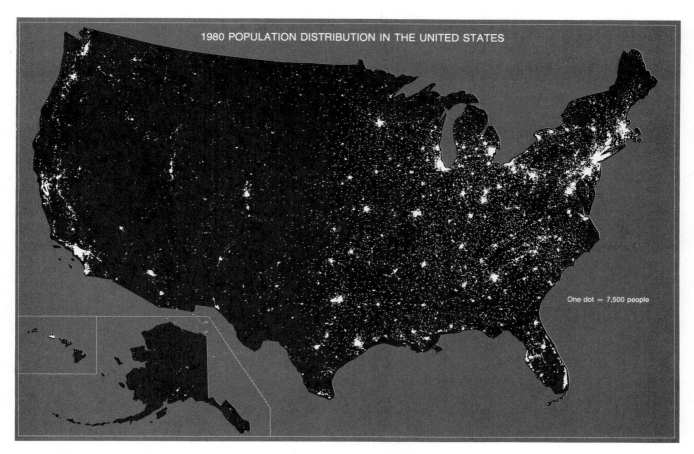

1980 POPULATION DISTRIBUTION IN THE UNITED STATES

One dot = 7,500 people

FIGURE 21.4   1980 population distribution in the United States.

Courtesy of U.S. Department of Commerce, Bureau of the Census.

Bureau of the Census.   The **Bureau of the Census** is a branch of the Department of Commerce. It produces a wide variety of maps, ranging from large-scale coverage of census subdivisions, including census tracts, blocks, and enumeration districts, to maps of incorporated places and other densely settled areas, including Standard Metropolitan Statistical Areas (SMSAs). The bureau also produces a map of U.S. counties and a variety of color-shaded and dot-distribution maps of U.S. census social and economic data (figure 21.4).

Computerized geographic coding of block-by-block census records is related to the TIGER system, which is described in chapter 19.

Detailed information regarding available maps and other census materials can be obtained from

Customer Services (DUSD)
Bureau of the Census
Washington, D.C. 20233
Phone: (301) 763–4100

Central Intelligence Agency.   Most of the maps produced by the **Central Intelligence Agency (CIA)** are not available to the public. A number of high-quality, multicolor, relief maps of foreign countries, however, are available from the Government Printing

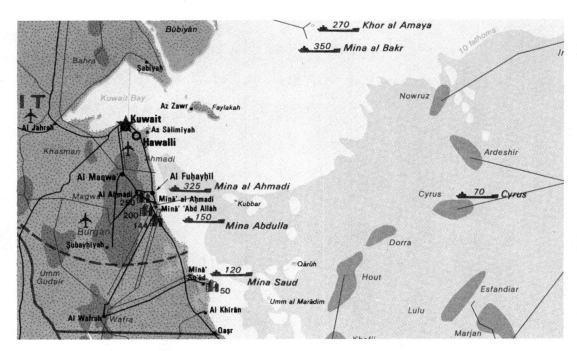

FIGURE 21.5   Portion of Central Intelligence Agency map. ("The Persian Gulf," 1:1,600,000, 1980.)

Office.[2] These maps sometimes include thematic insets that provide summary information about economic and social topics and features of the physical environment. An example of an economic activity map is shown in figure 21.5.

Department of Agriculture.   Three organizations within the U.S. **Department of Agriculture (USDA)** produce maps and other materials of interest to map users. These organizations are the Soil Conservation Service, the Agricultural Stabilization and Conservation Service, and the U.S. Forest Service.

The results of soil surveys, conducted by the USDA in conjunction with other federal and state agencies, are available from the **Soil Conservation Service** (figure

21.6). A copy of the publication *List of Published Soil Surveys* can be obtained from

> Cartographic Division
> Soil Conservation Service
> Department of Agriculture
> Federal Building
> 6505 Belcrest Road
> Hyattsville, MD 20782

The **Agricultural Stabilization and Conservation Service (ASCS)** produces aerial photos and photomaps of cropland areas (figure 21.7). These materials, as well as some satellite images, are available from

> Aerial Photography Field Office
> Agricultural Stabilization and Conservation Service
> Department of Agriculture
> (2222 West, 2300 South)
> P.O. Box 30010
> Salt Lake City, UT 84125

[2]Some of these maps, as well as other materials, are listed in "CIA Publications Released to the Public—Listing for 1972–1980," available from the National Technical Information Service, Springfield, Va., order number PB81–928003. The list was also printed in *The American Cartographer* 9, no. 1 (1982): 68 and 79.

FIGURE 21.6   Portion of Soil Conservation Service soil
survey map. (Crawford County, Pennsylvania, 1:20,000.)

FIGURE 21.7   Portion of National High Altitude Program
black-and-white photo (Colorado 1983).

Courtesy of U.S. Department of Agriculture, Agricultural Stabilization and
Conservation Service.

FIGURE 21.8   Map of Croatan National Forest, North Carolina.

Courtesy of U.S. Department of Agriculture, Forest Service.

The **U.S. Forest Service** publishes maps showing the location of national forests. The agency also publishes detailed maps of each national forest, usually at a scale of 1:24,000, as well as various visitors' maps and guides (figure 21.8).

Information regarding these maps can be obtained by writing to the following address or by contacting any U.S. Forest Service regional or national office.

U.S. Forest Service, Office of Information
Department of Agriculture
P.O. Box 2417
Washington, D.C. 20013

Department of Transportation.   In 1976, the **Department of Transportation (DOT)** produced a *U.S. Transportation Atlas,* which is available from the Government Printing Office. A map of "Federal-Aid Highways" published by the department is available from the USGS Distribution Branch. The department also provides information regarding sources of state highway maps. The address is

Federal Highway Administration, Department of Transportation
Public Affairs Office
Room 4210, 400 Seventh Street SW
Washington, D.C. 20590

National Aeronautics and Space Administration. A variety of aerial photographs, Landsat imagery, manned spacecraft imagery, Skylab imagery, and other materials resulting from programs of the **National Aeronautics and Space Administration (NASA)** are available from the EROS Data Center (described later in the chapter). An example of one of these products is shown in figure 2.1.

National Park Service. The **National Park Service** produces topographic maps, as well as visitors' maps and guides, for the national parks and monuments (figure 21.9). Information about these materials can be obtained from

National Park Service
Department of the Interior
Washington, D.C. 20242

National Weather Service. Examples of the climatic and weather maps produced by the National Meteorological Center are shown in chapter 15. Information about these products can be obtained from

National Weather Service
National Oceanic and Atmospheric
Administration
Department of Commerce
5200 Auth Road
Camp Springs, MD 20233

Tennessee Valley Authority. The **Tennessee Valley Authority (TVA)** produces various topographic, land-use, navigation, and recreation maps of the area within its jurisdiction. Information regarding these materials, examples of which are shown in figure 21.10, can be obtained from

Map Information and Records Unit
Tennessee Valley Authority
100 Haney Building
Chattanooga, TN 37401

or

Maps and Engineering Records Section
Tennessee Valley Authority
400 Commerce Avenue (WPA3)
Knoxville, TN 37902

MAJOR MAP SERIES

U.S. Geological Survey Topographic Maps

The USGS produces topographic maps in a wide variety of scales. Table 21.1 indicates the customary (English) system scales, as well as the metric system scales that are available.

Quadrangles are individual map sheets that are laid out as four-sided figures, each of which is bounded by lines of latitude and longitude.

Various map scales make it necessary to vary the extent of coverage of quadrangle maps. For example, a 1-degree quadrangle covers an area bounded by a line of latitude on the southern boundary and a second line of latitude, 1 degree greater in value, on the northern boundary. Similarly, the area is bounded by a line of longitude on the eastern boundary and a second line of longitude, 1 degree greater in value, on the western boundary. In the same fashion, a 30-minute quadrangle has boundaries that are thirty minutes apart on all four sides, and similar relationships hold for 15- and 7.5-minute quadrangles. A 1-degree quadrangle covers the same area as is covered by four 30-minute quadrangles, a 30-minute quadrangle the same as four 15-minute quadrangles, and a 15-minute quadrangle the same as four 7.5-minute quadrangles.

As discussed in chapter 2, lines of longitude converge toward the poles. In the Northern Hemisphere areas covered by the USGS, the shape of a quadrangle, which is bounded by two lines of longitude, is closer to a trapezoid because the northern boundary is somewhat narrower than the southern. The difference between this trapezoid and a true rectangle is extremely small, especially in the midlatitudes.

Another variation stems from meridian convergence in the high latitudes. If all quadrangles covered the same number of degrees and minutes in the east-west direction, those in Alaska would be significantly narrower than those in Texas. For this reason, and to keep sheet sizes relatively constant for printing and filing convenience, the east-west extent of quadrangles is sometimes adjusted. In Alaska, for example, 1:63,360 quadrangles cover 15 minutes of latitude (north-south) but cover as much as 36 minutes of longitude (east-west).

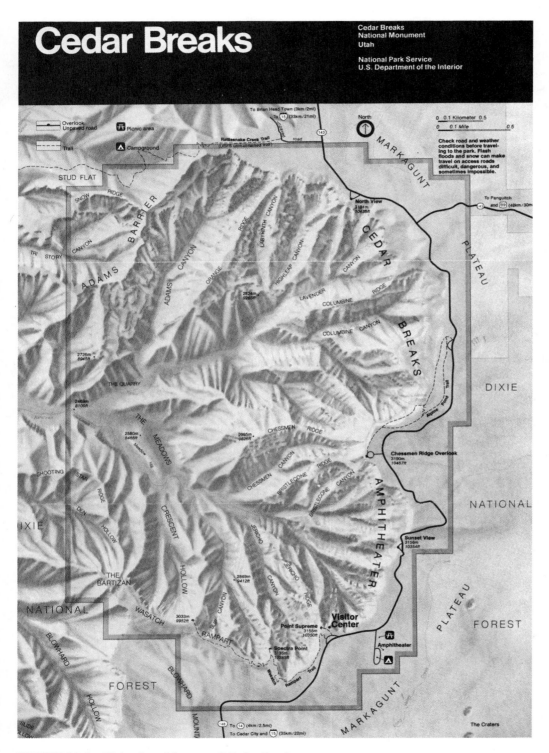

FIGURE 21.9   Visitor's guide map of Cedar Breaks
National Monument, Utah.

Courtesy of U.S. Department of the Interior, National Park Service.

(a)

(b)

FIGURE 21.10   Sample Tennessee Valley Authority
products. (*a*) Portion of Chickamauga Lake Recreation
Map (1982). (*b*) Portion of Navigation Chart 703,
Tennessee River, Chickamauga Lake (1968). (Not for
navigational purposes.)

TABLE 21.1   Publication Scales of U.S. Geological Survey Topographic Maps

| | | CUSTOMARY SYSTEM | |
Series	Scale	1 Inch Represents	Standard Quadrangle Size (Latitude × Longitude)
7.5 minutes	1:24,000	2,000 feet	7.5 minutes × 7.5 minutes
15 minutes	1:62,500	1 mile (approx.)	15 minutes × 15 minutes
1:63,360 Alaska	1:63,360	1 mile	15 minutes × 20–36 minutes
United States*	1:250,000	4 miles (approx.)	1 degree × 2 or 3 degrees†
State maps*	1:500,000	8 miles (approx.)	Not applicable‡
United States	1:1,000,000	16 miles (approx.)	4 degrees × 6 degrees

| | | METRIC SYSTEM | |
Series	Scale	1 Centimeter Represents	Standard Quadrangle Size (Latitude × Longitude)
7.5 minutes Puerto Rico	1:20,000	200 meters	7.5 minutes × 7.5 minutes
7.5 minutes × 15 minutes	1:25,000	250 meters	7.5 minutes × 15 minutes
Intermediate	1:50,000	500 meters	
Intermediate	1:100,000	1 kilometer	30 minutes × 60 minutes

Source: Adapted from National Cartographic Information Center pamphlet *National Mapping Program, Map Scales.*
*Coverage of Antarctica is also provided at this scale.
†Antarctic quadrangles are 1 degree × 3–15 degrees.
‡Antarctic quadrangles are 2 degrees × 7.5 degrees.

National Ocean Service Nautical Charts

The **National Ocean Service (NOS)** is a component of the National Oceanic and Atmospheric Administration (NOAA). Along with other responsibilities, the Office of Charting and Geodetic Services (C&GS), within NOS, produces nautical charts for U.S. oceanic coastal waters and the Great Lakes and connecting waterways. These charts are produced in different scales, ranging from small scales adequate for sailing between coastal ports and in the open ocean, to large scales that are needed to navigate in harbors and restricted channels. Chapter 6 provides information about the use of nautical charts and more details regarding their contents.

The two general series of charts are: (1) small-craft charts (figure 21.11) and (2) conventional charts (see figure 6.7). The small-craft charts are specially designed to meet the needs of small-craft operators. The conventional charts fall into the following categories:

1. **Harbor charts**, at scales of 1:50,000 and larger, are intended for navigation and anchorage in harbors and small waterways.
2. **Coast charts**, at scales from 1:50,000 to 1:150,000, are for coastwise navigation inside offshore reefs and shoals, entrance into bays and harbors of considerable size, and navigation of certain inland waterways.
3. **General charts**, at scales from 1:150,000 to 1:600,000, are for when a vessel's course is well offshore but its position can be fixed by landmarks, lights, buoys, and characteristic soundings.
4. **Sailing charts**, at scales smaller than 1:600,000, are for offshore sailing between distant coastal ports and for approaching the coast from the open ocean.
5. Special charts, such as **intracoastal waterway charts**, at a scale of 1:40,000, provide coverage of the inside route from Miami to Key West, Florida, and from Tampa to Anclote Anchorage, Florida. **Canoe charts** of the Minnesota-Ontario border lakes are designed to suit the needs of small, shallow-draft vessels.

Information regarding these products is included in a series of *Nautical Chart Catalogs.* Each catalog lists and describes the charts and other products, such

FIGURE 21.11   Portion of National Ocean Service small-craft navigational chart. (Chart 12324, original scale, 1:40,000—reduced, November 1986.) (Not for navigational purposes.)

as tide tables, coast pilots, current tables, tidal current charts, and Great Lakes water-level information, available for a particular region.

NOS charts and related publications may be ordered from

> Distribution Branch (N/CG33)
> National Ocean Service
> Riverdale, MD 20737

or from many authorized sales agents located in cities around the country.

NONFEDERAL MAP PRODUCERS

State Agencies[3]

Government agencies in the fifty states are involved in many mapping activities. The products that these agencies produce, which are generally available to the public, vary considerably in type and

quality from state to state. They have some common characteristics, however, because the needs of the various state governments tend to be very similar. All of the states, for example, are involved in site-specific functions, such as highway planning and construction. This type of work requires topographic coverage that is more detailed and larger scale than that provided by USGS quadrangle maps. On an entirely different front, the individual states vigorously promote tourism. One effective method of doing this is distributing promotional pieces, such as state highway maps or maps of state park facilities.

Products likely to be produced by every state include: (1) planimetric base maps of the counties, typically at a scale of 1 inch to 1 mile, with larger-scale coverage of metropolitan areas; (2) multicolor, folded, highway maps, which usually contain illustrations and promotional copy; (3) large-scale, photogrammetric, engineering maps for highway planning and construction; (4) maps showing the state's geologic characteristics; (5) outline maps of civil division boundaries and names; and (6) land-use maps.

Obtaining state-produced maps is not always straightforward because production and distribution responsibilities are often spread throughout several

[3]This section is based on Paul McElligott, "Mapping by State Governments," in Section 1, Government Mapping Activities, *U.S. National Report to ICA, 1984,* ed. Judy M. Olson (Falls Church, Va.: American Congress on Surveying and Mapping, 1984), 27–28.

agencies. Helpful information in this regard is provided by the list of addresses and phone numbers, by state, contained in the National Cartographic Information Center (NCIC) brochure *State Information Sources.* This brochure can be obtained from the NCIC, at the addresses given in appendix E.

Major Private Firms

Private companies produce many of the map products used in the United States. Some of the major private cartographic firms are listed in this section to provide a general overview of the types of maps and related products available from each producer. The list also provides a basis for searching out maps to serve special interests and needs. No evaluations, either pro or con, are implied by the inclusion or exclusion of a particular company from this listing or by the necessarily brief descriptions.

AAA Cartographic Services. The American Automobile Association (AAA) supplies a variety of travel-related publications to its members, including road atlases, tour books, camping guides, city maps, and regional and national road maps. **AAA Cartographic Services** produces all of these publications, as well as a road atlas available to the public. Information can be obtained from

American Automobile Association
1000 AAA Drive
Heathrow, FL 32746–5063

Donnelley Cartographic Services. Donnelley **Cartographic Services** is a custom mapping organization, a unit of R. R. Donnelley and Sons Company, the largest printer in the United States. Donnelley Cartographic Services offers a complete package of mapping services, including design, consulting, research, compilation, production, film processing, and color proofing. It specializes in high-quality color cartography for client ownership and print reproduction. Typical products consist of small-scale reference and thematic maps for clients in a number of markets, including textbook, reference-book, travel-directory, and road-atlas publishing. A sample telephone directory map is shown in figure 21.12.

Although Donnelley Cartographic Services is not a publisher in its own right (and does not offer a cat-

FIGURE 21.12   Map created for Southern New England Telephone Company by Donnelley Cartographic Services.

© 1988, all rights reserved, Southern New England Telephone Company. Reproduced by permission.

alog of printed products for sale), samples are supplied upon request. Information can be obtained from

Donnelley Cartographic Services
P.O. Box 3261
Lancaster, PA 17604

General Drafting Company, Inc. General **Drafting Company, Inc.** is a major map maker, having produced over 1 billion oil-company road maps since it first published a road map of Vermont in 1912. In addition, the company produces a variety of pictorial maps, airline maps, cruising guides, globes, and atlases (figure 21.13). In particular, it makes travel atlases, magazines, books, and guides for a number of clients and for its own distribution. The company also

FIGURE 21.13   Portion of General Drafting Company *TravelVision* road map of Minnesota and Wisconsin.
Courtesy of General Drafting Company, Inc.

creates locator maps for supermarkets, car-rental companies, motels, and other customers, as well as specialized maps for world's fairs and other events. Information can be obtained from

General Drafting Company, Inc.
Canfield Road
Convent Station, NJ 07961–0109
Phone: (201) 538–7600, (800) 367–6277

Gousha/Simon and Schuster, Inc.   Gousha/Simon and Schuster, Inc. produces highway maps of all fifty states, maps of all major U.S. metropolitan areas (figure 21.14), and a wide range of color-relief maps, and operates touring services for a number of major automobile clubs. In addition, the company develops custom maps and atlases for many car-rental companies, financial institutions, insurance companies, and others. Through its subsidiary, Jeppesen-Sanderson, the company also produces aeronautical charts. Gousha's Natural Color Relief Maps, created by Hal Shelton, noted geographer and artist, graphically represent temperature and rainfall zones, in conjunction with realistic shaded relief. Information can be obtained from

Gousha/Simon and Schuster, Inc.
2001 The Alameda
San Jose, CA 95150
Phone: (408) 296–1060

Hammond Incorporated.   Hammond Incorporated produces a comprehensive line of maps, world and road atlases, reference books, and wall charts. In addition, the company has a line of educational products for classroom use. Hammond also produces maps for the advertising and publishing markets. Information can be obtained from

Hammond Incorporated
515 Valley Street
Maplewood, NJ 07040–1396
Phone: (201) 763–6000

FIGURE 21.14   Portion of Gousha/Simon and Schuster
street map of San Francisco.

Courtesy of H. M. Gousha/Simon and Schuster, Inc.

National Geographic Society.   The Cartographic Division of the **National Geographic Society**
produces supplement maps that accompany the *National Geographic* magazine (60 million per year), as
well as smaller maps that illustrate the magazine's
stories. The Cartographic Division also produces atlases, physical and political globes, and mural maps.
The maps cover a wide range of topics, from general
maps that show cities and countries, to detailed maps
of historical events. National Geographic Society maps
are noted for their accuracy and attractive rendering.
Information is available from

National Geographic Society
Seventeenth and M Street
Washington, D.C. 20036
Phone: (202) 857-7000

Nystrom.   Nystrom produces physical and political maps (figure 21.15) and globes in various series
for different school-grade levels. The company's
Sculptural Relief Wall Maps feature a physical-
features base map without names, mounted on the
same roller with a political-information transparent
overlay. The company also produces laminated maps
for individual student use; raised-relief maps, both

wall-size and desk-size; maps for American and world
history; outline maps; and supplementary teaching
programs. Nystrom's vacuum-formed vinyl globes are
coordinated with the map series. Information can be
obtained from

Nystrom
3333 Elston Avenue
Chicago, IL 60618
Phone: (312) 463-1144, (800) 621-8086

Rand McNally and Company.   Rand McNally
and Company produces and markets a wide range of
map, atlas, directory/guide, and related cartographic
products and services for the consumer, business, and
education markets. Included in these products are
over 130 state and city road maps and 50 educational
wall maps. More than thirty atlases are produced,
ranging from classroom atlases to commercial and
marketing guides, and from a variety of road atlases
to fishing guides and a zip-code atlas. Information is
available from

Rand McNally and Company
Customer Service Department/Publishing Group
P.O. Box 7600
Chicago, IL 60680

FIGURE 21.15 Nystrom map of the world.

Courtesy of Nystrom, Division of Herff Jones, Inc.

INFORMATION SOURCES FOR MAPS AND RELATED MATERIALS

The greatest challenge facing the potential map user sometimes seems to be simply determining what maps and related materials are available. Almost equally difficult is the problem of how to obtain the items when their existence is known or suspected. This section outlines some of the more likely sources of both types of information.

Federal Sources of Information

Earth Science Information Center Network. The Earth Science Information Center Network (ESIC) is part of the U.S. Department of the Interior, Geological Survey (USGS). ESIC's mission is to help users gain better, faster, low-cost access to the cartographic holdings of federal, state, and private agencies. Several ESIC offices provide information about the availability, cost, and method of ordering almost any cartographic product (see appendix E).

A free *MiniCatalog of Map Data* can be obtained by writing or calling ESIC, and a more complete *Catalog of Map Data* is for sale by the Superintendent of Documents. These catalogs describe and give ordering information for such products as advance prints; color separates; feature separates; out-of-print maps; land-use, land-cover, and associated maps; slope maps; digital terrain tapes; maps on microfilm; orthophotoquads; aircraft photos of various types; manned spacecraft photos; Landsat imagery; geodetic control data; and a number of other materials.

National Geodetic Information Center. The National Geodetic Information Center provides information regarding the horizontal and vertical control networks established by the National Geodetic Survey and other federal and state agencies. The address is

National Geodetic Information Center
National Geodetic Survey, C18
National Ocean Service
National Oceanic and Atmospheric
Administration
Rockville, MD 20852

EROS Data Center. The **EROS Data Center**, in Sioux Falls, South Dakota, is part of the Earth Resources Observation Systems (EROS) Program of the U.S. Geological Survey. It is the national center for the processing and dissemination of photographic images and electronic data obtained from aerial photographic and space missions. Data from a number of programs are maintained at the center, including U.S. Department of the Interior aerial photography and National Aeronautics and Space Administration (NASA) photography and other remotely sensed data from research aircraft and from Skylab, Apollo, and Gemini spacecraft. The center previously maintained information from the Landsat program, but this function has been taken over by the Earth Observation Satellite Company (EOSAT), which is described later in the chapter.

The entire United States is covered by aerial photography produced in a coordinated program by the National High Altitude Program (NHAP). Starting in 1987, this program was redesignated the National Aerial Photography Program (NAPP), and some changes were introduced. NHAP photos were produced in black-and-white and in color-infrared. The nominal contact scale of 9-inch-by-9-inch NHAP black-and-white photos was 1:80,000. Each photo was centered on a USGS quadrangle and covered the entire quadrangle. Two or three color-infrared photos, at a nominal scale of 1:58,000, were required to cover a quadrangle. Enlarged paper prints of all of the photos were also available. Under NAPP, all photography is color-infrared, with photos centered on one-quarter quads, rather than on full quads. In addition, there is a wider range of choice in terms of enlargements and the season of the photography.

Inquiries about the availability of various types of coverage for a specific location and orders for photos

and images may be directed to the center at the following address

Users Service Unit
EROS Data Center
U.S. Geological Survey
Sioux Falls, SD 57198
Phone: (605) 594–6511

National Environmental Satellite, Data, and Information Service. National environmental data are maintained by the **National Environmental Satellite, Data, and Information Service (NESDIS)**. NESDIS manages U.S. civil meteorological and land remote-sensing satellite systems. These satellites monitor world weather conditions and conduct special monitoring of the Atlantic, Pacific, and Gulf coasts of the United States. The agency also formerly operated the earth-resources satellite Landsat, which is now operated by EOSAT (see chapter 18).

NESDIS also operates a worldwide environmental database, called the National Environmental Data Referral Service (NEDRES). This service provides global environmental data and information management and dissemination. Information is obtained from National Oceanic and Atmospheric Administration programs, as well as from other U.S. and foreign agencies, and is incorporated into the NEDRES environmental database. NEDRES is mentioned here because it includes geodetic, cartographic, and land-use/ground-cover information.

General information regarding NESDIS can be obtained from

Office of External Relations
Information and Communications Unit
E/ER3 NESDIS
NOAA
Room 3308, FB-4
Washington, D.C. 20233

The address for information about NEDRES is

NEDRES Program Officer
Assessment and Information Services Center
NOAA/NESDIS (E/AIx3)
3300 Whitehaven Street NW
Washington, D.C. 20235

Nonfederal Sources of Information

Publications.   Information about current maps is available in at least two journals. One source is the "New Maps" and "New Atlases" sections of *Cartographic Perspectives,* the journal of the North American Cartographic Information Society. Another source that has published similar information is the "Distinctive Recent Maps" section of some issues of *Cartography and Geographic Information Systems* (formerly *The American Cartographer*). Both of these journals are available in many libraries.

Earth Observation Satellite Company.   In 1985, the U.S. Department of Commerce signed a ten-year contract with the **Earth Observation Satellite Company (EOSAT)** to construct, launch, and operate Landsat satellites and to disseminate the collected data. EOSAT-supplied data from both past and present Landsat satellites are no longer in the public domain, so users must sign an agreement of nondisclosure and agree not to reproduce the data that they purchase.

Inquiries should be directed to

EOSAT Customer Services
4300 Forbes Boulevard
Lanham, MD 20706
Phone: (301) 552–0537, (800) 344–9933

SPOT Image Corporation.   The French, Belgian, and Swedish governments have undertaken the development of a satellite observation system called Systeme Probatoire d'Observation de la Terre (SPOT).[4] The system became operational in 1986, and images are commercially available in the United States from the SPOT Image Corporation.

Black-and-white images achieve a 10-meter ground resolution, whereas color images in three spectral bands have a 20-meter resolution. The full-scene format covers a 60-by-60-kilometer area on the ground, and images are available with differing degrees of correction and in the form of computer tapes or film or paper prints. Stereoscopic images are also available through the use of "off-nadir" stereoscopic pairs, which are two images of the same area recorded from different angles.

Inquiries should be sent to

SPOT Image Corporation
1897 Preston White Drive
Reston, VA 22091–4326

Map Collections

Some of the largest map collections in the United States are described here, as are several others of special interest (academic and state libraries are generally not discussed). More complete information is provided by specialized publications, such as the *Guide to U.S. Map Resources* (2d ed.) or *Map Collections in the United States and Canada* (4th ed.), which are listed in the "Suggested Readings" at the end of the chapter. A short discussion of the characteristics of the map storage and cataloging systems in map libraries is provided in appendix F.

Library of Congress.   The **Geography and Map Division** of the **Library of Congress** maintains "the largest and most comprehensive cartographic collection in the world."[5] Included in the collection are more than 3.9 million print and manuscript maps, 44,000 atlases, and 8,000 reference works. Over 300 globes, 2,000 three-dimensional plastic relief models, and a large number of other cartographic materials are also part of the collection. This collection may be consulted in the division's reading room. Specialists of the division are available to assist in the use of the collection, which emphasizes the United States and the other areas of the Western Hemisphere. The collection also includes historical holdings, such as Ptolemy's *Geography* (dated 1482) and some 700,000 fire-insurance maps.

The Library of Congress map collection is a treasure trove for anyone with an interest in maps. Persons interested in genealogical research, for example, often find that the collection of county and state maps and atlases provides valuable documentary information.

---

[4]For a detailed description of the system, see Michael Courtois and Gilbert Weill, "The SPOT Satellite System," in *Monitoring Earth's Ocean, Land, and Atmosphere from Space—Sensors, Systems, and Applications,* Vol. 97 of Progress in Astronautics and Aeronautics series, ed. Abraham Schnapf (New York: American Institute of Aeronautics and Astronautics, 1985).

[5]From a descriptive brochure published by the Geography and Map Division.

Similarly, persons interested in colonial America, the Revolutionary War, the War of 1812, and the Civil War find manuscript and printed maps that provide useful information.

The mailing address is

Library of Congress
Geography and Map Division
Washington, D.C. 20540

The location is

James Madison Memorial Building
Room LM B01
101 Independence Avenue SE
Washington, D.C. 20540
Phone: (202) 287–8530

National Archives. The U.S. **National Archives and Records Service** maintains a collection that includes 2 million maps and 100,000 aerial photographs produced by federal agencies. These materials include information pertaining to Indian treaties and related matters, surveys and settlement records compiled by the Bureau of Land Management, immigration and population growth and enumeration district maps from the records of the Census Bureau and the Bureau of Agricultural Economics, and other records related to urban development. The address is

U.S. National Archives and Records Service
Special Archives Division
Cartographic and Architectural Branch
Washington, D.C. 20408
Phone: (703) 756–6700

The American Geographical Society Collection. Located in the Golda Meir Library of the University of Wisconsin–Milwaukee, **The American Geographical Society Collection** is a major geographical reference and research collection. "The scope of the collection is broad, encompassing all aspects of geography and selected facets of related disciplines, such as economics, demography, regional science, urban studies, history, anthropology, archaeology, sociology, geology, earth science, oceanography, and meteorology. The materials collected range from the early travel narratives to the scientific results of polar and oceanographic expeditions to the technical reports and discussion papers on quantitative techniques that characterize much of contemporary research."[6]

Further information can be obtained from

The American Geographical Society Collection
Golda Meir Library
University of Wisconsin–Milwaukee
P.O. Box 399
Milwaukee, WI 53201
Phone: (414) 229–6282

Defense Mapping Agency. The map collection of the **Defense Mapping Agency Hydrographic/Topographic Center** contains close to 1,200,000 maps, in addition to books, atlases, and serials. The address is

Defense Mapping Agency Hydrographic/
Topographic Center
Scientific Data Department
Support Division
6500 Brookes Lane
Washington, D.C. 20315
Phone: (202) 227–2109

Specialized examples. Although they do not have the largest collections, the libraries discussed here exemplify the rich variety of specialized holdings that exist. A search of the various sources in the "Suggested Readings" at the end of the chapter may suggest map libraries with collections of particular personal interest.

The **Newberry Library** specializes in materials in the humanities, including a research collection in the history of cartography. Admission to the library's reading rooms is granted to researchers whose research projects require extensive use of the collections, and application for admission must be based on defined research needs.

The Hermon Dunlap Smith Center for the History of Cartography has been established at the library. The

---

[6]From a descriptive brochure, *The American Geographical Society Collection, The University of Wisconsin-Milwaukee Library*, Roman Drazniowsky, Curator.

center offers courses and lectures, publishes manuscripts, and participates in special projects related to the expansion of knowledge regarding the history of cartography.

Information can be obtained from

Newberry Library
Map Section
60 West Walton Street
Chicago, IL 60610
Phone: (312) 943–9090

The **John Carter Brown Library** contains a collection of primary map materials. These materials relate to virtually all aspects of the discovery, exploration, settlement, and development of the New World. The collection includes printed books, major collections of maps and prints, and a large number of textual manuscripts. The address is

Brown University
John Carter Brown Library
P.O. Box 1894
Providence, RI 02912
Phone: (401) 863–2725

CANADIAN GOVERNMENT MAPS

Topographic Mapping

The **Surveys, Mapping and Remote Sensing Sector** of the **Department of Energy, Mines and Resources** is Canada's principal topographic mapping agency. Among its products are maps at scales ranging from 1:1,000,000 to 1:25,000.

Maps of the **National Topographic System** of Canada are produced at scales of 1:1,000,000, 1:250,000, and 1:50,000. The 1:1,000,000-scale coverage is Canada's contribution to the International Map of the World (see Appendix D). The 1:250,000-scale maps provide the only complete topographic coverage of the country. These maps include detailed representation of relief, drainage, transportation, forest cover, and centers of population. Coverage of the more detailed 1:50,000-scale series is concentrated in the southerly, most densely populated portions of the country. Additional coverage at this scale is available for selected areas of particular interest. The system used to identify the separate sheets within these series is described in Appendix E.

Aeronautical Charts

Aeronautical charts are also produced by the Surveys, Mapping and Remote Sensing Sector of the Department of Energy, Mines and Resources. Charts are available in several formats suited for particular needs.

Visual flight rules aviation is served by three sets of charts. The first of these is the World Aeronautical Charts, at a scale of 1:1,000,000, on the Lambert conformal conic projection. These serve the needs of medium speed, medium range operations. The second set is the VFR Navigation Charts, at a scale of 1:500,000. They are on the Lambert conformal conic projection to 80° N, and on the polar stereographic from 80° N to the North Pole. These serve the needs of low and medium speed aircraft at low and intermediate altitudes. Currently, there are only four of the third type, which are VFR Terminal Area charts. These provide greater detail for the Vancouver, Winnipeg, Toronto, and Montreal terminal areas. They are at a scale of 1:250,000, on the transverse Mercator projection.

Charts for instrument operations, as well as a variety of supplementary data are also produced.

Defense Mapping

Topographic surveying and mapping for defense purposes is carried out by the **Mapping and Charting Establishment** of the **Department of National Defense**. A series of Military City Maps is available for civilian use. These color street maps are of selected urban areas is available for civilian use, at 1:25,000-scale.

Other Maps and Related Publications

Various special-topics maps are also available. These include sheets from the Canada Land Inventory Map Series. This series includes information about agriculture, forestry, wildlife/ungulates, wildlife/waterfowl, and recreation. These maps are principally at scales of 1:125,000, 1:250,000, 1:1,000,000.

In a different vein, descriptive publications on the national parks are available from

Canadian Government Travel Bureau
Department of Industry, Trade and Commerce
Ottawa, Ontario K1A OH6

National Geographical Mapping Program

The **National Geographical Mapping Program** provides geographical and spatially-referenced information. Topics include aspects of the natural environment and of the cultural make-up of Canada, at the federal government level. Publications of this program include the National Atlas of Canada and a geostatistical base map series. It also includes geographical names gazetteers and databases (see toponymy, below).

The *National Atlas of Canada* is now in its fifth edition. The atlas portrays information about the natural environment, man's use of resources, demography, and the historical development of the country. The current edition is an ongoing, coordinated series of single maps. Most of the maps are at a scale of 1:7,500,000. The atlas is not a bound volume, but is sold as individual sheets or as collected sets on specific topics. General subjects include geomorphology, climatology, hydrology, ecology, political geography, population, ethnography, agriculture, forestry, fisheries, mining, energy, transportation, employment, income, economic geography, administrative and geostatistical areas, internal affairs, communications, and defense. The fourth edition, which is a conventionally-bound product, is still available.

Map Information and Ordering

Index maps showing topographic map and aeronautical chart coverage are available from the **Canada Map Office**, as is information about the *Atlas of Canada* and the other maps listed above.

Canada Map Office
615 Booth Street
Ottawa, Ontario K1A 0E9
Phone: (613) 952-7000

Maps from Statistics Canada

Maps based on the 1986 Census of Canada, as well as other census years are available from

Statistics Canada
Marketing and Client Liaison
Phone: (613) 951-3889

Toponyms

Toponyms (geographical names) in Canada are coordinated by the **Canadian Permanent Committee on Geographical Names (CPCGN)** (see box, Names on Maps). The *Gazetteer of Canada* lists the approved names of features throughout the provinces and territories. The *Gazetteer* is available as bound volumes, but the information is also stored in the Canadian Geographical Names Data Base (CGNDB).

Inquiries regarding records on magnetic tape or diskettes should be addressed to

Toponym Section
National Atlas Information Service
Surveys, Mapping and Remote Sensing Sector
Department of Energy, Mines and Resources
615 Booth Street
Ottawa, Ontario K1A 0E9

Volumes of the *Gazetteer of Canada* are available from

Mail Order Services
Canadian Government Publishing Centre
Supply and Services Canada
Ottawa, Ontario K1A 0S9
Phone: (819) 956-4801

General information about the place name program is available from

Executive Secretary
Canadian Permanent Committee on Geographical Names
615 Booth Street
Ottawa, Ontario K1A 0E9
Phone: (613) 992-3405

NAMES ON MAPS

Occasionally, different maps attach different names to the same town, city, river, or other feature. In the case of maps produced in foreign countries, such differences may simply occur because of language differences. On the other hand, the same feature may have been given quite different names by different countries, so each country's maps are likely to follow the national preference.

Place-name difficulties that occur on maps of the United States, produced within the country, are usually a result of a name change. Old maps, of course, continue to show the earlier name. Even maps published after a change is made may mistakenly continue to use the earlier name. In extreme cases, a series of name changes may be involved, and considerable confusion may occur, as in the case of Cape Canaveral, Florida. The cape was renamed Cape Kennedy in 1963 but, after considerable controversy, the Cape Canaveral name was reinstated some ten years later. In this case, publishers who were slow to make the change to Cape Kennedy benefited because the former name was restored! Another occasional source of name confusion occurs when local usage differs from the officially recognized version, and a map publisher prefers one version to the other.

The names used on maps of other parts of the world, produced in the United States, sometimes vary considerably. Map producers may pick up different names from maps produced in other countries, for example, thus spreading confusion. Frequently, name confusion first came about because the English rendering of non-English place names by early explorers and travelers was inaccurate or inconsistent. It is not unusual, therefore, to encounter an English-language name for many cities, such as Vienna or Rome, even though the inhabitants of those cities know them as Wien and Roma. In fact, the local name was often simply ignored, and an unrelated English name substituted, such as Bangkok for Krung Thep in Thailand. In addition, because of language differences, foreign names may be incorrectly rendered, or may be rendered differently under different systems of transliteration. An example of this type of problem is the city of Guangzhou, China. Guangzhou is the currently accepted name of the city, which is better known in the United States as Canton. Other versions of the name of this city have included Kwangchow and Kuang-Chow. The tendency, in recent years, has been to give preference to the local version of such names, but to include the English version when it is well known.

The Board on Geographic Names (BGN) is the authority charged with establishing the official names of settlements and natural features in the United States. The names adopted by the BGN, both foreign and domestic, become the official names for use by U.S. government agencies. Because of the difficulties involved in connection with foreign place names, BGN decisions take into account the recommendations of the United Nations Group of Experts on Geographical Names. Although there is no legal requirement that private map producers follow BGN recommendations, many, if not all, do so. Because of this trend, maps produced by reputable concerns probably will contain few name conflicts in the future. When such conflicts are encountered, however, library-owned BGN gazetteers often can be consulted. Further information about available lists of geographic names can be obtained from Earth Science Information Centers (see appendix E).

In Canada, place name decisions are under the guidance and coordination of the Canadian Permanent Committee on Geographical Names (CPCGN). This committee consists of provincial and federal representatives. The Department of Energy, Mines and Resources provides a Secretariat for the committee. The actual place name decision process is decentralized. Each provincial or territorial government is responsible for geographic names decisions within its jurisdiction. Responsibility is shared with the appropriate federal government department in the case of federal lands. In reaching their decisions, the governments follow principles established by CPCGN. Decisions of the provincial and territorial authorities are provided to the CPCGN Secretariat. The Secretariat maintains the national toponymic data bank, which records the authorized names (see the list of Canadian maps and related products in this chapter).

Northern Land Use Information Series

Maps of the Northern Land Use Information Series present a wide variety of topics useful for managing natural resources in the Canadian North. General subjects that are mapped include wildlife resources, fisheries resources, native land use, ecological land classification, and socioeconomic and cultural data. Further information about this series can be obtained from

Director
Land Resources and Data Systems Branch
Environment Canada
Ottawa, Ontario K1A 0E7

and

Director
Environment Protection Branch
Indian and Northern Affairs
Ottawa, Ontario K1A 0H4

Aerial Photography

Extensive aerial photographic coverage is available in Canada. A large part of this coverage, especially for recent years, consists of standard 9″ × 9″ black-and-white photographs at a nominal scale of 1:50,000. Some color coverage is available, mostly in major metropolitan areas.

Aerial photographs are ordered by specifying geographic location. This may be done by listing the latitude and longitude, or by outlining the area desired on a topographic map. In addition, representative photographs of typical topographic features (eskers, for example) are available. Requests for aerial photographs are handled by

National Air Photo Library
615 Booth Street
Ottawa, Ontario K1A 0E9
Phone: (613) 995–4560

Hydrographic Charts

Hydrographic charts for Canadian waters are published by the **Department of Fisheries and Oceans** of the **Canadian Hydrographic Service**. There are two major chart series: standard nautical charts and small-craft charts.

Standard nautical charts are of three types. Relatively small-scale general and offshore charts are the least detailed and may not show all navigational aids. As the name suggests, they are not suitable for navigation close to shore. Larger scale, more detailed coastal and approach charts provide sufficient information for navigation close to shore. Finally, harbor charts are used for navigation in confined waters.

Small-craft charts are designed to serve the operators of recreational small craft. They generally cover rivers, lakes, and portions of other waterways heavily used for recreational purposes.

Indexes, charts, related publications, and ordering information are available from

Hydrographic Chart Distribution Office
Department of Fisheries and Oceans
1675 Russell Road, P.O. Box 8080
Ottawa, Ontario K1G 3H6
Phone: (613) 998–4931

Summary

The scope of production of maps and related products by major federal agencies coincides with their principal areas of responsibility. The largest producer, for example, is the U.S. Geological Survey (USGS). USGS, in addition to maps and reports on specialized geologic information, prepares standard topographic quadrangle maps. The Bureau of Land Management (BLM) publishes maps dealing with the survey of public lands, and the National Ocean Service (NOS) produces aeronautical and nautical charts and a variety of other maps and photos. The Bureau of Indian Affairs maps Indian lands, and the Bureau of the Census produces maps related to the acquisition and reporting of census data.

The Defense Mapping Agency (DMA) produces topographic maps, aeronautical and nautical charts, and related information, mostly for military use. Although it is a military organization, the Army Corps of Engineers makes charts and maps of navigable waterways in the United States for civilian use. Multicolor relief maps of foreign countries produced by the Central Intelligence Agency (CIA) are available to the public.

Various U.S. Department of Agriculture (USDA) agencies produce maps and other materials related to their missions. The Soil Conservation Service produces soil maps, the Agricultural Stabilization and Conservation Service (ASCS) supplies aerial photos and photomaps of croplands, and the U.S. Forest Service publishes maps of the national forests.

The Department of Transportation (DOT) produces a limited number of products related to the federal highways and provides information regarding sources of state highway maps. A variety of images from the National Aeronautics and Space Administration (NASA) missions are available from the EROS Data Center.

Among smaller producers, the National Park Service prepares maps of the national parks and monuments, the National Weather Service produces climatic and weather maps, and the Tennessee Valley Authority (TVA) makes maps of the TVA area.

Major federal map series include topographic maps and nautical charts. USGS topographic quadrangle maps are individual sheets, bounded by lines of latitude and longitude. They are published at various scales, and their extent of coverage also varies. NOS nautical charts are produced in different scales. Small scales are used for sailing in the open ocean, for example, and large scales are needed to navigate in harbors.

A variety of state agencies, especially those involved in geologic surveys, highway planning, and tourism and parks, commonly produce maps in their areas of interest.

Major private firms produce many map products, including street and highway maps, atlases, textbook and reference maps, airline maps, cruising guides, globes, and history, outline, and wall maps for classroom use.

Information about the availability of maps and related products can be obtained from a variety of sources. The preeminent federal source is the National Cartographic Information Center (NCIC). Also, the EROS Data Center and the National Environmental Satellite, Data, and Information Service (NESDIS) provide information about the availability of remote-sensing data.

Nonfederal sources include specialty reference books and the journals *Cartographic Perspectives* and *Cartography and Geographic Information Systems.* The Earth Observation Satellite Company (EOSAT) and the SPOT Image Corporation supply information about the availability of their remote-sensing data. Also, map and reference librarians are an excellent source of information. Map collections range from the

mammoth Geography and Map Division of the Library of Congress and the U.S. National Archives and Records Service, to much smaller individual, library, and university collections. The American Geographical Society Collection is a major private collection, and specialized collections are found at the Newberry Library and the Hermon Dunlap Smith Center for the History of Cartography. Many useful map libraries are located at universities and public libraries.

In Canada, the Surveys and Mapping Branch of the Department of Energy, Mines and Resources is the principal topographic mapping agency. It produces maps at scales ranging from 1:1,000,000 to 1:25,000.

Canadian aeronautical chart production is done by the same agency. Topographic surveying and mapping for defense purposes is carried out by the Mapping and Charting Establishment of the Department of National Defense.

Products of the National Geographical Mapping Program provide geographical and spatially-referenced information about the natural environment and the cultural make-up of Canada. Publications of this program include the National Atlas of Canada and geographical names gazetteers and databases.

Topographic maps and aeronautical charts, the *Atlas of Canada,* and maps from the National Geographical Mapping Program are available from the Canada Map Office.

Geographical names in Canada are coordinated by the Canadian Permanent Committee on Geographical Names (CPCGN). Approved names are listed in the *Gazetteer of Canada* and are stored in the Canadian Geographical Names Data Base (CGNDB).

Hydrographic charts are available for navigable waters and maps of the Northern Land Use Information Series present a wide variety of topics useful for managing natural resources in the Canadian North. In addition, extensive aerial photographic coverage is available in Canada.

SUGGESTED READINGS AND REFERENCE MATERIALS

American Geographical Society. *Current Geographical Publications, Additions to the Research Catalogue of the American Geographical Society.* Vol. 1 (1938–). New York: (1938–February 1978) and Milwaukee: American Geographical Society Collection (March 1978–).

Carrington, David K., and Richard W. Stevenson, eds. *Map Collections in the United States and Canada: A Directory.* 4th ed. New York: Special Libraries Association, 1985. (Provides information about 804 map collections. Includes the name of the head of the collection, address and telephone number, hours of operation, size, area and subject specialization, and so on.)

Cobb, David A., comp., 2d ed. *Guide to U.S. Map Resources.* Chicago: American Library Association, 1990. (A comprehensive guide to the holdings of U.S. federal, state, university, historical society, public library, and private map collections. Provides names, addresses, telephone numbers, size and areas of strength of the collection, access information, equipment available, and other characteristics.)

Ehrenberg, Ralph E. *Scholars' Guide to Washington, D.C. for Cartography and Remote-Sensing Imagery: Maps, Charts, Aerial Photographs, Satellite Images, Cartographic Literature, and Geographic Information Systems.* Woodrow Wilson International Center for Scholars, Scholars' Guide to Washington, D.C., no. 12. Washington, D.C.: Smithsonian Institution Press, 1987. (Provides information about the cartography-related holdings of over two hundred collections and organizations in Washington, D.C., including libraries; archives; galleries; museums; embassies; U.S. and international organizations; federal, state, and local government agencies; data banks; and academic programs and departments.)

Feild, Lance. *Map User's Source Book.* New York: Oceana Publications, 1982.

Hodgkiss, A. G., and A. F. Tatham. *Keyguide to Information Sources in Cartography.* New York: Facts on File Publications, 1986. (Part IV of this guide provides a directory of map-making agencies, as well as those that distribute or conserve maps, from which one may obtain information about their products or services. There is also an index of names, titles, organizations, topics, and geographical locations. Other portions of the book are also likely to be of interest: Part I includes a brief historical review of cartography in the Western world, lists the major map-producing agencies and map collections [primarily in Europe and the United States, but with some information about other regions as well], and discusses some of the major cartographic literature, both books and journals. It also provides information about map collecting, including cataloging, storage, and other related topics. Part II is an annotated bibliography of reference sources on the history of cartography, and Part III provides a similar bibliography on contemporary cartographic research.)

Kister, Kenneth F. *Kister's Atlas Buying Guide: General English-Language World Atlases Available in North America.* Phoenix, Ariz.: Oryx Press, 1983.

Makower, John, ed. *The Map Catalog.* New York: Vintage Books, 1986.

National Cartographic Information Center, National Mapping Program. *Map Data Catalog.* Washington, D.C.: U.S. Government Printing Office, 1981.

Olson, Judy M., ed. *U.S. National Report to ICA, 1984.* Falls Church, Va.: American Congress on Surveying and Mapping, 1984. (Published as a special issue of *The American Cartographer,* supplement to vol. 11 [Summer 1984]. The report to ICA [International Cartographic Association] includes information regarding government and nongovernment mapping activities; cartographic education; new products and automation; cartographic literature; societies, sources, and personnel; remote sensing; and other topics. Although it focuses on the period from January 1980 through December 1983, a considerable portion of the contents is useful for general reference purposes.)

Perkins, C. R., and R. B. Parry, eds. *Information Sources in Cartography.* New Providence, N.J.: K. G. Saur, 1991.

Rabenhorst, Thomas D., and Paul D. McDermott. *Applied Cartography: Source Materials for Mapmaking.* Columbus, Ohio: Merrill Publishing Company, 1989.

Shupe, Barbara, and Colette O'Connell. *Mapping Your Business.* New York: Special Libraries Association, 1983. (Despite the narrow focus suggested by its title, this is an excellent reference source for all map users. It includes lists of map collections in the United States, sources of remote-sensing imagery and federal, state, and foreign maps, and information regarding commercial publishers and firms and agencies involved in computerized cartography.)

U.S. Geological Survey. *New Publications of the U.S. Geological Survey.* Reston, Va.: U.S. Geological Survey, monthly. (A monthly publication listing books, maps, professional papers, reports, and other publications of the U.S. Geological Survey.)

U.S. Geological Survey, Kurt Dodd, H. Kit Fuller, and Paul F. Clarke, comps. *Guide to Obtaining USGS Information.* U.S. Geological Survey Circular 900. Washington, D.C.: U.S. Government Printing Office, 1986.

U.S. Geological Survey and Morris M. Thompson. *Maps for America: Cartographic Products of the U.S. Geological Survey and Others.* 3d ed. Washington, D.C.: U.S. Government Printing Office, 1987.

Wolter, John A., Ronald E. Grim, and David K. Carrington, eds. *World Directory of Map Collections.* International Federation of Library Associations (IFLA) Publications 31. New York: K. G. Saur, 1986.

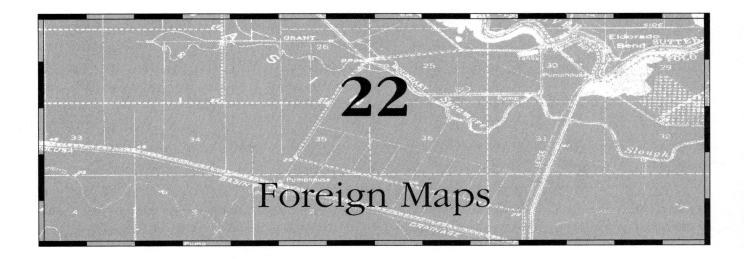

22

Foreign Maps

Using a map produced in a foreign country involves the same general techniques as using a map produced in one's own country. Special problems sometimes are encountered, however, especially when the map is printed in a language unfamiliar to us. Map content is more difficult to comprehend without the clues usually provided by an understanding of the printed language. Even when language problems are absent, other obstacles to map use include the use of unusual signs and symbols, alternative locational systems, or measurements expressed in uncommon units. When these difficulties are encountered, map interpretation requires additional effort.

LANGUAGE

Map use and interpretation is obviously difficult when the place names, legends, and other map information are printed in an unfamiliar language. The degree of difficulty depends on the characteristics of the language, as well as on the map's subject matter. If the map is a standard topographic sheet, for example, much of the content is likely to be self-explanatory. This is because the symbols used for coastlines, contours, and other features are frequently universal. Additional references for translating some of the words used on such a map, therefore, are often unnecessary because the symbols themselves are easily recognized.

An example would be a Hungarian map with many blue lines that obviously represent the drainage pattern. Each blue line is labeled with two words. One of the words changes every time and is apparently the name of the water course, but the other word is always

folyam. A Hungarian-English dictionary is not necessary to determine that *folyam* is the Hungarian word for some type of stream, although the specific type remains uncertain. The uncertainty is greater if there are two types of blue lines, with one set labeled *folyam* and the second set labeled *patak*. The comparative size and apparent importance of the streams might suggest that those labeled *folyam* are more important than those labeled *patak*. Only a dictionary, however, would reveal that *folyam* specifically means "river" and *patak* means "brook."

Thus, in a simple case, basic understanding of a foreign map is often possible without resorting to reference materials. When a more advanced level of understanding is required, however, additional reference materials are often needed. The need is especially acute when the map content is more unusual. In the case of a thematic map showing economic activity, for example, the symbols used to represent different types of factories, production levels, or other information may be anything but self-evident. In this type of situation, the user must expend additional effort if map content is to be adequately understood.

If the language on a map uses the Roman alphabet, the user can simply translate the terms of interest into English, using a foreign language/English dictionary. An even more useful reference is a **glossary** that concentrates on the definitions of geographical or cartographic terms that frequently occur on maps. Such glossaries are often included in the reference sections of atlases.[1]

---

[1]Useful glossaries are included in E. C. Olson and A. Whitmarsh, *Foreign Maps* (New York: Harper and Brothers, 1944), and U.S. Department of the Army, *Foreign Maps,* U.S. Department of the Army Technical Manual TM 5–248 (Washington, D.C.: Headquarters, Department of the Army, June 1956).

If the language in question does not use the Roman alphabet, translation is likely to be more difficult. The first step in the process is parallel to the previous example and requires looking for the repeated use of a certain character, or group of characters, in conjunction with a specific class of map features. The unfamiliar nature of the characters used often limits this approach, however, and a dictionary or glossary is usually necessary in all but the simplest cases.

Depending on the nature of the reference materials themselves, the use of dictionaries and glossaries may be either a one- or a two-step process. If the reference materials are presented in the characters of the original language, the only step needed is to look up the terms in the dictionary. Even this process may be somewhat difficult, however, because the structure of the characters needs to be understood before the method of listing them in the dictionary makes sense. In some cases, the dictionary contains a guide that assists in locating the characters and the needed translations.

Other dictionaries require an intermediate step known as **transliteration**, which means that each character used in the source language is converted into one or more Roman letters. The transliteration of some languages, such as Greek and Russian, involves the substitution, virtually letter for letter, of letters of the Roman alphabet for the original characters. After the transliteration is completed, the Romanized word and its translation are located in the dictionary, using standard alphabetization procedures. Thus, even though an extra step is involved, the transliteration of words prior to determining their meaning is often a fairly easy process, even for the user who is unfamiliar with the language.

The transliteration of some languages, such as Chinese and Japanese, is more difficult because the characters stand for whole syllables, words, or phrases. Locating these characters in a dictionary requires some study because their complex structure must be understood first.

Specialized glossaries are sometimes available, arranged so that common English terms for map features are listed alphabetically. Each of the English terms is followed by the equivalent foreign-language translation. In this case, the translation process consists of simply scanning the most likely English terms that describe the feature of interest until the foreign-language version that appears on the map is located.

This process is somewhat akin to searching for a needle in a haystack, but it at least has the advantage that some clues are provided regarding the likely location of the needle.

SIGNS AND SYMBOLS

One of the difficulties of interpreting signs and symbols is that they are often culturally related. This problem is similar to the difficulties encountered in the translation of culturally related words in a language. Many languages have an array of specialized terms that do not necessarily have direct equivalents in other languages. This is because each language has developed to meet the needs of the particular physical and social environment of its people.

The Eskimo people, for example, use a large number of specialized terms to distinguish a great variety of snow and ice conditions. This level of detail has evolved because differentiating between these conditions may be vital to survival. Similarly, the Arabic language includes a range of terms that describe particular types of desert-surface conditions.

In the same way, cultural factors often influence the types of features included on maps, as well as the amount of detail provided about them. Interest in certain features of the landscape may result in the development of specialized symbols to differentiate among them. Different types of windmills shown on maps of Holland are an example. Maps designed for people in other locations, and with other needs, might not show these specialized features at all or, at most, might present them much more simply. When specialized symbols appear on a map, some means of translating the legend description into a familiar language is mandatory.

LOCATIONAL SYSTEMS

There are two basic systems for designating locations on the earth's surface. One system involves the use of the latitude and longitude graticule, and the other involves the use of plane rectangular grids. Both of these methods were discussed in earlier chapters, but a few points should be added regarding their use on foreign maps.

Graticule

Using the latitude and longitude graticule is not always straightforward. In the United States and most other countries, maps are commonly based on the familiar 360-degree system of coordinates, called the **sexagesimal system**. This system is not universal, however, and some maps use a 400-unit system, called the **centesimal system**. In addition, no matter which system is used, the starting point for longitude designations is not always the same, so that the same place may have different longitude designations on different maps. A foreign map, then, may possibly use either the centesimal coordinate system, an unusual origin for longitude designations, or both.

Centesimal system. The centesimal coordinate system is sometimes encountered on maps produced in Europe, especially in France and Belgium. This system involves dividing the circle into four quadrants, with each quadrant further subdivided into one hundred units, called **grads**. In addition, in the centesimal system, there are a hundred minutes in each grade and a hundred seconds in each minute. Grads are sometimes indicated by a superscript g $(^g)$, in place of the degree symbol of the sexagesimal system.

Prime meridian. There is no obvious meridian to use as a starting point for measuring longitude. In general, most maps produced today adhere to the convention of measuring longitude from Greenwich. Some countries, however, still base their system of longitude on a prime meridian that passes through their capital or some other important city. This practice was even more common on older maps. The prime meridians that have sometimes been used by a number of countries are listed in table 22.1.

In general, on any map produced outside the United States, the user should check the prime meridian employed before using the longitude designations. (Even this is not entirely safe, however, because some older U.S. maps used a prime meridian based on Washington, D.C.) The origin point for the prime meridian is sometimes stated in the map's marginal information. If it is not, or if the information is in an inaccessible foreign language, the source map will need to be compared to other maps to determine the origin's location. The difference between the local meridian and the Greenwich meridian is then used to calculate the Greenwich longitude of the places of interest.

TABLE 22.1 Foreign Prime Meridians

LOCATION	GREENWICH LONGITUDE			
	°	′	″	
Amsterdam, Netherlands	4	53	01	E
Athens, Greece	23	42	59	E
Bern, Switzerland	7	26	22	E
Bruxelles (Brussels), Belgium	4	22	06	E
Helsinki, Finland	24	57	17	E
Hierro Island (Ferro Island), Canary Islands*	17	39	46	W
Istanbul, Turkey	28	58	50	E
Jakarta, Indonesia	106	48	28	E
København (Copenhagen), Denmark	12	34	40	E
Lisboa (Lisbon), Portugal	9	07	55	W
Madrid, Spain	3	41	15	W
Oslo, Norway	10	43	23	E
Paris, France	2	20	14	E
Pulkovo, U.S.S.R.	30	19	39	E
Roma (Rome), Italy	12	27	08	E
Stockholm, Sweden	18	03	30	E
Tiranë, Albania	19	46	5	E

Source: Modified from U.S. Department of the Army, *Map Reading*, U.S. Department of the Army Field Manual FM 21–26 (Washington, D.C.: Headquarters, Department of the Army, January 1969), 3–6.
*Often suggested as the datum for the prime meridian before the general acceptance of the Greenwich meridian in 1884. Adopted for French maps, for example, by Louis XIII, in 1634.

Plane Rectangular Grids

Topographic maps, in particular, often incorporate plane rectangular grids because they are relatively easy to use. In the past, there was considerable variation from country to country in the characteristics of these grids, but there is a tendency toward more uniformity in recent years. The Universal Transverse Mercator (UTM) system is often encountered, for example. On older maps, or in other rare cases, however, an unusual grid system is still possible. For this reason, a few comments regarding the characteristics of plane rectangular grid systems are in order.

Plane rectangular grid systems are universally based on the Cartesian coordinate concept, with measurements taken in the x and y directions from an origin point. The northeast quadrant is usually used for map purposes so that all coordinates are positive values, but this is not always the case. A brief examination of the grid designations on a map quickly reveals the use of any other quadrant because numbers in such a situation do not increase to the right and upward, and negative numbers may be encountered.

Grid origins are of two types: false origins and geographic origins. False origins are determined by measurement from some arbitrary starting point. This point might be a certain distance south of the region being mapped and, perhaps, a specified distance west of the central meridian of the map projection on which the grid has been superimposed. Geographic origins are based on a specific latitude and longitude location, usually outside the bounds of the area being mapped. The difference between the two is not likely to be of importance to a map user because the designation of grid locations is handled in the same manner under either system. One exception occurs when the origin is inside the region being mapped. This is rarely done, however, because it results in some positive and some negative coordinates.

Although numbers are almost always used to designate the grid lines, letters are sometimes used. In some cases, numbers may be used on one axis and letters on the other, or, rarely, letters may be used on both. The intervals between the grid lines are usually uniform so that the grid is square, but rectangular grids are sometimes encountered. Direct measurement of the spacing between the lines will quickly reveal the distances involved. Taking such measurements is especially important if letter designations are used.

Grids are used to designate either specific point locations or map areas. In the first case, the coordinates of the location are measured and specified, usually east and then north of the origin. If a location within a grid square is sufficiently accurate, the coordinates of the corner of the square nearest to the origin are given.

Finally, the method of stating a plane rectangular grid location may vary from system to system. These variations include the directional sequence—whether eastings are given first and then northings, or whether some other sequence is called for. Also, conventions vary with regard to the abbreviations of coordinates. Some systems routinely leave off initial digits, for example, and some omit trailing zeros.

If specifying a location in terms of an unfamiliar system, one need simply follow a method that is consistent and logical. All directions should be indicated, and abbreviations of numbers should be avoided. In particular, dividing coordinate pairs, possibly with a semicolon, helps to indicate the two elements of the coordinate (easting and northing, for example).

In summary, a bit of care and a few minutes spent examining the coordinates of the system shown around the map's neatline will pay off. Usually, understanding and using virtually any grid coordinate system with reasonable accuracy is not difficult. Information regarding the British National Grid, which is often encountered, is provided in appendix G.

UNITS OF MEASUREMENT

Units of measurement are fundamental to the mapping of features on the earth's surface. In the past, many different countries used their own specialized units, such as the Chinese *tang-su* (4.41 kilometers) or the Swedish *geografisk mil* (approximately 7.5 kilometers). In recent years, however, most countries have either adopted the metric system as a standard or continue to use units of the English system. For this reason, uncommon units are only likely to be encountered on older maps.

If a map with an unusual unit of measurement is encountered, one needs to determine the unfamiliar unit's equivalency in familiar units.[2] If this effort is unsuccessful, the problem can still be solved if the scale is stated as a representative fraction, which allows drawing of the user's own appropriately labeled, graphic scale. For example, a scale of 1:10,000 means that 1 unit on the map represents 10,000 units on the earth. A 10-centimeter line, therefore, represents 1 kilometer ($10 \times 10,000$ centimeters = 100,000 centimeters = 1 kilometer).

FOREIGN MAP PRODUCTS

An incredible variety of maps is produced worldwide. Virtually every country has at least one government agency that produces official maps (and many countries have literally dozens of such agencies). In addition, private companies throughout the world produce a multitude of maps. Simply finding out about the maps that these agencies and companies produce is a formidable task (and obtaining the maps is even more daunting). These aspects of worldwide mapping cannot be discussed in any systematic way in the space available here. Instead, the interested map reader should consult the specialized sources of information available.

[2]See, for example, the table in Olson and Whitmarsh, *Foreign Maps,* 169, or a table of measures in an encyclopedia.

An outstanding source of information about map coverage throughout the world is *World Mapping Today*. As the authors of this book indicate, they have attempted "to put together within one cover as much as possible of the various kinds of information needed for finding out about and acquiring modern topographic and thematic maps." The emphasis is on government mapping, but some information regarding commercial mapping is also included. A particularly helpful aspect is that many of the ins and outs of map acquisition are explained in chapter 3 of the book. *World Mapping Today* is listed in the "Suggested Readings," along with a number of other useful information sources.

Summary

Difficulties with language, unusual signs and symbols, specialized locational systems, or uncommon measurements are sometimes encountered on foreign maps.

Although a basic understanding of a foreign-language map is often possible through processes of association, such reference materials as dictionaries and glossaries are needed in more difficult circumstances, especially in the interpretation of specialized legends. If the language does not use the Roman alphabet, the additional process of transliteration is often necessary.

The signs and symbols found on maps produced in different nations are generally similar. In some cases, however, cultural or physical factors influence the types of features shown, and specialized symbols are introduced. When this occurs, interpretation of the symbol may require translation of the legend.

The latitude and longitude graticule is usually presented in a straightforward manner on foreign maps. The most frequent problem encountered in this connection is the substitution of a special meridian, such as the meridian of the nation's capital city, for the Greenwich prime meridian. A second difficulty is the occasional use of the 400-unit centesimal system, which divides the circle into four quadrants. Each quadrant is divided into one hundred grades, with one hundred minutes in a grade and one hundred seconds in a minute.

Plane rectangular grids may show considerable variation. Negative numbers or rectangular graticules may occur, for example. Also, unusual numbering systems and variations in notation sequence and abbreviations may be encountered.

Because many countries used their own measurement units in the past, historical maps are particularly likely to have unusual distance measurement units. Many maps produced in recent years, however, use metric or English units, sometimes in conjunction with local units.

SUGGESTED READINGS

Allin, J. *Map Sources Directory*. Downsview, Ontario: York University Libraries, 1982– (periodically updated).

Bibliographia Cartographica. München, W. Ger.: K. G. Saur, 1974– (annual).

Cartinform. Budapest, Hungary: Cartographia, 1971– (supplied with periodical *Cartactual*).

GeogKatalog. Stuttgart, W. Ger.: Geocenter ILH, 1977– (systematically updated).

Hodgkiss, A. G., and A. F. Tatham. *Keyguide to Information Sources in Cartography*. London: Mansell, 1983.

Kister, K. F. *Kister's Atlas Buying Guide*. Phoenix, Ariz.: Oryx Press, 1984 (first of a series).

Lawrence, G. P. "Maps, Atlases and Gazetteers." In *A Guide to Geographical Information Sources*, edited by S. Goddard. Beckenham, England: Croom Helm, 1985, 189–210.

Lock, C. B. M. *Modern Maps and Atlases*. London: Clive Bingley, 1969.

Olson, Everett C., and Agnes Whitmarsh. *Foreign Maps*. New York: Harper and Brothers, 1944. (Includes glossaries of foreign-language terms commonly encountered on maps.)

Parry, R. B., and C. R. Perkins. *World Mapping Today*. London: Butterworths, 1987.

Speak, P., and A. H. C. Carter. *Map Reading and Interpretation: New Edition with Metric Examples*. London: Longman Group Limited, 1970. (Provides sample color reproductions of official maps published in the United Kingdom.)

U.S. Department of the Army. *Foreign Maps*. U.S. Department of the Army Technical Manual TM 5–248. Washington, D.C.: Headquarters, U.S. Department of the Army, June 1956. (Includes translations and transliterations of many commonly encountered mapping terms in a variety of languages.)

Winch, K. L. *International Maps and Atlases in Print*. 2d ed. London and New York: Bowker, 1976.

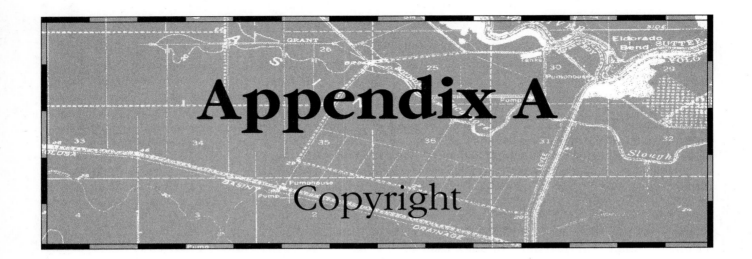

Appendix A
Copyright

Maps are protected under **copyright laws**, which means that it is illegal for anyone to reproduce copyrighted works, in whole or in part, without permission from the copyright owner. This is true regardless of the final purpose of the reproduction.

Essentially, all maps are copyrighted, including those published by foreign governments. The only notable exception to this rule are U.S. government publications, which are not protected by copyright.

Penalties for copyright violations can be severe and may include the payment of royalties, damages, costs, and fees. Avoiding such penalties requires scrupulously avoiding making unauthorized copies. This even extends to a single photocopy. In addition, a copy made from a previous copy is in violation, even if the copyright identification is not visible.

Requests for permission to reproduce a copyrighted map should be sent to the copyright holder. If permission is granted, a royalty fee may be required, depending upon the quantity of maps involved and the purpose for which they will be used.

Source: "Questions and Answers about Map Copyrights," with permission from International Map Dealers Association, P.O. Box 1789, Kankakee, IL 60901. (Copyright 1984 Wide World of Maps, Inc.)

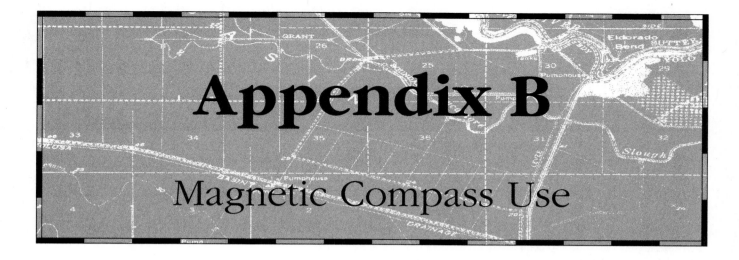

Appendix B
Magnetic Compass Use

Magnetic compasses are simple but useful devices. They contain a needle or dial that aligns with the magnetic force field of the earth and, hence, points to magnetic north. Although this basic concept is constant, compasses are produced in a variety of forms, each designed to be especially suitable for a particular task. In the end, however, *any* type of compass can be used for *any* of the tasks; you simply follow the procedures appropriate for the type available. This appendix is limited to providing basic information about the use of hand-held, magnetic compasses in conjunction with maps.

HAND-HELD, MAGNETIC COMPASS TYPES

The two primary types of hand-held, magnetic compasses are the floating-dial and floating-needle. A **floating-dial compass**, as the name suggests, contains a dial that is free to rotate. This dial has a north arrow printed on it, and degrees are printed clockwise around its periphery. A **lensatic compass** is of this type (figure B.1). A **floating-needle compass**, on the other hand, has a needle that is free to rotate within its housing. In some floating-needle compasses, degrees are printed in a clockwise direction around the periphery of a movable housing. An **orienteering compass** is of this type (figure B.2). Another type of floating-needle compass is called a **pocket transit**

(figure B.3). In this type, degrees are printed in a counter-clockwise direction around a fixed housing.

Directions are usually marked on modern compasses in degrees, although the cardinal directions (N, S, E, W) are often also indicated. Less expensive compasses are often calibrated in two-degree increments. More expensive models have finer calibrations and often have a sighting device built in so that directions can be determined more accurately. As with many other products, much better accuracy is obtained with a compass of good quality.

COMPASS TASKS

Two fundamental tasks—map orientation and azimuth determination—are performed with the help of compasses. When these tasks are mastered, they contribute to laying out and following specified routes, to locating the position of objects by intersection, and to determining one's position by resection. For simplicity sake, the discussion that follows assumes the use of the commonly encountered lensatic compass for these purposes. Differences involved in the use of other types will be apparent when you have them in hand. Also, the instructions that accompany a newly purchased compass provide additional guidance.

FIGURE B.1   Lensatic compass.

Source: John Kehoe photo.

FIGURE B.2   Orienteering compass.

Courtesy of Silva Division, Johnson Camping, Inc.

FIGURE B.3   Pocket transit.
Courtesy of Brunton Company.

Map Orientation

A map is oriented most simply by relating it to visible landmarks (see chapter 6). Often, however, there are no suitable landmarks within view, or more accuracy is required. In either case, map orientation is accomplished with the help of a compass.

Declination must be taken into account when orienting a map. The declination diagram on the map provides information regarding the amount and direction of local declination at the time the map was published. The direction and amount of annual change may also be included.

Before attempting to use a map in the field, do some preparatory work. First, calculate the current declination, and note it on the map. Second, add a magnetic-north reference line to the map. To do this, align a protractor with one of the meridians, measure the declination angle, and draw a pencil line across the face of the map. You may wish to add a series of parallel pencil lines, spaced about an inch apart, so that there will be a magnetic-north line handy to any map location. These steps will preclude having to make calculations in the field, where working conditions are often not ideal and confusion is more likely.

A tempting alternative method of obtaining a magnetic-north reference line is to simply extend the north magnetic line in the declination diagram. The preceding procedure is preferable for three reasons. First, the declination diagram does not take into account changes in declination since the map's publication date. Second, the declination diagram is usually quite small, and a slight drawing misalignment could result in considerable error. Third, especially in the case of small angles, the declination diagram may not be accurately drawn in the first place.

When the prepared map is taken into the field, orientation is easily accomplished. Select a location that provides a good view of the surrounding terrain and that is well away from automobiles, wire fences, or other metal objects, including your belt buckle. Place the map on a flat surface, open the compass out flat, and lay it on the map. Then, turn the map so that a magnetic-north reference line is aligned with the north arrow on the compass. (The compass sights can be used to provide a longer baseline and, therefore, greater accuracy of alignment.)

If you have not had the opportunity to draw magnetic-north lines on the map, simply lay the compass on the map so that its body is in alignment with a meridian. Then rotate the map until the north arrow matches the required declination.

Magnetic Azimuth Determination

Determining a magnetic azimuth from your location to a landmark is extremely simple. With the front and rear sights set vertically, hold the compass to your eye and line up the landmark with the rear peep sight and the vertical wire in the front sight. While maintaining this alignment, read the azimuth from the dial through the lens on the rear sight.

Route following.   You may wish to follow a particular azimuth that you have drawn on your map. Simply measure this azimuth with a protractor, using the magnetic-north reference lines for alignment. If you do not have a protractor, lay the compass flat on the oriented map. Align the compass body with the desired line, and read its azimuth at the zero mark on the case.

When you have determined the desired azimuth, hold the compass to your eye, and read the azimuth angle through the lens. Sighting through the front and rear sights, pick out a landmark along the indicated alignment, and walk to it. Repeat this procedure as necessary until you reach your destination or until a change in direction is required.

For quicker compass reference, set the compass before you start your route. First, align the zero mark on the compass housing with the north arrow. Then, holding the compass to this alignment, turn the bezel until the course marker on the cover (a short, radial line painted on the glass) is set at the desired azimuth. With this arrangement, whenever you need to take a sighting, simply hold the compass in front of you so that the zero mark is aligned with the north arrow, and sight along the course marker.

When following a route, you may also need to keep track of the distance you have traveled. Prepare for this ahead of time by pacing a measured distance, such as a football field, and determining the average length of your pace. Then, in the field, maintain a normal pace, and count your steps to determine the distance you have traveled.

Intersection and resection.   The methods of determining the map position of an object by intersection, and of finding your own position by resection, are discussed in chapter 6. All that needs to be noted here is that you can use your compass to determine the necessary azimuths for these procedures.

When locating an object by intersection, obtain magnetic azimuths from two known locations toward the object whose location you wish to map. Plot these azimuths on the map, using the magnetic-north reference lines to align the protractor. The intersection of the lines gives the map location of the object.

When you wish to determine your position by resection, determine azimuths from your location to two or three identifiable landmarks. Then, compute the back-azimuths (add 180 degrees to azimuths of less than 180 degrees; subtract 180 degrees from azimuths of 180 degrees or more). Identify the landmarks on the map, and draw the back-azimuths from each landmark, in turn. The intersection of these back-azimuths identifies your location.

SUGGESTED READINGS

Andresen, Steve. *The Orienteering Book*. Mountain View, Calif.: Anderson World, 1977.

Kjellstrom, Bjorn. *Be Expert with Map and Compass*. New York: Charles Scribner's Sons, 1976.

Muehrcke, Phillip C. *Map Use: Reading, Analysis, and Interpretation*. 3d ed. Madison, Wis.: JP Publications, 1992, 584–90.

Appendix C
Sources of Mapping Programs and Databases for Microcomputers

SOFTWARE EXCHANGES

The Association of American Geographers Microcomputing Specialty Group operates exchanges that offer very low-cost, noncopyrighted programs and databases, many of which have mapping applications. More information can be obtained from the following sources.

IBM-PC

Robert Sechrist
Department of Geography and Regional Planning
Indiana University of Pennsylvania
Indiana, PA 15705
Phone: (412) 357–2251

Apple II

James C. Hughes
Apple II Exchange Coordinator
Department of Geography and Environmental Studies
Slippery Rock University of Pennsylvania
Slippery Rock, PA 16057–9989
Phone: (412) 794–7309

Macintosh

Nancy B. Hultquist
Dept. of Geography and Land Studies
Central Washington University
Ellensburg, WA 98926
Phone: (509) 963–3571

SELECTED MICROCOMPUTER SOFTWARE

The range of software available for mapping and related applications on microcomputers changes rapidly, with new programs constantly appearing (and, not infrequently, with others disappearing). In addition, the available programs display a wide range of capabilities and an equally wide range of prices. This listing is, therefore, restricted to relatively well-established programs that were available at the time of writing. Only programs that run on microcomputers and that might be affordable for individual or introductory instructional use are included. Most of the programs run on IBM-PCs (or compatibles), and no computer-system designation is included in their description; those that run on other systems are appropriately identified. Programs with a dollar-sign ($) symbol after their name are priced in approximately the $500–$1,000 range. Those with a double-dollar-sign ($$) range from $1,000 to several thousand dollars in price. These more expensive programs are listed because discounts and other incentives are sometimes available to students and educators. A few programs with very low costs are marked with a cents (¢) sign.

Before considering the purchase of any program, you should obtain as much information as possible about the program. Developers and vendors will, of course, be happy to provide literature about their particular program. Such information should be supplemented, whenever possible, by reports from users of the program (again, developers and vendors will usually provide the names of users of their programs). In addition, reviews of some programs are available in journals such as *Cartography and Geographic Information Systems* (formerly *The American Cartographer*) and *The Professional Geographer*. Reading a review gives a good idea of the hardware requirements, as well as the capabilities and limitations of a program. Information about both of these aspects will help you to assess a program's suitability for your purposes.

THEMATIC MAPPING

Atlas Pro for DOS ($)
Atlas MapMaker for Windows ($)
Atlas MapMaker for Macintosh ($)

Strategic Mapping, Inc.
4030 Moorpark Ave., Suite 250
San Jose, CA 95117
Phone: (408) 985–7400

GIMMS-PC ($)

Chefford Canada Ltd.
9 Anatares Drive, Unit 110
Nepean, Ontario K2E 7V5
Phone: (613) 727–1738

Harvard GeoGraphics

Software Publishing Corporation
3165 Keifer Road
Santa Clara, CA 95051
Phone: (800) 345–2888

Map Collection, The

MapWare
P.O. Box 50168
Long Beach, CA 90815

MapInfo ($)
MapInfo for Macintosh ($)

Mapping Information Systems Corporation
200 Broadway
Troy, NY 12180
Phone: (518) 274–6000

Map-Master ($)

Ashton-Tate
20101 Hamilton Ave.
Torrance, CA 90502–1319
Phone: (310) 323–1403

MapViewer

Golden Software
P.O. Box 281
Golden, CO 80402–0281
Phone: (303) 279–1021

MicroCAM

AAG IBM Software Exchange

Multimap ($)

Planning Data Systems
1616 Walnut St., Suite 2103
Philadelphia, PA 19103
Phone: (215) 649–8701

SPSS/PC+Mapping ($)

SPSS Inc.
444 North Michigan Ave.
Chicago, IL 60611
Phone: (312) 329–3300

SURFACE MAPPING

SURFER

Golden Software, Inc.
P.O. Box 281
Golden, CO 80402–0281
Phone: (303) 279–1021

MAP PROJECTIONS

WORLD Projection and Mapping Program

Philip M. Voxland
Social Science Research Facilities Center
25 Blegen Hall
269 South Nineteenth Ave.
University of Minnesota
Minneapolis, MN 55455
Phone: (612) 625–8556

MicroCAM

AAG IBM Software Exchange

GEOGRAPHIC INFORMATION SYSTEMS

AGIS (Advanced Geographic Information System) ($)

Delta Data Systems, Inc.
131 Third St.
Picayune, MS 39466
Phone: (601) 799-1813

aMAP and pMAP (Map Analysis Packages)
(aMap for instructional use only)

Spatial Information Systems, Inc.
6907 Sprouse Court
Springfield, VA 22153
Phone: (703) 866-9458

ATLAS*GIS ($$)

Strategic Mapping, Inc.
4030 Moorpark Ave., Suite 250
San Jose, CA 95117
Phone: (408) 985-7400

EPPL7 (Environmental Planning and Programming Language) ($)

Land Management Information Center
Minnesota State Planning Agency
300 Centennial Office Building
658 Cedar St.
St. Paul, MN 55155
Phone: (612) 296-1211

GisPlus ($)

Caliper Corporation
1172 Beacon St.
Newton, MA 02161
Phone: (617) 527-4700

IDRISI

IDRISI
Graduate School of Geography
Clark University
950 Main St.
Worcester, MA 01610-1477
Phone: (508) 793-7526

MacGIS (Macintosh)

Business Manager
Cornell Research Foundation, Inc.
Cornell Business and Technology Park
20 Thornwood Drive, Suite 105
Ithaca, NY 14850
Phone: (607) 257-1081

macGIS 1.0 (Macintosh)

Dr. David Hulse
School of Architecture and Allied Arts
University of Oregon
Eugene, OR 97403
Phone: (503) 686-3634

MAP II Map Processor (Macintosh)

John Wiley and Sons Inc.
Order Department
Eastern Distribution Center
1 Wiley Drive
Somerset, NJ 08875
Phone: (908) 469-4400

MAP2000 ($)

Informed Management Environment, Inc.
3605 Katy Freeway, Suite 200
Houston, TX 77007
Phone: (713) 869-4630

MapBox ($)

Decision Images, Inc.
96 Tamarack Circle
Skillman, NJ 08558
Phone: (609) 683-0234

OSU-MAP-for-the-PC

Professor Duane Marble
Department of Geography
Ohio State University
Columbus, OH 43210-1361
Phone: (614) 292-2250

PAMAP ($)

PAMAP Technologies Corp.
3440 Douglas St., Suite 301
Victoria, British Columbia V8Z 3O5
Phone: (604) 381-3838

PC ARC/INFO ($$)

Environmental Systems Research Institute, Inc.
(ESRI)
380 New York St.
Redlands, CA 92373
Phone: (714) 793–2853

SPANS (SPatial ANalysis System) ($$)

in the United States

TYDAC Technologies Corp.
1655 N. Fort Meyer Drive, Suite 500
Arlington, VA 22209
Phone: (703) 522–0773

in Canada

INTERA TYDAC Technologies Inc.
2 Gurdwara Road, Suite 510
Nepean, Ontario K2E 1A2
Phone:·(613) 226–5525

VGA ERDAS ($$)

Erdas, Inc.
2801 Buford Highway, Suite 300
Atlanta, GA 30329
Phone: (404) 248–9000

IMAGE PROCESSING

DRAGON ($)

Decision Images, Inc.
96 Tamarack Circle
Skillman, NJ 08558
Phone: (609) 683–0234

IDRISI

IDRISI
Graduate School of Geography
Clark University
950 Main St.
Worcester, MA 01610–1477
Phone: (508) 793–7526

LANDSAT (¢)

AAG IBM Software Exchange

MIPS ($$)

MicroImages, Inc.
201 North 8th St., Suite 15
Lincoln, NE 68508–1347
Phone: (402) 477–9554

RSVGA ($)

EOSAT Customer Services
4300 Forbes Blvd.
Lanham, MD 20706
Phone: (800) 344–9933, ext. 537

or

Eidetic Digital Imaging Ltd.
1210 Marin Park Drive
Brentwood Bay, BC V0S 1A0
Phone: (604) 652–9326

VGA ERDAS ($$)

Erdas, Inc.
2801 Buford Highway, Suite 300
Atlanta, GA 30329
Phone: (404) 248–9000

COORDINATE CONVERSION

Tralaine

Mentor Software, Inc.
11534 Steele St.
Thornton, CO 80233
Phone: (303) 252–9090

DATA

DLG, TIGER

American Digital Cartography
715 West Parkway Blvd.
Appleton, WI 54914
Phone: (414) 733–6678

DLG, World Data Bank I and II

Micro Map & CAD
P.O. Box 621135
Littleton, CO 80162
Phone: (303) 973–2768

Thematic Mapper Subscenes

EOSAT Customer Services
4300 Forbes Blvd.
Lanham, MD 20706
Phone: (800) 344–9933, ext. 537

or

EOSAT
c/o EROS Data Center
Sioux Falls, SD 57198
Phone: (800) 367–2801

World Data Bank II
Micro Doc
3108 Jackson St.
Bellevue, NE 68005

DIGITIZING

Atlas Draw

Strategic Mapping, Inc.
4030 Moorpark Ave., Suite 250
San Jose, CA 95117
Phone: (408) 985–7400

DIGIT-II

Chefford Canada Ltd.
9 Anatares Drive, Unit 110
Nepean, Ontario K2E 7V5
Phone: (613) 727–1738

ROOTS ($)

Decision Images, Inc.
96 Tamarack Circle
Skillman, NJ 08558
Phone: (609) 683–0234

Appendix D

International Map of the World

The idea of a standardized, general-purpose map series of the world was suggested before the beginning of this century. Indeed, specifications for such a series, at a scale of 1:1,000,000, were established as early as 1909, but only limited actual mapping work was accomplished prior to World War II. Then, in 1962, a United Nations conference established specifications for the **International Map of the World (IMW) series** to provide a general-purpose map of the world and to serve as a base for the production of thematic maps.

Work on the IMW has been rather sporadic, largely because each country is responsible for the production of maps covering its own territory. In the Western Hemisphere, however, the American Geographical Society was originally responsible for the production of Latin American coverage.

Sheets of the series covering the United States are published by the U.S. Geological Survey. The Defense Mapping Agency (DMA) also produces 1:1,000,000-scale maps that do not, at the present time, adhere entirely to IMW specifications but that serve essentially the same purposes. Both of these products are based on information compiled from larger-scale maps, not from original surveys.

To have as much uniformity as possible in the series, the IMW conference established standards regarding the map projection, sheet coverage, and various stylistic matters. Elevations above sea level and depths of oceans and inland waters are shown in meters, for example. Principal and supplementary contour elevations are also established, as are the color progressions used for the hypsometric tints that indicate elevation zones on land and the bathymetric tints that indicate depth zones in the water.

Other standards include showing principal cities and towns, railroads, and political boundaries in black, roads in red, water features in blue, and topographic features in brown. Legend information is shown in French and English. Originally, a modified polyconic projection was used for the IMW. More recently, the Lambert conformal conic projection has been adopted.

The index system for the series begins at the 180th meridian (figure D.1). Sixty north-south zones are established, each 6 degrees wide. These zones extend eastward from 180°, with zone 1 immediately east of that meridian and zone 60 immediately west of it. Forty-six east-west bands are established, with each band 4 degrees wide (except for the bands around each pole, which cover 2 degrees each). The bands are identified by letters of the alphabet; the letters A to Z, excluding W, X, and Y, are used in each hemisphere, with A assigned to the band nearest the equator and Z adjacent to the poles.

An IMW sheet is designated, first, by the hemisphere (north or south) in which it is located. This is followed by the letter of the east-west band in which it falls, followed by the number of the north-south zone. The sheet that covers the Ottawa, Ontario, area, for example, is identified as NL–18. In addition, sheets are identified by name—in this case, Ottawa. Sheets are often combined, in areas close to the poles, because of the narrowing of the zones resulting from the convergence of the meridians. In the Canadian Arctic, for example, sheets NU—14 to 20 are combined on one sheet (Robeson Channel).

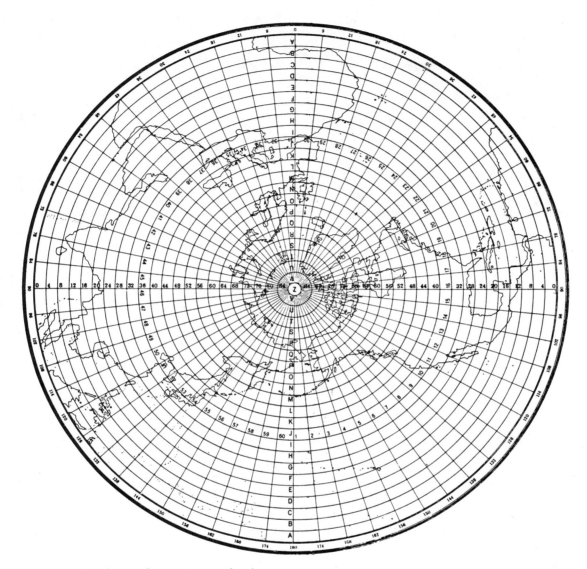

FIGURE D.1 Sheet reference system for the International Map of the World series (Northern Hemisphere).

Source: Morris M. Thompson, *Maps for America,* 3d ed. (Washington, D.C.: U.S. Department of the Interior, Geological Survey, 1987), 128.

Appendix E
Earth Science Information Center (ESIC) Network

NATIONAL HEADQUARTERS

Earth Science Information Office
U.S. Geological Survey
509 National Center
Reston, VA 22092
(703) 648–5912
Street address:
12201 Sunrise Valley Dr.
Room 2C123
Reston, VA 22092

EARTH SCIENCE INFORMATION CENTERS

Anchorage ESIC
U.S. Geological Survey
4230 University Dr., Room 101
Anchorage, AK 99508–4664
(907) 786–7011

Anchorage ESIC
U.S. Geological Survey
Room G84
605 W. 4th Ave.
Anchorage, AK 99501
(907) 271–2754

Denver ESIC
Distribution ESIC (Bldg. 810)
U.S. Geological Survey
Box 25286 Denver Federal Center
Denver, CO 80225
(303) 844–4169

Lakewood ESIC
U.S. Geological Survey
Rocky Mountain Mapping Center
Box 25046 Federal Center MS 504
Denver, CO 80225
(303) 236–5829

Menlo Park ESIC
U.S. Geological Survey
Room 3128 Building 3 (MS 532)
345 Middlefield Rd.
Menlo Park, CA 94025–3591
(415) 329–4309

Reston ESIC
U.S. Geological Survey
507 National Center
Reston, VA 22092
(703) 648–5920
Street address:
12201 Sunrise Valley Dr.
Room 1C100

Rolla ESIC
U.S. Geological Survey
1400 Independence Rd., MS 231
Rolla, MO 65401–2602
(314) 341–0995

Salt Lake City ESIC
U.S. Geological Survey
8105 Federal Building
125 S. State St.
Salt Lake City, UT 84138–1177
(801) 524–5652

San Francisco ESIC
U.S. Geological Survey
504 Custom House
555 Battery St.
San Francisco, CA 94111
(415) 705–1010

Sioux Falls ESIC
U.S. Geological Survey
EROS Data Center
Sioux Falls, SD 57198–0001
(605) 594–6151

Spokane ESIC
U.S. Geological Survey
678 U.S. Courthouse
West 920 Riverside Ave.
Spokane, WA 99201
(509) 353–2524

Stennis Space Center ESIC
U.S. Geological Survey
Building 3101
Stennis Space Center, MS 39529
(601) 688–3541

Washington D.C. ESIC
U.S. Geological Survey
Department of the Interior Bldg.
1849 C Street N.W., Room 2650
Washington, D.C. 20240
(202) 208–4047

Federal ESIC

Tennessee Valley Authority
Maps and Survey Branch
1101 Market Street
Chattanooga, TN 37402–2801
(615) 751–MAPS
Street address:
Room 100, Haney Bldg.

STATE ESICs

Alabama

Geological Survey of Alabama
ESIC Library
P.O. Drawer O
University Station
Tuscaloosa, AL 35486
(205) 349–2852
Street address:
420 Hackberry Lane
Walter B. Jones Hall

Alaska

Geodata Center
Geophysical Institute
University of Alaska–Fairbanks
Fairbanks, AK 99775–0800
(907) 474–7487

Arizona

Arizona State Land Department
Resource Analysis Division
1616 W. Adams
Phoenix, AZ 85007
(602) 542–4061

Arkansas

Arkansas Geological Commission
Vardelle Parham Geology Center
3815 W. Roosevelt Rd.
Little Rock, AR 72204
(501) 324–9165

California

Map and Imagery Laboratory
Library, University of California
Santa Barbara, CA 93106–9010
(805) 893–2779

Library Map Collection
San Diego State University
San Diego, CA 98182–0511
(619) 594–5650

California Department of Conservation
Division of Mines and Geology
Geological Information and Publications
660 Bercut Dr.
Sacramento, CA 95814–0131
(916) 324–7380

Connecticut

Natural Resources Center
Department of Environmental Protection
165 Capitol Ave.
State Office Bldg., Room 553
Hartford, CT 06106
(203) 566–3540

University of Connecticut
Map Library U-5M
Homer Babbidge Library
Storrs, CT 06268
(203) 486–4589

Delaware

Delaware Geological Survey
Cartographic Information Center
University of Delaware
Delaware Geological Survey Bldg.
Newark, DE 19716
(302) 451–8262

Florida

Florida Resources and Environmental Analysis
Center
361 Bellamy Bldg.
Florida State University
Tallahassee, FL 32306-4015
(904) 644–2883

Georgia

Geographic Information Center
Office of Government Information
Department of Community Affairs
1200 Equitable Building
100 Peachtree St.
Atlanta, GA 30303
(404) 656–5527

Hawaii

Office of State Planning
Governor's Office
State Capitol, Room 406
Honolulu, HI 96813
(808) 587–2894

University of Hawaii at Manoa
Thomas Hale Hamilton Library
Map Collection
2550 The Mall
Honolulu, HI 96822
(808) 956–6199

Idaho

Idaho State Historical Library
450 N. 4th St.
Boise, ID 83702–7695
(208) 334–3356

University of Idaho Library
Map Collection
Moscow, ID 83843
(208) 885–6344

Illinois

University of Illinois at Urbana-Champaign
Map & Geography Library
418 Main Library
1408 W. Gregory Dr.
Urbana, IL 61801
(217) 333–0827

Illinois State Geological Survey
Natural Resources Bldg.
615 E. Peabody Dr.
Champaign, IL 61820–6964
(217) 244–0933

Indiana

Purdue University
Laboratory for Applications of Remote Sensing
1158 ENTM 220
West Lafayette, IN 47907–1158
(317) 494–6305

Iowa

Iowa Department of Natural Resources
Geological Survey Bureau
123 N. Capitol St.
Iowa City, IA 52242
(319) 335–1575

Kansas

Kansas Geological Survey
University of Kansas
1930 Constant Ave.
Campus West
Lawrence, KS 66046–2598
(913) 864–3965

Kansas Applied Remote Sensing Program
Space Technology Center
University of Kansas
2291 Irving Hill Rd.
Lawrence, KS 66045–2969
(913) 864–7720

Kentucky

Kentucky Geological Survey
228 Mining and Mineral Resources Bldg.
University of Kentucky
Lexington, KY 40506–0107
(606) 257–5500

Louisiana

Division of Flood Control and Water
Management
Department of Transportation and Development
P.O. Box 94245, Capitol Station
Baton Rouge, LA 70804–9245
(504) 379–1473
Street address:
1201 Capitol Access Rd.
Room 401
Baton Rouge, LA 70821

Maine

Maine Geological Survey
State House Station #22
Augusta, ME 04333
(207) 289–2801

University of Maine
College of Forest Resources
The Map Store
South Annex A
Orono, ME 04469
(207) 581–6277

Maryland

Maryland Geological Survey
2300 St. Paul St.
Baltimore, MD 21218
(301) 554–5524

Massachusetts

University of Massachusetts
Cartographic Information Research Services
102D Hasbrouck Laboratory
Amherst, MA 01003
(413) 545–0359

Michigan

Land and Water Management
Michigan Department of Natural Resources
Steven T. Mason Bldg., Box 30028
Lansing, MI 48909
(517) 373-9123

Minnesota

Minnesota Department of Administration
Management Information Center
300 Centennial Office Building
658 Cedar St.
St. Paul, MN 55155
(612) 297-2490

University of Minnesota
S76 Wilson Library
John R. Borchert Map Library
Minneapolis, MN 55455-0414
(612) 624-4549

Mississippi

Mississippi Institutions of Higher Learning
MARIS
3825 Ridgewood Road
Jackson, MS 39211
(601) 982-6354

Missouri

Missouri Department of Natural Resources
Division of Geology and Land Survey
P.O. Box 250
Rolla, MO 65401
(314) 364-1752
Street address:
111 Fairgrounds Rd.
Rolla, MO 65401

Montana

Montana Bureau of Mines and Geology
Main Hall, Room 200
Montana Tech
Butte, MT 59701-8997
(406) 496-4167 or 4174

Nebraska

Conservation and Survey Division
University of Nebraska-Lincoln
113 Nebraska Hall
Lincoln, NE 68588-0517
(402) 472-2567 or 7523

Nevada

Nevada Bureau of Mines and Geology
University of Nevada, Reno
MS 178
Reno, NV 89557-0088
(702) 784-6691
Street address:
Scrughem Engineering-Mines Bldg.
Room 311
Reno, NV 89557

Government Documents Department Library
University of Nevada, Las Vegas
4505 Maryland Parkway
Las Vegas, NV 89154
(702) 739-3409

New Hampshire

Documents Library
Dimond Library
University of New Hampshire
Durham, NH 03824
(603) 862-1777

New Jersey

Department of Environmental Protection
New Jersey Geological Survey
CN-029
Trenton, NJ 08625
(609) 292-2576
Street address:
29 Arctic Parkway
Trenton, NJ 08368

New Mexico

Technology Application Center
University of New Mexico
2808 Central Ave. S.E.
Albuquerque, NM 87131
(505) 277-3622

New York

Map Information Unit
New York Department of Transportation
Bldg. 4, Room 105
Albany, NY 12232
(518) 457-3555

North Carolina

North Carolina Geological Survey
Department of Environment, Health and Natural
Resources
P.O. Box 27687
Raleigh, NC 27611-7687
(919) 733-2423
Street address:
512 N. Salisbury St.
Room 519C
Raleigh, NC 27611

North Carolina Geological Survey
Department of Environment, Health and Natural
Resources
59 Woodfin Pl.
Asheville, NC 28801
(704) 251-6208

North Dakota

North Dakota Geological Survey
600 E. Boulevard
Bismarck, ND 58505-0840
(701) 224-4109
Street address:
1022 E. Divide Ave.
Bismarck, ND 58505-0840

Ohio

Ohio Department of Natural Resources
Division of Soil and Water Conservation
Remote Sensing Section-ESIC
Fountain Square Bldg. E2
Columbus, OH 43224
(614) 265-6770

Oklahoma

Geology Library
University of Oklahoma
100 E. Boyd, Room R-220
Norman, OK 73019-0628
(405) 325-6451

Oregon

Department of Geology & Mineral Industries
(DOGAMI)
#28 Room 965
800 N.E. Oregon St.
Portland, OR 97232
(503) 731-4100

Oregon State Library
State Library Bldg.
Salem, OR 97310-0640
(503) 378-4368

University of Oregon Library
Map and Aerial Photography Library
165 Condon Hall
Eugene, OR 97403-1229
(503) 346-3051

Pennsylvania

Department of Environmental Resources
Bureau of Topographic and Geological Survey
Box 2357
Harrisburg, PA 17105-2357
(717) 783-8077
Street address:
916 Executive House
101 S. 2nd St.
Harrisburg, PA 17105

South Carolina

South Carolina Land Resources Conservation
Commission
Cartographic Information Center
2221 Devine Street, Suite 222
Columbia, SC 29205-2474
(803) 734-9100

South Dakota

South Dakota Geological Survey
Science Center
University of South Dakota
Vermillion, SD 57079-2390
(605) 677-5227

Tennessee

Map Library
Room 15, Hoskins
The University of Tennessee
Knoxville, TN 37996–4006
(615) 974–4315

Texas

Texas Natural Resources Information System
P.O. Box 13231
Austin, TX 78711–3231
(512) 463–8337
Street address:
1700 N. Congress Ave.
Steven F. Foster State Office Bldg., Room 428
Austin, TX 78701

Utah

Utah Geological and Mineral Survey
2363 S. Foothill Dr.
Salt Lake City, UT 84109–1491
(801) 467–7970

Vermont

University of Vermont
Bailey/Howe Library
Map Room
Burlington, VT 05405–0036
(802) 656–2503

Virginia

Department of Mines, Minerals and Energy
Division of Mineral Resources
Natural Resources Bldg.
Box 3667
Charlottesville, VA 22903
(804) 293–5121
Street address:
Natural Resources Bldg.
Alderman and McCormick Rds.
Charlottesville, Va 22903

Washington

Washington State Library
Information Services Division
P.O. Box 42478
Olympia, WA 98504–2478
(206) 753–4027
Street address:
Capitol Campus
16th and Water Sts.
Olympia, WA 98504–0111

Map Collection & Cartographic Information
Services
University of Washington Libraries
FM 25
Seattle, WA 98195
(206) 543–9392

West Virginia

West Virginia Geological and Economic Survey
West Virginia Cartographic Information Center
P.O. Box 879
Morgantown, WV 26507–0879
(304) 594–2331
Street address:
Montchateau Research Center
Cheat Lake
Morgantown, WV 26507

Wisconsin

State Cartographer's Office
160 Science Hall
550 N. Park St.
Madison, WI 53706–1404
(608) 262–3065

Wyoming

Geological Survey of Wyoming
Box 3008
University Station
Laramie, WY 82071
(307) 766–2286

Appendix F
Map Storage and Cataloging Systems

Map sheets are difficult to store and retrieve. They are also fragile and must be protected from damage. A typical storage system involves large cabinets containing horizontal file drawers (figure F.1). Individual maps, or groups of maps, are placed in large file folders. The file folders are then stacked in the appropriate drawers. Tubes or vertical files are sometimes used as alternative storage methods. Although the physical storage arrangements are important, the vital consideration, from the standpoint of the map user, is the *organization* of the system.

Assume, for example, that you are looking for a map showing the political subdivisions of Africa in 1970. In a small collection, you might simply go to a drawer labeled "Africa" and rummage through the maps to see if any of them suit your needs. If the collection is large, however, you would be involved in a time-consuming, physically tiring, and possibly frustrating search. Indeed, you might even overlook the map that you want because you failed to guess its file location. Some type of *cataloging system* would be of obvious assistance in locating and retrieving specific maps.

The catalog is an important component of the organization of any but the smallest map libraries because it provides a framework that facilitates the search for and retrieval of particular maps. A catalog eliminates the time-consuming and inefficient process of rummaging through random stacks of maps to locate the one needed.

The cataloging systems used in map collections vary in complexity, depending upon the anticipated needs of the users and the size and characteristics of

FIGURE F.1 Typical map storage drawers.
Courtesy of Hamilton Industries, Inc.

the collection. This appendix, therefore, does not describe the details of such systems but simply indicates the general approach typically involved.

One of the most commonly used map cataloging systems is the Library of Congress system. Maps are classified under *Class G* in this system, which is described in detail in the Library of Congress manual listed in the "Suggested Readings" at the end of the appendix. The other sources indicated in the "Suggested Readings" provide the detail necessary to fully understand some of the other commonly used systems.

CATALOGING

Map cataloging systems typically begin with the physical and political subdivisions of the world as an overall framework.[1] Each continent, for example, may be identified by a specific letter or number. Each country within the continent is then indicated by an additional letter or number code, with internal political subdivisions indicated by an extension of the call number. In a particular system, then, a map covering Racine County, Wisconsin, might be indexed as BA25.10. In this case, the *B* indicates that the area is located in North America, the *A* that it is in the United States, the 25 that it is in Wisconsin, and the 10 that it is Racine County.

The Library of Congress Class G schedule operates on a hierarchical numerical sequence. Under this system, world maps are designated G3200, and maps of the hemispheres are subdivisions (such as G3210 for the Northern Hemisphere). Maps of continents are given individual numbers (G3300 for North America, for example), and countries within each continent are given subnumbers (such as G3700 for the United

States). Within a country, each state or province has its own designation (such as G4120 for Wisconsin). A helpful map index of this schedule is available.[2]

In addition to the areal reference, the map's subject matter is usually indicated in the catalog. Typically, this involves a numerical system that identifies economic, physical, political, agricultural, and other topics or combinations of topics. The topics that appear on a specific map are indicated by assigning the appropriate code numbers. Each map is then recorded in the catalog, using a cross-referencing system. One entry, under the regional designation, would list the characteristics of the map and the topics that appear on it. Then, within each subject heading category, there would be a cross-reference to the map. Each map may be referenced by several entries, depending on the range of topics that it includes. Each reference specifies the number of the map to which it refers. In addition, the call number indicates the location of the map within the collection.

STORAGE

Once the index has identified the map of interest, the next problem is to physically locate the map. The arrangement of the map drawers and cabinets in the library is likely to be along the same basic lines as the index system. That is, areas may be set aside for maps of each continent, with cabinets or drawers assigned for maps of each country, and then of regions within the country.

Nonseries Maps

Some maps are produced as individual sheets, complete in and of themselves, and are not part of a series. This is particularly true of thematic maps, which often cover some political entity, such as a city, county, state, or country, or an area such as a continent or a hemisphere. Each individual thematic map

[1]It has been suggested that the main entry for cataloging maps should be the geographical area, followed by the subject. Other elements, such as date, scale, publisher, and so on, are likely to occur in a variety of sequences. See Arch C. Gerlach, "Geography and Map Cataloging and Classification in the Libraries," 317–22, and Joan Winearls, "Some Problems in Classifying and Cataloging Maps," 352–58, in *Map Librarianship: Readings,* comp. Roman Drazniowsky (Metuchen, N.J.: Scarecrow Press, 1975).

[2]Janice C. Lorrain and James A. Coombs, comps., *A Map Index to the LC "G" Schedule,* Open File Report 88–3, Map and Geography Round Table, American Library Association (Springfield, Mo.: Map Library, Southwest Missouri State University, 1988).

is usually filed according to the physical/political arrangement mentioned previously. Then, if there are a number of maps of the same area, they are placed in order, according to topic, within the area file.

Series Maps

Many maps, especially topographic maps, are produced as part of a series. Such series are often produced by government agencies and extend over an entire political entity. In addition, map series frequently cover areas outside of the region of origin, extending over continental areas or, even, the world.

The sheet outlines of series maps are usually systematically arranged, often along lines of latitude and longitude. The area covered by individual sheets in such a system is approximately rectangular, although the exact shape depends on latitude and the map projection used. This means that individual map sheets may cross political boundaries. When this occurs, it is not always clear where the map should be filed. For this reason, series maps are often filed together on the basis of the total extent of the series. A series that covers the entire world, for example, may be housed in one area of the library. An alternative is to break the series into parts, with each part filed with the maps of the appropriate region.

The main goal in filing the sheets of a series is to follow a procedure that allows individual sheets to be quickly identified, located, and retrieved. The producers of the series usually provide an identification and indexing system that allows users to organize their holdings systematically and to decide where each sheet belongs.

One common practice is to give each sheet the name of the most prominent feature located within its boundaries, whether it is a cultural feature, such as a city, dam, or town, or a natural feature, such as a river, lake, or mountain. The logical method of filing sheets identified by name is to simply put them in alphabetical order.

Obviously, the sequence of maps arranged in alphabetical order is not likely to bear any relationship to the geographical arrangement of the areas covered by the individual sheets. In the U.S. Geological Survey 1:250,000-scale National Topographic Map Series, for

FIGURE F.2 Arrangement of U.S. Geological Survey 1:250,000-scale topographic sheets for a portion of Texas.
Source: U.S. Geological Survey, "Texas Index to Topographic and Other Map Coverage."

example, the sheet named "Beaumont" is located just east of the one named "Austin" (figure F.2). On the other hand, the "Waco" sheet is located north of the "Austin" sheet, and the "Seguin" sheet is located south of it. When the Texas sheets are placed in alphabetical order, then, sheets from one area of the state are intermixed with sheets from other areas of the state and are not located next to one another. Furthermore, if the file contains sheets for the entire United States, the Texas sheets are further intermixed with sheets from all of the other states. Despite this apparent difficulty, the use of sheet names is a very common indexing method.

USGS Map Reference Code.   A useful method for filing USGS series maps is to use the **Map Reference Code** system as a guide. In this system, each map is assigned a unique reference code, based on its location (figure F.3). This code can be used to establish a filing hierarchy. In this approach, each element in the code is considered in sequence. Consider, for example, how maps that are part of a 7.5-minute topographic quadrangle series (scale 1:24,000) could be filed. The first two elements of the code for each map represent the latitude and longitude of the southeast

MAP REFERENCE CODE

U.S. Geological Survey maps are identified by name and series. In addition, a system has been initiated whereby each map is assigned a unique reference code which indicates the geographic coordinates, type, unit of measurement, and scale of map.

Various examples are illustrated at the right and a key to abbreviations is shown below.

MAP TYPES

AB - Alaska Boundary Series Index
AF - Alaska Boundary Series-National Forest System
AL - Alaska Boundary Series-Bureau of Land
        Management System
AP - Alaska Boundary Series-National Park System
AW - Alaska Boundary Series-National Wildlife
        Refuge System
CF - County (feet)
CM - County (metric)
EI - Ecological Inventory
LB - Land Use and Land Cover (base)
LM - Land Use and Land Cover (multicolor)
MM - Surface-Minerals Management Status
NS - National Atlas (separate sales)
OM - Orthophotomap
OQ - Orthophotoquad
PF - National Park, Monument (feet)
PL - Planimetric
PM - National Park, Monument (metric)
PR - National Park, Monument (shaded relief)
RA - Radar (airborne)
RF - Regional (feet)
RM - Regional (metric)
RP - Regional (planimetric)
RS - Radar (satellite)
SI - Satellite Imagery
SL - Slope Maps
SM - Surface Management Status
SP - State Base (planimetric)
SR - State Base (shaded relief)
ST - State Base (topographic)
TB - Topographic Bathymetric
TF - Topographic (feet)
TM - Topographic (metric)
UB - United States (base)
UG - United States (general)
UM - United States (magnetic)
UO - United States (outline)
UT - United States (topographic)
WB - World (base)
WG - World (general)
WO - World (outline)
WP - World (political)
WT - World (topographic)

7.5 MINUTE SERIES

Reference Code 30097-H1-TF-024
Latitude (30°)
Longitude (97°)
Index Number (H1)
Map Type (Topographic)
Unit of Measurement (Feet)
Map Scale (1:24 000)

7.5 x 15 MINUTE SERIES

Reference Code 30097-G3-TM-025
Latitude (30°)
Longitude (97°)
Index Number (G3)
Map Type (Topographic)
Unit of Measurement (Meters)
Map Scale (1:25 000)

15 MINUTE SERIES

Reference Code 30097-E7-TF-062
Latitude (30°)
Longitude (97°)
Index Number (E7)
Map Type (Topographic)
Unit of Measurement (Feet)
Map Scale (1:62 500)

30 x 60 MINUTE SERIES

Reference Code 30097-E1-TM-100
Latitude (30°)
Longitude (97°)
Index Number (E1)
Map Type (Topographic)
Unit of Measurement (Meters)
Map Scale (1:100 000)

1 x 2 DEGREE SERIES

Reference Code 30097-A1-TF-250
Latitude (30°)
Longitude (97°)
Index Number (A1)
Map Type (Topographic)
Unit of Measurement (Feet)
Map Scale (1:250 000)

MAP SCALES

020-1:20 000
024-1:24 000
025-1:25 000
050-1:50 000
062-1:62 500
063-1:63 360
100-1:100 000
250-1:250 000
500-1:500 000
01M-1:1 000 000
02M-1:2 000 000
25M-1:2 500 000

35M-1:3 500 000
05M-1:5 000 000
06M-1:6 000 000
07M-1:7 000 000
75M-1:7 500 000
08M-1:8 000 000
10M-1:10 000 000
11M-1:11 875 000
14M-1:14 000 000
16M-1:16 500 000
22M-1:22 000 000
30M-1:30 000 000
31M-1:3 168 000

NOTE: A file number, also unique to each published map, is assigned for internal USGS order filing purposes.

FIGURE F.3   USGS Map Reference Code System.

FIGURE F.4   Primary quadrangles of the National
Topographic System of Canada.

corner of the one-degree square quadrilateral in which
it falls. Thus, quadrangles between 30° and 31° N are
filed before those between 31° and 32° N. Then,
within each latitude group, the maps are arranged so
those between 97° and 98° E are filed before those
between 98° and 99° E. As is apparent from figure F.3,
sixty-four 7.5-minute quadrangles fall in each one-
degree square region. The sequence of filing these 64
maps is based on the next element of the map reference code. This element consists of a letter/number

pair, arranged in order from A1 to H8. It is worth men-
tioning that DLG data (see chapter 19) are often filed
on the basis of this map reference code.

National Topographic System of Canada Coding.
The coding used to identify quadrangles in the National Topographic System of Canada provides an excellent framework for map filing. In this system,
primary quadrangles are identified by a number based
on columns and rows that generally cover 4° north to
south and 8° east to west (figure F.4). (Because of the

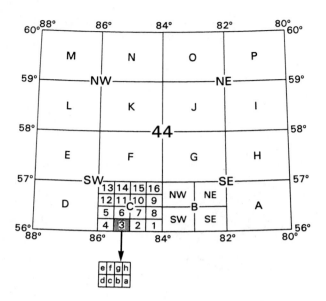

FIGURE F.5   Subdivision of a primary quadrangle of the National Topographic System of Canada.

convergence of the meridians, the columns are widened to 16° east to west, north of 80° N.) These quadrangles correspond to the coverage of the sheets of the 1:1,000,000-scale topographic series.[3]

Larger-scale topographic maps are identified by subdivision of the primary quadrangles (figure F.5). Within each scale group, the identification numbers provide a logical filing sequence. Thus, 1:500,000-scale sheets cover an area that is two degrees north-south by four degrees east-west. These sheets are identified by the primary quadrangle number, followed by the designation NE, NW, SE, or SW. 1:250,000-scale sheets cover sixteen one degree north-south by two degree east-west quadrangles within each primary quadrangle. North of 64° N there are eight subdivisions, which cover one degree north-south and two degrees east-west. North of 80° N there

[3]Note that these quadrangles do not correspond to the sheets of the 1:1,000,000-scale International Map of the World.

are four subdivisions, each covering one degree north-south and four degrees east-west. These sheets are identified by the primary quadrangle number, followed by the letters A through P, in the case of sheets south of 68° N, and A through H north of 68° N. Sheets at larger scales are identified by further subdivision, as indicated in figure F.5.

Series Indexes

A quick summary of the holdings in a map series is often useful and is provided by a series index. Such an index may be in the form of a table or a map. Each form has advantages and disadvantages.

A **tabular index** is simply an alphabetically or numerically ordered list of map names or identification numbers (figure F.6). Such a list is useful for inventory or ordering purposes. If an inventory is needed, a quantity indication is added next to the identifier for each map of the series in the collection. Those sheets that are not in the collection are then easily identified and, if desired, an order list can be created directly from the inventory sheet.

An **index map** is most satisfactory from the standpoint of determining the geographic coverage of the maps from a given series that are included in a collection. It consists of a base map of the area of interest, whether it is a county, state, country, continent, or the entire world. The outlines of the sheets that are published, or that are planned for publication, are drawn on this base map. The sheet name or number of each map is also indicated. An index map of this type is often available from the producer of the map series.

In use, the map librarian places appropriate marks on the index map to indicate the status of the series. The markings may simply indicate which sheets are in the collection. Often, however, they are more extensive and may indicate, for example, the edition or

7.5 MINUTE QUADRANGLES

43088–F3	Eden	43088–G4	Fond du Lac	43088–G8	Green Lake
44089–H8	Edgar	42089–F2	Footville	44088–C1	Greenleaf
42089–G1	Edgerton	45092–B3	Forest	44088–C5	Greenville
45091–F4	Edgewater	44087–F4	Forestville	44090–G5	Greenwood
45087–A3	Egg Harbor	42088–H7	Fort Atkinson	44088–G7	Gresham
45089–D2	Elcho	46088–A4	Fortune Lakes	46090–D5	Gurney
43088–G5	Eldorado	44091–B6	Fountain City	42091–G1	Guttenberg
44091–D4	Elk Creek	44091–A8	Four Corners		
44091–G6	Elk Creek Lake	46092–D3	Foxboro	46088–A7	Hagerman Lake
43088–G1	Elkhart Lake	42088–D2	Fox Lake	44089–G7	Halder
42088–F5	Elkhorn	43088–E8	Fox Lake	42088–H1	Hales Corners
44092–E1	Ella	43087–G8	Franklin	45089–A8	Hamburg
42090–G5	Ellenboro	42087–G8	Franksville	44089–B5	Hancock
45087–C1	Ellison Bay	45088–A5	Fredenburg Lake	45087–A7	Harmony
46091–C5	Ellison Lake	45092–F4	Frederic	43091–B2	Harpers Ferry
44092–F4	Ellsworth	44088–D3	Freedom	46089–C7	Harris Lake
44092–G3	El Paso	46092–A1	Frog Lake	45089–D5	Harrison
44088–F6	Embarrass	46092–E3	Frogner	45089–F6	Harshaw
45092–A3	Emerald	45089–B8	Fromm Lookout Tower	43088–C3	Hartford East

FIGURE F.6   Example tabular index of map series holdings.

Source: U.S. Geological Survey, portion of "Wisconsin Index to Topographic and Other Map Coverage."

editions that are in the collection, whether or not the hill-shaded version is included, the sheets that are on order, and so on (figure F.7).

When an index map is provided, it is a simple matter to locate the city, region, or other feature of interest and to determine the specific map that provides the desired coverage. Also, the index map shows at a glance the geographical extent of the coverage available for a general area, as well as what areas are absent from the collection. This is, therefore, often the most convenient form of index because typical map users almost always know what *area* or *feature* is of interest to them but are less likely to know the name or number of the map sheet(s) that provide the required coverage.

SUGGESTED READINGS

Akers, B. "Care and Handling of a Map Collection." *The Map Collector* 4 (1978): 2–5.

American Library Association. *Anglo-American Cataloging Rules.* 2d ed. Chicago: American Library Association, 1978.

Cartographic Materials: A Manual of Interpretation for AACR2. Chicago: American Library Association, 1982.

Larsgaard, Mary Lynette. *Map Librarianship: An Introduction.* 2d ed. Littleton, Colo.: Libraries Unlimited, 1987.

Neddermeyer, G. "Map Cataloging—An Introduction." *Drexel Library Quarterly* 9, no. 4 (1973): 18–25.

Nichols, H. *Map Librarianship.* Hamden, Conn.: Linnet Books, 1976.

United States, Library of Congress, Subject Cataloging Division. *Classification, Class G.* 4th ed. Washington, D.C.: Library of Congress, 1976.

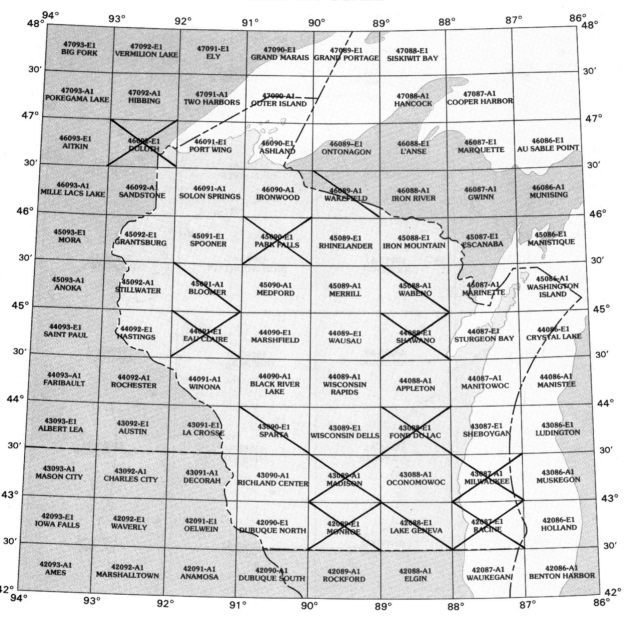

30 × 60 MINUTE SERIES
1:100 000 SCALE

 In collection   On order

FIGURE F.7   Series index map modified for use as index
of map series holdings. (U.S. Geological Survey
1:100,000-scale maps of Wisconsin and vicinity.)

Source: U.S. Geological Survey, ''Wisconsin Index to Topographic and
Other Map Coverage.''

Appendix G
British National Grid

A specialized grid reference system, called the **British National Grid**, is used by the British Ordnance Survey for maps of Britain. Similar systems are used in other parts of the world where British influence was strong.

The system involves major and minor grid squares (figure G.1). The major squares measure 500 kilometers on a side and are identified by a letter of the alphabet. The first major square is located north and west of Scotland and is lettered *H;* the last major square is located south and east of London and is lettered *T.*

Within each 500-kilometer square on the grid are twenty-five grid squares that are each 100 kilometers on a side. These 100-kilometer squares are lettered *A* to *Z* (with the letter *I* omitted), in a row-by-row pattern beginning in the northwest corner of the 500-kilometer square and ending in the southeast corner. The result is that each 100-kilometer grid square is uniquely identified by a pair of letters, with the letter that identifies the 500-kilometer square given first and the identifier for the 100-kilometer square given second. The Isle of Man, for example, is located principally in grid square SC.

Grid references for specific points within each 100-kilometer grid square are written as either four- or six-digit numbers. If a location is to be specified with an accuracy of 1 kilometer, the four-digit reference is used; this is called the Normal Kilometre Grid Reference. In essence, the Normal Kilometre Grid Reference identifies a square, 1 kilometer on a side, within which the point of interest is located. For example, the Normal Kilometre Grid Reference for a

FALSE ORIGIN OF NATIONAL GRID

FIGURE G.1 Major (100-kilometer) grid squares of the British National Grid, with letter designations. Numbers formerly used to designate each square are shown in parentheses.

Source: Reproduced from ''The Projection for Ordnance Survey Maps and Plans and the National Reference System,'' with permission of the Controller of Her Majesty's Stationary Office, © Crown copyright reserved.

FIGURE G.2   Grid references for a specific point.

point in figure G.2 is 4972. If the point is to be located to the nearest 100 meters, the Normal National Grid Reference is given as a six-digit figure—in this case, 498727. Because the numerical references could identify a point within *any* 100-kilometer grid square, the identifying letters for the appropriate square must be given if there is any possibility of confusion on the part of the map user. In the example given in figure G.2, since the point is within grid square SC, then the Full Kilometre Grid Reference is SC/4972, and the Full National Grid Reference is SC/498727.

Glossary of Selected Terms

Absolute altitude Altitude above the earth's surface, not above sea level.

Absolute scale Scale, on a graph, in which each unit of distance represents the same quantity of a given variable.

Accessibility In graph theory, how well connected places (nodes) are to other places.

Accumulative line graph (Lorenz curve) Arithmetic line graph used to illustrate the degree of concentration in one variable as compared to another.

Acre Unit of measurement in the U.S. Customary system. Contains 43,560 square feet.

Active remote-sensing system A remote-sensing system that includes special equipment that transmits signals of the required wavelength. For example, radar.

Admiralty nautical mile *See* **Nautical mile.**

Aerial photograph Remote-sensing product obtained by photography from an airborne platform.

Aerial survey camera Large-format camera used to take vertical photographs for mapping purposes.

Aeronautical chart A special map used for aerial navigation.

Agonic line Line on an isogonic chart that joins points of zero declination.

Agricultural Stabilization and Conservation Service, U.S. (ASCS) U.S. Department of Agriculture agency that produces aerial photos and photomaps of cropland areas.

Aliquot parts Division of a U.S. Public Land Survey section into various combinations of quarters (160 acres), quarter-quarters (40 acres), and halves (80 acres).

Alluvial fan Deposition feature formed as water slows where it leaves steep, restricted channels and empties into a valley bottom.

Alluvial plain Flat region where lakes or streams have deposited sedimentary materials.

Alpine features Distinctive landforms resulting from alpine glaciation.

Altitude of the sun Latitude that the sun is directly over on a given day.

American Geographical Society Collection Major geographical reference and research collection located in the Golda Meir Library of the University of Wisconsin-Milwaukee.

Analemma Figure-eight-shaped diagram that gives information about the latitudes at which the sun is directly overhead throughout the year and about the equation of time.

Aneroid altimeter Altimeter that, when properly calibrated, converts current barometric pressure into a direct altitude reading.

Annular drainage pattern Drainage pattern that results when streams flow in a ringlike, concentric pattern around a central dome or basin.

Apparent solar day The period between apparent solar noon on two consecutive days.

Apparent solar noon Time at which the sun passes over the meridian on which an observer is located.

Apparent solar time Time based on the passage of the sun.

Approximate contour Dashed or dotted line that joins points of approximately equal elevation.

Area cartogram (value-by-area cartogram) Maplike diagram on which the areas of the various regions are drawn in proportion to some value associated with them, such as income or population, instead of their actual area.

Areal averaging The situation in which the information presented on a map is the average value for each areal unit.

Areal scale Ratio between the area of a feature plotted on a map and the area of the same feature on the earth's surface.

Areal symbol Map symbol that represents a feature that is spread out over the earth's surface.

Arête Sharp-edged ridge crest formed by glacial action.

Arithmetic line graph Line graph in which equal distances (either vertical or horizontal) indicate equal changes in value, anywhere on the graph.

Army Corps of Engineers, U.S. Agency charged with maintenance of navigable waterways. Produces Mississippi River System nautical charts and maps showing small-craft facilities.

ASCS *See* **Agricultural Stabilization and Conservation Service**, U.S.

Associated number In graph theory, the topological distance from a given place (node) to the most remote place in the network.

Astronomic latitude Latitude based on the observation of astronomic bodies, such as Polaris.

Atmospheric window Wavelength region in which electromagnetic energy passes through the atmosphere with relatively little scatter or absorption.

Attribute code In computer-assisted cartography and geographic information systems, the set of characters by which a feature is identified.

Automated navigation Driving aids that automatically determine and display the current location of a vehicle, determine the best route to follow between selected locations, and/or provide en route guidance.

Azimuth (forward azimuth) Direction of line, defined at its starting point by its angle in relation to a meridian. Usually measured in a clockwise direction, starting from north.

Azimuthal equidistant projection Map projection on a plane, in which all points are plotted at their true distance from the center of the projection and are in their true global direction (azimuth) from the center.

Azimuthal projection Map projection made on a plane surface.

Back-azimuth A direction that is the exact reverse of an azimuth; that is, 180 degrees from an azimuth.

Back-bearing The direction that is the exact reverse of a bearing.

Bar chart Diagram on which bars of various lengths are used to express the values of the variables graphed. May use either absolute or percentage values.

Baseline Line that serves as the basis for a survey, with endpoints, direction, and length that are accurately known. Or, an east-west reference line used in conjunction with a U.S. Public Land Survey principal meridian.

Base map Background framework on which a thematic map is drawn.

Bathymetric map Map that shows water depths and the configuration of the underwater topography.

Bearing A direction, not exceeding 90 degrees, measured from either a north or south baseline, whichever is nearer to the direction being designated. May be expressed as a true, magnetic, or grid direction.

Bench mark Monument used to mark a point whose elevation above or below a specified datum has been established.

BGN *See* **Board on Geographic Names**, U.S.

Bifurcation ratio In graph theory, the ratio between the number of segments (links) of one order, in a tree, and the number of segments of the next higher order.

Bilateral graph Line graph that uses a single arithmetic scale to portray the values of two related variables so that the overlap of the lines indicates either positive or negative net values. For example, an excess of births over deaths yields a natural increase in population, whereas an excess of deaths over births indicates a natural decrease.

Bivariate map A map that shows the relationships between the values of two variables at once.

BLM *See* **Bureau of Land Management**, U.S.

Block diagram Pictorial representation of a portion of the earth's surface from an elevated, oblique point of view.

Board on Geographic Names, U.S. (BGN) Agency responsible for establishing official names for use on U.S. government maps.

Boyce-Clark radial shape index Measure of shape based on the lengths of radials extending outward from a node placed at the center of the shape.

Branching network (tree) In graph theory, a network that does not contain circuits (loops).

British National Grid Specialized grid reference system used by the British Ordnance Survey for maps of Britain.

Broad-band device Remote-sensing device that uses a sensor that receives electromagnetic energy of many wavelengths and integrates the information into a composite signal. For example, panchromatic film used in aerial photography.

Brown Library, John Carter Outstanding collection of primary materials relating to virtually all aspects of the discovery, exploration, settlement, and development of the New World. Located at Brown University, Providence, Rhode Island.

Bunge's measure Measure of shape based on a set of distance measurements taken between systematically placed vertices on the perimeters of the region.

Bureau of the Census, U.S. Department of Commerce agency that produces maps of census subdivisions.

Bureau of Indian Affairs, U.S. Agency that produces maps and surveys of Indian lands.

Bureau of Land Management, U.S. (BLM) Department of the Interior agency with extensive mapping responsibilities, including final authority on all matters pertaining to the survey of the public lands. Surveys and maintains U.S. Public Land Survey monuments and publishes township plats.

Butte Isolated remnant of a mesa, with very small surface area and clifflike sides.

Cadastral map Map that includes the location of property-ownership lines, along with their bearings and lengths, the ownership and size of land parcels, and similar information.

Cadastral survey Survey used to determine land-ownership boundaries and property descriptions. In the United States, preferably reserved for land-ownership surveys of the public lands.

Canada Land Survey System (CLSS) Survey system established in 1870 to provide an orderly land ownership framework in the prairies and mountains of western Canada. Uses principal meridians and base lines, townships, ranges, sections, and subdivisions of sections.

Canada Map Office Central office for ordering or obtaining information about government maps in Canada.

Canadian Permanent Committee on Geographical Names (CPCGN) Agency responsible for establishing official geographical names in Canada.

CPCGN *See* **Canadian Permanent Committee on Geographical Names**

Canoe chart Nautical chart of the Minnesota-Ontario border lakes produced by NOS. Designed to suit the needs of operators of small, shallow-draft vessels.

Carrying contour Single contour drawn to represent several contours that fall extremely close together in a particularly steep area.

Cartogram A special type of map in which a different standard of measurement, such as time or cost, is substituted for distance measurements, or in which the area of regions is made proportional to some other measure, such as population or income.

Cartography The art, science, and technology of making maps, together with their study as scientific documents and works of art. (Definition from International Cartographic Association.)

Cathode-ray tube (CRT) Television-like screen attached to a computer.

Centesimal system Coordinate system sometimes encountered on maps, especially French and Belgian. The circle is divided into four quadrants, with each quadrant subdivided into one hundred units, called grads. There are one hundred minutes in each grad and one hundred seconds in each minute.

Central Intelligence Agency, U.S. (CIA) Intelligence gathering and analysis agency, some of whose maps are available to the public.

Central-point linear cartogram Maplike diagram that shows travel costs or travel times from a single starting point to other locations in the region.

Centrifugal drainage pattern Drainage pattern that results when streams flow away from a central point, such as a volcanic cone.

Centripetal drainage pattern Drainage pattern that results when streams flow toward the center of a basin.

Change detection In remote-sensing analysis, detection of changed conditions by comparison of images obtained at different time periods.

Chart A special map used for navigational purposes.

Chi-square statistic Measure used to indicate the strength of association between two distributions.

Choropleth map A quantitative areal map in which the average magnitude of a phenomenon is indicated by a distinctive tone, pattern, or color applied over each unit area. Unit areas are delimited by state or county boundaries, or other arbitrary boundary lines.

Chronometer Extremely accurate clock. Essential for making longitude determinations before the development of radio time signals.

CIA *See* **Central Intelligence Agency, U.S.**

Cinder cone Conical, volcanic feature formed by the deposition of cinders blown from a central vent.

Circuit network In graph theory, a network that includes loops so that there is more than one possible path between some pairs of places (nodes).

Circular graph Graphic display often used to record information about events that occur during a specific time period, such as twelve hours or a year.

Cirque Glacier-carved basin at the head of a valley.

Classification Division of a range of data into groups. *See also* **Data classification.**

Classification error In remote-sensing analysis, classification of pixels into inappropriate categories.

Cliff Steep-faced escarpment.

Climate map Map of any climatic factor or of the climatic regions.

Climatograph Circular graph that shows climatic information, such as temperature or rainfall.

Clustered pattern Pattern in which many points are concentrated close together and outlying areas contain very few, if any, points.

Coast chart Nautical chart for coastwise navigation inside offshore reefs and shoals, entrance into bays and harbors of considerable size, and navigation of certain inland waterways.

Coefficient of areal correspondence Measure of the extent to which two distributions correspond to one another. Compares areas that fall into only one category, areas where the two categories overlap, and areas that fall outside either category.

Col Pass or saddle between two adjacent cirques that have cut into the arête that separates them.

Color emulsion Photographic emulsion that reproduces the range of colors seen by the human eye.

Color-infrared emulsion *See* **Infrared emulsion.**

Combination A means of map generalization in which two or more similar features are combined into one.

Compass deviation The difference between the direction to the north magnetic pole and the direction that the compass needle actually points.

Computer-assisted cartography Use of the computational power of the computer to improve the speed and accuracy of map production.

Cone Developable surface used for conic projections.

Conformality The retention of correct shapes of small areas on a map. Requires that the lines of latitude and longitude cross one another at right angles and that the map scale is the same in all directions at any given point.

Conjugate principal point On one photograph of a stereo pair, the location of the principal point of an adjacent photograph.

Connectivity In graph theory, a measure of the level of completeness of the graph, given by the connectivity index.

Connectivity index In graph theory, a comparison between the actual connections (routes) that exist in a given network, as compared to the total number possible.

Constant azimuth (rhumb line) A directional line that crosses each succeeding meridian at a constant angle.

Contiguous cartogram A cartogram in which the relationships between regions are retained but, of necessity, variations in the regions' shapes are introduced.

Continental glaciation Action of extensive ice sheets.

Continuously variable symbol A symbol, such as a circle, whose size is mathematically scaled in proportion to the value it represents.

Continuous surface A surface on which every point has a value connected to it.

Contour An imaginary line that joins points of equal elevation above or below some datum.

Contour interval Vertical distance between contours.

Control diagram Map based on a survey used to establish ground locations of control points for aerial photography.

Control network *See* **Geodetic control network.**

Controlled photomosaic Mosaic of aerial photos assembled with reference to ground control.

Conversion *See* **Digitizing.**

Conversion diagram Diagram used to assist in the change of azimuths from one reference direction to another.

Crater Depression formed at the top of a volcano or cinder cone.

CRT *See* **Cathode-ray tube.**

Cuesta Low ridge, similar to a plateau, formed by the erosion of a sloping, resistant layer.

Cut and fill Engineering process of balancing the amount of material removed from the high areas (cut) with that required to fill low areas.

Cut-line Path along which a profile is drawn.

Cycle On a graph with a logarithmic scale, a range of values with a multiple of ten (such as 1 to 10, or 10 to 100).

Cylinder Developable surface used for cylindrical projections.

Dasymetric map A quantitative areal map in which the variation in the magnitude of a phenomenon that occurs in a region is indicated by different tones, patterns, or colors applied over appropriate subdivisions of the region.

Data classification The process of grouping values so that each one is associated with others that have relatively similar characteristics and is separated from those with distinctly different characteristics. Applies to pixels in remote-sensing analysis or to data values in thematic mapping.

Data plane The computer equivalent of a map overlay. Each data plane contains information about the spatial arrangement of a specific variable.

Datum Fixed elevation, such as mean sea level, used as the starting point for a vertical survey.

Dead reckoning Method used by navigators for route planning or for keeping track of progress toward a destination. Depends on knowing (or predicting) the starting point and the direction, speed, and time of travel away from that point.

Declination diagram Diagram that shows the relationships between true, magnetic, and grid north.

Defense Mapping Agency, U.S. (DMA) Agency that provides mapping, charting, and geodetic support, including worldwide topographic maps, aeronautical charts, and nautical charts, to Department of Defense components.

Defilade A location that is hidden from view.

Deflection of the vertical The difference, at a given location, between a line drawn to the center of the earth and a line drawn to the earth's center of gravity.

Degree (of a slope) The angle of slope, measured in degrees.

Delta Fan-shaped, alluvial deposit at the mouth of a river.

DEM *See* **Digital elevation model.**

Dendritic Treelike drainage pattern.

Department of Agriculture, U.S. (USDA) Three organizations within USDA—the Soil Conservation Service, the Agricultural Stabilization and Conservation Service, and the U.S. Forest Service—produce maps and other materials of interest to map users.

Department of Transportation, U.S. (DOT) Agency that produced *U.S. Transportation Atlas* and that provides information regarding sources of state highway maps.

Dependent variable The value of a dependent variable is predicted on the basis of the value of an independent variable.

Depression contour Contour line drawn with short ticks at right angles to the contour line. The ticks point downslope, toward the bottom of the depression.

Depth curve (isobath) Underwater contour that shows the depth of water below a designated datum, such as mean low water.

Developable surface Projection surface, especially the cone and the cylinder, that is not flat at the time the projection is created but that can be flattened later.

Diameter In graph theory, the highest associated number in a network.

Digital data Tabular or locational information converted to digital form, especially for use with computer-assisted methods.

Digital elevation model (DEM) U.S. Geological Survey data base that contains elevation values in digital form.

Digital land-use and land-cover data U.S. Geological Survey digital data base that contains information on the location of up to thirty-seven categories of land-use and land-cover data.

Digital line graph (DLG) U.S. Geological Survey data base that contains digital map data in vector format.

Digitizing In computer-assisted cartography, the process of converting map data from their original visual form to a digital format that can be handled by a computer.

Dip In geology, the downward inclination of a bed or stratum relative to an imaginary horizontal plane.

Disrupted drainage pattern Drainage pattern in which streams run in many directions without visible pattern, often through areas of lake and marsh. Frequently the result of glacial action.

Dissection, type of Classification of drainage patterns into characteristic types.

Distance functions In a digital geographic information system, functions that produce information regarding, for example, the distance or the cost of access from a given point to every other point in the region.

Distance log *See* **Mileage table.**

Distance matrix Diagram that provides information about distances and/or travel times between major locations.

Distortion of concepts The use of carefully selected, misleading methods of map presentation for propaganda purposes.

DLG *See* **Digital line graph.**

DMA *See* **Defense Mapping Agency, U.S.**

Dominion Land Survey System *See* **Canada Land Survey System (CLSS).**

DOT *See* **Department of Transportation, U.S.**

Dot-distribution map Thematic map in which each dot represents a specified quantity of a particular variable.

Dot-matrix printer A computer output device that prints graphic images, including maps, in raster format (a pattern of dots).

Dot-planimeter method Method of areal measurement using regularly spaced pattern of dots.

Drainage pattern The arrangement of streams on the landscape.

Drumlin Lozenge-shaped hill, formed under continental glacier, with steep slopes facing in the direction from which the ice advanced and more gradual slopes in the opposite direction.

Drumlin field Extensive groups of drumlins.

Dune Feature formed by the deposition of wind-blown sand.

Earth Observation Satellite Company (EOSAT) Private agency that contracts with the U.S. Department of Commerce to construct, launch, and operate Landsat satellites and to disseminate the collected data.

Earth Science Information Centers (ESIC) Part of the U.S. Geological Survey, with mission to help users gain better, faster, low-cost access to the cartographic holdings of federal, state, and private agencies.

Ecliptic, plane of the The imaginary plane that passes through the sun and the earth at all positions of the earth's orbit around the sun.

Edge enhancement Image enhancement of remotely sensed data that increases the contrast between the values on either side of a dividing line, rendering shapes and details along the edges more conspicuous.

Electromagnetic spectrum Wavelengths of electromagnetic radiation.

Ellipsoid A regular solid formed by the rotation of an ellipse on its minor axis. It has a greater radius at right angles to the axis of rotation and a smaller radius along the axis. A better approximation of the shape of the earth than a sphere.

Energy, Mines and Resources, Department of (Canada) *See* **Surveys and Mapping Branch, Department of Energy, Mines and Resources.**

Engineering map Detailed map (plan) for guiding engineering projects.

EOSAT *See* **Earth Observation Satellite Company.**

Ephemeris Set of tables that gives information about the movements of the sun, moon, stars, and planets.

Equal-area (equivalent) projection A projection on which equal areas are retained, so that a unit area drawn anywhere on a map always represents the same area on the earth's surface.

Equation of time Measure obtained by subtracting mean solar time from apparent solar time.

Equator Great circle located midway between the poles of rotation.

Equidistance The retention of correct distance on a map.

Equivalence *See* **Equal-area (equivalent) projection.**

Eratosthenes Greek mathematician who, in 250 B.C., estimated the diameter of the earth using simple observations and geometric principles.

EROS Data Center U.S. Geological Survey facility in Sioux Falls, South Dakota, that serves as the national center for the processing and dissemination of photographic images and electronic data obtained from the Earth Resources Observation Systems (EROS) program and the National Aeronautics and Space Administration (NASA) program.

Escarpment Extensive line of marked difference in elevation.

ESIC *See* **Earth Science Information Centers.**

Estimated location Dead-reckoning location adjusted for the effects of winds and tides. Used if a locational fix cannot be obtained.

Exaggeration *See* **Locational shift and size exaggeration.**

Expected frequencies, table of Table that shows expected data combinations in the study area. Used in chi-square analysis.

Fall line Alignment, marked by waterfalls and rapids, where a river descends from an upland to a lowland.

False-color image In remote sensing, an image in which color bands are shifted away from the colors in the actual scene. For example, the green band may be reproduced in yellow, the red band in green, and the near-infrared band in red.

Fathom Nautical measurement that equals 6 feet (approximately 1.83 meters).

Fiducial marks Marks on an aerial photograph that are used to locate its principal point.

Fix Point of crossing of lines of position when plotted on a navigation chart, establishing the location of the vessel. *See also* **Line of position.**

Flight line A straight line between the principal point and the conjugate principal points on an aerial photograph. These are the consecutive points over which the airplane flew while the series of photographs was taken.

Flight plan Plan based on dead-reckoning procedures filed by aircraft crews prior to departure. Includes courses that will be flown, important landmarks, distances, estimated flying time, and altitude for each leg. In aerial photography, a flight path designed to provide the desired photographic coverage.

Floating-dial compass One of two primary types of hand-held, magnetic compasses that has a dial that is free to rotate within its housing.

Floating mark In a stereoplotter, a point of light that appears to be suspended over the stereomodel. Used to transfer locational information for both elevation (vertical) and planimetric (horizontal) features from the stereomodel to the manuscript map.

Floating-needle compass One of two primary types of hand-held, magnetic compasses that has a needle that is free to rotate within its housing.

Flood-control map Map that provides information about areas subject to flooding.

Flood-zone map Map showing zones subject to flooding under various conditions.

Flow map Map that uses quantitative linear symbols to represent connections or flows that exist between locations on the earth's surface.

Foot Unit of measurement in the U.S. Customary system, defined as 1:0.30480061 meter. Since 1959, also known as **U.S. survey foot.** *See also* **International foot.**

Forest Service, U.S. Department of Agriculture agency that publishes maps of national forests.

Form line A generalized contour frequently used on small-scale, less detailed maps.

Forward azimuth (azimuth) A directional designation. Usually measured in a clockwise direction from north.

GBF/DIME *See* **Geographic base file/dual independent map encoding.**

General chart Nautical chart for use when a vessel's course is well offshore but its position can be fixed by landmarks, lights, buoys, and characteristic soundings.

Generalization Process of adjusting the content of a map to provide as useful and recognizable a representation of the real world as is feasible within the map's space limits and scale.

Geocoding In computer-assisted cartography, assigning locational coordinates to map features based on an earth-based coordinate system, such as latitude/longitude, Universal Transverse Mercator, or State Plane Coordinates.

Geodetic control survey Detailed survey that takes into account the curvature of the earth and determines locations in terms of latitude and longitude. Used to provide the overall control, or framework, for mapping.

Geographical mile *See* **Nautical mile.**

Geographical north *See* **True north.**

Geographic base file/dual independent map encoding (GBF/DIME) files U.S. Bureau of the Census computerized records regarding addresses within urban areas. Supplanted by the TIGER system. *See also* **TIGER.**

Geographic information system (GIS) Spatial information system designed for data management, mapping, and analysis.

Geographic Names Information System (GNIS) U.S. Geological Survey digital index of standardized geographic names, as well as other information about the names.

Geoid Irregular shape of the surface of equigravitational potential of the earth.

Geological Survey, U.S. (USGS) Department of the Interior agency whose role is to gather, analyze, and make available information about the geological aspects of the United States. Probably the preeminent U.S. map producer.

Geologic map Map that provides information about the structure of the earth, such as types of rocks exposed at the earth's surface, types of bedrock that underlie the surface materials, aspects of the earth's thermal and magnetic characteristics, and many other characteristics.

GEOREF *See* **World Geographic Reference System.**

GIS *See* **Geographic information system.**

Glossary Table of definitions of specialized terms. Especially useful glossaries are those showing foreign-language designations for frequently encountered map features.

GNIS *See* **Geographic Names Information System.**

Gnomonic projection Map projection on a plane, with the light source at the center of the earth. All straight lines drawn on a gnomonic projection represent great circles.

Grad *See* **Centesimal system.**

Gradient (of a slope) Ratio between vertical distance (rise) and horizontal distance (run) on a slope.

Graduated circle Circular symbol whose area is proportional to the value of the data that it represents.

Graduated point symbol Map symbol used to indicate the value of the phenomenon (quantitative information) that occurs at a given location or within a given region.

Graph (network) Figure composed of points and lines.

Graphic scale Line drawn on a map whose length (and subdivisions) represents a specified distance on the earth.

Graph theory Method of analyzing the topology of a graph.

Graticule Pattern of meridians and parallels on the earth.

Great circle Line that is defined by the intersection of the earth's surface and a plane passing through the center of the earth.

Great-circle distance Shortest distance between two points on the earth's surface, represented by the path of a great circle.

Grid north The northerly direction of the lines of a locational grid, such as the Universal Transverse Mercator or State Plane Coordinate systems.

Grid-squares method Method of areal measurement using a superimposed, regular grid.

Grid tick Short line indicating the intersection of a grid or graticule line with the map neatline.

Ground control Known locations on the ground that are identifiable on an aerial photograph. Used for controlling the assembly of photomosaics or other aerial mapping processes.

Ground control points Easily identifiable points on the ground established to tie aerial photographs to ground surveys.

Ground resolution In remote sensing, the size of the area on the ground that is imaged at any one time. Determines the size of objects or areas that can be detected. *See* **Pixel.**

Guide meridian In U.S. Public Land Survey, north-south reference line established at 24-mile spacing.

Gyrocompass Nonmagnetic compass that indicates true north.

Harbor chart Nautical chart intended for navigation and anchorage in harbors and small waterways.

Hard copy Computer jargon meaning a tangible copy of computer information, including maps.

Hierarchic order In a branching network (tree), the level of importance of a segment (link).

High-low bar chart Diagram on which each bar represents a date or time and shows the high, low, and, sometimes, average values for the time period.

High-oblique aerial photograph Aerial photograph taken with the lens pointed at an angle away from the vertical so that the horizon is included in the image.

Highway map Map used for intercity road travel.

Hill shading (plastic shading) Gray values added to a map, as though illuminated by a northwest light source, so that the modeling of the surface is apparent.

Historical map Map produced in the past. Often provides useful insights into past knowledge and beliefs.

History map Modern map produced to show a situation from the past, including routes of exploration, battle diagrams, migration patterns, and many other topics.

Hogback Sharp-crested ridge formed by the eroded edge of steeply inclined strata.

Horizontal accuracy In National Map Accuracy Standards, accuracy of horizontal placement of well-defined points on the map.

Horizontal datum Starting elevation to which elevations on a map are referred.

Horn (matterhorn) Glacier-carved, pyramidal, rock pinnacle. Formed by the headward erosion of three or more cirques.

Hypsometric tints *See* **Layer tints.**

Illuminated contours Contours drawn as though illuminated by a northwest light source.

Image enhancement Computer-aided manipulations of remotely sensed data to improve the interpretation and classification of the image.

IMW *See* **International Map of the World.**

Independent variable The variable whose value is used to predict the value of a dependent variable.

Index contour Contour line that is accentuated and has elevation values inserted at intervals along its length.

Index map Base map showing outlines, and sheet numbers or names, of the sheets of a map series that are published or planned for publication. May be annotated to indicate the sheets that are in a map collection.

Index value An appropriate base period is selected, and index values are computed by dividing the individual data values by the base-period value and multiplying the results by 100.

Infrared emulsion In aerial photography, film emulsion that is sensitive to the infrared wavelengths. May be black-and-white or color.

Infrared wavelengths Wavelengths that fall outside the range of human vision. Particularly useful in remote sensing for the analysis of vegetation conditions and the identification of water bodies.

Inspection Process of orienting a map in the field by aligning recognizable features in the landscape with the same features on the map.

Instrument flight rules Rules that govern flights under conditions that prevent reliable visual contact and, therefore, require instruments to determine location, direction, and altitude.

Intermediate contour Contour line drawn in lighter line weight, usually without printed elevation values.

International Date Line Internationally accepted line, located near the 180th meridian, where one day ends and another day begins. The date line deviates from the meridian to avoid the occurrence of two different days of the week in a single nation.

International foot Defined as 1:0.3048 meter.

International Map of the World (IMW) Standardized, general-purpose map series of the world, at a scale of 1:1,000,000.

International nautical mile *See* **Nautical mile.**

Interpolation Method of logically determining the elevation of a point that is not on a contour or a spot height. Alternatively, method of determining the coordinates of a point not located on a grid or graticule line.

Interpretive key Logically organized listing of clues to assist a photo interpreter in the identification of features on an aerial photograph.

Interruption (of a map) Separation of a map projection along several dividing lines to show areas of particular interest (such as the continents or the oceans) with less distortion.

Interval scale Quantitative information that provides the exact value of some phenomenon on a standard scale with uniform intervals but an arbitrary zero value. For example, Celsius degrees.

Intervisibility Characteristic ascribed to two points that are mutually observable. Determined by the use of a profile.

Intracoastal waterway chart Nautical chart that provides coverage of the inside route from Miami to Key West, Florida, and from Tampa to Anclote Anchorage, Florida.

Isobar Line that joins points of equal barometric pressure.

Isobath *See* **Depth curve.**

Isogonic chart Map that shows magnetic declination.

Isogonic line Line on an isogonic chart that joins point of equal declination.

Isoline A line that joins points of equal value. *See also* **Isometric line** and **Isopleth.**

Isoline map A map that represents the values that occur on a surface by a series of lines that join points of equal value.

Isometric line An isoline based on values actually observed at control points located on a continuous surface.

Isopleth An isoline based on areal averages assigned to arbitrary control points that are not directly observable and are not located on a continuous surface.

Journalistic cartography Production of maps for use in newspapers, weekly newsmagazines, and general and popular weekly or monthly magazines.

Kendall's *Q* Statistic used in chi-square analysis to indicate the strength of the relationship between the variables in a 2-by-2 table.

Kettle Depression or lake formed in cavity left by melting of large fragments of ice lying within glacial debris.

Knot Speed of 1 nautical mile per hour.

Labeling In computer-assisted cartography, the process of attaching identification codes to the map elements.

Lacustrine plain Plain formerly occupied by lake bottom. Often formed behind terminal moraines.

Lambert conformal conic projection Map projection frequently used for midlatitude air charts because straight lines drawn on it closely approximate great-circle routes.

Landforms Topographic features on the surface of the earth.

Landsat Series of U.S. satellites in operation since 1972 that carry the multispectral scanner (MSS) and thematic mapper (TM) remote-sensing systems.

Landscape map Map that provides detailed site information and planting plans for gardens and parks.

Land survey A cadastral survey. In the United States, preferably used to describe such surveys outside the public lands.

Large scale Comparative term for map scale in which a relatively small area of the earth's surface is represented in considerable detail.

Latitude Angular measurement of north-south location, relative to the equator.

Latitude, line of *See* **Parallel.**

Layer tint (hypsometric tint) Tone or color used to fill in between contour lines or isobaths to indicate a zone of general elevation or water depth.

Leg In dead reckoning, the portion of a route traveled in a specific direction for a known length of time at a known speed.

Legal subdivision In the Canada Land Survey System, the division of a section into sixteen 40-acre subdivisions, which are the equivalent of quarter-quarter sections in the U.S. Public Land Survey.

Length, of a path In graph theory, the number of routes or links contained in a path between two nodes.

Lensatic compass A type of hand-held, floating-dial, magnetic compass.

Levee Elevated ridge along the bank of a stream. Natural levees result from the deposition of materials during floods. Man-made levees are built to constrain a stream during flood stage.

Leveling Method of establishing elevations relative to a starting level, or datum.

Library of Congress The Geography and Map Division maintains the largest and most comprehensive cartographic collection in the world.

Library of Congress system Commonly used map cataloging system. Maps are classified under Class G.

Linear cartogram Maplike diagram (also called a distance-transformation map or distance cartogram) designed to show relative distances, based on such measures as cost or time.

Linear contrast stretching Image enhancement of remotely sensed data that expands the range of tones so that they are easier to differentiate.

Linear interpolation On a contour map, logical method of estimating the unknown elevation of a point that falls between contours. Based on the assumption that the slope between contours is constant.

Linear symbol Map symbol used to represent a feature that has a linear path on the earth's surface.

Line graph Diagram consisting of a line or lines joining points plotted on a grid. Shows the value of one variable relative to the value of another.

Line plotter Computer output device that draws an image using continuous lines in the manner of traditional drafting.

Line of position Observation of known locations or alignments (ranges) by navigators operating within sight of land to monitor the location of their vessel. An application of the method of resection.

Line-route map Specialized cadastral map used by utility companies to show transmission line or pipeline routes and rights-of-way.

Link (route) In graph theory, a connecting line between two places, or nodes.

Locational shift and size exaggeration A means of map generalization in which the size of features is exaggerated to assure their visibility and their location is shifted to accommodate the larger-than-scale size.

Logarithmic scale On a line graph, a scale in which equal distances indicate the same percentage change in value.

Log-log graph Line graph that uses logarithmic scales on both axes. The shapes of lines plotted on the graph reflect percentage rates of change in both variables.

Longitude, line of *See* **Meridian.**

Loran Navigational, position-determination system based on radio transmission travel times from pairs of master and slave broadcast locations.

Lorenz curve *See* **Accumulative line graph.**

Loss-and-gain bar chart Bar chart with a central axis that serves as a zero line. Bars drawn on one side of the axis represent positive values (gains), and those on the other side represent negative values (losses).

Lot In U.S. Public Land Survey, subdivisions used when the normal system of fractional sections cannot be applied, such as along the northern and western edges of some townships, or along the shores of navigable streams or lakes 25 acres or more in extent.

Low-contrast image Remotely sensed image in which the values of the pixels fall in a relatively narrow range so that variations in the image's gray tones are difficult to discern.

Low-oblique aerial photograph Aerial photograph taken with the lens pointed at an angle away from the vertical, but not including the horizon.

Machine coordinates In computer-assisted cartography, locational coordinates of map features based on measurements (in inches or centimeters) from a control point, such as the corner of the digitizing board.

Magnetic declination The difference between true north and magnetic north at any given location.

Magnetic north The direction to the north magnetic pole.

Map inaccuracy Introduction of various errors into map products, which makes them less reliable sources of information.

Map measurer Instrument with tracing wheel. Used for measuring the length of curved or irregular lines.

Map orientation Alignment of a map so that the mapped features are in the proper relationship to the landscape.

Map-overlay analysis Technique that involves tracing and overlaying the outlines of variables of interest. Overlap of the areas shows the relationship between the phenomena mapped.

Mapping and Charting Establishment, Department of National Defence (Canada) Agency responsible for topographic surveying and mapping for defense purposes in Canada.

Map Reference Code (USGS) System by which a USGS quadrangle is identified based on the latitude and longitude of the southeast corner of the one-degree square quadrilateral in which it falls, and its location with that quadrilateral.

Map projection Systematic rendering on a flat sheet of paper of the earth's graticule (lines of latitude and longitude).

Matterhorn *See* **Horn.**

Maximum slope limitation Maximum permissible slope for a route. Established because of the limited capabilities of the equipment to be used.

Mean datum Vertical datum that averages long-term tidal variations.

Meander Sinuous route of a stream that is near grade.

Meander line In U.S. Public Land Survey, line surveyed along the mean high-water elevation of a navigable water body.

Mean solar time The average length of the day throughout the year. Equal to 24 hours. Required because the earth's speed on its elliptically shaped orbit varies, resulting in apparent solar days of different length from one part of the year to another.

Mental maps Generalized mental images of the physical world.

Mercator projection Conformal map projection that shows the world (less the polar regions) in a rectangular format. Useful for navigational purposes because all straight lines drawn on it are lines of constant compass direction.

Meridian Portion of a meridian circle located between the North and South Poles. Used to specify east-west location. A line of longitude. Meridians are spaced farthest apart on the equator and converge to a single point at the poles. Meridians and parallels are at right angles to one another.

Meridian circle Great circle that passes through the poles of rotation. *See also* **Meridian**.

Mesa Flat-topped, elevated feature similar to, but less extensive than, a plateau.

Meter Basic unit of measurement of the metric system. Originally defined as one ten-millionth of the great-circle distance from the earth's equator to the earth's pole. Since 1983, defined as the distance that light travels in 1/299,792,458 of a second.

Metes-and-bounds surveying Method of land survey used to describe unsystematic land ownerships. Records the direction and length of each portion of the boundary line of the property in sequence, often using distinctive markers, such as trees of particular species.

Metonic cycle Period of 18.6 years during which the complete cycle of relationships between the sun, moon, and earth evolves. Time period observed for the establishment of an accurate mean elevation datum.

Metric system System of measurement originally defined by the French Academy of Sciences in 1791.

Mile *See* **Statute mile** and **Nautical mile**.

Mileage table (distance log) Table consisting of columns of mileages between major locations.

Miller cylindrical projection Map projection drawn on a cylinder showing the world in a rectangular format. Distorts the size of areas less than does the Mercator.

Miller's measure Measure of shape based on the ratio between the area of a region and the area of a circle with the same perimeter as the region.

Modeling In digital geographic information systems, a logical sequence of analytical operations used to produce information, for example, regarding the alternative outcomes that would result from different courses of action.

Monument (survey) Plaque placed at survey control point to designate location and/or elevation.

MSS *See* **Multispectral scanner**.

Multiple-scale graph Diagram on which a separate scale is used to represent changes in each of two or more variables.

Multispectral device Remote-sensing device that simultaneously records radiation in two or more separate wavelength bands. For example, Landsat.

Multispectral scanner (MSS) Four-band, whisk-broom, remote-sensing system, with ground resolution of 79 by 79 meters, carried by Landsat.

Multivariate map A map that shows the relationships between the values of three or more variables at once.

Narrow-band device Remote-sensing device that uses a sensor that receives electromagnetic energy within a limited range of frequencies. For example, radar.

NASA *See* **National Aeronautics and Space Administration, U.S.**

National Aeronautics and Space Administration, U.S. (NASA) Agency that produces a variety of aerial photographs and spacecraft imagery (available from the EROS Data Center) from its space programs.

National Archives *See* **National Archives and Records Service, U.S.**

National Archives and Records Service, U.S. (National Archives) Agency that maintains a collection that includes 2 million maps and 100,000 aerial photographs produced by federal agencies.

National Defence, Department of, (Canada) *See* **Mapping and Charting Establishment, Department of National Defence**

National Environmental Satellite, Data, and Information Service, U.S. (NESDIS) Agency that maintains national environmental data and manages U.S. civil meteorological and land remote-sensing satellite systems.

National Geodetic Information Center U.S. agency that provides information regarding the horizontal and vertical control networks established by the National Geodetic Survey and other federal and state agencies.

National Geographical Mapping Program (Canada) Program that provides geographical and spatially-referenced information about the natural environment and the cultural make-up of Canada, at the federal government level.

National Map Accuracy Standards U.S. standards for evaluation of accuracy of vertical and horizontal locations on large-scale maps.

National Ocean Service, U.S. (NOS) Component of the National Oceanic and Atmospheric Administration (NOAA), U.S. Department of Commerce. Produces many types of maps, especially aeronautical and nautical charts and hydrographic surveys.

National Park Service, U.S. (NPS) Agency that produces topographic maps and visitors' maps and guides for the national parks and monuments.

National Topographic System of Canada Canadian government topographic maps, produced at scales of 1:1,000,000, 1:250,000, and 1:50,000. 1:250,000-scale maps provide complete topographic coverage of the country, including detailed representation of relief, drainage, transportation, forest cover, and centers of population.

National Weather Service, U.S. The National Meteorological Center of the National Weather Service produces climatic and weather maps.

Natural bridge Arch created by sideward erosion of a stone ridge.

Nautical chart A special map used for navigation at sea.

Nautical mile Unit of measurement used for measuring distances at sea. The former U.S. nautical mile (or geographical mile) measured 6,080.2 feet (1,853.24 meters), and the British

admiralty nautical mile equaled 6,080 feet (1,853.18 meters). The international nautical mile, established in 1959, equals 1,852 meters (6,076.12 feet).

NAVSTAR Global Positioning System (GPS) Navigational, position-determination system that depends on the time delay of signals transmitted from satellites.

NCIC *See* **National Cartographic Information Center (NCIC)**.

Nearest-neighbor analysis Point pattern measure based on comparison of the mean of the distances observed between each point and its nearest neighbor with the expected mean distance that would occur if the distribution were random.

Neatline The outline at which map detail terminates.

Negative In photography, an image on transparent film in which objects with a high level of energy reflection are recorded as dark images and those that reflect little energy appear as transparent areas.

NESDIS *See* **National Environmental Satellite, Data, and Information Service (NESDIS)**.

Network In general, a set of geographic locations interconnected in a system by a number of routes. In graph theory, a figure composed of points and lines.

Newberry Library Library that specializes in materials in the humanities, including a research collection in the history of cartography.

Node (place) In graph theory, a location.

Nominal areal symbol Map symbol that represents only the type or category and the location of some phenomenon.

Nominal linear symbol Map symbol used to indicate only the type or category and the alignment of some phenomenon.

Nominal measurement Qualitative information that divides a group into subgroups, with no implication that one subgroup is more or less important than another.

Noncontiguous cartogram Area cartogram that retains shapes by separating regions from one another.

Nonproportional point symbol Map symbol used to indicate only the type or category and the location of some phenomenon.

Nonspatial information system An information system that deals with data that have no locational component.

Nonsymmetric, nonplanar network Network with one-way connections in which a place where two or more routes (links) meet is not necessarily a connecting point (node).

Nonsymmetric, planar network Network with one-way connections in which every place where two or more routes (links) meet is a connecting point (node).

Normal orientation (of a projection surface) Commonly accepted standard arrangement of the projection surface relative to the globe. Normal orientations include the following: in cylindrical projections, the cylinder is tangent along the equator; in conic projections, the cone is tangent along a parallel, with its apex over the pole; and in azimuthal projections, the plane is tangent at the pole.

North Pole One of the earth's poles of rotation.

NOS *See* **National Ocean Service, U.S.**

NOTAM *See* **Notice to Airmen.**

Notice to Airmen (NOTAM) Publication of the Federal Aviation Administration (FAA) that provides up-to-date information about changed aeronautical navigational aids.

Notice to Mariners Weekly publication of the Defense Mapping Agency Hydrographic/Topographic Center (DMAHTC) that provides information needed to update nautical charts. Local notices are also published, as required, by U.S. Coast Guard District Offices.

NPS *See* **National Park Service, U.S.**

Null hypothesis Statement that there is no relationship between variables. If the null hypothesis can be rejected, some relationship exists.

Oblique aerial photograph Aerial photograph taken with the lens pointed at an angle away from the vertical. High obliques include the horizon; low obliques do not.

Oblique orientation (of a projection surface) Alignment of a projection surface at an angle somewhere between the normal and the transverse positions.

Observed frequencies, table of Used in chi-square analysis, table shows actual relationships between two variables in the study area.

100-year flood Level of flooding that has one chance in one hundred of being equaled or exceeded in any 1-year period.

Ordinal measurement Quantitative information classified on the basis of comparative values only (greater than, less than).

Orientation (of a projection surface) Arrangement of the projection surface relative to the globe. *See also* **Normal, Transverse, and Oblique orientations.**

Orienteering compass A type of hand-held, floating-needle, magnetic compass.

Orthodrome The direction of a great circle. Also known as the true azimuth.

Orthographic projection Map projection made with light source positioned at infinity.

Orthographic view View drawn as though every point were seen from directly overhead, such as a map.

Orthophoto Aerial photograph processed to remove the effect of planimetric shift. An orthophotograph has correct scale throughout.

Orthophotomap U.S. Geological Survey product, with same scale (1:24,000), coverage (7.5 minutes of latitude and longitude), and locational grids (Universal Transverse Mercator and State Plane Coordinates) as a regular quadrangle map. Color-enhanced orthophoto image with added contour lines and feature names.

Orthophotoquad U.S. Geological Survey product, with same scale (1:24,000), coverage (7.5 minutes of latitude and longitude), and locational grids (Universal Transverse Mercator and State Plane Coordinates) as a regular quadrangle map. Orthophoto image, printed in black and white, without contours.

Outline map Map that provides a framework for plotting information.

Output In computer-assisted cartography, the production of data.

Overlay analysis As used in computation of coefficient of areal correspondence, two distributions are mapped at the same scale, and the outline of one overlies the outline of the other.

Overlaying In digital geographic information systems, the digital equivalent of map-overlay analysis. Used for determining areas of overlap between categories on various data planes.

Oxbow lake Lake formed in a cut-off remnant of the changing river channel of a meandering stream.

Panchromatic emulsion Black-and-white photographic emulsion that is sensitive to a range of wavelengths within the electromagnetic spectrum similar to that seen by the human eye.

Parallax Difference in viewpoint of one eye versus the other, which results in a three-dimensional, stereoscopic image.

Parallel Set of locational lines used to specify location north or south of the equator. Parallels are true east-west lines, equally spaced between the equator and the poles, and always parallel to one another, so any two parallels are always the same distance apart. Parallels and meridians are at right angles to one another.

Passive remote-sensing system A remote-sensing system that relies on the detection of naturally generated energy that is either reflected or emitted by an object. For example, aerial photography.

Path In graph theory, a series of routes linking a series of places, or nodes.

Percent (of a slope) Vertical distance (rise) per 100 units of horizontal distance (run) on a slope.

Percentage scale In a graph, each unit of distance represents an equal percentage range.

Permanent Committee on Geographical Names *See* **Canadian Permanent Committee on Geographical Names.**

Perspective view View of a scene from a single viewpoint, such as an aerial photograph.

Peters projection Equal-area projection promoted for use in thematic mapping, despite its shortcomings in terms of shapes.

Photographic-overlay analysis Method of map-overlay analysis, developed by Ian McHarg in the late 1960s, aimed at finding "the solution of maximum social utility" for land-use applications.

Photo interpretation Recognition and identification, using aerial photographs, of the natural and man-made features on the earth's surface.

Photomosaic Composite image formed by piecing adjoining aerial photographs together to cover a larger area.

Physical model Three-dimensional model of the earth's surface.

Physiographic diagram Pictorial representation of the earth's surface, from an elevated, oblique point of view, using stylized representations of the various types of relief features.

Pie chart Circular diagram that is subdivided into proportional segments.

Pixel In remote sensing, small portion of an image that contains information about a specified area on the ground.

Place (node) In graph theory, a location.

Plan Detailed, large-scale map of a limited area.

Plane Flat surface used for azimuthal projections.

Plane of the ecliptic *See* **Ecliptic, plane of the.**

Plane rectangular grid (reference grid) System of lines superimposed on a map for locational purposes that does not take the curvature of the earth's surface into account.

Plane survey Survey of limited extent conducted without taking the earth's curvature into account. Contrast with **Geodetic control survey.**

Planimetric map Map that does not show relief features in measurable form.

Planimetric shift Variation in the planimetric location of objects in an aerial photograph due to differences in elevation. Results in scale variations within the photograph.

Plastic shading *See* **Hill shading.**

Plat Detailed map of a land subdivision.

Plateau Elevated feature formed when a relatively horizontal, resistant rock layer is gradually eroded and less resistant materials are removed more rapidly from its edges, leaving an escarpment on at least one side.

Pocket transit A type of hand-held, floating-needle, magnetic compass with degrees printed in a counterclockwise direction around a fixed housing.

Point symbol Map symbol used to represent a feature that occurs at a single location (point) on the earth's surface.

Polar flattening The result of the polar diameter of the earth being less than the equatorial diameter, due to the rotation of the earth on its axis. Amounts to about one part in 298, which is very close to a sphere.

Polaris Northern Hemisphere star, almost exactly overhead at the North Pole, that provides an excellent point of reference for determining latitude.

Polar planimeter Instrument that measures areas on a map.

Poles of rotation Location of points at which the earth's axis meets the surface (North Pole and South Pole). Poles provide the starting point for the system of latitude and longitude.

Polygon method Method of areal measurement based on subdividing area to be measured into regular geometric figures.

Population profile A graphic display of the age-sex distribution of a given region's population.

Population pyramid *See* **Population profile**.

Positive In photography, a print or transparency, usually made from a photographic negative, in which the areas in the original scene that reflect high levels of energy are light in tone and those that reflect little energy are dark in tone.

Preprocessing Computer-aided manipulations of the original remotely sensed data. Typically done prior to release of the data to the user.

Prime meridian Starting line for measurements of east and west longitude. On most modern maps, the prime meridian is the meridian of Greenwich, England.

Principal meridian North-south reference line used in a U.S. Public Land Survey zone.

Principal point Location on the ground at which an aerial camera is pointed. In a vertical photograph, coincides with the geometric center of the photograph. Located by joining the fiducial marks on the photograph.

Prism map A map drawn from an elevated oblique viewpoint that shows each region raised above the base level an amount proportional to the value, in that region, of the variable being mapped.

Profile Cross-sectional view through the terrain.

Propaganda Deliberate introduction of misleading information into map products.

Proportionality The comparison of the size of a reference feature on the map to the size of the same feature on the earth (or on a map of known scale).

Pseudoscopic effect In stereoscopic viewing of aerial photographs, the effect that causes hills to look like valleys and valleys to look like hills. Created when the photographs are oriented with shadows falling away from the viewer.

Psychological scaling Method of sizing proportional circles so that the symbols representing larger quantities are exaggerated in size, rather than being drawn in absolute proportion. Designed to offset a common tendency to underestimate the values represented by larger circles.

Public Land Survey, U.S. (systematic subdivision) Method of land survey, utilizing townships and ranges. Started in Ohio and ultimately extended throughout most of the western states and parts of the south. Originally known as the rectangular survey system.

Push-broom scanning In remote-sensing system, scanner that scans along the satellite's direction of movement.

Quadrangle Individual map sheet laid out as a four-sided figure bounded by lines of latitude and longitude.

Quadrat analysis Point pattern measure based on frequency count of points occurring within a superimposed grid (quadrats).

Quantitative areal symbol Map symbol used to indicate the magnitude of the phenomenon (quantitative information) occurring in a given region.

Quantitative linear symbol Map symbol used to indicate the alignment and magnitude (quantitative information) of the connection or flow that exists between locations on the earth's surface.

Radar An active remote-sensing technique involving the transmission, reflection, and detection of radio waves in the microwave wavelengths.

Radar image Remotely sensed image from a radar unit.

Radial drainage pattern Drainage pattern that results when streams flow away from (centrifugal) or toward (centripetal) a central point.

Radio direction finding Navigational, position-determination system that uses directional information obtained from radio signals.

Radio-type altimeter Altimeter that provides direct information about the absolute altitude of the aircraft above the earth's surface, instead of above sea level.

Random pattern Pattern in which a phenomenon is equally likely to occur at any location and in which the position of any point is not affected by the position of any other point.

Range In U.S. Public Land Survey and Canada Land Survey System, 6-mile-wide, north-south zone. In navigation, alignment of two known objects. *See also* **Line of position.**

Range-graded symbol Set of symbols, such as circles, in which each size represents a particular range of values.

Rapids Section of stream with swift current and interspersed with rocks and boulders.

Raster digitizing In computer-assisted cartography, digitizing map features on the basis of their presence or absence in a myriad of tiny cells (rasters).

Raster output In computer-assisted cartography, an image produced by creating a pattern of dots.

Raster plotter A computer output device that prints an image in the form of a pattern of dots.

Ratio measurement Quantitative information that provides the exact value of some phenomenon on a standard scale that has uniform intervals and a real (nonarbitrary) zero value. For example, distance in meters.

Realistic figures Symbols drawn in recognizable form, used instead of geometric figures to represent data values.

Real map Any tangible map product that has a permanent form and can be directly viewed.

Reclassification In digital geographic information systems, the replacement of the initial category designations on a data plane with new values based on specified criteria.

Rectangular drainage pattern Drainage pattern that results when tributaries join streams at approximately right angles.

Rectangular survey system *See* **Public Land Survey, U.S.**

Rectification In computer-assisted cartography and digital geographic information systems, the process of aligning the various data planes with one another.

Rectified print Aerial photographic print specially processed to correct irregularities due to tilt and variations in the altitude of the aircraft.

Reference grid *See* **Plane rectangular grid.**

Remotely sensed image Image gathered by means of a sensor that is not in contact with the objects in the scene being observed. Includes aerial photographs, images from radar and other airborne sensors, and satellite images.

Remote-sensing system Active or passive system that gathers information by means of sensors that are not in contact with the object being detected.

Representative fraction (RF) Expression of map scale as a ratio or fraction.

Resection Method of determining one's location by reference to three known features on the ground.

Rhumb line (constant azimuth) A directional line that crosses each succeeding meridian at a constant angle.

Rise Vertical distance between two points on a slope.

Road atlas Bound volume containing highway and/or street maps.

Robinson projection Compromise world map projection designed to minimize visually disturbing distortions of many world projections.

Roture Lot allocated to an individual farmer in the seigneurial land ownership system of French Canada.

Route (link) In graph theory, a connecting line between two places, or nodes.

Routed linear cartogram Maplike diagram that shows characteristics of specific paths from one point to another, such as average travel time.

Route map Map that provides information regarding bus, train, subway, or airline routes.

Run Horizontal distance between two points on a slope.

Sailing chart Nautical chart for offshore sailing between distant coastal ports and for approaching the coast from the open ocean.

Sand hills Area of stable sand dunes.

Sand spit Linear deposit of sand attached to shoreline at one or both ends.

Satellite image Remotely sensed image captured by instruments taken aloft in spacecraft, with or without a human crew.

Scale Ratio of the distance between two points on a map and the earth distance between the same two points.

Scale conversion Transforming a map scale from one form to another, such as from graphic to representative fraction.

Scanner Passive remote-sensing device that detects and records energy reflected or emitted from objects within its range. May be mounted on aircraft or space platforms.

Scatter diagram Graph used to display the relationship between two variables. Consists of a set of points plotted on the basis of paired, x- and y-values.

SCS *See* **Soil Conservation Service, U.S.**

Section In U.S. Public Land Survey and Canada Land Survey System, 1-square-mile (640-acre) subdivision of a township.

Sectional charts Aeronautical chart series, based on the Lambert conformal conic projection, with scale of 1:500,000.

Seigneur Nobleman, yeoman, or farmer who received a seigneurial land grant in exchange for promoting settlement and development.

Seigneury Seventeenth century French land grant in the region that is now Quebec and the Maritime provinces except Newfoundland. Granted for the purpose of promoting settlement and development.

Selection Means of map generalization in which the more important features in an area are retained and the less important ones are eliminated.

Semilogarithmic graph Line graph on which a logarithmic scale is used on one axis (usually the y-axis) and an arithmetic scale is used on the other. The shapes of lines plotted on the graph reflect rates of change in the variable plotted.

Semilog graph *See* **Semilogarithmic graph.**

Sexagesimal system Coordinate system in which the circle is divided into 360 degrees. Each degree is divided into 60 minutes and each minute into 60 seconds.

Shift *See* **Locational shift and size exaggeration.**

Signal source The origin of a signal that is detected by a remote-sensing system.

Signature Characteristic electromagnetic radiation pattern associated with a source object.

Silhouette graph Line graph on which the area below the curve is shaded or colored to give a silhouette effect.

Simplification Means of map generalization in which the shapes of the features retained on the map are presented in simplified form.

Sink Solution feature, often in limestone, resulting from the collapse of the roof of an underground stream or cavern.

Slope error Variation in horizontal distance introduced by surface undulations. The surface distance between two objects is longer than the map distance, except where the ground surface is perfectly flat.

Slope-zone map Map showing, by means of coloring or shading, areas of relatively similar slopes.

Small circles Circles created when a plane passing through the earth divides the earth into two unequal portions. Small circles parallel to the equator are called lines of latitude, or parallels.

Small scale Comparative term for map in which a generalized representation of a relatively large area of the earth's surface is shown in a relatively small space.

Smoothing Simplification of irregular lines because of generalization.

Soil Conservation Service, U.S. (SCS) U.S. Department of Agriculture agency that publishes maps of soil surveys.

Soundings Water depths at given points, printed on a hydrographic chart.

Spacing dividers Eleven-point dividers used for measuring interpolated locations.

Spatial (or geographic) information system An information system that allows each piece of data to be tied to some type of locational reference system.

SPC *See* **State Plane Coordinate system.**

Spectral range The range of wavelengths used by a remote-sensing device (broad-band, narrow-band, or multispectral).

Sphere Regular solid formed by the rotation of a circle on one of its diameters. A less-satisfactory approximation of the shape of the earth than an ellipsoid.

SPOT Push-broom remote-sensing system that carries sensors that operate in either panchromatic or three-band multispectral modes. Ground resolution is 10 by 10 meters in panchromatic mode and 20 by 20 meters in multispectral mode. *See also* **SPOT Image Corporation.**

Spot height Point symbol used to indicate the location to which an elevation value refers.

SPOT Image Corporation French, Belgian, and Swedish government consortium that operates a satellite observation system called "Systeme Probatoire d'Observation de la Terre" (SPOT).

Spring Flow of water issuing from the earth.

Standard parallel In U.S. Public Land Survey, east-west reference line established at 24-mile spacing. In normally oriented conic or cylindrical map projections, the parallel of intersection of the projection surface with the globe.

State Plane Coordinate System (SPCS) Plane rectangular coordinate system that is individually applied to zones in each state in the United States.

Statistical reports In digital geographic information systems, the production of statistical information from the data base.

Statistical surface Imaginary surface representing differences in the value of a nonphysical variable over a region.

Statute mile Unit of measurement in the U.S. Customary system. Defined as 5,280 feet (1,069.35 meters).

Stereographic projection Map projection made with light source positioned at the antipode (the point exactly opposite the point of tangency of the projection surface).

Stereomodel Apparent three-dimensional view of the terrain, as viewed in a stereoplotter.

Stereo pair *See* **Stereoscopic pair.**

Stereoplotter Plotting device that uses a stereoscopic image for the transfer of map information from aerial photographs.

Stereoscope Simple instrument that permits the simultaneous viewing of a stereo pair of aerial photographs so that the desired three-dimensional effect is achieved.

Stereoscopic image Three-dimensional image (especially of aerial photographs) seen through viewer that allows one eye to view one photograph and the other eye to see another, taken from a slightly different location.

Stereoscopic pair (stereo pair) Two adjacent aerial photographs showing the same scene from slightly different points of view. Used for stereoscopic (three-dimensional) viewing.

Stereoscopic viewing Method of looking at a stereo pair of aerial photographs through a stereoscope. Results in an apparently three-dimensional view of the scene.

Stilling basin Basin cut off from the direct influence of wind and waves used in the establishment of mean sea level.

Strahler method Method of assigning hierarchic order to the segments (links) in a branching network (tree).

Street map Map showing the road layout within a city.

Strike In geology, the compass bearing of the intersection of the surface of a bed or stratum with an imaginary horizontal plane.

Strip method Method of areal measurement using superimposed series of parallel lines.

Summer solstice Moment when the noon sun is directly overhead on the Tropic of Cancer.

Supplementary contour Additional contour, usually dashed or dotted, drawn between intermediate and index contours at intervals that are some regular fraction of the basic contour interval. Used to provide additional information in areas of flat terrain.

Surface Variation in elevation representing differences in the value of a (physical or statistical) variable over a region.

Surface graph Diagram on which values are expressed as spaces, or bands, between the lines on the graph.

Surveys, Mapping and Remote Sensing Sector, Department of Energy, Mines and Resources (Canada) Canada's principal topographic mapping agency. The agency's Topographic Mapping Division produces maps at scales ranging from 1:1,000,000 to 1:25,000.

Symbol distortion The introduction of exaggerated, often simplistic, symbols into map products for propaganda purposes.

Symmetric, nonplanar network Network with two-way connections, in which a place where two or more routes (links) meet is not necessarily a connecting point (node).

Symmetric, planar network Network with two-way connections, in which every place where two or more routes (links) meet is a connecting point (node).

Synoptic hours Times at which weather information is recorded by the worldwide network of reporting stations: 0000, 0600, 1200, and 1800 Greenwich Mean Time.

Systematic subdivision *See* **Public Land Survey, U.S.**

Table of expected frequencies *See* **Expected frequencies, table of.**

Table of observed frequencies *See* **Observed frequencies, table of.**

Tabular index An alphabetically or numerically ordered list of the sheet numbers or names of the sheets of a map series that are published or are planned for publication. May be annotated to indicate the sheets that are in a map collection.

Tangency (of a projection surface) Point or line at which the projection surface and the globe touch.

Tarn Small lake located in a cirque.

Tectonic activity Movement of the earth's crust.

Television map Map used in conjunction with television broadcasts. Often highly generalized.

Tennessee Valley Authority (TVA) Agency that produces topographic, land-use, navigation, and recreation maps of the area within its jurisdiction.

Terminal moraine Deposit of eroded material at the margin of furthest advance of a glacier.

Texture of dissection Describes the relative fineness of a stream pattern.

Thematic information extraction Image enhancement of remotely sensed data that provides information about conditions on the earth's surface.

Thematic map Map that shows information about a special topic, often statistical in nature.

Thematic mapper (TM) Seven-band, whisk-broom, remote-sensing system, with resolution of 30 by 30 meters, carried by Landsats 4 and 5.

Tick *See* **Grid tick.**

TIGER *See* **Topologically Integrated Geographic Encoding and Reference System.**

Till Unsorted deposit of glacial debris, including clay, sand, gravel, and boulders.

Time zones The twenty-four zones, each spanning 15 degrees of longitude, into which the earth is divided. All localities within a zone keep the same time as the zone's central (time) meridian. Zonal boundaries are adjusted to follow political boundaries or to fall in less-populated areas.

T-in-O map Medieval map that was not a literal representation of the true size and shape of the earth, but a stylized presentation used to support prevalent religious views.

Topographic map Map that shows the shape and elevation of the terrain.

Topography Configuration of the surface of the earth.

Topological distance In graph theory, the length of the shortest path (number of routes or links) between two places, or nodes.

Topologically Integrated Geographic Encoding and Reference System (TIGER) U.S. Bureau of the Census digital geographic and cartographic data file being developed for the 1990 Census of Population and future census operations. Supplanting the GBF/DIME system.

Topological positions Abstract relationships between the elements of a graph.

Toponym A geographical name.

Township Six-mile-wide, east-west zone in U.S. Public Land Survey and Canada Land Survey System. Also, 36-square-mile area formed by the intersection of an east-west township and a north-south range.

Township plat Detailed map of the land-ownership boundaries within a U.S. Public Land Survey township.

Trafficability The ability of an area to support vehicles of a specific type.

Transit system Navigational, position-determination system that depends upon the Doppler effect on satellite radio transmissions.

Transliteration Conversion of characters in a source language into one or more Roman letters.

Transparency *See* **Positive.**

Transverse Mercator projection Conformal map projection. Frequently used for topographical maps.

Transverse orientation (of a projection surface) Arrangement of the projection surface (relative to the globe) that is turned 90 degrees from normal.

Tree (branching network) In graph theory, a network that does not contain circuits (loops).

Trellis drainage pattern Drainage pattern that results when streams are arranged in a pattern of parallel tributaries.

Trend line Straight line superimposed over the cloud of dots on a scatter diagram representing the direction and strength of the relationship between the variables.

Triangle of error Triangle formed by failure of back-azimuth lines to intersect exactly during determination of location by resection.

Triangular graph Graphic display plotted on an equilateral triangle to show the mixture of three components of some total quantity.

Triangulation network Surveyed network established by measuring the angles between the baseline and additional observation points.

Trilateration network Surveyed network that serves the same purpose as a triangulation network. Based on measurement of distances, instead of angles.

True azimuth The direction of a great circle. Also known as an orthodrome.

True north (geographical north) The direction to the geographical north pole, along a line of longitude.

TVA *See* **Tennessee Valley Authority.**

Unclassed choropleth map A type of choropleth map that utilizes a separate symbol for each value represented. That is, the values are not classified or grouped.

Uncontrolled photomosaic Mosaic of aerial photos assembled without reference to ground control.

Underwater contour Contour that represents the land surface that was exposed before an area was flooded. Differs from **Depth curve**.

Uniform pattern Pattern in which every point is as far from all of its neighbors as possible.

Univariate map A map that shows the distribution of the values of a single variable.

Universal Polar Stereographic (UPS) grid system Plane rectangular grid system that covers the polar caps, north of 84° north and south of 80° south. Used in conjunction with the Universal Transverse Mercator (UTM) system, which covers the rest of the world. Civilian system uses only numbers, while U.S. Military Grid Reference System uses number/letter combinations to designate grid zones.

Universal Transverse Mercator (UTM) grid system Plane rectangular grid system that covers the earth's surface between 80° south and 84° north. Used in conjunction with the Universal Polar Stereographic (UPS) system, which covers the polar caps. Civilian system uses only numbers, while U.S. Military Grid Reference System uses number/letter combinations to designate grid zones.

Unsystematic subdivision Land-ownership pattern developed in an unplanned manner, using, for example, property boundaries established on the basis of settlers' claims.

U.S. Board on Geographic Names *See* **Board on Geographic Names**.

U.S. Customary Units Units of measurement, such as feet, inches, and miles, based on the units of the older English system.

USDA *See* **Department of Agriculture, U.S.**

USGS *See* **Geological Survey, U.S.**

U-shaped valley Typical valley profile resulting from glacial action.

U.S. National Map Accuracy Standards *See* **National Map Accuracy Standards**.

U.S. nautical mile *See* **Nautical mile**.

USPLS *See* **Public Land Survey, U.S.**

U.S. survey foot Defined as 1:0.30480061 meter.

Value-by-area cartogram *See* **Area cartogram**.

Variance As used in quadrat analysis, the variance compares the number of points in each grid cell with the average number of points over all of the cells.

Vector digitizing In computer-assisted cartography, digitizing map features on the basis of the coordinates of points or, in the case of linear features or the outlines of areas, a series of points.

Vertical accuracy In National Map Accuracy Standards, accuracy of designated elevation of well-defined points on the map.

Vertical aerial photograph Aerial photograph taken with the camera pointed as nearly perpendicular to the earth's surface as possible.

Vertical exaggeration Ratio between the vertical earth distance represented by a unit of map distance and the horizontal earth distance represented by the same measurement.

Virtual map Image that can be directly viewed but is not permanent, such as a map image on the screen of a cathode-ray tube (CRT), a mental map image, or information gathered by researchers in the field or by remote-sensing methods.

Visible spectrum That portion of the electromagnetic spectrum detected by the human eye.

Visual flight rules The simplest type of rules, governing flights under favorable weather conditions, in which visual references to landmarks can be used to reliably control the operation of the plane.

Volcanic cone Distinctive, often symmetrical, conical feature formed by the deposition of volcanic material.

Volumetric diagrams Apparently solid, three-dimensional figure, drawn so that the volume of each figure is proportional to the value it represents.

V-shaped valley Typical valley profile resulting from stream erosion.

WAC *See* **World Aeronautical Chart**.

Water gap Narrow notch in a ridge, through which the river has maintained its flow.

Weather map Standard weather map used for forecasting purposes. Depicts a wide range of information regarding the status of the weather at a specific time.

Whisk-broom scanning movement In remote-sensing system, oscillating mirror scanner that sweeps across the satellite's direction of movement.

Wind gap Narrow notch in a ridge through which the river has not maintained its flow.

Wind-rose Circular graph that shows the average frequency and direction of wind at one location over a given period of time.

Word statement (of map scale) Statement of scale ratio in words.

World Aeronautical Charts (WAC) Aeronautical chart series, with 1:1,000,000 scale, based on the Lambert conformal conic projection.

World Data Banks Two frequently used worldwide databases that contain data about coastlines, national boundaries, and place names. World Data Bank II, which is more detailed, also contains data about major rivers and national, state, and province boundaries.

World Geographic Reference System (GEOREF) System, primarily used for military air operations, that designates latitude and longitude by a simple set of letters and numbers.

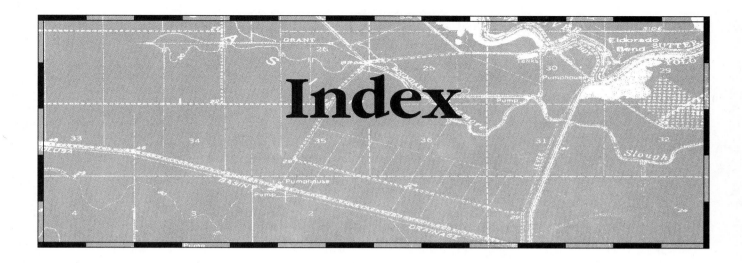

Index

A

AAA Cartographic Services, 350
Absolute
  altitude, 96
  scale, in line graph, 257
  value, bar chart, 265
Accessibility, in graph theory, 201
Accumulative line graph, 260
Accuracy, map, 66
Acre, 55
Action symbol, in propaganda, 231
Active remote-sensing, 88–89, 281
Activity, tectonic, 127
Admiralty nautical mile, 36
Aerial photo
  interpretation, 292–94
  photomosaic, 290–92
  print, 289–90
  scale, 287–88
  types, 17
Aerial photography, 38–41, 281–95
  in Canada, 360
Aerial survey camera, 38
Aeronautical
  chart, 93–98
    Canada, 357
  navigation, 92–98
Agencies, state mapping, 349–50
Agonic line, 78
Agricultural Stabilization and
    Conservation Service, U.S.
    (ASCS), 342
Agriculture, Department of, U.S.
    (USDA), 342–44
Airline map, 241
Air Photo Library, National, Canada,
    360
Albers equal-area projection, 46, 51
Aliquot part, 171
Alluvial
  fan, 143
  plain, 141
Alpine features, 135
Altimeter, 95, 96

Altitude
  absolute, 96
  of the sun, 30
*American Cartographer. See
    Cartography and
    Geographic Information
    Systems*
American Geographical Society
    Collection, 356
Analemma, 29–31
Aneroid altimeter, 95
Annular drainage pattern, 130
Antecedents of geographic
    information systems,
    323–25
Apparent solar time, 27, 30–31
Applications of
  computer-assisted cartography,
    314
  geographic information systems,
    334–35
Approximate contour, 103
Archives, National, U.S., 356
Area
  cartogram, 226–28
  data, 327
  determination, 71–75
  diagram, 270–73
  measurement, 55–56, 71–75
Areal
  averaging, 213
  correspondence, coefficient of,
    193–94
  distributions, spatial
    correspondence, 193–97
  scale, 71
  symbol, 211–20
Arête, 135
Arithmetic line graph, 256–61
Army Corps of Engineers, U.S., 339
Arpent, 175
Artificial drainage pattern, 130
ASCS, 342
Associated number, in graph theory,
    201
Astronomical observations, in water
    operations, 88

Astronomic latitude, 27
Atlas, road, 236
Atmospheric window, 299
Attribute code, in geographic
    information systems, 327
Automated navigation, automobile,
    240
Averaging, areal, 213
Aviation operations, 92–98
Azimuth, 48, 80–81
  back-, 81
  constant, 80
  conversion diagram, 80–81
  determination, magnetic, 372
  reference direction, 80–81, 84
Azimuthal
  equidistant projection, 47, 51
  projection, 42, 50

B

Back-azimuth, 81
Back-bearing, 81
Band, spectral, 301
Bar chart, 265–67
  absolute-value, 265
  high-low, 267
  loss-and-gain, 267
  percentage-value, 266
  symbol, 266
Baseline
  in CLSS, 177–78
  direction, 77
  in USPLS, 171
Base map, 7
Basic contour interval, 102, 114
Basin, stilling, 38
Bathymetric map, 10
Bearing, 81
  back-, 81
  in land survey, 170
  in water operations, 88
Bench mark, 100
BGN, 359
Bifurcation ratio, 203

Bilateral graph, 258–60
Bivariate map, 217
Black-and-white film, 284
BLM, 338
Block diagram, 109–10
Board on Geographic Names, U.S.
    (BGN), 318, 359
Bonne projection, 46, 51
Boyce-Clark radial shape index,
    185–87
Braided stream pattern, 130
Branching network, 203
Bridge, natural, 148
British National Grid, 395–96
Broad-band remote-sensing device,
    281
Brown Library, John Carter, 357
Buffer zone, 331
Bunge's shape measure, 183–85
Bureau
    of the Census, U.S., 341
    of Indian Affairs, U.S., 339
    of Land Management, U.S.
        (BLM), 338
Butte, 143

C

Cadastral
    map, 7
    survey, 169
Camera, aerial survey, 38
Canada
    Geographic Information System
        (CGIS), 325
    Land Survey System (CLSS),
        175–78
    Map Office, 358
Canadian
    Hydrographic Service, 360
    Permanent Committee on
        Geographical Names
        (CPCGN), 358, 359
Canoe chart, 348
Card, punched (Hollerith), 323
Carrying contour, 103
Cartogram, 15
    linear, 224–25
    value-by-area, 226–28
Cartographica, 320
Cartographic Perspectives, 355
Cartography, computer-assisted, 7,
    308–21
Cartography, journalistic, 248–50
*Cartography and Geographic
    Information Systems,*
    320, 355
Cataloging, map, 388
Cathode-ray tube, 3
Census, Bureau of the, U.S., 341
    digital products, 318–20
Centesimal system, 365
Central Intelligence Agency, U.S.
    (CIA), 341–42

Central-point linear cartogram,
    225–26
Centrifugal drainage pattern, 129
Centripetal drainage pattern, 129
Centuriation, 180
CGIS, 325
Change detection, in remote
    sensing, 306
Chart
    aeronautical, 93–98
        Canada, 357
    bar, 265–67
    isogonic, 78
    loran, 91
    nautical, 84–87, 348–49
    No. 1, 87
    pie, 267–70
Chi-square statistic, 194–97
Choropleth map, 13, 212–18
    unclassed, 217
Chronometer, 28
CIA, 341–42
Cinder cone, 146
Circle
    graduated, 270–72
    great, 22
    proportional, 270–72
    small, 23
Circuit network, 203
Circular graph, 276–77
Cirque, 135
Civilian system, in Universal
        Transverse Mercator grid,
        159–63
Classification
    in choropleth map, 214–17
    in remote sensing, 304
Cliff, 135
Climate map, 241, 243
Climatograph, 276–77
CLSS, 175–78
Clues, visual, in aerial photo
        interpretation, 292–94
Clustered pattern of points, 188,
        192–93
Coastal features, 134–35
Coast chart, 348
Code, attribute, in geographic
        information system, 327
Coefficient of areal correspondence,
        193–94
Col, 135
Collections, map, 355–57
Collection system, in remote
        sensing, 299–300
Color
    in aerial photo interpretation,
        294
    emulsion, 285–86
Coloring, hypsometric, 86
Columbus, Christopher, 248
Combination, in generalization, 63
Compass
    deviation, 79
    types, 369
    use, magnetic, 369–72
Compromise projections, 49

Computer-assisted
    area measurement, 74–75
    cartography, 7, 308–9, 321
        applications, 314
        format, 309
        implementation problems,
            309
        labeling, 310
        output, 311–12
    distance measurement, 68–70
Concave slope, 112
Concept distortion, 232–33
Cone
    in map projection, 42
    volcanic, 146
Conformal
    conic projection, Lambert, 45,
        50, 51, 93, 95
    projection, 51
Conformality, 45
Congress, Library of, 355–56
Conic projection, 50, 51
Conjugate principal point, 295
Connectivity index, 201–2
Constant azimuth, 80
Contiguous cartogram, 227
Continental glaciation, 138
Continuously variable scaling, of
        proportional circle, 270
Continuous surface, 220
Contour, 101–3
    characteristics, 112–16
    interpretation, 112–25
    interval, 101–2, 114
    types, 102–3
Contrast stretching, linear, 304
Control
    in aerial photography, 39
    geodetic survey, 26–28
    network, 35
Controlled photomosaic, 291–92
Conventional chart, 348
Conversion
    diagram, azimuth, 80–81
    to digital format, 309–11
    factors, units of measurement,
        57
    of scale, 61–63
Convex slope, 112
Coordinate, machine, 310
Coordinate Reader, Metric, 161–63
Copyright, 368
Corps of Engineers, Army, U.S., 339
Correspondence, coefficient of
        areal, 193–94
CPCGN, 358, 359
Crab, 286–87
Crater, 146
Cross section, geologic, 245–46
Crosswind, 92
CRT, 3
Cuesta, 143
Cultural influences of land
        subdivision, 178–79
Curve
    depth, 103
    Lorenz, 260
Cut and fill, 120–21

Cut-line, in profile, 117
Cycle
    in logarithmic line graph, 261
    metonic, 36
Cylinder, in map projection, 42
Cylindrical
    equal-area projection, 233–34
    projection, 49–50

D

Dasymetric map, 218
Data
    capture, in computer-assisted
        cartography, 309–11
    classification, in remote sensing,
        304
    digital, 7
        elevation model (DEM),
            317–18
        land-cover, 318
        land-use, 318
        line graph (DLG), 315–17
    forms, 327
    in geographic information
        system, 325–27
    grouping, 205. *See also*
        Classification
    in stereoplotting, 40
Data Bank, World, I and II, 320
Database
    in computer-assisted
        cartography, 314–21
    for microcomputers, 376–77
Data Center, EROS, 354
Date line, international, 31–32
Datum
    horizontal, 35
    mean, 36–38
    of nautical chart, 86
    North American (NAD), 35, 38
    vertical, 36–38
Dead reckoning, 92
Debris, glacial, 138
Decca system, 92
Declination
    diagram, 79
    magnetic, 78–79
Defense mapping, Canada, 357
Defense Mapping Agency, U.S.
        (DMA), 339
    Hydrographic/Topographic
        Center, 356
Defilade, 121
Deflection of the vertical, 35
Degree of slope, 122
Degrees of freedom, 196
Delta, 135
DEM, 317–18
Dendritic drainage pattern, 128
Department of
    Agriculture, U.S. (USDA),
        342–44
    Energy, Mines and Resources,
        Canada, 357

Fisheries and Oceans, Canadian
        Hydrographic Service,
        360
    National Defense, Canada, 357
    Transportation, U.S. (DOT), 344
Dependent variable, 196, 273–74
Depression contour, 103
Depth
    curve, 103
    indication, on nautical chart, 86
Detector location, in remote
        sensing, 281
Developable surface, 42
Deviation, compass, 79
Device, remote-sensing, 281
Diagram
    area, 270–73
    block, 109–10
    control, in aerial photography,
        39
    conversion, azimuth, 80–81
    declination, 79
    distance, 239–40
    physiographic, 108
    scatter, 273–74
    solid, 273
    volumetric, 273
Diameter, in graph theory, 201
Digital
    data, 7, 299, 309, 323, 376–77
        Census Bureau, 318–20
    database, 314–21
    land-cover data, 318
    land-use data, 318
    line graph (DLG), 315–17
    terrain tape (DTT), 318
Digital elevation model (DEM),
        317–18
Digitizing, 309–11
DIME. *See* GBF/DIME
Dip, 245
Direction, 77–81
    finding, radio (RDF), 90
    in map projection, 48
Direct methods of area
        measurement, 72–73
Displacement, planimetric, in block
        diagram, 109
Disrupted drainage pattern, 138
Dissection, 128–30
Distance
    diagram, 239–40
    function, in geographic
        information system,
        330–31
    great-circle, 47
    log, 239
    in map projection, 47
    matrix, 238–39
    measurement, 67–71
    topological, 201
Distortion
    in aerial photographs, 287–89
    in propaganda, 230–33
Distribution
    nominal, 212
    point, types of, 188
    quantitative, 212–20

Divide, drainage, 114
DLG, 315–17
DMA, 339
Dominion Lands Survey System,
        175–76
Donnelley Cartographic Services,
        350
Doppler effect, 89
DOT, 344
Dot-distribution map, 13, 205
Dot-matrix printer, 312
Dot planimeter, 73
Drainage
    divide, 114
    patterns, 127–30
Drift, 92
Drumlin, 138
DTT, 318
Dune, 148

E

Earth
    shape, 21, 23–25
    size, 25–26
Earth Observation Satellite
        Company (EOSAT), 355
Earth Science Information Center
        Network, U.S. (ESIC),
        353, 380–86
Ecliptic, plane of the, 30
Edge enhancement, 304
Electromagnetic radiation, 280,
        299
Elevation
    determination, 36
    estimation, 116
    model, digital (DEM), 317–18
Ellipsoid, 24–25
Emergency Management Agency,
        Federal, U.S. (FEMA), 117
Emulsion, photographic, 284–86
Engineering map, 10
Engineers, Army Corps of, U.S., 339
Enhancement, of remote sensing
        image, 304
EOSAT, 355
Ephemeris, 30
Equal-area projection, 46–47, 51,
        233–34
Equation of time, 29–31
Equator, 23
Equidistant map, 42, 47, 51
Equivalence, in map projection,
        46–47
Eratosthenes, 26
EROS Data Center, 354
Error
    classification, in remote sensing,
        304
    sources, in distance
        measurement, 70–71
    triangle of, 84
Escarpment, 135
ESIC, 353, 380–86

Estimated location, in navigation,
        92
Evaluation of classification
        in choropleth map, 215–17
        in remote sensing, 304
Events, imaginary, in propaganda,
        232
Exaggeration
        of size, in generalization, 63–64
        vertical, 107, 110, 117–20
Expected frequencies, table of, 196

F

Fall line, 148
False-color image, 300
False origin, 158
Fan, alluvial, 143
Fathom, 56, 86
Features, topographic, 127–48
Federal
        Emergency Management Agency,
                U.S. (FEMA), 117
        Highway Administration, U.S.,
                394
        map producers, 337–45
FEMA, 117
Fiducial mark, 295
Figure, realistic, 272–73
Film
        black-and-white, 284
        color, 285–86
Fisheries and Oceans, Department
                of, Canadian
                Hydrographic Service,
                360
Fix, in water operations, 88
Flattening, polar, 24
Flight
        line, in aerial photography, 295
        plan, in aerial photography, 286
        planning, 96–98
        rules, 96–97
Floating-dial compass, 369
Floating mark, 40
Floating-needle compass, 369
Flood, 100-year, 117
Flood-control map, 10
Flood-zone map, 117
Flow map, 14, 210–11
Foot, 54
Foreign maps, 363–67
Forest Service, U.S., 344
Format
        in computer-assisted
                cartography, 309
        in geographic information
                system, 327–28
        raster and vector, 309, 310
Form line, 104
Fraction, representative (RF), 58
Freedom, degrees of, 196
French Tract, 172–74

G

Gall's projection, 234
Gap, water and wind, 141
Gazetteer, National, U.S., 318
GBF/DIME, 319
General chart, 348
General Drafting Company, Inc.,
                350–51
Generalization, 63–64
Geocoding, 311
Geodetic control survey, 26–28, 35
Geodetic Information Center,
                National, U.S., 353–54
Geographic
        base file/dual independent map
                encoding (GBF/DIME),
                319
        information system (GIS), 7,
                323–25
                applications, 334–35
                attribute code, 327
                capabilities, 328
                components, 325–35
                data characteristics, 325–27
                distance function, 330–31
                format, 327–28
                labeling, 327
                map-overlay analysis,
                        323–25, 329–30
                modeling, 331–34
                output, 334
                reclassification, 328
                rectification, 327
                in remote sensing, 306
        mile, 56
        pole, 77–78
Geographical
        Mapping Program, National,
                Canada, 358
        Names, Canadian Permanent
                Committee on (CPCGN),
                358
Geographical north, 77
Geographic Information System,
                Canada (CGIS), 325
Geographic Names
        Board on, U.S. (BGN), 318
        Information System, U.S. (GNIS),
                318
Geographic Reference System,
                World (GEOREF), 156
Geoid, 25
Geologic
        cross section, 245–46
        map, 243–45
Geological Survey, U.S. (USGS),
                337–38
        Map Reference Code, 389–91
Geometric symbol, 272
GEOREF, 156
GIS. See Geographic information
                system
Glacial debris, 138
Glaciation, 135–38
Global Positioning System,
                NAVSTAR (GPS), 90

Globe characteristics, 45–48
Glossary, defined, 363
GNIS, 318
Gnomonic, 43, 51
        projection, 48, 49
Goode's interrupted homolosine
                projection, 46, 47
Gousha/Simon & Schuster, Inc.,
                351
GPS, 90
Grade, in angular measurement,
                365
Gradient, 121
Graduated
        circle, 270–72
        point symbol, 209
Graph, 200, 254–78
        circular, 276–77
        line, 254–64
        surface, 264–65
        triangular, 278
Graphic scale, 58–59
Graphs
        in geographic information
                system, 334
        maps as, 254–55
Graph theory, 200
Graticule, 23, 265
        on foreign maps, 365
Great circle, 22
Great-circle
        distance, 47
        planning chart, 85
Greenwich
        meridian, 22, 27, 31
        time, 28, 33
Grid, British National, 395–96
Grid
        azimuth, 80
        north, 79
        plane rectangular, 158–59
        reference, 158
        squares, in areal measurement,
                73
        systems, 158–68
Ground
        control, in aerial photography,
                39
        resolution, in remote sensing,
                300
Grouping of data, 205. See also
                Classification
Guide meridian, in USPLS, 175
Gyrocompass, 77

H

Hammond Incorporated, 351
Harbor chart, 348
Heartland, 232–33
Hierarchic order of trees, 203
High-low bar chart, 267
High-oblique photograph, 283
Highway Administration, Federal,
                U.S., 394

Highway map, 236–40
Hill shading, 104–6
Historical map, 246–47
History map, 247–48
Hogback, 141
Hollerith card, 323
Homolographic projection, 46
Homolosine projection, Goode's
    interrupted, 46, 47
Horizontal
    accuracy, 66–67
    datum, 35
    location, 36
Horn, 135
Hours, synoptic, 241
Hydrographic Service, Canadian,
    360
Hypothesis, null, 196
Hypsometric tint, 86, 95, 103–4

I

Illuminated contour, 104
Image
    classification, 304
    false-color, 300
    processing, 303–4
    radar, 17–19
    remotely-sensed, 17–19, 300
    stereoscopic, 38–39
Imaginary events, in propaganda,
    232
IMW, 378–79
Inaccuracy, map, 228–29
Independent variable, 196, 273–74
Index
    of connectivity, 201–2
    contour, 102
    value, in line graph, 260–61
Indexing, map, 392–93
Indian Affairs, Bureau of, U.S., 339
Indirect methods of area
    measurement, 73–74
Industrial site selection, in
    geographic information
    systems, 334
Information
    extraction, thematic, 304–6
    sources, map, 353–55
Infrared emulsion, 284–86
Inspection, in map orientation, 82
Instrument flight rules, 96–97
Intermediate contour, 103
International
    date line, 31–32
    foot, 54
    nautical mile, 56
International Map of the World
    (IMW), 378–79
Interpolation
    latitude and longitude, 152–56
    linear, 116
Interpretation
    of aerial photographs, 292–94
    of contours, 112–25

Interpretive key, in aerial photo
    interpretation, 294
Interruption, in map projection, 47
Intersection, by compass, 372
Interval measurement, 208
Intervisibility, 121
Intracoastal waterway chart, 348
Irregularities, in USPLS, 174–75
Isobar, 242
Isobath, 78, 103
Isogonic chart, 78
Isoline map, 14, 220
Isometric
    drawing, in block diagram, 110
    line, 220
Isopleth, 220–22

J

Journalistic cartography, 248–50

K

Kendall's Q, 197
Kettle, 138
Key, interpretive, in aerial
    photography, 294
Knot, 56

L

Labeling
    in computer-assisted
        cartography, 310
    in geographic information
        system, 327
Lacustrine plain, 138
Lambert conformal conic
        projection, 45, 50, 51,
        93, 95
Land
    navigation, 82–84
    subdivision, cultural influences
        of, 178–79
    survey, 169
        in Canada, 175–78
Land-cover data, digital, 318
Landforms, 127, 130–48
Land Management, Bureau of, U.S.
        (BLM), 338
Land-partitioning systems, 168–80
Landsat, 300–303
Landscape map, 11
Land Survey System, Canada (CLSS),
        175–78
Land-use data, digital, 318
Land Use Information Series,
        Northern, Canada, 360
Language, on foreign maps, 363–64

Large scale, 59–60
Latitude
    determination, 27
    interpolation, 152–56
    line of, 23
    position, 151–56
Layer tint, 103–4
Leg
    in aerial photography, 286
    in navigation, 92
Legal subdivisions, in CLSS, 178
Length of path, in graph theory,
    201
Lensatic compass, 369
Levee, natural, 143
Leveling, 36
Levels of measurement, 207–8
Library, Air Photo, National,
    Canada, 360
Library of Congress, 355–56
Light-source location, in map
    projection, 43
Limestone formations, 143
Line
    agonic, 78
    data, 327
    graph, 254–64
        digital (DLG), 315–17
    isometric, 220
    of latitude or longitude, 23
    plotter, 312
    of position, in water operations,
        88
    trend, 274
Linear
    cartogram, 224–26
    contrast stretching, 304
    interpolation, 116
    measurement, 54–55
    symbol, 209–11
Line-route map, 7–10
Link, 201
Location
    estimated, in navigation, 92
    horizontal, 36
Locational
    shift, in generalization, 63
    system, 21–23
        on foreign maps, 364
Log, distance, 239
Logarithmic line graph, 261–64
Log-log graph, 263–64
Longitude
    determination, 27–28
    interpolation, 152–56
    line of, 22
    position, 151–56
Long lot, 175–76
Loran, 90–92
Lorenz curve, 260
Loss-and-gain bar chart, 267
Lot, 171
    long, 175–76
Low-contrast image, 304
Low-oblique photograph, 283
Loxodrome, 85

M

Machine coordinate, 310
Mackinder, Halford J., 232–33
Magazine map, 250
Magnetic
 azimuth, 80–81, 84
  determination of, 372
 compass use, 369–72
 declination, 78–79
 pole, 77–79
Map. *See also* Map types
 accuracy, 66
 cataloging, 387–94
 collections, 355–57
 definition, 2–3
 foreign products, 366–67
 inaccuracy, 228–29
 index, 392–93
 information sources, 353–55
 measurer, 68
 misuse, 228–34
 orientation, 82, 371–72
 producers
  federal, 337–45
  nonfederal, 349–52
 projection, 42–51. *See also*
  Projection
 scale, 53, 58–59
 state agencies, 349–50
 storage, 387–94
Map Accuracy Standards, National,
 U.S., 66–67
Map libraries, 355–57
Map Office, Canada, 358
Map-overlay analysis, 323–25
Mapper, Thematic (TM), 303
Mapping
 agencies, state, 349–50
 firms, private, 350–52
 microcomputer, 312–14
 process, 26–28, 35–38
 software for microcomputers,
  373–77
 topographic, 38–41
Mapping and Charting
  Establishment,
  Department of National
  Defense, Canada, 357
Map projections. *See* Projections
Map Reference Code, USGS,
 389–91
Maps
 foreign, 363–67
 in geographic information
  system, 334
 as graphs, 254–55
Map types
 airline, 241
 base, 7
 bathymetric, 10
 bivariate, 217
 cadastral, 7
 choropleth, 13, 212–18

climate, 241, 243
dasymetric, 218
dot-distribution, 13, 205
engineering, 10
equidistant, 47
flood-control, 10
flood-zone, 117
flow, 14, 210–11
geologic, 243–45
highway, 236–40
historical, 246–47
history, 247–48
isoline, 14
landscape, 11
line-route, 7–10
magazine, 250
of Mars, 248
mental, 3–6
of moon, 248
multivariate, 217–18
newsmagazine, 250
newspaper, 248–50
outline, 7
of planet, 248
planimetric, 7–10
prism, 218–19
quadrangle, USGS, 345
real, 3, 7–20
route, 240–41
slope-zone, 123
street, 236, 240
surface, 220–22
television, 251–52
thematic, 11–15
T-in-O, 246–47
topographic, 10–11, 236–41
 Canada, 357
 USGS, 345
transportation, 236–41
univariate, 217
virtual, 3–7
weather, 241–42
Mariners, Notice to, 85
Mark
 bench, 100
 fiducial, 295
 floating, 40
Mars, map of, 248
Master station, in loran, 190
Matrix, distance, 238–39
Matterhorn, 135
Maximum slope limitation, 123–24
McHarg, Ian, 324–25
McNally, Rand, and Company, 352
Mean
 datum, 36–38
 solar time, 31
Meander, 143
Meander line, 172
Measurement
 area, 53–56, 71–75
 distance, 67–71
 levels of, 207–8
 linear, 54–55
 nautical, 54, 56

units, 54–57
 conversion factors, 57
 on foreign maps, 366
Mental map, 3–6
Mercator projection, 45, 49, 51, 85,
 232, 233, 251–52
 transverse, 43
Meridian, 22–23
 of Greenwich, 22, 27, 31
 guide, in USPLS, 175
 prime, 22
 on foreign maps, 365
 principal
  in CLSS, 177
  in USPLS, 171
Mesa, 143
Meter, 55
Metes-and-bounds survey, 169–70
Metonic cycle, 36
Metric Coordinate Reader, 161
Metric units of measurement,
 54–55, 56
Microcomputer
 databases, 376–77
 mapping, 312–14, 373–77
Microwave, 296, 300
Mile, 54–56
Mileage table, 239
Military
 applications, in geographic
  information systems,
  334–35
 system, in Universal Transverse
  Mercator grid, 163–65
Miller cylindrical projection, 49
Miller's shape measure, 183
Mils, 80
Misuse of map, 228–34
Mobility study, 334–35
Model (physical, terrain), 106–7
Modeling, in geographic
  information system,
  331–34
Moon, map of, 248
Moraine, terminal, 138
Mountains, 141
MSS, 301–3
Multiple-scale graph, 258
Multispectral
 remote-sensing device, 281
 scanner (MSS), 301–3
Multivariate map, 217–18

N

NACIS, 355
NAD, 35, 38
Names on maps, 318, 358–59
Narrow-band remote-sensing
  device, 281
NASA, 345

National
　Aeronautics and Space
　　Administration, U.S.
　　(NASA), 345
　Air Photo Library, Canada, 360
　Archives, U.S., 356
　Environmental Satellite, Data,
　　and Information Service,
　　U.S. (NESDIS), 354
　Gazetteer (U.S.), 318
　Geodetic Information Center,
　　U.S., 353–54
　Geographical Mapping Program,
　　Canada, 358
　Geographic Society, 352
　Grid, British, 395–96
　Map Accuracy Standards, U.S.,
　　66–67
　Ocean Service, U.S. (NOS), 338
　Park Service, U.S., 345
　Technical Information Service,
　　U.S. (NTIS), 320
　Topographic System, Canada,
　　357, 391–92
　Weather Service, U.S., 345
Natural
　bridge, 148
　levee, 143
Nautical
　chart, 84–87, 348–49
　measurements, 54, 56
Navigation
　aeronautical, 93–98
　automated (automobile), 240
　land, 82–84
　water, 84–93
NAVSTAR Global Positioning System
　(GPS), 90
Nearest-neighbor analysis, 190–93
Neatline, 152
Negative, photographic, 283
NESDIS, 354
Network
　control survey, 35
　in graph theory, 200–203
Newberry Library, 356
Newsmagazine map, 250
Newspaper map, 248–50
Node, 201
Nominal
　areal symbol, 212
　linear symbol, 209
　measurement, 207–8
Noncontiguous cartogram, 226–27
Nonfederal map producers, 349–52
Nonplanar network, 201–2
Nonproportional point symbol,
　205–6
Nonsymmetric network, 202
Noon, apparent solar, 27
Normal orientation, in map
　projection, 43
North, reference directions, 77–79

North American Cartographic
　Information Society
　(NACIS), 355
North American Datum (NAD)
　horizontal, 35
　vertical, 38
Northern Land Use Information
　Series, Canada, 360
North pole
　geographical or true, 77
　magnetic, 77, 78
NOS, 338
NOTAM, 93
Notice
　to Airmen (NOTAM), 93
　to Mariners, 85
NTIS, 320
Null hypothesis, 196
Number, associated, 201
Numerical shape indices, 182–87
Nystrom, 352

O

Oblique
　aerial photograph, 17, 281–83
　projection, 45
　view, 109–10
Observation, astronomical, in water
　operations, 88
Observed frequencies, table of, 195
Ocean Service, National, U.S.
　(NOS), 338
Omega system, 92
100-year flood, 117
Operations
　land, 82–84
　water, 84–93
Order, hierarchic, of trees, 203
Ordinal
　linear symbol, 210
　measurement, 208
Orientation
　map, 82, 247
　in map projection, 43
Orienteering compass, 369
Origin, false, 158
Orthodrome, 80
Orthographic, 43
　projection, 51
　view, 288
Orthophoto, 289, 292
Orthophotomap, 292
Orthophotoquad, 292
Outline map, 7
Output
　in computer-assisted
　　cartography, 311–12
　in geographic information
　　system, 334
　raster and vector, 312
Overlay analysis, 193–94, 323–24

Overlaying, in geographic
　information system,
　329–30
Oversized symbol, in propaganda,
　230–31
Oxbow lake, 143

P

Pair, stereoscopic, 39, 294–95
Panchromatic
　emulsion, 284
　film, 281
Parallax, 39
Parallel, 23
Park Service, National, U.S., 345
Part, aliquot, 171
Pass, 135
Passive remote-sensing system, 281
Path, in graph theory, 201
Pattern
　in aerial photo interpretation,
　　294
　of points, 187–93
Percentage
　change, on logarithmic scale,
　　262
　scale, in line graph, 257
　value bar chart, 266
Percent slope, 121
Permanent Committee on
　Geographical Names,
　Canadian (CPCGN), 358,
　359
Perspective view, 288
　in block diagram, 110
Peters projection, 233–34
Photograph, aerial, 17
　oblique, 17, 281–83
　vertical, 17, 38–41, 281
Photographic
　emulsion types, 284–86
　negative and positive, 283–84
　overlay method, 324–25
Photography, aerial, 38–41,
　281–95
　Canada, 360
Photo interpretation, 292–95
Photomosaic, 290–92
Physical
　model, 106–7
　surface, 220
Physiographic diagram, 108
Pie chart, 267–70
Pixel, in remote sensing, 300
Place names, 359
Places, in graph theory, 200–201
Plain
　alluvial, 141
　lacustrine, 138
Plan, 10

Plan, flight, in aerial photography, 286
Planar network, 201–2
Plane
    of the ecliptic, 30
    in map projection, 42
    rectangular grid, 158–59
        on foreign maps, 365–66
    survey, 35–38
Planet, map of, 248
Planimeter, 72–73
Planimetric
    data, 40
    displacement, in block diagram, 109
    map, 7–10
    shift, 288–89
Planning-chart, great-circle, 85
Plastic shading, 104
Plat, 171
Plateau, 141–43
Plotter, 312
Plotting, stereoscopic, 40–41
Pocket transit, 369
Point
    conjugate principal, 295
    data, 327
    pattern analysis, 187–93
    principal, 288, 295
    symbol, 205–6, 209
Polar
    flattening, 24
    planimeter, 72–73
Polaris, 27, 77
Poles, types, 27, 77–79
Polygon
    data, 327
    method, in areal measurement, 73
Population profile (pyramid), 274–76
Position
    determination
        in land operations, 83–84
        latitude and longitude, 27–28, 151–56
        in water operations, 87–92
    line of, 88
    topological, 200
Positive, photographic, 283–84
Preprocessing, in remote sensing, 303–4
Prime meridian, 22, 365
Principal
    meridian
        in CLSS, 177
        in USPLS, 171
    point, 288, 295
Print
    aerial photo, 289–90
    positive, 283–84
    rectified, 287
Printer, dot-matrix, 312
Prism map, 218–19
Private mapping firms, 350–52
Processing, image, 303–4

Producers, map
    federal, 337–45
    nonfederal, 349–52
Professional Geographer, The, 320
Profile
    map, 117–21
    population, 274–76
Projection process
    equivalence, 233–34
    interruption, 47
    light-source location, 43
    on surface, 42
Projection selection, 49–51
Projection, types, 42–51
    Albers equal-area, 46, 51
    azimuthal, 42, 50
        equidistant, 47, 51
    Bonne, 46, 51
    compromise, 49
    conformal, 51
    conic, 50, 51
    cylindrical, 50
    equal-area, 51, 233–34
    Gall's, 234
    gnomonic, 48, 49
    Goode's interrupted homolosine, 46, 47
    homolographic, 46
    homolosine, Goode's interrupted, 46–47
    Lambert conformal conic, 45, 50, 51, 93, 95
    Mercator, 45, 49, 51, 85, 232, 233, 251–52
    Miller cylindrical, 49
    of nautical chart, 85
    oblique, 45
    orthographic, 51
    Peters, 233–34
    Robinson, 49
    sinusoidal, 46–47, 51
    transverse Mercator, 50, 51
Propaganda, 229–34
Property description, in USPLS, 174
Proportional
    circle, 270–72
    flow map, 210
Pseudoscopic effect, 295
Psychological scaling, of proportional circle, 270–72
Public land, 171
Public Land Survey, U.S., (USPLS), 171–75
Punched card system, 323
Push-broom scanning, 303
Pyramid, population, 274–76

Q

Q, Kendall's, 197
Quadrangle map, USGS, 345
Quadrat analysis
    of areal distributions, 194–97
    of point patterns, 188–90

Quantitative
    areal symbol, 212–20
    linear symbol, 209–11
Quarter section, 56, 171, 178

R

Radar, 296
    image, 17–19
    side-looking airborne (SLAR), 296
    in water operations, 88–89
Radial drainage pattern, 129
Radial shape index, Boyce-Clark, 185–87
Radiation, electromagnetic, 280, 299
Radio
    altimeter, 96
    direction finding (RDF), 90
Rand McNally and Company, 352
Random pattern of points, 188, 190–91
Range
    in CLSS, 178
    spectral, 281
    in USPLS, 171
    in visual flight, 97
    in water operations, 88
Range-graded
    flow map, 210
    proportional circle, 270
Rapids, 146
Raster
    digitizing, 310
    format, 309, 310
    plotter, 312
Ratio
    bifurcation, 203
    measurement, 208
RDF, 90
Reader, Metric Coordinate, 161
Realistic figure, 272–73
Real map, 3, 7–20
Reclassification, in geographic information system, 328
Rectangular
    drainage pattern, 128
    survey system, 171
Rectification, in geographic information system, 327
Rectified print, 287
Reference grid, 158
Regression, 274
Relief shading, 104
Remotely-sensed image, 17–19
Remote sensing
    from airborne platforms, 280–97
    change detection, 306
    defined, 280
    from space, 299–306

Remote-sensing
active and passive systems, 281
devices, 281
Report, statistical, in geographic
information system, 334
Representative fraction (RF), 58
Resection
by compass, 372
in-land operations, 83–84
Reservoir capacity estimation, 116
Resolution, ground, 300
RF, 58
Rhumb line, 80
Ridge, 114
Rise, 121
Road atlas, 236
Robinson projection, 49
Rotation, pole of, 77
Roture, 175
Route, 201
following, by compass, 372
map, 240–41
selection, in land operations, 84
Routed linear cartogram, 224–25
Run, 121

S

Saddle, 135
Sailing chart, 348
Sand
hill, 148
spit, 134
Satellite
image, 19
observation, in water operations,
89–90
Scale, 53–63
absolute, in line graph, 257
of aerial photograph, 287–88
areal, 71
conversion, 61–63
determination, 60–61
large and small, 59–60
methods of stating, 58–59
percentage, in line graph, 257
vertical
in block diagram, 110
in physical model, 107
in profile, 117–20
Scaling
continuously variable, of
proportional circle, 270
of distance, 67–68
psychological, of proportional
circle, 270–72
Scanner
multispectral (MSS), 301–3
in remote sensing, 296–97
Scanning
push-broom, 303
whisk-broom, 302
Scatter diagram, 273–74

Sea level, 36–38
Section, 56
in CLSS, 177–78
in USPLS, 171
Sectional chart, aeronautical, 95–96
Seigneury, 175
Selection
in generalization, 63
of projection, 49–51
Semilogarithmic (semilog) graph,
262–63
Series index, 392–93
Sexigesimal system, 365
Shading (hill, plastic, relief,
terrain), 104
Shadow, in aerial photo
interpretation, 294
Shape
in aerial photo interpretation,
294
of earth, 21, 23–25
in map projection, 45
indices, 182–87
subjective description, 182
Shift
locational, in generalization, 63
planimetric, 288–89
Shorelines, 134–35
Side-looking airborne radar (SLAR),
296
Signal source, in remote sensing,
281
Signature, in remote sensing, 280
Signs, on foreign maps, 364
Silhouette graph, 260
Simplification, in generalization, 63
Sink, 143
Sinusoidal projection, 46–47, 51
Site selection, industrial, in
geographic information
systems, 334
Size
in aerial photo interpretation,
294
of earth, 25–26
exaggeration, in generalization,
63–64
SLAR, 296
Slave station, in loran, 90
Slope, 112, 121–25
error, in distance measurement,
70–71
maximum, 123–24
measurement, 121–23
percent, 121
Slope-zone map, 123
Small
circle, 23
craft chart, 348
scale, 59–60
Smart map, 308
Smoothing error, in distance
measurement, 70
Software exchanges, for mapping
with microcomputers,
373–77
Solar time, 30–31

Solid diagram, 273
Solstice, summer, 26
Solution features, 143
Sounding, 86
Source, signal, 281
Spacing dividers, 155
Spatial correspondence of areal
distributions, 193
SPCS, 166–68
Spectral
band, 301
characteristics, in remote
sensing, 299
range, 281
Spectrum, 280
Spherical shape, 21
Spot height, 100
SPOT Image Corporation, 355
SPOT system, 303
Spring, 146
Standard parallel, in USPLS, 175
State mapping agencies, 349–50
State Plane Coordinate System
(SPCS), 166–68
Statistical
report, in geographic
information system, 334
surface, 220
Statistics Canada, 358
Statute mile, 54
Stereographic, 43, 51
Stereomodel, 39–40
Stereo pair, 39, 294–95
Stereoplotter, 39
Stereoscope, 39, 295
Stereoscopic
image, 38–39
plotting, 40–41
viewing, 294–95
Stilling basin, 38
Storage, of maps, 388–92
Strahler method, 203
Stream
ordering, 203
patterns, 127–30
Street map, 236, 240
Stretching, linear contrast, 304
Strike, 244–45
Strip method, in areal
measurement, 73
Subdivision
of degrees, 156
legal, in CLSS, 178
systematic, 171–75, 176–78
unsystematic, 169–70
Summer solstice, 26
Sun, altitude of the, 30
Supplementary contour, 103
Surface
continuous, 220
data, 327
developable, 42
graph, 264–65
map, 220–22
physical, 220
for projection, 42
statistical, 220

Survey
    cadastral, 169
    foot, U.S., 54
    geodetic, 35
    land, 169
        in Canada, 175–78
    metes-and-bounds, 169–70
    plane, 35–38
    system, rectangular, 171
Surveys, Mapping and Remote
        Sensing Sector,
        Department of Energy,
        Mines and Resources,
        Canada, 357
Symbol
    areal, 211–20
    distortion, 230–32
    geometric, 272
    linear, 209–11
    point, 205–6, 209
Symbols
    on foreign maps, 364
    on nautical charts, 86–87
    in propaganda, 229–34
Symmetric network, 201–2
Synoptic hours, 241
Systematic subdivision, 171–75

T

Table
    of expected frequencies, 196
    of mileage, 239
    of observed frequencies, 195
Tabular index, 392
Tangency, in map projection, 43
Tarn, 135
Technical Information Service,
        National, U.S., 320
Tectonic activity, 127
Television map, 251–52
Tennessee Valley Authority (TVA),
        345
Terminal moraine, 138
Terrain
    analysis, 314, 334
    model, 106–7
    representation, 100–125
Texture
    in aerial photo interpretation,
        294
    of dissection, 130
Thematic
    information extraction, in
        remote sensing, 304–6
    map, 11–15
Thematic Mapper (TM), 303
TIGER, 318–20
Till, 138

Time
    apparent solar, 30–31
    equation of, 29–31
    Greenwich, 28, 33
    mean solar, 31
    of travel, 240
    zone, 31, 33
T-in-O map, 246–47
Tint hypsometric (layer), 95,
        103–4
TM, 303
Tone, in aerial photo interpretation,
        294
Topographic
    features, 127–48
    map, 10–11
    mapping, 38–41
    maps
        Canada, 357
        USGS, 345
Topographic System, National,
        Canada, 357, 391–92
Topography, 127
Topological
    distance, 201
    position, 200
Topologically Integrated
        Geographic Encoding and
        Reference system
        (TIGER), 318–20
Toponyms. *See also,* Geographic
        Names
    in Canada, 358, 359
Township
    in Canada, 176
    plat, 171
    in USPLS, 171
Trafficability, 125
Transit
    pocket, 369
    system, 89
Translation, 364
Transliteration, 364
Transparency, positive, 283–84
Transportation, Department of, U.S.
        (DOT), 344
Transportation map, 236–41
Transverse projection, 43
    Mercator, 50, 51
Travel-time, 240
Trees
    in graph theory, 203–4
Trellis drainage pattern, 128
Trend line, 274
Triangle of error, 84
Triangular graph, 278
Triangulation network, 35
Trilateration network, 35
True
    azimuth, 80
    north, 77
TVA, 345

U

Unclassed choropleth map, 217
Uncontrolled photomosaic, 290–91
Underwater contour, 103
Uniform
    pattern of points, 188, 192–93
    slope, 112
U.S.
    Board on Geographic Names,
        318
    customary units of
        measurement, 53, 54, 55
    National Map Accuracy
        Standards, 66–67
    nautical mile, 56
    Public Land Survey (USPLS),
        171–75
Units of measurement, 53–57
    on foreign maps, 366
    on nautical chart, 86
Univariate map, 217
Universal
    Polar Stereographic (UPS) grid,
        159
    Transverse Mercator (UTM) grid
        civilian, 159–63
        military, 163–65
Unsystematic subdivision, 169–70
UPS, 159
USDA, 342–44
USGS. *See* Geological Survey, U.S.
U-shaped valley, 114, 135
USPLS, 171–75
UTM, 159–65

V

Valley, 114
Value, index, in line graph, 260–61
Value-by-area cartogram, 226–28
Variable
    dependent and independent,
        196
    in graphs, 254
Variance, in quadrat analysis, 188
Vector format, 309, 310
    plotter, 312
Vertical
    accuracy, 67
    aerial photograph, 17, 38–41,
        281
    datum, 36–38
    deflection of, 35
    exaggeration
        in block diagram, 110
        in physical model, 107
        in profile, 117–20

View
    oblique, 109–10
    orthographic, 288
    perspective, 288
        in block diagram, 110
Viewing, stereoscopic, 294–95
Virtual map, 3–7
Visible spectrum, 280
Visual
    clues, in aerial photo
        interpretation, 292–94
    flight rules, 96–97
Volcanic features, 146
Volumetric diagram, 273
V-shaped valley, 114, 143

W

WAC, 93
Water
    features, 146
    gap, 141
    navigation, 84–93
Waterway chart, intracoastal, 348
Weather map, 241–42
Weather Service, National, U.S., 345
Whisk-broom scanning, 302
Wind
    features, 148
    gap, 141
Window, atmospheric, 299

Wind-rose, 277
Word statement, of scale, 58
World Aeronautical Chart (WAC),
    93
    Data Bank I and II, 320
    Geographic Reference System
        (GEOREF), 156

Z

Zone
    buffer, 331
    time, 33